Constructing Democratic Governance

An Inter-American Dialogue Book

Constructing Democratic Governance: Latin America and the Caribbean in the 1990s
edited by Jorge I. Domínguez and Abraham F. Lowenthal

Available in separate paperback editions:

Constructing Democratic Governance: Latin America and the Caribbean in the 1990s—Themes and Issues
edited by Jorge I. Domínguez and Abraham F. Lowenthal

Constructing Democratic Governance: South America in the 1990s
edited by Jorge I. Domínguez and Abraham F. Lowenthal

Constructing Democratic Governance: Mexico, Central America, and the Caribbean in the 1990s
edited by Jorge I. Domínguez and Abraham F. Lowenthal

Constructing Democratic Governance

Latin America and the Caribbean in the 1990s

edited by
Jorge I. Domínguez and
Abraham F. Lowenthal

The Johns Hopkins University Press
Baltimore and London

The Johns Hopkins University Press
2715 North Charles Street
Baltimore, Maryland 21218-4319
The Johns Hopkins Press Ltd., London

Library of Congress Cataloging-in-Publication Data

Constructing democratic governance: Latin America and the Caribbean
   in the 1990s / edited by Jorge I. Domínguez and Abraham F. Lowenthal
      p.   cm.—(An Inter-American dialogue book)
   Includes bibliographical references and index.
   ISBN 0-8018-5385-0 (alk. paper)
   1. Latin America—Politics and government—1980– . 2. Democracy—
Latin America. 3. Caribbean Area—Politics and government—1945– .
4. Democracy—Caribbean Area. I. Domínguez, Jorge I., 1945– .
II. Lowenthal, Abraham F. III. Series.
JL966.C677   1996
321.8′098—dc20   96-12421
                                                                      CIP

A catalog record for this book is available from the British Library.

Contents

Part V. Conclusion

Foreword

There is no more important challenge in the hemisphere today than building effective democratic governance. The understandable celebrations associated with the transition to constitutional, elected governments in Latin America over the past fifteen years have now yielded to growing concern that persistent obstacles stand in the way of constructing and consolidating genuine democracies. Free and competitive elections are no longer noteworthy events in the region. Yet progress is lagging behind in other key areas such as establishing civilian control over armed forces, fully protecting human rights, advancing the rule of law, strengthening the role of the legislature and the judiciary, fostering citizen participation, improving the performance of political parties, and redressing sharp social inequalities and ethnic divisions.

Analysts make many claims about the state of democracy in the hemisphere—and policymakers make decisions based on such assessments—but there have been few, if any, systematic attempts to understand and explain prevailing conditions in Latin America and the Caribbean. This volume is just such an effort. The editors commissioned twenty-one country studies and five chapters on crosscutting issues relevant to a number of the national cases. Abraham F. Lowenthal, the Inter-American Dialogue's founding executive director and currently a board member, and Jorge I. Domínguez, who is a member and associated fellow of the Dialogue, succeeded in attracting first-rate analysts from Latin America, the Caribbean, Canada, and the United States to prepare these studies.

The chapters went through several drafts. They benefited from the comments of the editors as well as from a major two-day conference held in Washington, D.C., in September 1994 that brought together U.S. and Latin American senior government officials, representatives of multilateral institutions, congressional staff, policy analysts, and key leaders from many nongovernmental organizations. The conference prompted rich discussion on both the country and the thematic papers and helped bridge the worlds of policy and academia.

Many others deserve credit for their role in this project. Jeanne Kinney Giraldo, a doctoral student in political science at Harvard University, provided detailed, critical commentary on all the chapters. We would also like to extend our appreciation to Javier Corrales and Robert Hemmer for their fine translations and to the Dialogue interns who contributed to this project: Robert Bettman, Corrine Castagnet, Sarah Connelly, Cindy Garret, Alex Gross, Robyn Prinz, James Rogan, Eduardo

Romo, and John White. Special thanks are in order for Nicola Lowther, who skillfully performed the countless editing and other tasks that finishing such a volume entails, and to Jenny Pilling, for her unfailing patience and dedication in coordinating the project.

The Inter-American Dialogue's research and publications are designed to improve the quality of public debate and decision on key issues in western hemisphere affairs. The Dialogue is both a forum for sustained exchange among leaders and an independent, nonpartisan center for policy analysis on U.S.–Latin American economic and political relations. The Dialogue's one hundred members—from the United States, Canada, Latin America, and the Caribbean—include prominent political, business, labor, academic, media, military, and religious leaders. At periodic plenary sessions, members analyze key hemispheric issues and formulate recommendations for policy and action. The Dialogue presents its findings in comprehensive reports circulated throughout the Americas. Its research agenda focuses on four broad themes: democratic governance, inter-American cooperation, economic integration, and social equity.

The Inter-American Dialogue wishes to express its gratitude to the National Endowment for Democracy and the A. W. Mellon Foundation for their support for commissioning the papers, the September 1994 international conference in Washington, and the publication of this volume. Mead Data Central–Lexis/Nexus Research Information Services gave us crucial research assistance. We are also pleased to acknowledge the broader support that the Dialogue has obtained from the Ford, A. W. Mellon, and William and Flora Hewlett foundations and the Carnegie Corporation of New York.

Michael Shifter
Program Director, Democratic Governance
Inter-American Dialogue

Peter Hakim
President
Inter-American Dialogue

Contributors

Diego Abente Brun is professor of political science at the National University of Asunción and the Catholic University of Asunción, Paraguay, and was formerly professor of political science at Miami University in Ohio. He has written various articles and books on Paraguay and the democratic transition in Latin America such as *Paraguay en transición* (1993). Dr. Abente Brun received his Ph.D. in political science from the University of New Mexico and in 1993 was elected senator to the Paraguayan National Congress.

Alan Angell is a fellow of Saint Antony's College and a former director of the Latin American Centre, University of Oxford. He has written extensively on Chilean politics and more recently has been working on the politics of social sector reform.

Jorge G. Castañeda is professor of political science and international affairs at Mexico's National Autonomous University (UNAM). He was previously senior associate of the Carnegie Endowment for International Peace in Washington, D.C., and a visiting professor at Princeton University and the University of California, Berkeley.

Michael Coppedge is associate professor in the department of government at the University of Notre Dame. He previously taught at the Nitze School of Advanced International Studies of Johns Hopkins University and at Princeton University. His research interests include the governability and performance of democratic regimes, the evolution of Latin American party systems, politics in Venezuela and Mexico, and the measurement of democracy. His latest book is *Strong*

Parties and Lame Ducks: Presidential Partyarchy and Factionalism in Venezuela (1994). Dr. Coppedge received his Ph.D. from Yale University.

Ricardo Córdova Macías is the executive director of the Fundación Dr. Guillermo Manuel Ungo in El Salvador. He also is president of the Central American Sociology Association.

Liliana De Riz is currently a senior researcher at the Instituto de Investigaciones de la Facultad de Ciencias Sociales of the Universidad de Buenos Aires, where she remains a professor of political science. In addition to writing numerous articles on Argentina and comparative politics, Dr. De Riz has edited *Retorno y derrumbe: El último gobierno peronista*, in its second edition (1987); *Radicales y Peronistas: El Congreso Argentino entre 1983 y 1989* (1994); and *Argentina since 1946*, which she co-authored. She holds a Ph.D. in sociology from the Ecole Pratique des Hautes Etudes, Université de Paris.

Jorge I. Domínguez is Frank G. Thomson Professor of Government at Harvard University. Previously he was visiting senior fellow at the Inter-American Dialogue, of which he is a founding member. A past president of the Latin American Studies Association and member of the Council on Foreign Relations, he is a member of the editorial boards of *Mexican Studies, Cuban Studies, Political Science Quarterly*, and the *Journal of Inter-American Studies and World Affairs*. Dr. Domínguez is a leading authority on Cuban and Latin American politics and is widely published on these topics. With James McCann, he recently co-authored *Democratizing Mexico: Public Opinions and Electoral Choice*.

Denise Dresser is professor of political science at the Instituto Tecnológico Autónomo de México (ITAM). Dr. Dresser has been a visiting research fellow at the Center for U.S.-Mexican Studies, University of California, San Diego, and a postdoctoral fellow at the Center for International Studies, University of Southern California. In 1994 she was a senior visiting fellow at the Inter-American Dialogue in Washington, D.C. She is the author of *Neopopulist Solutions to Neoliberal Problems: Mexico's National Solidarity Program* and of numerous articles on Mexican politics and U.S.-Mexican relations. She received her Ph.D. from Princeton University.

Rosario Espinal is associate professor of sociology at Temple University. She has published widely on Dominican politics and democratization in Latin America. Professor Espinal has written *Autoritarismo y democracia en la política dominicana* (1987, 1994) and scholarly articles published in the *Journal of Latin American Studies*, the *Bulletin of Latin American Research, Electoral Studies, Development and Change, Revista Nueva Sociedad*, and in several edited books. She has been a fellow at the Kellogg Institute for International Studies at the University of Notre Dame and at the Centre for Latin American Studies at Oxford University. She was a Fulbright Scholar in 1995.

Eduardo A. Gamarra is acting director of the Latin American and Caribbean Center and associate professor of political science at Florida International University. His research interests include civil-military relations, democratization, legislatures and political parties in Latin America, narcotics trafficking, and U.S.–Latin American relations. His recent publications include *Entre la Droga y la Democracia* (1994); *Democracy, Markets, and Structural Reform in Latin America: Argentina, Bolivia, Brazil, Chile, and Mexico* (1994); and *The Administration of Justice in Bolivia: An Institutional Analysis* (1991). He holds a Ph.D. in political science from the University of Pittsburgh.

Edward L. Gibson is assistant professor of political science at Northwestern University. He previously taught at the University of Michigan, was an academy scholar at Harvard University's Academy for International and Area Studies, and served as assistant director of the Industry Council for Development from 1981 to 1985. He is the author of *Class and Conservative Parties: Argentina in Comparative Perspective* (1996). He holds a Ph.D. in political science from Columbia University.

Jeanne Kinney Giraldo is a Ph.D. candidate and has been a teaching fellow in the department of government at Harvard University. Her papers include "Democracy and Development in Chile: Alejandro Foxley and the Concertación's Economic Policy," which she presented to the Latin American Studies Association in March 1994.

Lowell Gudmundson is professor and chair of Latin American Studies at Mount Holyoke College. He taught for more than seven years in the Costa Rican university system in the 1970s and 1980s. His major publications include *Costa Rica before Coffee* (1995); (with Héctor Lindo-Fuentes) *Central America, 1821–1871* (1995); and (co-edited) *Coffee, Society and Power in Latin America* (1995). He holds a Ph.D. in history from the University of Minnesota.

Frances Hagopian is associate professor of political science at Tufts University. She has taught at the Massachusetts Institute of Technology and Harvard University. Professor Hagopian's research has focused on Brazilian politics and democratization in Latin America. She is the author of *Traditional Politics and Regime Change in Brazil* (1996) and several articles on democratization in Brazil and South America which have appeared in such journals as *World Politics* and *Comparative Political Studies.*

Anita Isaacs is associate professor of political science at Haverford College in Pennsylvania and previously taught at Oxford University and New York University. She has served as program officer for the Ford Foundation and as a consultant to the Canadian International Development Research Centre (IDRC). Her publications include *The Politics of Military Rule and Transition in Ecuador* (1993); "Ecuador," in *Oxford Companion to World Politics* (1993); and "Problems of Democratic Consolidation in Ecuador," *Bulletin of Latin American Research* (1991). Dr. Isaacs holds a Ph.D. in politics from Oxford University.

Harvey F. Kline is the director of the Latin American Studies Program at the University of Alabama, where he is professor of political science. Previously he taught at the University of Massachusetts-Amherst and the Universidad de los Andes. Among his many publications are *Colombia: Portrait of Unity and Diversity* (1983); *The Coal of El Cerrejón: Dependent Bargaining and Colombian Policy Making* (1987); and *Colombia: Democracy under Assault* (1995). A Phi Beta Kappa graduate of the University of North Carolina, Dr. Kline received his Ph.D. from the University of Texas.

Bolívar Lamounier founded and was first director of the São Paulo Institute of Social, Economic, and Political Research (IDESP), where he remains a senior researcher. He was previously a member of the Brazilian Presidential Commission for Constitutional Studies (the Arinos Commission) and a member of the Academic Council of the Woodrow Wilson International Center for Scholars Latin American Program. Dr. Lamounier has written extensively on Brazilian and comparative politics for both academic and journalistic publications. He received his Ph.D. from the University of California, Los Angeles.

Abraham F. Lowenthal is president of the Pacific Council on International Policy and director of the Center for International Studies at the University of Southern California. From 1982 to 1992 he was the Inter-American Dialogue's founding executive director. He was previously the founding director of the Latin American Program at the Woodrow Wilson International Center for Scholars and director of studies at the Council on Foreign Relations. He is widely published.

Anthony P. Maingot is professor of sociology at Florida International University. He is founding editor of *Hemisphere Magazine,* the university's publication on Latin American and Caribbean studies. He has taught at Yale University and the University of the West Indies in Trinidad, has served as a member of the Constitutional Reform Commission of Trinidad from 1971 to 1974, and has worked at the RAND Corporation. His most recent book is *The United States and the Caribbean: Challenges of an Asymmetrical Relationship* (1994).

Richard L. Millett is senior research associate and director of the Washington-based National Linkages Program of the North-South Center. He is a specialist on civil-military relations, democratization, Central America, and Panama. Dr. Millett is also professor of history and chair of Latin American Studies at Southern Illinois University, and senior advisor on Latin America for political risk services and adjunct professor at the Defense Institute of Security Assistance Management.

Trevor Munroe is reader in government and politics at the University of the West Indies, Mona. A major leader in Jamaica's labor movement and a civic activist, Dr. Munroe was a Fulbright Fellow at Harvard University and has been widely published. He holds a doctorate from Oxford University where he attended as a Jamaican Rhodes Scholar.

Marifeli Pérez-Stable is associate professor of sociology at the State University of New York at Old Westbury and the author of *The Cuban Revolution: Origins, Course, and Legacy* (1993). Her research interests include origins of Latin American revolutions, development paths in the Spanish-speaking Caribbean, and the impact of U.S. intervention on national and state formation in the Caribbean and Central America. She is president of the Institute of Cuban Studies and vice-president of the Cuban Committee for Democracy.

Juan Rial is senior researcher at the *Peitho* Society for Political Analysis in Montevideo, Uruguay, and currently works as a consultant for electoral processes in Latin America and Africa. He has published extensively in his fields of expertise. He was one of the editors of *The Military and Democracy* (1990) and *Elecciones y democracia en América Latina* (1992).

Mark B. Rosenberg is acting dean of the College of Urban and Public Affairs at Florida International University. He was a Fulbright Research Scholar in Honduras and has written numerous articles and essays on Honduran affairs. He is currently completing a book on Honduran politics.

J. Mark Ruhl is Glenn and Mary Todd Professor of Political Science and chair of the department of political science at Dickinson College in Carlisle, Pennsylvania. He has written extensively on political and economic change in Honduras and has published *Colombia: Armed Forces and Society* and *Party Politics and Elections in Latin America* (co-authored with R. H. McDonald).

Timothy R. Scully, C.S.C, is senior faculty fellow and associate professor of government and international studies at the University of Notre Dame, where he directs the Latin American Studies Program. He also serves as the university's vice-president and associate provost. Among his many publications are *Rethinking the Center: Party Politics in Nineteenth and Twentieth Century Chile* (1992) and *Building Democratic Institutions: Party Systems in Latin America* (1995), which he co-authored and co-edited. Father Scully holds a Ph.D. from the University of California, Berkeley.

Rose J. Spalding is professor of political science at DePaul University, where she codirects the Latin American Studies Program. The editor of *The Political Economy of Revolutionary Nicaragua* (1987) and author of *Capitalists and Revolution in Nicaragua: Opposition and Accommodation, 1979–1993* (1994), Dr. Spalding is widely published. She received her Ph.D. from the University of North Carolina, Chapel Hill.

Susan Stokes is assistant professor of political science at the University of Chicago, where she concentrates on comparative politics and the political economy and development of Latin America. She previously taught at the University of Washington. Dr. Stokes is widely published and serves on the editorial board of *Politics and Society.* She holds a Ph.D. from Stanford University.

Edelberto Torres-Rivas is professor of social sciences in the graduate program on Central America at the University of Costa Rica and Professor Emeritus of the Facultad Latinoamericana de Ciencias Sociales (FLACSO), Ecuador. He works on the themes of violence and fear in authoritarian cultures. His most recent book is *History and Society in Central America.*

Deborah J. Yashar is assistant professor of government and of social sciences at Harvard University and a faculty associate of Harvard's Center for International Affairs. Dr. Yashar is the author of *Demanding Democracy: Reform and Reaction in Costa Rica and Guatemala* (forthcoming) and of a number of articles on democracy, representation, and protest in Latin America. She holds a Ph.D. from the University of California, Berkeley.

Acronyms and Abbreviations

General

CEPAL • Economic Commission for Latin America

EC • European Community

ECLA • Economic Commission for Latin America

ELG • export-led growth

FBIS • Foreign Broadcast Information Service

FDIC • Federal Deposit Insurance Corporation

GATT • General Agreement on Tariffs and Trade

GDP • gross domestic product

GNP • gross national product

ISI • import-substituting industrialization

LDCs • lesser developed countries

MDCs • more developed countries

MERCOSUL/R • Southern Cone Common Market

NAFTA • North American Free Trade Agreement

NGOs • nongovernmental organizations

OPEC • Organization of Petroleum Exporting Countries

PSOE • Socialist Workers Party of Spain

SOFRES • French polling association

VAT • value added tax

International Organizations

IDB • Inter-American Development Bank

IMF • International Monetary Fund

NACLA • North American Congress on Latin America

OAS • Organization of American States

UN • United Nations

UNDP • United Nations Development Program

USAID • United States Agency for International Development

Anglophone Caribbean

CARICOM • Caribbean Common Market

JCF • Jamaican Constabulary Force

OECS • Organization of Eastern Caribbean States

PNP • People's National Party (Jamaica)

Argentina

CGT • General Confederation of Labor

FG • Left-of-center political organization

FREPASO • Center-Left coalition

MID • Movement for Integration and Development

MODIN • Movement for National Dignity and Independence

PJ • Peronists

UCEDE • Union of the Democratic Center

UCR • Radical Civic Union

Bolivia

ADN • Democratic and Nationalist Action

AP • Patriotic Accord

CBN • Bolivian National Brewery

COB • Bolivian Worker Central

COMSUR • Mineral Company of the South

CONDEPA • Conscience of the Fatherland

COPAP • Political Council of the Patriotic Accord

ENAF • National Smelting Company

ENDE • National Electricity Company

ENFE • National Railroad Enterprises

ENTEL • National Telecom Enterprises

FELCN • Special Counternarcotics Force

LAB • National Airways

MBL • Free Bolivia Movement

MIR • Revolutionary Movement of the Left

MNR • National Revolutionary Movement

MRTK • Tupac Katari Revolutionary Movement

NPE • New Economic Policy

RTP • Popular Radio and Television

UCS • Solidarity Civic Union

YPFB • National Hydrocarbons Enterprises of Bolivia

Brazil

ARENA • National Renovating Alliance

"Diretas-Já" • Direct Elections Now campaign

IBOPE • Brazilian Institute of Public Opinion

IDESP • Institute of Social Economic and Political Research

MDB • Brazilian Democratic Movement

OAB • Brazilian Bar Association

PCB • Brazilian Communist Party

PDS • Democratic Social Party

PDT • Democratic Labor Party

PFL • Liberal Front Party

PMDB • Brazilian Democratic Movement Party

PMDB+PFL • Democratic Alliance

PRN • Party of National Renovation

PSDB • Brazilian Social Democratic Party

PT • Workers' Party

PTB • Brazilian Workers Party

Chile

CD • Concertation for Democracy

CODELCO • National Copper Corporation

MIDA • Communist Party

PPD • Party for Democracy

RN • National Renovation

UCC • Center-Center Union

UDI • Independent Democratic Union

Colombia

AD M-19 • Democratic Alliance M-19

ANAPO • National Popular Alliance

ANDI • National Association of Industrialists

ANIF • National Association of Financial Institutions

CAMACOL • Colombian Chamber of Construction

CGT • General Confederation of Labor

CRIC • Regional Indigenous Council of the Cauca

CSTC • Syndical Confederation of Workers of Colombia

CTC • Confederation of Colombian Workers

ELN • National Liberation Army

ELP • Popular Liberation Army

EPL • Popular Army of National Liberation

FARC • Armed Forces of the Colombian Revolution

FEDECAFE • National Federation of Coffee Growers

FEDEMETAL • Colombian Federation of Metallurgical Industries

FEDESARROLLO • Foundation for Higher Education and Development

FENALCO • National Federation of Merchants

M-19 • Nineteenth of April Movement; *see also* AD M-19

MSN • National Salvation Movement

NFD • New Democratic Force

PEPES • Persecuted by Pablo Escobar

SAC • Colombian Agricultural Society

UP • Patriotic Union

UTC • Union of Colombian Workers

Costa Rica

CBI • Caribbean Basin Initiative

OIJ • Judicial Police

PLN • National Liberation Party

PUSC • Social Christian Unity Party

TSE • Supreme Electoral Tribunal

Cuba

CCD • Cuban Committee for Democracy

CODEHU • Human Rights Organizations Coordinating Committee

PCC • Cuban Communist Party

Dominican Republic

PLD • Dominican Liberation Party

PRD • Dominican Revolutionary Party

PRI • Independent Revolutionary Party

PRSC • Social Christian Reformist Party

PUCMM • Pontifical Catholic University "Madre y Maestra"

Ecuador

CONAIE • National Confederation of Indigenous Nationalities of Ecuador

FUT • United Federation of Workers

PSC • Social Christian Party

PUR • United Republican Party

El Salvador

ABECAFE • Salvadoran Association of Coffee Cultivators and Exporters

ASCAFE • Salvadoran Coffee Association

ANSP • National Academy of Public Security

ARENA • Nationalist Republican Alliance

CD • Democratic Convergence

COPAZ • Commission for the Consolidation of Peace

FAES • Armed Forces of El Salvador

FMLN • Farabundo Martí National Liberation Front

FPL • Popular Liberation Forces

ILO • International Labor Organization

IUDOP • University Institute for Public Opinion

MAC • Christian Authentic Movement

MNR • National Revolutionary Movement

MSN • National Solidarity Movement

MU • Unity Movement

ONUSAL • United Nations Mission in El Salvador

PCN • Party of National Conciliation

PDC • Christian Democratic Party

PN • National Police

PNC • National Civilian Police

SIRES • applications for an identification card

TSE • Supreme Electoral Board

Guatemala

CACIF • Chambers of Commerce Industry and Finance

CERJ • Council of Ethnic Communities "We Are All Equal"

CONAVIGUA • National Steering Group of Guatemalan Widows

FDG • Guatemalan Republican Front

GAM • Mutual Help Group

INC • National Instance for Consensus

MLN • Movement of National Liberation

PID • Institutional Democratic Party

UCN • National Center Union

URNG • Guatemalan National Revolutionary Unity

Haiti

CEP • Provisional Electoral Commission

FNCD • National Front for Democratic Convergence

KID • Convention for Democratic Initiatives

KONAKOM • National Committee of the Congress of Democratic Movements

MOP • Organizing Movement of the Nation

OPL • Popular Organization Lavalas

PLB • Barye Workers Party

VSN • Volunteers for National Security

Honduras

BANFAA • Armed Forces Bank

CCIC • Chamber of Commerce and Industry of Cortes

DNI • National Investigative Directorate

FPM • Morazanista Patriotic Front

HONDUTEL • telecommunications monopoly

IPM • Military Pensions Institute

PDC • Christian Democratic Party

PINU • Innovation and Unity Party

PL • Liberal Party

PN • National Party

Mexico

AC • Civic Alliance

EZLN • Zapatista National Liberation Army

FDN • National Democratic Front

IFE • Federal Electoral Institute

ISI • import-substituting industrialization

IVA • value added tax

PAN • National Action Party

PARM • Authentic Party of the Mexican Revolution

PPC • Popular Christian Party

PPS • Popular Socialist Party

PRD • Democratic Revolutionary Party

PRI • Institutional Revolutionary Party

PRONASOL • National Solidarity Program

Nicaragua

AMNLAE • Nicaraguan Women's Association Luisa Amanda Espinosa

ATC • Farmworkers Association

COSEP • Superior Council of Private Enterprise

CST • Sandinista Workers Federation

EPS • Sandinista Popular Army

ESAF • Enhanced Structural Adjustment Facility

FISE • Emergency Social Investment Fund

FNT • National Workers' Front

FSLN • Sandinista Front for National Liberation

IEN • Institute of Nicaraguan Studies

MRS • Sandinista Renewal Movement

PALI • Authentic Liberal Party

PLC • Liberal Constitutionalist Party

PLI • Independent Liberal Party

PLIUN • Liberal Party for National Unity

PLN • National Liberal Party

UNAG • National Union of Farmers and Ranchers

UNO • National Opposition Union

Panama

ARI • Inter-Oceanic Regional Authority

FP • Public Force (national police)

MOLIRENA • National Liberal Republican Movement

PDF • Panamanian Defense Forces

PRD • Democratic Revolutionary Party

Paraguay

ANR • Colorado Party

EN • National Encounter

PLRA • Liberal Radical Authentic Party

Peru

APRA • American Popular Revolutionary Alliance

CCD • Democratic Constitutional Congress

FREDEMO • Democratic Front

IFI • International financial institutions

IU • United Left

PPC • Popular Christian Party

SIN • National Intelligence Service

Uruguay

FA • Broad Front

PIT-CNT • Interunion Workers Council–Workers National Caucus

Venezuela

AD • Social Democratic Party

Causa R • Cause R (a new unionist party)

CN • a personal vehicle for Rafael Caldera

CONINDUSTRIA • Council of Industrial Producers

CONSECOMERCIO • Council of Commercial Enterprises

COPEI • Christian Democratic Party

CTV • Venezuelan Workers Confederation

FEDECAMARAS • Federation of Chambers of Commerce and Production

MAS • a democratic party of the Left

MEP • People's Electoral Movement

RECADI • Foreign Exchange Agency

UNO • Ordíst National Union

URD • a personal vehicle for Jóvito Villalba

I

Introduction

Introduction: Constructing Democratic Governance

Abraham F. Lowenthal and Jorge I. Domínguez

Democratic political norms and procedures are increasingly common throughout Latin America and the Caribbean. But effective democratic governance—the daily practice of constitutional rule under law with stable political institutions that mediate among power contenders, restrain the dominant, and protect the weak—is far from consolidated; in many countries it is not even gaining strength. In fact, effective democratic governance has yet to be constructed in most countries of the region.

That mixed message is the main finding of this project on the state of democracy in the Americas in the mid-1990s. We aim neither to celebrate democracy's recent progress in the hemisphere nor to lament its continuing shortfalls. Rather we seek to analyze the sources of Latin America's current democratizing tendency as well as the remaining obstacles to democratic governance, to understand what has been achieved and how, and to illuminate what remains to be done.

In commissioning essays for what we hope will be a benchmark survey for the mid-1990s, we turned primarily to specialists on the politics of individual countries of Latin America and the Caribbean, often na-

This introduction draws on points made in various chapters of *Constructing Democratic Governance*. It also draws on a vast literature about democratic transitions, consolidation, and construction. We have been influenced by many other authors of whom we would cite the following, in alphabetical order, as particularly helpful: Giorgio Alberti, Nancy Bermeo, Catherine Conaghan, Robert Dahl, Larry Diamond, Jonathan Fox, Manuel Antonio Garretón, Jonathan Hartlyn, Samuel P. Huntington, Terry Karl, Juan Linz, Scott Mainwaring, Guillermo O'Donnell, Robert Putnam, Adam Przeworski, Karen Remmer, Aníbal Romero, Philippe Schmitter, Ben Ross Schneider, Alfred Stepan, J. Samuel Valenzuela, and Laurence Whitehead. We are especially grateful to Michael Shifter for his comments on this and several other chapters in this collection.

We would like to express our special appreciation to those at Harvard's Center for International Affairs and David Rockefeller Center of Latin American Studies and at the Center for International Studies of the University of Southern California who help us try to keep up, in both cases, with too many projects. We are also very grateful to all those mentioned in the Foreword by Peter Hakim and Michael Shifter.

tionals of these countries. In order to facilitate comparability, we asked the authors of country chapters to address a common set of issues. Among the topics we posed were the nature of the electoral process; the condition of parties and other political institutions; executive-legislative, civil-military, and church-state relations; the rule of law and the state of the judiciary; the roles of civic, professional, business, and labor organizations and of the media; the treatment of minorities and women; the impact of socioeconomic inequities; and the challenge (when relevant) of incorporating into politics those who until recently had employed violence to secure their objectives. We also asked contributors to highlight special issues salient in particular countries, such as the impact of ethnic movements, the narcotics trade, or gross corruption. No one chapter in this collection addresses all these questions in detail, but most of them take up many of the topics, with the result that the collection as a whole provides a nuanced set of appraisals.

To capture some of the important insights to be gained from cross-national analysis, we invited essays on central issues faced in several countries: the challenge for constructing democracy of incorporating the formerly extraconstitutional Left and the equally thorny task of taming the extraconstitutional Right; the difficulties of building effective democratic governance in fundamentally unjust societies; the issues posed by the growing and more active indigenous movements; and the tension between traditional power structures and the modern political forms they still sometimes dominate. Because our project permitted the exchange of drafts over many months, authors of these crosscutting chapters were able to draw on evidence from the country studies, and many of the authors of country studies, in turn, were able to incorporate insights from the topical essays into their final drafts; we believe these "conversations" among contributors have considerably enriched our efforts.

The positive side of our mixed message should not be underestimated or taken for granted. It is noteworthy that politics throughout Latin America and the Caribbean has moved unevenly but steadily toward electoral democracy. U.S. president George Bush surely overstated matters in 1992 when he proclaimed the western hemisphere, apart from Cuba, as the "first completely democratic hemisphere in human history," and Clinton administration officials engaged in similar hyperbole at the December 1994 Miami summit of democratically elected heads of governments. But, such flights of politically motivated rhetoric aside, it is undeniable that one Latin American nation after another has moved from authoritarian rule toward democratic politics.

In 1975 only two countries in all of South America had elected presidents, while Central America was still governed by praetorian dictators in every nation but Costa Rica. Since that time, governments of force have almost everywhere given way to regimes chosen in national elections, most of them reasonably free and fair, and the elected authorities have almost without exception served out their constitutionally stipulated terms. Whenever an internal attempt has been made to overthrow an elected government during the past decade, the attempted coup has been put down immediately or soon thereafter reversed. In the more ambiguous case of Peru, where an elected government itself closed down democratic institutions to rule by decree, internal and external pressures combined to produce a gradual restoration of democratic legitimacy; a similar *autogolpe* (auto-coup) in Guatemala was reversed even more quickly.

Acting through the regional organization the Organization of American States, Latin American governments have reduced strict doctrinal adherence to the norm of nonintervention in order to make a meaningful regional commitment to collective action in defense of democracy. The internationally endorsed multilateral effort to restore President Jean-Bertrand Aristide to office in Haiti was a stunning display of the new regional consensus. If Cuba's personal autocracy still persists in the mid-1990s, it is ever more conspicuous as an anachronistic exception. And even Cuba has undertaken some political reforms in a democratic direction, albeit modest ones.

The core democratic idea—that, to be legitimate, government authority must derive from periodic free, fair, broadly participatory, and genuinely contested elections—has gained broad acceptance throughout the Americas. Both elites and masses from many different perspectives and ideological backgrounds have come to support the fundamental democratic notion of popular sovereignty as well as the understanding that, for democratic elections to be legitimate, there must be freedom of opinion and of association and a free press to which all competitors have access. People from across the political spectrum—military officers and former guerrillas, peasants and industrial workers, intellectuals and industrialists—agree on the desirability and feasibility of democratic governance.

It was not always thus. Just thirty years ago, even twenty-five years ago, vanguards on the Left and guardians on the Right openly proclaimed their disdain for democratic institutions, and each current had considerable support. It was often argued that cultural and religious traditions predisposed Latin Americans toward authoritarian rule and that democracy was a foreign transplant, bound to be rejected by the body politic.

Throughout the chapters of this collection, there is ample evidence that Latin Americans today want democratic governance and are trying to build it. Perhaps the most dramatic illustration of this transformation came in Chile and Nicaragua, where entrenched rulers let power be taken from them as a result of internationally observed elections they certainly could have prevented. But less dramatic examples abound. The presidency has been turned over from incumbents to oppositions in numerous countries. Where that has not yet occurred, it has become imaginable. Elected civilian presidents have survived military coup attempts in half a dozen nations during the past few years. And military coups have become unlikely in several other countries where it was still a ready option, frequently invoked, just a generation ago. Even in Central America, where military officers have for so long dominated politics, the growth of civilian institutions is clearly taking place.

All this is true and important. Latin America's broad and forceful transition toward democratic governance is a paradigm shift of historic dimensions. Whatever the shortfalls of performance or the detours and reversals along the way, these chapters emphasize the significance of Latin America's turn toward democracy. That this turn has occurred and been sustained during a period of major economic stress and structural change is all the more impressive.

But what is equally evident in these chapters and just as significant is that holding fair elections and avoiding successful coups are not by themselves sufficient to produce effective and enduring democratic governance. Effective democratic governance requires not only that the governing authorities be freely and fairly elected but that the public share the expectation that the rulers will remain subject to periodic popular review and that they can be replaced through equally fair elections. It also implies that executive authority is otherwise constrained and held accountable by law, by an independent and autonomous judiciary, and by additional countervailing powers.

Effective democratic governance involves clear and consistent subordination of the military and the police to civilian political institutions, especially parties, that are autonomous, stable, and powerful enough to express and aggregate social interests and also to constrain self-aggrandizing power grabs by the executive. It implies the organizations and procedures of civil society, of intermediary institutions engaging in the interests and values of diverse individuals and groups. Yet for democratic governance to work well, government officials must also have enough authority and legitimacy to take and implement decisions that are intended to privilege public and national interests over those of sectors, classes, regions, or private actors. The tension between effective authority and accountability is built into democratic governance and provides a constant challenge, even in those societies where democracy has been most fully achieved.

These chapters suggest that it is premature and indeed misleading to talk about "consolidating" democratic governance in Latin America and the Caribbean. Electoral procedures are being institutionalized in a number of countries, to be sure, but all too often these coexist with pervasive clientelism, imbedded injustice, massive corruption, flagrant impunity, and reserved domains beyond the authority of government or the rule of law. Throughout much of the region, the frustrations in advancing effective democratic governance have at times shaken Latin Americans' confidence in and commitment to democracy itself.

In most nations, effective democratic governance is still incipient, inchoate, fragile, highly uneven, incomplete, and often contradicted. Democratic governance in Latin America needs to be nurtured, constructed, and reinforced, bit by bit and country by country. In their assessment of Latin America's progress toward democracy, these essays underline that a great deal remains to be accomplished.

How hard it is to build effective and enduring democratic governance is highlighted by considering the United States, the hemisphere's most established democracy. Effective democratic governance in the United States has been deteriorating in recent years with the marked decline in public respect for parties and virtually all other political institutions; the deep rejection of professional politicians and incumbents; the decline of interconnectedness among citizens in the communities where they live; growing struggle over identity, culture, and values that cannot be resolved by compromises over "more or less"; consistently high levels of violent crime; the privatization of security and the use of deadly force; and an erosion of confidence in law, courts, and access to equal justice. Any inclination to think that democracy in the western hemisphere is close to being consolidated must be challenged throughout the Americas, North and South.

This is not the place for extended comments on what can be done to strengthen the prospects of constructing democratic governance.[1] But one strong implication of these essays is that we should rethink the sharply dichotomous categorization of "democracies" and "non-democracies." The tendency to think about democracy in "on-off" terms focuses too much international policy attention on holding and monitoring elections and on preventing or reversing coups. Elections and attempted coups are clearly defined moments of decision, and the steady reinforcement of international norms in favor of free elections and against coups has certainly been important in making democratic governance possible.

But effective democratic governance depends fundamentally on the quotidian building, exercise, and maintenance of democratic political

1. We have dealt with this issue in an Inter-American Dialogue Policy Brief, *The Challenges of Democratic Governance in Latin America and the Caribbean: Sounding the Alarm,* and the Dialogue has recently published an entire volume on international efforts to promote Latin American democracy: Tom Farer, ed., *Beyond Sovereignty: Collectively Defending Democracy in the Americas* (Baltimore: Johns Hopkins University Press, 1996).

practice. The most urgent and important task today is to help make democracy in the Americas work day to day: to maintain order peacefully with the consent of the governed, to represent the interests of all citizens fairly and effectively, and to extend the rule of law to all corners and all issues in the hemisphere. These are the challenges all true democrats must confront.

II

Themes and Issues

1

Incorporating the Left into Democratic Politics

Alan Angell

> Historically the Left . . . has always presumed the existence of an objective,
> a program, an organized force capable of carrying out that program, and a
> theory that explained the logic of the system. The program may have been
> improvised, the objective unreal, and the organized force nothing of the
> kind, but this was how the Left thought about change, at least how it legiti-
> mized its activities. All this is now open to question.[1]

This quotation from José Aricó well captures the ideological dilemma
that faces the Left in Latin America since the collapse of international
communism in the late 1980s. The Latin American Left always sought
legitimation in an appeal to a broader context than the purely national
one. This was partly the heritage of a Left that was firmly rooted in
Marxism as its ideological model and Leninism as its political practice.
It is difficult, for example, to explain the important political role of
communist parties in Latin America, in spite of their limited popularity, and even more limited success as promoters of revolution, unless
this international and ideological dimension is taken into account.
Communist parties in Latin America were seen as the direct representatives of an international movement of world revolution, giving them
an importance beyond their specific electoral appeal or political power.
It is true, of course, that the impact of the Cuban Revolution on the
Latin American Left was shattering, not least on those orthodox communist parties that claimed a monopoly of the truth. But in a sense
what happened was that the center of the Latin American Left was
transferred from Moscow to Havana, and Marxism became combined
with a kind of revolutionary voluntarism rather than with strict Leninism. The Latin American Left still had its international reference point
and its revolutionary orthodoxy.

The collapse of international communism profoundly changed the
Latin American Left. The significance of what happened after the revolutions of 1989 in Eastern Europe was as important for the Latin American Left as the Bolshevik revolution of 1917. No longer could the Left
claim a special significance as part of an international movement. No
longer could the Left appeal to a particular ideology as containing the
inevitable laws of historical development. With the collapse of inter-

national communism, the Left lost the mobilizing vision of a socialist society to be achieved by revolution. In the words of Jorge Castañeda, the idea of revolution became not simply unimaginable but even undesirable.[2]

The Left in Latin America now found itself facing a newly defined political context that was national rather than international. This might be seen as an advantage. The Left would no longer have to justify or excuse the undemocratic practices of the Communist bloc.[3] It no longer had to defend regimes that offended liberal democratic beliefs. The Left no longer had to face the same degree of hostility from the United States. It could begin to free itself from the charge that the Left in power will automatically degenerate into authoritarianism.

But no movement changes completely overnight in response to external events. The Left in Latin America did not suddenly become social democratic. Old practices persisted, not least that of an elitist Leninism still practicing a style of party government that was far from democratic and participatory. The far Left saw in the collapse of communism not the result of an excess of Marxist practice but, on the contrary, a lack of it. There are still practitioners of revolutionary violence. There are still adherents of a state-centered doctrine of economic planning.

These groups might be seen as remnants of the past fighting a rearguard action against the social democratic modernizers. This interpretation would be more plausible if the modernizers had a clear ideological program and widespread support. But the prevailing ideological climate in Latin America is not favorable to the Left, in whatever form. In the first place, the prevailing economic doctrine of the free market runs counter to the idea of central state planning, which has dominated the thinking of the Left since its inception. If the idea of state planning is discredited, then the Left has somehow to make its long-term objectives compatible with a free market system. But in practice the Left has little credible alternative to offer to the casualties of the economic adjustment packages that had in many cases stabilized national economies, though at great social cost. Second, the Left still faces the electoral dilemma that had haunted its history: how can it move outside its core of organized labor and leftist intellectuals to reach social sectors previously indifferent to its message, but necessary for any prospect of electoral success? Third, given the dismal record of the Left in power—for whatever reasons, the economic performance of Allende's Chile, Castro's Cuba, or Sandinista Nicaragua was not inspiring—how can the Left establish credibility as competent administrators?

The perplexity of the Left in facing this conjuncture is well expressed in this statement by José Pasos, deputy chief of the FSLN's (Sandinista Front for National Liberation) international department, after the Sandinista defeat in 1990.

We have to become a modern party. There are some principles that don't change: political pluralism, non-alignment, mixed economy. Our anti-imperialism stays the same, but it is not the anti-imperialism of Marx or Lenin. For us, it means non-interference in our internal affairs and it's the United States that interferes. We continue to believe in socialism as the goal. But it's definitely not the socialism that has come up in the East, nor the socialism of Cuba, nor perestroika. Perhaps the most acceptable for us would be Swedish socialism, but it's very expensive. What kind of socialism a poor country can have is a discussion that we're now going to begin. (*Guardian* [London], April 30, 1990, interview)

The previous models of socialism widely prevalent in Latin America have lost their appeal, and there is little consensus on a new model. There is a problem of defining the aims of the Left in the new order.

There is also a problem of defining the means by which the Left can effectively gain power. How can the Left mobilize the poor effectively? What strategy of alliances should it pursue to win power in a way that still leaves intact some identifiable socialist project? How can the Left relate to the social movements of Latin America without arousing suspicion of political manipulation by the Left?

There is, in addition, the issue of the appropriate form of organization for mobilizing support for the Left. There are serious questions about whether this can be done simply by continuing with the same kind of party organization and structure as in the past, not least because of the need to respond to changes in social structure which have weakened the traditional base of the Left, namely, the dramatic reduction in the power and influence of the trade union movement in countries as diverse as Bolivia and Argentina, for example.

The Shadow of the Past

The present crisis has to be seen in the context of the historical development of the Left in Latin America. What were the weaknesses of the Left, and which of those weaknesses survive to the present? What were the strengths of the Left, and which of those strengths survive?

The Left historically has been characterized by deep and bitter divisions and has rarely, if ever, been united. In most countries one should talk not of the Left, but of the Left*s*. The most public manifestations of disunity were differences, often bitter and violent ones about ideology and strategy, about who could legitimately be included as being "on the Left."[4] There is less fundamental disagreement today about ideologies: battles between orthodox communists, Trotskyists, and Maoists are increasingly irrelevant. There is more agreement today on the need for unity and consensus on the Left, for building wider coalitions, and for working with other parties. In some countries, notably Chile, this tactic has been pursued with some success by one part of the Left, namely, the socialist parties, but was opposed with catastrophic effects on its own following by the other part, the communist movement. In most countries, however, the unity of the Left is, if not so far away as it was in the days of heated ideological debate, still an objective to be achieved rather than something attained.

However, the disunity of the Left has never been a function of purely doctrinal issues. The Left in most countries is best seen as a combination of a variety of parties, social movements, and ideologies, and these three elements do not necessarily overlap nor agree. The ideology of the Left, of Marxism, has always been much more influential than the organized parties of the Left, and often the adherents of the doctrine were among the strongest critics of the leftist parties.[5] The real influence of Marxism in Latin America was felt not so much through the parties of the Left, but at the level of ideology and as a stimulus to political mobilization and action, not least in the trade union movement and among students and intellectuals, including, from the 1960s, radical Catholics.

The problem that faces the current Left is precisely how to regain that sense of ideological commitment, and how it can do so to rival the enhanced ideological commitment and appeal of the Right with its doctrine of the free market.[6] One of the major strengths of the Left was precisely its firm belief in the validity of its ideas. In order to recover that strength, the Left needs to develop ideas appropriate to the era of post-Marxism—and that is a challenge that faces the Left worldwide, not just in Latin America. The Left can no longer behave as if the logic of historical development is on its side.

To talk of redefining ideologies, of devising policies, and of making tactical alliances implies a Left structured around political parties and associated organizations such as trade unions. Yet this pattern of political organization applies to relatively few countries, notably to Chile and Uruguay, and (to a lesser extent since 1989) to Venezuela. But in other countries, the Left is relatively diffuse, similar to the Mexican Left which encompasses a large number of parties, political groups, labor unions, organized popular movements, and mass publications that continually fluctuate in both form and composition. Such dispersion can be a source of strength, if there is a broadly unifying party or movement (such as the PT [Workers' Party] in Brazil and, more questionably, the PRD [Democratic Revolutionary Party] in Mexico). But if this unifying factor does not exist, then such dispersion can be a source of weakness (as in Peru or Bolivia).

Historically, the Left sought its base in the union movement which, in its turn, sought to act as representative of the urban, if not the rural, poor. But the recent period has seen the decline of unions in general, and those that remain powerful are in the public sector and do not always enjoy broad social support for their demands. There has also occurred the growth of community-based organizations, often suspicious of manipulation by political parties, including those of the Left. These grass-roots movements express powerful demands for citizenship rights; they draw some inspiration from radical Catholicism; and they incorporate groups that had not been politically active in the past, especially women and the unemployed. Their demands are rarely political in the first instance, but when the political environment is unresponsive or even hostile, then a general demand for democracy is inevitably linked to their specific aims. Popular movements tend to be of protest and opposition. They flourished when military dictatorships limited political participation. They created a powerful opposition consciousness, with a strongly corporatist element: they believe in the state and not in the market.

These so-called new social movements are not always hostile to parties. In Brazil the role of the Left, especially the PT, in the neighborhood organizations is important. The PT helped these organizations transcend their immediate material perspectives, fostered coordination on a broader scale, and raised general political issues. But in other countries these social movements can, and often do, express an explicit rejection of, or disillusionment with, political parties. In Peru, areas where the Left and APRA (American Popular Revolutionary Alliance) had been traditionally strong voted in 1990 for the politically unknown Fujimori as president and for his untried party, Cambio 90. Fujimori received 40 percent of his total Lima vote from the twelve poorest districts, far exceeding the vote for the left-wing coalition, the Izquierda Unida (United Left).[7]

The electoral challenge to the Left from these movements is formidable for these populist figures are often capable of winning considerable support from the urban or rural poor. In societies where class structures are less firm, and certainly less institutionally expressed through class-based organizations, the Left faces a strong challenge. What can it offer to the urban poor that is more attractive than the promises of an effective populist politician? One partial answer at least is that of efficient local government, and this is an area where the Left is trying to establish a distinctive profile to contrast with the clientelism and corruption that are held to be characteristic of local government generally in Latin America.[8]

The problem that the Left has faced in mobilizing the poor of the shantytowns is part of a broader problem that has faced and still faces the Left in Latin America, that is, the electoral and popular challenge of the populist parties. The political space traditionally occupied in Europe by social democracy was occupied in Latin America by nationalist populist parties. These parties were never constrained by ideological orthodoxy and in the past drew heavily upon the ideas and practices of the Left. A crucial and continuous political problem for the Left was, and in many ways still is, the nature of its relationship with such parties of greater ideological flexibility, greater political appeal, and broader social support.[9] The Colombian Left has never been able to establish a continuing electoral presence outside an alliance with the Liberal party, in part a consequence of the Colombian electoral system which penalizes small independent parties. One of the reasons why sectors of the Colombian Left have preferred violent tactics has been the overwhelming political weight of the two traditional parties.

However, populism in Latin America has recently emphasized its hostility to political parties as such. This has been manifested not only at the national level by leaders such as Fujimori in Peru or Caldera in Venezuela, but also at the local level where a number of mayors of major cities have been elected on antiparty tickets. This presents real problems for the Left. Not only does it have to combat the appeal of genuinely popular leaders, but it also has to combat a widespread indifference to, or even rejection of, the political party as such.

One of the most enduring divisions of the Left in Latin America has been over the justification of the use of violence to achieve political objectives, a tactic that was given an enormous boost by the Cuban Revolution. The election of Allende in Chile was an equally dramatic moment for the Left and seemed to legitimate the peaceful road to socialism. This was the first experiment in trying to create a socialist society through peaceful, constitutional means and posed a question of universal relevance for the Left: could there be a peaceful transition to socialism in a pluralistic and democratic society? This was no imposition from above of a rigid revolutionary dogma, but a pluralist and democratic government attempting to win popular support for the most part by argument and persuasion.

With the coup of 1973, however, other questions were posed: what could the Latin American Left learn from the mistakes of the Chilean Left? How could the Left anywhere hope to attain power in the face of opposition from the national and international Right? The effect of the failure of the Unidad Popular (Popular Unity) government was to polarize the Left in Latin America. The more radical groups, such as the Sandinistas in Nicaragua and pro-Cuban groups elsewhere, resolved to intensify armed conflict. Their argument was that the coup showed that a peaceful road to socialism was simply an illusion. The far Left argued that in face of the opposition of the Right, the military, and the United States, armed revolution was the only hope of achieving power.

If one response of the Left to the coup was to advocate the need for violence, another response was diametrically opposite—arguing that the Left should now moderate its policies and actions so that the conditions that gave rise to coups would not occur. The revisionists argued that the Left should stop visualizing power exclusively in terms of force, as something to be physically possessed. The Left should stop concentrating on property relations to the exclusion of other factors: a simple transference of ownership to the state would not solve anything and could indeed create more problems than it resolved. The military could not be defeated by force. A radical government had to achieve such widespread legitimacy that the conditions that gave rise to military intervention—social disorder, political conflict outside the parliamentary and electoral arenas—did not occur. That meant concessions to the Right and a determined effort to win the support of the middle classes and to achieve a working relationship with the business sectors. Political alliances were seen as necessary, and democracy was seen as a value in its own right.

In a way the modern debate on the Left in Latin America began with the Chilean coup and is not yet concluded. Some parties of the Left, not least the Chilean Socialist party, can be placed firmly in the camp of the revisionists. But other movements of the Left, notably guerrilla groups in Colombia and Peru, still pursue the armed struggle. Yet others, such as the Sandinistas in Nicaragua or the former guerrilla groups in El Salvador, are making an uneasy transition from armed movement to political party.

This debate was conducted largely clandestinely or in exile for much of the 1970s and 1980s as the Left was a passive witness to forces that it could barely influence. Military authoritarian governments brutally attacked the Left. Parties and unions were suppressed, and many leaders were killed or exiled. Intellectual debate was stifled. The period of authoritarianism saw changes in society and the economy that were unfavorable to the Left: the growth of informal as opposed to formal employment, the emergence of free market economics as the dominant mode, the reduction in the size of the state. These trends continued into the period of transitions to democracy. And, if this state of organizational weakness and ideological uncertainty was not enough, then to the misfortunes of the Left was added the collapse of international communism.

The Latin American Left in the 1990s

It should be clear from the analysis so far that, in common with many other parts of the world, the Left in Latin America in the 1990s faced multiple challenges, and faced them from a position of organizational weakness, ideological uncertainty, and minority electoral support. Yet the Left in some countries had strengths that it could draw upon. The Left had opposed, often with great courage, the authoritarian governments of the 1970s and 1980s and could claim a greater democratic credibility than the movements of the Right. The Left in some countries, notably Brazil, organized the new movements in the unions and neighborhoods and acted as the representative of the poor. In others, the Left had a tradition of organization and had created a subculture of socialism that resisted the drift to the Right. There are also the seeds of future growth of the Left in the twin failures of many of the restored democracies of Latin America: the failure to create adequate safety nets to deal with the social costs of the economic adjustment programs and the failure to halt the corruption of the governing elites. The Left owes its origins to protest above all, and given the social condition of the poor in Latin America, there is still a great deal to protest about.

How far can we identify general trends? How far can we say that the Left in Latin America unambiguously accepts democracy? How far is the Left a serious political force in Latin America? The answers to these questions are not easy, and to some extent national diversity is greater now, in the postcommunist era, than in the past. If there are no completely uniform trends, it is still possible to make some distinctions that are broader than the national level.

There is a strong social democratic Left in a number of countries. In these countries—Chile, Venezuela, Uruguay, Brazil, Mexico are the leading examples—there are parties firmly committed to the democratic system, and with significant electoral support. They each have a popular leader, though not policies for dealing with economic and social issues which are substantially different from the predominant free market ones.

In other countries, notably those of Central America and Colombia, there is a Left emerging from the guerrilla experience, forced by a mixture of necessity and rethinking to accept the rules of competitive party politics. The commitment of these movements is much more conditional, and they contain within them groups that prefer the armed method of seizing power.

Yet there still exists an active tradition of leftist insurgency. This is most sharply present in Peru with the Maoist-inspired Sendero Luminoso movement. It is true that this movement has suffered a sharp reversal of its power with the arrest of its leader, Abimael Guzman. But it is equally characteristic of such movements that they can appear suddenly and with little advance warning, as happened with the Zapatista movement in Chiapas in Mexico.

Other countries are characterized by the eclipse of the Left and its electoral and political insignificance. Peronism in Argentina has turned its back upon its leftist past and has created a vacuum on the Left. In Bolivia, a once powerful leftist movement based on the unions, above all the mining unions, has collapsed as the unions have been decimated.

The political influence of the Left in any country will be at maximum when four factors coincide and reinforce each other: a united party, widely based social support, ideas that are seen as relevant and credible, and a popular leader. These factors rarely coincide in this neat fashion, but some Latin American countries combine them, notably those where political parties are reasonably well structured and where, arguably, there is a social democratic tradition of some weight. In these countries it can be argued that the commitment of the Left to electoral politics is not just a matter of expediency but of principle. Indeed, perhaps it is given that if the violent road is ruled out for a variety of reasons, then the only alternative open to the Left is through the maximization of electoral gains. It could also be argued for these countries that the incorporation of the Left into democratic and constitutional politics is less problematic and less conditional than is that of the Right.

The Social Democratic Left

One response to the decline of orthodox communism, and the increasing unattractiveness of the Cuban model—and in contrast to the violence associated with the guerrilla movements of countries such as Peru, Colombia, and El Salvador—was a renewal of interest in socialism of an essentially parliamentary and electoral form. The reaction to years of military dictatorship, and the suppression of basic freedoms of the Left, was a much more positive evaluation of the benefits of formal democracy. The growth of social democratic movements in Europe, notably the Spanish socialist party of Felipe González, provided a source of inspiration. The work of the Socialist International in Latin America provided international links, further encouragement, and some financial assistance. Closer analysis of the social structure of Latin America led the more moderate Left to realize the importance of appealing to the middle classes and to the growing popular organizations that were not trade unions, nor expressions of class struggle, and that owed more to church-inspired institutions than to the Marxist Left.

These parties in the 1990s advocated a number of policies very different from those of previous decades. Instead of the centralized state, they advocated decentralization and participation of the community in local decision making. Instead of a Leninist model of internal party government, they emphasized inner party democracy and positive discrimination for women. Instead of concentrating power in the executive, they emphasized the need for checks and balances and turned their attention to issues such as an independent judiciary and an independent central bank. They sought to establish their credentials by efficient administration of the local governments they controlled. They emphasized that, against the corruption that had emerged so much into the open with the return to democracy, they would be, by contrast, honest and accountable if elected. What is happening in practice falls short of the rhetoric, but there are countries where the Left is trying to present itself, with some success, as a modern, capable, and incorrupt political force.

The countries where the social democratic model of the Left prevails have a number of features in common. They are all countries with relatively strong institutional frameworks, and with reasonably developed party systems. These systems have allowed the Left to develop as an institutional force and to learn the rules of political competition and party behavior. They are all countries with relatively modern economic and social structures, providing a social base for the Left to develop electoral and political support. Though all countries have seen periods of repression—indeed of intense repression in some cases—it has not been continuous, nor has it been the norm. And, in all of them, the ideas of socialism and Marxism have been vigorous and widespread.

The Chilean Socialist party, though always containing a variety of ideological factions, had moved to the left during the 1960s, partly under the influence of the Cuban Revolution. During the Popular Unity government, it was more radical than the Communist party and supported worker and peasant takeovers of factories and farms. It was savagely repressed after the 1973 coup, and most of the leadership of the party was forced into exile, where the party divided into a moderate wing and a Marxist-Leninist wing. This difference partly reflected the experience of exile. Those exiled in France, Italy, or the Scandinavian countries were influenced by the changes taking place in European social democracy, and they came eventually to dominate the whole party. The party was forced to a profound reconsideration of the meaning of democracy.[10]

The Chilean socialists embraced a political alliance with the Christian Democrats in opposition to Pinochet in the plebiscite in 1988. After the elections of 1989 they entered the government coalition. They shed the dogmas of the past and embraced the market and modernization of the economy with even greater enthusiasm than the Christian Democrats. Both entrepreneurs and the military found the newly fashioned socialists more congenial politically than the Christian Democrats. The socialists are divided into two parties, but this enhances rather than diminishes their appeal. The Socialist party appeals to the traditional subculture of socialism in Chile, based on the trade union and the local party. The Party for Democracy (PPD), founded to fight the 1988 plebiscite, appeals to the less ideological sector of the electorate, to a wide spectrum of middle-class urban groups, and gains support through the leadership of the socialist politician most credible as a future president, Ricardo Lagos. In the 1993 elections the socialists combined gained just under 24 percent of the vote. What the Chilean socialists have done, and done very effectively, has been to establish themselves as efficient administrators, as a party of government and not just of opposition.

The Venezuelan Movimiento al Socialismo (MAS, Movement to Socialism) was formed in 1971 by dissident members of the Communist party, and many of them had participated in the 1960s guerrilla movement. Though the party has rarely gained more than 5 percent of the vote, its importance in the political system has been greater than that figure would suggest, for the ideas it has disseminated have been influential, and it helped to consolidate democracy in Venezuela by lending its support to the system established in 1958. The MAS was influenced by the experience of the Italian Communist party and by the Eurocommunist movement. It emphasized that there must be individual and national roads to socialism and rejected the idea that there was one correct model. It was critical of the Leninist style of party organization and argued for a participatory party structure. It criticized the Communist party for underestimating the role and importance of the middle classes in the Venezuelan political system. Although many of the members of the MAS came from the Communist party and the far Left, the party committed itself to democracy, both for the country and in its own internal structure. The MAS emphasized the need for honesty and accountability in public life, and sought to present itself as the true representative of the values that the major parties—AD (Acción Democrática [Democratic Action]) and COPEI (Comité de Organización Política Electoral Independiente [Committee for Independent Electoral Politics])—had once embodied but had compromised in the struggle for political power.

In the 1988 elections, running in alliance with another left-wing party, the MAS won 10.2 percent of the vote, and in the first direct elections for state governors held in 1989, it took the industrial state of Aragua and came second to AD in several others. But the MAS suffered from its lack of a popular and union base, and its decision to support Caldera in the 1993 presidential election was seen by many as succumbing to the temptation to gain power at the cost of principle. It has been challenged on the left by Causa R, a trade union–based party from the provinces. Causa R takes as its model the Brazilian PT. It has established a powerful presence in the union movement, achieved popularity as an efficient and honest government of the state of Bolívar, and has an attractive leader in the trade unionist and governor of the state of Bolívar, Andrés Velásquez. Causa R gained 20.5 percent of the vote in the 1993 congressional elections compared with 28.2 percent for AD, 28.6 percent for COPEI, 12.8 percent for the MAS, and 11.8 percent for the coalition supporting Caldera.[11]

The Venezuelan Left has not established credibility as a party of central government as in Chile. But it has done so at the local level. It emphasizes honest government in contrast to the rampant corruption of the major parties: it emphasizes participation in contrast to the elitism of the major parties. This appeal has prospered as the economy in Venezuela went into decline, as accusations of corruption multiplied, and as Causa R was able to break the stranglehold of AD in the trade union movement.

The Left in Uruguay was unusual in the way that it seemed less affected in its ideas and strategy by the long years of military dictatorship than the Left in Brazil or Chile. However, more than the other countries of the Southern Cone, the restoration of democracy in Uruguay was precisely that, a restoration of the previous system. In fact, the Left changed rather more than the two dominant parties in Uruguay, Colorado and Nacional. The Left made a strong showing in the 1971 elections when, organized as the Frente Amplio (FA, Broad Front), it won 18 percent of the vote. In the first elections following military rule in 1984, it won 21.3 percent of the vote and in 1989, 21.2 percent. But there were changes in the composition and politics of the FA.

In 1973 the main parties in the FA were the communist, the socialist, and the MLN (National Liberation Movement)-Tupamaros. By 1984 the vote going to the radical Left, the MLN, fell as a proportion of the total Left vote from 23 percent to 6.7 percent; to the Communists from 32.9 percent to 28.2 percent; while the major gainers were a new moderate Christian Democratic–inspired party, the Movimiento por el Gobierno del Pueblo (Movement for the People's Government), which won 39.3 percent of the FA's vote compared to the 10.3 percent that had gone to moderate parties in 1971. The FA was clearly less extreme than in 1971, and its commitment to electoral politics was firm. It lost the support of the most moderate group in 1989, which formed the Nuevo Espacio (New Space) party that took 9 percent of the popular vote, but its share of the vote remained constant. Moreover, the FA won a plurality in Montevideo, with 37 percent of the vote, and elected the mayor there.

The FA, as its name implies, is a broad coalition held together by the peculiarities of the Uruguayan electoral system, which encourages broad coalitions of many parties. It gained support partly because it was the only credible alternative to the traditional two-party dominance at a time when those parties were increasingly unpopular for their handling of the economy. The FA consolidated its hold on the Left by its opposition to the law that grants amnesty to military officers for human rights abuses. The FA benefited from the Uruguayan union system which, in contrast to most countries of Latin America, has a history of autonomous development unincorporated into the state machine and not colonized by one of the two major parties.[12] But the FA is weak outside Montevideo, where it gained only 9 percent of the vote, and unionized workers who vote heavily for it constitute only 19 percent of the adult population of Montevideo and are insignificant elsewhere. The exit from the FA of the moderate parties reduced its overall chance of electoral gains.[13] To some extent the FA's survival was testimony to the overall immobility of the Uruguayan political system rather than to the development of a new and innovative leftist movement.

Like Venezuela, the Left in Uruguay benefited from disenchantment with the two dominant parties, established a reputation for efficient local government, has a popular leader in the former mayor of Montevideo, Tavaré Vásquez, has significant support in the union movement, and also mobilized support around the human rights issue. In the 1994 elections the FA won 30 percent of the national vote, but what was impressive was that it made significant gains in the interior of the country as well as in Montevideo. It elected a new mayor of Montevideo, in part a vote of confidence in the record of the previous FA administration. Its overall national support is now more or less equal to those of the traditional parties, though like those two parties it also has divisions and factions. The FA's experience demonstrates the benefit the Left can derive from efficient local administration.

The most important development on the Left in Latin America came with the formation of the Brazilian Partido dos Trabalhadores (PT, Workers' Party). The PT grew out of the new unionism that developed in the massive metallurgical industries of the São Paulo region. By 1978, after a year of labor militancy, the new union leaders, especially Luis Inacio da Silva (Lula), came to believe that workplace militancy was inadequate to achieve their broader aims. In Lula's words:

> In my view the Brazilian left has made mistakes throughout its history precisely because it was unable to comprehend what was going on inside the workers' heads and upon that basis elaborate an original doctrine. . . . I do not deny that the PCB [Brazilian Communist Party] has been an influential force for many years. What I do deny is the justness of telling the workers that they have to be Communists. The only just course of action is to give the workers the opportunity to be whatever suits them best. We do not wish to impose doctrines. We want to develop a just doctrine which emanates from the organization of our workers and which at the same time is a result of our own organization.[14]

The PT has become the largest explicitly socialist party in Latin America. Its electoral support increased from 3 percent of the total vote in 1982 to 7 percent in 1986. In the 1988 elections for mayor, PT candidates took control of thirty-six cities, notably São Paulo, where the candidate was a woman migrant from the impoverished northeast, Luiza Erundina. The PT's vote overall in Brazil's one hundred largest cities was 28.8 percent of the total. Though the party had its roots in the urban union movement, it has also grown in the rural areas where it has the support of the radical Church and the local base communities. In the first round of the 1989 presidential elections, Lula, the PT candidate, won 16.08 percent of the vote, narrowly winning the second place over Brizola (PDT, Democratic Labor Party) with 15.74 percent. In the second round, Lula (37.86%) was defeated by Fernando Collor de Mello (42.75%), despite the party's having moderated its radical political platform in order to appeal to the Center—a tactic that almost worked. In the 1993 presidential elections, the PT was again the major challenger, and indeed for months was the frontrunner in the opinion polls. In the end it lost to the social democratic candidate, Fernando Henrique Cardoso, but increased its first ballot vote to 27 percent and gained a larger representation in Congress.

The PT also sought to adopt a new model of internal organization that would, unlike that of the PCB, respect the autonomy of the union movement. The party was not to lead the workers but to express their demands in the political sphere. The organization of the party emphasized participatory democracy. The core organization of the party would be the *núcleo de base*, composed of affiliated members from either a neighborhood, professional group or workplace, or social movement, and engaged in permanent political, rather than occasional electoral, activity. The party was meant to dissolve the differences that normally exist between social movement and party. If, in practice, many nuclei do function largely as electoral bodies, the level of participation of the estimated 600,000 members of the PT is still extraordinarily high by Brazilian party standards.

Such a participatory structure was very appropriate for the oppositional politics made necessary by the imposition of military rule. It is less clear that such a structure is functional for a competitive democracy. Many of the members and leaders of the party came from Catholic radicalism rather than Marxism, and they were more concerned to maintain the autonomy of union and popular organizations than they were to create a disciplined political party. There were many conflicts inside the PT, not least between the PT members of Congress and the party leaders outside Congress. The three Brazilian Trotskyist parties all worked within the PT, even though the largest of them, the Convergência Socialista (Socialist Convergence), conceives of the PT as a front to be radicalized under the direction of a revolutionary vanguard, combating in the PT the influence of the church and the parliamentary group.[15] Such a variety of political positions did not lead to party discipline, but the defeat of the Trotskyists in the 1991 Congress led to a more unified party.

The PT is undoubtedly novel, not just among the parties of Brazil but even among the socialist parties of Latin America. It is firmly rooted in the working class and controls some 60 percent of unions in the public sector, and only slightly fewer in the private sector. In Congress the PT is the party with the largest proportion of deputies linked to organized labor and social movements. It has tried to develop new policies and practices, for example, 30 percent of seats in the Central Committee of the party are to be held by women. But there are problems that it faces for further development.

The PT is an ideological party in a party system that is very un-ideological. It faces the challenge of other parties on the Left, notably the old radical populist party of Brizola, and the social democratic PSDB (Brazilian Social Democratic Party). It reaches out to the organized poor in town and countryside, but most poor Brazilians are neither members of unions nor of social organizations, and in 1989 these sectors voted more heavily for the right-wing Collor de Mello than for Lula. Like all parties of the Left, the PT has difficulties in proposing policy alternatives for dealing with the economic crisis which do not look either like the unsuccessful formulas of the past or simple imitations of the orthodox neoliberal policies. While the PT's attachment to a radical ideology helps to develop committed party members, that very commitment limits its ability to compete in the fluid and populist world of Brazilian party politics.

For all the differences between political systems, there are parallels in Chile, Venezuela, Uruguay, Brazil, and elsewhere in Latin America in the emergence of a socialism that stresses participation and democracy, rejects the past orthodoxy of one correct model, and is firmly based on national structures rather than international doctrines.

As usual in Latin America, it is difficult to fit Mexico into any comparative category, but with the 1988 presidential election, a new party of the Left did emerge to shake the political dominance of the PRI (Institutional Revolutionary Party). The political coalition put together to support the presidential candidature of Cárdenas was a heterogeneous coalition of dissident members of the PRI, the independent parties of the Left, and the satellite leftist parties that had traditionally revolved around the PRI (such as the PPS, Popular Socialist Party). In the 1988 elections it was the satellite Left that saw its vote sharply increase while that of the independent Left fell. Although normally these parties gained only a small vote—4.7 percent in 1979 and 2.96 percent in 1982—their vote rose to 21.04 percent in 1988 when they were supporting the candidature of Cárdenas in the FDN (National Democratic Front) coalition.

The attraction of this coalition was based on the popularity of its leader, Cuauhtémoc Cárdenas, the son of the reformist president, on its revolutionary nationalism, and on its being an effective vehicle for anti-PRI protest. The coalition emphasized political democracy and the autonomy of mass organizations, but its message was vague enough to create uncertainty as to whether it was simply the Left of the PRI or a genuinely new socialist departure. The coalition was a fragile combination of very disparate elements from the anti-Communist PARM (Authentic Party of the Mexican Revolution) to the Stalinist but opportunist PPS. It faced bitter opposition from the PRI because it competed directly for those groups and voters that have been the backbone of the PRI. It is also similar to the PRI in its rather undemocratic internal practices, and it suffers from continuous internal dissent and disagreement.

In March 1990 the renamed PRD (Partido Revolucionario Democrático [Democratic Revolutionary Party]) agreed to incorporate popular movements into the party, but the relationship between the party and the movements is by no means clear and is unlikely to parallel the close organic relationship between the social movements and the PT in Brazil. What is novel about the rise of *neocardenismo* for the Mexican Left is that it involves a repudiation of attempts to establish a clear separation between the socialist agenda and the ideology of the Mexican Revolution. The eternal dilemma for the Left in Mexico, and this applies to the PRD as well, is how to free the mass organizations such as the unions from control by the state, without looking as if they are just seeking to replace PRI control with their own.

Unlike the Brazilian PT, however, the Mexican PRD did badly in its second presidential campaign, coming a poor third in the contest. The history of the Left in Latin America is a constant story of advance and reversal, and in the case of Mexico reversals are usually greater than the advances. The PRD faced problems of lack of internal unity and, above all, lack of an alternative economic strategy.[16] Moreover, in an age when electioneering is increasingly dominated by television, the PRD's leader did not prove to be an effective media performer.

What explains the relative strength of the Left in the countries we have examined? In all cases, there was a tradition of leftist political activity on which to build. There was and is a trade union and popular movement influenced by socialism. In all these countries there is a competitive electoral system that does not discriminate blatantly against the Left (even in Mexico, the system did not disguise the support for Cárdenas in 1988, though it probably did diminish it). In all cases there is a relatively free and vigorous press that allows the Left to make its case. In all the countries (except Chile) there is opposition to the existing government for neglecting the suffering of the poor and for abuse of power. Popular feeling on these issues has translated into support for the Left. And, in the case of all the countries examined, the Left has shown, in central or local government, that it is capable of exercising power with restraint and efficiency. These conditions are not present in most of the other countries of Latin America.

The Insurgent Left

Very different from any other country in Latin America is Peru, with its Maoist-inspired Sendero Luminoso guerrilla movement. Sendero professes admiration for the ideas of Mao at the height of the cultural revolution, when some of the Sendero leadership had been present in China. It also drew on the *indigenista* ideas of Mariátegui. Its largely mestizo leadership is hostile to any grass-roots organization other than the party. It recreated the authoritarian structures of Andean society, replacing the rule of the landlords with that of the party. It is organized in a highly secretive cell structure, which is difficult to penetrate. It is extremely ruthless and violent and uses terror to impose its rule.

Sendero made a substantial shift in strategy in 1988, declaring that the cities were "necessary" rather than "secondary." Sendero gained some support in the urban shantytowns of Lima and in some industrial unions. The capacity of Sendero to wreak havoc on the fragile political system in Peru was not in doubt; but what is in doubt is whether the movement could do more than that. The capture of its leader, Guzmán, in 1993 is undoubtedly a setback for the movement, but such a powerfully organized clandestine movement is hardly likely to disappear unless the conditions that gave rise to it are addressed.

The growth of Sendero created problems for the mosaic of other parties—orthodox communist, Trotskyist, pro-Chinese, Castroite—that make up the Left in Peru. The story of the Left in Peru is a never-ending process of temporary and fragile unification followed by division. The Left did well in the 1978 elections for the Constituent Assembly, with 29.4 percent of the vote. But the withdrawal of the Trotskyists weakened the coalition, and there were five separate leftist slates competing in the 1980 elections with a combined vote of only 14.4 percent. Most groups on the Left combined to form the Izquierda Unida (IU, United Left) in 1980, and the Left vote rose to 29 percent in the Council elections of 1983, with the leader of the IU, Alfonso Barrantes, taking control of Lima with 36.5 percent of the vote.

Yet the Left was far from united. As mayor of Lima, Barrantes faced a spate of land invasions organized by the far Left within his coalition. This lack of unity led to a fall in the leftist vote to 21 percent in 1985, though it was still the second electoral force. But the divisions intensified, reflecting on the part of important elements of the IU coalition an ambiguous attitude toward democracy (shared, it should be said, by some groups on the Right and even by the APRA government). The issue of political violence remained a dividing line between those who wished to collaborate in the democratic process, for all its faults, and those who wished to bring it down and replace it with a different order. Barrantes was criticized by those who argued that the major focus of activity should be the streets and factories and not the Congress. The first national congress of the IU in January 1989 led to a decisive split as Barrantes took with him moderate delegates to form a rival coalition, the Izquierda Socialista (Socialist Left). The leftist vote in the council elections in 1989 collapsed to 11.5 percent, and the two leftist candidates contesting the presidential election in 1990 gained only 11 percent of the vote between them.[17] In the 1995 elections the Left was virtually eclipsed, as indeed were all the traditional political parties.

Any explanation of the peculiarities of the Left in Peru has to be rooted in the sharp economic decline in that country, arguably the worst in all of Latin America. More than 50 percent of Peruvians in Lima live in poverty, 10 percent in extreme poverty. Conditions are even worse in the countryside. Added to that is ethnic antagonism, a series of governments that since 1968 have made extravagant promises of reform exceeded only by the extravagance of their failures, persistent inflation developing into hyperinflation, and a left subculture in which the dominant ideology became Maoism. This combination of features is peculiar to Peru and accounts for the failure of Sendero to set off would-be imitators in other Latin American countries.

The political fortunes of any party in Peru—whether of the Right, the Center, or the Left—look bleak at present. It is not so much that the democratic Left is rejected in Peru, but that all forces of democracy are weak while the initiative lies with an authoritarian president who rejects parties as such.

The Left Lays Down Its Arms, Conditionally

The experience of the Left in the countries of Central America and Colombia has been rather different from that of the rest of Latin America. The Left in Central America really gained power only through force and still feels it needs arms to defend itself against possible future attacks from the Right. It is not entirely clear that it can evolve into some kind of social democracy. Its history has been marked by more prolonged and sustained repression than has occurred in other countries in Latin America.

The loss of the elections in 1990 faced the Sandinistas with the task of creating a political party in opposition. The Sandinistas were at core a vanguard party, and one that had held neither a congress nor conducted internal elections during its entire existence. While it had avoided many of the normal Leninist traits, it retained a strong *dirigiste* impetus, not least because its original guerrilla origins had been reinforced by the need to fight a war against the Contras. Defending a successful revolution against attack calls for characteristics very different from those of a party competing for power in competitive elections in a formally democratic system. As yet elements of both party and vanguard military force coexist uneasily in a political system that itself is far from seeing the end of violence used to advance political positions.

The same kinds of dilemmas face the insurgent movements in El Salvador. How do you move from guerrilla force to political party when you do not entirely trust the other forces to abandon the use of violence? How far will movements such as the FMLN (Farabundo Martí National Liberation Front) accept electoral results if they are unfavorable to them? How far will the ex-guerrilla movements resist the provocations of the Right? How far can movements like the FMLN, whose discipline has been enforced by military necessity, accept the kinds of internal disagreements that affect all political parties? The FMLN achieved a fairly remarkable set of agreements in the peace accords in

1992, demonstrating a high degree of political skill. But constructing a viable leftist party while simultaneously creating a viable democratic system and rebuilding a war-devastated economy are enormously formidable tasks.

There has been a notable change in the language of the leaders of the guerrillas. In the words of one of the leading Salvadoran guerrilla leaders, Joaquín Villalobos, "We Salvadorean revolutionaries at first were ideologically rigid, by necessity, in order to survive and develop. But later new conditions were created which offered the opportunity to develop our own thinking. The FMLN is proposing an open pluralist project, which will be pragmatically inserted in our domestic and geopolitical reality. What is fundamental is not its ideological definition but whether it resolves El Salvador's problems or not."[18] The question then remains, what if it does not solve El Salvador's problems? Although the FMLN did well in the 1994 elections, its candidate for the presidency, Rubén Zamora, gained only 24 percent of the vote in the first ballot and 32 percent in the second; and the FMLN has only twenty-one out of eighty-four congressional seats. It faces a formidable challenge not only to overcome the ascendancy of the Right, both politically and ideologically, but also to overcome its own internal divisions.

The Colombian Left has faced dilemmas similar to those of the Left in Central America. On what conditions do you lay down arms and at what cost? Like Peru, Colombia has its peculiarities that render comparisons difficult. Political violence has not been used only by the Left. On the contrary, the major parties, the Liberals and the Conservatives, have a much longer and more sustained tradition of political insurrection. The Left has, in a way, only conformed to one powerful tradition in a country where a weak state has been unable to control political insurgency.

The Colombian Communist party had a small guerrilla arm, the Fuerzas Armadas de la Revolución Colombiana (FARC, Armed Forces of the Colombian Revolution), though rather more as a result of conformity to political practice in the republic than an indication of a desire to seize state power. The FARC controlled some isolated rural municipalities, thus allowing the Communist party to claim that it was pursuing a revolutionary strategy while in practice finding that electoral politics was a more congenial occupation.[19] The participation of the FARC in the peace process in Colombia has been rather ambiguous because the dispersed organization of the group makes it difficult to impose any central direction. Guerrilla leaders may decide that the time has come to lay down arms, but they cannot guarantee that their commands will be followed locally.

The success of Castro set off many would-be imitators in Colombia. The Ejército Popular de Liberación Nacional (EPL, Popular Army of National Liberation) was a small Maoist group. The Ejército de Liberación Nacional (ELN, Army of National Liberation) was a Castroite group founded in Cuba in 1963–64 and advocated the *foco* approach of Che Guevara, but had more success and gained a considerable fortune by its attacks on internationally owned oil installations. If the motives for the violence of the traditional parties have been sometimes obscure, so it is for the guerrilla groups as well. In part, guerrilla violence has become a business in which the language may be that of a rather stale Marxism or Maoism, but the reality looks more like that of the Mafia.

The most important of the recent guerrilla groups to emerge in Colombia was the M-19, formed in 1970 in protest at alleged electoral fraud that prevented the former dictator, General Rojas Pinilla, from taking power. Such antecedents hardly qualify the M-19 to be counted as a leftist movement, and its program amounted to little more than a combination of vague nationalism and spectacular armed actions. The M-19 accepted participation in the peace process and gained considerable public support as a result, securing strong representation in the Constituent Assembly called to frame the Constitution of 1991. But as the M-19 showed itself to be little different in practice from the other parties, it lost its identity and suffered increasing electoral reversals. As Chernick and Jimenez write, the M-19's

> deep seated vanguardist and exclusionary sensibilities presented serious obstacles to the development of a strategy combining electoral coalitions with popular nonviolent mobilization in order to implement the historic leftist program of dismantling elite economic and political power. In the absence of a political party with an organizational base of support and participation, the ground swell of enthusiasm for the M-19 leading up to the constitutional assembly could thus prove as ephemeral as the vote for ANAPO [National Popular Alliance] in the presidential elections of April 19, 1970.[20]

Subsequent elections have borne out this prediction.

While a relatively weak Colombian state was unable to repress the guerrillas, they did not amount to a serious threat to the status quo— much less than the traditional parties did when they, too, entered the armed struggle to compete for power. The guerrillas undoubtedly gained some local support in certain areas, such as the banana zone of Uraba with its harsh labor regime, and Arauca where the newly found oil wealth brought few benefits to the poor. But support for the guerrillas remained local, their aims confused, their rivalry endemic, and their power infinitely inferior to the real threat to Colombian democracy that developed with the illegal drugs trade in the 1980s.

The conditions for the development of a successful social democratic Left in these countries looks more doubtful than for the countries examined in the first part of this section. The social base for the development of the Left is weaker in these societies that are more rural and less industrial. The Left has suffered almost continuous repression and has responded by developing insurgency as its main tactic. Even in Colombia with a much stronger electoral tradition, many of the leftist guerrillas who went into politics were assassinated by their former enemies, by the drug cartels, and by paramilitary groups. The Colombian FARC set up the Unión Patriótica (Patriotic Union) in 1985 to contest elections. In the next few years some fifteen hundred members of the party were assassinated. It is hardly surprising that the FARC mistrusts the democratic process. In such circumstances, to expect a Left to develop along the lines of the Chilean Left looks most unrealistic. The Left does not determine its own fate. In the case of Central America, if democracy really results from the present phase of pacification, then the Left may be transformed into a conventional party or parties—but that depends upon an equally massive transformation of the other political forces.[21]

The Left in Retreat

It is less easy to group developments on the Left in other countries into neat categories. In a number of countries, parties that were once on the Left have virtually abandoned any resemblance to their former allegiances. Such would be the case, for example, of the Peronist movement in Argentina, the MIR (Revolutionary Movement of the Left) in Bolivia, or the formerly leftist parties in Ecuador. In these countries it can be argued that a series of factors has reduced the Left to a marginal role at best. Hyperinflationary experiences, combined with structural adjustment programs, erode the organizational basis of the Left, namely, the union movement, and popular preoccupation with solving the problem of inflation takes precedence over any concern with social justice. Indeed, in the case of Bolivia the ability to combine a successful anti-inflationary program with a relatively successful safety net program for the poor has strengthened the government and reduced the influence of the Left even further.[22]

It would be premature to assume that the Left has no future in countries such as Argentina or Bolivia. Indeed, one of the big surprises of the elections in Argentina for a constituent assembly in 1994 was the 12 percent of the national vote, and the 37 percent of the Buenos Aires vote, that went to a new leftist coalition, the Frente Grande (FG, Broad Front). This, however, was more of a protest vote against the Menem government by disaffected Radical party voters than the birth of a new Left in Argentina. Although the newly named leftist coalition, FREPASO (Frente Solidario País [National Solidarity Front]), gained almost 30 percent of the vote in May 1995, this once again represented the collapse of the Radicals. FREPASO is a very fragile alliance with no real coherent program or organization.

The Left in Argentina and Bolivia, among other countries, has suffered with the decline of the union movement. Successful control over hyperinflation has brought benefits to the government in power, not least from the poor who suffer most from the process. The Left in these countries looks like a remnant from the past, without ideas or policies to confront the future. Protest movements in these countries are equally likely to be apolitical, or rightist-linked, as they are to be an expression of support for the Left. The Left has been discredited by its past excesses, from Monontero violence in Argentina to militant syndicalist protest in Bolivia.

Conclusion

What role can the Left play in the consolidation of democracy in Latin America? Does it, in fact, have a significant role to play? In some parts of the world, ethnic strife or religious fundamentalism have pushed the Left off the political stage. Some parties of the European Left have moved so far from their original positions that it strains credibility to call them parties of the Left any more: the Spanish PSOE (Partido Socialista Obrero de España [Socialist Workers' Party of Spain]) is a case in point.

This has not been the fate of the Left in Latin America. It is true that the Left in the 1990s has no distinctive policies to offer that are politically attractive and represent a true alternative to those of the neoliberal Right. The agenda for debate on the Left looks rather unoriginal (though this is far from saying that it is unimportant). Questions of inner party democracy go back to the very formation of mass political parties. Methods of strengthening popular participation through decentralizing government functions is hardly a novelty. Many of the issues on the Left in the developed world, especially concern for the environment and gender discrimination, hardly feature yet in any real sense on the Latin American Left.

But the strength of the Left in Latin America drew traditionally more upon the unacceptable nature of life for the majority of the people than upon the viability of policy options. The Left has drawn upon a powerful tradition of protest. The factors that brought the Left into being in the first place have hardly disappeared. The economic recession of the 1980s accentuated inequality and worsened poverty in Latin America. Political power is still disproportionately controlled by forces of the Right. The poor and dispossessed have little recourse to justice within existing legal and institutional systems. Corruption has eroded the legitimacy of government in Brazil and Venezuela.

In this sense the Left has a dual task: to seek a way of aggregating social demands into effective political ones, and to do so in a way that consolidates the fragile democratic systems on the continent. Indeed, it could be argued that unless the Left is able to channel potentially explosive demands into reasonable political options, then the democratic systems will be further undermined.[23] In other words, the evolution of the Left will inevitably affect the nature of the transition to democracy, especially in regard to two central challenges: consolidating democratic rule and complying with popular demands for socioeconomic development and distributive justice. The Left's response will influence not only the prospects for the survival of democracy, but also the type of democracy that emerges by shaping the character and content of socioeconomic and political structures. That response so far has been uneven, though in view of the international upheavals, and the national repression that have affected the Left in almost all countries, a limited response so far is hardly a cause for surprise. But there does seem to be a shift toward commitment to democracy as a value in itself, toward creating a stable and inclusive political order even in war-torn Central America, and toward establishing the Left's reputation as honest and efficient administrators.

The Left may be short of ideas at present, but that too may be inevitable as the Left struggles to adapt itself to a new political framework and a new institutional order. No doubt the temptation to revert to an authoritarian Leninist past will be too great to resist for some sectors, and there is the terrible example of Peru where the major force on the Left embodies all the worst features of dogmatic, violent revolution. No doubt in some countries the Left will continue to be politically irrelevant. In most countries, however, the Left is not now predominantly insurrectionary, nor irrelevant, but on the contrary attempting to contribute positively to building a new political and social order that, while not reverting to the central state model of the past, seeks to redress the social costs associated with the new model of economic development.

2

Conservative Party Politics in Latin America: Patterns of Electoral Mobilization in the 1980s and 1990s

Edward L. Gibson

In the 1980s a new and unexpected phenomenon swept much of Latin America: conservative electoral activism. This was a development that few could have predicted from past historical experience, especially in countries that had recently emerged from authoritarian rule. The expectation of most observers had been conservative electoral estrangement rather than activism. The literature on democratization thus tended to address the likely political action of the Right as a potential problem of democratization, particularly where powerful socioeconomic and political actors, incapable of effectively organizing themselves for the electoral struggle, might exercise the many options for "exit" available to them in nondemocratic realms. As such, the Right was seen as a force to be "pacified" or "neutralized" while democratic agendas became consolidated. This view was nicely captured in a quote from one of the most influential scholarly texts on democratization in the early 1980s:

> Put in a nutshell, parties of the Right-Center and Right must be "helped" to do well, and parties of the Left-Center and Left should not win by an overwhelming majority. . . . The problem is especially acute for those partisan forces representing the interests of propertied classes, privileged professionals, and entrenched institutions. . . . Unless their party or parties can muster enough votes to stay in the game, they are likely to desert the electoral process in favor of antidemocratic conspiracy and destabilization.[1]

The worst fears of these political observers were not borne out by events. In fact, the view of conservatism as an estranged or at best passive player in electoral politics was contradicted by events. In the 1980s the Right did well in the electoral game without much "help." It won power outright through the electoral process in Brazil, Uruguay, Ecuador, and El Salvador. It also had a major impact on the political process, shaping the terms of the political debate as well as the policymaking process, in Peru, Mexico, Chile, and Argentina. Furthermore, toward the end of the crisis-ridden 1980s, conservative leaders and their core constituencies emerged as major coalition partners of governments embarked upon free market reforms, even in countries where they had lost the elections to populist or nonconservative governments. Democracy in the 1980s, therefore, revealed surprising capacities for conservative electoral mobilization. However, what is striking about this experience is that, just as this mobilization was effective, it also appears to have been institutionally ephemeral in a number of important cases. New coalitions between the state, conservative political leaders, and business groups have now emerged on the scene. In the process, the conservative party institutions that gained visibility in the 1980s have receded from view in the seemingly more governable democratic politics of the 1990s.

The experience of the previous decade of democratic politics thus raises a number of key questions: what conditions facilitate the emergence of conservative parties in the region?[2] To what extent has the conservative electoral mobilization of the 1980s led to the institutionalization of participation by socioeconomic elites in democratic politics? What might all this indicate about the future relationship between the political action of social elites and democratic governance?

Democracy and the Right: From "Lost Decade" Mobilizations to Governing Coalitions

In rough terms, the political evolution of the Latin American Right since the start of the democratization wave of the 1970s and 1980s can be divided into two phases. The first of these can be labeled the "lost decade" mobilizations, which saw the rise of new mass-based movements advocating free market economic reform.[3] This catapulted new parties onto the political stage and made the Right an important player in electoral politics. Party politics thus became a central arena for both advancing the agendas of conservative movements and expanding its leadership and constituent base. The second phase of the political evolution of Latin American conservatism might be labeled the "governing coalition" phase. While still in its infancy, a number of trends seem already to have emerged from this phase. The first of these is the forging of new governing coalitions between the state and socioeconomic elites that have provided vital social support for the market reform process and have stabilized the civilian governments carrying out these reforms. These reforms have been followed by new sociopolitical arrangements highly favorable to socioeconomic elites. If, as Ruth and David Collier suggest, state-labor relations served as a "coalitional fulcrum" during previous crucial phases of Latin American political development, then it can be argued that, in this period of regime restructuring, the coalitional fulcrum has shifted from state-labor relations to state-business relations.[4]

In terms of the political evolution of conservatism, the effect of this phase has been ironic. It has resulted in highly favorable political and economic conditions for the core socioeconomic constituencies of conservatism. It has also resulted in the withering or outright collapse of conservative party organizations that had played such a prominent role during the "lost decade" mobilization in the 1980s.

These developments also render the relationship between governability and conservative political action somewhat ambiguous. In the short to medium term, they have provided important political stability to governments embarked upon wrenching economic reforms. Today economic elites support democratic governments and are pivotal coalitional partners. Democracy is thus more stable because it counts on the vital support of the propertied and socially powerful. In the long run, however, the withering of conservative parties and electoral movements raises questions about the future institutional capacity of elites to influence politics through democratic channels. Much of this depends on whether these coalitions will result in longer-term electoral alliances, or whether they prove to be another instance of the ephemeral marriages of convenience between populists and plutocrats that have long marked the region's checkered political history.

Democratic Stability and Conservative Parties in Latin America: The Historical Argument

Stable democracy in Latin America, as everywhere else, has historically been linked to the existence of strong national party systems. Strong national party systems have historically been linked to viable conservative parties. Logically, this should not be surprising. The importance of conservative parties to democratic stability lies in the pivotal social position of their constituencies and in the fact that they will be inevitable and important participants in the struggle for power. The organizational forms of their political participation will have major consequences for the relevance of different political institutions. If the organizational forms of upper-class power are weakly linked to political parties, regimes—or the major decision-making arenas of regimes—will be structured accordingly. Democracy in Latin America has endured where elites have possessed the institutional means to control it and where the challenges of mass politics could be regularly addressed through elite-controlled democratic institutions.

The argument here is not that conservative parties have made democracy "better" or more representative, only more stable. This proposition is supported by evidence from a growing number of comparative-historical studies of social conflict and political development in Latin Amer-

Table 1 **Conservative Parties and Democratic Rule in South and Central America: From the Advent of Mass Politics to 1990**

	Competitive National Conservative Party(ies) Prior to Mass Politics?	Years of Democracy (restricted or full)	Years of Nondemocratic Rule	Ratio Years Democratic/ Years Nondemocratic
Chile	Yes	45	24	1.9
Colombia	Yes	45	9	5.0
Costa Rica	Yes	48	2	24.0
Uruguay	Yes	67	20	3.4
Average				8.6
Argentina	No	40	38	1.1
Brazil	No	24	36	0.7
Ecuador	No	25	40	0.6
Peru	No	30	30	1.0
Venezuela[a]	No	35	20	1.8
Bolivia	No	20	40	0.5
Mexico	No	8	62	0.1
El Salvador	No	6	53	0.1
Honduras	No	24	18	1.3
Nicaragua	No	0	54	0
Guatemala	No	14	45	0.3
Panama	No	15	35	0.4
Average				0.7

Source: Edward Gibson, *Class and Conservative Parties: Argentina in Comparative Perspective* (Baltimore: Johns Hopkins University Press, 1996).

[a]The Christian Democratic Party (COPEI) plays a crucial role as the founding conservative party in interparty agreements for democratic regime inaugurated in 1958. Thereafter, upper-class representation is gained in the two major parties, Acción Democrática and COPEI.

ica.[5] It is also supported by the data presented in Table 1, which compares two groups of countries with different historical legacies of conservative party organization. The first group is characterized by strong historical legacies of conservative party organization. National oligarchic competitive party systems were established in the nineteenth century, when political competition was restricted to the socially privileged. As a result, conservative party structures were in place to deal with the challenge of mass politics when the expansion of popular participation took place. In the second group of countries such legacies of oligarchic competitive parties were largely absent, and national conservative party organization during the advent of mass politics tended to be weak or fragmented. Taking the initiation of mass politics as the historical point of departure, we can see that the durability of democratic regimes during the twentieth century was affected by this "genetic legacy" of conservative party organization. Those countries where national conservative parties were in place during the expansion of participation tended to experience significantly longer periods of democratic rule than those countries where conservative party organization was weak.

The data in Table 1 indicate the importance of historical legacies of conservative party organization to the continuity of democratic institutions. Countries that had viable, competitive national conservative parties in place at the start of democratic politics exhibited far greater democratic stability during the twentieth century than countries that did not. The average ratio of years under democratic rule to years under authoritarian rule for the four countries with strong legacies of conservative party organization was almost 9 to 1. For countries with weaker legacies of national conservative party organization at the start of mass democracy, the average ratio was 0.7 to 1.[6]

The point to be stressed here is that, regardless of the multiple arenas available for the organization of elite interests, one of the massive facts of democratic development in Latin America has been its positive association with stable upper-class participation in party politics. For countries with legacies of authoritarianism and weak conservative party organization, the development of new conservative parties is thus a central issue in the study of democratization.

Latin American Conservatism and the Lost Decade Mobilizations

The question asked by much of the Latin American Left in the early 1980s as it faced transitions to democracy might well have been asked by Latin American conservatism: "why participate?"[7] In fact, democracy posed even thornier dilemmas for conservatives as they pondered their options during the return to democracy. In contrast to the Left, neither the leaders nor the core constituencies of conservatism had traditionally needed the protection of democratic institutions to prosper as political or economic actors. Their control over economic influence, and the privileged access they enjoyed to the institutions of state power, raised doubts about their need for democratic institutions as well as the advantages of devoting resources to the tasks of electoral mobilization.

Two factors played a role in changing the calculus of participation for conservative leaders. The first of these was the negative experience of authoritarian rule. The second was exclusion from state power during the early periods of democratic government.

The authoritarian experience that preceded the recent transitions to democracy in many countries raised doubts about the "certainty" of benefits from authoritarian rule for the leaders and constituencies of Latin American conservatism. One of the distinguishing features of this authoritarian period was that it produced important strains in the system of quid pro quos that governed conservative-authoritarian alliances in the past. Conservative political leaders had accepted control of the state by authoritarian powers in exchange for privileged access to its most important policymaking institutions, usually economic policymaking institutions. Similarly, business leaders abstained from autonomous political action in exchange for the benefits that discretionary state power under authoritarian rule could provide: the repression of competing claims from labor and a privileged position for business in channels of access to the state.

This is what snapped in the 1970s and 1980s. Conservative leaders and the upper classes learned a common lesson during this period: discretionary state power under authoritarian rule can be a double-edged sword. While an effective check against popular challenges, it had also proven to be a growing threat to the interests of political and economic elites. Argentina provides a telling case. The military had proved an uncontrollable partner, driven by its own agendas and internal conflicts. The effective implementation of policy under these conditions was problematic, to say the least. Business elites also often found channels to state policymakers closed. Ultimately, the military led the country to a reckless war against Argentina's historic trading partner and cultural referent. The subsequent collapse of the armed forces as a political actor also meant that it would not be available as a source of pressure against nonconservative governments.

Additional incentives for party building were provided by the fact that, during the government of the Radical president, Raúl Alfonsín, access to state power was completely closed off to conservative leaders. There would be no room in the top institutions of economic policymaking for the technocratic elite that had filled the leadership functions of the Argentine conservative movement. If influence was to be exercised over governmental decisions, it would have to be from without, through the mobilization of opinion and the construction of electoral coalitions.

This pattern of disenchantment with authoritarian rule and exclusion from state power also spurred conservative party building in other countries in the region. In Peru the leftist turn of the armed forces during the 1968–75 period of rule by General Velasco Alvarado introduced a major rupture in the conservative civil-military relationship. The country's first elected president after the transition, Fernando Belaúnde Terry, had himself been overthrown by the armed forces in 1968 and had based his comeback campaign in the founding elections of 1980 on a platform of opposition to the military regime.[8] The exclusion of conservatives from the 1985–90 APRA (American Popular Revolutionary Alliance) government of President Alan García, and the markedly populist cast of its economic policies, gave impetus to new strategies of conservative organization. During the late 1980s, party politics became a major arena for conservative political action in the country's chaotic democratic regime. This was bolstered by the mobilization of business behind party politics in the late 1980s, as business elites turned to the electoral arena in opposition to a government that exhibited growing hostility to business interests.

For Mexican conservatives, embracing the agenda of the Partido Acción Nacional (PAN, National Action Party) for political democratization was vital to challenging the ruling party's monopoly over political decision making. It also became important to business elites made wary by government-sponsored antibusiness campaigns and an increasingly systematic use of discretionary state power against business interests during the 1970s and early 1980s. Electoral politics thus became a vehicle for political leaders and business elites alike for challenging the actions of an increasingly antagonistic state.

In all these cases, therefore, the impetus for conservative party building lay in a break in state-elite relations. Support for democracy was spurred by the new uncertainties associated with authoritarian rule and the hopes for more favorable contexts for state-elite relations under democratic governments.[9] Exclusion from state power by democratic governments after the transition from authoritarianism made party politics a much-needed vehicle for reasserting influence over state decision making.

In many countries these developments sparked the rise of new leadership within conservative movements. They opened the way for the emergence of a more diverse conservative political class that saw in the manifold ideological and organizational tasks of party politics a route to influence and political advancement. In Argentina a new conservative party, the Unión del Centro Democrático (UCEDE, Union of the Democratic Center), was founded in 1982 by liberal ex-technocrats closely linked to previous authoritarian governments. Within a few years the internal pluralization of the party sparked challenges to established leaders and set internal struggles in motion that transformed the UCEDE's power structure and its appeals to the electorate. The new leaders that flocked to conservative party politics gave it a new ideological content. They introduced new agendas and discourses that permitted the party to appeal to a broader cross-section of supporters. Their interest in gaining access to tightly controlled leadership structures also made them advocates for internal democratization, and increased the importance of *political* liberalism as an ideological banner for rallying their followers. In addition, and most important for the electoral Right's growth, they sought to challenge established leaders by building new bases of support outside their parties' traditional electorate through strategies of electoral popularization.

The combination of ideas, organization, and political practice that came to be known as *la nueva derecha* was thus an outgrowth of internal struggle. The transformation of Latin American conservatism was not generally carried out by its established leaders. It was the synthesis of a clash between old and new, between traditional leaders and newly politicized activists contesting them for primacy.

In Mexico the PAN's protagonism in the democratization process attracted new activists and business elites into the party. Catholic *solidarista* currents that had dominated the PAN were displaced by *neo-panista* currents that gave the party's ideological orientation a far more liberal content.[10] They also expanded the party's prodemocracy platforms with new antistatist appeals and agendas of liberal economic reform.

The Peruvian electoral Right's transformation in the late 1980s was marked by struggle between the liberal activists and intellectuals that rallied behind Vargas Llosa's Movimiento Libertad and the veteran party leaders of the long-established Acción Popular and the Partido Popular Cristiano (PPC, Popular Christian Party). Libertad's activists were generally new to party politics. They brought new agendas of anti-statism and "popular liberalism" that clashed with the "social-Christian" doctrines of the PPC and with the paternalistic orientations of Belaúnde's Acción Popular. The new activists eventually came to shape Peruvian conservatism's appeals to the electorate in the late 1980s, but before reaching that stage they had to impose their agenda on a resistant conservative movement.

Business and the Lost Decade Mobilizations

Throughout the early 1980s, as *la nueva derecha*'s appeals gained ground in the electorate, a major question loomed over their prospects for growth: would they succeed in mobilizing the support of business for their free market, antistate, coalitions? Historical evidence gave them few reasons for optimism: generally, stable business-party ties have been weak in the region. Latin American business has remained an aloof ally in the electoral struggles of conservative parties. At election time conservative parties may do well among the upper social strata; as individuals, business executives may vote for such parties and contribute financial support to their campaigns. But the organizational expressions of Latin American business, such as trade associations, large companies, or even prominent business elites, have rarely identified themselves with electoral politics. The political action of Latin American business has been focused directly on the state either through firm-state contacts or corporatist institutions.

The most important reason for this lies in the historical evolution of Latin American business, particularly the region's industrial sectors. Business development has taken place largely under the protection and tutelage of the state. State dependence has strongly conditioned business patterns of collective action and has made business elites wary of identification with partisan political action. In Argentina this wariness persisted throughout the 1980s, in spite of efforts by conservative parties to enlist business support. Despite the severity of the economic crisis, the Radical government of Raúl Alfonsín carefully maintained working relations with the business community. Continued business access to policymaking institutions hindered conservative efforts to mobilize active business support for its antistate agendas of economic reform.

In other countries, however, this pattern was broken. Three democratizing countries—Peru, Mexico, and El Salvador—experienced significant business electoral mobilization during the 1980s. In each of these cases the cause of that mobilization was a break in relations between business and the state. In addition, this mobilization helped to make conservative parties national electoral contenders. It catapulted Peru's new Frente Democrático (FREDEMO, Democratic Front) coalition and Mexico's PAN to the fore of national politics. It also led to the capture of national power by El Salvador's Alianza Republicana Nacionalista (ARENA, Nationalist Republican Alliance).

Long-standing ties between the state and the business community deteriorated progressively in each of these countries in the years preceding the late 1980s business mobilization. In Peru, relations between APRA president Alan García and the business community, initially cordial when García came to power in 1985, became marked by open hostility. The government intensified its populist policies, and business groups became increasingly reluctant participants in the government's plans for industrial development.[11]

In Mexico the business community had historically acted as a "stealth actor" in the nation's politics. It abstained from open political activity in exchange for informal but regular access to policymaking elites within the state, and to the rent-seeking opportunities that such access could provide. This arrangement came under strain during the 1970–76 administration of President Luis Echeverría, whose populist orientation and antibusiness rhetoric marked a change from the previously collaborative stance of earlier governments toward business. These business-state tensions continued into the 1976–82 government of President López Portillo. By the late 1970s and early 1980s, business took to increasingly open forms of political mobilization through interest associations and support for the growing party of opposition, the Partido Acción Nacional.[12]

In El Salvador, previously close ties between the state and business were broken by the reformist turn of the state after 1982 and the advent of the reformist Christian Democratic government of Napoleón Duarte in 1984. In an effort to consolidate popular support, and to counter the growing support of leftist opposition, the Christian Democratic government initiated socioeconomic reforms that, while imperfectly implemented, put business and agricultural elites on the defensive. Under siege by a powerful leftist movement demanding radical change, and excluded from a government committed to social reform, economic elites embarked upon major organizational and ideological mobilization. Business leaders also began to flow toward a party linked to agrarian elites and controlled by paramilitary groups, the Alianza Republicana Nacionalista.

The spark that crystallized the business-conservative party alliance in all these countries was the attempted nationalization of the banking system by the reformist governments, which took place in Mexico and El Salvador in the early 1980s and in Peru in 1987. Activated business elites found willing allies in the once-distant pro-free market politicians that were transforming the conservative party landscape. The party leadership's antistate agendas, once in tension with the business community, now became an effective ideological vehicle for challenging the dangers of discretionary state power. They also provided the ideological glue for linking business concerns to a more diverse set of democratization and economic growth issues capable of generating multiclass support.

The electoral mobilization of business galvanized conservative party politics. The open support of the Peruvian business community for the electoral challenge mounted by Mario Vargas Llosa's Movimiento Libertad endowed the movement with resources and credibility that allowed it to assert its hegemony over other parties in the conservative movement and emerge as a major contender in the 1989 presidential elections.[13] In Mexico, the defection to the PAN by important national business interests after the 1982 nationalizations solidified *neo-panista* control over the party and gave major credibility to the party's pro-democracy and pro-free market challenge against the governing party. During the 1980s the PAN became a serious electoral contender in a number of regional elections and, for the first time in its history, presented a credible national challenge to the governing PRI (Institutional Revolutionary Party) in the 1989 electoral campaign.[14] In El Salvador the mobilization of business behind ARENA produced an important leadership change in the party, as Alfredo Cristiani, a figure linked to agricultural and business interests, displaced the party's paramilitary leader, Roberto D'Abuisson. After a series of ARENA advances in congressional elections during the 1980s, the party captured the presidency in the elections of 1989.[15]

Just as business-state ties can break, however, they can also be mended. As Soledad Loaeza wrote regarding the later years of de la Madrid's presidency in Mexico, "all that the de la Madrid government [1983–89] needed to do was to restore harmony between the state and business for the latter to abandon its support for party opposition."[16] Under the presidency of Carlos Salinas de Gortari, the state overtures toward business intensified, resulting in an open alliance between the government and business groups behind the Salinas administration's program of economic reform. These developments produced a hemorrhage of business support from the PAN, particularly by the larger business and industrial interests that had mobilized behind it after the attempted bank nationalizations of 1982. Similarly, amid the general deflation of conservative party activity in Peru that followed the rise to power and the embrace of free market economic reform by Alberto Fujimori, there has been a renewal of state-business ties and a dissolution of the business party links that had characterized the post-1987 period. Only in El Salvador, where ARENA continues to control the national government, have the links forged between the conservative party and business during the 1980s endured.

A comparative look at the Latin American experience in the 1980s thus suggests that the potential for the electoral mobilization of business is negatively associated with the strength of the state-business relationship. Furthermore, where conservative parties are poorly institutionalized, the electoral fortunes of such parties are particularly sensitive to fluctuations in this relationship. Where significant ruptures in state-business ties take place, business can become a powerful force for the expansion of conservative party influence in electoral arenas. However, the withdrawal of business support can impose major constraints on the institutionalization of these parties and can prevent the maintenance of viable strategies of opposition. This vulnerability to the fickleness of business support constitutes one of the most important impediments to the development of conservative parties in the region.

Governing Coalitions and the Deinstitutionalization of Conservative Party Politics

The new conservative parties that emerged from the lost decade mobilizations were essentially forgers of protest coalitions. Their coalition-building process reached a climax in the presidential elections that swept the region in the late 1980s. But now we must take a step further and ask, what has happened after those elections? To what extent have these coalitions, born out of protest, been forged into stable conservative electoral coalitions?

The institutionalization of these parties depends a great deal on what party leaders do *between* elections. This is especially important for those parties that failed to win presidential elections and cannot now benefit from the fruits of power. If these parties are to become consolidated, a considerable degree of leadership specialization and continuity will be required. Coalitions must be stabilized, organizations built, financial resources mobilized, and ideological appeals reforged. These are the tasks of political leaders. In Latin America, however, the incentives for sustained strategies of party opposition tend to be weak.

There are many reasons for this. The hyper-presidentialist nature of most Latin American regimes, and the often attendant marginalization of the legislative branch, remove an important potential arena that could provide incentives for sustained strategies of party building and political opposition between elections.

Since the last elections, however, another development has posed a threat to conservative party continuity: in countries where conservative parties lost, governments adopted their agendas of liberal reform and in many cases brought conservatives back into the state to help implement those programs. In Peru much of President Fujimori's economic team was taken from the conservative FREDEMO coalition he had just defeated. In Mexico the PAN "cogoverns" with the PRI by rubber-stamping its economic reform initiatives in the National Assembly and controlling regional power bases. It has, however, lost the national initiative it once possessed as the country's most important electoral advocate of free market reform and democratization.

One of the most dramatic instances of this was Argentina, where the Peronist government's economic policymaking institutions became a veritable revolving door of conservative party appointees. What impact did this development have on the UCEDE? The Peronist government's economic reform program, with which conservatives had cast their political fortunes, has been an important success.

Ironically, conservatives did not share in any resulting electoral benefits. In fact, the period of economic reform has been marked by a massive decline in the electoral fortunes of the country's most important conservative party, the UCEDE. Between 1989 and 1991, the UCEDE lost more than 60 percent of its electoral support. In the 1993 elections the UCEDE did not even register a chemical trace in the national elections, and in its home base of Buenos Aires only received 8.7 percent of the vote, the lowest percentage in its short history.

The reason for this is quite simple, beyond the identity crisis caused by the appropriation of a party's agenda by a government in power. As governments controlled by other parties open their doors to conservatives, this produces a drain of leaders from the activities of party organization, who join the government in technocratic roles. The parties become demobilized.

What the postreform period seems to indicate is that, in the tentative institutional context of democratizing regimes, just as leaders can choose to become involved in party politics as a means of gaining influence over the political process, so too can they choose to abstain from party politics once new opportunities to gain access to state decision making are opened to them.

The primary victim of this process is the institutionalization of conservative party politics. As long as conservative parties remain merely part of a varied arsenal for pressure against the state, rather than as institutions permanently organized for the capture of power through elections, it is difficult to foresee their consolidation as shapers of the political process in Latin American democratic politics.

Conclusion: The Possible Futures of Conservative Political Organization

After almost two decades of democratization in Latin America, the institutional forms of upper-class representation are still very much in question. The early fears of upper-class subversion of democratic government have by and large receded, as new and more favorable arrangements in the economic and political realm have emerged from the turbulent experiences of the 1980s and early 1990s. The propertied and the socially powerful today support democratic governments. However, their connection to democratic institutions continues to be tenuous.

As a possible scenario for the future of conservative political organization, the consolidation of existing conservative parties as influential and regular players in democratic politics should by no means be ruled out. El Salvador's ARENA has shown signs of moving in this direction. Its hold on power since 1989, reaffirmed by its comfortable victory in the presidential and local elections of 1994, has given it the opportunity to evolve beyond its pre-electoral status as an elite-based opposition movement.[17] In Mexico the PAN has, after fits and starts, established itself as a major challenger to the PRI's hegemony in key regions of the country. If it is able to forge ties with national business, and build to a critical mass from incremental regional gains, it may challenge the PRI's hold on national power. However, in most of the countries discussed here, the possibilities for such an institutionalization scenario seem more remote. Thus three other scenarios might be advanced as plausible futures for conservative political organization.

The first scenario is merely a return to the time-tried pattern of state-centered pressure politics (relying on economic power, military power, or both). In this case, the current state-conservative coalitions will serve only as temporary marriages of convenience, leaving no lasting institutional legacies in the party realm, other than the erosion of the party institutions built in the 1980s.

However, things have changed in much of Latin America, and there are reasons to hope that the current disarticulation of conservative party politics does not merely represent a return to old historical patterns. The combined experiences of disastrous military rule and lost decade mobilizations have left their mark on the structure of politics and the incentives guiding conservative political action. Burned bridges with erstwhile military allies, as well as the surprising effectiveness of the electoral routes chosen in the 1980s, may have rendered old conservative ways unfeasible or unattractive to political leaders and much of the business community. Conservatives jumped into the arenas of electoral politics and mass persuasion in the 1980s, and there may be powerful factors preventing easy exit. Thus, while the deinstitutionalization of conservative parties seems to be a widespread phenomenon, it might well be part of a transition to "something else" in the electoral realm rather than a return to past patterns of electoral marginalization.

Thus a second and more hopeful scenario for the consolidation of Latin American democracies might be termed the "conservatization of populism." It would be a sequel of sorts to the ideological and programmatic "conservatization" of populist parties that shaped policymaking in the aftermath of the lost decade mobilizations. Where this leads to successful economic policies and favorable electoral dividends, it may help to bring about deeper changes at the institutional and coalitional levels. The "populist conservatization" scenario would involve (and in several cases has already involved) the absorption of conservatives into the leadership ranks of populist parties. More fundamentally, however, it would be driven by a shift in the social bases of these parties.

Changes in the region's political economy, particularly the lessening of business-state dependence as developmentalism yields to new economic models, would lead to new patterns of upper-class political representation. In this scenario, the formerly "populist" parties could become the electoral carriers of conservatism—the modern guarantors of market stability with a ready-made popular base. Historic state-business ties would yield to more stable party-business ties. The ideological and pragmatic convergences that have brought populist leaders together with business groups today would thus lead to longer-lasting institutional unions.

In this scenario, the social base of populist parties would become increasingly transformed by the addition of upper- and upper-middle-class voters. At the interest group level, the support of business groups for populist parties would become solidified and increasingly open, making business a pivotal base of financial and political support and displacing the parties' more traditional labor and middle sector constituencies. In effect, this development would constitute a core constituency shift for populist parties, rendering them effective advocates of upper-class political agendas while maintaining mass support for these agendas.

Trends in this direction are already visible in Argentina, where the Peronist party has succeeded in mobilizing important electoral support from upper-income voters and has deepened its ties with the large business community. This budding core constituency shift appears now to be prompting a leadership union, as important conservative party leaders have joined the Peronist party ranks. The PRI in Mexico has also shown signs of moving in this direction. In Chile the reformist Christian Democratic Party's promarket and probusiness stand in the last few years has eroded support in both the electorate and the business communities for the country's traditional conservative parties. The election to the presidency of Christian Democrat Eduardo Frei, an economic conservative with close ties to the business community, leaves open the possibility for such a shift in the social bases of support for the party. The ideological and coalitional shifts experienced by the Bolivian Movimiento Nacional Revolucionario (MNR, National Revolutionary Movement) in the last decade may provide another instance of populist conservatization.[18]

However, the realization of a populist conservatization scenario is fraught with obstacles. Any such transition would be marked by considerable conflict. Old guard elements on both the populist and the conservative side stand ready to undermine the union at every turn. Victory by radical populist leaders in internal elections could split the alliances apart. In addition, loyalties to old party labels and standards can prove surprisingly resilient. In these situations, economic success might not be a strong enough glue to keep the pragmatic alliance from unraveling before the power of entrenched ideological and institutional legacies.

A third scenario would thus fall between the two mentioned above: a new "rapid deployment" model of conservative party politics. The 1980s gave important lessons to conservatives. In a very short period of time they proved able to change the terms of the political debate and gain support for their agendas through the electoral process. They did so without the help of their erstwhile uniformed allies and, in many cases, without prior party structures. Given the structural power of their core constituencies, control of vital mass media outlets, contacts with influential intellectual circles, international ties, and the now tested financial power of a mobilized business community, conservatives have found themselves to be quite adept at mobilizing national electoral movements quickly and when crisis conditions warrant them.

That they have proven equally willing to abandon party building when possibilities for state-centered strategies emerge does not preclude a return to electoral mobilization if conditions change. In a future post-Fujimori crisis, a new conservative coalition might well emerge from the ashes of the short-lived FREDEMO and Movimiento Libertad, with familiar leaders wearing new and unfamiliar party labels. Rapid deployment for presidential elections might also be an effective strategy for conservatives that are institutionally weak nationally but have strong regional parties that safeguard their interests between presidential elections.[19] Knitting together the familiar constellation of regional conservative party networks and business interests behind new candidates and institutional facades, Brazil's regionally fragmented conservatives may, again and again, thwart the long and hard-fought bid of the Workers' Party for national power.

As a model of conservative political action, "rapid deployment" might blend the old and the new of conservative party politics in Latin America. It remains true to its historic institutional fluidity in much of the region, yet it also incorporates the significant changes in political practice that came with the lost decade mobilizations. Its impact on democratic development in the region, however, is hard to foretell. On the one hand, it would represent an advancement over previous military coup models of conservative political action. On the other, it is just as much a crisis-driven form of political action, one that does little to solidify the institutional bases of democratic politics.

It can be said that conservatives "discovered" party politics in many countries during the 1980s. It might be too much, however, to expect that the stable institutionalization models of party development imported from other regions or countries should result from this. Rather than the long-term development of conservative parties, we might see electoral mobilization emerge as a new and potent weapon in a varied arsenal of elite-based political resources, one whose relevance will rise and fall in response to changing opportunities that present themselves to conservative leaders and their core constituencies.

3

Democracy and Inequality in Latin America: A Tension of the Times

Jorge G. Castañeda

Democratization in Latin America has been the object of a great deal of study, introspection, and doubt over the years. Every wave of democratic institution building has been accompanied by analysis and speculation about its origins, duration, and inevitability; every rush of dictatorships has generated endless reflection about its motivations, contingent nature, or fatal rooting in the political culture, history, or social configuration of the hemisphere. When, in the 1950s, it seemed that a recently created middle class had finally laid the ground for the emergence of democratic rule, great emphasis was placed on this social determinism as an explanatory factor. In the 1960s the Alliance for Progress and the Venezuelan and Colombian paradigms were rapidly explained by economic and social change, as well as by international considerations. Together with the ideological justification of two-party systems, they were quickly prescribed as the best antidote to the spread of the Cuban Revolution. More recently and with much more sophistication, the transitions from authoritarian rule that began in the early 1980s and came to fruition mostly in the course of that decade were analyzed and theorized with much detail and substance. Many authors attributed the new wave of democracy to the application this time around of the well-learned lessons of the past. The transitions would be successful and lasting on this occasion, it was hoped, because the factors that contributed to democracy's ephemeral nature in previous eras were neutralized by maturing leaders, a fortified civil society, and more responsible international partners.

Whatever the nuances—and they were not unimportant—one of the central points stressed by the transition theorists as well as by the politicians in charge of or involved in the transitions themselves was that the just-born democracies not be "overloaded" by political, but mainly economic and social, demands. The concern of nearly all observers and participants was that emerging, fragile, and "thin-skinned," so to speak, political systems not be suddenly and immediately submitted to overwhelming demands of an economic and social nature that would strain them to the breaking point. These demands, if presented and insisted upon, it was thought, would lead to a breakdown of the infant democracies and entail, however unwittingly, serious prejudice to the very sectors of society that would be most favored by the satisfaction of the demands that short-circuited the system. Whether this involved retribution for past human rights abuses, a rapid repayment of the social debt, or a more general redistributive economic policy, it was believed—not unreasonably—that by insisting upon these demands and not allowing the new regimes a breathing spell, something like a honeymoon, they simply would not last.

Largely because in nations like Chile, Argentina, Brazil, and to a lesser extent Uruguay many of these conditions for successful transitions were met, the new democracies did endure, or, more specifically, the transitions from authoritarian rule were consummated. And despite sporadic or localized setbacks—Peru after April 1992, Venezuela during that same year, perhaps Chile as long as Augusto Pinochet remained in place—Latin America was by and large considered, quite rightly, to have begun to consolidate its democratic regimes and credentials. One after another, elected presidents were succeeded by other elected administrations, human rights were to a large extent respected, a free press flourished, basic freedoms were safeguarded, and most of the trappings of representative democracy were preserved. But three preoccupations rapidly surfaced both in the literature and in real life, all pointing to the same dilemma.

Problems with Democratic Consolidation

First, many naysayers and pessimists wondered whether the virtuous identity established between the consolidation of democratic regimes and the implementation of economic reforms along radical free market lines (that came to be known in Latin America as the neoliberal program) would not be sundered by a populist backlash. Would not demagogues or those nostalgic for bygone times take advantage of the short-term discontent provided by unpopular economic policies and of the democratic openings guaranteed by the liberalization dynamic to jeopardize the entire process by pressuring for redistributive policies or running on populist programs? What, they asked, could be done to retain the economic reforms on the one hand and democracy on the other, given that some were using the latter to fight the former? Many doubted that the current reforms and marvels of free market Latin America would last, given the region's penchant for doing the wrong things and its proverbial incapacity to stay the right course, tough as it may seem at first glance.

Second, others—more knowledgeable, sophisticated, and less enchanted by the market for the market's sake—expressed doubts about the depth of the democratization process in the light of what appeared to constitute the indispensable conditions of its success. It seemed that the only way for the nascent democratic regimes to last was if they guaranteed the permanence of the economic and social policies that had been carried out by the dictatorships that had preceded them. The example of Pinochet's Chile was often waved by these skeptics: the necessary (and indeed, sufficient) condition for a return to more or less democratic rule in Chile lay in the absolute maintenance of the free market, free trade policies pursued during more than fifteen years by the military regime. Democracy was fine, as long as it did not make too much of a difference insofar as economic and social matters were concerned. But how long could this sort of arrangement last, given the pent-up social demands accumulated during and the economic biases built up by the long period of authoritarian domination?

Third, and perhaps most crucially, many observers of the current democratic interlude in Latin America asked a harder question. Was the region's ancestral, abysmal inequality no longer the apparently insurmountable obstacle to democratic rule that it had been in the past? Inequality has been a permanent fixture of Latin American reality since independence. Alexander von Humboldt had made the point as early as 1802: "Mexico is the country of inequality. Perhaps nowhere in the world is there a more horrendous distribution of wealth, civilization, cultivation of land and population." The bishop of Michoacán, Fray Antonio de San Miguel, had written at the same time: "On the one hand, we see the effects of envy and discord, of skill, theft, and the penchant for hurting the rich in their interests; on the other, we see the arrogance, the hardness, and the wish always to abuse the weakness of the Indians. I do not doubt that these ills are born everywhere from great inequalities. But in America they are even more horrendous because there is no intermediate point; one is rich or miserable, noble or infamous in law and in deed."[1] Was this inequality not the cause of the absence of democratic rule, had the situation improved, or was the interminable inequality of Latin America no longer the obstacle to democracy it always had been?

After some soul-searching and much hand-wringing, a certain consensus began to emerge among students of the region's politics in relation to the type of question that needed to be asked, even if broad disagreements remained over the answer that the question called for. How compatible, it was asked, could democracy and widespread inequality and injustice be? Could representative democracy coexist with poverty of one sort or another affecting between half and two-thirds of the population? Could democratic rule survive in conditions of growing and acute inequality? And if not, wherein could the right answer to an ultimately perverse question be found?

This drawn-out preamble is justified by the need to emphasize that the current debate in Latin America about the nature of the region's new democracies and the possible tensions between the latter and the type of economic and social structures presently in place is not totally new. Nor is it limited to present-day discussions regarding the compatibility, or lack of it, between free market programs and democratization processes. Indeed, what is perhaps most interesting about the contemporary worries over the precarious nature of the region's institutions and advances is that they reproduce previous debates and doubts. And they reflect an underlying commonality: somewhere in the abstract thinking about and the everyday politics of Latin America there is a tension between the region's social configuration and its political aspirations. That tension is at the center of the discussion addressed here.

Before proceeding with that discussion, and having noted that it is not an entirely new one, it is nonetheless important to warn that a significant dose of today's tensions between these two trends is novel. The problem is no longer exactly what it was in the 1950s, when the identity of an emerging middle class and the possibility of two-party alternation was posited by numerous students of the region. The tension is greater than ever before because, on the one hand, the numbers are worse, yet on the other, the aspirations for and the roots of democracy are deeper.

There is a great deal of current debate in Latin America and in the multilateral agencies that deal with the region over exactly what occurred in the hemisphere during the 1980s in relation to inequality. There are undeniable problems of lack of reliable data, noncomparable series, baselines, and underreporting. In some countries the data is sufficient and illustrative, such as in Mexico and Brazil, and it is distressing. If in 1960 in Brazil the poorest 50 percent of the population received 17.7 percent of national income, in 1970 its share dropped to 15 percent, by 1980 to 14.2 percent, and in 1990 to 10.4 percent. In Mexico a similar process took place: in 1984 the poorest 50 percent of the population received 20.7 percent of national income; by 1989 the proportion had fallen to 18.7 percent, and by 1992 to 18.4 percent. Conversely, the richest 10 percent saw its share rise from 32.7 percent in 1984 to 37.9 percent in 1989 and 38.1 percent in 1992. According to the World Bank, of the twelve countries of Latin America for which comparative figures exist, in eight "the income distribution—measured by the Gini coefficient—deteriorated in the 1980s."[2] According to a review of other studies and sources of information regarding income distribution in Latin America before and after the "lost decade," "while most groups during the adjustment process saw their share in total income falling . . . the top ten percent—the richest to begin with—improved their relative position (with the exception of Colombia)."[3]

If data were available in relation to distribution of wealth and no longer simply of income, the early 1990s would almost surely show the same process of concentration as with income, or even worse. This is particularly true in countries with significant formerly state-owned sectors of the economy that were largely privatized in the first years of this decade. Regardless of the merits and motivations of these privatizations, given that they virtually all were carried out by sales to existing private sector conglomerates and without any of the share dispersion that at least nominally took place in Britain, for example, there is little doubt that they further concentrated assets in nations where small numbers already controlled huge chunks of the national patrimony. Suffice it to say that the thirteen Mexican billionaires on the *Forbes* list of the world's richest individuals own upwards of 10 percent of the nation's annual gross domestic product.

But there is not only more inequality; it is of a different nature. There is a new inequality, and a new poverty, in the hemisphere produced by the conjunction of the rush to the cities and the disappearance of economic growth at the rates most of Latin America became accustomed to between 1940 and 1980. The large majority of the poor and excluded are now in the cities, even if a greater proportion of the total number of each nation's rural inhabitants is poor. The new urban poor labor in the informal economy, on the streets and corners of the sprawling metropolises of a now overwhelmingly urban hemisphere. They live in the shantytowns overlooking the hills and in the increasingly segregated "poor" neighborhoods of cities removed from the ocean. They are, more recently, the laid-off or part-time employees of shutdown plants or streamlined bureaucracies that perhaps did not need them and that left them indigent in the streets.

But these urban poor are no longer the first generation to have left the countryside. In many cases, they are the sons and daughters of the originators of the rural exodus of previous decades; they have gone at least to grade school, they read and write and watch television, and are directly exposed to the trappings and opulence of middle-class and wealthy urban life. They do not live in another world; they live in the metaphorical cellars and tenements of the same high rise the penthouse occupants dwell in.

Yet, at the same time that the deterioration in income distribution was occurring, the democratization processes of Latin America were coming to fruition. Democracy did come to Brazil during this period, if by it we understand at least the prevalence of basic freedoms, alternation in power by different parties, competition for power exclusively through electoral means, the rule of law, and so on. It did not come to Mexico, although the demands for it were rapidly building. In both cases the pressure being built by the deterioration in the distribution of income, as good an indicator of inequality as any other, was rapidly growing. Thus while rights and choices were being granted to broader sectors of the population, the inequality that breeds growing demands and tensions was also increasing. Little wonder that the democratic transition was being resisted by Mexican officials, or that the fiscal crisis of the Brazilian federal government and of virtually every state government reached astronomical dimensions.

The fact that the democratic institutions of Latin America *are* more firmly rooted than in the past is another innovation. The national security dictatorships of the 1970s and early 1980s, the dirty wars and torture chambers, did leave a chilling lesson that was mostly well learned. It is better to build strong institutions that protect democracy than to do without them. Civil society is stronger, the middle class is larger, respect for human rights more widespread. Third, the international context is different. It is far from certain that the United States has, after the cold war, truly become a force for democracy in Latin America. But it has probably ceased to be a force against democracy, no longer combating it when it threatens its economic or, more important, geopolitical interests, as it did from the 1950s to the 1970s in much of the region. Finally, the ramshackle Latin American welfare states of the past are being dismantled today and are often being replaced by radical free market policies that, in addition to cutting inflation, tend to aggravate existing inequalities, at least in the short run. Thus the entire inequality/democracy debate, while not just born in Latin America, and though unquestionably part of the region's political and ideological tradition, is cast in a new light today.

Simply stated, the dilemma is that the kind of representative democracy that Latin America has sporadically enjoyed, and that it seems to be consolidating today, is not compatible with the region's social structures, and particularly with the enormous gaps between rich and poor, black, brown, and white, town and country, industrial powerhouses and rural backwaters. Whatever stance one may want to adopt regarding the causality and sequence between the emergence of some sort of broad middle class constituting a majority of the population and the viability of representative democracy, a certain simultaneity must prevail for the latter to endure. Because in Latin America today there is more inequality than before, and because Latin America was already more unequal than any other part of the world, the fragile democracy whose birth or resurrection it has witnessed in the past decade is likely to be short-lived.

Before proceeding any further, it is crucial to distinguish between the analytical statement that in principle and in the region today there is a tension between poverty and/or inequality on the one hand and democracy on the other, and the political call for the postponement of

democracy until the continent's economic and social lags are sur-
mounted. One statement is strictly analytical in nature and has no pre-
scriptive value in itself other than to imply, as we shall see, that
without progress in the attempt to reduce inequalities, there is a risk
for democratic rule. The other statement—that democracy should wait
until poverty is eradicated, as has been so often argued, tacitly or explicitly, by authoritarian regimes in Latin America of all ideological inclinations, but mainly by those on the Right—is politically motivated.
It can mean that democracy should be suspended until inequality is
reduced, or it can imply that given inequality and poverty, certain
shortcomings in the organization and functioning of democratic rule in
Latin America are more or less inevitable. But there is no causal or substantive link between the two types of statements. One can both detect
the tension between inequality and democracy *and* be a firm supporter
of democracy; or one can be a committed opponent of democratic rule
in Latin America, for whatever reasons, and at the same time not believe there is any incompatibility between inequality and democracy.
In fact, the political statement subsumes and implies the analytical
judgment, but not the other way around.

The reasons for the presumed incompatibility mentioned above are
clear. Democracy means giving free rein to the expression of pent-up
demands of downtrodden or even marginalized sectors of society, and
then finding and implementing solutions or giving satisfaction to at
least part of those demands soon, if not immediately. The demands
cannot be forestalled: they are too pressing. And satisfaction cannot be
indefinitely postponed because those who do so proceed at their own
peril given that they can be removed from office just by losing the next
election. The gradualism and various virtuous cycles that made democracy and capitalism compatible in Europe and North America since late
last century do not operate in Latin America today, at least from this
perspective.

There is every reason to believe that the problem thus stated does
exist, and in order for democracy and existing inequalities to cohabit in
Latin America, it is the second term that must be addressed in order for
the first one to survive. "Something special," that is, changes beyond
what inertia and "natural" mechanisms will provide, must take place
in order for the tension between both terms not to become unmanageable. But it is worth stressing that this incompatibility is not impervious to time and circumstance; it is so abstract a statement that its
verification in practice can be a drawn-out matter. The dilemma must
be formulated as a general principle or premise that will materialize
only if a certain number of circumstances coincide. Conversely, if certain conditions of a different nature are all present, the consequences of
the incompatibility can be avoided, though generally only for a set period of time.

Recent empirical work carried out by economists—and even by the World Bank—shows that there is a clear link between democracy, inequality, and economic growth. The traditional Kaldorian or Kuznetsian approach, whereby it was believed that inequality fostered growth because the rich saved more than the poor, and consequently high rates of investment demanded a greater concentration of wealth and income among the rich, has fallen into disfavor. A different and contrary correlation is currently posited, and some empirical evidence seems to indicate that it is more accurate. According to this view, most recently researched, among others, by Alberto Alesina and Roberto Perotti for the National Bureau of Economic Research, high inequality correlates with political instability, which then generates low investment rates. Working with data from seventy countries for the period between 1960 and 1985, these authors have found that "income inequality increases socio-political instability which in turn decreases investment," which obviously leads to lower growth.[4] They add that more acute inequalities also make for stronger pressures in favor of fiscal redistribution, which can act as a deterrent to investment.

Prospects for the Construction of Democracy

In Latin America the recurrent cycle of democracy, overwhelming social and economic demands, public spending, inflation, devaluation, and middle-class and power elite disenchantment followed by a tragic outcome is well known. The reasons for this cycle, regardless of whether on occasion they are identified with a simplistic assessment of mere economic policy mistakes, are quite evident. The inequities in Latin American society, the information available to broad sectors of the population about how matters could be different, and the obvious injustice prevailing throughout the region are all such that most lasting democratic experiences give way to elections that bring to office governments or leaders that try to satisfy these aspirations. But given the scarcity of resources and the overall economic obstacles existing throughout the region, it is impossible to satisfy virtually any demand in a significant manner without engaging in some sort of redistributive exercise. This implies alienating or ostracizing the powerful sectors of society from which the resources to be redistributed must be obtained.

In most Latin American nations this signifies turning these sectors against the democratic process that brought up the redistributive issue in the first place. Given this dynamic, which has actually appeared in Latin America on multiple occasions, some have reached the conclusion—self-serving or sincere—that until the gaps between rich and poor are reduced, and thus the intensity of the poor's demands is defused, democracy will simply not work. It is not so much a question of the *desirability* of having inequalities and democracy coexist, but of the *impossibility* of that coexistence. Thus the political statement previously made explicit encloses the substantive premise: the reason democracy should be suspended until inequality is reduced is that otherwise it simply will not work.

This dilemma is specific to the region and to the contemporary era. It is, in a sense, a strictly historical problem and largely located in Latin America, the "middle class" of world societies as Alain Touraine has often said. It is a historical problem because of the compressed nature of modern evolution in Latin America, and it is a localized problem because of the specific traits of Latin America.

First, it is a localized problem. In the world's industrialized nations, although inequalities do subsist and are probably widening, they are sufficiently narrow to be manageable. A large enough majority of the population is equal unto itself, and democratic institutions are sufficiently old and well rooted that the undeniable contradiction that does persist between the basic premise of equality in principle before the law and the market, and the inequality that in fact prevails in much of modern society (between poor and rich, black and white, foreign and national, men and women, adults and children, and so on) remains within the bounds of what democracy will countenance. In the wealthy nations, the tension between democracy and inequality is just that: a tension that can be adequately managed or has been from the end of the last century until now.

Latin America has always been the most unequal of the world's poorer regions. Even in 1978, for example, just as the period of the continent's sustained economic expansion came to a close, the share of total income received by the poorest fifth of the population was lower than for any other area: 2.9 percent compared to 5 percent for southern Europe, 6.2 percent for East Asia, 5.3 percent for the Middle East and North Africa, and 6.2 percent for sub-Saharan Africa.[5] If, in many Latin American countries, the richest 10 percent of the population obtains today between 40 and 50 percent of national income, in East Asia the average is in the mid-30 percent range.

In the utterly destitute nations of the world—Africa and most of Asia—either inequality is far less dramatic than in Latin America, though poverty may be much more acute, or, more commonly, democratic governance is a relatively new phenomenon whose vicissitudes are understandable, given youth and the awesome challenges of economic development. Most of the nations of Asia and Africa did not exist as independent entities as recently as forty years ago. The others either have democratic governance and a high standard of living— Japan, for example—or low levels of inequality, even though they have not enjoyed democratic rule—China, Korea—or have levels of inequality below those of Latin America and something like electoral democracy at work—India, of course. It is useful to recall that India, despite its abject poverty, has a ratio of income shares of the richest 20 percent of the population and poorest 20 percent far lower (better), at around 10 percent, than countries such as Mexico (15–17%), Colombia and Venezuela (20%), or Brazil and Ecuador (25% and 45% respectively).[6] One reason for this difference might be the Indian political system and the redistribution that the lasting existence of even as skewed a system of representative democracy as India's entails.

Only in Latin America are the degree of inequality, the size and existence of a middle class, the level of economic development, and the sufficiently consummated process of nation building all far enough along to explain the number of attempts to establish democratic rule over the past century and a half. And only in Latin America have those attempts proved so frequently unfruitful that the issue is truly a burning one. In a nutshell, only in Latin America is there both enough democracy for it to be at risk and so much inequality for it to be a problem.

But the tension we are dealing with is also a historical phenomenon. It did not occur elsewhere in other times, although conceivably it could have. In principle, the immensely poor and unjust societies of nineteenth-century Western Europe or the United States could have been forced simultaneously to live with emerging democratic rule and social forms of organization and economic development that excluded vast sectors of the population from the benefits of the market, employment, mass consumption, and so forth. What difference is there truly between Dickens' England and the suburbs of São Paulo?

The answer lies in the different historical rhythms involved. Democratic rule expanded only at a slow pace, and sector by sector of the population, in most of Western Europe until after World War I. The franchise itself was extended by segments of society; in England it was only granted to all males late in the century. For practical purposes, democracy and incorporation into the modern market economy went hand in hand, and while early attempts did emerge to push democratic rule further ahead than the economic and social situation of the "dangerous masses" warranted (the Chartist movement, the revolutions of 1848 on the continent, even the Paris Commune of 1871), the little they temporarily achieved was swiftly rolled back. A certain contemporaneity prevailed: no idea or reform was truly "ahead of its time."

But in Latin America, of course, matters were quite different from the very caricatured outset. Just after independence, nations that virtually did not exist adopted sophisticated, enlightened liberal constitutions inspired by French philosophers and American founding fathers. And this diachronic feature continued through the first hundred, then hundred and fifty years of independence, although often certain formulas were employed to alleviate the pressures it generated. Thus elections were scheduled now and then, and, in some countries at some moments in time, power was actually contended for at the ballot box; in fact, extraordinarily few people voted.

As late as 1960 in Brazil, for example, there were only 16 million registered voters, of which barely 11.7 million actually voted in federal elections.[7] This was in a country of 80 million inhabitants at the time. In the 1940s the situation was of course much worse, not only in Brazil but throughout Latin America: where elections were held, only few voted. Still, the franchise was extended to everyone, and as democratic regimes consolidated in the early 1980s they awoke to a paradox illustrated, again, by the Brazilian example. In the 1989 presidential elections in that country, there were 75 million registered voters, a large majority of which went to the polls. But only 7.5 million Brazilians paid taxes; that is, schematically, only a tenth of the electorate was actually incorporated into one of the basic aspects of citizenship and modernity. Throughout Latin America the same paradox surfaced: on the one hand, the hemisphere had adopted, nearly across the board and from a historical perspective virtually overnight, the political structures for governance and transferring power of the industrial democracies, but the social structure of those nations was anything but present in Latin America.

The gradual extension of involvement in the market economy, the construction of a social safety net, and the granting of the franchise could not all occur in Latin America little by little or more or less simultaneously. No one can be easily denied the right to vote in the late twentieth century either because they cannot read or write, or because they do not own property, or because they are black, or because they are women. In a sense, the right to vote is either denied to everybody by authoritarian rule or afforded to everyone thanks to the ongoing democratic transitions. But nothing could be done as rapidly on the social front: the 60–70 percent of the population in nearly every Latin American country that is poor, devoid of formal employment, decent education, health, and housing, that does not pay taxes, and whose level of consumption is just above the minimum possible cannot be transformed overnight into a European or Canadian middle class.

Hence the *historical* nature of the problem. The gradualism of the nineteenth century and parts of this one is not applicable in Latin America. Indeed, the immediacy of the situation is even worse than just described, if one factors in another contemporary ingredient absent in previous eras. The impoverished masses who can now vote, organize, demonstrate, and demand in Latin America are part of a more informed world than the one their nineteenth-century predecessors lived in. Television, urbanization, literacy, the global flow of information, all enhance the tension between democracy and inequality today as compared to before. The demands generated by the perception of widening social gaps are greater and more intensely felt because there is far more information available today to the destitute and excluded about how desperate their fate actually is.

The "overload syndrome" that characterizes Latin American economic, social, and political life today is thus specific and historical. This also means that the solution to the problem, once accurately described, must also be solidly anchored in the region's traits. An additional effort to circumscribe the issue with greater precision is consequently in order. It implies addressing the exceptions, lags, and alternatives (at least theoretical in nature) that the problem involves.

One apparent exception to the hypothesis whereby Latin American democracy only barely survives under conditions of severe and worsening, or in any case not improving, inequality lies in the more or less prolonged periods following either hyperinflation or authoritarian rule. In both cases, it would seem that, despite growing inequality, poverty, and injustice and the implementation of economic policies that severely concentrate wealth and income, democratic institutions and regimes tend to thrive, enjoy broad popular support, and acquire an enhanced capacity to pursue their agendas. The more well known examples of this are Argentina under Carlos Menem in relation to hyperinflation, Chile under Patricio Aylwin with regard to a return to democracy, as well as Bolivia since Víctor Paz Estenssoro's stabilization experiment began in the early 1980s. Some might conclude, in the light of these examples, that by resorting to the market and establishing democratic rule, a virtuous cycle was set in motion in these countries whereby the two pillars of enlightened societies—democracy and the market—reinforce each other and render matters such as the inequality of outcomes irrelevant because equal opportunity is extended to all.

Actually it can be argued that, in the case of a victory over hyperinflation, the honeymoon that some democratic regimes enjoy despite widespread, standing injustice can be explained by the fact that runaway inflation is precisely inequality-generating par excellence, and thus its elimination provides a respite from, and in some cases an improvement in, overall inequality. The poor and the harassed middle class can come to perceive an easing of inflation as not only improving their lot in absolute terms but even in relation to other sectors of society.

This is particularly true when price stabilization is linked with trade liberalization and local currency appreciation, as was the case in Mexico between 1989 and 1992, in Chile from 1977 through 1981, and in Argentina from 1990 onward. Access to imported goods generally identified with upscale consumption, the possibility of traveling abroad and saving in dollars, all are contributing factors to this sentiment. The popularity of regimes that implement draconian adjustment programs right after serious bouts with hyperinflation does not negate the tension between inequality and democracy. If anything, it reaffirms this tension by showing how a perceived, if only temporary, bettering of the affliction of inequality reinforces democracy. It also does not demonstrate that the success in fighting inflation will forever discourage the tensions discussed here. It is reasonable to expect that, after a certain period of time after which memories of high inflation fade, reality weighs in, and that when unsatisfied demands for other forms of reducing inequality—higher salaries, social spending, jobs—kick in, the enthusiasm for democratic institutions and their elected regimes will begin to wane.

A return to democratic rule is also a motivation for a honeymoon. Often, after lengthy periods of dictatorship and repression, electorates and various social movements are willing to grant newly installed democratic governments a breathing spell. They do not press all their pent-up demands immediately; they do not "overload" the system overnight, particularly if there is a widespread belief that such overloads led to authoritarian rule in the first place. This is clearly relevant to the Chilean case today, where after sixteen years of military dictatorship and sweeping inequalities, the people of Chile did not insist on the prompt satisfaction of their aspirations for justice, higher salaries, and more social spending. The return of democratic rule in Uruguay in 1983 under Julio María Sanguinetti can also be interpreted in this fashion.

But again, appearances can be somewhat deceiving. In fact, the government of Patricio Aylwin in Chile did raise social spending and increased taxes to finance it, and did reduce part of the poverty generated in Chilean society by a decade and a half of radical free market policies. And as time went by, the honeymoon wore off, with the traditional militancy of the Chilean labor and popular movements resurfacing, albeit under new, different forms. This led to a greater emphasis on social spending with the inauguration of the new administration headed by Eduardo Frei. If anything, the social honeymoon in Chile and the relatively rapid, though still incomplete, restoration of Chilean democracy owe part of their existence to the modest but undeniable redistributive policies of the Aylwin-led Center-Left coalition.

A third explanation for certain apparent exceptions regarding the democracy-inequality tension involves the type of countries just referred to. It can be surmised that there is a certain threshold of inequality: below it, tensions are almost always present; above it, they can be avoided or postponed. It may be no coincidence that three of the countries mentioned as exceptions—Argentina, Uruguay, and Chile—are, together with Costa Rica, the least unequal nations of Latin America (despite degrees of injustice that are far greater than those of the industrialized world) and those that suffer from the smallest volume of ethnic, regional, racial, and social disparities. It is true that, in relative terms, the deterioration in at least two of these nations—Chile and Argentina—has been as marked as elsewhere, if not more, and that it is small consolation to the poor of greater Buenos Aires or Santiago that they are "less unequal" than their counterparts in Recife or Mexico City. But there may well be a question of an absolute level here: the starting point for the decline in these nations is clearly higher than in the rest of Latin America, and thus the capacity to absorb broader inequality without "overloading" a newly reestablished democratic system is also greater.

Finally, there is the question of time. On many occasions in Latin America, particularly in the nations with a strong pre-Columbian heritage, time moves differently—some would say more slowly—than in other regions and countries. Immediate reactions, quick responses, rapid cause-and-effect relationships are rarely the case. Time lags, delayed reactions, and an often incomprehensible patience tend to be much more common. The famous Mexican saying "In Mexico nothing ever happens until it happens" is a symptom of this: the quick pace of causes is not always matched by an equally fast rhythm of effects. Where it may seem that a given cause—say, growing inequality—should produce a determined effect rather quickly, the absence of which suggests that there may not be much of a cause in the first place, in fact the explanation for the apparent mismatch is time, not the lack of causality. On many occasions the effect is simply slow in coming: it will happen, in time.

The exceptions, then, are explainable. Nothing in these examples lessens the substantive contradiction between democracy and a given threshold of inequality, and a given evolution of it. This last point is essential: if Albert O. Hirschman is right in positing a "tunnel effect" whereby it is more important for matters to be moving in the optimal direction, and that there be a perception among those affected that things are improving, then the opposite is also true. If there is a reverse "tunnel effect" and people sense that their lot is deteriorating and in reality it probably is, the "overload syndrome" will almost certainly come into play at some stage. The main thrust of this line of reasoning is that, other than under exceptional circumstances such as those outlined above, and in the absence of a "tunnel effect," democracy and the levels of inequality prevalent in Latin America are not compatible, and the tension between the two will become exacerbated. At some point the elastic band will be stretched too far.

The fundamental difficulty in untying this knot lies in another Latin American dilemma, which touches on the heart of the matter, the redistributive question. There are two indisputable premises for reducing inequality in Latin America: producing new wealth and distributing it differently than existing wealth. Without growth, no redistribution is possible. But distributing new growth the same way as before will only ensure that existing disparities are maintained: there is no automatic way of reducing inequality just by generating new wealth. To reduce injustice in Latin America, given growth, implies a redistributive imperative.

There is a growing body of literature suggesting that there are sound economic and political reasons for redistribution in highly unequal societies, in addition to the obvious ethical justifications. The first, mentioned in the previously quoted work by Alesina and Perotti,[8] stresses the countervailing pressures exerted by redistribution. The old approach emphasizes the discouraging effects on investment generated by high taxation, which is still the most efficient instrument of redistribution. But these authors note that redistribution through taxation, if effective, makes for less unequal societies, which in turn makes for more stable political systems that generate certainty, guarantee property rights, and so forth, which finally implies higher levels of investment and thus of growth. Another twist to this same argument is that more just societies permit sounder and more accountable governance because it is more democratic. Any comparison or counterfactual exercise involving higher or lower levels of taxation and redistribution has to take into account the deterrent effect on savings, investment, and growth generated by high degrees of social inequality and the political instability that generally accompanies it. The fundamental question is how to set in motion the trends toward redistribution and lesser inequality in a context where these two trends have been mostly absent.

Here is where the issue of democracy comes into play. In principle, there are several ways of redistributing wealth, income, opportunity, achievement, and ultimately capability, to use Amartya Sen's enumeration. Universal suffrage is not the only one: revolution, command capitalism along Korean lines, or outside intervention—the American factor in Japan, Taiwan, and also Korea in the late 1940s and 1950s—are among them. Unfortunately none of these other ways is quite suitable or viable for Latin America. Revolution has certainly worked from a redistributive perspective: Cuba is the least unequal country in Latin America by any definition, and, until a few years ago, this was not simply equality of the destitute. But that road does not seem to remain open in the post–cold war world, and few in the region today would find it attractive.

Command capitalism, with a strong authoritarian state, an honest civil service, and an agreeable private sector, has been tried too, also with some success as far as growth and reducing poverty are concerned, but with much less to show for itself as far as reducing inequality. The Brazilian model from 1964 onward, and even the case of Mexico, are good examples, up to a point. But here again, given current aspirations for democracy, and the bittersweet taste left by those experiences, it seems unlikely that redistribution from above can truly function in Latin America today. Nor does redistribution from abroad appear to be functional: it has never worked too well in the past—the Alliance for Progress precedent is ambiguous at best—and it is difficult to conceive of conditions under which the United States could actually take charge of land reform or other distributive mechanisms in Latin America, as it did in Japan under the occupation after World War II.

Indeed, there is every reason to believe not just that the only path conducive to some sort of redistribution today—democratic governance—is also the one whose absence explains a fair share of the inequality prevailing in the region today, or even a decade ago, after what Hirschman has called *les trente glorieuses.* We now know that even high levels of economic expansion, such as those Mexico and Brazil enjoyed from the 1940s through the early 1980s, in the context of undemocratic governance does not substantially improve distribution and may have worsened it. Conservative economists or commentators have argued that the explanation for the paradox of high growth and poor distribution lies in the *type* of economic growth that countries like Mexico and Brazil experienced: protected, subsidized, with an overpowerful state-owned sector of the economy that encouraged rent-seeking and concentration of assets and income. While there is no doubt that the type of growth in question was clearly of that nature, it is less evident that therein lies the cause of the inequality. The best counterexample is Chile from the mid-1970s through the late 1980s, a sufficiently extended period to warrant comparisons with other cases. Chile did achieve high growth during this period, particularly after 1984 and before 1981; and the type of growth it enjoyed was precisely the kind that radical free market advocates prescribe: nonsubsidized, unprotected, private sector-driven. Yet by every indication and source, Chile was a far more unequal nation and society in 1990 than in 1970, or in 1975 when the Pinochet experiment truly got under way.

Unfortunately for the perspective suggested here, Chile is not a much more egalitarian society today, after five years of democratic rule, than it was before. Without democracy in Latin America today, it seems nearly impossible to achieve the aim of alleviating gaping disparities. But one should not exaggerate the extent to which democracy alone can accomplish this task; this thesis should be posited only with caution and wide-open eyes.

Since 1988 Chile has negotiated a difficult transition to democratic rule. It has done so successfully, although serious handicaps and restrictions endure. Not only are the former military rulers still in command of the armed forces; not only are several institutions still not subject to any type of democratic accountability; in fact, a not insignificant share of the national budget remains automatically and unmovably allocated to the military. Nonetheless, just about by any standard that is relevant to Latin America, Chile no longer suffers from one of the most atrocious episodes of authoritarian rule the region has ever known. Largely as a consequence of this transformation, the social policies of the dictatorship have been overhauled. Spending on education, health, housing, and the poor has increased. In order to finance this "repayment of the social debt," as it is known in Chile, taxes have been raised, not as much as they should be, but Alejandro Foxley, Aylwin's finance minister, was the only Latin American technocrat in favor of higher taxes, not lower. Chile is, for practical purposes, the only country in the hemisphere pursuing some sort of redistributive effort, chiefly as a result of the drastic shift from authoritarian rule to representative democracy.

The emphasis on social spending has partly paid off. The number of officially poor Chileans dropped between 1990 and 1993 from 5 million to 3 million. But income distribution has barely budged: it remains stuck at roughly the same levels as in 1988, in turn far worse than in the early 1970s. In other words, a significant effort, in a country enjoying high rates of economic growth and an undeniable democratization process, has left in four years a scant trace in terms of redistributing income and thus in reducing inequality. There are, of course, plausible explanations. One is time: four years is simply not enough, perhaps. Another is the locked-in nature of the economic policies of the dictatorship. Despite the social effort, wages remain low and must continue to be in order to attract investment; trade liberalization and the absence of subsidies make it difficult to transfer resources from the rich to the poor. Furthermore, so much ground was lost in this area during the previous fifteen years that simply arresting the decline is an accomplishment; reversing trends is a much more difficult task. Finally, the tax system, given trade policies, capital mobility, and political restraints, has not been stretched very far. The increase in revenues remains low. Yet the Chilean case cannot but make one wonder: is any sort of redistribution possible, even under favorable political conditions?

The Chilean case also opens another line of discussion. Is the main impediment to democratic rule inequality or poverty? Or, conversely, may it be possible to consolidate democracy if extreme poverty is significantly alleviated, even if inequality stays the same (i.e., if the bottom ranks of the income scale improve their lot in absolute terms, even if in relative terms they do not)? This is a central question in Latin America today, precisely because it does seem possible to reduce absolute levels of poverty, at least among the most destitute sectors of society, but it is much more difficult to redistribute wealth and income.

Indeed, many students of the region are suggesting that the new forms of combating poverty—highly targeted programs, the efforts of nongovernmental organizations, philanthropic work, and so on—are the modern equivalent of previous, now obsolete efforts at Keynesian redistribution. It is important to distinguish two issues here. One is that combating extreme poverty does not necessarily alter the income distribution structure of a nation, or, in any case, it mostly affects the bottom rank in the scale by subtracting from the share of the lower middle-class ranks. This is basically what occurred in Chile from the late 1970s through the late 1980s. Poverty and inequality are not the same. As we already saw, India may be poorer than any country in Latin America, but it is less unequal.

A different issue is whether combating poverty can be an adequate and effective substitute for reducing inequality as far as its effects on democracy are concerned. If the key issue is poverty, and not inequality, then the current democratization boom in Latin America might be consolidated simply by following well-planned antipoverty programs, at the same time that income and wealth remain highly concentrated.

The benefit of this alternative is that it does not alienate the wealthier and more powerful sectors of society, alienation that is, after all, the single most prejudicial and counterproductive by-product of traditional redistributive schemes. The problem in Latin America has always been that any attempt at reducing the wealth, power, and impunity of elites, be this attempt democratic or authoritarian, conservative or revolutionary, has inevitably provoked their wrath and reaction. The latter has in turn unleashed a series of uncontrolled forces that either did away with democratic institutions or forced a clampdown on them, leading to exile, plotting, and the *contra* syndrome. Whether the redistributive exercise was accomplished with moderation (Guatemala, 1951–54) or excess (Cuba, 1959–61), democratically (Chile 1971–73) or by the military (Peru, 1968–74), it has systematically brought a negative, antidemocratic, and visceral counterattack by those affected by it. If it were possible simply to reduce poverty—without diminishing inequality in the short term—and the antipoverty effort were to have virtually no redistributive effect, there would be a painless, effective, and democracy-stabilizing solution to the age-old dilemma. No wonder that, in theory, this silver bullet has received the blessing of all the powers that be, from the Washington Consensus to Chicago Boys in Santiago.

There is little empirical evidence yet available in one direction or another in this regard. The new microtargeted antipoverty programs in Mexico, Chile, and Argentina are either too recent or insufficiently studied with proper data to permit any evaluation either of their actual, lasting effects on reducing poverty or on their impact on the stability of the democratic (or not-so-democratic) institutions in the countries in question. It may well be, however, that instead of its being necessary to redistribute income from the rich to the middle class, and transforming the poor in general into a widening middle class in order to stabilize democratic institutions, it is enough to shift the extreme poor into the next higher category—just poor, period—in order for the virtuous cycle of democracy, justice, and so on to be set in motion.

While this possibility cannot be ignored, it seems safer to believe that democracy without reducing inequality can endure only under great stress and given exceptional conditions; at the same time, only democracy can reduce the disparities that make it untenable. It seems safer to say that the only way to consolidate democratic rule in Latin America today is by redistributing wealth and income by combining economic growth—virtually of any type: the variable is not the nature of the growth but its existence and the context in which it takes place—with a sufficiently democratic political system that allows those sectors of society that have been heretofore excluded from most of the fruits of previous growth to fight for and achieve a larger share of the pie.

Federal, state, and municipal elections, tax reform to finance higher expenditures on education, health, and housing, labor rights, a more vigorous civil society, land reform in those regions where it is still relevant, urban reform in other areas: all of these are, among other things, redistributive factors operating through democratic channels. Workers do obtain higher wages if they are allowed to negotiate collectively, to organize unions, and, when useful, to strike. Citizens can vote for parties and measures that raise taxes to finance greater social spending; municipal authorities that do not steal do redistribute wealth from their potential pockets, or those of their predecessors, to society in general.

There is little disagreement here. That democracy can redistribute, even in Latin America, seems a truism. Any sustained alternation in power through elections with the broader trappings of democratic rule will, in Latin America, generate almost unavoidably a redistributive effect. The mechanics of how to proceed are also well known: investment in human capital (education, training, and health), other forms of social spending (housing, child care, and so forth), jobs, and development of infrastructure to promote growth—there is no great mystery about what must be done. The problem always has lain in finding the money to achieve these goals, not in the exact nature of the goals. The fact that today the fiscal option—as opposed to direct public sector involvement in the real economy—is the preferred option does not alter matters greatly, nor does it imply that the taxation avenue does not lead to a certain state presence in the economy in the medium term. Nor does this imply that ideological and policy fads will not shift again, sometime.

The main point is that the trick is political, not technical. The problem lies in the consequences, for both democratic rule and redistribution, of "going too far" and in the difficulty of defining "too far." The scope of the latter phrase is by definition in the eyes of the victim: what is "too far" for a landed oligarch may be acceptable for an ECLA (Economic Commission for Latin America)-born industrialist, whose definition is in turn narrower than that of a telecommunications magnate who got rich in the sobering years of the debt crisis. And all of their estimates of the acceptable breadth of reform may be far less broad than that implicitly or explicitly held by the presumed beneficiaries of the reforms themselves. Normally that is what elections, debate, congressional accountability over the budget, and collective bargaining are for: determining in a democratic, universally accepted fashion what is "too far" and what is not. In Latin America, this has not truly been the case ever, anywhere, with the possible exception of Costa Rica since 1947.

But there are some grounds for being optimistic in this regard. The persistence in time—as opposed to the actual rooting—of democratic institutions makes it more difficult for them to be overthrown; a return to military rule in countries like Brazil, Chile, or even Venezuela (a more complicated case) seems improbable. There is a virtuous gradualism in this. The discredit of the military, the attachment of broad sectors of society to the democratic paradigm, and the international context make a simple destruction of democratic institutions à la Chile or Guatemala more unlikely than ever.

The new international context is also a deterrent to the refusal of the powerful sectors of society to accept some form of redistribution. Short of conspiring and succeeding in overthrowing the institutions of representative democracy, the privileged instrument of resistance to redistribution is capital flight, refusal to invest, or both. Greater capital mobility in the globalized economy of today would seem to make this a more potent weapon and a nearly impossible one to defend against. At the same time, to the extent that there is beginning to be a shift in beliefs in the world regarding the need to reduce inequalities in certain regions, and there are growing possibilities of achieving new forms of international cooperation on taxation of assets abroad, for example, that weapon may begin to lose its effectiveness.

Moreover, if other conditions in the world, the region, and a given country are favorable to investment, the exact behavior of certain domestic private sector members may no longer be as relevant as before. In the same way that speculative capital has flowed in, in nearly identical proportions, to "best students" Mexico, Chile, and Argentina as it has to macroeconomic basket cases such as Brazil, it is quite possible that if the overall fundamentals are kept sound, foreign investment would continue to flow into nations that made a serious redistributive effort, even if domestic investment were to dry up for a time as a form of resistance to that effort.

Finally, there is the greater evil-lesser evil dynamic. There are important sectors of Latin American elites that still believe they have no need to countenance any redistributive intent. Either through ideological windmills, such as what is currently called neoliberalism, or good old-fashioned cynicism, they continue to maintain that under no conditions will they accept any reduction in their wealth, income, privilege, and power. But other sectors are beginning today, as they did in some nations in the aftermath of the Cuban Revolution in the early

1960s, to understand two facts, one of convenience, the other of indifference.

Certain segments of the rich and powerful today realize that their profits are so huge, that the difference between the rates of return on their investments in Latin America and elsewhere is so great, and the gaps between their situation and that of the vast majority of the region's inhabitants are so broad, that there is much room for painless concessions. Accepting higher taxes, paying higher wages, tolerating lower profits is not the end of the world; it might even be a way of making the world as it is somewhat more livable. Other sectors are beginning, once again, to be frightened by the specter of violence, armed uprisings, crime and drug trafficking, and the gaping inequalities from which all these blights ultimately stem. They are beginning—just barely—to acknowledge that while a revolution along Bolshevik, Chinese, or Cuban lines is no longer a realistic threat, armed chaos and popular fundamentalism is, and whatever the final result of such outbursts might be, in the meantime the current way of life of the wealthy and powerful in Latin America would become untenable.

The vicious cycle of democratization, social pressures, reforms, and counterreaction/end of democracy is precisely what has made democratic rule such a sporadic and unlikely feature of Latin American life. The only way to break the cycle is, of course, to attack all its links simultaneously: make democracy deeper and broader, so that it is more firmly rooted and more difficult to destroy; reduce inequalities as quickly and as decisively as possible, so as to defuse social pressures to go "too far"; encourage and implement reforms bold and substantive enough to reduce inequalities and give satisfaction to social demands and moderate enough to bring at least part of the business and foreign elite along, all the while neutralizing the military so they do not act on behalf of those who do not go along; at the same time bring to bear sufficient international cooperation to forestall capital flight or at least obtain some benefit from it, while insisting on welcoming foreign investment with tax rates that are higher than before but still lower, given overall rates of return, than in the wealthier and poorer nations.

The increments in leeway or breathing space one obtains through each of these changes and cautious steps enhance the maneuverability on the next turn around of the cycle: more democracy, in order to channel greater social pressures into more redistribution, thus defusing additional pressures and enabling the continuation of a moderate pace of reforms, consequently allowing the process to maintain allies in the business and international communities. Until this effort is undertaken in this manner, or one similar to it, with a sustained political will to proceed in this direction and at the same time the support and skill to stick to such a course, we will not know if it is simply a naive aspiration or a realistic blueprint for change.

In this way the vicious cycle can become the beginning of a virtuous dynamic that can make the two terms of our tension self-reinforcing instead of antagonistic. If democracy lasts long enough, and is accompanied by at least moderate but sustained economic growth, it can be a fulcrum for redistribution. If so, the institutions and mechanisms that bring about a reduction in inequality will be credited with this success, and will also enjoy the popularity and backing that comes not only from their intrinsic merits and from the evils of authoritarian rule, but from a specific improvement in the lives of millions. If democracy and growth coincide, and the former redistributes the fruits of the latter, democratic rule and inequality can be compatible for a while. If democracy does not coincide with growth or with redistribution, in all likelihood it will not last in Latin America during these last years of our century.

4

Traditional Power Structures and Democratic Governance in Latin America

Frances Hagopian

Among the challenges confronting democratic regimes in Latin America in the 1990s, the persistence of traditional power structures in the region stands out as critical. In an area long plagued by economic inequality, traditional elites historically have denied the fruits of full citizenship to peasants and other lower-class groups through coercive labor systems and various formal and informal political mechanisms that limit mass political representation. Today the power of traditional elites and the economic and political structures buttressing that power gravely threaten what Jorge Domínguez and Abraham Lowenthal urge us in the introduction to this collection to ponder: the capacity of institutions within democratic regimes to govern effectively and with accountability in response to the expressed concerns of the electorate. In those countries in which traditional power structures are strongest, democracy is arguably the most fragile. More specifically, the deficiencies of democratic governance highlighted by the contributors to this collection—weak political parties, incomplete state reform, and ineffective governments—are most in evidence.

This chapter examines the manifestations, causes, and consequences for democratic governance of the persistence of traditional power structures. In several countries where power is narrowly concentrated in closed circles of "traditional elites," or elites related by kinship or personal connections who dominate outside of industrial sectors and the largest cities, agrarian structures are egregiously unequal. "Traditional" parties command a sizable vote in elections and seat delegations to national and provincial legislative bodies large enough to exert a profound influence on public policy. Traditional elites dominate the political arena through blunt coercion exercised in the private sphere, through state institutions, and through more subtle mechanisms, especially the dispensation of state patronage. During the period of transitions to democracy, these elites preserved their access to state institutions and patronage resources, as well as their prerogatives to block constitutional reforms and ordinary legislation inimical to their interests, through negotiations with prodemocratic forces. Democratization has not so much threatened the persistence of traditional power structures as traditional elites have threatened democracy.

This chapter argues that while the electoral participation of "conservative" forces may enhance the stability of elective regimes, the residual power of traditional elites threatens the democratic process by undermining both the *effectiveness* and *accountability* of democratic governments. Patronage politics, the hallmark of governance by traditional elites in an era of mass politics, have driven government deficits sky-high and hampered the ability of states to deliver social services efficiently and on a universal basis. In some cases, traditional elites have even worked to block market-oriented reforms. They have also diminished democratic accountability by deforming democratic institutions and diluting mechanisms for political representation and participation in the decision-making process. Moreover, the limits on political, economic, and social reform they often exact as a price for their tolerance of formal democratic procedures ultimately weakens the attachments of nonelites to democracy. I conclude with the recommendation that political reforms be initiated to eliminate nondemocratic institutional arrangements and ensure that traditional elites compete electorally on a fair basis with other social forces, particularly those on the Left. Democratic governance has been most problematic where the opponents of traditional elites are weakly organized.

Traditional Elites and Democracy: The Problem Elaborated

A long tradition in the social sciences, most successfully articulated by Barrington Moore Jr., sees ridding the economic and political orders of the "aristocracy" as a necessary prerequisite for successful democratization.[1] Where landed elites were able to resist the erosion of their powers through opportune alliances with rising industrial and commercial elites, the road to democracy in the modern world was blocked. John Johnson's classic 1958 text extolling the political role of the middle sectors in Latin America made the same assumption.[2] Although Johnson's optimism and faith in the potential of the middle classes to challenge the power of the "oligarchy" and bring democracy to the region's most developed countries in the 1950s was in retrospect misplaced, it is true that where "middle sectors" allied with urban lower classes to pry open their political systems, competitive if ultimately unstable democracies were established in this century. Where, on the other hand, revolutionary and populist alliances were unsuccessful, as in El Salvador and Peru before 1968, democracy remained an elusive goal. Most observers agree that it was only after Peru's reformist military regime undermined the power of the country's landed oligarchy that the potential for a fuller democracy to take root became real.[3]

The breakdown of democratic regimes that pushed reform agendas upon recalcitrant elites and the violence of the counterrevolution that swept the region from the mid-1960s to the mid-1980s has led some observers to urge that this traditional view about the desirability of strategies that attempt to defeat traditional elites outright be revised. These observers believe that the strength of traditional elites during the process of redemocratization and in the early years of a democratic regime should be seen as a positive development insofar as it allows those elites to negotiate policies and procedures favorable to their interests that will ultimately secure their attachment to a democratic order.[4] They contend that giving the "Right" an electoral voice and a credible chance to win elections, as long as it is willing to play by the rules, is preferable to more perfectly constructed democracies that may not underrepresent the Right but will surely drive it to extra-electoral means to protect its interests.

Comparative evidence supports the view that compromise with traditional elites can serve to stabilize democracy. In Argentina, conservative elites, sensing the futility of participating in and respecting the outcomes of elections that they were bound to lose, instead enlisted the support of the military in 1955, 1962, 1966, and again in 1976 to remove governments that injured their economic interests. Since the late 1980s, Gibson's tentative conclusion that the growth of the rightist UCEDE (Union of the Democratic Center) had "reduced the uncertainty of democratic politics for Argentina's upper classes and, thus, . . . helped to integrate them into the democratic process"[5] has rung true. Similarly, in Venezuela, an Acción Democrática (Democratic Action) government that "took a direct stance against the traditional authoritarian alliance" lasted only three years, but when the interests of all elites were safeguarded in the political pacts that reestablished democracy in 1958, democracy was consolidated on a more solid foundation.[6] More recently, in Spain, a "third wave" democratizer,[7] a political consensus in favor of democracy was forged through a series of political and economic pacts that purchased the loyalty of the traditional pillars of the Franco regime to the democratic order as well as peace between labor and capital.

The Venezuelan and Spanish precedents in particular have buoyed the hope that negotiated settlements between democrats and conservative political elites will not only purchase a short-term truce permitting fragile democracies to survive but also lay the foundations for a stronger democracy in the medium and long term. Advocates of such a strategy of reconciliation expect that the formerly nondemocratic Right will become more faithful to democracy once it gets better at the game of democratic politics. Most important, they expect that the political generations that follow, socialized into competitive electoral politics, will have a stronger attachment to democracy than their predecessors for whom the acceptance of democracy was conditional upon the preservation of their interests. Such a scenario, it is claimed, unfolded in the postwar German Federal Republic.[8]

After a decade or more during which this advice has been heeded and democracy has been reestablished via negotiations that left traditional elites in power in several Latin American countries, most notably Brazil, Ecuador, and El Salvador, the time is ripe for a reassessment of this new orthodoxy. This chapter undertakes such a reassessment through an examination of the influence of traditional elites on the early phases of democratization. I proceed by first distinguishing traditional power structures and traditional elites from the Right and other conservative economic and political elites (who are capably discussed in the chapter by Edward Gibson in this collection).

Traditional Power Structures in Latin America

"Traditional power structures" serve as the economic and political foundations of the power of traditional elites. "Traditional elites," sometimes referred to as oligarchs, are most frequently defined socioeconomically as agrarian or rural-based elites and politically as "conservative" and "rightist" forces. They are "rural-based" in that they or their families, at least at one time, enjoyed the concentrated ownership of land, especially in those countries where land is scarce. Also, as Blachman and Sharpe have persuasively argued in the Central American context, they have benefited from coercive labor systems: debt peonage, sharecropping, and other labor-repressive institutions.[9] Today's traditional elites are the "heirs," as Zeitlin and Ratcliffe put it in writing of the Chilean elite, "of their own political families' landed political power and propensity to rule."[10]

Nonetheless, these common definitions of traditional elites often obscure more than they clarify. Many "traditional" rural-based elites, including the coffee oligarchies of Central America and the cattle ranchers and grain producers of the Pampas, have in fact long employed "modern," productive agricultural techniques in large-scale commercial agriculture for domestic and foreign markets. They can no longer be equated with "landed elites," moreover, because they have diversified their economic activities, a step that has allowed them to survive agricultural modernization, urbanization, and industrialization in the postwar period. The overlapping of agricultural and commercial interests makes it impossible to restrict the "traditional" label to rural-based, agricultural elites.[11] Finally, traditional elites are not the only political groups that hold conservative beliefs, promote a conservative agenda, and organize political parties of the Right.

Traditional elites in Latin America today, not readily identifiable purely by a common economic condition, are perhaps most accurately conceived as closed circles of power holders that dominate a range of state institutions and political processes, and that concentrate political as well as economic power within a limited number of families.[12] It is their control of *political* resources that has enabled traditional elites to preserve their economic power and resist the meaningful expansion of political competition and participation. The most important of these political assets was, until recently, their alliance with the military. Historically and in the contemporary period, traditional elites have also effectively used judicial, bureaucratic, and legislative power to win favorable state policies and to deny the extension of a broad range of citizenship rights to the lower classes, most notably the right to organize. Today, exercising tight control over several political parties, they also control political recruitment; membership in or alliance with these families is often key to political advancement.

Although the power base of traditional elites lies in local and regional politics, they have enjoyed ample success in national-level politics. At minimum they have gained sufficient electoral support to gain entry into governing coalitions and, not infrequently, their parties have won outright legislative majorities and even control of the executive branch. Historically Latin American traditional elites dominated the electoral arena through coercion, particularly of dependent peasant populations. Although they still resort to coercion in some places, in recent years they have demonstrated their capacity to survive in increasingly more participatory and competitive electoral systems by employing newer, more subtle forms of political domination, in particular, the distribution of state patronage. Traditional elites use clientelism more than any other method of competing in elections and governing, and they do so more extensively and regularly than any other set of politicians. What distinguishes the "traditional" from the "nontraditional" use of patronage is that it is exercised through highly personalized, family-based, clientelistic networks. Personalism, in fact, is as much a hallmark of traditional politics as is limited political competition.

Although there is considerable overlap between the economic power of the agricultural sector and the electoral success of traditional parties, this correspondence is not perfect. In some countries, the power of traditional elites has been ravaged by social revolution or moderated by the rise of parties of the Left and the cultural predisposition of elites to compromise. In Mexico, Bolivia, Nicaragua, and Cuba, social revolution and the land reforms of revolutionary governments deprived prerevolutionary traditional elites of their principal source of power. A new, postrevolutionary political elite consolidated power to such an extent in Mexico that it is possible to speak of a political oligarchy, but this elite cannot be considered "traditional."[13] In Bolivia the pre-revolutionary white, Spanish-speaking, landed aristocracy was stripped of its landholdings by a sweeping agrarian reform. Minifundismo and military intervention, however, rendered the effects of social revolution less thorough and permanent than in Mexico and Cuba and permitted a new agricultural and mining elite to arise. In nonrevolutionary settings, political reform and economic differentiation sometimes served the same end. In Peru the military-sponsored agrarian reform of 1969, however incomplete, broke the power of the landed elite.[14] As Lowenthal put it, "most of Peru's former oligarchs have fallen from unquestioned authority to oblivion or even ignominy."[15] In Venezuela, agrarian reform finished what the conversion to an oil economy had begun: the shift of power away from traditional, rural elites.[16] In Costa Rica a tradition of small-holder agriculture and a political class that embraced democratic principles made agrarian reform less essential for democratic development than elsewhere on the continent.[17]

In the agriculturally fertile countries of the Southern Cone, the power of traditional rural-based elites was tempered by the successful organization of urban-based competitors, especially those in the popular classes. In both Argentina and Uruguay, highly commercially oriented agrarian elites shared power early in the twentieth century with middle sector groups. In Argentina they irrevocably lost their political hegemony after 1912, but after 1930 they did not hesitate to back extraparliamentary means to remove populist governments that manipulated exchange rates to favor industrial interests over their own. In Uruguay, traditional elites were committed to a democratic order that combined electoral dominance for their two political parties with the most progressive package of social welfare policies in the hemisphere. Traditional elites in Chile accepted democratization as long as their property rights were secure and the peasantry was excluded from political participation. Until the 1960s these elites used their congressional veto to block legislation that would have permitted rural organizing efforts, the dismantling of harshly labor-repressive agricultural systems, and measures to redistribute land. Subsequently, in the early 1970s, they fought to overthrow an elected government that redistributed their assets. In the mid-1970s a "counterreform" reversed much of the agrarian reform of the late 1960s and early 1970s, but did not restore the pre-1962 agrarian system. Nonetheless, today the National Agricultural Society remains a powerful interest group, the Renovación Nacional (National Renovation) remains a powerful political party, and the interests of traditional elites are well represented in the current Congress by a thin majority in the Senate that includes Pinochet appointees and a substantial minority in the directly elected lower Chamber.

Elsewhere the power of traditional elites has been preserved, even after economic modernization, by the ability of traditional elites to deny outright basic rights of citizenship or to manipulate state resources and representative networks to their advantage. In Brazil, Colombia, Ecuador, El Salvador, Guatemala, and Honduras, traditional elites control several branches of government: they might occupy the presidency, command a working legislative majority, or make or approve appointments to the judiciary and civil service. They also control important political parties and the policy agenda to such an extent that a mass democratic politics has hardly taken root. These are countries in which traditional power structures persist at high rates. In Brazil, traditional elites exercise a great deal of control over the national congress and state and local governments, several major political parties, and, to a large extent, the design of political institutions and economic and social policy. In Honduras and Colombia, "traditional" parties enjoy virtually uncontested electoral hegemony. The National and Liberal Parties in Honduras have captured at least 92 percent of the vote in every election held since 1980. With the singular exception of the vote for the M-19 in the Constituent Assembly elections of 1991, the Conservative and Liberal Parties in Colombia have captured more than 90 percent of the vote in every election since the restoration of democratic rule in 1958, allowing them to control the presidency, the legislature, and all other state positions appointed by these powers. The leadership of these parties has remained for decades in the hands of the same families, and even in the 1980s this "patrimony of traditional elites" had apparently only moderately diminished.[18] In Ecuador a resilient oligarchy based in Guayaquil that "worked closely" with all five constitutional regimes between 1948 and 1963[19] has survived military rule and oil-financed industrialization. Even today, it exercises significant influence in the Ecuadorian Congress and Supreme Court.[20]

The persistence of traditional elite power is even more pervasive in the Central American nations of El Salvador and Guatemala. In El Salvador, the oligarchy has retained control of the judiciary and has organized a formidable political party, ARENA (Nationalist Republican Alliance), that defeated the reformist Christian Democrats in the 1989 presidential election and captured nearly half of the seats in the Legislative Assembly two years later. Even when out of office during the Christian Democratic administration of Napoleón Duarte (1984–89), the coffee elite of El Salvador collectively battled, and ultimately defeated, the establishment of a coffee marketing board, and it also managed to dilute the agrarian reform. More obviously consequential for democratic consolidation, traditional elites blocked crucial reforms of the judicial system and civil-military relations that most observers feel are prerequisites for the full integration of all democratic players in the Salvadoran political system.[21] In Guatemala the oligarchy has for half a century used whatever means necessary to fend off the multiclass coalition that would restrain its powers. Increasingly unable to impose a settlement, it has accepted the protection of the Guatemalan military and military-written constitutions to preserve its hegemony.

In the Dominican Republic, Haiti, Paraguay, and prerevolutionary Nicaragua, personalistic dictatorships and intermittent occupation by U.S. forces served both to prop up and to attenuate the dominance of regionally based traditional elites. Elites in these countries sacrificed absolute domination for economic opportunity, restrictions on mass organizing, and insulation from the pressures to expand the limited opportunities for political participation. In the Dominican Republic where, until the death of Rafael Trujillo in 1961, "the primitive bureaucracy was concerned almost entirely with supporting the personal interests of the ruling oligarchy,"[22] a legacy of the Trujillo dictatorship was the excessive centralization of power and personalism today evident in the persistent political dominance of Joaquín Balaguer. In the late 1970s, in the Dominican Republic, traditional power holders joined with industrial elites to fashion a democratic regime. In Haiti, a decade later, they conspired with military elites to overthrow one. The Paraguayan Colorado Party, which served as the electoral vehicle for the dictator Stroessner and elected two-thirds of the representatives to both chambers in 1983, emerged from authoritarian rule in the 1989 elections with 74 percent of the vote. Its vote total slipped to 40 percent in the 1991 municipal elections, but it is still the largest party.[23]

The remainder of this chapter focuses on the cases of "high" and "medium" traditional elite persistence. The next section elaborates how traditional elites in these countries were able to survive both the reigns of increasingly professional and autonomous militaries that came to power to "modernize" their countries and the transitions to fuller, more participatory democracies to such a degree that it is meaningful to consider their impact on democratic governance today. The experience of these elites with military rule and its demise also contributes to our understanding of how their attitudinal and behavioral predispositions toward democratic government were shaped.

Traditional Elites, Military Rule, and Democratization

The conventional wisdom used to be that military rule in Latin America benefited traditional elites. As Charles Anderson long ago pointed out, military coups took place precisely to assure the holders of important power capabilities that their position in society would not be endangered,[24] a claim best evidenced by the historic marriage between the ruling families and military establishments of Central America. Alfred Stepan's work on the Brazilian military, which demonstrated a considerable level of military institutional autonomy, perhaps forever shattered the image of the military as the storm troopers of the oligarchy.[25] His thesis was only strengthened when the Peruvian military proclaimed itself "anti-oligarchic" and when militaries in "bureaucratic-authoritarian regimes" subsequently did not relinquish power to civilians. Instead, they empowered technocrats and insulated them from political representatives in order to stabilize economies in crisis and to promote industrial development. These regimes most zealously attacked the interests of labor, but they also were perceived as betraying the traditional and modern upper classes that had supported the overthrow of elected presidents. In many lesser developed countries in the region as well, rifts opened between military establishments and civilian elites.

Whether military regimes were committed to reform or restoration, the effects of their economic policies and political strategies altered the power of traditional forces. In some countries, traditional elites were strengthened, and in others they were weakened by the economic policies adopted by militaries to stabilize or restructure their economies. They were also affected by the political strategies these militaries pursued to maintain themselves in power or fashion the polity to conform to their vision even after their departures. Thus, in Peru, twelve years of military rule eroded traditional power structures and the influence of the traditional landed families and their financial institutions,[26] whereas in Ecuador traditional elites survived a nominally reformist military regime "virtually unscathed."[27] The Ecuadorian regime had a less profound commitment to reform, it was less cohesive, and traditional elites were able to mount an effective opposition to agrarian reform and other military-sponsored programs. Traditional elites also benefited from the marginalization of political parties under military rule. While all parties were weakened, those new parties that were only beginning to make inroads among the country's popular sectors were disadvantaged to a larger degree than already established traditional parties.[28]

Most bureaucratic-authoritarian regimes excluded the political representatives of civilian elites from decision making at the same time that these regimes supported the economic interests of these groups. The result was a variable pattern of influence on the persistence of traditional power structures. In Brazil, agricultural elites benefited from real negative interest rates on loans from the state-owned Bank of Brazil, and agrarian reform was effectively removed from the political agenda for two decades. Agricultural modernization proceeded quickly in the southern parts of the country and on the southern and western frontiers, but traditional elites retained their control of land in the northeast of the country. The Brazilian military regime was also the only bureaucratic-authoritarian regime to offer political protection to the traditional elite. Because the military needed the skill, networks, and support of the traditional political elite to win legislative and local elections, it favored traditional elites who organized politically well-integrated state clientelistic networks and who could effectively dispense state patronage. Traditional elites in Brazil emerged from the period of military rule stronger than they were at its outset, and perhaps stronger than they would have been otherwise.

In the more politically repressive military regimes of the Southern Cone, the effects of military rule on traditional power structures are more ambiguous. In Argentina and Chile these effects may not have been significant. Exchange rates meant to favor exports strengthened the hand of the grain exporters of the Argentine Pampas but, as Edward Gibson argues in his chapter in this collection, civilian elites learned that the military, driven by its own agenda and internal divisions, was an "uncontrollable partner that could not effectively implement policy." In Chile, favorable policies for the "modern" agricultural sector, in particular for "nontraditional" exports that helped to sustain traditional elites, also helped to offset the adverse political consequences that might have followed from the decision of the Chilean military to retire political parties, including the then leading party of the Right and representative of the traditional elite, the Partido Nacional (National Party).

In Uruguay, on the other hand, military rule may have served to weaken traditional power structures. The military governors declared traditional parties, which had competed and governed for decades on the basis of their ability to distribute state patronage to their constituents, to be in "recess." By depriving traditional party leaders of positions in state administration and the opportunity to compete in electoral campaigns in which they typically exchanged pork for votes— in other words, of their ability to practice political clientelism—the military may have eroded their electoral dominance. The leftist Frente Amplio (FA, Broad Front) and Nuevo Espacio (New Space) coalitions increased their electoral representation from 18 percent in the 1971 and 1984 elections to 30 percent in 1989. Nonetheless, despite the improved electoral performance of coalitions of leftist parties, the traditional parties continue to control the presidency.

Most analysts agree that South American militaries experienced a loss of power and prestige as a result of their most recent governing experiences. By contrast, military establishments in Central America have gained power. When he assumed office as the elected president of Guatemala in 1985, Vinicio Cerezo was subject to numerous restrictions on his power by the military.[29] The militaries in Honduras and Guatemala in recent decades have acquired unprecedented levels of autonomy from their traditional allies,[30] and their alliance with economic elites is now an alliance of equals.[31] In a 1991 interview, General Héctor Gramajo spoke of the Guatemalan military's desires for greater autonomy and claimed that "The Army no longer plays an electoral role . . . [nor] are we any longer the redeemers for the right-wing *latifundistas.* . . . They no longer dominate the Army. The Army doesn't ask them for food rations [for the soldiers], but it doesn't do their dirty work for them either. We are not concubines, we are professionals."[32] In Honduras, Guatemala, and Ecuador, independence from civilian elites was achieved to a significant degree because of the active involvement of the military in the economy. The military in Honduras has a hand in public utilities, transportation, and, through its own pension institute, is a major player in financial markets.[33] The Ecuadorian armed forces, as Isaacs reports, "have amassed a vast and diverse economic empire."

The trend toward growing military autonomy in both Central and South America prompted many Latin American traditional elites not to attempt to block the return of civilian rule and, once established, not to support attempts at military coups.[34] Where militaries attempted to govern autonomously, there were two principal reasons for the conversion of traditional elites to the virtues of democratic governance. First, in Peru, Ecuador, Nicaragua, and Panama, authoritarian rulers did not govern consistently in the interests of the elite. Second, in these countries as well as in Honduras, the Dominican Republic, and Argentina, traditional elites wearied of their lack of access to top policymakers. In both cases, they embraced democracy as a means to *expand* their influence. In Argentina, in particular, traditional elites also dropped their customary resistance to democratic governance because, as Gibson notes, the military led the country into a "reckless war," and because they believed that the economic constraints of the 1980s would eliminate any possible reversion to anti-agrarian, anti-exporting, populist policies. In several Central American countries, reigning oligarchies additionally embraced elections in order to win international support in their bid to stave off impending revolution.

Whatever their motives, since the transitions to democracy, traditional elites have by and large made commitments to electoral politics, though to different degrees and for different stakes. In Argentina, for example, the traditional elite invested considerable resources and effort in organizing a credible electoral alternative on the political Right for the first time in fifty years, primarily through uniting the conservative provincial parties of the interior with the Buenos Aires–based UCEDE in the Alianza de Centro (Alliance of the Center).[35] In the late 1980s the modest success of this electoral alliance won for the Right influence in government[36] and, together with the estrangement between civilian and military elites, reduced the potential for an authoritarian regression. In El Salvador, the incorporation of one faction of the traditional right into the ARENA party moved the resolution of political conflict from the military toward the electoral arena. With nearly half the seats in the legislature occupied by ARENA delegates, ex-president Alfredo Cristiani, representing a faction of the traditional Salvadoran elite willing to compromise on democracy, was able to make credible moves toward democratization.[37]

On the other hand, whether traditional elites initiated the transitions to democratic regimes or merely embraced the ideas of civilian rule and competitive elections at some point during the transition process, their role in the democratization process has contributed to the preservation of traditional power structures. Through their participation in coalitions to end authoritarian rule they carved out spaces for themselves in the political arena, which they might have otherwise lost through the "natural" processes of socioeconomic and electoral change. From these strongholds, they exercise veto power over many political and economic reforms at the top of the political agenda in new and newly reestablished democracies. In this respect, recent negotiated transitions to democracy in several Latin American countries—Brazil and Ecuador chief among them—have more closely followed the Colombian precedent than the Spanish one. The consociational agreements forged in Colombia in 1957 in the aftermath of a decade of political violence, praised by many for securing democracy, also fortified traditional power structures *and* limited democracy. In the decades that followed the establishment of the National Front, the "gentlemen" who governed Colombia were able to limit popular mobilization, limit access to higher education, and stymie agrarian reform.[38] These developments were not merely undesirable features of a stable democracy. They have threatened democracy itself, leading to a Colombian state so weak that it cannot respond adequately to challenges to its authority.[39]

Does this mean, then, that the participation of traditional elites in political pacts is bad for democratic consolidation? The evidence suggests that the new common wisdom about broadly inclusive negotiated transitions should not be discarded altogether, but it should be qualified. Advocates of political pacts base their argument that political pacts provide an auspicious beginning for democratic regimes on three assumptions: (1) that key players participate in pacts; (2) that pacts solve procedural questions, and occasionally substantive issues (the former are crucial for strengthening democratic institutions, whereas the latter, Przeworski argues, are binding only on the signatories, not their political heirs);[40] and (3) that each side is strong enough that no one actor can dominate the outcome. Where traditional elites dominate, these assumptions are only partly true.

In model pacted transitions such as those that took place in Venezuela and Spain, political transitions were supported by leaders of established political parties, business, and labor organizations. Backed by their constituents and members, these civilian elites struck a series of political settlements that distributed fair chances for all parties to compete for power in the electoral arena and socioeconomic pacts that reduced the uncertainty of democracy and guaranteed economic "rights" for all actors. In Brazil and Ecuador, by contrast, leaders of corporate groups did not participate in negotiations that were dominated by traditional elites. In these countries as well as the Dominican Republic, democratic regimes were brought into being without class compromise. As Conaghan and Espinal put it in writing of Ecuador and the Dominican Republic, "These democracies did not emerge as a political arrangement to negotiate the relations between labour and capital, but as a vehicle for restructuring domination by economic and political elites."[41] In none of these cases was social peace or institutional reform achieved as a result of pact making.

In those countries where traditional elites reemerged from military rule with substantial reservoirs of economic and political power, they insisted, as a price for their cooperation with the democratic opposition, on limiting policy reform. They also undermined, rather than strengthened, democratic political institutions, including political parties. In Brazil, for example, in exchange for supporting the civilian opposition candidate for president, traditional politicians were able to negotiate their continued access to the high-level state posts and patronage resources that underlay their political power. They also flooded and won seats on the governing bodies of all major political parties except the Workers' Party (the PMDB [Party of the Brazilian Democratic Movement] was transformed from a party posed to represent popular classes into an oligarchical vehicle), thus robbing several of budding programmatic identities. In the early years of the New Republic, social policy and constitutional issues were bartered for personal political gain. The votes of traditional elites to preserve the presidential system of government, for example, were won with generous allocations from the housing and other ministries. In short, the price of constructing a temporary majority for the purpose of accelerating the departure of the military was that traditional clientelistic networks and other antidemocratic modes of political representation were revitalized, and forces that might have challenged military prerogatives were weakened.

A similar chain of events transpired in Ecuador. In Ecuador, the formation of governing coalitions involved "the distribution of an inordinate amount of patronage, which in turn mortgaged the president's ability to govern effectively. . . . The particular way in which patronage politics has dominated bargaining and compromise . . . has served more to undermine than to bolster the democratic process." In short, "tenuous party loyalties, party fragmentation, a surfeit of patronage politics, and persistent conflicts between the president and the congress" continue to plague Ecuador despite the "crafted transition."[42] While it is too soon to assess the outcome of the peace process in El Salvador, its success may depend on whether the negotiations indeed move away from settling who should hold power and resolve what the mechanisms and forms should be for competing for power, as Córdova Macías hypothesizes, in his chapter in this collection, has been the case. The "Forum on Socio-Economic *Concertación*," he reports, to date has not moved beyond defining an agenda.

One feature that may work to the advantage of the Salvadoran transition which was absent in the Brazilian and Ecuadorian cases is the presence of a Left in the negotiations that is strong enough to bargain effectively. If a "too strong" electoral Left—one that can form a government without "centrist" allies to moderate a program of radical reform—is threatening to democracy because the traditional elite is likely to back military force to safeguard its interests (e.g., Venezuela in 1948; Chile in 1973), a "too weak" electoral Left poses different but no less serious dangers to democracy. In both Ecuador and the Dominican Republic, where the lower-class population was not effectively mobilized or otherwise threatening, traditional and modern sector elites created postauthoritarian regimes that Conaghan and Espinal have characterized as "democratic-authoritarian" hybrids.[43] The participation of the Left in the electoral process appears to enhance rather than detract from the prospects for establishing stable, competitive democracies. In Chile the participation of the Socialist Party and the socialist-leaning Party for Democracy in the 1988 "Campaign for the No," in the subsequent negotiations over the establishment of a democratic regime, and indeed, beginning in 1990, government, has contributed to one of the continent's most effective and accountable democracies. The role in the negotiations to bring about the democratic transition and the subsequent electoral success of the Uruguayan Left in the 1980s, after years of frustration at the polls and the military defeat of the Tupamaros, has augmented, not harmed, the prospects for democracy in Uruguay. In one of his last writings on the state of democracy in Uruguay, Gillespie was sanguine that democracy was well on its way toward being reconsolidated.[44]

What the evidence from these examples suggests is that pacts can be valuable under three conditions: (1) when they are negotiated among near political equals, and thus each party must concede something of value; (2) when they resolve economic, social, or cultural conflict (as, for example, between capital and labor, landed and landless, or ethnic or linguistic majorities and minorities); and (3) when they safeguard the opportunity for all segments of society to participate politically. When, instead, they satisfy none of these conditions but preserve traditional elite power, often at the expense of democratic institutions, they can result in defective democracies that govern poorly, as we see below.

The Impact of Traditional Power Structures on Democratic Governance

The contention that where traditional power structures are strong, democratic governance is the least effective and accountable is supported by an obvious set of correlations. Where traditional elites are strongest, political parties are weakest, executive-legislative relations are at their worst, and economic reforms have lagged. Where the power of traditional elites has been broken or attenuated, economic reform has been made possible or secured under democratic regimes, political parties are healthier, and democratic institutions have been strengthened since the return to democracy, even if they have not made a full recovery from military rule.

The obvious question which these observations raise is whether or not such failures should be attributed to the persistence of traditional power structures or if they could more accurately be viewed as caused by any one of a number of factors frequently cited by other analysts: faulty institutional design; poorly devised electoral laws; and a nondemocratic political culture. Exaggerated federalism, strong presidents, and congresses too weak to govern effectively but strong enough to obstruct executive initiatives (the institutional flaws aptly cited in the chapter by Lamounier in this collection as underlying what he describes as Brazil's "hyperactive paralysis syndrome"), as well as permissive party legislation, have undeniably contributed to governance problems in several countries across the region. But it is problematic to treat deficient institutions and electoral systems as the *independent* source of the most acute of these governance problems.

If faulty institutional design were the foremost cause of the disappointing performance of democratic government, then how is it to be explained that some countries with otherwise similar institutional features exhibit different governance problems? All Latin American countries, for example, have presidential systems of government, but presidents in Brazil and Ecuador are more often vulnerable to the lack of adequate support in congress and less effective than are their counterparts in Chile, Argentina, and Costa Rica. Electoral and party laws that discourage party discipline and allow the number of political parties to proliferate, moreover, are not equally damaging in all countries. Party discipline is surely eroded in Brazil by the unique combination of open list proportional representation and large, multimember districts.[45] Yet Uruguay's "double simultaneous vote," which by design should be just as threatening to party unity and the programmatic integrity of its parties, has not weakened Uruguay's parties to nearly the same extent. Uruguayan parties are able to retain their leaders and voters and frame accountable policies. The harm done by permissive party legislation per se is also unclear. While the proliferation of parties to feed the ambitions of politicians has undoubtedly fragmented many party systems, "political entrepreneurs" such as Luis Inácio "Lula" da Silva and Fernando Henrique Cardoso in Brazil and Carlos "Chacho" Álvarez in Argentina that have founded new parties based on programmatic alternatives have enhanced the representativeness of their party systems without necessarily diminishing the effectiveness of their governments.

There are in fact several reasons to believe that where the institutional and cultural problems highlighted by many analysts as threatening many Latin American democracies do tend to coincide with a specific cluster of governing problems—such as congressional inaction, fragile governing coalitions, and a rapidly declining public faith in democratic institutions—these institutional defects are themselves epiphenomenal, brought on by traditional elite power. Behind weak presidents, ineffective legislatures, and unfulfilled popular expectations most often lay weak parties with volatile bases of public support and undisciplined congressional delegations that are generally associated with high levels of traditional elite power. "Government gridlock" and policy immobilism can be attributed to traditional elites using their power base in the legislature to check the executive, often when they have failed to control the presidency, although it would be inaccurate to view traditional elite-dominated congresses as uniformly ineffective. Congresses in countries in the grip of traditional elites are readily able to pass legislation in areas that do not affect the power base of traditional elites, but stall measures that would redistribute wealth and income or redesign institutions along lines that would make democratic governments more accountable to mass electorates and less accountable to traditional elites. Similarly, the "consociational" pull away from the center highlighted by Lamounier, embodied in governmental federalism and parties with strong provincial governing bodies, are themselves in the Latin American context creations of strong, preindustrial regional elites seeking to maximize their power. Federalism has persisted where traditional elites are strong, as in Brazil, and declined to the advantage of the center where they are not, as in postrevolutionary Mexico.

Aspects of political culture that are deemed unsupportive of democratic governance, too, are shaped by the beliefs and political practices of traditional elites. Historically, the dominant strains of the political cultures of Brazil, Ecuador, and Colombia were personalism, clientelism, and regionalism. Today mass publics breaking out of traditional patterns of deference not surprisingly hope that democracy will bring material rewards as well as freedom from fear of repression, but the reason why the Brazilian and other electorates expect an "unreasonable" amount from their democracies is probably because parties that can neither frame nor pursue a coherent program of government raise rather than discipline popular expectations. When they fail to satisfy public appetites for government outputs, they also erode public confidence in democratic political institutions.

In what specific ways, then, have traditional elites with high levels of political power, either directly or through parties, undermined the performance of democratic government? First, because these elites depend on distributing patronage resources to compete in democratic political systems, they have fueled patronage inflation, politicized the delivery of social services, inhibited policymaking, and strained government budgets with their profligate spending patterns.[46] In the first few years of democratic government in Brazil, regionally based political elites, most of them traditional, went on a spending spree that resulted in a debt of U.S.$57 billion that the federal government was later forced to assume. The inefficient delivery of scarce social resources such as education and health might also be attributed to the excessive clientelism practiced by traditional elites. In the Dominican Republic, Rosario Espinal points out that the education, health, and agricultural ministries, as well as the judiciary, have been grossly underfunded in recent years.

A second way in which traditional politicians have reduced the effectiveness of democratic government has been to either slow or block market-oriented reforms, or to negotiate even more patronage resources in exchange for supporting reform in areas that affect them least, such as systems of wage and salary compensation, trade liberalization, and the regulation of foreign investment. This has occurred more often than market-oriented economic reforms have undermined the power base of traditional elites. In Brazil the earliest portion of an economic reform program that has lagged by regional standards to be completed was trade liberalization, and traditional politicians readily lent their support in the Congress to anti-inflation legislation that restrained wages in exchange for the government "opening its coffers."[47] These same politicians, however, have most stubbornly and to date effectively resisted state reform that would reduce the state payroll, restrain the spending of state governments, and reform the social security system, all of which most experts feel are required to complete Brazil's fiscal stabilization. In Colombia, according to Matthew Shugart, elites of the traditional parties posed such an obstacle to economic liberalization that former president Virgilio Barco lent his support to a referendum initiative to stage an extraordinary election of a Constituent Assembly that would otherwise not have been held. The new constitution promulgated in 1991 was designed to reduce the clientelistic basis of economic policymaking.[48] In Ecuador the president has lacked support for his economic program in the Congress and most significantly from within his own party. According to Anita Isaacs, all other legislation, including judicial reform, has been postponed pending the passage of economic reforms. The legislature has not even produced a budget in fifteen months.

Where traditional power structures persist at high levels, moreover, democratic accountability is limited at best. In Guatemala, Honduras, and El Salvador, the forces of the traditional Right are so strong that they have twisted democracies into what critics have called "façade democracies" in which, despite the staging of elections, ruling groups do not lose power.[49] The most blatant distortion of democracy has been a lack of constitutional guarantees for those segments of the population that elites would prefer to exclude from the electoral process. Opponents of traditional elite dominance have been denied equal access to the media and public during electoral campaigns, and they have even been physically intimidated. In El Salvador, in 1993, the United Nations estimated that close to 800,000 eligible voters, or 27 percent of voting-age Salvadorans, were without electoral identification cards. The unregistered, as Córdova Macías points out, were overwhelmingly from two zones: the largest urban areas and the rural areas that had formerly experienced high levels of armed conflict. Although the UN believes that today the largest obstacles to voter registration are lack of citizen mobilization and technical inefficiencies, the hypothesis cannot be discounted that for some time opponents of traditional elite power were systematically disenfranchised.

Elsewhere, democratic accountability is undermined by distortions of electoral law. While it may be customary in democracies to over-represent underpopulated regions in one chamber (usually the upper), the state of São Paulo is grossly underrepresented in the *lower house* of the Brazilian Congress (the Chamber of Deputies) as well as the Senate. A deputy needs only 14,000 votes to be elected in Amapá, 180,000 in Rio Grande do Sul, and 300,000 in São Paulo.[50] The underrepresentation of São Paulo, designed by the military to give electoral advantage to its supporters among the traditional elite in Brazil's northeast, persists to this day because those who benefit, a majority in the Congress, can block any attempts to redress this inequity.

Even when these political systems appear to be operating according to democratic rules, democratic accountability is limited by the appropriation by traditional power holders of mass political parties. In an era of mass politics, the strategies that parties representing traditional elites employ to compete with one other and nonelite parties, mobilize their electoral supporters, and even govern—all based on clientelism— weaken political party programs, deny mass political representation in the political and policy arenas, and almost always underrepresent the collective interests of the mass electorate. The country studies in this collection attest to the fact that, in those countries in which traditional elites are strongest, political party attachments in the electorate are weak; parties have short lives; they do not readily distinguish themselves from one another by program; and they are the least effective in fulfilling their interest-aggregating functions.

Weakened parties are especially evident in Brazil, Ecuador, and Guatemala. In both Brazil and Ecuador, analysts have employed the same metaphor of "shirt-changing" to describe the frequency with which traditional politicians move from one party to another.[51] In Brazil, once the opposition elected the president in 1985, state and local politicians deserted the pro-military PDS (Democratic Social Party) en masse for the ranks of the newly created PFL (Party of the Liberal Front) and the former opposition party, the PMDB; in the early 1990s, the fortunes of the PRN (Party of National Reconstruction) similarly rose and fell with the star of Fernando Collor de Mello. In Ecuador, according to Isaacs, by April 1994 one-third of those elected to Congress had deserted the party for which they ran, many lured away by the promises of government patronage. The problem for democratic governance when politicians frequently change parties is that they can be held accountable only for their constituency service, not for the passage or blockage of issue-based legislation. When parties are extremely short-lived, this problem is exacerbated. In his chapter in this collection, Edelberto Torres-Rivas decries that parties in Guatemala have only a "precarious temporal existence" (eight of the sixteen parties contesting the 1984 election for a Constituent Assembly had been created within one month of the election, and another five were less than one year old); their programs are vacuous; and they lack roots in the electorate. It is little wonder that in Guatemala political parties do not represent the social and economic interests of the political community and have little say in actual governance. As another observer of contemporary Guatemala has written, "since 1954 the political realm has not been where accords are defined and solutions sought to the fundamental problems of the nation. . . . The ruling authority negotiates directly with special interests and establishes political accords with them. Thus, the power dynamic of personal authority has replaced the power of the political party. Parties merely bless decisions already made in the political black market, decisions made beyond any legal authority or regulatory process."[52]

Finally, more often than not, traditional elites extract as a condition for their support for democratic regimes limits on policy reform. Agrarian reform, scuttled in Colombia in the 1960s, Ecuador in the 1970s, and El Salvador and Brazil in the 1980s, is only the most obvious of a longer list of impermissible public policies. Such limits threaten democracy because the absence of anticipated reform weakens the attachment to democracy of potential beneficiaries whose support for democracy is often instrumentally based.[53]

Where weak parties have not effectively represented popular interests and policy reform has been limited—precisely in those countries in which the persistence of traditional power structures is most pronounced—there are apparent declining rates of electoral participation and shallow commitments on the part of the masses to democracy.[54] In Brazil, voter turnout in only four years (1986–90) plunged from 95 percent to less than 70 percent, and the number of blank and spoiled ballots cast rose sharply in 1990 to 31.5 percent, a level even higher than that registered at the height of the dictatorship in 1970, when the opposition was encouraging such symbolic protest. In the 1993 plebiscite to choose a form of government, less than 55 percent of the population cast a valid vote for either presidentialism or parliamentarism.[55] In Ecuador voter absenteeism exceeded 25 percent in the 1984 presidential elections.[56] In Honduras, 35 percent of voters abstained from casting a ballot in the 1993 presidential elections, compared with just 6 percent in the 1985 election.[57] In El Salvador, voter absenteeism was 67.4 percent in the 1989 presidential election.[58] In Guatemala, turnout for the runoff election for president in 1990 was 42.9 percent of registered voters,[59] and in the 1993 municipal elections abstentions rose still higher to 70 percent of registered voters.[60] These tendencies toward declining voter turnout conform to a longer trend in Colombia where, according to Kline, rates of participation have been low since the 1950s. With the exception of the presidential election of 1970, they have fallen within the range of 34–50 percent of the electorate. In the March 1994 congressional election, abstention rates reached 70 percent.[61]

Public opinion in these countries also explicitly evaluates the performance of democracies and democratic institutions poorly. In 1989, ten years after the transfer of power to civilians, public opinion in Guayaquil and Quito was sharply divided about the desirability of democracy and its ability to solve problems. Less than a majority of respondents to polls conducted by the Institute of Social Studies and Public Opinion in Guayaquil found democracy preferable to, and better at solving problems than, dictatorship.[62] Five years later, in April 1994, 64 percent believed democracy was not the best form of government for Ecuador, and 80 percent felt that political parties did not serve the public interest.[63] Eighty percent of respondents in Quito were without strong party loyalties (up from 38 percent in 1989).[64] In Brazil in late 1993, in the midst of a corruption scandal, according to Lamounier, 55 percent of a national sample interviewed by DataFolha rated the Congress as "bad" or "very bad," 31 percent as "fair," and only 8 percent as "good" or "excellent." The proportion saying that the country "could do well without the Congress" had climbed to 43 percent. The failure to make progress on economic and political inclusion has, moreover, fueled rebellions in Guatemala, El Salvador, and even Colombia that certainly threaten democracy. Less dramatic but also potentially destabilizing protest has also been registered in Paraguay, according to Diego Abente Brun, in his chapter in this collection, as a result of long-repressed social demands.[65]

In sum, if securing the attachment of politically powerful traditional elites to the democratization process has accelerated the timetable of transition to democracy and in essence solved "the Argentine problem," it has also hindered democratic governance by undermining the effectiveness and accountability of democracy. With traditional elites retaining positions of preeminence as a result of military rule and the democratization process, and exercising that preeminence in the political parties and the legislature, a new series of problems has been created: "façade" democracies (the "Central American problem"); policy immobilism (the "Colombian problem"); the conversion of political parties into vehicles for the private use of oligarchies (the "Brazilian problem"); and the concomitant alarming reduction in popular political participation.

Conclusions and Recommendations

This chapter has suggested that the challenges of democratic governance are qualitatively different and immeasurably more severe in countries that exhibit "high" levels of traditional political elite persistence than in those with "medium" and "low" levels. In the former set of countries, expedient alliances formed between democratic oppositions and traditional elites to exit from military rule that often postponed or abandoned outright the reform of social policy, agrarian structures, political institutions, and constitutions and that awarded the perquisite of filling government posts to the forces of the traditional right, have temporarily quieted the real divisions between elite and nonelite and rural and urban citizens. However, these simmer beneath the surface. Without sufficient guarantees to participate in the electoral process and a credible expectation of sharing power, the Left could turn to open rebellion, as it did in Guatemala since the 1950s, in Colombia in the 1970s and 1980s, and in El Salvador in the 1980s. The attachment of the Right to democracy is no less secure.

Democratic regimes in Latin America today inevitably find themselves attempting to navigate a treacherous course between the Scylla of confrontation and the Charybdis of accommodation. Confronting traditional elites surely risks the familiar military coup, or what O'Donnell has called a "sudden death" for democracy.[66] However, the persistent strength of traditional forces permitted by accommodationist strategies also poses a risk that democracy will expire via the steady erosion of its effectiveness and accountability, leading ultimately to the rejection of democratic institutions on the part of mass publics—a "slow death" different from that envisioned by O'Donnell but just as final. Is there a way out of this dilemma? Can the power and antidemocratic tendencies of traditional political elites be attenuated without pushing them to adopt antisystem behavior as they did so often in the past in response to developmental-populist coalitions?

A probing examination of the role played by traditional elites in the early years of democratic rule suggests that where political institutions and procedures are relatively unfettered by negotiated settlements and where the nonelite democratic opposition is strong, and traditional elites must learn to defend their interests in competition with a credible Left in the electoral arena, the prospects are much improved for their positive contribution to the process of democratization. Where, on the other hand, traditional forces are relatively unrestrained and their hegemony uncontested, they pose grave threats indeed to democracy. This is especially true where they are still closely allied with military establishments. If this argument is correct, negotiation and delayed or gradual reform is not a panacea to consolidate democracies plagued by traditional power structures. More important than pacing reform to conform to a gradual schedule is to strengthen the forces with which they must negotiate.

I conclude with two sets of recommendations for reform. The first is to reduce the economic power of traditional elites and strengthen nonelite groups through poverty alleviation, not asset redistribution. The recent history of Latin America shows that measures that threaten to harm the economic interests of traditional elites are the first that will provoke them to antisystem behavior, but that traditional power holders will not today bring down Center-Left governments that respect their economic interests. Although the government of Peronist Carlos Menem in Argentina has done little that a government of the Right would not have, that of the Concertación in Chile has. Since the transition to civilian rule, the governing Center-Left coalition of Christian Democrats and Socialists in Chile has pursued policies that have not redistributed assets but that, through taxation (and sound fiscal policy) have improved social services and reduced poverty. With the economy growing, there is little basis for traditional elite discontent. Such a strategy could serve as a model for reform in other countries in which traditional elites can be electorally defeated but not discounted.

The second proposal is to curb traditional power structures through political reform. My recommendation here falls into three parts. The first is to pursue whatever steps are politically feasible to deepen the wedge between militaries and traditional elites created by the most recent episodes of military rule. This proposal may ultimately be as important as the more frequently sounded ones to reduce military budgets and assert civilian control over both military and police forces.

Second, priority should be assigned to enacting ordinary and constitutional legislation that guarantees formal democracy. Most obviously, legislation that supports coercive labor systems and that limits the ability of popular classes to organize for either economic or political goals should be repealed. In many countries, a fuller democracy will require substantial judicial reform and guarantees of physical safety, as most of the authors of the country studies in this collection have stressed. In other countries, a revision of electoral laws may be required. What makes sense in contexts of electoral dominance by traditional power holders is to revise electoral laws in such a way as to expand the opportunities for political representation of other social groups in decision-making arenas. Where the opportunity still presents itself, it is important to represent the Right, but not to overrepresent it. If traditional elites exercise their strongest authority at the regional and local levels of the political system, extreme caution should be exercised before proceeding with reforms that would *decentralize* power and decision making. The best chance to advance democratizing reforms may be at the national level.

Third, once formal institutional rules are made more democratic, the most important task is to strengthen the avenues for political participation and representation, in particular political parties that speak to the issues and defend the interests of their constituents, whether defined by social class, ethnic group, gender, or neighborhood, in ways that enhance democratic accountability. The corollary to this recommendation is to decrease, by whatever means, the strains of personalism, clientelism, and corruption that prevail in precisely those countries in which traditional elites are strongest. Contrary to the oft-heard claim that clientelism and democracy are perfectly compatible and that clientelism can even be a means by which disadvantaged classes gain access to state resources, recent trends toward rising voter disillusion in Brazil, Ecuador, and elsewhere in Latin America have shown that the excessive resort to patronage politics has weakened parties, damaged the competence of governments to manage the economy, and eroded public faith in democratic institutions. It is no longer only the naysayers who ask if democracy can survive such distortions of political representation and governance.

Traditional political elites are certainly not the only ones who dip their hands into public coffers to buy votes. But this practice, a prop of the traditional order in the modern polity, has been the only basis upon which they have created parties, run electoral campaigns, and governed in the formal democracies in which they enjoy their greatest strength, and it has gravely threatened democratic governance. Alternative methods of representation that can safeguard, to a reasonable degree, the interests of elites without sacrificing the form and substance of democracy are urgently needed at this time. If adopting these reforms jeopardizes a quick death for democracy, it may be the case that probability will increase rather than decrease over time, and there may be no better time to strike than now.

5

Indigenous Protest and Democracy in Latin America

Deborah J. Yashar

On New Year's Day 1994 the Chiapas rebellion captivated Mexico and the rest of the Americas. Shocked by the well-planned and executed military maneuvers, analysts were left wondering where this movement had come from, whom it represented, and what it wanted. Yet, from a comparative perspective, the Chiapas uprising represents perhaps only the most dramatic and internationally followed example of organizing within indigenous communities. Indeed, in the 1980s and 1990s, there has been a rise in indigenous organizing and mobilizing in Latin America, including international campaigns for the five hundred years of resistance and the 1993 Year of Indigenous People, the emergence of Indian organizations in Ecuador, Bolivia, Colombia, and Guatemala, the rise of autonomy movements in Panama and Nicaragua, the 1993 election of Víctor Hugo Cárdenas, a prominent indigenous leader, as vice-president of Bolivia, and the awarding of the 1992 Nobel Peace Prize to Rigoberta Menchú, a Mayan Indian leader from Guatemala.

The codevelopment of the increasing organization of indigenous communities and the hemispheric embrace of political democracy in the 1980s and 1990s present the opportunity and responsibility to reevaluate the relationship between ethnic cleavages and democracy in Latin America.[1] Why have indigenous communities become increasingly politicized along ethnic lines in recent years? What are the conditions under which strong ethnic identities are compatible with, and even supportive of, democracy?[2]

This chapter argues that these movements are primarily a response to the twin emergence of delegative democracies and neoliberal reforms.[3] Democratization in the 1980s provided greater space for the *public* articulation of ethnic identities, demands, and conflicts. Nonetheless, indigenous communities have experienced a new stage of political disenfranchisement as states fail to uphold the individual rights associated with liberal democracy just as neoliberal reforms dismantle state institutions that had previously extended legal corporate class rights, representation, and social welfare. Building on social networks left in place by prior rounds of political and religious organizing, indigenous groups have mobilized across communities to demand rights and resources denied them as Indians.

Confronted with the lost momentum of traditional leftist parties and popular movements that have yet to define a political vision that resonates in indigenous communities, newly mobilized indigenous communities have organized and gained a new domestic and international presence. Yet, in contrast to the examples of the former Yugoslavia, Sri Lanka, Rwanda, and Burundi, indigenous mobilization in Latin America has rarely been a prelude to civil war struggles to capture the state; Sendero Luminoso, the guerilla movement in Peru, is the obvious exception, although even here the combatants do not see their struggle as part of an ethnic conflict. Rather, Latin America's indigenous movements have largely demanded greater democracy, including greater political representation in and access to national political institutions as well as greater local autonomy.

This chapter constitutes, therefore, a springboard for preliminary ruminations and discussions about a topic that has received scant attention within the Latin American context. It is sure to overgeneralize and misrepresent, particularly given the multiple meanings associated with ethnicity and democracy. These are problems associated with delineating ethnic identities, boundaries, and relations in the different Latin American countries, and analyzing the intersection of ethnic and democratic politics from a macrocomparative perspective when very little work to date has explored these issues in a systematic, reliable, and crossnational framework. Yet, against the history of exclusion, denial, and repression of Latin American indigenous peoples coupled with the knowledge that the failure to address ethnic cleavages elsewhere has unleashed a politics of xenophobia and a xenophobia of violence, it is important to begin addressing the future of democracy in pluri-ethnic states in Latin America. I begin with two descriptive overviews of the ways in which Latin American states have interpreted ethnic relations, followed by a discussion of the recent mobilizations within and by indigenous communities. The final two sections explain why these movements have emerged and how to bridge ethnic cleavages in a way consonant with greater indigenous representation and the deepening of democracy.

The "Indian Question" in Latin America

The history of ethnic relations in Latin America has been one of violence, subordination, denial, and assimilation.[4] With the arrival of Columbus and the ensuing conquest by Spanish and Portuguese settlers, indigenous communities were subsequently subordinated to the political authority of newly created Latin American states and the spiritual authority of the Catholic Church.[5] Military expeditions against the indigenous population were particularly brutal in Uruguay, Argentina, Chile, and to a lesser degree in Brazil.[6] These same countries, like many others in Latin America, enacted legislation to attract European immigration, arguing that this would improve the racial composition and therefore the economic and political prospects of the new states. Latin American states treated indigenous peoples as heathens, a threat to security, an impediment to economic development, and a source of cheap, if not free, labor. The various states enacted corresponding, if at times internally contradictory, policies to address these fears, perceptions, and goals. They killed those perceived as a threat to an emerging nation-state, isolated or denied the existence of those in remote areas, coerced populations for their labor, and promoted a policy of assimilation.

Indeed, in the twentieth century, goals of assimilation informed educational programs and state policies designed to construct a homogeneous nation.[7] Most politicians and scholars assumed that the existing state was legitimate but that the construction and identification of primary identities, be they around the mestizo nation or class, needed fixing. To this end, Latin American governments created Indian institutes to study indigenous populations—much as one would analyze national folklore—and to create the mechanisms to assimilate them into the national (read modern mestizo) population. While Brazil formed an Indian office in 1910, other Latin American countries founded these offices in the 1930s and 1940s.[8] Moreover, in 1940, the first Interamerican Indigenista Congress was held and led to the founding of the Interamerican Indigenista Institute. This policy was designed in places like Mexico, Guatemala, Peru, and Bolivia to incorporate people perceived as backward into the ranks of a new, presumably more civilized nation.[9] States encouraged indigenous men and women to discard any public display of indigenous identity, encouraged the adoption of a mestizo identity, and thus publicly encouraged miscegenation to "whiten" the population.[10]

Latin American states, therefore, promoted ethnic assimilation (and often miscegenation) to arrive at a mestizo national identity where population reflected ideology. According to positions articulated by state officials and intellectuals, mestizaje allowed for social mobility as one's ethnic status changed from indigenous (other) to mestizo (us); this process presumably depoliticized ethnic cleavages. Yet, if ideologically, ethnic identity became fluid, states and landlords often continued to repress these same communities (particularly when rebellious in the face of state colonization, development plans, and repressive rural labor relations) according to a rigid understanding of the appropriate ethnic and class rights of the assimilated population.[11] Consequently, economic mobility of the newly assimilated rarely advanced beyond a relatively low ceiling.[12]

The dominant paradigms in the social sciences after World War II tended to reinforce nineteenth-century liberal discourse in Latin America regarding the primordial, transitory, and atavistic nature of indigenous groups. The social sciences, in general, tended to devalue the salience and contemporary character of ethnicity in Latin America and elsewhere. While anthropologists conducted invaluable ethnographic work in the region, much of this work drew from paradigms that assumed that ethnic identities, particularly among indigenous groups, were an expression of a past world. Whether informed by traditions as diverse as modernization or Marxist theory, scholars tended to reduce ethnic identity to primordialism. They often assumed that, with economic development and the further integration of ethnic groups into an industrializing capitalist economy, presumed atavistic identities would and should subside.[13] One anthropologist, writing in the early 1970s, stated that "Ecuador is not a country inhabited by white folk, for as an ethnic minority they only add up to scarcely one-tenth of the total population. Neither is it a country of Indians, for in that case its history would be one of regression, or else, of stratification . . . the nation is Mestizo. . . . Once the Indians enter civilized life . . . the Mestizo part of the population will be more homogeneous."[14]

Modernization theorists posited that, with economic growth, the proliferation of technology, and social mobilization, individuals would transcend ethnic ties and become, among other things, more individuated, secular, and eventually more committed to the nation-state. Marxists, however, tended to argue that, with the increasing impoverishment associated with capitalism and the increasing integration of ethnic groups into the labor market, primary ethnic identities would subside as economically exploited individuals realized that the more salient and liberating corporate identity would revolve around class.[15] In short, the expression of ethnic identities was seen as a problem. In practice and ideology, states and intellectuals identified ethnicity and the ethnic problem as coterminous with the indigenous and the indigenous problem. From this perspective, getting rid of Indians (through assimilation or repression) was necessary to arrive at and sustain modernity on the basis of a mestizo nation.

The Rise in Indigenous Organizing and the Articulation of New Agendas

Against this backdrop, indigenous men and women seem to disappear, responding passively to the incursion of new states, markets, and clerics whose very purpose to undermine the political structures, economies, and cosmologies of indigenous groups remains unchallenged. Yet these assumptions regarding the passivity and obsolescence of indigenous peoples have been repeatedly challenged, particularly in the 1980s and 1990s. First, while economic development has often occurred at the expense of indigenous communities, and while many indigenous men and women outwardly assimilated into mestizo culture—severing or weakening ties with their local communities and practices—self-identified indigenous communities have survived, albeit as with all communities, they have changed over time.

While current, reliable, crossnational data is hard to find, it is commonly stated that approximately four hundred ethnic groups live in Latin America, composing 35–40 million people, 6–10 percent of the total Latin American population, and an estimated 10 percent of the world's more than 300 million indigenous peoples. The Andean region and Mesoamerica claim 90 percent of Latin America's indigenous peoples. These populations, which have been largely agricultural and sedentary, are the ones that the colonists made the greatest effort to incorporate and dominate in Latin America. By contrast, the other 10 percent of indigenous peoples are located in Orinoguia, Amazonia, Mato Grosso, Gran Chaco, Araucania, and Patagonia. Their economies have historically revolved largely around hunting, gathering, fishing, and occasionally small-scale agriculture. This great diversity of regions and economies coincides with great cultural and numerical differences between indigenous communities within and across regions.[16]

It is commonly argued that indigenous peoples constitute the majority of the population in Bolivia and Guatemala, followed by substantially large populations in Ecuador, Mexico, and Peru. In absolute terms, the largest numbers of Indians reside in Mexico, followed by Peru, Guatemala, Bolivia, and Ecuador (see Table 2). The estimated, though not terribly reliable, figures in Table 2 do not reveal the ways in which indigenous communities have changed with respect to the meaning, content, scope, and form of identities, practices, or goals of indigenous peoples. Nor do these figures intend to stipulate a shared identity among indigenous peoples. Indeed, the very idea of an "indigenous people" is predicated on the arrival of "settlers" against whom indigenous peoples identify themselves and are identified. Hence there is a dual image that needs to be kept in mind. While indigenous peoples differ substantially among themselves with respect to primary identities, practices, and so on, often leading to conflict or competition, they have often shared common opposition to those who have tried to dominate them as a people.

By the mid-1980s, indigenous organizations had emerged in almost every country and had begun developing nationally and internationally recognized personas. Particularly important examples of these first organizations included the Shuar Federation of Ecuador, the Regional Council of Cauca in Colombia, and the Kataristas in Bolivia.[17] From the outside looking in, the most striking pattern seemed to be the increasingly public and vocal position articulated by indigenous leaders and

Table 2 Estimates of Indigenous Peoples in the Americas, 1979–1991

	Estimated Population	% of Total Population
Argentina	477,000	1.5
Belize	15,000	9.1
Bolivia	4,985,000	71.2
Brazil	325,000	0.2
Canada	892,000	0.8
Chile	767,000	5.9
Colombia	708,000	2.2
Costa Rica	19,000	0.6
Ecuador	3,753,000	37.5
El Salvador	500,000	10.0
French Guyana	1,000	1.2
Guatemala	5,423,000	60.3
Guyana	29,000	3.9
Honduras	168,000	3.4
Mexico	10,537,000	12.4
Nicaragua	66,000	1.7
Panama	194,000	8.0
Paraguay	101,000	2.5
Peru	8,097,000	38.6
Surinam	11,000	2.9
United States	1,959,000	0.8
Uruguay	0	0.0
Venezuela	290,000	1.5

Source: Stefano Varese, "Think Locally, Act Globally," in North American Congress on Latin America, *Report on the Americas: The First Nations, 1492–1992* 25, no. 3 (1991): 16; computed from Enrique Mayer and Elio Masferrer, "La población indígena en América en 1978," *América Indígena* 39, no. 2 (1979), World Bank, *Informe sobre el desarrollo mundial 1991,* and United States and Canada census. A slightly different set of numbers is provided in James W. Wilkie, Carlos Alberto Contreras, and Christof Anders Weber, eds., *Statistical Abstract of Latin America,* vol. 30, pt.1 (Los Angeles: UCLA Latin American Center Publications, 1993), table 662, 150; data also derived from Mayer and Masferrer, "La población indígena," quoted in *Intercom, International Population News Magazine of the Population Reference Bureau* 9, no. 6 (1981).

the increasing scope of indigenous networks and mobilization outside of state- or party-initiated mobilization. Indeed, the organizations of largely indigenous communities were new insofar as the emerging movements generally emerged from within and across indigenous communities; publicly articulated demands in opposition to state-defined national (assimilationist) and development goals (that seemed to be taking place at the material and cultural expense of the communities); and began challenging the failure of class-based parties or peasant movements and coalitions to address the demands, practices, and identities of indigenous members.

From the inside looking out, however, the emergent organizations are quite diverse with respect to goals, strategies, representativeness, and scope of networks. These differences are played out within and between indigenous organizations over the primacy of material versus cultural orientation of the organization and its demands, alliances with popular movements and political parties, and tactics for change.

Despite the diversity within coalitions of indigenous peoples, one can discern an emerging agenda. In what follows, I discuss four inter-related demands[18]: land rights, human and civil rights, spaces for greater political participation, and rights to political and cultural autonomy. It is important to reiterate that not all indigenous groups work toward each of these goals addressed here, nor are all indigenous groups working in coalition. Indeed, as with any political organization, there are internal debates over goals, allies, strategies, tactics, and related conflicts. Rather, in what follows, I paint a canvas in broad brush strokes to highlight issues that have emerged in one form or another in various parts of the region.

One of the most pressing and pervasive issues articulated by indigenous groups has revolved around land or property rights. Demands have included agrarian reform, land titling, and territorial demarcation.[19] In Mexico, Guatemala, and Peru, for example, a number of indigenous groups have mobilized for agrarian reform. Associated demands also include access to credit, technology, and other agricultural resources. In each of these three countries, the state alienated land from the indigenous population and coerced indigenous communities into providing labor for plantations, mining, and so on. Subsequent land reforms did not have a lasting effect on these communities. In Guatemala the 1952 land reform was largely reversed with the 1954 counterreform. In Mexico the land reform of the 1930s seems to have had the least effect in regions with the largest indigenous populations, amply documented in the discussions of the Chiapas rebellion. In Peru the 1960s land reform was not implemented evenly in all regions.[20]

Land reform in these cases has historically been articulated and understood largely as a class issue—to redistribute land to peasants or small farmers—even if "objectively" the beneficiaries have included a large number or even a majority of indigenous men and women. Moreover, traditional land reform projects have looked at land reform as a way to distribute private property to individuals rather than to indigenous corporate communities.[21] More contemporary indigenous movements, however, have demanded land on the basis of ethnic, community, and class-based identities.

Indigenous movements in Argentina, Chile, Costa Rica, and Panama, which are considerably smaller in both absolute and relative terms to those in Mexico, Guatemala, and Peru, have largely demanded land titling. For example, in April 1993 approximately 7,000 Kuna and 15,000 Embera Indians in Panama organized to protest the slow deliberations of a land titling bill by blockading the highway and briefly taking hostage the governor of the province of Panama. While the Kuna and Embera are each demanding around 180,000 hectares of land, the Guaymí and Buglé are demanding title to around 11 million square kilometers.[22]

Land reform and titling defer to the state to arbitrate and regulate property rights. However, other demands for land rights have emerged which challenge the state's right either to influence all political relations within a certain territory or to assume property rights to natural resources. Demands for territorial demarcation, as in Brazil, Colombia, and Panama, and for rights to natural resources within a given territory, ultimately refer to issues of political and cultural autonomy in addition to material well-being. With these ideas in mind, the 1991 Colombian Constitution referred to indigenous lands as "territorial entities" in article 286; according to this article, existing political authority structures assume governing capacity, including criminal and civil jurisdiction, in these territories; moreover, the territories are responsible for determining their own development strategy and for administering public resources as if they were municipalities. At the time of this writing, complaints have emerged within the Colombian indigenous community that the actual distribution of these territories remains undecided and that the regulation of disputes between the national government and the future territorial entities remains unclear.[23]

These demands for a clearly demarcated territory and for control over the resources contained within those boundaries have become particularly salient as developers, ranchers, settlers, poachers, and the like increasingly penetrate areas that previously had been the de facto home of indigenous communities, as in the Amazon. In Ecuador and in Chiapas, Mexico, indigenous groups have protested the acquisition of titles over land and resources acquired by foreign oil companies. This increasing encroachment on Indian lands has not only resulted in the decline in indigenous-held territories but also in the decline of populations as violence, environmental destruction, and new diseases threaten indigenous people residing in these areas. The human rights commission of the American Anthropological Association, referring to the Awa-Guaja Indians in Amazonia, forecasts that they face extinction.[24]

In addition to land-related demands, a second set of demands implores the existing government to uphold and protect human and civil rights. In Mexico, Guatemala, and Peru, the governments have often orchestrated or turned their back on human rights abuses targeting indigenous peoples. Human rights groups have documented nationwide abuse of indigenous communities in Guatemala and Peru. In these two countries, military and paramilitary practice have tended to suspect indigenous communities as sympathetic to, if not members of, the guerrillas. In Mexico, human rights abuses occur in regions with large indigenous populations, as in Chiapas and Oaxaca.[25] Stavenhagen notes that while the constitutions of many Latin American countries have stipulated the juridical equality of its citizens, that in fact indigenous men and women do not experience a continual respect for human rights.[26] These human rights abuses obviously mock the rights constitutive of democracy.

A third set of demands addresses issues of political representation in national politics. The constitutions of Latin America, in fact, do not directly discriminate against Indians as individuals (although they have been discriminated against historically through literacy requirements for suffrage). However, legislation has often treated Indians as wards of the state. For example, despite comparatively liberal Brazilian legislation, indigenous men and women are often discussed in statutes referring to legal minors and the juridically handicapped.[27] Pedro Balcúmez, a Mayan Indian leader with the Consejo de Organizaciones Maya stated: "We do not want protection but effective participation in society and the economy."[28]

In the 1990s there have been scattered albeit important advances in indigenous participation in national positions. Indigenous leaders have assumed prominent national positions including the 1993 election of Bolivian vice-president Víctor Hugo Cárdenas;[29] the Guatemalan minister of education, Celestino Tay Coyoy, as the first Mayan cabinet appointment in that country; and indigenous representation in Colombia's Constituent and Legislative Assembly.[30] The inclusion of indigenous representatives has been a significant advance over the near, if not total, exclusion in the past of indigenous participation at the national level. However, electoral participation has served to highlight the diversity of ethnic groups (in countries such as Ecuador and Bolivia) and the salience of often conflicting agendas. Indeed, in the significant example of the Bolivian vice-president, he was able to win office by forming an electoral alliance with the MNR (National Revolutionary Movement), leaving some to question the integrity and endurance of the vice-president's party.

Finally, indigenous communities have called for autonomy and self-determination, widely used concepts that in fact mask a diversity of demands from cultural to political to developmental. Calls for cultural autonomy and self-determination are reacting against the assimilationist policies discussed earlier. They are reacting against the image projected abroad by tourist offices of quaint Indians marketing ethnic artifacts. Against pressures to assimilate and folkloric images presented by tourist offices,[31] many indigenous leaders have begun to define their own culture, both for themselves and others. Hence, in Guatemala, for example, a number of indigenous groups have emerged to promote cultural autonomy, integrity, and respect that the state has traditionally denied them. Mayan priests have come forth to announce and to celebrate Mayan cosmology and history, as illustrated by the 1990 gathering at Iximché; projects promote indigenous language study; women who had stopped wearing indigenous clothing have begin to wear *traje*. These demands and actions highlight the changing boundaries of identity that are transcending localized communities to embrace a broader Mayan identity. Hence women who have chosen to wear *huipiles* again now often do so irrespective of the community from which their families originate. This seems to be the case particularly for women who now live in the city.

Demands for political autonomy present, along with demands for territory, the most dramatic challenge to Latin American states as some communities want indigenous jurisdiction over a given territory, as in the Nicaraguan case of the Miskito and the Colombian case of territorial entities. Finally, calls for increased autonomy over and input into development projects have taken place through international and national forums. Throughout the region, indigenous communities have applied for and some have received funding from international nongovernmental organizations committed to local development projects. Moreover, indigenous communities have called for increased access to participation in state development agencies.

In Chile, for example, indigenous communities have attempted to increase access to state programs and funding for the increased economic, political, and cultural autonomy of the Mapuche (160,000), Aymara (170,000), and Easter Islanders (3,000). According to the *Latin American Weekly Report* (February 11, 1993), Chilean Indians acquired "a national development corporation of their own, a fund for land and water, and a fund for 'ethno-development,' to help them preserve their language and their culture. Already one Mapuche organization is pressing for more official recognition that they are a 'people,' not just another sector of society."

Demands for recognition as a people have raised legal eyebrows, for fear that recognition as a people is the first step toward secession or a threat to the power of the national state.[32] This might be the case among a few groups, but it appears to be uncommon. Miguel Sucuquí, a Mayan organizer in the governing board of the Council of the Ethnic Communities "We Are All Equal" (CERJ), a largely indigenous human rights organization, for example, said:

> So our most immediate task is organization and unification, and this must be done on the basis of our culture and our traditions. With that unification, we Mayans would have an enormous capacity to build our own life within the Guatemalan state. We are not forming a state within another state—we want that to be well understood. But were there freedom of organization, of expression, of religion, the Mayan people could unite, strengthen ourselves, and create the proper institutional expressions for sustaining our lives as a people.[33]

This set of demands around land, human and civic rights, political representation, and political autonomy has been articulated at the national as well as international level. Indigenous groups have gained access to international forums where they have influenced political agendas. The United Nations, for example, created in 1983 a working group on indigenous peoples that has included representation from member states and indigenous organizations to draft a declaration of indigenous rights; this working group declared 1993 the Year of Indigenous People. Indigenous peoples have formed transnational organizations such as the South American Indian Council, the International Indian Treaty Council, and most dramatically for the Campaign for Five Hundred Years of Indigenous, Black, and Popular Resistance that culminated in 1992. And they have gained a presence in international environmental movements, displayed with fanfare at the 1992 Earth Summit in Rio de Janeiro, Brazil.[34] Indigenous communities have also found an institutional space within transnational environmental groups, which have worked in coalition to promote equitable and sustainable development.[35]

Why the Increase in Indigenous Mobilization?

Why have indigenous communities mobilized in increasing numbers and scope in the past decade? Given the widely divergent types of groups that we have discussed and the as yet limited comparative information available on ethnic relations in Latin America, the following comments are initial observations that form part of an ongoing research project.

Ethnic and Class Conflict

It is a given in Latin America that indigenous populations experience ethnic discrimination, marginalization, material deprivation, and economic exploitation. "World Bank and other development agencies indicate that Indians remain the poorest and most destitute of the region's population, with the highest rate of infant mortality and childhood malnutrition and the lowest rates of literacy and schooling."[36] Carlos Fuentes, speaking of the inextricable fusion of ethnic and class identities among the Mayas in Chiapas, said: "What has an extremely long lifespan is the sequence of poverty, injustice, plunder and violation in which, since the sixteenth century, live the Indians who are peasants and the peasants who are Indians."[37]

These structural conditions have disadvantaged indigenous communities for centuries and constitute a constant source of conflict and object of change. Resistance has assumed multiple forms from sporadic rebellions to everyday forms of resistance embedded in dances, stories, and rituals that are an integral part of indigenous communities.[38] The dance of the conquest, for example, has been amply studied by anthropologists who have highlighted the ways in which the dance is a vivid reminder of an ongoing process of colonization, anger toward the land-lord, and expression of resistance. Similarly, the Popul Vuj weaves many complex tapestries of meaning, one of which is the oft-repeated phrase: "May we all rise up, may no one be left behind." Violent resistance and everyday forms of resistance against these conditions will continue so long as sharp discrepancies between ethnic and class communities continue to be delineated so sharply.

Yet, looking at these structures alone cannot explain why in recent years there has been a continentwide rise in indigenous organizing along ethnic-based demands. Indeed, if we want to explain the recent increase in indigenous organizing, we need to look beyond these constant causes to the new conditions that have led these dominated groups to resort to what Albert O. Hirschman has called voice (in its legal and violent forms), as opposed to exit or loyalty.[39]

Democratic and Neoliberal Reforms: The Changing Role of the State

The recent round of democratization has created the legal space for the expression of new identities as the resort to repression has become more problematic, although certainly not altogether absent. Indigenous groups have occupied these legally sanctioned spaces, which are not always respected by the militaries of the different countries. Indigenous groups have assumed this space particularly in the wake of popular movements and leftist political parties, many of which had played an important role in anti-authoritarian struggles but rarely succeeded in proposing viable political and economic alternatives.[40]

Yet, if indigenous communities have largely applauded the recent wave of democratization and efforts at demilitarization, they have remained wary of other efforts to dismantle the state in response to neoliberal reforms.[41] Indeed, the 1980s and 1990s have witnessed a change in state-society relations in ways that have affected indigenous communities in contradictory and often adverse ways. As Latin American states dismantle many of the social programs, they take away corporate benefits and representation that had previously defined state relations with indigenous communities. The move toward privatization, for example, has affected de jure and de facto indigenous lands. In Mexico the state's decision to withdraw protection of *ejidos* has generated anxiety, and rightfully so, over indigenous communities' loss of previously communal lands to large agribusiness. In Brazil the opening up to foreign direct investment has resulted in an increased number of developers (and illegal poachers) who have encroached on Amazonian lands that had (often by default) effectively been the domain of indigenous communities. In Ecuador, austerity measures, agrarian development laws, and oil exploration threaten indigenous land tenure and the environmental standards of the region.

Many indigenous leaders, alongside others in the popular movement, therefore, interpret the consequences of neoliberal reforms as an assault on physical, material, and cultural well-being. For example, efforts by Ecuadorian president Sixto Durán-Ballén to pass an agricultural development law prompted widespread protests by the National Confederation of Indigenous Nationalities of Ecuador (CONAIE), which opposed the law on the grounds that it would break up communally owned land and that it sold water rights. The threat of nationwide protests led the government to amend the law to limit the sale of land by communities and to allow for the expropriation of private property if carried out for a social reason, among other things.[42] CONAIE has also participated in coalitions with workers in general strikes to protest neoliberal reforms and the granting of further oil exploration licenses. They have called for study of the environmental impact of any future oil exploration and for research into alternative development strategies.[43]

With the implementation of neoliberal reforms, the corporate basis of state-society relations is being renegotiated. Rather than finding economic interests articulated through corporate laws and through more populist parties, indigenous peasants (and workers alike) are facing a situation in which social welfare issues are not being addressed by the state or through political parties. This has weakened representation for indigenous communities that had previously articulated demands (however feebly) with the state as peasants, as in Mexico and Bolivia.

Finally, the neoliberal concern for the individual in theory has not always translated into concern for the individual in practice. O'Donnell has analyzed this phenomenon in his discussions of the uneven ways in which democracy is experienced in Latin America. This is in large part because efforts to downsize an overbearing and inefficient state have often neglected to strengthen those parts of the state that are necessary for the effective functioning of democracy. Indeed, the uneven practices of judicial and bureaucratic branches of the state have been particularly disadvantageous to indigenous peoples who often remain subject to the political power of local and regional elites.[44]

In the absence of state reforms, individuals cannot necessarily practice their theoretically state-sanctioned civil and political rights that the new democratic regimes claim to uphold; unsurprisingly, the excluded tend to include the indigenous, the impoverished, and women. In this sense, the dismantling of corporate forms of representation and protection, without establishing more effective forms of individual representation and mediation, has left many indigenous communities and individuals without effective access to state resources and with an unreliable judicial and bureaucratic state apparatus. This has proven particularly disadvantageous for the poor, indigenous, and women.

Building upon Existing Organizational Networks

Indigenous organizations appear to have mobilized against changes in state and social relations by building upon and drawing strength from existing institutional networks left by groups that had previously organized in rural areas. The Catholic Church, followed by peasant union and leftist parties, has left a particularly significant institutional legacy.[45] The church, alongside the military, has traditionally been seen as one of two institutions that most successfully penetrated rural areas and historically attempted to control indigenous areas. As is now well known, following Vatican II and inspired by liberation theology, representatives of the church promoted new forms of organization within and across urban and rural communities.

Indigenous lay leaders, drawing on consciousness raising, community networks, strategizing, and the legitimacy and resources of the church, emerged to promote community organizations. These originally revolved around material struggles within a Christian framework and were often subsumed within class-based popular movements and leftist parties. They also provided a forum for subsequently strengthening indigenous networks and developing a generation of indigenous leaders with authority often within and beyond traditional community-based authority structures. This was clearly the case in Guatemala and Mexico and likely played a role in other countries inspired by liberation theology or with previously strong leftist movements or parties. I suggest that indigenous communities particularly capitalized on these institutional legacies with the recent wave of democratization and neoliberal reforms.

The New International Moment

While international communication among organized indigenous groups began in the early 1970s, it accelerated in the late 1980s with the approach of 1992 and with the increased concern of transnational organizations and lending agencies for equitable and sustainable development, environmental protection, and human rights.[46] On the one hand, the struggles to redefine 1992 as five hundred years of resistance rather than five hundred years of celebration sparked continentwide conferences that grew in size and scope with each meeting. The meetings provided the forum for indigenous leaders to gather together and in the process appears to have both heightened and deepened awareness of an "Indian" identity *shared* by indigenous groups throughout the Americas. Moreover, it increased networks between and within indigenous communities. In response to a question as to whether Mayan rites had become more widespread or more public in recent years, Miguel Sucuquí of the CERJ said:

Actually, it is both. . . . But when Spain and the Latinamerican countries started to make a lot of noise about celebrating the Columbus Quincentenial [*sic*], this caused a restlessness, a curiosity, in our people, and an investigation of the Mayan religion began, and more people began to consult with priests and elders about what had happened. The message of these leaders has been received by the people with great interests, and our Mayan religious practices are being revived publicly, and are being accepted by our people.[47]

On the other hand, international organizations and lending agencies have become more receptive to and supportive of indigenous groups and their demands. Indigenous people have gained an increased presence within the United Nations and its working groups. International coalitions with nongovernmental organizations and advocacy groups have significantly increased access to material resources, information, and the media. Moreover, international lending agencies have created and strengthened new programs that have increased funding possibilities for indigenous groups. Lending programs that include environmental and democratic conditionalities have also created new political opportunities for indigenous groups to pressure their respective governments.[48] Alison Brysk notes, however, the very severe limitations for promoting domestic citizenship when work is focused on the international arena.[49] Local- and national-level organizing continues to be an essential component in indigenous struggles for more equitable citizenship rights.

Deepening Democracy as Part of Bridging Ethnic Cleavages

Increased indigenous mobilization coincided with the hemispheric transition from authoritarian rule. However, by the end of the 1980s and the beginning of the 1990s, many of the countries that had ethnically heterogeneous societies experienced political closure. Witness, for example, the successful coup attempts in Peru and Haiti and failed ones in Guatemala and Venezuela.[50] Yet it would be foolhardy to conclude that ethnically heterogeneous societies and political democracy are incompatible.[51] Indeed, if we assume that a strong civil society is important to democracy, then we should embrace many of these mobilizations while thinking about the creation of institutional arenas for expressing dissent and conflict as well as consent and compromise.

To return to the final question raised at the beginning of this chapter, what are the conditions under which this increased articulation of indigenous communities is compatible with, and even supportive of, democratic practices and consolidation? The following suggests ways in which we need to reconceptualize citizenship in Latin America while looking at institutional mechanisms for creating more participatory, representative, and durable political democracies in ethnically heterogeneous societies.

Reconceptualizing the Nation

First, at an ideological level, Latin American states need to begin by reconceptualizing the very idea of a homogeneous mestizo nation. As Stefano Varese has noted, the emergence of indigenous movements and their denunciation of assimilationist policies challenge the conception in Latin America that a mestizo nation does or should correspond to the existing states.[52] Indeed, the very process of nation building in the late nineteenth and most of the twentieth century is being fundamentally questioned as people begin to talk about difference and equality. The challenge becomes to articulate a way in which democracy can emerge and endure in multi-ethnic states.

Rustow, in his pathbreaking essay, argued that one needs a sense of national unity to achieve democracy: it provides the sense of loyalty that glues the pieces together in the face of societal conflict.[53] Yet it is questionable if one needs "national" loyalty or loyalty to a "state" to achieve and sustain democracy. If Latin American indigenous communities are to develop or sustain commitment to democratic regimes, then multi-ethnic states need to revise the ideology of a mestizo nation to account for the more diverse composition of a given country's citizenry. This is particularly the case given that citizenship rights in practice are often derivative of whether one is conceived of as part of the nation. In some countries, such as Colombia, Paraguay, Mexico, and momentarily in Peru, constitutional changes have been made.[54] These are important steps.

Rethinking the Institutions of Political Representation

A discursive and constitutional recognition of a pluri-ethnic population is an important beginning. However, without institutional changes, it remains a symbolic advance. Indeed, the new Latin American governments need to redesign political institutions in creative ways to allow for greater and more effective political representation. In this spirit, I tentatively highlight issues of institutional design that merit additional research and analysis.

How does one provide for democratic representation and governance in ethnically divided societies in which ethnic cleavages seem increasingly politicized? This is largely a question of who is to be represented and how. In the case of indigenous communities, this question encompasses the dilemma of how to balance respect for individual and corporate representation.

A first and older set of arguments originally called for consociationalism. The simplified argument was that elite representation of the major ethnic groups needed to be institutionally guaranteed; the ensuing "cartel of elites" would defuse conflict over who controls the state while increasing the spaces for discussion and compromise over issues that had been particularly contentious. In recent years, this approach has been criticized on the following grounds.[55] First, this political arrangement assumes the primordial nature of ethnic identity and institutionalizes these very differences. Second, a political cartel of elites can and does lead to antidemocratic behavior; in turn, it inhibits democratic participation by groups whose identities and interests are assumed rather than expressed. The cases of Venezuela and Colombia, which implemented consociational-like solutions (although ones that revolved around partisan rather than ethnic identities), have highlighted the limits of this kind of institutional approach, as has Lebanon. Finally, it assumes that ethnic conflicts are vertically organized with varying ethnic groups vying for state power. Yet in Latin America, as we have seen, ethnic groups overwhelmingly remain horizontally organized and geographically concentrated, often seeking input or power over more local or regional politics rather than control over national politics.

A different set of arguments has highlighted the need to redesign district boundaries to increase indigenous electoral representation. The mechanisms for doing so vary according to the district magnitude of electoral regions, whether and how these regions coincide with ethnic groups, and the methods for calculating representation (proportional representation versus plurality voting). Redesigning electoral boundaries to coincide with indigenous territories or majority indigenous populations should compel politicians, be they indigenous or not, to begin to respond to varied demands as they are articulated by communities in a given district.

An alternative way of envisioning increased representation and participation within ethnically heterogeneous societies, therefore, is to decentralize political control. Decentralization can accommodate calls for more localized control and cultural autonomy while maintaining centralized decision making over issues that affect the country as a whole. While this boundary between local and national issues is clearly a source of tension itself, a more decentralized system at least allows for a more heterogeneous and changing vision of identity, provides more control over regional political economies, and might increase local participation.[56] This type of system would require tax reform to protect against the increasing economic disparity between regions and to ensure relatively comparable provision of social services. However, for this system to function differently than it already does, say in Mexico, we need to look at reforming clientelist control over regional politics that occurs through corrupt party systems, privatized power holdings, and inefficacious state apparatuses.

Reforming the State

In many of the countries, reforming the military institution to prevent human rights abuses, particularly in the countryside, is a necessary measure for consolidating democracy and bridging ethnic cleavages. On the one hand, human rights abuses are clearly inimical to democracy. On the other hand, military repression itself often compels groups to resort to violence as they find limited legal spaces for organizing and confront democratic practices subverted by the military's presence and practices in the countryside.

Moreover, the issue of state capacity has to be further problematized in Latin America. At the very moment that Latin American regimes are negotiating the retreat of the state from the economy, fairly little is being done to increase the transparency, efficiency, and legal practices of such central state institutions as the courts, the bureaucracy, and the police—all essential to the rule of law and one's rights as a citizen.[57] The absence of more pervasive and functional courts and bureaucracies has particularly affected indigenous sectors as they are located in areas in which political power is often exercised independently of and often in disregard for the law. As O'Donnell and Lehmann have both indicated, constitutional political equality is symbolically meaningful but substantively meaningless without the state capacity to make it a reality for sectors that have been marginalized along class, ethnic, and gender lines.[58]

Indeed, in the absence of the functioning of the rule of law, responsive bureaucracies, and military and police forms subordinated to democratically elected civilian rule, it is difficult to practice the rights of political citizenship. From this perspective, political order is not just a question of the organization and representation of social groups but also about creating states with the capacity to carry out their respective functions in the presence of competing private power centers. In the absence of effective reform, participation remains what O'Donnell has called low-intensity citizenship, contributing, I contend, to the increasing politicization of ethnic cleavages in cases such as Guatemala, Mexico, and Peru.[59]

Material Conditions and Citizenship

T. H. Marshall, echoing a refrain from Tocqueville, argued three decades ago that the political equality associated with liberal democracy was at odds with the social and economic inequalities associated with class/capitalism. The welfare state was the response. In Europe and parts of Latin America, political coalitions sought to alleviate the poverty and conflict produced by capitalism and articulated an ideology in which the state was responsible for ensuring that its citizens sustained a certain standard of living.

With the move toward market-oriented macroeconomic reforms, and fiscal and political limits of social welfare spending, many countries have cut back on social programs originally intended to alleviate poverty. While these reform programs are associated with macroeconomic growth in some countries, they have also coincided with increasing impoverishment among the poor, a pattern that has particularly affected indigenous communities. In each of these states, this dramatic retreat of the state has compounded already serious problems related to property relations and living standards within indigenous communities.

If this increasing impoverishment continues (particularly if government measures are seen as a threat to land access or sustainable development) *and* indigenous communities conclude that they are left without legally assured and functioning state channels to influence policy and access resources, more indigenous communities will be left with little option but to take to the streets in protest, as in Ecuador and Guatemala, or turn to violence as in Mexico. From this angle, it is essential to address those "constant causes" mentioned earlier and to redress conditions of poverty and political marginalization as part of a respect for and pillar of democratic citizenship (as opposed to an explanation of rising mobilization, per se).

Here, of course, the issue of land—its distribution, titling, and political jurisdiction—reemerges as the central issue and dilemma. Where indigenous groups demand land, traditional elites are sure to bristle, and in the past this bristling has never been good for the maintenance of democracy. At a minimum, therefore, countries with strong elites need to find creative fora to address these issues directly, involving both indigenous communities and elites in the process of developing political solutions. Moreover, more integrated development strategies are needed that allow not only for local participation in their design, but that promote economic sustainability, credit, investment, training, and infrastructure. With this thought in mind, we return to the Chiapas uprising. As the Indigenous Revolutionary Clandestine Committee of the Zapatista General Command stated in a January 6, 1994, communiqué, its central goal after all is "making known to the Mexican people and the rest of the world the miserable conditions in which millions of Mexicans, especially we indigenous people, live and die."[60] At a minimum, governments need to democratize politics and promote an idea of citizenship in which the provision for basic economic needs is seen as a right and not a privilege.

Notes

Chapter 1 Incorporating the Left into Democratic Politics (Angell)

1. From an interview with José Aricó, in NACLA (North American Congress on Latin America), *Report on the Americas: The Latin American Left* 15, no. 5 (1992): 21.

2. This theme is brilliantly developed in Jorge Castañeda, *Utopia Unarmed: The Latin American Left after the Cold War* (New York: Alfred A. Knopf, 1993). The merit of this book is not only that it is an acute and perceptive account of the development of the Left in a number of Latin American countries, but that it is also a thoughtful presentation of a social democratic alternative for the Left in Mexico. For a shorter, more historical account and an extensive bibliographical essay, see Alan Angell, "The Latin American Left since the 1920s," in Leslie Bethell, ed., *The Cambridge History of Latin America*, vol. 6 (New York: Cambridge University Press, 1994).

3. Even Cuba arouses little enthusiasm on the Latin American Left any more, except as a kind of residual anti-Americanism. The exception to this statement is in Central America, where solidarity with Cuba is a much stronger force. But even here there is no longer any desire to emulate the "Cuban model."

4. Defining the Right is no less difficult. A recent authoritative book on the Right defines it as including "many different elements of society and many different political agendas. The term refers to different combinations in different contexts, but they would usually include, among others, the holders of traditional wealth in land and minerals, anti-populist businessmen and economists, the conservative wing of the established Church, anti-communist international elites and, in most countries, much of the military." Douglas Chalmers et al., eds., *The Right and Democracy in Latin America* (New York: Praeger, 1992), 4. As a working definition, this is vague and ambiguous and begs as many questions as it answers, but it does highlight the difficulty of trying to define such imprecise terms as *Left* and *Right*.

5. Marxism as an ideological force has been very influential in Mexico, for example, even at the level of government during the presidency of Cárdenas, while Marxism as an organized party has been weak and mostly marginal. As Barry Carr writes: "It would be unwise to equate the left only with formal political parties and currents. . . . There is a broader Mexican left wing tradition comprised of contradictory positions. This tradition, embracing radical nationalism, statism, syndicalism and a history of struggles against corruption and for popular democracy, is not easily identifiable with the actions of particular parties. Non party, and sometimes anti-party manifestations of these tendencies have always been present in the union movement. . . . Since the late 1960s radicalized variants of this tradition have also come to dominate the ideology and practice of social movements outside organised labour." Barry Carr, "Labor and the Left," in Kevin Middlebrook, ed., *Union Workers and the State in Mexico* (San Diego: Center for U.S.-Mexican Studies, 1991).

6. An interesting suggestion for the Left in Europe, but that could be applied to Latin America, comes from the *Economist:* "Social democrats may be better equipped with lots of small ideas than with a few big ones, so long as those ideas offer an alternative to the ideas of the right—essentially by upholding the

belief that societies should be judged not by the well-being of their richest members but by the fate of the less well off." *Economist*, July 11, 1994, 25.

7. The growth of evangelical movements can be seen as part of this same process of rejection of the traditional forms of social organization, whether it be the political parties or the Catholic Church. In Peru an important base of support for Fujimori came from the evangelical churches.

8. I am grateful to Carol Graham for raising this point.

9. Although to describe these parties as populist begs many questions, it does point to features that differentiate them from the orthodox parties of the Left. They had a stronger desire for power, enjoyed broader social appeal, and had more flexible and politically astute leaders. Examples of such parties include APRA, Acción Democrática (Democratic Action) in Venezuela, the Partido Peronista (Peronist Party) in Argentina, the Colorados (Colorados) in Uruguay, the Partido Trabalhista Brasileiro (PTB, Brazilian Workers' Party) of Vargas in Brazil, and the Liberal party of Colombia.

10. Haya de la Torre had written about Chilean socialists in 1946 that "they have contempt for democracy because it has not cost them anything to acquire it. If only they knew the real face of tyranny." After 1973 they did indeed know the real face of tyranny. Quoted in Jorge Arrate, *La fuerza de la idea socialista* (Santiago: Ediciones del Ornitorrinco, 1989), 23.

11. Figures from the chapter by Michael Coppedge in this collection. This chapter explains very well the loss of popularity of what had been a very stable two-party system, giving rise to support, on the one hand, for a new Left party, Causa R, and on the other, for an old-style populist now campaigning against the parties, Rafael Caldera.

12. But as Juan Rial points out in his chapter in this collection, the union movement in Uruguay is less centralized and disciplined than it was, and is divided between a radical and moderate faction.

13. Rial (ibid.) describes the former guerrilla movement, the Tupamaros as fully—if negatively—integrated into the democratic system and as the "bearers of a high voltage discourse that defends the main tenets of the ideology of the extreme left."

14. Quoted in an interview with Lula in *Adelante* (London) (January 1981): 6.

15. It is perhaps too easy, in a rather bleak panorama, for the Left overall to praise the PT. A cautionary note is sounded by Bolivar Lamounier: "The PT is neither a disciplined party of the old Soviet-inspired variety, nor an European style labor or social-democrat party. It is not even a relative of Argentine justicialismo, ready to follow any president as long as he comes from the peronista ranks and seems to be succeeding. Unlike the rank-and-file of these other left of center varieties, the PT's dedicated militancy is characterized by a diffuse and somewhat messianic intent of substituting a 'good' for the now defunct 'bad socialism.'" Bolivar Lamounier, "Brazilian Democracy from the 1980s to the 1990s: The Hyperactive Paralysis Syndrome" (paper for the Inter-American Dialogue, Washington, D.C., 1994), 52.

16. In the words of Denise Dresser, writing about the 1994 campaign: "Cárdenas is attempting to shed his statist image and reinvent himself as a modernizer with a social conscience. He has vehemently disavowed suggestions that he would nationalize the banks, and return to the protectionist policies of the past. What he does propose is the need for a revised role of the government in the promotion of economic growth, employment and the design of an industrial policy. Cárdenas offers continuity with 'revisions.'" Denise Dresser, "Mexico: Twilight of the Perfect Dictatorship" (paper for the Inter-American Dialogue, Washington, D.C., 1994), 10.

17. Lewis Taylor, "One Step Forward, Two Steps Back: The Peruvian *Izquierda Unida* 1980–1990," *Journal of Communist Studies* 6, no. 1 (1990): 74.

18. Quoted in James Dunkerely, "The Pacification of Central America," Institute of Latin American Studies, Research Paper no. 34 (University of London: 1993), 103.

19. Christopher Abel and Marco Palacios, "Colombia since 1958," in *The Cambridge History of Latin America* (Cambridge, 1991), 8:655.

20. Marc Chernick and Michael Jimenez, "Leftist Politics in Colombia," in Barry Carr and Steve Ellner, eds., *The Latin American Left* (Boulder, Colo.: Westview Press, 1993).

21. James Dunkerely describes the current political situation in Central America as pacification rather than democratization. He makes the point that the Left's exclusion from previous elections works to its disadvantage: "It is worth noting that even parties such as the Guatemalan Christian Democrats that have participated in deeply flawed electoral systems have thereby acquired operational skills and systems lacking in excluded organisations. Age and the attendant familiarity and loyalty have been core assets for established parties even where failure to win office has precluded the distribution of rewards or threatened a sense of impotence and exhaustion." Dunkerely, "Pacification of Central America," 48. It remains to be seen, then, how the Left in Central America will react to persistent electoral defeat if that occurs.

22. Successful stabilization policies can bring immediate popularity to an incumbent government, whatever its politics. But crucial to the long-term success of those measures are widespread poverty alleviation programs. If governments can combine both, then the outlook for the Left is poor. For a detailed and illuminating account of the Bolivian ESF (Emergency Social Fund), see Carol Graham, *Safety Nets, Politics and the Poor: Transitions to Market Economies* (Washington, D.C.: Brookings, 1994).

23. In discussion, Alex Wilde pointed out that the democratic agenda in Latin America is incomplete in the sense that some issues are not included in the debate on democracy, notably those involving distributional issues. One function of the Left, then, should be to ensu: to address are put on the political agenda.

Part III

ch. 2

Part II
ch. 4 & 5

Chapter 2   Conservative Party Politics in La

I thank Jeanne Giraldo for her very help this chapter.

Parts of this article are taken from my b *ties: Argentina in Comparative Perspective* sity Press, 1996).

1. Guillermo O'Donnell and Philippe C. Schmitter, *Tentative Conclusions about Uncertain Democracies*, part IV of *Transitions from Authoritarian Rule: Prospects for Democracy*, ed. Guillermo O'Donnell, Philippe C. Schmitter, and Laurence Whitehead (Baltimore: Johns Hopkins University Press, 1986), 62–63.

2. For the purposes of this analysis, conservative parties are defined as parties that draw their core constituencies from the upper strata of society and are thus defined by their social base rather than by their ideology. This helps to distinguish this type of party from other parties or movements that are often considered to be part of "the Right." In this chapter, "the Right" refers to one end of a Left-Right ideological continuum that conservatism might well share

with movements of different sociological bases. Fringe groups on the Right, quasi-fascists, or paramilitary party groups are thus excluded from this analysis unless they are characterized by this strategic relationship with socioeconomic elites. For a more detailed theoretical discussion of this issue, see Gibson, *Class and Conservative Parties: Argentina in Comparative Perspective.*

3. The phrase "lost decade" refers to the 1980s, which is known in common parlance as Latin America's lost decade of development. This period, which saw the region's most impressive historical wave of democratization, also represented its worst and most generalized socioeconomic crisis since the Great Depression.

4. For the Colliers' argument about the pivotal importance of state-labor relations in the evolution of political regimes in Latin America, see Ruth Berins Collier and David Collier, *Shaping the Political Arena: Critical Junctures, the Labor Movement, and Regime Dynamics in Latin America* (Princeton: Princeton University Press, 1991).

5. See, for example, Collier and Collier, *Shaping the Political Arena;* Dietrich Rueschemeyer, Evelyn Stevens, and John Stevens, *Capitalist Development and Democracy* (Chicago: University of Chicago Press, 1992); and Karen L. Remmer, *Party Competition in Argentina and Chile* (Lincoln: University of Nebraska Press, 1984).

6. The figures for Costa Rica skew the average for the first group of countries considerably. In this case, the median ratio is probably a fairer measure. The median ratio for the group of countries with strong conservative parties is 4.2, while the median ratio for countries with weak historical legacies of conservative party organization is .55. If only the South American cases are taken into account (the Central American cases providing the extreme values on both ends), the average ratios are 3.43 and 0.9. Whatever measure is chosen, however, the conclusion remains the same: countries with viable national conservative parties in place at the start of democracy experienced far greater democratic stability throughout the twentieth century than countries that did not.

7. For an exploration of this question by a prominent member of the Brazilian Left, see Francisco Weffort, "Why Democracy?" in Alfred Stepan, ed., *Democratizing Brazil: Problems of Transition and Consolidation* (New York: Oxford University Press, 1989), 327–50.

8. For an account of Belaúnde's strategies on his return to power, and the symbolic strength of his campaign as a repudiation of the experience of military rule, see Julio Cotler, "Los partidos políticos y la democracia en el Perú," *CEDES/CLACSO Grupo de Trabajo de Partidos Políticos, Documento de Trabajo 9* (Buenos Aires: 1989).

9. This phenomenon was not limited to the above-mentioned countries. It was also present in such countries as Ecuador and Bolivia, where a profound deterioration in business-state relations occurred, even without the drama of bank nationalizations. As Catherine M. Conaghan, James M. Malloy, and Luis A. Abugattas point out, business concern over the unpredictability of military rule was a major factor shaping postauthoritarian politics in all Central Andean countries. See their article, "Business and the 'Boys': The Politics of Neoliberalism in the Central Andes," *Latin American Research Review* 25, no. 2 (1990): 3–30. For Argentina see also Carlos Acuña, "Intereses empresarios, dictadura, y democracia en la Argentina actual (O, sobre porqué la burguesía abandona estrategias autoritarias y opta por la estabilidad democrática)," *Documento CEDES 39* (Buenos Aires: Centro de Estudios de Estado y Sociedad, 1990).

10. See Roberto Tirado, "Los empresarios y la política partidaria," *Estudios Sociológicos* (Mexico City: El Colegio de México) 15 (1987).

11. The evolution of business-government relations during the García government is analyzed in detail by Francisco Durand in *Business and Politics in Peru: The State and the National Bourgeoisie* (Boulder, Colo.: Westview, 1993).

12. See Blanca Heredia, "Can Rational Profit-Maximizers Be Democratic? Business and Democracy in Mexico," paper presented at conference of "Business Elites and Democracy in Latin America," Kellogg Institute, the University of Notre Dame, May 3–5, 1991, p. 2. See also Leticia Barraza and Ilán Bizberg, "El Partido Acción Nacional y el régimen político mexicano," *Foro Internacional* 30, no. 3 (1991): 418–45.

13. Mirko Lauer, "Adios conservadurismo, bienvenido liberalismo: La nueva derecha en el Perú," and Francisco Durand, "The National Bourgeoisie and the Peruvian State: Coalition and Conflict in the 1980's," in *Business and Politics in Peru: The State and the National Bourgeoisie* (Boulder, Colo.: Westview, 1993).

14. Heredia, "Can Rational Profit-Maximizers be Democratic?"; Barraza and Bizberg, "El Partido Acción Nacional."

15. Gabriel Gaspar Tapia, *El Salvador: El ascenso de la nueva derecha* (San Salvador: CINAS, 1989).

16. Soledad Loaeza, "Derecha y democracia en el cambio político mexicano, 1982–1988," conference paper no. 24 (New York: Columbia University–New York University Consortium, April 1990), 47.

17. For an analysis of factors behind ARENA's performance in the 1994 elections, see Liesl Haas and Gina M. Perez, "Voting with Their Stomachs: 'Las Elecciones del Siglo' in El Salvador," *LASA Forum* (Latin American Studies Association) 25, no. 3 (1994): 3–6.

18. For an analysis of recent developments in Bolivian politics, including policymaking and coalition building by the MNR under presidents Paz Estenssoro and Sánchez de Lozada, see the chapter by Gamarra in this collection.

19. I am indebted to Jeanne Giraldo for this point.

Chapter 3 Democracy and Inequality in Latin America (Castañeda)

1. Fernando Benítez, "Desigualdad," *La Jornada*, January 8, 1994.

2. Nora Lustig, "Introduction," in *Coping with Austerity: Poverty and Inequality in Latin America* (Washington, D.C.: Brookings, 1995).

3. Rafael Rodríguez Castañeda, "El reparto de la riqueza en tiempos de Salinas de Gortari," *Proceso* 971 (July 12, 1992): 6–9.

4. Alberto Alesina and Roberto Perotti, *Income Distribution, Political Instability, and Investment* (Cambridge, Mass.: National Bureau of Economic Research, October 1993).

5. Sebastian Edwards, *Latin America and the Caribbean: A Decade after the Debt Crisis* (Washington, D.C.: World Bank, 1993), 118.

6. *World Development Report 1992* (Oxford: Oxford University Press, 1992): 236.

7. Thomas E. Skidmore, *Politics in Brazil* (Oxford: Oxford University Press, 1970): 192.

8. Alesina and Perotti, *Income Distribution.*

Chapter 4 Traditional Power Structures and Democratic Governance in Latin America (Hagopian)

I am grateful for the helpful comments I received from Jorge Domínguez and Jeanne Giraldo on an earlier version of this chapter.

1. *Social Origins of Dictatorship and Democracy* (Boston: Beacon Press, 1966).

2. John Johnson, *Political Change in Latin America: The Emergence of the Middle Sectors* (Stanford: Stanford University Press, 1958).

3. Cynthia McClintock, "Peru: Precarious Regimes, Authoritarian and Democratic," in Larry Diamond, Juan J. Linz, and Seymour Martin Lipset, eds., *Democracy in Developing Countries: Latin America* (Boulder, Colo.: Lynne Rienner, 1989), 355, advances the argument that changes in social structure— of which expropriating virtually all the major interests of the oligarchy stands out—were advantageous to the establishment of democracy in Peru. Although democracy is weak in Peru today, the threats to democracy in the early 1990s are attributable to causes other than a rebellion of the traditional Right.

4. John Higley and Richard Gunther's *Elites and Democratic Consolidation in Latin America and Southern Europe* (New York: Cambridge University Press, 1992), for example, assumes that democratic consolidation and ulti-mately the stability and survival of democratic regimes depend critically upon a broad elite consensus concerning the rules of the democratic political game and the worth of democratic institutions. See the volume's introduction by Mi-chael Burton, Richard Gunther, and John Higley ("Introduction: Elite Transfor-mations and Democratic Regimes"), p. 3. In his contribution to the volume ("Spain: The Very Model of the Modern Elite Settlement"), Gunther applauds the participation of members of the Franco regime in the construction of a new democracy in Spain, judging it preferable that they play "active roles in the reform process, rather than sitting on the sidelines as embittered opponents of change or as vengeful victims of a political purge" (p. 52).

5. Edward L. Gibson, "Democracy and the New Electoral Right in Argen-tina," *Journal of Inter-American Studies and World Affairs* 32, no. 3 (1990): 213.

6. Terry Lynn Karl, "Petroleum and Political Pacts: The Transition to De-mocracy in Venezuela," in Guillermo O'Donnell, Philippe C. Schmitter, and Laurence Whitehead, *Transitions from Authoritarian Rule: Latin America* (Baltimore: Johns Hopkins University Press, 1986), 203.

7. Samuel P. Huntington, *The Third Wave: Democratization in the Late Twentieth Century* (Norman: University of Oklahoma Press, 1991).

8. Ibid., 264–65.

9. Morris J. Blachman and Kenneth E. Sharpe, "The Transitions to 'Electoral' and Democratic Politics in Central America: Assessing the Role of Political Parties," in Louis W. Goodman, William M. LeoGrande, and Johanna Mendelson Forman, eds. *Political Parties and Democracy in Central America* (Boulder, Colo.: Westview Press, 1992), 35.

10. Maurice Zeitlin and Richard Earl Ratcliffe, *Landlords and Capitalists: The Dominant Class of Chile* (Princeton: Princeton University Press, 1988), 207.

11. The Guayaquil-based "agroexport" oligarchy in Ecuador controls im-porting and even industrial interests; see Osvaldo Hurtado, *Political Power in Ecuador* (Albuquerque: University of New Mexico Press, 1989), 176, 178–79. In Guatemala, El Salvador, Nicaragua, and Honduras, traditional, agriculturally based elites had commercial and financial dealings; see Blachman and Sharpe, "Transitions," 33. In Chile, an interlocking web of agricultural, industrial, and financial interests within families led Zeitlin and Ratcliffe, *Landlords and Cap-italists*, to refer to them as "landed capitalists" rather than traditional elites.

12. A long tradition narrowly identifies as the nucleus of the "traditional elite" of El Salvador a limited number of governing families that range from fourteen to twenty. Elsewhere I have argued that political elites in Brazil who

are descended from a small number of governing families might be considered "traditional" even if they no longer base their power primarily or exclusively on land or agricultural activities; see my *Traditional Politics and Regime Change in Brazil* (New York: Cambridge University Press, 1996). Writing of the Chilean agrarian elite, Zeitlin and Ratcliffe, *Landlords and Capitalists*, 206, asserted that "to belong to a landed capitalist family is to be marked for political prominence."

13. Peter H. Smith, *Labyrinths of Power: Political Recruitment in Twentieth-Century Mexico* (Princeton: Princeton University Press, 1979).

14. For the effect of the 1952 revolution on the power of the landed aristocracy in Bolivia, see James M. Malloy, *Bolivia: The Uncompleted Revolution* (Pittsburgh: University of Pittsburgh Press, 1970), 188–215; and Antonio García, "Agrarian Reform and Social Development in Bolivia," in Rodolfo Stavenhagen, ed., *Agrarian Problems and Peasant Movements in Latin America* (Garden City, N.Y.: Anchor, 1970), 301–46. In the Peruvian case, McClintock, "Peru," 355–58, has argued that even if it fell short of its distributional goals—land reform reached only between one-fifth and one-fourth of the potential beneficiaries—military-sponsored agrarian reform broke the back of the landed oligarchy and created new classes of small farmers and wealthy rural workers. See also Abraham F. Lowenthal, "The Peruvian Experiment Reconsidered," in Cynthia McClintock and Abraham F. Lowenthal, eds., *The Peruvian Experiment Reconsidered* (Princeton: Princeton University Press, 1983); and Laura Guasti, "Clientelism in Decline: A Peruvian Regional Study," in S. N. Eisenstadt and René Lemarchand, eds., *Political Clientelism, Patronage, and Development*, Contemporary Political Sociology 3 (Beverly Hills: Sage, 1987), 217–48.

15. "The Peruvian Experiment Reconsidered," 425.

16. John Duncan Powell, *The Mobilization of the Venezuelan Peasant* (Cambridge, Mass.: Harvard University Press, 1971); Karl, "Petroleum and Political Pacts," 199–203.

17. John A. Booth, "Costa Rica: The Roots of Democratic Stability," in Diamond, Linz, and Lipset, eds., *Democracy in Developing Countries*, 387–95.

18. John D. Martz, "Party Elites and Leadership in Colombia and Venezuela," *Journal of Latin American Studies* 24, no. 1 (1992): 96, 99.

19. Hurtado, *Political Power in Ecuador*, 179.

20. Appointments to the Supreme Court, which, according to Anita Isaacs, in this collection, are highly politicized, are made by the Congress.

21. Jeffrey M. Paige, "Coffee and Power in El Salvador," *Latin American Research Review* 28, no. 3 (1993): 7–40.

22. Richard C. Kearney, "Spoils in the Caribbean: The Struggle for Merit-Based Civil Service in the Dominican Republic," *Public Administration Review* 46, no. 2 (1986): 145.

23. Carina Perelli and Juan Rial, "Partidos políticos y democracia en el Cono Sur" (Montevideo: PEITHO, September 1991), 15.

24. Charles W. Anderson, *Politics and Economic Change in Latin America: The Governing of Restless Nations* (Princeton: D. Van Nostrand, 1967), 96–97.

25. Alfred Stepan, *The Military in Politics: Changing Patterns in Brazil* (Princeton: Princeton University Press, 1971).

26. Lowenthal, "The Peruvian Experiment Reconsidered," 425.

27. Anita Isaacs, *Military Rule and Transition in Ecuador, 1972–92* (Pittsburgh: University of Pittsburgh Press, 1993), 60.

28. Ibid., 124–26.

29. Richard L. Millett, "Politicized Warriors: The Military and Central American Politics," in Goodman, LeoGrande, and Mendelson Forman, eds., *Po-*

litical Parties, 67. In a press conference at the Carnegie Endowment in Washington, D.C., Cerezo estimated that he entered the presidency with 30 percent of the power, a figure he hoped to increase to 70 percent by 1989.

30. Mark Rosenberg, in this collection, speaks of a forty-year tradition of military autonomy in Honduras.

31. According to Millett, "Politicized Warriors," 64–65, modernization of these militaries, U.S. assistance, and the emergence of divisions within the officer corps all contributed to these developments.

32. Jennifer Schirmer, "The Guatemalan Military Project: An Interview with Gen. Héctor Gramajo," *Harvard International Review* 13, no. 3 (1991): 12–13. It is worth quoting Gramajo at length: "This generation of military officers is more professional. . . . The success of Guatemala depends on wresting power from the economic elite. In 1954, groups from the economic elite and the Army overthrew the government with a counterrevolution. A new Army was created and joined forces with the right wing. With the rise of the insurgency in 1960, this alliance drew even closer together, such that between 1970 and 1978, they were almost one and the same. . . . In 1982, the money of the right staged a coup against Lucas to replace him with Ríos Montt, who then brought in his own people, and the two split apart once again. General Mejía tried to bring the two groups together again between 1983 and 1986, but the economic situation was bad and the right treated him badly, as they remained separated. . . . Now . . . the structure [of our autonomy] is in place."

33. See the chapter by Rosenberg in this collection.

34. An example would be the failure of civilian elites to support the attempted military coup in Guatemala in 1993.

35. Gibson, "Democracy and the New Electoral Right," 197.

36. Ibid., 185, 187–88, 189–92, 198.

37. The coffee millers (represented by ABECAFE [Salvadoran Association of Coffee Cultivators and Exporters]) and two factions contesting the leadership of the association of coffee growers (ASCAFE [Salvadoran Coffee Association], or La Cafetalera) are not; see Paige, "Coffee and Power in El Salvador," 7–40. According to Paige, from 1984 to 1989, la Cafetalera was directed by a faction led by Orlando de Sola that shunned any notion of compromise and democratic development in El Salvador; a more moderate faction now holds power, yet still has little commitment to the steps that would be required to bring a stable democracy to El Salvador.

38. The characterization of the political oligarchy of Colombia as "gentlemen" is from Alexander Wilde, "Conversations among Gentlemen: Oligarchical Democracy in Colombia," in Juan J. Linz and Alfred Stepan, eds., *The Breakdown of Democratic Regimes: Latin America* (Baltimore: Johns Hopkins University Press, 1978), 28–87. The view of the consequences of the National Front is that of R. Albert Berry and Mauricio Solaún, "Notes toward an Interpretation of the National Front," in R. Albert Berry, Ronald G. Hellman, and Mauricio Solaún, eds., *Politics of Compromise: Coalition Government in Colombia* (New Brunswick, N.J.: Transaction Books, 1980), 439–45.

39. See Jonathan Hartlyn, "Colombia: The Politics of Violence and Accommodation," in Diamond, Linz, and Lipset, eds., *Democracy in Developing Countries*, 329–30.

40. Adam Przeworski, "Some Problems in the Study of the Transition to Democracy," in O'Donnell, Schmitter, and Whitehead, *Transitions from Authoritarian Rule: Comparative Perspectives*, 59–60.

41. Catherine M. Conaghan and Rosario Espinal, "Unlikely Transitions to Uncertain Regimes? Democracy without Compromise in the Dominican Re-

public and Ecuador," *Journal of Latin American Studies* 22, no. 3 (1990): 555; also cf. Isaacs, *Military Rule*, 120.

42. Isaacs, *Military Rule*, 128–29.

43. Conaghan and Espinal, "Unlikely Transitions," 554–55.

44. Charles Guy Gillespie, "The Role of Civil-Military Pacts in Elite Settlements and Elite Convergence: Democratic Consolidation in Uruguay," in Higley and Gunther, eds., *Elites and Democratic Consolidation*,

45. This argument has best been made by Scott Mainwaring, "Politicians, Parties, and Electoral Systems: Brazil in Comparative Perspective," *Comparative Politics* 24, no. 1 (1991), 23–28.

46. Barry Ames ("Electoral Strategy and Legislative Politics in Brazil, 1978–1990: A Progress Report," Washington University, a paper circulated at the International Congress of the Latin American Studies Association, April 1991, 6) has also linked the fact that in Brazil "electorally successful parties embrace distant, hostile portions of the ideological spectrum, and many if not most deputies spend the bulk of their time getting jobs and pork-barrel projects for their constituents" with the fact that "the national congress is weak and ill-suited for policy making on issues of national concern." He anticipates that in the long run "the ability of Brazil's congress to grapple with social and economic issues could be hindered—perhaps crippled—by the inability of the parties to organize around national-level issues."

47. The expression is that of the powerful former governor of Bahia, Antonio Carlos Magalhães.

48. "Economic Liberalization with Constitutional Reform in Colombia," in Leslie Elliott Armijo, ed., *Conversations about Democratization and Economic Reform: Working Papers of the Southern California Seminar* (Los Angeles: Center for International Studies, University of Southern California, 1995), 248–49.

49. Blachman and Sharpe, "Transitions," 34, 43. These features distinguish what the authors refer to as "pseudo" and "limited" democracies.

50. *Visão*, January 20, 1993, 6.

51. For the case of Brazil, see David Fleischer, "O Congresso-Constituinte de 1987: Um Perfil Sócio-Econômico e Político," paper presented at the University of Brasília, 1987. For the case of Ecuador, see the chapter by Isaacs in this collection.

52. Héctor Rosada Granados, "Parties, Transition, and the Political System in Guatemala," in Goodman, LeoGrande, and Mendelson Forman, eds., *Political Parties*, 105.

53. Evidence of such views on democracy can be found among sugar workers in Brazil (Anthony Pereira, "Regime Change without Democratization: Sugar Workers' Unions in Pernambuco, Northeast Brazil, 1961–89" [Ph.D. diss., Harvard University, 1991]), and also among residents of coastal cooperatives in Peru (McClintock, "Peru," 360).

54. Perhaps for a lack of reform, though not due to traditional elite persistence, a similar disturbing pattern is evident in Peru. Despite rather consistent support for democratic governance in public opinion polls in Lima for much of the decade of the 1980s, in April 1992, two days after President Alberto Fujimori rolled out the tanks and closed Congress for its refusal to back his proposed economic reform, 73 percent of those surveyed in the capital by the Peruvian Enterprise of Public Opinion supported the president's usurpation of power. Reported in *Folha de São Paulo* (Brazil) April 8, 1992, sec. 2, 1.

55. A higher percentage cast valid ballots in the 1994 presidential elections (67 percent), but the number of valid votes was less than had been cast in 1989.

56. James Wilkie, Carlos Alberto Contreras, and Christof Anders Weber, eds., *Statistical Abstract of Latin America*, vol. 30, pt. 1 (Los Angeles: UCLA Latin American Center, 1993), table 1051, 301.

57. See the chapter by Rosenberg in this collection.

58. Wilkie et al., eds., *Statistical Abstract*, 305.

59. Rosada Granados, "Parties, Transition, and the Political System," 107.

60. See the chapter by Torres-Rivas in this collection.

61. See the chapter by Kline in this collection.

62. Isaacs, *Military Rule*, 134.

63. Ibid., 21.

64. See the chapter by Isaacs in this collection.

65. See the chapter by Abente Brun in this collection.

66. Guillermo O'Donnell, "Transitions, Continuities, and Paradoxes," in Scott Mainwaring, Guillermo O'Donnell, and J. Samuel Valenzuela, eds., *Issues in Democratic Consolidation: The New South American Democracies in Comparative Perspective* (Notre Dame: University of Notre Dame Press, 1992), 25–33.

Chapter 5 Indigenous Protest and Democracy in Latin America (Yashar)

I thank Jorge I. Domínguez and John Gershman for their constructive criticism on an earlier version of this chapter, Donna Lee Van Cott for sharing her work in progress, and Daniela Raz for her research assistance.

1. The rise in indigenous organizing coincided with the rise in the black consciousness movement, particularly in Brazil. However, given significant historical and contemporary differences between the black consciousness movement and the varied indigenous movements, I limit the scope of this chapter to indigenous organizing and its relationship to democracy. Hence all references here to ethnic identity or organizing refer to the politicization of indigenous organizing alone.

2. See Donald L. Horowitz, *Ethnic Groups in Conflict* (Berkeley: University of California Press, 1985) and "Democracy in Divided Societies: The Challenge of Ethnic Conflict," *Journal of Democracy* 4, no. 4 (1993): 18–38. In his earlier work, Horowitz noted that in Africa and Asia increasing ethnic conflict tended to rise in tandem with the decline of democracy. While indigenous groups in Latin America did emerge in the early 1970s under authoritarian conditions, they have grown in size and reputation under the period of democratization. Horowitz later noted that, in fact, there is a more ambiguous relationship between the articulation and politicization of ethnicity and democracy.

3. See Guillermo O'Donnell, "Delegative Democracy?" *Journal of Democracy* 5, no. 1 (1994): 55–69, for his suggestive discussion of delegative democracies and the retreat of the state in Latin America. In characterizing the former he notes (ibid., 59–60): "Delegative democracies rest on the premise that whoever wins election to the presidency is thereby entitled to govern as he or she sees fit, constrained only by the hard facts of existing power relations and by a constitutionally limited term of office. The president is taken to be the embodiment of the nation and the main custodian and definer of its interests. The policies of his government need bear no resemblance to the promises of his campaign. . . . Typically, winning presidential candidates in DDs [delegative democracies] present themselves as above both political parties and organized interests. How could it be otherwise for somebody who claims to embody the whole of the nation? In this view, other institutions—courts and legislatures, for instance—are nuisances. . . . Accountability to such institutions appears as a mere impediment to the full authority that the president has been delegated to exercise."

4. Ethnicity, like democracy, is a highly contested concept and would require a lengthy monograph to explore and delineate its meaning(s). Nonetheless, for the sake of clarity, I follow the definition articulated by Esman and

Rabinovitch who "define ethnicity in its broadest meaning—as collective identity and solidarity based on such ascriptive facts as imputed common descent, language, custom, belief systems and practices (religious), and in some cases race or color." See Milton J. Esman and Itamar Rabinovitch, *Ethnicity, Pluralism, and the State in the Middle East* (Ithaca: Cornell University Press, 1988). Individual members do not have to possess the bundle of characteristics associated with an ethnic identity, nor does an ethnic group have to possess a "true" or "unchanged" heritage. Rather, following the work of scholars such as Benedict Anderson, *Imagined Communities: Reflections on the Origin and Spread of Nationalism* (London: New Left Books, 1980); Howard Winant, "Rethinking Race in Brazil," *Journal of Latin American Studies* 24 (1992): 173–92; and Arturo Escobar and Sonia Alvarez, eds., *The Making of Social Movements in Latin America* (Boulder, Colo.: Westview Press, 1992), it is important to see these identities as a construction of group solidarity coincident with a belief of shared peoplehood, historical lineage, and customs; it is as much "imagined" as "real." For the sake of this chapter, it differs from the idea of the "nation" insofar as the latter coincides with a state or a struggle for a state.

5. See Florencia E. Mallon, "Indian Communities, Political Cultures, and the State in Latin America, 1780–1990," *Journal of Latin American Studies* 24, quincentenary suppl. (1992): 35–53, and David Maybury-Lewis, "Becoming Indian in Lowland South America," in Greg Urban and Joel Sherzer, eds., *Nation-States and Indians in Latin America* (Austin: University of Texas Press, 1991), 207–35, for a discussion of the varied ways in which nineteenth-century states set out to control indigenous communities through violence, isolation, and assimilation. See Steve J. Stern, "Paradigms of Conquest: History, Historiography, and Politics," *Journal of Latin American Studies* 24, quincentenary suppl. (1992): 1–34, for a sobering discussion of the need to adopt a more nuanced understanding of the colonization of the Americas and the multiple roles and actions of the colonizers and indigenous peoples in this process.

6. See Rodolfo Stavenhagen, *Derecho indígena y derechos humanos en América Latina* (Mexico City: El Colegio de México, Instituto Interamericano de Derechos Humanos, 1988), 29, and Maybury-Lewis, "Becoming Indian."

7. European elites viewed mestizos in the nineteenth century as low life, just a rank above Indians. By the twentieth century, intellectuals had created a mythology around the mestizo who came to symbolize the Latin American nation in countries with multi-ethnic populations.

8. Stavenhagen, *Derecho indígena*, 105, and Maybury-Lewis, "Becoming Indian."

9. See Rodolfo Stavenhagen, "Challenging the Nation-State in Latin America," *Journal of International Affairs* 45, no. 2 (1992): 421–40, for an overview of Latin America. See Mallon, "Indian Communities," for a discussion of the varied contexts and forms that this policy took in Mexico, Peru, and Brazil. This attempt to create a more homogeneous population contrasted with U.S. history where more rigid social lines were drawn between the Indian, black, and white population.

10. Ethnic relations in Latin America have played out historically in quite different ways from African and Asian countries that gained independence almost a century and a half later than in Latin America. Because Latin America gained independence more than a century earlier than Africa, independence and national liberation became associated in the historiography with the European settlers who subsequently set out to construct a nation-state coincident with the ethnicity of the conquerors (i.e., themselves). In Africa and parts of Asia, where many countries maintained colonial status through the 1950s and 1960s, independence movements developed within indigenous communities

against settler populations. National liberation movements set out not only to capture state power but also to refashion a "truer" national identity to coincide with the postcolonial state. Following independence, any semblance of national unity within many African countries broke down and gave way to ongoing conflict between ethnic groups, as in Nigeria, Rwanda, and Burundi. Hence, while pluri-ethnic states compose both Latin America and Africa, ethnic relations and conflict have played out on different terrains.

In Latin America, ethnic conflict has tended to occur between horizontal groups, in which it is seen as conflict between white/mestizo groups that effectively occupy the state and indigenous groups that do not. In Africa, excluding important examples such as South Africa and Eritrea, ethnic conflict since independence has tended to play out between more vertically integrated groups competing, when democratic conditions prevail, to gain political power. For this reason, Horowitz's important 1985 study of ethnic groups in conflict (Horowitz, *Ethnic Groups*) does not apply to Latin America, for he limits his analysis to vertically integrated ethnic groups.

11. Pierre Van den Berghe, "Ethnicity and Class in Highland Peru," in David L. Browman and Ronald A. Schwarz, eds., *Peasants, Primitives, and Proletariats: The Struggle for Identity in South America* (The Hague: Mouton, 1979), 264–65.

12. Pierre-Michel Fontaine, *Race, Class, and Power in Brazil* (Los Angeles: University of California Press, 1985). Fontaine's volume on race relations finds a common pattern for Afro-Brazilians.

13. Given the scope of this chapter, I have simplified the approaches developed to address ethnic identities and conflict. Clearly, both modernization and Marxist approaches dominated intellectual discourse but did not wholly define it. Moreover, both approaches were more complex and varied than I have indicated here. For example, different theorists operating within the modernization paradigm argued that modernization would overcome ethnic primordialism, be impeded by ethnic primordialism, and produce ethnic conflict; in all cases, however, the progress and future of modernization was assumed to rest on transcending and/or controlling ethnic conflict. For a more detailed overview, see, in particular, John Stack, *The Primordial Challenge: Ethnicity in the Contemporary World* (New York: Greenwood Press, 1986). See also Horowitz, "Democracy in Divided Societies" and *Ethnic Groups in Conflict*, chap. 3; and Stavenhagen, "Challenging the Nation-State" and his *The Ethnic Question: Conflicts, Development, and Human Rights* (Tokyo: United Nations University Press, 1990).

14. Norman E. Whitten Jr., "Jungle Quechua Ethnicity: An Ecuadorian Case Study," 240.

15. Through the 1970s and 1980s, many academics and politicians alike tended to reduce discussion of indigenous peoples in Latin America to a discussion of economic issues. Indeed, if one sets out to gather basic demographic information on Latin America, there are a host of economic indicators, broken down by country, class, and sex. Yet it is virtually impossible to gather reliable, continuous, contemporary, and crossnational data on indigenous populations. With the increased awareness of the socially constructed nature of ethnic identity, one could argue that this is actually advantageous. But, within the positivist assumptions held by many of the demographers throughout the 1980s, this absence of information highlights the insignificance attributed to race and ethnicity. For example, the 1984 *Statistical Abstract of Latin America*, suppl. ser. 8, *Latin American Population and Urbanization Analysis: 1950–1982*, ed. Richard W. Wilkie (Los Angeles: UCLA Latin American Center, 1984), does not even make reference to the fact that there is an indigenous population in Latin

America. The statistical abstract on Latin America as a whole does not include ethnicity as one of its main variables; indeed, the 1993 abstract includes only one table, drawing from late 1970s data, that refers to the Amerindian population.

16. See Browman and Schwarz, eds., *Peasants, Primitives, and Proletariats*, 251; Stavenhagen, *Derecho indígena*, 32, 145; Urban and Sherzer, eds., *Nation-States and Indians*; Wilkie, ed., *Statistical Abstract*, 150; NACLA (North American Congress on Latin America), *Report on the Americas: The First Nations, 1492–1992* 25, no. 3 (1991): 16; and *Latin American Weekly Reports*, June 10, 1993.

17. For an overview of these movements, see collections of essays in Donna Lee Van Cott, ed., *Indigenous Peoples and Democracy in Latin America* (New York: St. Martin's Press, 1994).

18. See also Stavenhagen, "Challenging the Nation-State" and *The Ethnic Question*; Van Cott, ed., *Indigenous Peoples*, 11–21; and Urban and Sherzer, eds., *Nation-States and Indians*.

19. In particular, see Stavenhagen, "Challenging the Nation-State," 435. According to Manuela Tomei of the International Labor Organization, Latin American states have adopted new legislation to address indigenous peoples and rights, particularly with respect to land rights. She notes that Colombia and Ecuador are in the forefront but that legislative developments have also occurred in Bolivia, Brazil, Chile, Guatemala, Paraguay, and Peru. Of course, legislation and implementation are two separate issues. See *Latin American Weekly Reports*, June 10, 1993.

20. Cynthia McClintock, "Peru's Sendero Luminoso: Origins and Trajectories," in Susan Eckstein, ed., *Power and Popular Protest: Latin American Social Movements* (Berkeley: University of California Press, 1989).

21. In either case, land reform is not just about gaining access to land; by definition, it is also about decreasing resources of the landed elite and therefore changing rural relations. This raises an interesting dilemma. On the one hand, many studies have shown that a strong landed elite is inimical to democracy as it exercises nondemocratic control over regions. On the other hand, efforts to weaken the latter's control have also proven inimical to democracy, as landed elites have often moved to undermine the democratic regimes that create the political opportunities upon which land reform proposals are often articulated and at times implemented. See Moore's classic statement to this effect: Barrington Moore Jr., *Social Origins of Dictatorship and Democracy: Lord and Peasant in the Making of the Modern World* (Boston: Beacon Press, 1966). Hagopian's chapter in this collection notes that where traditional elites (read landed elites) are strong, democracy appears most fragile.

22. *Latin American Weekly Reports*, May 13, 1993.

23. See U.S. Department of State Dispatch "Colombia Human Rights Practice in 1993" (Washington, D.C., 1994).

24. Information from the American Anthropological Association and Amnesty International, reported in *New York Times*, Week in Review, January 2, 1994.

25. See Amnesty International Reports, Minnesota Advocates for Human Rights 1993 report on Chiapas, and *Boston Globe*, January 16, 1994.

26. Stavenhagen, *Derecho indígena*, 343.

27. See ibid., 344–45, and Maybury-Lewis, "Becoming Indian," 218–26.

28. *Latin American Weekly Reports*, February 2, 1993.

29. Of course, the Bolivian case is ambiguous. On the one hand, it highlights the achievement of high office by a Bolivian indigenous man who has specifically organized around ethnic issues and demands. On the other hand, he and his party have had an extremely low electoral success, highlighting the

limited success of indigenous leaders and parties in mobilizing the Bolivian electorate at the polls.

30. Information from Van Cott, ed., *Indigenous Peoples*, 14–19, and *The Report on Guatemala* 14, no. 3 (fall 1993).

31. Indigenous women do seek to sell textiles and wares to tourists and do benefit materially in the short run from tourism. Nonetheless, the production of daily household clothing and goods for a tourist market has distorted the domestic market for indigenous consumption. In Guatemala, for example, many indigenous women can no longer afford to wear or buy the *huipiles* produced for the international market.

32. For example, upon discovering a document from the Confederation of Indigenous Nationalities of Ecuador (CONAIE), Mariano González, the agriculture minister of Ecuador, claimed that the indigenous organization hopes to set up a state within a state; reported in *Latin American Weekly Reports*, February 18, 1993.

33. Reported in *Report on Guatemala* (fall 1993), 11.

34. See Stavenhagen, *The Ethnic Question*, 35, for a discussion of the United Nations.

35. For a discussion of indigenous participation in transnational nongovernmental organizations, see Alison Brysk, "Acting Globally: Indian Rights and International Politics in Latin America," in Van Cott, ed., *Indigenous Peoples*, 29–54.

36. Shelton Davis and William Partridge, "Promoting the Development of Indigenous People in Latin America," *Finance and Development* 31 (March 1994), 38–40.

37. *New York Times* op-ed article, reprinted in *Boston Globe*, January 11, 1994.

38. For example, see James Scott, *Domination and the Arts of Resistance: Hidden Transcripts* (New Haven: Yale University Press, 1990).

39. As I discuss in the final section, if the terms of class and ethnic subordination do not explain the recent rise in ethnic mobilization, one cannot begin to respond to the demands of these communities without redressing these very structures.

40. As the social movements literature has highlighted, traditional popular movements proved incapable of maintaining their momentum in the new democracies as political parties displaced them in the political arena and as they failed to articulate a politics of proposition rather than protest. See, for example, the final three chapters of Arturo Escobar and Sonia Alvarez, eds., *The Making of Social Movements in Latin America* (Boulder, Colo.: Westview Press, 1992). Similarly, leftist political parties have generally fared poorly in the political arena.

41. Chile appears to be the exception here in two respects. Pinochet implemented comprehensive neoliberal reforms under authoritarian rule, that is, prior to the democratic governments of Aylwin and Frei. Moreover, the Mapuches, as noted, have been able to manage their resources and to channel their profits into a foundation. However, further research is needed to determine why and how this foundation was founded; if and how it is related to the timing and/or the consequences of the neoliberal reforms; if this recourse to international lending is part of a broader pattern to develop autonomous organizations with international funding in the absence of state support; and how the response of indigenous groups in Chile to the neoliberal reforms compares to that of other indigenous communities in Latin America.

42. See *Latin American Weekly Reports*, June 30, 1994, 277; July 14, 1994, 309; and July 28, 1994, 335. Also reported on the British Broadcasting Corpora-

tion, summary of world broadcasts, on June 22, 1994, and Reuter Textline from BBC Monitoring Service, June 24, 1994.

43. See the chapter by Isaacs in this collection and *Latin American Weekly Reports*, February 10, 1994, 52.

44. O'Donnell, "Delegative Democracy?"

45. A related hypothesis suggests that the failure of the Left to articulate and organize around ethnic concerns led indigenous communities to mobilize new ethnic-based organizations. At this stage, however, this hypothesis cannot explain why the Left was able to mobilize indigenous communities along material demands in earlier periods; when ethnic identities appear to have gained more political salience than other types of demands; and why contemporary indigenous organizations predated the decline of the Left.

46. See Brysk, "Acting Globally."

47. *Report on Guatemala* (fall 1993), 7.

48. Davis and Partridge, "Promoting the Development of Indigenous People," 39–40. Note that the World Bank and other international lending agencies have held regular meetings with one another as well as with El Fondo Indígena, The Indigenous Fund (founded by a number of Latin American countries in 1992) to address issues of land regularization and resource management, technical assistance and training, and access to credit and investment.

49. Brysk, "Acting Globally," 45.

50. Note that it is difficult to assess the success of a coup attempt. It is often unclear what coup plotters intended or what they gained in backroom negotiations.

51. Indeed, it appears that the origins of the two coup attempts had less to do with ethnic conflict and more to do with political paralysis resulting from the election of a president without any partisan support in the legislature, a legislature that did not legislate but was beholden to corrupt political parties, and the military's fear of the escalation of the civil war. Under these conditions, in both countries, the respective presidents (Fujimori in Peru and Serrano in Guatemala) created an alliance with the military to get rid of the legislature.

52. See Stefano Varese, "Think Locally, Act Globally," in North American Congress on Latin America, *Report on the Americas: The First Nations, 1492–1992*: 25, no. 3 (1991): 13–17.

53. Dankwart Rustow, "Transitions to Democracy: Toward a Dynamic Model," *Comparative Politics* 2, no. 3 (1970): 337–63.

54. See Van Cott, ed., *Indigenous Peoples*, 15–16.

55. See Hans Daalder, "The Consociational Democracy Theme," *World Politics* 26 (October 1973): 604–21, and Ian Shapiro, "Democratic Innovation: South Africa in Comparative Context," *World Politics* 46 (October 1993): 121–50, among others.

56. Bolivia passed a law on decentralization and popular participation on April 21, 1994. According to *Latin American Weekly Reports* (May 12, 1994, 196): "The participation law enables the central government to share out revenues between municipalities, provinces, and departments in accordance with their populations, and thereby favor traditionally neglected regions and groups. Responsibility for maintaining the physical infrastructure of schools, clinics, roads, and services is transferred from central government to the 301 municipalities. The law has also given legal recognition to Indian communities and other local organizations."

57. See O'Donnell, "Delegative Democracy?" and David Lehmann, *Democracy and Development in Latin America: Economics, Politics and Religion in the Postwar Period* (Philadelphia: Temple University Press, 1990), whose arguments regarding state-society relations and citizenship in Latin America have largely informed this discussion.

58. Guillermo O'Donnell, "On the State, Democratization and Some Conceptual Problems: A Latin American View with Glances at Some Postcommunist Countries," *World Development* 21, no. 8 (1993): 1361, and Lehmann, *Democracy and Development.*

59. O'Donnell, "On the State."

60. *New York Times,* January 17, 1994.

Index

III

South America

1

Venezuela: The Rise and Fall of Partyarchy

Michael Coppedge

Venezuela, once the most governable democracy in Latin America, is now a very fragile one. This chapter describes the formula that made Venezuela governable in the 1970s, traces that formula's emergence in the 1960s, and explains why it broke down in the 1980s, leaving the democratic regime in danger in the 1990s. This historical perspective is necessary for anyone seeking to understand the prospects for democratic governability in the Caldera government, for it will be expected to provide an alternative to the old formula but will also be judged by comparison with the old formula's achievements. If Caldera's democratic alternative is judged a failure, many Venezuelans will be inclined to give the nondemocratic alternative a second look.

The historical perspective is also useful for generating several lessons for other Latin American democracies. First, because Venezuela's formula worked well for a while, it helps identify the elements of democratic governability. Second, the crisis of governability yields insights into the strengths and weaknesses of one formula that is often held up as a model for other countries. Finally, only the long-term view can provide an appreciation of the challenges faced by any formula in a dynamic social and economic context. Even successful formulas for governability must adapt to survive. The guardians of Venezuela's formula adapted too little at first, but perhaps not too late.

Elements of Democratic Governability

Governability is best understood by analyzing the relationships among strategic actors, that is, organized interests with sufficient control of some power resource—factors of production, mass membership, public office, armed force, moral authority, or ideas and information—to disturb public order or economic development.[1] Whether they actually cause disturbances, merely threaten to do so, or take advantage of an implicit understanding of their potential for disturbance, they are the only actors whose behavior is relevant for governability. In Latin American democratic regimes there are generally three kinds of strategic actors. Some are state actors, specifically the military (and police), the permanent bureaucracy, and the government (those temporarily holding public office and providing direction to the state). Some are social actors: the church, private sector associations, labor unions, the media, organized peasants, indigenous movements, even guerrillas and terrorists. Finally, political parties are usually strategic actors as well, not acting exclusively in the state or society, but attempting to mediate between them by contesting elections, staffing the government, and representing civil society in the legislature.

Governability is the degree to which relations among these strategic actors obey formulas that are stable and mutually acceptable. Some formulas are formalized in law, such as constitutions, labor codes, or provisions for tripartite representation on the boards of state enterprises. Many other formulas are informal, such as coalitions, party pacts, or the tendency of policymakers to consult with private sector associations. When the formulas are stable and mutually acceptable, violence is minimized, conflicts are resolved peacefully, actors "play by the rules of the game," and interactions build trust. In short, governability reigns. When the formulas that govern relations among strategic actors are not stable and mutually acceptable, manifestations of ungovernability occur as some actors reject old formulas, try to impose new ones, or withhold consent from any formula while they build up their own power or attempt to undermine the power of other actors. Examples of such manifestations range from cabinet crises, stalemate, and electoral fraud to violent protest, terrorism, and military coups.

Venezuela's Formula: Partyarchy

Venezuela practiced a formula for governability that worked exceptionally well in the 1970s. It was a formula that gave a central role to the two largest political parties, the social democratic Acción Democrática (AD) and the Christian democratic COPEI (Comité de Organización Política Electoral Independiente). Many Venezuelans came to call this formula *partidocracia* (from *partido* and *democracia*), which I translate as "partyarchy."[2] The guardians of the formula, so to speak, were the leading *adecos* and *copeyanos*, whom some Venezuelans called the *"status" adecopeyano* and I will call the Adecopeyano establishment, or simply the establishment.

The terms of the partyarchy formula were as follows:

1. *Inclusive representation.* AD and COPEI represented almost all groups in society. The card-carrying membership of these two parties was larger (up to 31% of total voters) than party membership in any other democratic country in the world, with the possible exceptions of Costa Rica and Chile. Because most nonmembers were at least sympa-

thizers, these two parties also shared about 80 percent of the legislative vote and 90 percent of the presidential vote from 1973 to 1988, even though dozens of other parties appeared on the ballot. Party organization was extensive: every small town in Venezuela had a party headquarters for AD and COPEI. Moreover, the leadership of practically all organizations of civil society (other than the church and private sector associations) was chosen in elections using slates identified with AD and COPEI. About 80 percent of the peasant federations and at least 60 percent of the labor unions were controlled by leaders affiliated with AD.

2. *Electoral competition.* Citizens and social actors not affiliated with the Adecopeyano establishment at least recognized elections, whose fairness was a source of pride, as the legitimate mechanism for deciding who would occupy public office. Election campaigns were civic festivals lasting nearly a year, mobilizing millions in canvassing, parades, car caravans, and open-air mass meetings, always flooded with campaign paraphernalia. Abstention never exceeded 12.4 percent before 1988.

3. *Party discipline.* AD and COPEI practiced iron discipline: militants at all levels of the party organization risked expulsion if they disobeyed decisions made by the small inner circle of leaders, or *cogollo*, at the head of each party. The Leninist principle of democratic centralism was even explicitly endorsed by AD party statutes. Consequently, senators and deputies, state legislators, and municipal council members strayed from the party line so infrequently that congressional leaders did not even bother to tally or record votes; only the relative sizes of the parties mattered. Labor leaders usually refrained from holding strikes when their party was in power, and the politicized officers of professional associations, student governments, peasant federations, state enterprises, foundations, and most other organizations used their positions to further their party's interests. The two parties therefore acted as powerful and readily mobilized blocs.

4. *Concertación (consensus-seeking).* The leaders of AD and COPEI made a habit of consulting one another, and usually leaders of other parties and social organizations as well, whenever controversial issues arose.[3] Policies concerning defense, foreign affairs, and the oil industry were usually made by consensus, and even when consensus proved impossible, the attempt to reach it mollified the opposition. Party leaders were openly committed to the principle that no conflict could be allowed to escalate to the point of threatening the democratic regime. Although conflicts did occur, the leadership always stepped back from the brink in time to save the regime.[4]

5. *Wider relations.* The parties also hammered out good working relations with other strategic actors—the military and the private sector.[5] In exchange for noninterference in political questions, AD and COPEI

governments rewarded the armed forces with high salaries, ambitious educational programs, frequent promotions, and expensive equipment. The private sector associations FEDECAMARAS (Federation of Chambers of Commerce and Industry), CONSECOMERCIO (Commercial Council), and CONINDUSTRIA (Confederation of Industry), while often critical of government policies, also became dependent on high subsidies, low taxes, and protectionist tariffs. These associations were often included in the concertación process, and it was understood that the finance minister would be designated in consultation with one or more of the huge holding companies owned by the wealthiest families.

Governability was therefore ensured by the Adecopeyano establishment which, because it controlled large, popular, and tightly disciplined parties with influence over most other organizations, had the authority to bargain with other parties and other strategic actors and the power to enforce the deals that it made.

The Rise and Decline of Partyarchy

The formula just described was typical of the 1970s in Venezuela but existed only in a much weakened form by 1990. While the leaders of the democratic transition in 1958 benefited greatly from many aspects of their emerging partyarchy, the formula did not become fully consolidated until about 1970. Therefore, the 1970s represent a peak in the rising and declining life cycle of Venezuelan partyarchy.

Challenges and Consolidation in the 1960s

Acción Democrática had been a large, broad-based, and tightly disciplined party since its founding in 1941, but the other elements of partyarchy were missing before 1958.[6] Only two fair, full-suffrage national elections had been held before that year, and they were in 1946 and 1948, long since interrupted by the military dictatorship of Marcos Pérez Jiménez. COPEI had come into existence during the 1945–48 Trienio but was not a likely partner for concertación with AD; indeed, the Copeyanos and the church hierarchy had supported the coup that ended the first AD government in 1948.[7] The military had been persecuting AD for the last decade, and some business leaders were wary of a return to AD rule because of its left-of-center orientation. When Pérez Jiménez was overthrown in an internal coup, negotiations among AD, COPEI, Unión Republicana Democrática, (URD, Democratic Republican Union), and a business leader culminated in the 1958 Pact of Punto Fijo, which first put the other elements of partyarchy in place. Under the leadership of Rómulo Betancourt and Rafael Caldera, AD and COPEI formed a united front to demand elections, thus beginning a long tradition of concertación. Relying on its party discipline, AD promised labor quiescence if business leaders would support elections, and they agreed, which left the military with no choice but to complete the transition.[8] The pact expressly committed party leaders to use their organizations to moderate political conflict, and although Betancourt was the clear winner in the 1958 presidential election, he honored his commitment to form a national unity government in which the three parties were represented equally.

The formula that made the transition to democracy possible encountered several serious challenges in its early years but defeated them all. The military was not completely united in support of democracy, but Betancourt's assiduous courtship of the military enabled him to survive four coup attempts.[9] Guerrilla movements threatened democracy in Venezuela in the wake of the Cuban Revolution, but civilian presidents from AD took responsibility for the brutal campaigns to defeat the armed Left, and in the process earned the military's respect and loyalty. The guerrillas themselves found little support for their efforts among peasants, who were benefiting from an extensive land reform passed by the AD-COPEI governing coalition in 1961. Politically isolated and militarily besieged, the guerrillas ended their armed struggle in the mid-1960s. Some ex-guerrillas participated in the elections of 1968, and President Caldera granted them amnesty in 1969. A split in the communist party in 1970–71 gave birth to the Movimiento al Socialismo (MAS, Movement to Socialism), which committed itself to the electoral path to power. Thus the threat from the Left was neutralized.

Three factions within AD in the 1960s were opposed to close cooperation with COPEI and therefore challenged the formula from within, but each one was expelled and then rendered irrelevant at the next election.[10] As late as 1968 some voters, especially in urban areas, remained enamored of Pérez Jiménez or other right-wing populist candidates, and the combined vote for AD and COPEI declined over the first three elections. But in 1968, when Caldera won the presidency in a close race and AD recognized his victory, it became clear that the only realistic alternative to AD was COPEI.[11] In the next election, the two parties won nearly 80 percent of the vote, and continued to do so for the next fifteen years.

By about 1970, therefore, the Adecopeyano establishment had defeated challenges from the Left, the Right, and within, leaving itself at the head of a very effective formula for governability. The legitimacy of this formula was bolstered by the quadrupling of oil prices during the 1974–79 AD government of Carlos Andrés Pérez, who had the good fortune to be elected at the beginning of the OPEC oil embargo. The fantastic windfall of petrodollars made it easier for the establishment to "buy" support with patronage, consumer subsidies, an overvalued currency, wage increases, and high rates of economic growth.

The Emergence of New Challenges in the 1980s

Over the next decade, however, Venezuela's partyarchy developed pathological tendencies: a loss of direction, corruption, and obsession with control. It was as though new terms had been added to the formula for governability, too shameful to acknowledge, but nevertheless very real.

Loss of Direction. In the twenty years following the Pact of Punto Fijo, AD and COPEI governments had accomplished most of the policy goals their parties had discussed in the early 1960s: land reform, nationalization of the oil industry, expansion of public education, job creation, and the consolidation of democracy. If debate over policy had continued within or among the parties during those two decades, they would have set new goals for themselves, but such was not the case: AD's *Tesis Política* has not been updated since 1964. Party discipline stifled the expression of controversial ideas within each party, and *concertación* filtered the controversy out of interparty debate.

With the threat of expulsion, made credible by a series of party splits in the 1960s, and therefore the end of one's political career hanging over every militant's head, few party leaders were willing to suggest new ideas that might turn out to be controversial. The most daring leaders had already been expelled; those remaining in the party were the ones who had learned to keep quiet and wait for the national leadership to tell them what to think.

Furthermore, AD and COPEI both drifted toward the center, and the more similar they became, the fewer questions of substance they found to debate. Presidential campaigns relied more and more on personal attacks, mudslinging, and nice-sounding but meaningless slogans. It became hard for voters to support parties as a means to some honorable end; increasingly, they came to be seen as ends in themselves.

Corruption. Venezuela had never been entirely free of corruption, not even during the early years of the democratic regime when the government was prosecuting the former dictator for corruption. But two developments caused an increase in corruption in the late 1970s—the oil bonanza and partyarchy. As Terry Karl has reported, oil revenues earned during the Pérez government (1974–79) were 54 percent greater, in real terms, than those received by all previous Venezuelan governments since 1917 combined.[12] In this incredible deluge of wealth, it was inevitable that some public officials would divert part of the flow into their own pockets and that financial accountability would grow lax.

What is harder to understand is why corrupt practices continued to flourish even after the country went deeply into debt and oil prices fell, plunging the country into economic crisis. The continuation of corruption required a climate of impunity, which was a by-product of partyarchy. The courts, like the bureaucracy, the universities, and most other institutions, were thoroughly politicized along party lines and seemed never to find sufficient evidence to justify a trial or a conviction. There had to have been complicity between AD and COPEI as well, because they behaved as though there were a secret clause of the Pact of Punto Fijo prohibiting prosecution for corruption. The practice of *concertación*, intended to moderate political conflict, served equally well to conceal abuses of power by the Adecopeyano establishment. The practitioners of impunity no doubt rationalized their actions on the grounds that full disclosure of the magnitude of corruption would endanger the democratic regime; in retrospect, ironically, they appear to have been correct.

Obsession with Control. In the hands of increasingly unprincipled party militants, the party founders' dedication to the moderation of conflict was transmogrified into an obsession with controlling other actors in civil society. Governments by and large respected the freedom of organization; but to the parties, the founding of any new independent organization was a call to arms. Efforts would be made to co-opt its leadership. If this tactic was successful, the organization would be subject to party discipline. If unsuccessful, party activists would sometimes secretly infiltrate the organization, win control of it, and then hand it over to their party. If all else failed, they would create a parallel organization with the same mission and outcompete the independent organization with the assistance of fellow partisans in the local government, eventually causing the independents to fail. This tactic was employed so commonly that the word *paralelismo* gained currency to describe it.

At first the parties were successful in preserving their control, but here and there independent organizations gained a foothold—unions in the state of Bolívar, some neighborhood associations in the cities, and in the late 1980s, human rights and ecology nongovernmental organizations (NGOs).[13] Such social movements should have been welcomed because they represented a strengthening of civil society and posed no more threat to governability than Christian base communities did in Brazil, or peasant *coordinadoras* in Mexico, or the mothers of the Plaza de Mayo in Argentina. But rather than welcoming and encouraging this newly flourishing civil society and opening the system to more genuine participation, the parties treated independent groups as threats to party control. An opportunity to deepen Venezuelan democracy was thus lost, and the independent organizations responded by linking their aims to an antiparty, anti-establishment agenda.

During the 1980s the new challenges to partyarchy gained enough strength to harm governability. The economic decline of 1979–90 acted as a catalyst for the opposition to the establishment.[14] When the debt crisis hit in 1983 and when oil prices fell, particularly after 1985, the parties' capacity to control civil society diminished. Fewer resources were available for patronage or for simply meeting the state's routine obligations; public services declined, and infrastructure was allowed to deteriorate. The parties lost some of their ability to fulfill their promises, to co-opt new organizations—particularly the neighborhood associations that sprang up to clamor for better public services—and to provide government jobs for friends and (former) enemies.[15] As living standards declined, disenchantment grew, made bitter by the knowledge that the country had seen tremendous wealth and let it slip away. For most of the decade, however, most Venezuelans were willing to channel their discontent into the electoral process just as they had for years, driving the alternation of AD and COPEI in power.

Two developments during the second Pérez government (1989–93) transformed the anti-incumbent anger into an anti-establishment anger. First, the economic policies of the Pérez government were powerfully disillusioning. Many people voted for Pérez in 1988 hoping that he would somehow return Venezuela to the boom it had enjoyed during his first government, and Pérez' campaign did little to discourage that hope. For example, a poll taken in January 1989, just before the inauguration, showed that 45 percent of Venezuelans believed that their own situation would be better by the end of the Pérez government, and the president-elect's approval rating was 79 percent favorable.[16]

One of Pérez' first acts as president, however, was to announce a drastic *paquete* of structural adjustment measures, including many price increases, with insufficient explanation of their necessity. The day they took effect, the widespread feeling of betrayal and desperation exploded in the three days of looting and riots known as the *Caracazo*. People had pinned their hopes on an election and a change of government, and it seemed only to make things worse. In the short term, that was true: 1989 gave Venezuela its worst economic performance since the Depression, with an 8.3 percent drop in production and inflation topping 80 percent. By May 1992, between the two coup attempts, only 28 percent believed their situation would improve by the end of the Pérez government, and the president's approval rating had plunged to 69 percent unfavorable.[17]

In the long run, these policies were responsible for a dramatic economic recovery beginning in 1991, but before that could happen a second development turned the popular anger against the entire political class. In 1989–90 the increasingly independent press gave constant, high-profile coverage to corrupt activities that had taken place during the previous administration. There were frequent revelations about how the foreign exchange agency RECADI had been used to manufacture illegal profits for politicians and businessmen with connections to former president Jaime Lusinchi (1984–89) and his secretary and mistress, Bianca Ibáñez (whom he later married). When Venezuelans, in the depths of economic crisis, were bombarded with reports of millions of dollars being spirited away, they drew the understandable (though certainly exaggerated) conclusion that they were suffering because the politicians had stolen their country's riches.[18]

For example, when a 1984 poll asked Venezuelans what factor contributed most to the country's large foreign debt, the top two responses were "bad administration of the nation's funds" (36%) and "administrative corruption" (33%). Similarly, in response to a 1985 question about the causes of the economic crisis, 86 percent assigned "much responsibility" to corruption, as did 74 percent to "bad administration of national resources" and 50 percent to the "decline of moral values."[19]

Despite the continuing scandalmongering, only one minor character in the scandal was punished. This synthesis of the anger over the economy and the anger about corruption was more potent than either issue taken separately. It was made even more galling by the fact that now the government was asking everyone to sacrifice to help pay for these crimes. This time they directed their anger at both parties because COPEI, led by Eduardo Fernández, supported Pérez' economic policies. (Pérez pursued his policies despite muffled protests from the dominant faction of his own party, AD, but AD was blamed for his policies anyway.) In this way the Adecopeyano establishment came to be blamed for the corruption, the impunity, and the economic crisis itself.

The Search for a Viable Alternative

Initially some of this anger was turned against democracy itself. After all, it was hard to tell where the establishment ended and democracy began; they were born at the same time and grew up together, and the establishment liked to equate *itself* with democracy. This helps explain why the leaders of the coup attempt of February 1992 enjoyed such popularity: the loss of this particular "democratic" regime struck 26–32 percent of the population as a small price to pay to get rid of a hated president.[20] But the second coup attempt, in November 1992, was a turning point in the definition of an alternative to partyarchy. Its visible spokesmen were not the clean-cut, articulate, and patriotic young officers from February, but scruffy and incoherent revolutionaries. The idea of being governed by them scared away much of the support for a coup and gave new urgency to the search for a democratic alternative.

That alternative was defined in two stages over the next fifteen months. The first stage was the impeachment of Pérez in May 1993 and the selection of an interim president, Ramón J. Velásquez. As befitted a transitional figure, Velásquez was neither a party militant nor an anti-establishment figure. (He was one of Venezuela's many "independents" who never actually joined a party but were known to sympathize with one; in his case, AD, because of a close friendship with Betancourt.) Governability actually improved during the interim government, because a tax reform, a new banking law, and other urgent bills that had been put on the back burner until the impeachment vote were passed quickly with the support of AD and COPEI, knowing that the independent president would be held responsible more than either party.[21]

The second stage was the process leading up to the general elections of December 5, 1993. For their part, AD and COPEI tried to define the alternative to the establishment as a renovated AD-COPEI establishment. An electoral reform passed in 1988 had instituted direct elections for mayors and governors, and state elections in 1989 and 1992 had begun a turnover in and revitalization of the party leadership at the state and local levels.[22] A new generation of Adecos and Copeyanos, as well as MASistas and a few leaders of the Causa R, a new-unionist movement, were building a base of genuine support at these levels and challenging the dominance of the *cogollos* in their parties. The renovation of the parties took a startling leap forward when two members of this generation unexpectedly won the presidential nominations of AD and COPEI. In AD the nominee was Claudio Fermín, a former mayor of Caracas; and in COPEI, Governor Oswaldo Alvarez Paz of Zulia came from behind in the party's first open primary to defeat Eduardo Fernández and other prominent national leaders. Because they were officially nominees of AD and COPEI, however, and both identified with the economic policies of the Pérez administration, they were at a disadvantage against the leading candidate, Rafael Caldera.

As the founder of COPEI, a signer of the Pact of Punto Fijo, a former president, and a key participant in all of the *concertación* of the previous thirty-five years, Caldera would seem a most unlikely beneficiary of the anti-establishment sentiment, but he was. Two actions made his political image makeover possible. First was an electrifying speech he made in the Senate following the February 1992 coup attempt. In that speech, broadcast live throughout the nation, he stopped short of endorsing the coup attempt but expressed the popular frustration with Pérez, his policies, and unresponsive politicians so movingly that he was instantly acknowledged as the principal spokesman for the opposition. His second act was to bolt his own party in early 1993 to run for president as an independent candidate with the backing of MAS, a personalistic vehicle called Convergencia Nacional (National Convergence) and sixteen other small parties. This was the most dramatic break with the establishment possible, not simply because he abandoned (and was expelled by) the party he founded, but because such defections had become unthinkable in Venezuela. Caldera won the election with 30.45 percent of the vote, to 24 percent for Fermín,

23 percent for Alvarez Paz, and 22 percent for Causa R founder Andrés Velásquez.

The First Two Years of the Caldera Government

The beginning of the Caldera government was a critical moment for democratic governability in Venezuela: the Adecopeyano establishment had, for the first time in thirty-five years, lost power, and an anti-establishment figure was searching for a new formula for governing. His search was bound to be frustrating because of: (1) his weak base of support, (2) the potential strength of the opposition, (3) declining confidence in elections, (4) conflict with governors, (5) a wary and divided military, (6) difficult relations with organized labor, and (7) an uneasy private sector. Venezuela is far less governable during the Caldera government than it was in the 1970s. It has not, however, reached some theoretical extreme of ungovernability; it has merely lost all the advantages that used to distinguish it from its neighbors. To put the situation in perspective, Venezuela has become "Latin Americanized." Some comparisons with aspects of governance in other Latin American countries are helpful for assessing Venezuela's prospects.

Base of Support

With 30 percent of the vote in 1993, Caldera did not have much of a mandate to govern. (Indeed, after factoring in the 43.8% abstention rate, he was elected with the support of only 17% of the registered voters.) His initial governing coalition was composed of the leftist MAS plus the Convergencia Nacional and minor parties, which together controlled barely a quarter of the seats in Congress. To make matters worse, the coalition was a patchwork of sixteen tiny parties ranging from the far Left to the far Right, fleshed out by a few disaffected Adecos and Copeyanos. In his effort to distance himself from AD and COPEI and the technocratic "IESA Boys"[23] of the Pérez government, Caldera passed over both known politicians and the policy elite, leaving himself with a cabinet dominated by second-string technocrats.

While AD and COPEI were harshly punished at the polls, they still controlled a majority of the seats in Congress (see Table 1). Simple arithmetic makes it clear that Caldera could not create a legislative majority without either AD or COPEI. Conflict between the old establishment-dominated Congress and the anti-establishment president was not long in coming: in June 1994 Caldera suspended constitutional guarantees of certain civil liberties, ostensibly to deal with a banking crisis and those responsible for it. (However, the government also took advantage of the situation to crack down on street crime, suspected insurrection plotters, and annoying journalists.) When Congress balked at ratifying the emergency powers, Caldera bullied it into acquiescence

Table 1 **Venezuela: Seats in Congress by Party, 1993**

	Chamber of Deputies		Senate	
	N	%	N	%
AD	56	27.9	18	34.6
COPEI	54	26.9	15	28.8
Causa R	40	19.9	10	19.2
MAS and Convergencia Nacional	51	25.4	9	17.3
Total	201	100.0	52	100.0

Source: NotiSur, February 4, 1994.

by threatening to convene a constituent assembly with the authority to dissolve Congress. The president then held civil liberties hostage until July 1995, when Congress finally approved a financial emergency management law giving the president a freer hand in setting economic policy.

In the meantime, executive-legislative relations were smoothed out by an unexpected coalition. In August 1994 an "orthodox" faction led by Luis Alfaro Ucero gained control of AD and removed almost all of the younger, reformist, neoliberal leaders from the National Executive Committee. This was the most visible manifestation of a top-to-bottom purge of AD that restored party unity and left it more closely aligned with Caldera's skeptical approach to economic policy. Without formally becoming a coalition partner, AD supported most of Caldera's initiatives in Congress, making it possible for several major pieces of legislation to pass. As the December 1995 gubernatorial and mayoral elections approached, however, with growth stagnant, inflation still over 50 percent, and Caldera's approval rating dipping below 40 percent, AD ended its cooperation and the tiny parties of the coalition one by one began to distance themselves from the government, leaving it ever more isolated.

Caldera's coalition alternatives were practically nonexistent. COPEI, despite lingering rank-and-file devotion to Caldera, was led after December 1994 principally by General Secretary Donald Ramírez (an ally of former president Luis Herrera Campíns), who was an opponent of reconciliation with his party's founder. To Ramírez, Caldera betrayed the party he founded by running as an independent candidate in 1993; to Caldera, the leaders of COPEI betrayed him personally by not supporting his candidacy. The only other significant party was the Causa R, which followed an obstructionist line in Congress, routinely abstaining on and voting against government bills, and sometimes breaking quorum and boycotting sessions. There were, therefore, no other realistic coalition possibilities.

There were two ways to govern without a formal presidential coalition. First, Caldera could try to assemble ad hoc majorities for specific legislative initiatives, appealing directly to the people to pressure the Congress. This strategy did not serve him well during his first administration, when he also refused to form a coalition despite having won the presidency with 29 percent of the vote, and was stalemated by the Congress during 70 percent of his time in office.[24] This strategy could work only if he were a very popular president like Fujimori, so it ceased to be a viable option by mid-1995. If Caldera were to boost his popularity by, for example, taking some dramatic action against corruption, his relations with Congress would be easier for a while. But until that happened, the fates of less popular presidents with similarly narrow bases of support—Belaúnde (first term), Febres Cordero, Velasco Ibarra, Sarney, Collor, Illia, Allende—presaged either stalemate or a *pugna de poderes* (power struggle) with the Congress.[25] Caldera early on expressed a desire to amend the constitution to obtain the power to dissolve Congress. The Congress was hardly likely to place such a powerful weapon in his hands, and the prospect that Caldera might attempt to seize it for himself inspired speculation about a possible *Calderazo* (presidential coup led by Caldera).

The second way to govern without a presidential coalition was to form an opposition coalition in the Congress, most likely composed of the two former establishment parties. The last time AD and COPEI were both in the opposition was 1957, and they signed a pact to oppose military rule. This time a pact could lead to an opposition majority and stalemate. There are precedents for such opposition majority coalitions in both Venezuela—where the AD-led coalition legislated over Caldera's head during his first government—and Peru, where APRA (American Popular Revolutionary Alliance) and Odría's UNO (Odríist National Union) cooperated to stalemate Belaúnde from 1963 to 1968. There remained, then, two ways to avoid executive-legislative stalemate, but both carried the risk of escalating confrontation and constitutional crisis.

Confidence in Elections

Despite electoral reforms, elections lost some of their legitimacy as the sole path to power during the 1980s. Abstention was triple what it was fifteen years before, despite mandatory voting, and charges of electoral fraud were increasingly common. While the numerous upsets and the fragmentation of the vote among several parties indicated that elections were fair, many Venezuelans came to suspect that the largest parties routinely divided among themselves any votes cast for parties that were not represented at the voting station.[26] López Maya documents unsuccessful attempts by AD to steal gubernatorial elections from the Causa R.[27] Two of the gubernatorial elections of 1992 had to be held again in 1993 to resolve questions about their fairness, and both Caldera and Andrés Velásquez claimed that AD, COPEI, and the military conspired to deprive them of hundreds of thousands of votes in the last presidential election.[28] Whether these claims were true or not, they were a symptom of declining governability. Nevertheless, the issue did not become as heated as it has been in Nicaragua, El Salvador, Honduras, Paraguay, or other less consolidated democracies. Democratic regimes such as Chile and Colombia have survived for many years despite occasional disputes over election results, so this issue alone would not place Venezuelan democracy in any immediate danger.

Conflict with Governors

Venezuela's twenty-two elected state governors were in a position to make trouble for the national government because they were politicians with a base of support independent of both president and party. Conflicts with Pérez were frequent because governors were directly elected for the first time in 1989 and the division of powers between federal and state governments was still murky. Procedures for resolving disputes had to be improvised for each issue that arose. Conflicts intensified during the Caldera administration because the most effective governors, the ones reelected in 1992, became lame ducks as the 1995 gubernatorial elections approached, with the potential to challenge Caldera's authority by launching presidential candidacies. Their potential for disruption should not be exaggerated, however, because their resources were quite limited, and because independent governors do not seem to cause serious problems of governance in the other federal presidential democracies of the hemisphere, Argentina, Brazil, and the United States.

Relations with the Military

Caldera was perhaps the best candidate to mollify the rebellious junior officers: on the second anniversary of the February 4, 1992, coup attempt, he promised to free the seventy rebel officers still in prison in Venezuela and to invite back the fifty-two still in exile in Peru and Ecuador. Such acts, however, only exacerbated the tensions within the military between the junior officers and the high command, which had already virtually severed the chain of command at bases throughout the country. Caldera asserted his authority by dismissing the defense minister and service chiefs ahead of schedule as soon as he took office, but this act created further resentment toward the new president and new divisions in the military. Some officers were also antagonized by Caldera's accusations of military involvement in vote fraud, and were apprehensive about his ability to govern for the next five years. Upon resigning, outgoing defense minister Radamés Muñoz León said:

This situation has infuriated me. This cannot be the reward we receive for the democratic struggle we have waged within the Armed Forces. I am crying inside over my people because I do not know what will happen to the country with a precarious government that was elected by scarcely 8 percent of the population, or 16 percent of the potential voters, and whose first act was to strike an institution that is at the service of the fatherland and not of political parties, personalities, or economic or political interests.[29]

The divisions in the armed forces did not appear to be as deep as those typically found in the Bolivian, Argentine, or Peruvian militaries, but they were deep enough to warrant concern about future coup attempts like those of 1992 should Caldera find himself as isolated and unpopular as Pérez was.

Relations with Organized Labor

Caldera was destined to have an acrimonious relationship with Venezuela's unions. On the one hand, he promised them much, both as the candidate with the populist image and as the author of the labor law, which was reviled by the private sector for being too generous to workers. But on the other hand, Venezuela's fiscal deficit made it impossible for the state to provide workers many of the benefits to which the labor law entitled them. (A telling indicator: oil revenues, which used to cover 70% of public expenditures, covered only 40% in 1994.) And should the unions become disappointed and angry, Caldera would have no way to restrain them because he had virtually no institutional connection to the unions. Instead, most of the unions were allied with the parties in the opposition—AD, COPEI, and Causa R. (A minority sector of organized labor was affiliated with MAS and MEP [People's Electoral Movement], but it tended to follow the lead of the Venezuelan Workers Confederation [CTV], which was dominated by AD.) When AD was in the opposition in the past, it encouraged its unions to be militant, either to embarrass the government or to gain credibility for its claim to be a social democratic party.[30] There were some indications that the AD union movement was asserting its independence from the party in the 1980s and 1990s. But whether the unions were independent or not, they would have no reason to hold back their members for Caldera. Increased strike activity was therefore inevitable. Nevertheless, strike rates have always been comparatively low in Venezuela, so Venezuelan unions were unlikely to become as disruptive as their counterparts have sometimes been in Bolivia, Argentina, Chile, or Peru.

Relations with the Private Sector

The process of structural adjustment of the economy also adjusted the political relationship between the state and the private sector in Latin America. Many firms that had grown dependent on protectionism, state subsidies, and political connections found it difficult to survive in a more open market economy and lost their political influence; other firms that welcomed competition prospered and increased their influence. This Schumpeterian process of creative destruction increased conflict within the private sector in the early stages of adjustment. But where the process was allowed to proceed long enough, as in Colombia, Chile, Bolivia, and Mexico, the competitive firms became dominant and developed a more mutually satisfying, transparent relationship with the state that enhanced governability in the economic arena. In Venezuela the election of Caldera interrupted this process before the competitive firms gained dominance.

Caldera's election was an interruption because his campaign sent out mixed and vaguely worrisome signals. Some businessmen were concerned by his alliance with MAS and the communists; others were confused by the inconsistent policies advocated by his closest advisors; still others were disturbed by campaign promises to renegotiate the terms of the debt servicing agreement and to defend a fixed exchange rate when measures to fight inflation were not being discussed. After the election, Caldera's support for limited price controls, the suspension of the retail portion of the value added tax, and the lack of a clear plan to reduce the fiscal deficit added to their uneasiness. Some of the fears were alleviated by Caldera's inaugural address, but by that time a new fear had overwhelmed all the others: the fear of a financial collapse brought on by the failure of Banco Latino.

Banco Latino can be seen as a remnant of the unreformed private sector—a bank that traded on connections and corruption. It was the second largest and fastest-growing bank in Venezuela, but its success was built on political connections and lax regulation that allowed it to offer unsustainably high interest rates, and its efforts to cover its liabilities eventually degenerated into a massive Ponzi scheme. When the scheme collapsed in January 1994, U.S.$1.5 billion in deposits—20 percent of the market—was at risk, affecting not only a million small depositors but also the pension funds of Petróleos de Venezuela, the national electric company, the armed forces, and, most scandalously, nearly half of the funds available to the Venezuelan equivalent of the Federal Deposit Insurance Corporation (FDIC). This failure, when combined with the problems of other weakened banks, required a U.S.$5 billion bailout and swelled the fiscal deficit to 12 percent by 1995.[31] The overall health of the Venezuelan economy is probably better than that of some other Latin American nations, but this crisis created profound uncertainty about the country's medium-term economic future, and therefore undermined much of the progress toward governability in the economic arena that had been achieved before 1993.

In summary, the potential for governability in Venezuela was poor in the 1990s. Compared to its highly governable past, society was more polarized, the new governing coalition was fragmented and divided, and the former establishment parties, recently forced into the opposition, seemed either unable or unwilling to help the new president succeed in the long term. This does not mean that democracy is about to break down. There is little enthusiasm for a military government, and most strategic actors were willing to give Caldera a chance to prove himself. But in the meantime, Venezuela encountered increased symptoms of ungovernability: strikes and protests, disputed election results, conflict between governors and the federal government, economic uncertainty, and especially confrontation between the president and Congress.

2

Colombia: Building Democracy in the Midst of Violence and Drugs

Harvey F. Kline

Colombia has usually been considered one of the most democratic countries of Latin America by both foreign scholars and proud Colombians themselves. The basis for this familiar claim has been that civilian governments have predominated and there have been only five years of military rule in this century.

Yet there are at least three serious problems with this conventional view. First, as former president Alfonso López Michelsen has suggested, instead of a national military tyranny, the country had thousands of small tyrannies as large landowners ruled in an authoritarian fashion despite the formal democratic regime. Second, Colombian history is replete with violence and the violation of human rights, including that most basic one, the right to life. By the late 1980s both the subnational tyrannies and violence had become worse, with the latter coming from the new "small" tyrants—a combination of guerrilla groups, drug dealers, and paramilitary squads. Homicide became the most common cause of death (about 85% by "common criminals"), and Colombia with 33 million inhabitants had twice as many murders as the United States. Further, the same bands controlled a large percentage of the national territory, constituting de facto governments that were more powerful within those areas than officials of the national government.

Third, drug money has completely infiltrated Colombian politics. No one knows how many candidates have received such funds, how many did so knowingly, and what the effects have been on public policies. When the treasurer of President Ernesto Samper's 1994 campaign alleged that money from the Cali drug group had been used in electoral activities, the debate that followed in August and September 1995 led to the resignation of the minister of defense (who had been the director of Samper's campaign), as well as suggestions that either the president resign or step aside temporarily so that the influence of the drug money could be objectively studied.

As a result of the first two problems, a Constituent Assembly met during the first half of 1991 and a constitution, replacing the one of

1886, was proclaimed on July 4, 1991. One important part of the reform was the attempt to make Colombian democracy more open, so that people who were guerrillas would have no reason for violent conflict. Another part was to strengthen the justice system, so that impunity would no longer rule. This chapter, after describing the historical context of Colombian politics, considers how successful or unsuccessful this constitutional reform is likely to be in bringing democracy to that nation.

The Three Models of Governance in Colombia

Democracy has never been completely achieved during the three regimes of Colombian history. The first period of "sectarian democracy" (1849–1953) began with the founding of the Liberal and Conservative parties in midcentury and continued until its breakdown in 1953. While civilian governments were the norm during this period, fraud and violence were used to keep the respective parties in power, while the party out of power often started civil wars to oust the incumbent government, albeit seldom with success. After the frequent civil wars, the losers were given amnesty.

Despite the changes of the party in power, traumatic international events such as the loss of Panama, and dramatic social and demographic changes in the country, this basic regime persisted for more than a century because of several factors that added intensity to it. A religious context was added to politics when the Roman Catholic Church sided with the Conservative party. The civil wars were so frequent that each generation had memories of party "martyrs" from the previous one. After 1930 the government became more involved in the economy, increasing the stakes of the conflict. All this led to a culmination of the regime in a period of partisan violence so long and intense that Colombians refer to it as La Violencia. During the period between 1946 and 1965, at least two hundred thousand Colombians died in this nationwide civil war between the Liberals and Conservatives.

The second period of "consociational democracy" came when, as a way to end this violence (and the only military dictatorship of the twentieth century), Conservative and Liberal party leaders agreed on power sharing. The original duration was 1958–74, during which the National Front shared all political power equally between the two traditional parties. The presidency alternated every four years, while elective and appointive positions were divided equally. Only the Liberal and Conservative parties could hold office. Power sharing was continued after 1974 by the constitutional requirement that the president give "adequate and equitable" participation in the executive branch to the second largest political party.

The National Front was successful in ending the partisan violence, with the latter years bringing the democratic election of mayors in 1988. The consociational period seemed to have ended when President Virgilio Barco (1986–90), a Liberal, ruled with his party only. The Conservatives refused the cabinet seats offered them.

During the consociational period, however, other forms of violence replaced that between the parties. Marxist guerrilla groups appeared in the first half of the 1960s, some with direct connections to earlier liberal groups of La Violencia. Landowners formed paramilitary groups when the government failed to protect them from the guerrillas. Drug dealers began violent tactics against the government in the 1980s and, having bought agricultural land with their profits, in some cases took over the paramilitary groups.

The 1980s were so violent in Colombia (with death rates reaching higher levels than during La Violencia) that leaders of political parties, economic interest groups, and university students called for the Constituent Assembly that brought Colombia to the current period of "participatory democracy." Among the features of this newest stage, which began with the Constitution of 1991, are the following:

The president is now elected by an absolute majority, unlike the previous plurality, and can have only one term.

The Congress is given new powers (including the right to censure cabinet officials), while its members are also more controlled than before as to holding other elective positions (previously a member of the Congress could concurrently be a member of a departmental assembly and/or a municipal council), attendance, and pork barrel legislation.

No longer can a president declare an indefinite "state of siege," during which certain rights were suspended. Now the president can declare a "state of emergency" for only ninety days of a calendar year; the Congress can extend it by another ninety.

Electoral rights were changed, with election of departmental governors added. Further, the district for the national Senate was changed to a national one from departmental ones.

In addition, voters have initiative and recall rights.

The judicial system was changed from the traditional Napoleonic model to one more like that of the United States, with a national prosecutor who is to coordinate all law enforcement in the country.

A new national Congress and governors were elected under these rules in October 1991 and March 1994, and the first presidential election was held in May 1994. A popular initiative did lead to the consideration and passing of a new law on kidnapping in 1993. But there have yet to be recall elections. In late 1993 consideration for doing so in the case of the mayor of Bogotá ran into the obstacle that, although the right of recall was in the new constitution, the Congress had not yet passed enabling legislation for a recall election.

Current Status of Governance in Colombia

The current conditions in Colombia demonstrate that democratic governance is still a distant goal. Although the Constitution of 1991 is still only partially implemented, this chapter provides predictions of likely results.

Nature of the Electoral Process

The two historic political parties still dominate Colombian elections, but, at least since the National Front, they no longer effectively aggregate interests in such a way that Colombian voters can choose candidates on the basis of programmatic identity. Rather, both the Liberals and the Conservatives include a variety of ideological persuasions, including traditional conservatives with ties to the landed elite, neoliberals, populists, and welfare state liberals.

While Colombian political parties were based on the intensity of the conflict during the sectarian period, after the National Front the system became one based on personalities, images, and campaign expenditures because of the cooperation of the two parties during the consociational period, the gradual loss of inherited ascription to the parties, and the absence of distinctive party programs.

The ramifications of these changes have been seen in the current splintering of the Conservative party into at least three groups: a group still calling itself the Conservative party; the National Salvation Movement (MSN) led by Alvaro Gómez; and the New Democratic Force (NFD) led by Andrés Pastrana. Gómez supported the Pastrana presidential campaign, and Pastrana has been the most important Conservative leader since then.

Although the Liberal party has remained united, it is illuminating that its leader, octogenarian former president Alfonso López, used a "wasp swarm" strategy in the two congressional elections. Using this approach, López recruited key regional leaders to be on the party's senatorial list, leading to a majority of a disunited party.

A significant third party is the Alianza Democrática (AD, Democratic Alliance) M-19. Founded by the M-19 guerrilla group upon its demobilization in 1989, AD M-19's presidential candidate, Antonio Navarro, received 12.5 percent of the 1990 vote, by far the highest for any party of the Left in Colombian history. With nineteen seats, AD M-19 was second to the Liberals (twenty-five) in the number of seats in the Constituent Assembly, and Navarro was its co-president. Yet in the October 1991 elections, the AD M-19 won only nine of the one hundred senatorial seats and none in March 1994. As its presidential candidate for 1994, Navarro won 4 percent of the vote.

Another smaller party is the Unión Patriótica (UP, Patriotic Union), which was founded by the Fuerzas Armadas de la Revolución Colombiana (FARC, Armed Forces of the Colombian Revolution), the largest guerrilla groups in Colombia, during the democratic opening of President Belisario Betancur (1982–86). The UP's electoral success has been slight, in part because of the assassinations of its militants, including its presidential candidate in 1990.

Rates of participation in Colombian elections have been very low since the 1950s. Although there were exceptions (such as the hotly contested presidential election of 1970), most commonly participation in presidential elections has been in the 34–50 percent range. The 1986 presidential election had an abstention rate of 54 percent, while that of 1990 had 57 percent. Fifty-eight percent of the potential electors did not vote in the Constituent Assembly election in December 1990. Seventy percent did not vote in the March 1994 congressional elections, which included the Liberal "popular consultation" to choose the party's presidential candidate.

Since the particular form of proportional representation used does not punish parties with many lists, Colombian legislative campaigns are characterized by a multiplicity of slates. Most have few individuals elected from them, making the position on the list of greatest importance. Power is in the hands of departmental leaders rather than national ones. Changing the system to have a national list for the Senate was intentionally designed so that small groups, distributed widely over the country, could get some representation. Yet the chaos of congressional elections was seen in March 1994. Thirty-six political parties offered lists of candidates; there were 674 lists (with 3,355 hopefuls) for the 163 lower house positions; there were 251 lists of candidates (with 1,978 aspirants) for the 100 Senate seats, with 96 lists electing one senator and two lists winning two seats.

The traditional method that parties have used to choose presidential candidates has been a national convention controlled by regional leaders. However, in the 1980s a group of young Liberals, led by Luis Carlos Galán and calling themselves the New Liberalism movement, split from the party after the 1982 convention and chose Alfonso López to be the presidential candidate. Part of the deal to get Galán back into the Liberal party in 1990 was a kind of open primary for the selection of its presidential candidate. Under this system, individuals vote for a Liberal candidate for president at the same time that they vote in congressional elections. To guard against voters who are not Liberals from having a key say in the party's presidential candidate, the rule is that a candidate must win by at least 5 percent.

The Colombian government gives a financial supplement to candidates according to the number of votes they receive, but most campaign money is private and not controlled by the government. There is no doubt that drug money is important to many Colombian politicians. While the day has passed when someone like Pablo Escobar can be elected an alternate in the lower house of Congress from Antioquia, as he was in 1982, an unknown number of politicians are supported by drug money.

Vote counting in Colombia is done by the National Registry. Monitoring procedures include the right for all parties and candidates to have representatives at the polling places and at places where votes are counted. Charges of gross electoral fraud have been rare, although the 1970 presidential election did include them. There is a definite danger in running for public office and voting for the UP, especially in certain areas of the country.

After the intentional limitation of democratic representation during the National Front, three issues of representation became salient in Colombia. The first had to do with the bias of the traditional voting system. From 1978 until the new Constitution of 1991, various groups argued that this system kept their interests from being represented, although it was never very explicit how that was the case in a proportional representation system. The second had to do with the murder of candidates from parties of the Left, especially the Unión Patriótica; more than two thousand of its militants have been killed.

The final issue of representation had to do with the relationship of politicians to the drug trade. With the Medellín group, the problem was the danger to politicians who had opposed the illicit commerce. Along with journalists, judges, and law officers, politicians were assassinated by the Medellín group, including Luis Carlos Galán, the leading Liberal candidate in 1990, as well as two other presidential candidates in that bloody election (one each from the AD M-19 and the UP). The problem with the Cali group, on the other hand, was the degree to which *narco* money had corrupted politicians. Some analysts have even suggested that the Cali corruption of politicians became much more serious than the Medellín terrorism ever was.

While Colombia has a long way to go to take care of the problems of drug money and UP candidate assassination, the system is clearly much more open than before, perhaps too much so with the confusion for the elector. The 1994 election for the Senate shows this, with the following number of senators elected: Liberals, fifty-eight; Conservatives (including NFD and MSN), twenty-seven; Indians, two; Christians, two; and other movements, thirteen.

Executive-Legislative Relations

As a way to avoid excessive executive power, checks and balances have never worked well in Colombia. The constitutions have appeared to be much like that of the United States; however, under the Constitution of 1886, this ideal was not reached for two reasons. First, the Congress did not exercise the powers that it had, for example, waiting over a decade after the Constitutional Reform of 1968 to set up a committee to work on economic planning with the executive branch. In large part, no doubt, this had to do with the part-time nature of being a member of Congress. Second, during much of the time after 1946, Colombian presidents governed under "state of siege" provisions of the constitution. Although the Congress continued meeting, and executive decrees had to be declared constitutional by the Council of State, the president was able to rule by decree.

The Constitution of 1991 seeks to correct both of these problems. Members of Congress can no longer hold other elective positions, and no longer are there alternates to attend Congress in their stead. Missing six votes in the Congress, without excuse, leads to a member's being removed from office.

The new constitution also controls the state of siege powers. Now a president can decree a "state of exception" for only ninety days of a calendar year; the Senate can extend it for another ninety. For some, this begs the question of effective government, as the causes for states of siege (guerrilla groups, drug dealers, and paramilitary squads) are present all 365 days of the year.

The change of congressional power was far from immediate after the new constitution was approved. Perhaps because more than half of the members elected in 1991 had been in the Congress before, in its first two years the legislature showed many patterns held over from the past. Semantic sleight of hand made pork barrel legislation possible; the Liberal party was no more united than previously; and the first opportunity to use the censure power, after the escape of Pablo Escobar, was lost. The August 1995 lower house investigation of drug money in the Samper campaign does suggest, however, a gradual increase of congressional power, while executive power decreases.

The same tendency is likely to be seen in relation to the state of emergency that President Samper proclaimed during the drug investigation. While some alleged that the proclamation was a smoke screen to divert attention from the investigation, others pointed out that violence was at higher levels than usual. The key question is whether the Senate will be willing to extend the emergency after the first ninety days.

The Rule of Law and the Judiciary

With problems coming from guerrilla groups, drug dealers, paramilitary squads, in addition to "common crime," the Colombian judicial system became seriously overloaded during the 1980s. Of all the crimes reported in 1983, only 10 percent led to verdicts, according to the government, while the Inter-American Commission on Human Rights put the figure at 4 percent in 1990. Impunity became the rule rather than the exception.

One particularly serious problem of the judicial system after the 1980s came from the immense wealth of the drug leaders, who were seldom successfully adjudicated because they either bribed, threatened, or killed judges. While the guerrilla groups have had less effect on the judicial system, a notable exception to this was the M-19 seizure of the Palace of Justice in Bogotá in November 1985. The guerrilla group's stated motivation was to try President Belisario Betancur, although some would argue that it was to destroy records on drug leaders instead. Whatever the motivation, when the national military regained control of the building, more than a hundred civilians were dead, including half of the Supreme Court.

In an attempt to solve the myriad problems of the justice system, President Virgilio Barco initiated a system of "anonymous judges." To prevent retribution against the judges, the idea was that testimony would be taken in such a way that neither defendants nor witnesses would see the judge or hear his or her unaltered voice. While this had some success, the fact that some of the anonymous judges were summarily executed, apparently by drug groups, indicated that the system was not a total success.

Two other novel approaches begun in the Colombian judicial system during the Barco years were plea bargaining and rewards for informants. These policies were carried further during the government of César Gaviria (1990–94), most notably in the case of the surrender policy for drug dealers and paramilitary squad members. Under that policy, any person could receive a reduced sentence if he or she surrendered and confessed one crime. Since the maximum sentence in Colombia was thirty years at the time, the most a defendant could receive was fifteen years, even if he or she did not obtain additional reductions through studying or starting a business during the confinement.

The 1991 Constitution instituted a dramatic change for the Colombian judicial system. Rather than the traditional Napoleonic code, in which some judges do the investigation of crimes and others the adjudication, the new judicial system includes a National Prosecutor's Office (Fiscalía Nacional), with the functions of investigating and prosecuting cases as well as coordinating the activities of all military and civilian agencies gathering evidence on crimes. After the first two years, the new system was processing 50 percent more cases than the old one did, although, in a country in which impunity had become the rule, it will be at least several more years before one can definitively conclude that the legal impasse has been ended.

Civil-Military Relations

In comparative terms, civilians control the military more in Colombia than in most other Latin American countries. After all, there has been only one case in this century when a civilian was overthrown by the military (Laureano Gómez by General Gustavo Rojas Pinilla in 1953). However, the complexity of the relationship of elected presidents to the military is greater than the mere fact of having elected civilian presidents. For example, the apparent power of the military in Colombia was shown by the fact that between 1958 and 1991 the minister of war was always a ranking member of the armed forces. Further, the leadership of the military branches has largely been left up to the officers, and they have generally followed seniority in selecting leaders.

Of greater importance is the question of whether the civilian presidents are really making decisions in national security policy. During the "Security Statute" of President Julio César Turbay (1978–82), newspaper pundits alleged that many decisions were made by General Camacho Leyva rather than by the president. Likewise, members of Congress later charged that decision making was carried out by the military, although President Betancur was making the public statements, during the taking of the Palace of Justice in November 1985. The same accusations are made about the military attack on the headquarters of the Fuerzas Armadas de la Revolución Colombiana in December 1990: ranking military officers made the decision, not President Gaviria, who was not even informed of the attack beforehand. For all these declarations there are denials by both military and civilian leadership.

There have been, however, more public disagreements between the president and military officers. One major question has been about the role the military is to play: should it remain apolitical, true to Colombian tradition? Or should it speak up about the social and economic problems of the nation? On at least three occasions (the first in 1965 and the last in 1981), individual military leaders have seen it necessary to talk about the basic problems of the society. For example, in 1981 the commander of the army, General Landazábal Reyes, wrote in *Army Review,* "We are convinced that the army can militarily destroy the guerrillas, but we are also convinced that even with this, subversion will continue as long as the objective and subjective conditions in the economic, social, and political areas, which daily impair and disrupt stability, are not modified." The first two military leaders who made similar statements were relieved of their posts; Landazábal, too, was later replaced.

There was substantial military opposition to the Betancur National Dialogue. During it, military officers increasingly assisted paramilitary groups through supplies, training, and, in some cases, active participation of military personnel in the groups. Likewise, the armed forces have always felt at a disadvantage against the guerrillas, as the representatives of the Colombian state have to respect human rights (or be criticized by international groups), while the guerrillas do not have to show respect for the same rights.

The July 1992 escape of Pablo Escobar from prison near Medellín made it obvious that some members of the military have been corrupted by drug money. Although there have been instances of large groups of officers being caught taking drug money, no one has an accurate estimate of how large that group might be in the entire country.

Finally, the August–September 1995 presidential crisis led some observers to suggest that President Samper had been forced to enter a coalition with army generals and large business interests. He needed the armed forces with him in face of all the criticism from civilians, it was said. But adding the military to his coalition meant that Samper was not so reformist as before, and indeed that could be the explanation of his state of emergency to combat crime and guerrillas.

Two major conclusions seem warranted. First, the Colombian president does have real power in relation to the military. In August 1991, for example, when President Gaviria named the first civilian minister of war since 1949, there were no objections from the military. Second, it seems unlikely that the Colombian military will take over power directly. Although remarks of many political leaders, including former president Misael Pastrana, indicated their concern that a military takeover would occur during the deterioration of public order in the 1980s, the military stayed in its barracks even when the death rate surpassed that of La Violencia.

The Roles of Civic, Professional, Business, and Labor Organizations

A few economic interest groups have joined the traditional parties as the most powerful forces in Colombian politics since the beginning of the National Front. Today some even suggest that the economic groups (*gremios*) are of greater importance than the parties.

All major producer associations come from the upper sector; all seek to maintain the status quo. Although they might sometimes disagree with the policy of a government, they have supported the political regime, whether it was the National Front or the system in place since the end of the Front. The associations tend to react to governmental policy rather than initiate it. With the growth of the executive branch, in both the ministries and the decentralized institutes, the associations have developed strong ties with that branch. This does not mean, however, that they will not use connections within the Congress if that is the preferable way to block government policy.

All economic sectors of the upper- and middle-income groups are organized. The most powerful seem to be those "peak" organizations of economic activities, the National Federation of Coffee Growers (FEDECAFE) and a few other producer associations.

Probably the most politically powerful of the economic interest groups is the National Association of Industrialists (ANDI). ANDI approximates an overall peak organization of all producer associations as it includes not only the large industrialists, but also firms from the agribusiness, insurance, financial, and commercial sectors. It is the leading advocate of free enterprise in Colombia and has important roots in the industrialists of Medellín, its power coming from its wealth and social prestige, the common overlapping of membership of the group with that of the government, and the fact that industrialization has been a major goal of almost all Colombian presidents during the last half century. ANDI tends to oppose anything that might negatively affect the private sector, but historically has supported the government when there is opposition to the basic system of government.

FEDECAFE was founded in 1927 and is open to any person interested in developing the coffee industry, although it is dominated by the large coffee growers. The federation collects various taxes on coffee and has used its wealth to invest in banks and shipping. It has a close relationship with the government, given the importance of coffee to economic policy. One big difference between Colombia and other Latin American countries is the degree of "privatization" of certain key functions. Nowhere else would a legally private organization be allowed to do what FEDECAFE does; the governments would do it directly.

With the lack of differentiation of the political parties and their factions, interest articulation and aggregation increasingly have been done by the *gremios* (who have made efforts to be bipartisan) and by the church and the military. For example, in April 1981 the *gremios* stated the position of some of them when the Frente Gremial (Trade Association Front) published an analysis of Colombian problems. Composed of the presidents of ANDI, the Colombian Chamber of Construction (CAMACOL), the Colombian Federation of Metallurgical Industries (FEDEMETAL), the National Federation of Merchants (FENALCO), and the National Association of Financial Institutions (ANIF), the Frente did not limit itself to issues directly affecting the economic activities of the *gremios*. Rather, general issues such as inflation, lack of housing for the poor, and the minimum wage were considered and solutions were proposed.

The continued importance of the *gremios* was shown in 1991 when, for the first time in the history of the country and with the support of President Gaviria, the principal production *gremios* agreed to form a special entity that would have the responsibility of negotiating with the government on issues of international trade, foreign investment, and world cooperation. The National Gremial Council was supported by thirteen organizations: ANDI, SAC (Colombian Agricultural Society), FENALCO, FEDEMETAL, CAMACOL, the National Association of Exporters, the National Federation of Livestock Raisers, the Union of Insurers of Colombia, the Banking Association of Colombia, the Association of Producers and Exporters of Sugarcane, the Colombian Association of Plastic Industries, the Popular Association of Industrialists, and the Colombian Association of Automobile Parts Manufacturers. The idea of creating the council came from a suggestion of the minister of development, Ernesto Samper, who said that the business groups complained about the lack of negotiations with the government, but the latter lacked channels through which to negotiate. It was announced that the council would have a coordinating committee that would make recommendations to the government and would make statements about any step the government might take in the "economic opening."

While the activity of the Frente Gremial had not been well received by President Turbay in the early 1980s, President Gaviria had a completely different idea. Further, one should not discount the power of the *gremios* in the interim. These economic interest groups have always had considerable power in public policymaking.

Organized labor is a weaker political force in Colombia. In part this is because of the small percentage of the work force that is unionized. Divisions among labor federations, some of which are along traditional political party lines, are another cause. Several other factors also contribute to labor's weak position in Colombian politics. Labor leaders are still required to be full-time workers in their industries, a requirement that is enforced selectively. The percentage of the force that is unionized is small, only 17–19 percent in 1974, falling to 9 percent ten years later, 8 percent in 1989, and 5 percent in 1992, although the percentages were higher in industry, utilities, transportation, and communications. Further, labor legislation has promoted the development of enterprise unions and weakened the possibilities of industrywide unions.

Finally, strikes in manufacturing are limited legally to a maximum of forty days before the compulsory introduction of binding arbitration. This stipulation of the law, which has led some to conclude that Colombia has adopted many of the policies of the bureaucratic authoritarian regimes of the Southern Cone without the large-scale repression of them, weakens that key power resource of organized labor—the ability to paralyze the economy through strike actions.

The first national labor federation was the Confederation of Colombian Workers (CTC), founded in 1936 during the administration of Liberal Alfonso López Pumarejo. With the end of the Liberal hegemony in 1946, the CTC was repressed by the government of Conservative Mariano Ospina. As a rival organization, the Union of Colombian Workers (UTC) was founded by the Jesuits. The UTC was allowed to flourish during the Conservative years.

Two other labor federations emerged in the 1960s and 1970s. The Syndical Confederation of Workers of Colombia (CSTC) was formed in 1964 when numerous communist-oriented unions banded together after having been ejected from the CTC. The General Confederation of Labor (CGT), a socialist and radical-Christian labor federation, was formed in 1971. Both the CSTC and CGT existed without legal recognition until it was granted by President López in 1974. There are still other labor unions at the enterprise level, but they remain unaffiliated with any of the four federations. Estimates in 1992 gave the following breakdown of union membership: the new Central Unica de Trabajadores, 60 percent; CTC, 7 percent; CSTC, 10 percent; CGT, 18 percent; and unaffiliated, 19 percent.

Relevant Aspects of Church-State Relations

Traditionally Colombia has been one of the most Roman Catholic of Latin American nations, with the power of the church in the nineteenth century based on land and on a concordat between the Colombian state and the Vatican. As Colombians have become more urban, the power of the church has declined. Various Protestant groups, especially of the evangelical movement, have also appeared, particularly in the cities.

The church hierarchy, however, has continued to speak out when politicians raise the possibility of changes in areas considered to be church domain. When candidate López in 1982 suggested the possibility of easier divorce, the bishops' reply suggested that good Catholics should not vote for candidates with such programs. The sentiments of the church hierarchy were very similar during the Constituent Assembly in 1991. As Archbishop Pedro Rubiano Sáenz of Cali stated, "However much it is said that the Constitution approved divorce for Catholic marriage, we affirm and will always teach in accord with Catholic faith and doctrine, that valid matrimony is indissoluble and that the annulling of civil effects of sacramental marriages cannot destroy the relationship."[1]

Yet it seems that the Constitution of 1991 demonstrates what experts had already concluded: the political power of the hierarchy of the Roman Catholic Church is much less than before. This, of course, does not mean that it has disappeared. Individual Roman Catholic priests have played important roles in guerrilla demobilization, in the surrender of Pablo Escobar, and in the denunciation of human rights abuses.

The Role of the Media

Colombia has one of the strongest media in Latin America, with the notable exception to that generalization coming at those times in recent years when states of siege have included media censorship. It should also be acknowledged that the Colombian "dirty war" has affected the media. Journalists have been killed by drug dealers, by paramilitary groups, by guerrillas, and by "unknown people." In all cases the effect is censorship, as seen in the case of Gabriel Cano, the publisher of *El Espectador*, assassinated by drug groups in Bogotá on December 17, 1986. Cano's only transgression was having written articles against illicit drugs.

Media freedoms should now increase because of the state of siege limitation in the new constitution and the end of drug terrorism. Yet so long as guerrilla and paramilitary violence continue, complete media freedom is tenuous at best.

Minority Rights

Minority rights in Colombia include those of religious and racial groups. In the religious case, there has long been discrimination against non-Catholics. During La Violencia, it was assumed that all Protestants must be Liberals, hence giving Conservatives justification for killing them. Yet, with urbanization and the end of partisan violence, there is greater religious tolerance than before. One member of the 1991 Constituent Assembly was elected by an evangelical list, and the same group elected a senator in both 1991 and 1994. With the possible exception of the very isolated regions of the country, non-Catholic religions are unlikely to be the victims of violent discrimination.

Colombians are racially diverse, with large numbers of pure or nearly pure Spanish background (and a smattering of other Europeans), as well as Indians and Colombians of pure African descent. There are also combinations of the three races. The British geographer Peter Wade suggests that Colombian racial relations be visualized as a triangle whose uppermost point is white and whose bottom corners are black and Indian. The white apex is associated with power, wealth, civilization, government, and high degrees of urbanity, education, and culture. The bottom two corners are seen from above as primitive, dependent, uneducated, rural, and inferior. Blacks are stereotyped as lazy, having an abnormal family structure because of the absence of male role models, and a love for music, dancing, and celebration. Indian culture is perceived by whites as even more foreign and distinct than black culture, especially in life-style and language.[2]

It is impossible to state the exact racial categories in Colombia and to number the individuals in them, as no recent census has included a question about "race"; hence using that characteristic for statistical analysis of education, income, or anything else is simply impossible. Further, it is not a factor analyzed in public opinion polls. Nor is there enough agreement to make self-identification valid. As Wade argues, the national racial order is based on "the contradictory but interdependent coexistence of blackness, indianness, mixedness, and whiteness."

There is no legal discrimination by race. No laws have ever been passed to end such discrimination simply because laws allowing discrimination never existed. Likewise voting has never been restricted by race per se, although until literacy was removed as a requirement for voting in the 1930s, many people of color could not vote. Of course illiterate whites could not either. Many blacks and Indians still do not vote because they live in isolated areas where the Colombian government has no effective presence. The respective organizations claim that there are 3.5 million blacks and 700,000 Indians, although it is clear that most of the former do not live in such isolated areas.

This is not to say that racial prejudices do not exist. The archconservative President Laureano Gómez (1949–53) stated that Indians and blacks were inferior and that the "Spanish spirit" guided Colombian character. In more general terms, the system of *blanqueamiento* (whitening), while pointing out racial and cultural differences, is one that gives value to whiteness and disparages blackness and Indianness.

The Colombian Andes are different from Ecuador, Peru, and Bolivia because many people, especially in the Andean Central region, who might be racially native Colombian, are not culturally so. They are not considered *indios* because they dress in a fashion similar to other inhabitants, and they speak Spanish rather than an indigenous language. Likewise people of pure African-American heritage racially do have alternatives to escape blackness. First there is the possibility of race mixture, but there is also "social whitening" by living in the cities and integrating oneself into nonblack networks.

Government statistics indicate that there are 411,803 Indians in the country (or about 1.5 percent of the population). The National Indian Council, possibly having more reliable statistics than the government, claims to have organized 80 percent of the 700,000 Indians in the country (2.3 percent of the national population); it is of note that it was only in 1982 that the council was founded, indicating both the status as a small minority in the country and the difficulty of organizing such a dispersed group. From the perspective of the native people, there are issues that need to be addressed, most notably their traditional tribal lands. A regional indigenous organization appeared in the Cauca area in the early 1970s, with three objectives: reestablishing Indian reservations, increasing the authority of their local governments, and reaffirming the autonomy of their regions. After the leadership of this Regional Indigenous Council of the Cauca (CRIC) was jailed by the local authorities or assassinated by thugs hired by large landowners, native American members joined various guerrilla groups. In 1984 an Indian guerrilla group was formed, the Quintín Lame Armed Movement, which for the next six years was to average between one hundred and three hundred members.

At least in part because of these unsettled traditional demands of indigenous groups, made more noticeable as the commemoration of the five hundredth anniversary of the arrival of the Europeans approached, the *indígenas* were assigned two seats in the 1991 Constituent Assembly and the new constitution gives them two seats of the one hundred in the national Senate. The constitution gave no such special seats for blacks, perhaps reflecting the fact that solidarity for blacks is a hard goal to achieve in Colombia. Unlike Brazil or Cuba, Colombia has few cultural remnants of the African heritage, and, as Peter Wade points out, the boundaries of the black category are "fuzzy and shifting"; some blacks make the most of their opportunities to "escape from blackness."

Perhaps for these reasons, it was just before the signing of the constitution in 1991 that the participants of the Fifth Afro-American Encounter raised three issues: that Afro-Americans be recognized as a cultural group, that Afro-American territories be given the same status as indigenous ones, and that social justice be established for the 3.5 million Afro-Americans in Colombia. Rather than these demands being considered by the Constituent Assembly and incorporated into the new constitution, the matter was left for the consideration of the national Congress. In 1993 it passed a law that would give two seats in the lower house of Congress to the black communities.

Hence members of the ethnic minorities who remain in traditional communities will be represented in the Congress. However, these communities are likely to continue disappearing simply because the quality of life in a "mixed" urban setting has the appearance of being better to most Colombians.

Gender Discrimination

As in most of Latin America, male domination is present in Colombia, although it might be decreasing over time. Increasingly women are economically active in the work force, making up an estimated 43 percent of the work force in 1989 compared to 38 percent in 1980, 26 percent in 1973, and 19 percent in 1951. Studies do indicate that women are paid less than men, even when education is the same, and that women are more likely to be unemployed than men.

The most recent data available indicate that university education is increasingly a possibility for women. Of women holding employment, 18.7 percent had postsecondary education in 1990 compared to 15.8 percent in 1984, 14.7 percent in 1980, and 11.6 percent in 1976. The percentage of public education students who are women has increased over past decades, suggesting that even middle-income women are experiencing mobility through education.

Political rights for women came much more slowly. Postindependence leaders stressed the role of women in the family and home. During the nineteenth century, women did receive the right to vote in the province of Vélez, but attempts to make that a national right failed in 1886, 1936, 1944, and 1946. Women were granted legal capacity to administer their property in 1932, rights to access to higher education in 1933, and the right to hold nonelected public office in 1936.

Women received the vote only in 1954, not because of a feminist movement but as a gift from dictator Gustavo Rojas Pinilla. His Constituent Assembly had included two women. But women did not vote until the 1957 constitutional plebiscite, article 1 of which said "Women will have the same political rights as men." Most recent data indicate that they vote less often than men, and women seldom hold political office. Between 1958 and 1972, only 2.1 percent of the senators, 4.2 percent of the chamber members, 7.4 percent of the members of the departmental assemblies, and 6.4 percent of the municipal councils were women. In 1991 these figures were 1 percent of the Senate, 5.2 percent of the Chamber, and 2.5 percent of municipal councils. Women, however, have had more representation in cabinets of recent presidents. Both Virgilio Barco and César Gaviria appointed female foreign ministers, with Noemí Sanín during the Gaviria government becoming a "star" of the cabinet.

Most of the changes benefiting women have come from presidential initiative, responding to societal demands but not consulting with women's groups. In 1974 President Alfonso López fulfilled his campaign promises to women by abolishing *potestad marital* (the husband's marital rights over the wife and children). In 1990 President César Gaviria created the Council for Youth, Family, and Women, although he appointed a man to head it. In 1991, paid maternity benefits were extended from eight to twelve weeks for women covered by social security.

The writing of a new constitution in 1991 seemed to give women new opportunities. However, only 8 of the 119 lists were headed by women, and just 4 were elected to the Constituent Assembly of 70 members. Two notable cases were the all-feminist list headed by Rosa Turizo, prosecutor of the Superior Tribunal of Medellín, and the list presented by nongovernmental organizations and headed by Helena Páez, former minister of labor and advisor to Gaviria's Council for

Youth, Family, and Women. Neither was elected. Many women supported the AD M-19, and two of the four women elected were from that list. The other two were a Liberal and a leader of the Central Workers Union elected by the Unión Patriótica.

Feminist groups were active in letting the Constituent Assembly know its proposed changes, which can be best summarized as getting the UN statements on women's rights into the Colombian constitution. While there was some success in this effort, as with the other changes to the constitution, only time will tell if the formal stipulations will be translated into real ones. Perhaps indicative is that sexual harassment became a national issue for the first time in late 1993.

Reincorporation into Democratic Politics

In the Colombian case, the question of "reincorporation" of those who until recently employed extraconstitutional means, including violence, to secure their objectives must be divided into different discussions of the three sets of groups: the guerrilla groups, the drug dealers, and the paramilitary squads. The challenge differs for the three.

Currently, according to figures of the Colombian government, there are 7,500 guerrilla troops, two-thirds from the Fuerzas Armadas de la Revolución Colombiana and one-third from the Ejército de Liberación Nacional (ELN, National Liberation Army). This is probably about one-half of the highest level of guerrilla groups, as it has been estimated that there were fifteen thousand when Belisario Betancur became president in 1982. During the peace negotiations in Caracas, Venezuela and Tlaxcala, Mexico in 1991–92, the government was prepared to offer a reincorporation package similar to that offered to the M-19 and the Ejército de Liberación Popular (ELP, Popular Liberation Army): amnesty for political crimes and support for either education or starting a legitimate economic activity.

The first major difficulty this policy has faced in the cases of the smaller M-19 and ELP is that amnesty on the part of the government is not necessarily translated into forgiveness on the part of aggrieved Colombians. Each amnesty since the years of Belisario Betancur has been followed by the assassination of demobilized guerrilla fighters. Further, in the absence of an effective national police force, this is likely to be an even greater problem in the case of the larger FARC and ELN who, during their longer histories, have left many more Colombians with hopes of revenge.

The second problem with this policy has been the inability of the Colombian government to keep its financial promises to demobilized guerrillas. This would be an even greater problem with the FARC and ELN because they are so much larger. More important, both guerrilla groups have substantial income from the coca and poppy activities of the FARC and from various kinds of extortion from them and the ELN. In short, the comparison is between continuing as a guerrilla or demobilizing and having fewer economic resources and a probability of death that is no lower than the current one.

The case of the drug violence is far from clear. Most of the narco-terrorism connected to the drug dealers came from the Medellín group, and especially two of its leaders, Pablo Escobar and José Gonzalo Rodríguez Gacha. The violence ebbed even before Escobar's surrender in June 1991, and it did not approach its previous level during the period between July 1992 and December 1993, when Escobar was once again free. Now that he is dead, it is not clear who the new leaders of the Medellín group will be and whether or not they will use violent tactics.

The Cali drug group, now the largest in Colombia, has never used violent tactics against the government to the extent that the Medellín group did. The Gaviria policies intentionally had to do with drug *terrorism* and not drug *trade*. Although the Gaviria government used the same sort of plea bargaining it used with Escobar with the Rodríguez Orejuela group in Cali, few leaders of the latter group surrendered. Ironically most of the major Cali leaders were captured and put in jail under the presidency of the man they allegedly helped to elect.

The Gaviria plea bargaining had success with some of the paramilitary groups, notably with the surrender of Fidel Castaño in Córdoba and Ariel Otero in Puerto Boyacá. The two combined turned in more than seven hundred weapons, and 250 members of the Otero group surrendered, all of whom were investigated and are to be tried. Further, Otero was optimistic that the paramilitary group's war was over and that they would not take up arms again.

Yet one might not be quite so optimistic about the demobilization of the paramilitary groups for at least three reasons. First, the government knew that many members of the Otero and Castaño groups had not surrendered, nor had they turned in all their weapons. As stated by Commander Julio César of Puerto Boyacá, self-defense groups would be marginal only as long as the army and the police guaranteed that Puerto Boyacá remained free of guerrillas. So far the Colombian government has not established a military presence to do so.

Second, by July 1992 the Otero group was once again active, this time as they sent troops to combat guerrillas in the Casanare region. There, with recent petroleum discoveries, the ELN appeared for the first time. The paramilitary groups followed, completing the ingredients for a new dirty war in yet another part of Colombia. The third reason for pessimism came when Castaño began paramilitary activities again in 1993, in this case as a leader of the PEPES (Persecuted by Pablo Escobar), a group trying to kill the escaped drug leader. Of course the reason for this paramilitary group disappeared when Colombian army troops killed Escobar on December 2, 1993.

In short, it seems likely that individual groups in Colombia will use vigilantism as long as the Colombian government is not capable of maintaining law and order in the country. Although some progress toward that goal was made during the Gaviria years, large parts of the country (which neither governmental nor other experts have defined precisely) are still not effectively under control of the government. Vast areas of Santander are still controlled by the ELN; of the Amazon region by the FARC; of Magdalena Medio and Urabá by paramilitary groups; of Medellín and other large cities by youth gangs; and of Antioquia, Valle, the Amazon region, and the Orinoco plains by drug dealers. While the majority of the people might live in parts of cities controlled by the government, the majority of the territory is controlled by others.

The Significance for Democratic Governance of Gross Socioeconomic Inequities and Programs to Overcome Them

Colombia is in the middle range of Latin American countries in income distribution, neither as equitable as Southern Cone countries nor so inequitable as Brazil, Mexico, and Peru. While the percentage of Colombians living in poverty has decreased in recent decades (40% of the population in 1991 compared to some 70% thirty years ago), poverty is now more visible in the cities. In 1988 the lowest 50 percent of the people received only 18.9 percent of the income, while the top 10 percent had almost twice that much. What this means for many Colombians, as shown in a 1983 study, is that 54 percent of the households had incomes below U.S.$200 a month, and those in the lowest quintile spent more than their total official income for food alone.

The same maldistribution is seen in the ownership of land. In 1960, 62.5 percent of all agricultural holdings were less than 5 hectares (12.3 acres), 4.5 percent of all agricultural land. At the other extreme, 0.07 percent of the holdings were greater than 2,500 hectares (6,173 acres), making up 20.2 percent of the land. In 1970–71, after more than a decade of agrarian reform, even though there were fewer *minifundios,* there were more *latifundios* of more than 2,500 hectares. In effect, after a decade of land reform there were more large areas occupying more, in absolute terms, of the national territory.

In the past twenty years, land reform has not been a priority of Colombian governments. It appears that land might be more inequitably distributed than it was in 1971. With the new violence of leftist guerrilla groups and paramilitary bands, some landowners have fled to the cities. At the same time, drug dealers have bought more land in order to grow their coca crops, to be "gentlemen farmers," and to launder their drug profits.

To this point, these economic inequities have not been translated into political issues, in large part because the multiclass Liberal and Conservative parties have not found it necessary or useful to do so. President Virgilio Barco pledged his government to abolish "absolute poverty," an unrealistic goal in which he failed. Indeed, analysis by the independent think tank FEDESARROLLO (Foundation for Higher Education and Development) suggested in the early 1990s that the government's expenditure on social programs, including education and health, was decreasing in the 1980s, in part because of reallocation of funds to the military.

It was clear in the 1991–92 negotiations with the government that the guerrilla groups thought that the Gaviria neoliberal *apertura* (opening) would lead to an economic crisis of such magnitude that the poor could be mobilized. In 1994 one presidential candidate, Enrique Parejo, strongly criticized the *apertura,* but he lost the Liberal primary.

Conclusions: Specific Difficulties Salient in the Narcotics Trade

As the above has made clear, the drug question is paramount in Colombia. Not only has there been narcoterrorism, but guerrilla groups are difficult to negotiate with because they have coca and poppy fields. In the 1980s many paramilitary squads that had been set up by landowners were taken over by the drug lords as the new landowners, especially in Magdalena Medio. In August and September 1995, for the first time in Colombia, the question for debate became whether Colombian "democracy" had become a *narcodemocracia.*

The ways that this confrontation of the media and the drug lords distorts Colombian democracy have been discussed by María Jimena Duzán, herself a victim of it. As she has written, "Colombians, especially journalists, who deal with these themes [drugs] know that at such times our democracy itself is at stake in the form of our freedom of expression and our right to dissent." Duzán made it clear that the problem was more widespread when she added:

> Perhaps the most dramatic effect of the drug business can be seen in the decomposition and uncertainty that it has provoked on all social levels. For the nation's large middle class, including politicians, judges, soldiers, journalists, and police, drug money has inundated economic life with a flood of corruption, wiping out any semblance of a code of ethics or a value system. . . . This is a terrorized political class that has delivered itself to the designs and money of the drug dealers. Those who stand up to the bosses and challenge them have fallen victim, brave politicians such as Luis Carlos Galán, Carlos Pizarro, and Bernardo Jaramillo.[3]

The journalist concluded that if Colombia could not manage to rebuild its justice system and reopen its stagnant political system, "then the capture and extradition of individual drug bosses will mean very little indeed. We need true social reform, so that democracy—and not murder with impunity—will be universal."[4]

During the August–September 1995 debate, Duzán added: "This is the first time in Colombian history that the political establishment is being investigated. We have a restricted democracy that has been corrupted not just by drug traffickers, but by the power that the political class has held for the past 30 years. The idea was that whoever wins, everybody wins. Now, opening a Pandora's box is very difficult because everyone was involved."[5] While one might quibble with the idea that the political establishment has been in power for only thirty years, observers in the U.S. government have been concerned with the contents of this Pandora's box for a number of years.

Hence the death of Pablo Escobar was at best the beginning of the establishment of the rule of law in Colombia—and not the conclusion. At present, high officials in the Colombian government have not come up with a realistic plan of law enforcement that would allow the government to maintain that most basic human right, that of life. Vigilantism continues from the paramilitary groups, and at least 90 percent of the murders committed by them have not been punished. As long as that continues, as concluded by the Inter-American Commission on Human Rights, it "not only damages the international image of the justice system in Colombia, but also tarnishes the images of recent administrations, despite their obvious and genuine efforts to control the violence rampant in Colombia."[6]

The next Colombian governments might have a new opportunity to solve many of these problems as new revenues from petroleum become available to them. Since subsoil resources belong to the state, future governments will not have to redistribute wealth (something that Colombian governments have either not tried or failed in their efforts to do). Potentially the Cusiana petroleum earnings could be large enough to allow the governments to construct an effective national police force and to make a reality out of the promises of the 1991 Constitution of health care and education for all. However, both of those policies might have inflationary effects, and the history of Colombian politics in the 1970s and 1980s was that governments sacrificed growth to avoid inflation.

The other obvious matter that must be dealt with has to do with drug money in politics. Outsiders have long had the impression that drug money has much power in the country. Beginning in August 1995 for the first time Colombians debated that possibility. Pandora's box has been opened and cannot be closed sucessfully without a complete investigation of all Colombian politicians. That is precisely what the National Prosecutor's Office had begun in mid-1995, even before the accusations about Samper's campaign. Perhaps we will one day look back at this debate as the real beginning of more meaningful democracy in Colombia.

3

Ecuador: Democracy Standing the Test of Time?

Anita Isaacs

At first glance, democratization in Ecuador may seem irreversible. The first country in the region to complete a transition, the country has since witnessed four successive democratic presidential elections, with power alternating in almost rhythmic fashion between representatives from the political Center-Left and Right. Conflicts that have arisen between the legislature and the executive have been resolved without provoking an *autogolpe* or a military intervention, as they so often did in Ecuadorian history and, more recently, in neighboring Peru. To date, rumored and attempted coups alike have failed to materialize, suggesting that the armed forces are indeed reluctant to resume the reins of power they relinquished in 1979. Civil society has been strengthened, most notably through the emergence of the Confederación de Nacionalidades Indígenas del Ecuador (CONAIE, National Confederation of Indigenous Nationalities of Ecuador), an organization that speaks for a substantial segment of the 40 percent of the population that is Indian, with an increasingly powerful voice that the government ignores at its own peril. Finally, the recognition of the need for economic, judicial, and political reform indicates that there exists the political resolve to sustain and deepen Ecuadorian democracy.

Upon closer examination, however, these promising signs mask a system in severe crisis, plagued by a seeming inability to establish a framework for effective democratic governance. Thus, while conflicts between Congress and the president have yet to produce breakdown, the institutional reforms that accompanied the transition have also still to bear fruit. Confrontation among the political leadership continues to create gridlock, thereby preventing the enactment of critical reform. Although the growth of civil society is a welcome sign, its expression nevertheless also reveals the persistent difficulties that the country's poor and ethnic majorities face in seeking formal, regular channels of political participation. More generally, civilian disillusionment with a democratic system that has failed to deliver and to incorporate vast sectors of the population is on the rise, matched by ever louder grumblings of discontent from military quarters, whose apparent reluctance to intervene should not be equated with unwavering support for the elected civilian rule.

In this chapter I expand on these elements by exploring the state of democratic governance in Ecuador. First I examine the political, economic, and social dimensions of the current crisis and then reflect on the prospects for sustained and deepened democratic rule, emphasizing that it has become increasingly difficult for the political leadership either to shrug off or to meet the current challenges.

The Political Situation

Having promised to "arrive at democracy as a step forward," Ecuadorian transition architects dedicated three years (1976–79) to a process of concerted analysis, dialogue, and accommodation in an attempt to fulfill that pledge. Key political players, including members of the armed forces, the political leadership, representatives of the union movement, and entrepreneurial associations participated alongside members of the country's scholarly and legal communities in a prolonged process of consultation and negotiation. Political rather than social or economic reform dominated the transition agenda, with discussion centered on how to enhance the effectiveness and inclusiveness of a system in which politics was traditionally the preserve of the country's elite. Political parties and political party attachments were weak, and perennial conflicts between the executive and the legislature crippled the policymaking process. Because of the disproportionate strength of entrepreneurial groups as contrasted with that of popular sector organizations, as well as the relative health of the Ecuadorian economy at the time, participants paid scant attention to socioeconomic reform or accommodation. To the extent that economic development concerns were addressed at all, therefore, they were placed on the agenda by the military, concerned about ensuring a continued role for itself in a future democratic system.

Participants applauded the outcome, yielding as it did a set of reforms, pacts, and promises of ongoing pact making that provided the Ecuadorian transition with many of the ingredients viewed as essential stepping stones on the path toward sustained democratic rule. A new constitution approved in a referendum, and an accompanying political party law, contained political reforms designed to remedy what were perceived to be the most serious shortcomings of democratic politics as practiced historically in Ecuador. The framers of the new charter and party law (scholars and legal experts heeding the recommendations emerging from the consultative process) broadened political participation by expanding the franchise to include the illiterate population.

Participants similarly sought to strengthen the political party system. On the one hand, they hoped that the extension of suffrage would provide a natural constituency for a promising new generation of reformist political parties. But they also took direct steps, including the drafting of regulations that restricted participation in elections to legally recognized parties and to candidates who were affiliated with an official party. Finally, to guard against conflicts between the president and the Congress, as well as the ensuing policy paralysis, they introduced the concept of a second ballot. Ideally, the electoral process itself would stimulate pact making, while the election of a president with solid congressional backing would permit the passage of legislation.[1]

The political leadership and the armed forces also agreed on a set of pacts designed to ensure the military's exit without unduly limiting democracy. Having avoided the kind of repression that characterized authoritarian rule in the Southern Cone and Central America, the issue of retribution and accountability did not plague the Ecuadorian transition, as it did transitions elsewhere in the region. Rather, the Ecuadorian armed forces seemed more preoccupied with protecting the substantial economic interests they had acquired during the years of military rule and of assuring that they retained a minimal degree of political influence. This was achieved by using the relationship between security and development to justify inclusion of a clause in the new constitution recognizing the military's responsibility to "assist in the social and economic development of the country."[2]

Elected democratic governments that have come to power since 1979, however, have not lived up to the expectations generated by the transition process, as politics in the post transition era bears an uncanny resemblance to the political status quo ante. Institutions remain fragile, conflicts continue to plague executive-legislative relations, and the country's poor and indigenous communities are still effectively excluded from the political process.

The Ecuadorian experience reveals the difficulties inherent in any attempt to draft into existence a set of rules and an institutional framework that can sustain democratic governance in the absence of an ongoing commitment by the political leadership. Indeed, in the post-transition era, Ecuadorian political elites have tended to abide by the letter rather than the spirit of the well-intentioned reforms, reverting for the most part and whenever possible to traditional political practices. Thus, for instance, the vagueness of the legislation governing the participation of parties in elections has hampered its enforcement, thereby frustrating any hope of constructing a solid party system centered around a small number of political parties with a well-defined program, ideology, and constituency.

Remarkably little headway has also been made in securing the loyalty of either those who run for office under the banner of any given party or a grass-roots base, and, as much as ever, parties continue to be used as electoral vehicles by their leadership. Whereas, for example, six slates competed in the transition elections, those numbers climbed to nine by 1984, ten by 1988, and twelve in the 1992 election, in anticipation of which some sixteen parties had been granted recognition. Political attachments, moreover, often last only as long as the mandated electoral period. In a practice so common that it is referred to as a *cambio de camisetas* (shirt changing) elected deputies frequently switch parties or choose to sit as independents, enticed less by ideological conviction than by personal political calculation.

This process is well illustrated by the campaign, election, and government of Sixto Durán. Durán was elected to the presidency in July 1992 as the candidate of the Partido Unidad Republicana (PUR, United Republican Party), a conservative organization hastily put together just before the elections as a result of a split in the Partido Social Cristiano (PSC, Social Christian Party), under whose auspices Durán had unsuccessfully run in both the 1979 and 1988 elections. Only a year and a half after the elections, however, the PUR had all but disappeared. Disgruntled deputies, dissatisfied with the absence of patronage and discouraged by the declining popularity of their leader, abandoned the party. The remains of the organization have recently been absorbed into the Conservative party, in an attempt to construct a more solid base of congressional support for presidential initiatives. PUR deputies are not the only ones to have "changed shirts" in the past year and a half. Indeed, at the time of this writing, one third of those elected to Congress in 1992 have deserted the party for which they ran, many lured away by promises of government patronage.

The ephemeral nature of political parties and political party attachments has severely hindered efforts to build a mass constituency. Indeed, according to opinion polls conducted in the two major urban centers of Quito and Guayaquil, the numbers of individuals who feel strong attachments to any given political party have dwindled considerably in the past several years. Whereas an already significant 47 percent of those surveyed in Guayaquil claimed no specific party affiliation in 1989, that percentage had climbed to 67 percent by 1993. The results are even more striking for Quito, where the numbers of those without strong party loyalties has jumped from 38 percent to 88 percent of the population during that same period.[3]

Confrontation rather than cooperation also still clouds the political atmosphere, as the politics of *concertación* (governance by consensus) continue to elude Ecuador. Although the political reform process has ensured that presidents are now elected with majoritarian support, once elected, congressional support is anything but guaranteed. Congressional coalitions exist, but these rarely involve the same groupings that joined ranks in anticipation of the runoff ballot. Instead, new coalitions are forged, shaped less by a common ideological bond than by a shared crude desire to undermine the president. This is achieved either by blocking legislation or by engaging in a process of *juicio político* (political trial), in which ministers are first called to account for "abuses of authority" and, if found guilty, subsequently stripped of their authority. Occasionally, the process of *juicio político* has exposed corruption and other illegal practices. But more often than not, it has replaced debate and discussion over policies, serving merely as an oppositionist device, designed to weaken and discredit the executive.

The result is policy paralysis. For instance, for much of the Durán administration, and despite a flurry of executive activity, Congress refused to approve virtually any legislation, thus postponing the enactment of a major economic reform program. Sadly, because of the prevailing spirit of confrontation between the two branches of government, any serious discussion of revisions to legislation is impeded. Debate and compromise are precluded, for concessions are viewed as amounting to political surrender. Furthermore, because of the priority attached to economic restructuring, other key reforms of the judiciary and the political system itself can receive the attention they deserve only after the economic legislation has been dealt with.

The president also shares blame for the politics of confrontation and ensuing gridlock. Presidential responsibility for fomenting conflict was most apparent during previous administrations, in which presidents responded aggressively to initial baiting from the legislature. While more conciliatory, Durán's leadership can also be faulted for political missteps, policy incoherence, and political indecisiveness. It was, for example, Durán's commitment to radical economic restructuring that justified his selection of an economic team composed of technocrats and members of the business community rather than the political faithful who had joined his party in the hope of securing access to plum government positions. By doing so, however, he paid a heavy political price, antagonizing key members of his own party and providing an impetus for the emergence of an opposition bloc that would include former PUR deputies.

Making matters worse, Durán's ministerial appointees were not all of the same mind as to the pace and character of economic reform. This contributed to the incoherence with which economic reforms were introduced and to the eventual stalling of the reform process itself, while the political leadership floundered in the face of mounting congressional and popular opposition. Yet, despite the obvious clashes among his ministers, Durán would wait one full year before shuffling his cabinet.[4]

Persistent conflicts between the Ecuadorian executive and the Congress have done more than paralyze the legislative process. They have also had a dangerous spillover effect on the administration of justice, circumscribing the independence of the judiciary. Appointments to the Supreme Court—a right that Congress reserves—are highly politicized, mirroring the specific character of congressional alliances and the depth of congressional-executive antagonism at any given moment. The dispute triggered over the nomination of Supreme Court justices during the Febres Cordero administration (1984–88) is perhaps most illustrative.

In 1983 the Congress amended the constitution, reducing the term of sitting judges from six to four years. Two years later, in an effort to seat a court favorable to the dominant opposition alliance in the legislature, Congress claimed that the measure should apply retroactively. This produced a confrontation between the president and the opposition bloc, in which troops were actually deployed to surround the Supreme Court building in order to deny access to the newly appointed justices. Although less intense, the 1993 appointment of a new president of the Supreme Court was also caught up in party bickering, as congressional kingpins disgruntled by political losses suffered in the legislature reacted by vetoing potential candidates for the court presidency.[5]

The effectiveness of the judicial system has also been dangerously compromised. The Ecuadorian judiciary cannot rely on a constitutionally mandated portion of the budget, but rather must enter the political fray on an annual basis to lobby Congress for its share. Furthermore, it is woefully underfinanced. It consistently receives less than 1 percent of the national budget, which is very low by Latin American standards, less than even the judicial systems of Central America. Understandably, the administration of justice, already plagued by its own internal inefficiencies and hampered by the "civil law process," has suffered as a result. Salaries are insufficiently high to attract a sufficient number of well-qualified judges, there is a dearth of public defenders, and case loads are excessive.[6]

In addition, the Ecuadorian political system has yet to incorporate the country's poor majorities. Universal suffrage notwithstanding, and despite the heralded emergence of a new generation of reformist parties in recent decades, a substantial segment of the population remains marginal to the political process. Of no group is this truer perhaps than of the indigenous community. Despite their size and potential political clout, no organized party has yet to reach out to Ecuadorian Indians. Political parties of both the Right and Left instead tend to regard the indigenous community as an obstacle to modernization.[7]

The political consequences of this neglect are several and significant. First, Ecuadorian Indians have been forced to organize and to pressure largely outside the formal political system. Demonstrations and protests have thus been staged to voice indigenous demands for cultural recognition, bilingual education, and land reform—demands that might have found room on one or another political party and government agenda. Moreover, the nonviolent strategy first espoused has gradually been relinquished. Mounting frustration over the continued neglect and marginalization of the country's poor and ethnic majorities has triggered an increase in violent action on the part of indigenous organizations. As the government and landowners react in turn through repression and violent confrontation, that violence has tended to spiral dangerously.

Second, and along similar lines, in the past year a new guerrilla organization, Puka Inti (Red Sun), has also captured the headlines through acts of sabotage. At present the government appears to have gained the upper hand in battling Puka Inti. Still, one need not look too far afield to recognize that the continued economic and political marginalization of the country's Indian population could well enhance the appeal of such guerrilla organizations.

Third, the military has distinguished itself as the only organized institution to endeavor to respond to indigenous demands, suggesting that the ghost of the military pacts negotiated during the transition may have come back to haunt Ecuadorian politics after all. Faithful to its constitutionally sanctioned responsibility for social and economic development, and shocked by the depth of the rage, poverty, and neglect of the country's Indian population, the military has sought to provide development assistance. The armed forces have moved into the countryside where they have worked actively alongside the indigenous population, delivering public services and undertaking infrastructural development.[8]

The Socioeconomic Situation

Continued faith in petroleum-induced economic recovery, coupled with the election of several governments of the political Center-Left and the set of powerful political interests aligned in opposition to economic restructuring, helps explain why Ecuador for so long bucked the Latin American trend toward greater privatization and economic openness, as a means of emerging from the economic quagmire of the 1980s. Eventually, however, the pressure to restore international confidence in an economy desperately in need of renewed foreign credit and heightened investment has proved impossible to resist. Fulfilling his campaign pledge, therefore, the incumbent government of Sixto Durán presented Congress with a draft law of economic modernization in February 1993.

The proposed legislation calls for a sweeping overhaul of the Ecuadorian economy. According to the law, the public bureaucracy would be drastically reduced, strategic sectors of the economy, previously reserved for the state, would be opened to private competition, and a massive program of privatization of state enterprises would be undertaken under presidential regulation and supervision. Sectors of the petroleum industry and a set of enterprises controlled by the country's armed forces figure among the areas targeted for privatization. The modernization law has been accompanied by complementary legislation, including the passage of a revised foreign investment code and new hydrocarbons legislation, both intended to enhance foreign investor interest in the Ecuadorian economy.[9]

While there is an acutely felt sense that the political leadership must take immediate steps to resolve the economic crisis, the character and the course of the proposed legislation have generated considerable opposition among large segments of the population. To begin with, there is a genuine concern that the process of privatization will merely open the gateway to further corruption. Most Ecuadorians are already persuaded that corruption among the political leadership is pervasive. In a recent survey, for instance, almost 90 percent of those polled noted that the principal accomplishment of the process of *juicio político* was to expose rather than to check against corruption. Understandably, many fear that the dismantling of the state will involve even more bribes and illicit payoffs as potential investors seek to buy up public firms. Arguably, those fears have already been realized, although not entirely in the manner envisioned. Indeed, during the summer of 1995, Vice-President Dahik, who was the inspiration behind the economic reform initiative conceded to having been blackmailed into granting money and special favors in exchange for congressional support in securing the passage of the economic legislation.

Popular sectors vehemently object to further economic adjustment and reform of the sort envisioned in the law. To be sure, the Ecuadorian poor have suffered a substantial swelling of their ranks in recent years, with roughly 50–60 percent of the population now deemed to live below the poverty line. Furthermore, the already precarious existence of the country's poor has deteriorated considerably in recent years. According to some estimates, the passage of the initial structural adjustment program in September 1992 triggered as much as a 50 percent decline in living standards and a 15 percent rise in official unemployment during the first year of the Durán administration alone.

Current estimates suggest that only 28 percent of the economically active population of 3.6 million earn a minimum wage which, at U.S.$30 a month, is far from sufficient to buy a basic basket of goods for an average family, which costs approximately U.S.$250 a month.[10] In labor's view, poverty would only be exacerbated further by the passage of the modernization law, not least by the massive layoffs resulting from bureaucratic downsizing and privatization, which could affect as many as 120,000 workers in a public sector labor force that currently employs 400,000. Having already witnessed the effects of Durán's austerity programs, therefore, labor representatives have brushed off government promises to cushion the blow through the enactment of a variety of social programs. Rather, they have insisted that Ecuadorian workers simply cannot afford either continued austerity or the loss of jobs that would be occasioned through reform of the state sector.[11]

The rural poor have equally good reason to oppose the reform package. The existence of the rural poor, estimated to comprise two-thirds of the rural population in a country where some 45 percent of the population still lives in the countryside, is as precarious as that of the urban poor. Indeed, despite the passage of two agrarian reforms during the military regimes of the 1960s and 1970s, the pattern of land ownership in Ecuador remains highly skewed. Eighty-three percent of the land is held by the wealthiest 20 percent of the population, while the poorest 40 percent controls a mere 3 percent. *Minifundia* and landlessness also abound. The average holding of 58 percent of the population is a meager 0.4 hectares, and one of every four rural Ecuadorians is landless.[12] To complete the picture, the problems of the rural poor, most notably those indigenous communities located in the Ecuadorian Amazon (Oriente), are compounded by the insecurity of their land titles and by the environmental destruction resulting from unregulated oil exploration. The pollution of lakes, lagoons, and rivers has threatened the health and livelihood of those Indian communities who live near these waterways.

The rural poor thus fear the impact that reforms will have on their living standards. Subsistence will be jeopardized further, as austerity takes its toll and the modernization push attracts private investors anxious to strike it rich in the Oriente. Renewed challenges to indigenous land tenure and environmental destruction are likely to result from the rush to exploit the full economic potential of the region.

So often at odds with each other, labor and indigenous organizations have spoken in remarkable unison in opposing the reforms. Not only have both groups focused on the intolerable economic impact of the reforms, but they have denounced the undemocratic character of the reforms. They have criticized both the concentration of economic decision-making power in the hands of the executive as well as the absence of popular input into the economic development process, a long-standing demand of indigenous groups. They have also urged the government to subject the law to a popular referendum before its enactment.

Popular discontent has not been limited to public appeals but has also given rise to widespread social unrest. Here again, labor and Indian groups have on occasion managed to collaborate in staging strikes and demonstrations. Worthy of note in this regard is the general strike of June 1993, launched jointly by the Federación Unitario de Trabajadores (FUT, United Federation of Workers) and CONAIE, with the additional support of students and white collar workers. Although the FUT's decision to call off the protest prematurely angered fellow strikers, the action nevertheless broke with a pattern of heretofore uncoordinated labor and Indian protests. Moreover, that action also set a precedent that would be repeated several months later when CONAIE also endorsed a bitter teachers strike.[13]

The Durán government's response, moreover, has served to exacerbate social and political tensions. Strikes have occasionally been settled, with the government acceding to some of the requests of striking workers. But more often than not, whenever negotiations occur, they usually do so only after a period of confrontation provoked by the government labeling the strike a national security threat, thereby justifying the dispatch of troops and subsequent arrest and dismissal of striking workers. This was the case, for instance, during both strikes mentioned above: the general strike of June 1993 and the prolonged teachers strike, which dragged on through the fall and winter of 1993. Along similar lines, the imposition of a state of emergency following the outbreak of a border war with Peru in January 1995, and that would remain in place long after the hostilities ceased, had the effect of justifying the government's hard line toward strike and protest activity.

Furthermore, the strikes reveal a conditioned response to popular grievances that has characterized the past several Ecuadorian administrations. When questioned, for instance, about the objectives of the general strike, Durán's labor minister responded by noting that the action was designed to bring about "anarchic internal commotion." The description was surprisingly reminiscent of that attached to labor unrest by ministers in both the Borja (1988–92) and Febres Cordero governments, who also deployed troops to quell strikes launched to protest the effects of economic crisis. Under conditions such as these, therefore, where strikes and demonstrations tend not to be viewed as legitimate democratic mechanisms for voicing popular discontent, but rather as subversive forms of political activity, the preferred response has favored repression over negotiation, with attendant social and political costs.[14]

The tensions generated may also have been aggravated by the business community's attitude toward economic reform and the relationship between business, labor, and government. For the most part, Ecuadorian entrepreneurial groups welcomed the proposed reform package, which they viewed as long overdue and which several of their representatives helped craft from positions in the administration. But while private sector support for the program remains high, the popular opposition that it has triggered and the slow-moving, uncertain process of legislative approval have proved disheartening to many. Fear of antagonizing the country's economic elites will certainly heighten pressures for a probusiness government to continue to pursue economic restructuring in a swift and steadfast manner, albeit at the risk of further alienating popular sector organizations. It is at times such as these, moreover, that the absence of a tradition of socioeconomic pacts is most sorely felt. Pacts might have served to temper the conflict produced by the conjuncture of severe crisis, reform, and difference of opinion between strengthened popular sector organizations and ever influential entrepreneurial groups.

Complicating matters even more, the government feels disquieting pressures from another politically powerful source, pressures that are undoubtedly linked to the tenacity with which Ecuador confronted Peru during the border clashes of 1995. For a variety of reasons, the Ecuadorian military has joined the chorus of voices objecting to the proposed reforms. In a process that began during the era of military rule (1972–79), the Ecuadorian armed forces have amassed a vast and diverse economic empire, the holdings of which range from textile manufacturing, agricultural exports, munitions plants, a merchant fleet, and oil tankers to banks, airlines, travel agencies, and hotels. As the current government has already made it quite clear that many of those enterprises are slated for immediate privatization, the military has sprung into action, mobilizing to defend its economic interests against attack.

In addition to the very real material interests that are at stake, the armed forces also have opposed the reforms on more ideological grounds. After all, it was in the name of nationalism and reform that the military leadership of the 1970s expanded dramatically the economic responsibilities of the state while curtailing those of foreign investors. Consequently, it should come as no surprise to hear the current defense minister warn that "there are enterprises of strategic value that cannot be handed over to monopolistic foreign hands and capitalists." For the armed forces, therefore, it is more than their economic interests that are at stake: so, too, is the legacy of the Rodríguez Lara dictatorship. Finally, much as they did during the period of military rule and transition, the Ecuadorian military continues to draw a connection between security and development, still insisting today that security is threatened by excessive poverty and injustice. The heightened poverty and aggravated social discontent that has been a hallmark of the years of civilian rule is not lost on the armed forces, who fear a dangerous escalation of both as a result of the selected course of economic reform.[15]

The armed forces have been straightforward, in both voicing their opposition to the modernization law and discussing the range of actions they could pursue to block the effort. To date they have chosen to engage government officials and the public in dialogue about the direction of the proposed reforms. After years of silence, and indicative of the legitimacy they still command as both individuals and leaders of a military regime, retired officers who served in the military regime have been drafted into political action. With the apparent blessing of their colleagues in active service, several of this group's members—including the nationalist minister of natural resources, Admiral Jarrín Ampudia, and General Rodríguez Lara himself—have wandered the halls of Congress lobbying its members and have appeared on television to explain their objections to the reforms. In these and other fora, they have highlighted the social and economic threat posed by the modernization law. But they have also mused about the possibility of more concerted military action, justified in their view by the fact that the proposed dismantling of the economic apparatus of the state violates the constitution and by their constitutionally mandated responsibility for national security and development.[16]

Brinkmanship and the Possibilities for Reform

Efforts at political reform have thus far been frustrated in Ecuador, as the political leadership remains wedded to traditional patterns of political behavior. Despite attempts to use the transition to establish a framework for a more representative and effective democratic system, institutions remain weak and the politics of exclusion and conflict have prevailed. Fragile political parties lack a strong internal organization, rank and file, or mass constituency. The vast majority of Ecuadorians continue to stand outside the formal political system, and the process of governance has again been crippled by a seemingly endless series of personal conflicts between the executive and the legislature.

Nevertheless, and despite the attendant social and economic consequences, elected civilian rule has survived for a decade and a half. Somehow the political class has muddled through, pulling back as democratic governance veered perilously close to provoking breakdown. Ultimately, political conflicts have been resolved, permitting constitutional alliances to be forged, albeit at the last moment. Rumors of military intervention have also come to naught, and attempted coups have been aborted. Poor and ethnic majorities have found alternative means to organize and to pressure the system. Given the proliferation of political parties, there has been no dearth of new political organizations willing and able to take the place of a governing party that tends to exit in disgrace at election time.

Another critical political juncture appears to have been reached today. The imperative of economic and political reform, coupled with intense disagreements over how to proceed, has produced renewed confrontation between old adversaries: the Congress and the president. As it has on so many previous occasions, the policymaking process has been paralyzed, impeding the enactment of necessary economic reform as well as the serious consideration of other critical legislation.

Just as important, the discussion of economic reform has done more than fan the flames of congressional-executive conflict. It has also brought other influential political actors into the fray, whose opposition could prove potentially explosive. The increasingly shrill voices of the strengthened labor and indigenous organizations have still not found effective formal means of expression, with the result that greatly exacerbated sociopolitical conflict is not easily contained. Complicating matters further, they have found an ally in the armed forces, who are equally vociferous in resisting the enactment of the proposed economic legislation and who have refused to rule out direct forms of intervention.

Time, therefore, once more appears gradually to be running out on democratic governance. As we have seen, popular frustrations have mounted, giving rise to an almost constant pattern of strikes and protests. The business community has grown increasingly disenchanted with a political class that does not lead. And the armed forces have become impatient, preoccupied by the likely impact of economic crisis and reform on both the armed forces as an institution and on national security for which they feel responsible. Popular confidence in the capacities of the elected political leadership and of the democratic system is at a particularly low ebb. Recent opinion polls reveal that more than 80 percent of the population feel that political parties do not serve the public interest; some 64 percent believe that democracy is not the best form of government for Ecuador; the majority argue that some form of dictatorship is necessary to halt corruption; and the armed forces, along with the Catholic Church, are listed as the institutions most respected by Ecuadorians.[17]

As it has so many times before, the political leadership has again responded to crisis by recognizing the need for reform. Several members of Congress concede the need to move forward on economic reform and to begin to consider other key political reforms. Their public declarations reveal an understanding of the gravity of the political, social, and economic situation and an awareness of the importance of demonstrating the political leadership's capacity to enact effective and meaningful reforms. There is thus growing pressure to revise the economic legislation to take into account popular grievances and to begin to review pending legislation that would address the inefficiencies of the judicial system.

Discussions have also begun in earnest over a set of proposed constitutional reforms passed in a popular consultation held in late August 1994. The Ecuadorian electorate approved several politically significant measures, including a proposal that would permit the reelection of deputies to consecutive terms, another that would allow independents to compete for political office, and a third that would transfer responsibility over the budget from Congress to the executive. Although congressional passage of these reforms is by no means guaranteed, their approval and subsequent enactment would represent an effort to attack some of the central problems plaguing Ecuadorian politics. Measures such as the election of independents and the reelection of members of Congress are thus seen as necessary to tackle the corruption and political opportunism that seem to drive Ecuadorian politics as much as ever today, as evidenced in phenomena such as the *cambio de cami-*

setas. In addition, the reelection of deputies is viewed as contributing to the creation of an experienced and professional political class, able to view the policymaking process in longer terms than permitted by the current two-year congressional cycle.

These advantages notwithstanding, the reforms currently under consideration are unlikely either to tackle or to resolve other (arguably the key) critical problems afflicting Ecuadorian politics today. First, the proposed reforms do little, and indeed may well exacerbate, the conflicts between the executive and the Congress that produce the logjams that cripple the policymaking process and that understandably serve to discredit democratic governance. As things stand at present, Congress has relatively little responsibility for the formulation of policy. Its power resides essentially in its capacity to veto legislation passed on to it for approval by the executive branch. It is thus not entirely surprising that congressional coalitions seem to form for little other than the express purpose of preventing the enactment of legislation, a process that is only likely to intensify should the executive also gain full control over the budget.

Seen from this perspective, moreover, it could be argued that constitutional reforms that transfer greater powers to the legislature would contribute more to the enhancement of democratic rule than those that seek to heighten the role of the executive. If awarded greater policymaking responsibilities rather than even fewer, members of Congress might be encouraged to engage in coalition building with a view to formulating acceptable and sound policies rather than merely to vetoing legislation. Politically constructive pacts that at present appear only to accompany electoral campaigns might thus either survive the election itself or be extended to include additional players during the period of democratic governance.

Second, the proposed reforms ignore the acute problem of political marginalization of the majority of Ecuadorians. Transition architects were very much concerned with introducing reforms that would render Ecuadorian politics more inclusive. As we have seen, the failure of those efforts has taken a toll on the system, contributing to the intensification of violence and repression that accompanies persistent protest today. The key to greater inclusiveness is not self-evident. Nevertheless, it is worth noting that, despite the emerging concern over how to reform the state so as to preserve, or indeed buttress, certain critical social and economic capacities, little similar concern has been articulated surrounding the political capacities of the state. In an era in which the concept of civil society has been reified, however, the stability of democratic governance surely demands that commensurate attention be paid to enhancing the political effectiveness of governments in the region, if only to ensure their ability to respond to demands placed upon them by civic organizations.

In emphasizing as it does the absence of a strong commitment both to democratic governance among the country's political leadership and, increasingly, to sustained democratic rule among a majority of Ecuadorians, the above discussion underscores the importance of undertaking creative and more precisely targeted domestic political reforms. It also thereby highlights the secondary nature of international democracy assistance efforts, including those pursued by governmental, nongovernmental, and multilateral institutions.

Bearing those limitations in mind, there are nevertheless several targets of opportunity for members of the international community concerned with assisting Ecuadorians to overcome some of the most immediately apparent obstacles to sustained and deepened democratic rule. Targeted poverty alleviation programs, similar to those undertaken in recent years in neighboring Bolivia, could cushion some of the worst effects of prolonged austerity for the neediest Ecuadorians. Other measures could strengthen the hand and the capacities of those elements in the political leadership most genuinely committed to enhancing democratic governance through institutional reform. First, financial and technical assistance for judicial reform is both timely and essential. Second, legislative exchange programs and other forms of assistance to parliamentarians could encourage serious thinking about creative and effective political mechanisms that might address the more structural obstacles to effective democratic governance.

There may also be opportunities in the Ecuadorian case to provide international assistance in ways that serve multiple purposes: attenuating some of the deep-seated resentment that has been a cause of the heightened sociopolitical tensions of the past several years; enhancing popular participation in and, by extension, popular commitment to the democratic political process; and in the process also reducing inequalities over the longer term. For instance, an innovative legislative assistance program focusing on indigenous political organization could address the problem of continued marginalization of indigenous communities by all major political groupings as well as capitalize on the emerging interest of indigenous leaders in organizing themselves into a political party.

International efforts might also explore ways of drawing Ecuadorian nongovernmental organizations into discussions of economic and political reform. This could be achieved by rendering academic and educational research and study opportunities, as well as opportunities for internships with counterpart organizations abroad, more readily accessible to Ecuadorian nongovernmental organizations. Arguably, this would have the effect of bolstering the analytical and organizational capacities of these organizations and, by extension, their ability to have a demonstrable impact on the policymaking process. Along similar lines, the international community might also continue to encourage and indeed sponsor dialogue among representatives from nongovernmental organizations and the Ecuadorian government as well as, where relevant, members of international organizations.

Although to be effective such efforts must occur in tandem with domestic initiatives, taken as a package they could together have the combined effect of addressing the strongly articulated popular demand for inclusion in the decision-making process and contributing to making necessary reform more widely acceptable. In the process, democratic governance in Ecuador might stand the test of time and find itself both sustained and deepened.

4

Peru: The Rupture of Democratic Rule

Susan Stokes

Peru is the only Latin American country since the most recent wave of democratic transitions where a consolidated democratic regime was destroyed by a coup d'état, only to be revived after the April 1995 presidential and legislative elections and the installation of the elected government in July 1995.[1] The hiatus in democratic rule and the re-emergence, however brief, of de facto government make Peru unique in South America. But the forces that destroyed democracy in Peru are not unique to that country. The reasons for the breakdown of democracy in Peru, the nature of the de facto regime, and the processes and pressures pressing it back onto a course of democratization will therefore all be of considerable comparative interest.

Democracy in Peru, 1980–1992

The Democratizing Legacy of Populist Military Rule

The election of a civilian leadership in 1980 made Peru the second Latin American country to return to civilian rule in the most recent wave of democratization. Economic crisis and internal divisions within the military lay behind this transition. At a deeper level, populist military rule under General Juan Velasco Alvarado (1968–75) sparked political mobilization of industrial workers, shantytown residents, and peasant communities, and unintentionally breathed life into political parties of the Center and Left that sought to lead this mobilization. Populist military rule, then, had a certain contradictory quality: it left in its wake a level of from-the-bottom participation and a broadened party system that were inconsistent with continued military control.

These features of the military period carried over into the period of renewed civilian rule. A Constitutional Assembly was elected in 1978 in which the Center-populist APRA (American Popular Revolutionary Alliance) was the largest party and in which socialist and Marxist parties controlled a powerful bloc. This distribution foreshadowed a three-party (or three-force) system that crystallized in the 1980s: the Right (AP, Popular Action; PPC, Popular Christian Party) won presidential elections in 1980, was a majority of the legislature in 1980–85, and won many local elections; the Center (APRA) won the presidency in 1985, controlled the legislature in 1985–90, and controlled many local governments; and the Left was the second force in the legislature in 1985–90 and won many local elections, including the mayorship of Lima (1983–86). This party system, though eventually unstable, was broader and more socially representative than Peruvian party systems of earlier periods. The Peruvian military, moreover, proved more tolerant of traditionally antagonistic parties than it ever had before. Finally, Peruvian civil society emerged, ironically, enriched by the period of military rule: the peak business associations were joined by an enlivened labor movement and other organized expressions of Peruvian society. Since the founding of the republic, never had Peruvian civil society been as rich or as broad.

Fragilities in the Democratic System

But Peruvian politics faced serious challenges. First among them were guerrilla movements. The largest was Sendero Luminoso (Shining Path), itself a by-product of the mobilization and radicalization of the Velasco years, but a by-product that parted ways with most of the Left when the latter adopted an electoral strategy. Successive governments failed to win over Sendero's support bases, and halfhearted peace initiatives foundered on its intransigence. In the apt words of an Americas Watch report, the response to Sendero of Peru's first elected administration (Belaúnde, 1980–85) was to "abdicate democratic authority" and turn over not just the implementation but the conceptualization of the counterinsurgency to the armed forces. The García government initially tried to assert civilian direction over counterinsurgency but returned to a militarized approach after a prison massacre in June 1986.

By 1990 the Peruvian military, after a decade of internal warfare, had succeeded only in driving the guerrillas out of parts of its native territory. But Sendero dug in in new areas, such as the coca- and cash-rich Upper Huallaga Valley, and made inroads in poor communities in Lima. The human costs of the insurgency were twenty-five thousand dead at the hands of both Sendero and the military; five thousand "disappeared," and more than one hundred extrajudicial executions; a string of massacres by military and paramilitary groups that tarnished the government's image; the enduring involvement of the military in shoring up the civilian government's power and authority; and a gnawing sense of insecurity of which no Peruvian was free.

Peru was unique among Latin America's new democracies in facing a serious guerrilla threat. But other fragilities in the democratic system were common to many South American countries. One was the concentration of significant power in the hands of the president. This concentration rested on some constitutional supports. The Constitution of

1979 gave more power to the executive than did the Constitution of 1933, such as in allowing presidents to make laws by decree when the legislature was out of session. The 1979 drafters enhanced presidential power because they perceived that impasses between a minority president and the legislature were a cause of the military coup of 1968. But in the 1980s even presidents from parties commanding majorities in the legislature (Belaúnde, García) relied on decree powers to make law. It is not clear why this was so, although the perception of the legislature's ineffectiveness probably played a role.

Excessive executive power exacerbated another frailty of Peruvian democracy, weaknesses of political parties. Seats in the upper and lower chambers were apportioned by the D'Hondt formula of proportional representation, with Chamber of Deputies seats apportioned by votes in departments and Senate seats by votes in the nation as a whole. This system broadened the representation of parties in the legislature but weakened the representational link between constituents and legislators. The ranking of candidates within party lists was established by popularity with the voters, giving individual candidates an incentive to campaign as personalities rather than as party members.

Thus, although the party system was broader and more accurately reflective of the electorate's preferences, with weak mechanisms of accountability, these signals were far from guarantees of the course of policy once candidates were elected. At worst, then, party affiliation was a superficial label that politicians adopted and sloughed off at will. And parties were organizations without discipline, as activists could not control leaders (evidenced by the erratic behavior of Alan García as president) and party leaderships could not impose order in the ranks (evidenced by the rupture of the fractious United Left coalition in 1989).

With these preexisting weaknesses in the party system, and with a grave economic crisis and other factors discrediting governing parties in 1980–85 (AP) and 1985–90 (APRA), it took little additional tinkering with the electoral system for Alberto Fujimori to render Peru a country virtually without real political parties (see below). Ironically, the partyless society, the ideal of Latin American military rulers of the previous period, was nearly achieved in Peru with little repression.

Guerrilla movements enhancing the role of the military and eroding the sense of civilian authority, presidents facing few institutional checks, a deteriorating party system—all of these were political precursors to the breakdown of democratic rule in Peru. Our picture would be incomplete without mentioning the dire economic conditions that Peru suffered for most of the recent period of civilian government. Crossnational research shows that the likelihood of coups d'état is a function of both level of income and rate of growth: coups are more likely among poor countries and those with slow growth.[2] Given the

Table 2 **Peru: Some Economic Indicators, 1980–1990**

	1980–84[a]	1985	1986	1987	1988	1989	1990
GDP[b]	22.8	22.3	24.7	27.1	25.1	22.0	21.5
GDP growth	0.4	1.7	10.8	9.7	−7.4	−12.4	−2.4
Per capita GDP growth	−1.9	−0.5	8.5	7.4	−9.3	−14.1	−4.3
Consumption growth	1.4	0.8	14.3	9.2	−8.8	−16.6	−2.2
Inflation	84.5	169.8	78.9	81.5	580	2,821	7,417
Foreign debt[c]	11.2	13.7	14.5	15.4	16.5	16.8	17.4
Real wage in Lima[d]	95	148	185	194	134	110	57
% change demand for labor	27%	12%	3%	−45%	−21%		

Source: Richard Webb and Graciela Fernández Baca de Valdez, Perú en Números 1991.
[a]Average.
[b]In billions of 1986 U.S.$.
[c]In billions of U.S.$.
[d]Average monthly real wage in millions of 1990 intis

economic decline reflected in Table 2, perhaps we should be surprised that Peru experienced only one successful coup and one serious coup attempt (November 1992, see below) in recent years.

Alberto Fujimori: From Election to Coup

The Peruvian electorate's choice of Alberto Fujimori in 1990 represented a mandate to resolve the country's economic crisis without the harsh measures proposed by the Right. Mario Vargas Llosa, the leading candidate and the only one backed by traditional parties with a chance of winning the election,[3] campaigned for a neoliberal revolution: immediate price adjustments and removal of subsidies, withdrawal of the state from the economy, an early and substantial reduction in the number of public employees, privatization and trade liberalization. Campaigning against Vargas Llosa, Alberto Fujimori charged that an orthodox price shock would exacerbate inertial causes of inflation. Fujimori called instead for concerted wage and price agreements to fight inflation, a downsized but activist state, and an economic model emphasizing labor-intensive "microindustries." What little organized support Fujimori had came from socially progressive evangelicals, representatives of the informal sector, and the Japanese-Peruvian community.

Fujimori placed a strong second in the first round of the elections, forcing the dispirited Vargas Llosa into a second round. Fujimori won the runoff, 57 percent to 35 percent. Immediately the president-elect came under intense pressure from domestic and international sources to abandon the neo-Keynesian model he had outlined in the election campaign. New advisors who gained access to the president-elect, some of them erstwhile associates of Vargas Llosa, pressed for an orthodox stabilization policy. In late June 1990 Fujimori, a new figure in Peruvian public life and decidedly without international stature, made a visit to the United States and Japan. At meetings with officials at the highest level of the international financial institutions in the United States and with the Japanese prime minister, the president-elect was repeatedly pressed to reach an agreement with the International Monetary Fund (IMF).

The Fujimori government's economic policies in the end were closer to those of his former opponent than to those outlined in his own campaign. If the 1990 election had represented a mandate to stabilize while eschewing economic orthodoxy, that mandate was violated. On August 8 the price adjustments were announced: the price of 84 octane gasoline rose by 3,140 percent; the price of kerosene, widely used by the lower classes for cooking, rose by 6,964 percent. Subsidies for many basic foodstuffs were removed, and the prices of these soared: bread by 1,567 percent, cooking oil by 639 percent, sugar by 552 percent, and rice by 533 percent. Medicine prices rose on average by 1,385 percent. During the first eighteen months, the following structural reforms were implemented: exchange rate unification and liberalization, reduction and simplification of tariffs on imports, elimination of tariffs on exports, capital market liberalization, reduction of employees in government ministries and state-owned enterprises, elimination of job security laws, elimination of wage indexation, and liberalization of labor relations. Gone was any sense of policy implementation through *concertación* or negotiations with the representatives of labor and business; in fact, Fujimori frequently bypassed even the legislature, using decree powers to make laws.

This episode is important not only because it points to the weakness of mechanisms of accountability in Peru but also because it is likely that at this point Fujimori began to adopt a style of leadership uncontrolled by any constraints from other branches of government or political parties. He began to sense that public opinion could be mobilized in support of actions that violated the commonly understood rules of the game.

The constitutional period of Fujimori's rule (July 1990–April 1992) was also one of growing reliance of the president on military officials, and officials in his newly created National Intelligence Service (SIN), for information, protection, and support. This reliance grew in part because Fujimori's own pre-election institutional sources of support, thin though they were, were lost to the president as a result of his economic policy shift. Thus the evangelicals broke with Fujimori in the wake of his orthodox price shock in mid-1990. And his initial multiparty cabinet, reflecting the support of APRA and the Left in the second round of the presidential election, gave way fairly quickly to a succession of cabinets of independents of rightist orientation.

Thus Fujimori increasingly turned to the military to fill the void of organized support for his presidency. After the June 1990 election, Fujimori took up residence in a military residential zone in a suburb of Lima. He spent considerable time cultivating military personnel and made numerous public appearances at military events, from commemorations of battles to cadet graduation ceremonies. By the second year of his term, Fujimori's closest advisor was Vladimiro Montesinos, a shadowy former army captain, lawyer, and now head of the National Intelligence Service. Fujimori's reliance on the military and its intelligence service left him increasingly insensitive to foreign and domestic pressures to curb and investigate human rights abuses.

The immediate backdrop to the coup d'état of April 5, 1992, was a conflict between the president and the Congress over executive powers and counterinsurgency and economic policy. In November 1991 Fujimori issued a package of 126 decree laws, including measures limiting press freedoms, extending military powers over civilian authorities in emergency zones, and a "national mobilization law" declaring that any person residing in Peru was obliged to collaborate in the fight against terrorism and drug trafficking. The military was given free access to the universities, and a "national defense system" was established, allowing the military to intervene in the production, marketing, and consumption of goods. Critics of the measures limiting press freedoms noted that a recent massacre by paramilitary groups could not have been reported had the law been in place. Critics from across the political spectrum decried the militarization of the Peruvian state.

At the same time the measures strengthened the president's control over the military, provoking dissent among constitutionalists in the armed forces. The measures provided that the president would nominate the chiefs of the armed forces and retain them in office past their age of retirement. Retired General Luis Cisneros Vizquerra complained that the package of measures "militarizes the population while politicizing the armed forces."[4]

A retrospective look at the record leaves the impression that (as was later reported) Fujimori and a close group of advisors planned the April coup for months in advance. In early 1992 Fujimori embarked on an apparent campaign to poison the public's opinion of the Congress. He suggested that Congress was beholden to drug traffickers and money launderers, he virtually ignored the constitution by refusing to accept the resignation of a minister whom the Chamber of Deputies had censured, and he reminded Congress of his constitutional right to dissolve that body and hold new elections under certain circumstances.[5] For its part, congressional leaders reminded the president of their right to declare him morally incapacitated and call for new presidential elections, and they attempted to block some antiterrorist and fiscal reform measures.

The struggle between Congress and the president was also over aspects of economic policy. Congress was balking at a proposed fiscal reform and objected to the government's agricultural policy, leading to the censure of Enrique Rossl Link, the agriculture minister. Carlos Boloña, Fujimori's economic minister, who had served as a World Bank official and had close ties with the international financial community, complained that congressional interference threatened the stabilization and economic reform programs and violated agreements the government had reached with multilateral lending institutions. (In fact, as noted above, a long list of structural reforms had already been put in place without significant congressional resistance.) Just as the conflict of powers intensified, the World Bank issued a statement endorsing Fujimori's economic program, noting the government's achievements in trade liberalization and claiming that the policy was yielding results faster than those of Chile and Mexico. The international financial institutions further signaled support of Fujimori when the IMF's Michel Camdessus scheduled a visit to Lima in February 1992.[6]

This conflict of powers culminated in the April 5, 1992, coup d'état. With the support of the military, public opinion still favorable, and the prospect of a mild international response, Fujimori orchestrated a self-coup: he dissolved Congress, placed congressional and party leaders and some journalists under house arrest, jailed some members of the former García administration, interrupted judicial functions, and censored major newspapers. Fujimori declared that he would head an "emergency government of national reconstruction." In the weeks following the coup, the regime dismissed 135 judges and prosecutors, threatened opposition politicians with long prison terms if they continued to exercise "public functions" (a threat extended to his own previous vice-presidents), and launched an attack on terrorist suspects at the Canto Grande prison outside Lima that left thirty-six prisoners dead.

The Interlude of De Facto Rule and the Trend toward Redemocratization

Between April 1992 and July 1995, Peru has been ruled by a civilian-military government, one that begrudgingly succumbed to pressures to liberalize and to return to a formal state of constitutional rule.[7] The gradual shift toward reconstitutionalization and liberalization was the result of international pressure (comforted by high public opinion ratings, Fujimori was immune to domestic pressures). In the week following the coup, the OAS (Organization of American States) held an emergency session to consider the Peruvian crisis, issuing strong statements of condemnation and suspending Peru from the Rio Group. But it could not muster support for economic sanctions. U.S. Secretary of State James Baker noted the fallacy of destroying democracy to save it, and U.S. Assistant Secretary of State for Inter-American Affairs Bernard Aronson worked actively to reverse Fujimori's actions. The Peru Support Group, a group of eleven industrialized countries that were to help Peru secure loans to pay off arrears to the IMF, suspended these loans.

The international financial institutions (IFIs), in contrast, sent ambiguous signals after the coup. There can be little doubt that they were dismayed by the coup and saw it as threatening the reinsertion of Peru into the international financial community. Still, these institutions gave signals that Peruvian leaders could well have interpreted as meaning that, if forced to choose between the two, the IFIs valued economic reform over democracy. Indeed, the data shows that the coup slowed the disbursement of funds for several months, but by the end of 1992, the Inter-American Development Bank (IDB) had disbursed U.S.$390 million, the amount independent analysts had predicted before the coup would be forthcoming from that institution.[8] The IDB representative announced in Lima in September 1992 that full resumption of loans was not conditional on a return to democracy.

The IMF and the World Bank also sent mixed signals. The World Bank proceeded with several missions to Peru in the months following the coup. Soon after the coup the IMF let it be known that a standby agreement could still be reached if economic targets were met by the end of the year. In September the IMF found that Peru had achieved goals laid out in a 1991 Letter of Intent, giving Peru access to loans.[9]

Toward Reconstitutionalization (April 1992–November 1993)

Between mid-April 1992 and November 1993 the new authoritarian regime, pressed by the OAS and foreign governments, entered into a process of limited reconstitutionalization. This period encompassed three sets of elections: in November 1992 delegates were elected to a Democratic Constitutional Congress (CCD), in January 1993 voters elected municipal governments nationwide, and in November 1993 they voted in a referendum on the new constitution.

Two facts about these elections should be noted. First, they were carried out under rules modified by the de facto regime, rules that were designed to augment the power of the regime and about which there was no negotiation with political parties or other political actors. Thus the government announced that delegates to the CCD would be barred from holding office for two subsequent terms; this and a sense of the illegitimacy of the process led most of the major political parties to abstain.[10] In the January 1993 municipal elections, the regime considerably lowered the number of signatures required on petitions allowing candidates to appear on the ballot. The intended effect was to drown the traditional political parties in a flood of novice candidacies. Thirty-eight candidates appeared on the ballot for mayor of Lima, and seventy-seven for the provincial city of Huaura, with an electorate of about twenty-five thousand.

But the regime's efforts to eliminate parties and to aggrandize official party power were not entirely successful, which brings us to the second fact about post-coup elections worthy of note: never did the regime register sweeping electoral successes. In elections for the CCD the two pro-regime lists received only 40 percent of the vote. In January 1993 municipal elections the Cambio '90 candidate for mayor of Lima was so low in public opinion polls that he withdrew from competition two weeks before the election, and the incumbent mayor, who later became openly hostile to Fujimori, was elected in a landslide. Candidates tied to traditional parties, although not necessarily representing those parties, were elected in Arequipa, Cuzco, Callao, Trujillo, Chiclayo, and many smaller cities and towns. Finally, in the November 1993 referendum on the constitution, the "yes" vote barely beat the "no" vote by a margin of 52 percent to 48 percent. Only Fujimori himself managed to mobilize large margins of victory, as in the 1995 presidential elections.

Although pro-Fujimori forces failed to win an absolute majority of votes in elections for the CCD, they controlled forty-three of eighty seats in the constitutional body. Thus, although the CCD was a forum where opposition views were voiced, the constitution that was produced and eventually ratified was a faithful reflection of the regime's desires. The 1993 Constitution is considerably more politically authoritarian and socially conservative than the 1979 Constitution. It expands the president's powers to dissolve Congress (article 134) and to declare states of exception (article 137), and places promotion of military personnel in the hands of the president, without requiring congressional ratification (article 118). The 1993 Constitution introduces presidential reelection (article 112),[11] and the death penalty (article 140), which Fujimori showed interest in applying retroactively. It removes state commitment to free elementary education and job security, and places new barriers in the way of labor organization (article 28).

Constitutional Rule (November 1993–April 1995)

This period was one in which the regime's commitment to constitutional rule, now under a constitution of its own design, was tested. Although ultimately the regime did permit national elections in April 1995, events in 1994 gave rise to questions regarding the regime's independence from the military and its commitment to the rule of law.

A February 1994 political crisis occurred when the CCD majority and the president intervened to move the prosecution of military officers accused of extrajudicial executions from a civilian to a military court.[12] A Supreme Court justice had earlier ruled that the case of officers implicated in the massacre of nine students and a professor from La Cantuta national teachers university should be heard in civilian court.[13] The CCD majority hurriedly wrote a law allowing a simple majority of the Supreme Court to decide cases of jurisdiction, and the law (dubbed "Ley Cantuta" by critics) was quickly signed by the president. A majority on the Supreme Court then voted to turn the case over to a military court (recall that Fujimori had drastically altered the composition of the Supreme Court after the coup). The action appeared to violate separation of powers, as laid out in the 1993 Constitution. The upshot was international condemnation, the resignation of the prime minister, and declining support for the president in public opinion polls.

A second incident in 1994 raised further questions in Peru and abroad about the government's capacity to respect the rule of law and human rights. In April, as part of a counterinsurgency campaign in the Upper Huallaga Valley known as Operation Aries, the military carried out aerial attacks against civilian targets, resulting in widespread casualties. Military officials in the region barred access by journalists and by the International Committee of the Red Cross. The number killed in the attacks may never be known.[14]

The significance of these events was to suggest that the Fujimori government, despite the return to constitutional rule, was heavily bound by its allies in the military. The events throw into relief the cross-pressures Fujimori faced. On one side he was pressed by foreign governments, domestic political leaders, the opposition press, and public opinion to return to democracy. But at the same time he was involved in a delicate and potentially destructive operation of courting and controlling the military. The sense of Fujimori's enduring obligations to the military at the expense of democratic procedures was reinforced again when, soon after his reinauguration in July 1995, he announced an amnesty for all military officials accused of human rights abuses.

Earlier I noted that Fujimori had turned to the Peruvian military as his primary, in a real sense his only, institutional source of support. Fujimori's late 1991 efforts to militarize the state and exert direct control over the armed forces strained his relations with the military; these relations were further complicated by the April 1992 coup. Although the military establishment on the whole has remained loyal to the president, in fact Fujimori relies on a small group of high-ranking officers. Fujimori relied on General Nicolas de Bari Hermoza, the army commander and chief of the Joint Command of the Armed Forces, retaining him in that position after his scheduled 1992 retirement. This caused discontent among other officers. Also controversial among the military establishment was Fujimori's close association with Vladimiro Montesinos, the former army captain and lawyer who has been accused of disloyalty and ties to drug traffickers.

Military discontent twice erupted into open revolt. On November 13, 1992, a high-level group of active and retired officers attempted a coup to return the country to constitutional rule. Later from their jail cells the would-be coup-makers complained that Fujimori "demoted or retired professionals, while promoting a clique of corrupt officers and shadowy security advisors."[15] Then, in early 1993, members of the military provided opposition members of the CCD with evidence leading to the discovery of graves of nine students and a professor "disappeared" from La Cantuta in September 1992. The officers' apparent motive was to undermine General Hermoza by linking him with human rights violations.

In April 1993 Army General Rodolfo Robles, a constitutionalist suspected of being the source of the incriminating information, was removed from his position as chief of army instruction. Robles later went into exile in Argentina, issuing a statement condemning military officials for human rights violations. In late April and early May, tanks appeared on the streets of Lima in support of Hermoza, who had made controversial statements accusing CCD members investigating the La Cantuta case of being apologists for terrorism.

Economic Performance, Public Opinion, and International Response

International opposition to the Peruvian coup d'état was harsher than the coup-makers anticipated and amounted to effective pressure for a return to some sort of constitutional rule. But international opposition was more muted than it might have been because of some common misperceptions about the Peruvian situation. Before moving to the policy implications of my analysis, I address three "facts" that have softened international criticism of Peru's departure from a democratic course.

No Democracy to Interrupt

"Democracy has not been destroyed in Peru for the simple reason that, in any meaningful sense, it never existed." The reasoning in this case of Caleb Rossiter appeared in several influential newspapers in the United States.[16] Many accounts enumerated Peru's problems—"economic ruin, cocaine traffickers, disease, starvation and a civil war with Shining Path terrorists"[17]—and concluded that (1) a country with such problems could not be a democracy, and (2) a drastic change in the political system was justified as a way of resolving those problems.

The fallacy is to confuse "democracy" with a just society. Moreover, although some critics were correct in their Aristotelian observation of the degrading effect of deep poverty and inequality on democracy, it does not follow that poverty and inequality are likely to be eliminated if democracy is eliminated. Here Jorge Castañeda's formulation is apt: "Democracy without reducing inequality can only endure under great stress and given exceptional conditions; but only democracy can reduce the disparities that make it untenable."[18] Caleb Rossiter went so far as to suggest that poor "Indians and mestizos" inhabiting Lima's shantytowns are "disenfranchised." In fact, about 85 percent of the adults in those shantytowns voted in eight separate elections between 1978 and 1990, and many voted for candidates for president, Congress, and mayorships whose party programs called for the redistribution of wealth.

Fuzzy analyses abounded in the days following the coup. In a news analysis, Thomas Friedman wrote "does it make sense to tell an impoverished country whose courts are widely believed to have been corrupted by drug traffickers, and whose capital is under attack from vicious Maoist guerrillas that the only way out of its problems is to restore the democracy that existed before the Government crackdown?"[19] The difficulty is that Fujimori did not carry out the coup to resolve these problems. His actions are better understood as arising from an intolerance for checks on executive power by Congress and the judiciary. Mistaken accounts of the motives behind the coup led U.S. analysts to "hope . . . that with a little time" to "get his country back under control . . . public pressure will ensure that whatever [Fujimori] does he does quickly and then restores democracy."[20] The scenario lacked credibility.

Fujimori's Resolution of Peru's Security and Economic Crises

One of the disputes between the president and Congress leading up to the coup was Fujimori's controversial antiterrorist laws. These laws were not proposed as a serious effort to reorient a failing counterinsurgency campaign; indeed, they represented a hardening of a policy that had already been in place for a decade, with paltry results. All serious analyses noted that the proposals were intended to solidify Fujimori's support among the military. Later successes in counterinsurgency since the coup (the capture of Abimael Guzmán and Sendero's top leadership) were the result of good police work by a special police investigative unit that had been at work for many years before the coup. Furthermore, politicians from across the political spectrum, lawyers' associations, the press, and all democratic forces found Fujimori's proposed antiterrorist laws anathema.

Those who justify the move away from democracy because of Peru's recent economic successes have their chronology wrong. Most of Fujimori's economic reforms were put in place during the first year after his election: these included price liberalization, deficit reduction, and trade liberalization. Still on the agenda at the time of the coup were fiscal reform and privatization. By the time of the coup, structural adjustment was a fait accompli; although congressional opponents might have tinkered with economic policy, they would not have fundamentally undermined it or altered its course.

Public Opinion in Peru in Support of Fujimori

Nothing has inhibited international critics more than Fujimori's much-touted popularity and that of his coup. According to public opinion polls, Fujimori's approval ratings have varied between about 30 percent and about 80 percent. The high point in his approval ratings came after the coup. But polls immediately after the coup showed that large majorities wanted a quick return to democracy. So Peruvians supported the coup and democracy at the same time. What does this mean? It is likely to mean that they felt deep frustration and insecurity because of Sendero Luminoso and because of the economic recession (note that recession, and the perception of economic crisis, persisted well into the Fujimori administration). This frustration and insecurity left many open to the claim that Congress lay at the root of all problems; they were reassured by a decisive show of authority by the chief executive. But there is little indication in public opinion polling that Peruvians favored an authoritarian form of government over a democratic one. Indeed, when faced with the brutal and arbitrary side of authoritarian systems, as in the La Cantuta massacre and cover-up, Fujimori's support ebbed.[21]

Those who wished to moderate international criticism after the coup noted Peruvians' disdain for political parties, implying that Fujimori was the country's only available popular leader. But the decline of political parties has been overstated. First, as noted earlier, for a full decade after the return to civilian rule, Peru enjoyed a broad and relatively stable party system. The 1990 elections, rather than indicating a collapse of the party system, reflected the fact that one of the traditional parties (APRA) was the discredited incumbent and a second force (the IU, United Left) had divided. The third traditional force backed a candidate whose policy positions failed to win him majority support. The decline of Peru's political parties in the 1990s is not only a result of disaffection among voters but also of intentional manipulation (lowering barriers to entry for candidacies, lowering incentives to participation for legislators, post-coup exile, and arrest for political leaders).

Likely Future Developments and Policy Implications

In a formal sense, democracy was restored in Peru after the April 1995 elections (elections, however, that were not free of irregularities). One hopes for a certain liberalization of the political system during Fujimori's second term (1995–2000).[22] Liberalization would require a reduced role of military tribunals in what are properly civilian cases; a return to regularized processes of promotion within the military; election rules that promote a stable party system, and hence a strengthened legislature; and the vigorous protection of human rights.

The reelected Fujimori government is unlikely to initiate such liberalization, however, of its own accord, and the government's military allies press it in the opposite direction, as the postelection amnesty for those accused of human rights abuses indicates. International policymakers must give very clear signals of their unwillingness to accept curtailments of democratic rights, even though they might be tempted to think of these curtailments as the price of policies they approve. Precisely the opposite signals were transmitted in the past. Policymakers and international institutions with strong preferences for the Fujimori government's economic reform program must be steadfast in support of true political liberalization. Similarly, international actors must realize that true political liberalization does not threaten to breathe new life into Peru's now nearly vanquished guerrilla movements, just as the turn toward authoritarian rule did not produce victory over those movements.

Signals emanating from the international community must be strong and unambiguous. What U.S. officials and representatives of international financial institutions say today enters into the Peruvian leadership's calculations of what it can and cannot do tomorrow. Past actions have been tainted by ambiguities. That international financial institutions eschew formal political conditionality should not lead them to believe that they play no role in politics. The IMF, World Bank, IDB, and other institutions have strong policy preferences; when they support politicians who advocate the policies they prefer, they can alter the domestic balance of power in developing countries. When such favored politicians destroy democratic institutions and justify their actions as necessary to sustain reforms, the IFIs are dragged, whether they like it or not, to the center of the arena of political conflict. In short, international actors cannot simultaneously hold policy preferences and remove themselves from any political role. The responsible alternative is to combine policy preferences with some general criteria for acceptable modes of governance.

5

Bolivia: Managing Democracy in the 1990s

Eduardo A. Gamarra

For the first time since the transition to democracy began in 1978, on June 6, 1993, Bolivians voted and elected a president on the same day. With almost 35 percent of the vote, the Movimiento Nacionalista Revolucionario's (MNR, National Revolutionary Movement) Gonzalo Sánchez de Lozada and his Aymara running partner, Victor Hugo Cárdenas scored a fourteen-point victory over the ruling Acuerdo Patriótico (AP, Patriotic Accord). Under the terms of a constitutional provision (article 90), however, when no candidate achieves an absolute majority, the national Congress must elect a president from the top three contenders. On August 6 Sánchez de Lozada won the congressional round and was sworn into office.

Things did not go as well for Sánchez de Lozada in 1989. Despite winning the elections, he was denied the presidency after a congressional coalition of the second and third place parties, Acción Democrática y Nacionalista (ADN, Democratic and Nationalist Action) and the Movimiento de Izquierda Revolucionaria (MIR, Revolutionary Movement of the Left) respectively, elected the latter's chief, Jaime Paz Zamora. That election, in turn, was a replay of 1985 when the ADN's General Hugo Banzer Suárez lost the presidency to the MNR's Víctor Paz Estenssoro despite winning the elections. This sequence highlights the complexity of the democratization process in Bolivia.

Transition, Governance, and Economic Reform

In a country where turbulent political change had been the norm, the 1993 electoral context may appear anomalous. In fact, democratization has not been easy. The transition to democracy came only after three decades of profound turmoil sparked mainly by the dynamics unleashed by the 1952 revolution. Between 1952 and 1964, the MNR nationalized the mining industry, declared universal suffrage, and approved an agrarian reform law. Moreover, the MNR initiated a state-led development strategy that, despite its overthrow by a military junta in 1964, lasted until the mid-1980s.

Throughout most of the 1960s and 1970s, a period that coincided with the most extreme days of the U.S.-directed national security doctrine, Bolivia was ruled by a variety of military rulers. While these military governments generally followed the contours of the state development strategy introduced by the MNR, they were distinct from one another mainly in terms of ideological and generational differences. Between 1978 and 1982, seven military and two weak civilian governments ruled the country. Coups and countercoups characterized one of the darkest and most unstable periods in Bolivian history. The unsolved dilemmas of the MNR-led revolution, worsened by decades of military dictatorships, accounted for Bolivia's convoluted transition to democracy.

Not surprisingly, the transition to democracy came during Bolivia's worst-ever economic crisis. Hernán Siles Suazo, the first civilian elected president to assume office, could do little to control hyperinflation, respond to pent-up social demands, overcome an opposition-controlled Congress, put down military coup attempts, and satisfy a hostile private sector. Even his own ruling coalition, the Unidad Democrática y Popular (Popular and Democratic Union), turned on the president. Among the many conspirators against the government was then vice-president Jaime Paz Zamora, who entertained the opposition's offers to topple Siles in a so-called congressionally sanctioned constitutional coup. The hapless Siles government was also trapped by demands from the international financial community for greater economic austerity and from the United States to carry out a controversial interdiction-based counternarcotics strategy.

Considering the magnitude of the crisis facing Bolivia, in the mid-1980s the challenge for any government was first and foremost to control the spiraling economic crisis. But the political challenges were equally pressing. Institutions, such as legislatures and parties, were undisciplined and constantly conspired to end prematurely Siles Suazo's mandate. Whoever came to power faced the impossible task of producing a government with both an executive and legislative force.

Between 1985 and 1993 Bolivia had two governments whose style of rule set in motion significant trends, which may not have solved the country's deep structural problems but fundamentally transformed the pattern of governance. The elections of 1985 brought back to the presidency for the fourth time Víctor Paz Estenssoro, one of the major leaders of the revolution of 1952 and arguably the most important statesman of twentieth-century Bolivia. Paz Estenssoro's government successfully introduced the Nueva Política Económica (NPE, New Economic Policy), until then, one of the most profound stabilization programs in Latin America. After sustaining his NPE for four years and ending the country's record-setting hyperinflation, in August 1989 Paz Estenssoro handed power to Jaime Paz Zamora. The NPE was judged so successful that with a few nuances, such as calls for social spending, all of the major contenders in subsequent elections in 1989 and 1993 pledged to uphold the program.

The key to the NPE's success was largely rooted in the deal president Paz Estenssoro struck with General Hugo Banzer Suárez to form the Pacto por la Democracia (Pact for democracy) between the MNR and the ADN. The pact was not a program of cogovernment but a legislative pact to support the Paz Estenssoro government and the imposition of the NPE. Behind the rhetoric about patriotism and newfound commitment to democratic values, the pact was an agreement through which ADN would share in state patronage by assuming control of a number of state corporations. A secret addendum (signed in May 1988) provided for the MNR to support Banzer's candidacy in the next election. In short, the pact provided the Paz Estenssoro government with an important device to end the gridlock between executive and legislative authority in Bolivia.

The pact institutionalized an important decision-making style that was arguably antidemocratic. In the national Congress, the members of the pact rubber stamped most executive initiatives, legitimating a policymaking process that gave no room for an open debate about economic policy. The pact also enabled the Paz Estenssoro government to control any challenges to the counternarcotics agreements signed with the United States. In many ways, this pattern of policymaking was reminiscent of the exclusionary processes of previous authoritarian experiences. The governing style introduced by the MNR called for an executive-centered system to "manage" the economy in much the same way in which a chief executive officer (CEO) manages a large corporation.

The decision-making style that resurfaced in 1985 was built upon a long tradition of recruiting "apolitical" technocratic advisors to bolster and lend credibility to the actions of a strong executive. In the 1970s, for example, military rulers surrounded themselves with civilian technocrats to implement an exclusionary decision-making process. As Malloy notes, Bolivian policymakers in 1985 reproduced the decision-making style of the authoritarian rulers they replaced by recruiting civilian technocrats to deal with the crisis and imposing a closed policymaking process.[1] Bypassing Congress, utilizing the military to impose states of siege, and neglecting or postponing the demands of social groups, the style of governance of these leaders clearly restricted access to the decision-making process. Because of its success, however, this decision-making style was perceived as the only way to implement Bolivia's highly touted NPE successfully.

In the 1980s the policymaking process allowed a number of business groups and other social actors greater access to the policymaking process. The common factor is that both authoritarian and democratic rulers determined the degree and the nature of access to the decision-making process. Defined narrowly, the key to governing Bolivia rests with how rulers frame access to the policy process.[2]

Not surprisingly, the most prominent person to emerge from this governing style was Gonzalo Sánchez de Lozada, a wealthy mining industrialist, who is owner and manager of the Compañía Minera del Sur (COMSUR, Mineral Company of the South), one of Bolivia's largest private mining enterprises. Sánchez de Lozada was not only one of the principal intellectual architects of Bolivia's NPE, but as the MNR's minister of planning between 1986 and 1989, he was the man charged with implementing neoliberalism. "Goni," as he is popularly known, became Bolivia's corporate-style CEO who slashed public spending, called for decentralization, deregulation, and privatization, and carried out most of the neoliberal reforms of the 1980s. His success as minister catapulted him to prominence and thrust him into the limelight as the MNR's presidential candidate in 1989.

The elections of 1989—basically a three-way race between Sánchez de Lozada (MNR), Banzer (ADN), and Jaime Paz Zamora (MIR)—produced no clear winner with Sánchez de Lozada winning a slight plurality of 23.07 percent, followed by Banzer with 22.70 percent, and Paz Zamora with 19.64 percent. For a number of reasons neither Banzer nor Paz Zamora would deal with Sánchez de Lozada, and hence they were left with each other. In a bizarre arrangement dubbed the Acuerdo Patriótico, which was either an act of statesmanship or of opportunism, Banzer and the ADN struck a deal with Paz Zamora and the MIR. This time it was a two-step arrangement first to elect Paz Zamora to the presidency and then to form a government in which Banzer would play a major role as head of a so-called Consejo Político del Acuerdo Patriótico (COPAP, Political Council of the Patriotic Accord), a bipartisan policy board that would oversee both political and governmental affairs.

Between 1989 and 1993 Bolivia was governed by the Acuerdo Patriótico. In contrast to the Pacto por la Democracia, this formal alliance lacked any real economic plan of its own and was largely perceived as the caretaker of the NPE policies introduced by Sánchez de Lozada and the MNR. The new pact emulated many of the dimensions of the MNR-ADN pact. First and foremost, it pushed through Congress legislation designed to deepen NPE economic reforms. Moreover, throughout its four-year period in office, the performance of the Acuerdo Patriótico, especially the MIR, was clouded by widespread accusations of corruption. As in most of Latin America, corruption associated with political parties had a tremendous impact on the fortunes of incumbents. The lack of any innovation in economic policy combined with corruption were key factors in the dramatic ascendance of Sánchez de Lozada in 1993 and also in the emergence of two key outsiders.

The Emergence of New *Caudillos*

Public perception regarding the nature of the three principal parties led to the emergence of two leader-dominated and populist-style parties, Conciencia de Patria (CONDEPA, Conscience of the Fatherland) led by Carlos Palenque and Unidad Cívica Solidaridad (UCS, Solidarity Civic Union) headed by Max Fernández. As in other Latin American countries, these neopopulist parties emerged outside of the political mainstream and delivered mainly an antipolitics message. Because they are led by strong men, both are reminiscent of old-style Bolivian *caudillismo*. It is probably a mistake, however, to explain their emergence solely as a result of the inability of the traditional parties to channel the interests of marginal sectors of Bolivia's population. The reasons are more complex and varied.[3]

One possible explanation is suggested by Guillermo O'Donnell's notion of "delegative democracy." Owing to the state's incapacity to enforce the law, the popular classes become disenchanted with the ineffectiveness of democratic institutions in resolving their problems. This disenchantment translates into political withdrawal and mass apathy. As these groups become more marginal, they "delegate" their grievances to these new leaders whose commitment to representative democracy is largely suspect. Through traditional mechanisms, such as clientelism and appeals to populism, these new leaders convey to the citizenry that participation within the framework of representative democracy is obsolete and undesirable. Moreover, they offer a more direct and unmediated channel of representation. In a direct way, these leaders offer some hope for the displaced sectors.

CONDEPA was successful because of the appeal of its founder, Carlos Palenque, a popular radio and television announcer revered by the Aymara-speaking working classes of La Paz. Palenque's nickname, "el Compadre," revealed that the basic logic of Bolivia's party system was still patrimonial. CONDEPA made huge inroads in the lower-class sectors of Bolivia's capital city. Through his Radio y Televisión Popular (RTP, Popular Radio and Television), for example, Palenque offered a unique alternative to Bolivia's often discriminatory administration of justice. Palenque's RTP programs, especially one called "La Tribuna del Pueblo," provided a quick "resolution" to the myriad social problems afflicting recent non-Spanish-speaking arrivals to the capital city, domestic servants, and the vast population of the informal sector that encircles La Paz. "Palenquismo," as Lazarte called it, provides the only linkage these groups have to the system.[4]

Since the 1989 elections, Palenque has attempted to develop a broader crossregional, crossclass, and interethnic base of support. After demonstrating his party's ability to win municipal elections (in 1989, for example, CONDEPA defeated all three major parties in La Paz and also won the race for mayor again in December 1991), Palenque moved decisively on several fronts. First, he expanded his base of local La Paz support by recruiting prominent defectors of the agonizing Left. He also attracted many members of the old nationalist Right. The most significant pillar of support was drummed up through the airwaves of RTP. Finally, to contest the national elections he courted prominent members of the Santa Cruz business sector.

The other threat to the traditional parties came from Max Fernández and his UCS. Beginning in 1989, Fernández converted the UCS into a mechanism to deliver promises and prebends to vast and remote sectors of Bolivia. The slogan "Max obras" (Max[imum] [public]works) became more than a simple political statement. Throughout the country, Fernández built hospitals and schools, paved roads, and handed out sporting equipment and generators.[5]

Fernández first made his appearance in 1986 when he purchased enough stock to control the Cervecería Boliviana Nacional (CBN, Bolivian National Brewery), Bolivia's largest brewery. Fernández, a Cochabamba native of humble background, claimed that his business skills enabled him to establish a monopoly over the commercialization and distribution of beer in Santa Cruz, which he then used to control the entire company.[6] It is worth noting that control over the commercialization and distribution of beer in Bolivia of the mid-1980s was indeed a very profitable venture. During the hyperinflationary period of 1984–85, for example, rumor had it that the government could pay its salaries only when the CBN paid its taxes.

Much speculation has surrounded the origins of Fernández' fortune. Until recently the U.S. embassy was obsessed with indicting him for alleged ties to the narcotics industry. Little evidence to indict Fernández was ever produced. In 1993 U.S. embassy officials considered it imprudent to go after Fernández primarily because of the increase in his popular support.[7] This contrasts with the obstacles placed in his path during the 1989 elections, when U.S. embassy pressure forced the National Electoral Court to prohibit him from running for office.

Because Fernández' UCS was not allowed to run in the 1989 elections, it held no seats in the National Congress. The Acuerdo Patriótico government and the opposition parties used this as an excuse to exclude him and his party from all major and minor negotiations. This exclusion ended abruptly during the December 1991 municipal elections when the UCS showed its strength on a national scale. Since then the UCS has been a part of every attempt to negotiate reforms to the electoral law reform, and Fernández has played a prominent role in all political party agreements to reform the constitution signed since 1989.

Fernández runs the UCS in an authoritarian manner, and, in classic populist style, control over his political party is determined by his capacity to deliver prebends. His wealth has enabled him to establish a wide network based on old-style vertical and hierarchical patron-clientelism. Fernández names the party leadership; no assemblies or elections are held to elect the governing body of the UCS. Most striking, however, is Fernández' rather unappealing personality. He lacks charisma, speaks Spanish poorly, and is unable to articulate any party platform coherently. To overcome these shortcomings, Fernández has hired prominent members of the political class, who generally present UCS campaign promises. As Lazarte argues, however, Fernández resembles Gonzalo Sánchez de Lozada in many ways. Both are entrepreneurs, CEOs, and pragmatic men of action rather than words.[8] Although both appeal to the same social sectors—the lower middle classes and the urban proletariat—Fernández' humble social origins may give him an electoral advantage.

Most appealing to the working classes was Fernández' innovative employer-worker relations at his brewery. Workers in the CBN enjoy high wages and other benefits not available to blue collar employees elsewhere in the private or public sector. Reportedly, on one occasion when the Acuerdo Patriótico government decreed a wage increase, Fernández doubled the salaries of his workers. Periodically newspapers carry declarations from grateful workers who defend him from his political opponents.[9]

In short, Fernández and Palenque resorted to patrimonial methods to mobilize support during elections. Like all other parties in the system, however, the central objective of CONDEPA and UCS is to penetrate the party system and obtain access to state patronage through the formation of alliances with the three principal parties.[10] The irony of these neopopulist parties is that, while they have emerged partially in response to the patrimonial practices of the traditional parties, Fernández and Palenque use the same methods.

Palenquismo and Maxismo shared the same constituency, and the electoral battle demonstrated that this was, in fact, a most important political battle. Palenque, and not the traditional parties, for example, often raised charges of Fernández' alleged links to the drug industry. In 1993 Fernández slapped a libel suit against Palenque and, true to form, announced that if he were to win the suit he would donate the U.S.$10 million to homeless children and to senior citizens.

In any event, both Palenquismo and Maxismo may have been born out of public disdain for the three principal political parties resulting from their inability to aggregate the demands of the popular sectors. They became key national political options that are unlikely to disappear, although their support will ebb. Yet their actions, rhetoric, and personal histories demonstrate only a vague commitment to democratic values. Moreover, as Lazarte notes, the social sectors that support both parties are only superficially committed to democracy because no other option is available.[11] Of course, the same could be said about nearly every social sector and political group in the country. Palenquistas and Maxistas have organized neither in favor nor against representative democracy, but outside of the democratic process. Hence, although Fernández and Palenque can play a positive role by attempting to integrate these excluded sectors into the institutions of the democratic process, they could also tilt the balance against democracy.

In sum, the popular sectors attracted to Palenquismo and Maxismo may be reluctant to accept the logic of representative democracy and may also be swayed by the promises of a more direct form of democracy. Uncomfortable with the mediation of parties, these sectors in Bolivia have historically displayed an affinity for a direct relationship with the leader. It is important to note, however, that Palenquismo and Maxismo may have played a crucial role in the stability of Bolivian democracy and may have become the only mitigating force that has prevented the emergence of radical groups among the marginal sectors of Bolivia.

Sánchez de Lozada and the Agenda for the Mid-1990s

Gonzalo Sánchez de Lozada's campaign in 1993 raised a great deal of expectations across the social spectrum mainly because of the image he had developed over the previous eight years. To vast sectors of the electorate, "Goni" was a man of action who would deliver all of the promises made during the campaign. To the working class, the MNR platform offered the best hope that, in some measure, demands for higher wages and the alleviation of the levels of critical poverty brought about by the economic crisis of the 1980s would be met. Sánchez de Lozada's campaign platform, dubbed "el Plan de Todos," promised to reduce the impact of market-oriented reforms introduced in 1985 that stabilized the economy but brought only low growth rates.[12] Most of the electorate, but especially the middle class, believed his promises that corruption in government would be eliminated.

The election of Víctor Hugo Cárdenas of the Movimiento Revolucionario Tupac Katari (MRTK, Tupac Katari Revolutionary Movement) as vice-president constituted a significant watershed. The symbolism associated with the MNR's ticket is worth noting. In the MNR's campaign, Sánchez de Lozada and Cárdenas were portrayed as "children of the revolution" in a calculated attempt to tap into those social sectors that were once strongly identified with the MNR, such as the peasantry, but that had long abandoned the party. As the first Aymara to achieve such high office, Cárdenas brought with him a great deal of expectations of the indigenous sectors of Bolivia. Cárdenas delivered a huge voting bloc of mainly rural Aymara *campesinos* to the MNR. Moreover, to prevent the growth of guerrilla-type movements that used ethnic symbols to mobilize support, Cárdenas represented the most important hope for bridging ethnic and linguistic cleavages and extending Bolivia's young democracy to the indigenous masses.[13]

Despite its obvious margin of defeat, the ruling AP did not immediately concede the víctory to Sánchez de Lozada and Cárdenas. General Hugo Banzer Suárez, the AP's candidate and former de facto president, refused to recognize the MNR's victory, correctly claiming that the constitution still gave them the option of contesting the presidency as no candidate had achieved 50 percent of the vote. As the results filtered in, confirming an embarrassing defeat, the old general's grip over ADN, his own party, faltered.

One sector of Banzer's ADN initiated negotiations with CONDEPA to give the presidency to the populist Carlos Palenque, who had won only 14 percent of the vote. Another reportedly entered into talks with Sánchez de Lozada. By mid-June, internal disputes between members of ADN became public and in some cases vicious. A similar situation developed inside the MIR, as factions positioned themselves for the next four years. About the only clear trend was the dissolution of the AP and the almost certain fragmentation of ADN and the MIR, its component parties.

The first confirmation of the MNR victory came when Antonio Araníbar of the Movimiento Bolivia Libre (MBL, Free Bolivia Movement) announced his unconditional support for Sánchez de Lozada. With only 5 percent of the vote, the MBL lent its support, expecting some role in the future government. The MBL's announcement had an immediate impact. On June 8, Banzer took the face-saving but belated decision to congratulate Sánchez de Lozada and promised that the AP would vote for the MNR in Congress in August. Paz Zamora, in turn, delivered an impassioned speech stressing the need for a peaceful transition and the development of a stable ruling coalition to ensure the governability of Bolivian democracy and the continuity of economic reforms.[14]

Sánchez de Lozada's search for a governing partner culminated in yet another surprise. On July 2 the MNR struck a deal (dubbing it the "Pacto de la gobernabilidad," Governability Pact) with Max Fernández, Bolivia's controversial beer baron and chief of the UCS. As in all previous pacts, the distribution of key government posts in exchange for the UCS's twenty-one seats in Congress sealed the agreement.[15] Moreover, Sánchez de Lozada was able to broker the first visit by Fernández with the U.S. ambassador since accusations had surfaced of his alleged ties to narcotics trafficking. The MNR's deal making did not end there. On July 7 Sánchez de Lozada signed a Pacto por el Cambio (Pact for Change) with the MBL doling out yet another set of government posts.[16] With his election in Congress assured, Sánchez de Lozada departed for Washington to sell his new government to the State Department and other U.S. government agencies that closely followed the deal making in Bolivia.

Implementing El Plan de Todos

On August 6, 1993, Gonzalo Sánchez de Lozada became the fourth democratically elected president of Bolivia since the transition from military rule to be sworn into office. At issue was how the Sánchez de Lozada government and the new ruling alliance would deliver their campaign promises and press ahead with market-oriented reforms. Despite having had two months to prepare an orderly transition and hit the ground running, the new government stumbled and staggered in its first few months in office. On his first day in office, Sánchez de Lozada named only ten ministers as part of an ambitious project to reduce the size of the executive branch. The actual plan as such did not go into effect until September 17; the opposition promptly accused the government of creating a tremendous power vacuum. Of the ten ministries, three areas—finance, services, and production—became "super" ministries and were turned over to prominent members of the private sector.[17] Filling the nearly one hundred other posts in the ten ministries, however, took a long time mainly because the government failed to secure the congressional approval of the decree regulating the reorganization of the ministries. Fernando Illanes, one of the "super" ministers, made a stir when he claimed that the delay in filling posts was a result of the lack of honest and capable candidates in Bolivia.[18]

The MNR's ambitious Plan de Todos, which promised a social-market economy alternative to the rigid continuity of the New Economic Policy, must be evaluated with a degree of caution. The plan included seven "pillars": attracting investment; job creation; ensuring economic stability; improving health and education; popular participation; changing the role of government; and combating corruption. The key to the MNR's investment proposal rested on the "capitalization and democratization" of public enterprises, a significant departure from the dogma of privatization. Contrary to privatization advocates, the MNR proposed to "increase the capital of the principal state enterprises [YPFB, National Hydrocarbons Enterprises of Bolivia; ENAF, National Smelting Company; ENDE, National Electricity Company; ENTEL, National Telecom Enterprises; LAB, Bolivian National Airways; and ENFE, National Railroad Enterprises] through foreign investment, but maintaining a majority participation of Bolivian citizens in said enterprises to convert them into the effective owners. . . . At least 51 percent of stock holdings in these enterprises will remain in Bolivian hands, while foreign partners will own up to 49 percent of stock."[19]

In February 1994 the Bolivian Congress approved a capitalization law that essentially authorizes a joint venture association in which a state enterprise contributes its assets and a private investor contributes an equivalent amount in capital. In theory, this would double the original value of the enterprise. Once an enterprise is capitalized, the investor would receive 50 percent of the company's stock and sole management control. The remaining stock would be distributed evenly among the 3.2 million Bolivians over the age of eighteen.[20] The government also claimed that this program would result in the creation of half a million new jobs. According to government consultants, besides capitalizing six state enterprises, the government would also privatize the state retirement system by partially funding the establishment of private pension funds.[21]

The government also promised that revenue from the sale of state enterprises (expected to reach about U.S.$8 billion) would be employed in a pension fund for all Bolivians over the age of eighteen. Government economists argued that the capitalization of state enterprises would be equivalent to investing approximately 35 percent of Bolivia's GDP (gross domestic product). In 1993 foreign investment dropped relative to 1992, and public investment more than doubled overall private investment.

While turning over the ownership of state assets to Bolivian citizens and workers and the establishment of a pension fund were an important shift from pure privatization, its feasibility was questionable. Nevertheless, the very notion of workers becoming shareholders of former state companies was a unique innovation in the current Latin American neoliberal era. Whether this arrangement will serve to attract foreign and national investors is still doubtful. Nearly two years after the law's enactment, even the promise of granting national and foreign capital the administration of former state monopolies has yielded few takers.

In his first two years in office, Sánchez de Lozada discovered that it was quite difficult to govern efficiently and simultaneously deliver the promises made during the electoral campaign. In fact, the new president has not modified the general thrust of austerity policies. One of the government's first acts was to "relocate" nine thousand middle-class workers. Almost immediately the government faced major confrontations with the Central Obrera Boliviana (COB, Bolivian Worker Central), which regained some of the strength it lost in its battles against the two previous administrations. Opposing Sánchez de Lozada's relocation of workers plans and his efforts to "capitalize" state enterprises, the COB staged general strikes and stoppages and forced the new government into church-mediated negotiations. To quell labor unrest, the government announced a so-called Relief Plan (Plan Alivio). Additionally, the government opened a "Bolsa de Trabajo," where workers who made less than Bs.1,000 monthly would receive a stipend of Bs.500. The only problem has been that most workers make less than Bs.1,000 and the Bolsa de Trabajo never found a steady funding source. The government produced several innovative programs aimed at reducing the state's payroll. In late 1993 the government offered a U.S.$1,000 bonus per year of service to workers who chose to retire voluntarily from the mining sector. At closing time on February 28, 1994, the deadline established by the government, about one thousand workers had taken the government's offer. These measures, however, were not enough to satisfy labor's demands. As will be seen later, the recurring plot of the conflict with the COB—threatened and actual general strikes, failed negotiations, and church mediation—eventually forced the government's hand.

The health of the economy was probably the most pressing aspect of governance facing the Sánchez de Lozada government. Years of austerity under the NPE and falling social indicators led to deteriorating conditions throughout Bolivia. In the rural areas, for example, 90 percent of the population lives in poverty compared to about 40 percent in the urban centers. Basic services such as potable water are not available to 65 percent of the population in rural areas. To revert these trends in Bolivia, it is clear that more than just "good governance" will be required.

Basic economic indicators, however, point out that at least in terms of growth rates, inflation, interest rates, exchange rates, and international reserves, the situation is at least stable. In 1993 inflation reached only 9.31 percent, the lowest in South America, and the economy grew a moderate 3.18 percent. Open unemployment continued to drop, reaching only 5.4 percent in 1993. The government has had a very difficult time keeping its electoral promise of creating 250,000 new jobs and improving the working conditions of another 250,000. But Bolivia's basic problem is the concentration of wealth in a very reduced sector of the population. With a poverty rate exceeding 70 percent of the population, social tensions are likely to explode if the trend is not reverted. Events in April 1995 revealed that ten years of economic stability and GDP growth had not alleviated the social situation and led instead to great unrest.

Legislative Successes

During the first twelve months of the Sánchez de Lozada government, five significant laws were passed by Congress including the cabinet restructuring law, the capitalization law, the popular participation law, the education reform law, and the constitutional amendments law. As far as government officials were concerned, this body of legislation provided a reform agenda as far-reaching as Bolivia's 1952 National Revolution.

The most innovative of these laws was the popular participation law (discussed in the following section). As mentioned above, the cabinet restructuring law reduced the number of cabinet ministries from seventeen to twelve. The new cabinet included a politically correct Ministry of Human Sustainable and Economic Development that served to launch Bolivia's successful bid to host the 1996 Presidential Summit of the Americas on Sustainable Development. The approval of the capitalization law signified the beginning of a unique new plan to dismantle state enterprises. As of this writing, the National Electricity Company (ENDE, Empresa Nacional de Electricidad) has been capitalized, and government officials were optimistic that the remaining five enterprises would be capitalized in the future. The proposed pension plan, however, was another story, as the concept has been developed but not fully implemented.

The education reform law was aimed at strengthening Bolivia's public school system, which has been in a severe crisis for the better part of the last two decades. In some measure the reform intended to decentralize school management by turning over these responsibilities to elected municipal governments and other legally recognized community groups. The law also links municipal, provincial, departmental, and national citizens' groups with the national education secretary. The new law established mechanisms to monitor teacher qualifications and academic standards, and promised to increase teacher compensation. Government officials noted, however, that the intent of the new law is to establish an educational system that reflects local "cultural, linguistic, and ethnic identities, stressing primary education, the education of young girls, and early education in the native language of pupils." This, of course, is an opinion not shared by most of the unionized teachers around the country, who oppose the new law. In March—and, as will be seen, in April 1995—the Teachers Union held the government at bay and prevented the implementation of the law by literally taking over the streets of La Paz.

President Sánchez de Lozada's intention during his second year in office was to dedicate time to "govern in detail," to enact and implement his "revolutionary" set of five laws. Sánchez claimed that while his first year was filled with legislative successes, he had not been able to govern effectively. Sensitive about these shortcomings, Sánchez intended to "govern" for the rest of his term. His record in 1994–95 was not remarkable, and his leadership came increasingly under heavy scrutiny.

The Popular Participation Law

The popular participation law, promulgated on April 21, 1994, may radically change the territorial, economic, and democratic conditions of local government in Bolivia. The government claims that the transfer of political and economic power to municipal governments, along with increased social participation, is a revolutionary process equivalent to the 1952 transformation of the country.[22] Territorially, the new law defines the municipality as a section of a province and places every rural and urban square inch of the nation under the political-administrative jurisdiction of one of about three hundred municipal governments. It also provides a relatively large amount of financial resources to municipal governments on a per capita basis. In short, the popular participation law may eventually ensure that central government resources that have been accumulating in the central bank since early July 1994 will be disbursed to the newly constituted municipalities. Moreover, it grants legal status to traditional citizens' groups at the grass-roots level, arguing that it will facilitate their participation in and oversight of municipal government.

According to the government, during the law's first year more than three hundred municipal governments were established. With the resources they receive from the state, these have initiated the construction of more than one thousand schools, sanitary posts, roads, public bathrooms, and the like nationwide. The government expected nearly eight thousand such projects to be completed in 1995. As of April 1995, approximately three thousand communities and neighborhood associations had been recognized with an additional seven thousand pending.

The popular participation law proved to be quite popular internationally, as extensive media coverage of its implementation painted a very positive picture of a law intended to empower local government and allow citizens to decide how revenues would be spent. Domestically, however, the law was a much more difficult sell. The principal accusation was that the so-called territorial base communities and the vigilance committees were less instruments of "accountability" and more MNR mechanisms to control local government. The truth probably lies somewhere in between; however, the opposition used this as a rallying cry against the government. Moreover, the popular participation law appeared to go against the grain of previous administrative decentralization initiatives. In addition, the law bypassed the powerful civic committees in each city and department, who considered the new law a potential threat to their vision of decentralization. Civic committees called for an elected prefect in each department and a weaker municipal council. In April 1995 this debate came to a head with a severe confrontation, with regional civic committees from Tarija, Santa Cruz, and elsewhere demanding the implementation of a decentralization law.

Sánchez de Lozada and the Armed Forces

Sánchez de Lozada's relations with the military have also been problematic. His difficulties with the armed forces should not have been surprising given that the commanders of the armed forces did not welcome the MNR's victory in the June 1993 elections for at least two reasons. First, the commanders feared a full-blown investigation into charges of corruption by members of the armed forces and their allies in the outgoing Paz Zamora administration. Second, the armed forces were wary of both Sánchez de Lozada's lack of expertise in civil-military relations and the MNR's historic favoritism toward the police. Sectors within the institution believed the MNR would attempt to politicize it.

For the Bolivian armed forces, the process of adapting to democracy has been quite difficult as it faced a tremendous reduction in its prerogatives and waged a battle with the police over the scarce foreign economic resources provided by the counternarcotics campaign. In contrast, the national police adapted quickly to the new democratic process and regained prerogatives it had lost during the military period and, in fact, appropriated several additional prerogatives normally reserved for the armed forces. With Sánchez de Lozada and the MNR in office, the armed forces feared a continuation of this trend.

In October 1993 Sánchez de Lozada sacked the entire armed forces command, bypassed the next *tanda* (graduating class) in line for command, sent thirteen generals into early retirement, and named a new command comprised of officers deemed to be free of corruption. Older officers publicly expressed their outrage and voluntarily retired. General Carlos Casso Michael, for example, noted that while a "soldier must obey the orders of the captain general of the armed forces, as a person I cannot allow myself to be under the command of a promotion that was younger than mine."[23] The response from both the sacked officers and those sent into retirement sent a clear message that the Bolivian armed forces are still a major power contender. General Moisés Shirique, who was in line for commander of the army, retreated into the Estado Mayor and refused to follow the president's directive. In the tense days that followed, Shirique was rumored to be preparing a coup attempt. Although Shirique eventually desisted and accepted a new position as chief of staff, the confrontation was severe enough to warrant concern over the course of civil-military relations in Bolivia.

The changing of the guard may have come at a particularly problematic moment for the armed forces, especially the army. Within the institution several groups—such as Vivo Rojo of Trotskyist leanings, Tres Estrellas, a self-described institutionalist movement, and Movimiento Boliviariano (Bolivian Movement) of nationalist tendencies—have made their demands known publicly. Pamphlets and other items have circulated widely, revealing a great deal of internal turmoil. At least three issues appear to be generating internal dissent. First is the increasing reliance on U.S. military assistance tied exclusively to the counternarcotics effort. At issue more specifically is the increasing presence of U.S. military personnel in civic action exercises. Second is a general sense that democracy has not been generous to the institution. Officers argue that there is an inverse relationship between the military's support for democracy and the benefits it has derived. In other words, instead of being rewarded for defending democracy, the institution has been severely penalized through budgetary restrictions and attempts to privatize its enterprises.

Related to this issue is what many military officers consider another inverse relationship between their support for democracy and improvements in the conditions of the police forces. In the past decade, the police institution has increased in size, its budget has expanded, it has had virtually unlimited access to U.S. funds, and, at least according to disgruntled military officers, the MNR government has covered up corruption within the police force. Moreover, some officers are convinced that the time is ripe in Bolivia for the emergence of subversive groups and that the military is now unprepared to respond.

Despite these problems, the naming of the new military command in October 1993 averted a major investigation into charges of corruption and may have indeed prevented an even more serious confrontation with the armed forces. In the following months the armed forces appeared satisfied with the deal worked out with Sánchez de Lozada. But tensions with civilians resurfaced in January 1994 when the *Bolivian Times*, an English-language newspaper owned by foreign journalists based in Bolivia, revealed that military lodges (*logias*) tied to Colonel Luis Arce Gómez, the former minister of interior under García Meza who is currently serving a thirty-year sentence in a U.S. prison, had placed a bomb in an airplane that crashed in 1969 and carried out the murder of two prominent journalists who were about to uncover an alleged arms trafficking network.[24] A few days later, however, the story took a bizarre turn when it became clear that the reporters from the *Bolivian Times* had been sold a fictitious story by none other than Antonio Arguedas, the man who, after a stint on the CIA's payroll, sold Che Guevara's diary to Fidel Castro. The incident was dismissed as an attempt to discredit the armed forces; the commanders, in turn, reiterated their commitment to protecting the constitution. No perceivable danger of a military coup is visible in the near future, but it is clear that civil-military relations require constant nurturing.

The unraveling social situation in early 1995 forced the Sánchez de Lozada government to rely on the armed forces for a great number of missions. As was already the case under previous governments, the MNR has increased its reliance on the armed forces for maintaining order in the Chapare, Bolivia's largest coca growing area. And, as was also the case under the two previous governments, the military was charged with enforcing a state of siege imposed on April 18, 1995. The armed forces were given added public security roles that included the right to arrest and detain hundreds of striking labor leaders.

A Fragile Ruling Coalition

Few would dispute that Bolivia's institutional and legal matrix made governing the country difficult, and it is no wonder that president Sánchez de Lozada made institutional reform the centerpiece of his government. To understand the institutional dilemmas, it is important to review some of the principal features of the process of transition to democracy and the place of institutional dynamics in the democratization process that followed.

The difficulties faced by Bolivia during the transition to democracy highlight the current debate about constitutional reform and gave ample ammunition to those who advocated replacing presidentialism with a parliamentary system. Yet the continuity of the Bolivian experience demonstrates that ways out (or *salidas*) of severe crises were not the product of an abstract debate among political scientists but the result of the creativity of political leaders responding to a specific set of circumstances. In other words, Bolivian political leaders produced hybrids between old-fashioned tools of governing and the "modern" thrust of neoliberalism and democratization.

To reiterate a point made earlier, to govern Bolivia in the context of a severe political and economic crisis and demands from the international community to carry out counternarcotics programs, decision makers had to deal with several issues simultaneously. Perhaps most significant was the necessity of dealing with pressing institutional questions ranging from electoral laws to constitutional reform. A recurring issue involved relations between the branches of government: every president since 1982 has had to face and attempt to resolve executive-legislative impasses.

This task translated into a crucial need to build coalitions not only of groups in civil society but also among the political parties that had fought intense and bitter electoral battles. Coalition building in Bolivia has required three aspects: electoral coalitions, required to compete for formal power; congressional coalitions to achieve control of the executive branch following the vote in Congress; and ruling or sustaining coalitions to support governments and specific policy lines. The important characteristic of this process has been the ability of some leaders to craft coalitions both to get elected and to govern.[25]

Political coalitions, such as the Pacto por la Democracia (1985–89) and the Acuerdo Patriótico (1989–93) and the current Pacto por el Cambio (Pact for Change) (with the Movimiento Bolivia Libre, MBL [Free Bolivia Movement]) and the Pacto por la Gobernabilidad (Governability Pact) (with the UCS), played several key roles. They linked the domestic arena with international themes, such as market-oriented reforms, provided support for governments, and enabled these to carry out specific policy initiatives. Since the mid-1980s the dynamics of coalition formation and competition have driven the process of democratization.

The recurrent need for political coalitions institutionalized a quasi-parliamentary feature, which has essentially converted Bolivia's political system into a hybrid form of presidentialism. This has been the key to governance in Bolivia. The hybrid nature of the country's presidential system facilitated the implementation of stabilization measures and contributed to the continuity of the democratization process.

As of this writing, most relevant political actors perceived that they had a stake in the system and pursued strategies aimed at coalition formation. Some analysts point to the recurrent practice of coalition formation as a sign of the maturing of the Bolivian political party system.[26] As discussed elsewhere, political parties are still primarily vehicles to capture and circulate state patronage among the dependent middle classes. Political parties are driven more by issues of access to patronage than in constituting programmatically focused governments. Nevertheless, parties are an essential part of governing Bolivia not only because they are the principal source for the recruitment of future leaders but because they are responsible for bringing democratic governments into and out of office. The paradox is that political parties are both the principal source of the difficulties of governing and the only real source of a potential solution.

Given this immediate legacy, Sánchez de Lozada faced the critical task in 1993 of forging an alliance that could resist any challenges from the opposition. Unlike 1985, however, the governing pacts the MNR entered into with the MBL and UCS were extremely fragile. Despite this fragility, Sánchez managed to carry out a great deal of his agenda, albeit at a snail's pace. Most of the government's problems rested with the nature of the ruling coalition, which had difficulty controlling its ranks as both interparty and intraparty disputes proved destabilizing. A recurring conflict between the president's party and the cabinet was problematic, leading to at least three major cabinet shifts in two years. Sánchez de Lozada's first cabinet was comprised of technocrats and businessmen, while Congress was left in the hands of the MNR's old guard. A joke circulating among the opposition in the early months illustrates the problem. According to this version, Sánchez de Lozada forgot that to govern Bolivia one must always make a pact with the MNR. These tensions eventually produced a cabinet crisis in March 1994 forcing Sánchez de Lozada to replace the private sector members with members of the MNR. Predictably, as problems occurred with its private sector allies and with the political parties in the coalition, the government charged ahead with the *movimientización* (the movement to staff the cabinet with MNR members). In 1995, with only one notable exception—foreign minister Antonio Araníbar—the entire cabinet was made up of MNR personnel.

The ruling coalition proved extremely unstable. On any given week, unsubstantiated rumors abounded about a split or defection. Fernández, who felt excluded from the decisions taken by the government, lashed out often against the MBL and the MNR. He was finally ushered out of the coalition in late 1994, and his party showed serious internal splits. More important, however, the defection showed serious problems of stability in the ruling coalition.

By the same token, the MBL found itself in the difficult position of having to defend policies it had opposed over the previous eight years, such as U.S.-designed counternarcotics programs and deepening "neoliberal" economic reforms. A "national summit" held in January 1994 with Sánchez de Lozada cemented the MNR-MBL relationship, and the coalition is still together as of this writing (February 1996). Antonio Araníbar, the MBL foreign minister, performed extremely well and, at least according to opinion polls, was the most popular member of the cabinet. A more accurate picture would reveal that the MNR has engulfed the MBL and that its fate may be entirely in the hands of Sánchez de Lozada and the MNR. Despite attempts by members of the MBL to retain their identity independently of the MNR, the fact remains that the future of this small band of well-intentioned former leftists is tied intimately with the fortunes of this government.

In the early phases of the Sánchez de Lozada period, it appeared that if these alliances held, the MNR could garner enough power to make all other parties irrelevant and achieve single-party status to close out the twentieth century. This statement can be understood, however, only by explaining the crisis of the opposition political parties. The origins of the crisis are rooted deeply within the confines of a vast web of political corruption that unraveled in early 1994.

Corruption and Political Parties: Toward a Hegemonic Party?

President Sánchez de Lozada faced an all-out battle with opposition political parties from the very day he took office. In November 1993, for example, a few members of the two former ruling parties (ADN and MIR) called for his impeachment and/or the convocation of early elections. Then in December, when the MNR-controlled Congress amended the electoral law, the opposition parties charged Sánchez with attempting to rig the rules of the game to favor his party. Despite the absence of a constitutional mechanism to shorten his term, the opposition repeatedly called for a revocation of the president's mandate.

But these moves were not significant as these parties faced internal crises that could force their disappearance. The unraveling of the opposition warrants more concern because it is intrinsically linked to the explosion of political corruption that has plagued Bolivian democracy and that has serious repercussions for the governability of the country.

After it left office in August 1993, ADN became engulfed in a tremendous internal political battle as a result of General Banzer's retirement from politics in November of that year. Banzer's retirement confirmed the institutional weaknesses of ADN, especially the inability of the party to name a viable successor. No single individual appeared capable of bringing the party together in time for the 1997 elections. ADN's internal crisis was fueled by speculation of widespread corruption during the 1989–93 period. In late 1994, to avert the complete collapse of ADN, General Banzer returned to politics and will apparently run for office in 1997.

Concern for corruption in office became the single most significant factor in the total collapse of the MIR. Since August 1993 former president Paz Zamora attempted to distance himself from his party and attempted to pursue lofty international objectives that included possible stints at the Wilson Center in Washington, D.C., and serving on the International Peace Commission in Chiapas, Mexico. These goals, however, were dramatically altered with the March 1994 accusations by the Special Counternarcotics Force (FELCN, Fuerza Especial de Lucha Contra el Narcotráfico) that widespread linkages between the MIR and narcotraffickers have existed since at least 1987.[27] These accusations extended to the entire leadership structure of the MIR and put a serious damper on the party's quest for a return to political office at mid-decade. In a dramatic sequence of events, drug traffickers described in painful detail before congressional committees the manner in which Paz Zamora and the MIR had allegedly come to rely on the cocaine industry to finance their electoral campaigns. The impact of these accusations was great. On March 25, 1994, Paz Zamora resigned from politics claiming that "errors were made during his administration but no crimes occurred."

Paz Zamora's own appearance before the congressional committee added an important dimension to the process. In a four-hour-long testimony, the former president accused the United States of conspiring to unravel the MIR because Paz Zamora had dared to invite Cuban president Fidel Castro to the August 1993 inaugural ceremonies. Whatever the merits of the MIR's defense, the alleged linkages between the MIR and traffickers appeared to confirm previous charges of widespread corruption when that party was in office.

In December 1994 the FELCN indicted, arrested, and imprisoned Oscar Eid Franco, the MIR's second in command, for charges related to the party's linkages to the drug industry. In early 1995, despite the accusations against him, Paz Zamora surprisingly reemerged as the only person capable of saving the MIR and, along with Banzer, the only one capable of unifying the opposition. While polls did not favor him—he barely received a 5 percent rating in most polls—the average person in Bolivia in early 1995 believed that Paz Zamora would run for office in 1997.

With the demise of the Acuerdo Patriótico and the troubled future of ADN and MIR, the only real opposition force was CONDEPA, the populist party headed by Carlos Palenque, which in the December 1993 municipal election expanded its support outside of the department of La Paz and again won the mayor's office in the capital city. In 1995 CONDEPA appeared to be the only party capable of posing a serious challenge to the MNR. During Sánchez de Lozada's first year in office, all signs were that the MNR could achieve hegemonic party status. But impressions in Bolivia do not last long. By April 1995 the MNR was well on its way to its own unraveling, and the Sánchez de Lozada government appeared headed for a very rough final two years.

Constitutional Reform

The principal challenge in Bolivia in the 1990s was to determine whether the ad hoc arrangements of the 1980s and early 1990s, which were dependent on specific personalities and conjunctures, could be transformed into stable institutional changes. Both the Paz Estenssoro and Paz Zamora governments generated central authority by reducing the power and influence of other institutions such as legislatures, parties, labor unions, and the judiciary. This appeared to be the trend in the Sánchez de Lozada government as well. In his first two years in office, Sánchez de Lozada relied mainly on his cabinet to design and implement policies and used Congress merely as a rubber stamp mechanism. Paradoxically, these exclusionary practices resulted in high support for democracy among the Bolivian masses but overwhelming rejection of parties, legislatures, and judiciaries, the principal institutions of representative democracy.

It became increasingly clear, however, that the Bolivian government would have to consult with the very same institutions that were so denigrated in the previous years. It was also clear, however, that substantial reforms would have to be considered and effected by political institutions in the next few years. These could enhance the process of democratization; they could also serve to create more trouble for whomever sits in the Palacio Quemado.

Two reforms are illustrative of this dilemma. The first involves yet another reform to the electoral law. Aimed at resolving both the difficulties in electing a president and garnering a majority in Congress, the new electoral law proposed a German-style system whereby 50 percent of the lower house will be elected by single-member district norms and the rest will be allotted by the current proportional representation system.[28] The single-member pattern may indeed ensure a majority in the Chamber of Deputies, which would in turn facilitate the election of a president. At the same time, however, the new law may limit the access to the system of smaller parties and erode the faith in the system of larger parties that lose in single-member districts, leading to an un-willingness to enter into pacts. Critics note, for example, that the single-member district would facilitate the election of a majority in the lower house reinforcing the rubber stamping role of the Congress.

A second debate over constitutional reforms is illustrative of the pattern of confrontation faced by the Sánchez de Lozada government. In April 1993 the three principal parties signed a law "on the necessity to reform the constitution." Signed into law by then vice-president Luis Ossio, the law paved the way for proposals such as a five-year presidential term, the eighteen-year-old vote, the congressional election of a president from only the top two vote-getters, and the establishment of a constitutional tribunal that would perform a judicial review function.

In January 1994 this law became a great source of controversy as two conflicting interpretations emerged. On one side, members of the opposition parties argued that a constitutional convention must be elected to reform the constitution. The government argued that the April 1993 law passed with the deliberate intention of avoiding a constitutional convention that could throw out the entire constitution instead of focusing on only a few articles.[29] In any event, this debate was resolved in the government's favor in the early part of 1994 as it took its case before the national Congress it controls. Sánchez de Lozada achieved the reforms he had long sought; however, the outstanding question was whether these would make governing Bolivia any easier.

The answer to the previous question does not lie in the judiciary, which became engulfed in the worst crisis of the century. Owing largely to allegations of corruption at every level, the judiciary was one of the least respected institutions in Bolivia. Notwithstanding the prevalence of corruption, the most serious problem facing the judicial system was still Bolivia's multiethnic population and the lack of access most of the population has to the country's courts. By law, all proceedings must be conducted in Spanish, even though this is not the primary language for a substantial percentage of the population. It is not surprising, therefore, that a large proportion of the population bypasses the judicial system and seeks an alternative form of justice. Until now, the principal alternative has been the emergence of Carlos Palenque, the populist presidential candidate and radio and TV talk show host.

Proposals to reform the judiciary abounded, but the government's aim to adopt a constitutional tribunal prevailed. Such a tribunal would presumably become an "apolitical" chamber for judicial review handling all constitutional claims and thus averting the type of debilitating interbranch confrontations that have characterized Bolivia's political system in the past several years. The constitutional tribunal would simultaneously serve as a constitutional complaint council where individual citizens would bring charges of human rights violations and the like.[30] Opponents of the tribunal argued that it would establish a fourth branch of government that would essentially undermine the judiciary. Whether this new institution will resolve the kinds of problems of access and unfairness that have characterized the system remains to be seen.

In August 1994 thirty-five articles of the constitution were amended through the constitutional amendments law including: direct election of half of the members of the lower house of Congress from single-member districts; an increase in the terms for presidents, members of parliament, mayors, and municipal council members to five years, with general and municipal elections alternating every two and a half years; clear procedures favoring the direct election of the president and all mayors; voting age lowered to eighteen; increased powers to departmental prefects; departmental assemblies composed of national representatives doing double duty as the only assembly members of the department from which they were chosen by the single-member district procedure; the establishment of an independent human rights ombudsman; and the establishment of a constitutional tribunal. These reforms are significant and warrant an extended discussion beyond the scope of this chapter. Suffice it to say that the most significant in the medium to long term may have to do with the way in which members of the lower house of Congress will be elected. If the reform is successful, legislators may indeed become more like the districts they ostensibly represent. Opposition to these reforms is also evident. Charges abound that two types of legislators have been created: those elected through single-member districts who will see themselves as true representatives and the rest who will be seen as pure party hacks. Moreover, there is no guarantee that this reform will foster coalition building, the only strength of the Bolivian system.

Coca and Cocaine: The Principal Foreign Policy Issue

Despite promises to the contrary, the Sánchez de Lozada government pursued the same U.S.-designed counternarcotics strategy of its predecessors. Given the fact that the government had to implement outstanding agreements with the United States, this was no surprise. Between August 1993 and January 1994, Bolivia was one of the principal recipients of civic action missions related to drug control missions; moreover, U.S. presence in the country increased. Initially, things appeared to go well on the bilateral front. The Bolivian government unveiled a new so-called Option Zero that called for industrial projects and mass training programs for coca growers in exchange for the complete eradication of illegal coca leaf crops. These efforts and programs received extensive praise from Lee Brown, the U.S. government's drug czar. But all was not well on the counternarcotics front.

In 1993 and again in 1994, the cultivation of coca crops expanded, and the government again failed to meet established eradication goals.

As a result, for two consecutive years the White House recommended to the U.S. Congress that Bolivia be granted only a "national interest certification," a probationary type of certification. Future noncertification could result in a complete cut-off of U.S. economic assistance and a negative U.S. vote on multilateral agency support for Bolivia.

Sánchez de Lozada faced an all too familiar dilemma: comply with agreements with the United States and, at the same time, prevent any civil unrest in the coca-growing regions. The government's initial response was forceful; for the first time since the coca-cocaine theme came to dominate U.S.-Bolivian bilateral relations, a Bolivian government recognized that the coca crops in the Chapare region were grown exclusively to provide raw material for the cocaine industry. Predictably this fueled a major confrontation with the peasant unions of the Chapare. The government's policy to eradicate coca forcefully headed toward an all-out confrontation with peasant coca growers. In early March 1994, for example, eradication workers clashed violently with peasants in the Chapare. For the Bolivian government, things did not appear to work out at any level.

Then in early September 1994, confrontations with peasants in the Chapare increased as the government arrested prominent union leaders. Coca growers unions staged a march on La Paz demanding an end to eradication policies, police and military actions in the coca-growing regions, and a broader set of issues including greater funding for alternative development programs. The coca growers march stirred a national debate that in some measure prompted a reexamination of bilateral agreements with the United States. This strategy, however, did not pay off as Washington simply tightened the noose.

The U.S. national interest certification of Bolivia in 1995 stirred numerous other conflicts with coca growers and in some measure contributed to the launching of a state of siege in April. The United States issued an ultimatum that in no uncertain terms stated that the government must reach a specific eradication goal by July 1, 1995, and approve an extradition treaty or face a withdrawal of economic assistance. In its haste to satisfy U.S. demands, the Bolivian government agreed to the eradication terms and negotiated an extradition treaty. The Chapare coca growers, however, were not pleased with the U.S. ultimatum. In short, the confrontation between the government and coca growers could escalate considerably in 1995 and lead to unpredictable outcomes.

The Future of Democratic Governance in Bolivia

In April 1995 Bolivia faced a general strike by the COB, a teachers strike demanding an end to educational reform, an incipient separatist movement from the southernmost department of Tarija, and a potential insurrection by coca-growing peasants in the Chapare Valley. Responding to these pressures, president Sánchez de Lozada declared a state of siege on April 18 for a ninety-day period. Shortly before midnight on April 18, the military and police arrested hundreds of union leaders and confined them to remote jungle towns in northern Bolivia.

The problems confronting the Sánchez de Lozada government had dragged on for six weeks. Demanding that the government rescind the educational reform law that would ostensibly leave them unemployed, striking teachers erected roadblocks, threw dynamite sticks at police, and, in general, paralyzed life in the capital city. In the Chapare, coca growers unions organized a movement, presumably to resist the government's attempts to enforce a voluntary and involuntary coca eradication program.[31] The COB, in turn, was in its thirteenth day of a general strike to protest low salaries and the government's refusal to give in to demands for higher levels of social spending. Finally, after staging a march with twenty thousand or so supporters, civic leaders in the city of Tarija threatened to secede from Bolivia if the central government refused to implement a decentralization law that would establish stronger local governments.

Throughout most of Bolivia, public opinion had little or no sympathy for the striking workers and teachers. Most Bolivians wondered when and if the government would take decisive action to end the strikes that prevented them from going to work or walking the streets without dodging tear gas, rubber bullets, and rocks. President Sánchez de Lozada's attempts at establishing dialogue with the strikers, with the mediation of the Catholic Church, were seen mainly as a reflection of the weakness and indecisiveness of the government.

On April 19, 1995, the day after the state of siege was declared, public opinion in general favored President Sánchez de Lozada's decision to mobilize the armed forces and arrest labor leaders. Television "man on the street" interviews reflected a sense of relief and support for the reestablishment of order in the streets. Most did not question why the rules of exception had been implemented; instead, they wondered why the government had taken so long to react. A taxi driver quoted in the *Miami Herald* captured this generalized sentiment and highlighted an all too common reaction throughout Latin America: "What we need here is a Fujimori who, as in Peru, will enforce the principle of respect for authority, will put things in their place, and will resolve the country's problems without cutting any political deals."[32]

It is still too early to make any assessment of the impact of the state of siege under way in Bolivia. If the past will be repeated, then labor unions will be weakened considerably and will resurface in a few years to contest the process of neoliberalism that the government has promised to sustain for the rest of the century. The likelihood of greater unrest is high, however, as this is the first time that any government—military or civilian—has targeted coca growers, unions, and civic committees simultaneously. All three sectors have legitimate claims that will not go away.

If President Sánchez de Lozada's statement to the military academy a day after launching the measures of exception, that in modern democracy the role of the armed forces is to sustain the legally constituted regime, is a sign of things to come, then Bolivia can expect an even greater reliance on the military to carry out public security matters.

What can be learned from the recent Bolivian experience? First, we now know that imposing and sustaining market-oriented reforms in a small and poor country is a very difficult task indeed. A decade after the imposition of Decree 21060, Bolivia has reached a critical juncture. Although the country's economy has grown steadily, averaging 2.5 percent per year, this has not been enough to deal with declining socioeconomic conditions in the country. Three democratically elected governments since 1985 have imposed states of exception to deal with labor and other social unrest. In the process, they have relied on the armed forces to engage in public security missions.

Second, the Bolivian experience suggests that decision making must be largely executive-centered, with legislatures playing little or no legislative role other than approving executive initiatives. To achieve this, stable ruling coalitions are essential to avoid executive-legislative impasses. In some sense, however, this style of rule has resulted in a profound crisis of all major political institutions. Political parties are perhaps more disconnected from society in 1995 than at any time since the transition to democracy in 1982. The legislature and the judicial branch rank at the bottom of citizen confidence. Third, the Bolivian case suggests that profound constitutional reforms are difficult to enact but even more difficult to implement. The Sánchez de Lozada administration's promise to resolve age-old problems of representation and administration of justice will take time to take hold and have an impact. Few in Bolivia, however, are willing to give the reforms a chance to succeed, as the only term that is of significance there is the short term.

Fourth, it is clear that successive Bolivian governments have done quite a bit over the course of the past decade to fit into the neoliberal wave that has engulfed the Americas. Yet the relative insignificance of the country in regional affairs has resulted in little international interest or investment. Innovative ideas, such as the capitalization initiative of the current government, have received extensive praise from international financial institutions, but the program cannot survive on praise alone.

Finally, the Bolivian experience reiterates what Central American countries learned in the 1980s. Countries that are the target of U.S. security concerns will have an even more difficult time with governance. Every government in Bolivia will continue to be trapped by numerous domestic and international ramifications of the counter-narcotics issue. In 1995, confrontations with coca growers reached their highest level ever, and given current trends there appears no short-term solution. This trend is likely to aggravate if U.S. insistence on eradication persists. The state of siege measures that were imposed in April 1995 were but the beginning of what is likely to escalate into a full-blown confrontation between the government and coca growers. All proposals to solve the problem, ranging from the Bolivian government's zero option to Washington's renewed focus on targeting the supplying countries, are infeasible and will invariably translate into a major problem of governance for any Bolivian president.

6

Chile: The Political Underpinnings of Economic Liberalization

Timothy R. Scully, C.S.C.

In terms of the two axes of economic and political liberalization, Chile differs in a number of important ways from other contemporary cases in Latin America. First, more than a "transition" to democracy, Chile (along with Uruguay) should be considered a case of "redemocratization," of reviving previously well-established democratic practices and political institutions. Institutional legacies from Chile's democratic past continue to shape contemporary politics in decisive ways. Second, though comparatively tardy in returning to democratic rule, Chile's move toward economic liberalization was by far the earliest and probably the most far-reaching in Latin America. Moreover, with respect to sequencing, Chile constitutes the region's only unambiguous example of a regime transition *following* substantial economic liberalization.

This distinctive path serves notice that lessons from Chile may be difficult to draw in a way that travels comfortably from one context to another. Rather than drawing lessons from the Chilean case, this chapter explores the political underpinnings of Chile's rather comprehensive economic liberalization. More precisely, I seek to analyze the relationship between Chile's democratic political heritage, its authoritarian interlude and continuing authoritarian *amarres* (ties), and the exemplary economic policies and performance of contemporary Chile.

In many ways, Chile has been extraordinarily fortunate. I argue that the contemporary consensus over economic policymaking, and the government's capacity to implement these policies effectively, rest not only upon Chile's democratic heritage, nor entirely upon certain legacies of the authoritarian period, but rather precisely upon the combination of these experiences. Strong political institutions arising from the democratic past, made in part more conducive to consensus policymaking by authoritarian holdovers built into the 1980 Constitution, have endowed Chile's democratic government with a remarkable capacity to implement and sustain coherent economic policy.

After a brief review of the results of economic policies in today's Chile, this chapter explores key elements of the political context that have facilitated its success. I argue that Chile is able to sustain a profound process of economic liberalization better under democratic conditions than would have been possible under dictatorship, in part because of the reappearance of Chile's well-institutionalized party system, and in part because of a crucial shift in the ideological center of gravity toward moderation. Ironically, certain nondemocratic limits built into the democratic game by the dictatorship of Augusto Pinochet, for the time being at least, have also contributed to making democracy and economic reform both possible and compatible in Chile.

Beyond Liberalization: Growth with Equity

By now the turbulent story of economic restructuring designed and carried out from the mid-1970s through the 1980s by the most repressive regime in Chile's history is familiar enough. The fruits of the relatively orthodox shock therapy applied to Chile's economy were first visible mostly in terms of the deep economic and social dislocations it produced. After almost a decade of rather freewheeling neoliberal experiments in the 1970s and early 1980s, brief cycles of economic boom and bust had resulted in virtually no growth in per capita income. However, by the mid-1980s a more pragmatic set of economic policies had restored overall macroeconomic balance to the economy, resulting in steady growth from 1985 onward.

Though almost certainly more disruptive than it needed to be,[1] the overall program of economic liberalization carried out by the Pinochet government nonetheless endowed the country with a relatively solid foundation for economic growth. The expansion and diversification of the export sector, and the emergence of a more dynamic and competitive business class—largely legacies from the Pinochet era—contributed decisively to the country's newfound status as the region's showcase economy.[2] In 1992 the Chilean economy outperformed even optimistic government predictions, growing at the brisk annual rate of 10.3 percent, with unemployment at a remarkably low 4.9 percent of the work force and inflation at a reasonable level (12.7%). During 1993 growth remained high at 6 percent, yielding an average growth rate for the Aylwin period (1989–93) of more than 6 percent. By the end of the Aylwin period, practically every macroeconomic indicator, including inflation (11.5%), unemployment (4.6%), investment in fixed capital (27.2% of GDP [gross domestic product]), domestic savings (21% of GDP), productivity and wage rates (both growing more than 4.5% annually), all pointed to the same phenomenon: Chile is booming.[3] The first years of the Frei government have been marked by the same success: inflation in single digits and falling, foreign reserves at U.S.$14.8

billion and rising, a booming export sector (growing more than 25 percent in 1994), and foreign investment continuing to pour in. Though Chile surely experienced a painful and disruptive economic adjustment, in 1995 Chile had an economy that it was difficult to find fault with. Indeed, the Pinochet experience has raised larger comparative questions about the relationship between authoritarianism, democracy, and the possibilities for successful economic restructuring.

While there is little argument that the opening of the economy and the deliberate drive to pursue export-led growth have positively affected growth, there is likewise no room for doubt about the effects of these changes on distribution under Pinochet. As many authors have shown, there was a seamy side to Chile's "economic miracle."[4] By the end of the Pinochet period, income distribution had worsened considerably: the poorest 40 percent of households in Santiago saw their share of consumption fall from 19.4 percent in 1969 to 12.6 percent in 1988, while the share of the richest 20 percent rose from 44.5 percent to 54.9 percent. By all measurements, the proportion of families defined as living in poverty and extreme poverty had risen dramatically during the years of authoritarianism. For example, in 1987, 44.7 percent of all Chileans lived in poverty; 16.8 percent were classified as indigent.[5] From 1970 to 1988, total social expenditures per capita fell 8.8 percent; health expenditures alone fell by nearly 30 percent.[6] As Eugenio Tironi put it, by the end of the military regime, Chile had become in some respects a "dual society" wherein a large portion of the population was left without the benefits of the miracle.[7]

Observers have emphasized the many ways in which post-Pinochet economic policy simply mimics that initiated by the Chicago Boys. However, these assertions are unfair. A central component of the Aylwin administration's economic strategy sought to demonstrate that growth need not necessarily come at the expense of equity. The first major piece of legislation enacted by the new democratic government in 1990 was tax reform, which collected an additional 2 percent of GNP (gross national product) and boosted tax revenues by approximately 15 percent, making it possible to increase government spending on social programs from 9.9 percent to 11.7 percent of GDP.[8] Between 1989 and 1995, government social spending rose by 50 percent in real terms.[9] Chile's government was spending unprecedented resources on social programs, including training and vocational programs for youth, an expanded public health program, and an ambitious public housing initiative. Perhaps most strikingly, at the same time that Aylwin's government sought to address the more urgent social demands inherited from the Pinochet regime, the public sector experienced growing budget surpluses every year he was in office. Income distribution improved during the Aylwin administration, with the income share of the wealthiest one-fifth of the population falling from 59.9 percent in 1989 to 54.7 percent in 1991.[10] The numbers of Chileans living in poverty fell between 1990 and 1995 by more than one million people, from 40.1 percent of the population to 28 percent.[11] Though far from eliminating the enormous social debt incurred during the military dictatorship, the Aylwin and Frei administrations have made important progress in bringing about a more equitable distribution of the fruits of economic growth.

Chile's born-again conversion to private initiative and the market has been remarkably complete, but it would be misleading to suggest that privatization has removed the state entirely from the market scene. The conversion to private initiative and markets requires a strong state with ample initiative and regulatory capacity, and Chile is endowed with a relatively coherent state apparatus with a long-standing developmentalist tradition. The Chilean state continues to play a key role in coordinating economic activity, but it is undergoing its own transition from the predominantly entrepreneurial state dating from the years of import-substituting industrialization to the contemporary regulatory state.[12] In fact, several fundamental aspects of the precise role the state will play in Chile's future development, such as the nature of state involvement in the giant (as yet still nationalized) Chilean copper industry, have yet to be resolved and still haunt the political landscape like ghosts from another era.

The Reemergence of Strong Democratic Political Institutions

I argue that the restoration of what was previously a long-standing democratic regime endowed the Aylwin administration with unusual leverage to craft coherent economic policy. And, perhaps more than any other feature of this transition, the recovery of strong, viable, and relatively well-institutionalized political parties provided the Aylwin government both the legitimacy and the initiative capacity to do so.[13] Despite the vast social debt left by the Pinochet regime and earlier blistering critiques of neoliberalism by those who now comprise the leadership of the Concertation Alliance, the Aylwin government has not deviated from the authoritarian regime's fundamental free market orientation.[14]

With the return of competitive politics after 1988, parties resumed their role as the backbone of the Chilean political system.[15] The reappearance of Chile's institutionalized party system facilitated the possibility for coherent policymaking in the post-Pinochet era because it allowed for political participation and conflict in ways that did not overwhelm the political system.[16] Faced with seventeen years of pent-up popular demands, Chile's institutionalized party system has been key, together with organized labor, in helping government policymakers express and channel social conflict, directing it toward recognized institutions. Where party systems are less well institutionalized, such as is the case in Brazil, Ecuador, and Peru, presidents may enjoy widespread backing in congress—and therefore broad executive initiative capacity—at moments of peak popularity. Yet such backing often evanesces in the legislature with signs of diminishing public approval. Chile's institutionalized party system by no means assures congressional support for government initiatives, especially given its problematic multiparty presidential character, but it increases the likelihood.[17]

The degree to which a party system is institutionalized provides an important key for understanding success or failure of efforts at economic restructuring in many Latin American countries. It is no accident, for example, that the leadership of Chile's Concertation government (as well as the political leaderships of Costa Rica and Uruguay) have eschewed rule by executive decree (*decretismo*) for carrying out economic policy. Where parties and other political institutions, such as congress and the judiciary, are well established, presidents must deal with them and negotiate major policy directions. These political institutions help orient economic actors by laying down clear and legitimate rules of the game, and for this reason they help ensure a framework of predictability for economic decision making. With well-established political institutions such as coherent and well-organized parties, actors are more likely to know the rules of the game and generally have some sense of how to pursue their interests, even when surprises occasionally confront them. Institutionalized parties are certainly not a sufficient condition for explaining successful economic policymaking in new democracies, but they may be necessary. However, in addition to the degree of institutionalization present within a party system, it is also important to explore the kinds of parties and the ways they interact.

The reappearance of a highly institutionalized party system is a key legacy from Chile's democratic past, but the dynamics that characterize the contemporary party system differ in significant ways from its pre-coup predecessor.[18] Several of these differences greatly affect the capacity of the democratic government to formulate and pursue coherent policy. First, current party leaders, with the exception of the communists and a minority of socialist leaders on the Left, and to some extent the Unión Democrática Independiente (UDI, Independent Democratic Union) on the Right, now try to emphasize the centrist nature of their positions and programs. Renovación Nacional (RN, National Renovation) insists repeatedly that it is a "Center-Right" party, and the Unión del Centro Centro (UCC, Center-Center Union) puts this notion into its very label. This reorientation toward the center is especially striking among a majority of the socialists. Whereas in the late 1960s and early 1970s the predominant group in the party was influenced by the Cuban Revolution and espoused positions generally considered to be to the left of the communists, most—and in the case of the socialist-inspired Party for Democracy (PPD), virtually all—are now close to the current, more liberal outlook and policies of the Spanish socialists.[19] As a result of these changes, the Chilean party system—at least during the years of the democratic transition (from 1988 to the present)—is no longer characterized by the same sharp ideological cleavages between the main parties as was the case before the 1973 breakdown, and therefore is not currently subject to the centrifugal pulls of polarized pluralism.[20]

Crucially, today there is a rough consensus over fundamental issues pertaining to the nation's socioeconomic institutions, and voters are not asked to choose between radically different models of development. This general ideological convergence toward the Center and, in terms of economic policy, toward export-led growth and free markets, has sharply reduced conflict, thereby making it far easier to formulate and implement coherent policies. This is not to suggest that dissenting voices, such as that of the (now greatly diminished) Communist Party (MIDA), are completely absent. Notwithstanding, there is perhaps as much or more ideological consensus on the appropriateness of the current economic model in Chile today as there was correspondingly widespread agreement in the 1940s on the correctness of import-substituting industrialization led by a strong developmentalist state.[21]

Second, and equally consequential for the Aylwin government's capacity to shape successful economic policy, the pattern of party alliances during the Aylwin years is very different from what it was in the late 1960s and early 1970s. Whereas in the earlier period the Christian Democrats were at loggerheads with the parties of the Left and the Radicals, and in the early 1970s the Christian Democrats struck an alliance with the Right to oppose the Popular Unity government of Salvador Allende, the Concertation government is comprised principally of Christian Democrats and parties that were formerly part of the Popular Unity government, except for the communists. Two decades ago the coalitional patterns were determined mainly by support or opposition to the left-wing government of President Allende, while more recently they have been determined by party acceptance or rejection of the military regime.

This change in the pattern of political coalitions is of the utmost importance. By introducing a new dimension of party division along the lines of support or rejection of the military government, it has submerged—at least for the time being—traditional sources of conflict between the parties, contributing to the decrease in ideological distance between them.[22] The current Chilean party system has been recreated in a manner reminiscent of the Popular Front governments in the late 1930s to late 1940s, when there was also a Center to Left alliance, but an alliance in support of a very different socioeconomic model (that of import-substituting industrialization). The principal differences in terms of political support between the Concertation and the Popular

Front coalitions are that the Christian Democrats, and not the Radicals, now act as the fulcrum of the party system at the Center, and that the Communist Party, whose vote is a fraction of what it was then, does not belong to the present coalition. The differences separating the two periods in terms of economic policy are far greater, replacing a state-directed development model with Latin America's most liberal, market-oriented economy.

These changes in Chile's political landscape have powerfully reinforced the capacity of the democratic government to pursue a strategy of pacts and *acuerdos* (agreements) leading to successful economic policies. The symbolic importance of Finance Minister Alejandro Foxley, a Christian Democrat, and Economics Minister Carlos Ominami, a socialist, both early and intractable opponents of the Chicago Boys, reinforced the first Concertation government's efforts to strengthen Chile's export-led growth strategy. Their leadership lent to the current economic model legitimacy that it never enjoyed under the military regime. Since both the Christian Democratic and socialist parties have traditionally identified themselves as opponents of unbridled capitalism, the fact that they now find themselves leading the efforts to sustain inherited liberal economic policies places them in some respects in an even stronger position vis-à-vis economic liberalization than the Chicago Boys![23] At home their economic policies commanded the support of practically the entire spectrum of political opinion, and abroad they became a model for developing countries undergoing economic and political liberalization.

Recovering Democracy within the Framework of the 1980 Constitution

Democratic governance returned to Chile with the inauguration of Patricio Aylwin in March 1990, yet the battle toward full recovery of a consolidated democratic political regime has been a difficult and, to date, unfinished one. The institutional framework inherited by the Aylwin government is loaded with features built into the 1980 Constitution that constrain and potentially undermine the authority of the democratically elected government.[24] Though much of the 1980 Constitution restores familiar republican elements to Chile's democratic institutional order, it also includes institutional privileges for the military and its political allies that are inimical to the democratic process.

Within the framework of the 1980 Constitution, Pinochet and his supporters ostensibly sought to craft a "protected" capitalist democracy and to resolve once and for all the most fundamental conflicts that had rocked twentieth-century democratic politics in Chile. While economic managers Sergio de Castro and Miguel Kast were busy designing and implementing dramatic policies aimed at liberalizing the economy, the regime's chief ideologist, Jaime Guzmán, and others were drawing up the legal framework to support them.

Perhaps more crucial than any other feature, the inviolability of private property enshrined in the 1980 Constitution resolved, at least for the time being, a central axis of decades of social and political conflict in Chile and a key source of uncertainty in the economic arena. Ever since the new constitution took effect, the Supreme Court has consistently given a narrow interpretation to the constitutional provision that "protects the right to private property of all persons" (article 19). In contrast to the 1925 Constitution, expropriation is now possible only by legislation specifically "authorizing expropriation by virtue of public utility or national interest." "In all cases," the constitution continues, "the owner will have the right to indemnification for any alienated property," the total compensation being fixed by common agreement or adjudicated by a decision of the appropriate court. Given the interpretation of these clauses by the Supreme Court, any expropriation must be compensated at market value and with full cash payment in advance.

The sacrosanct status of private property enshrined in the 1980 Constitution, combined with constitutional provisions placing strict limits on the role of the state as entrepreneur, in a country where laws traditionally carry a great deal of weight, has contributed mightily to resolving the problem of economic credibility and has contributed to a positive climate for domestic and foreign investment. This provision, together with the creation within the constitution of an independent central bank and important changes in the ideological climate referred to above, reinforced confidence among entrepreneurs that the parameters of economic policy will not fluctuate unexpectedly. That none of the major political actors in post-Pinochet Chile has challenged either the fundamental inviolability of private property or the limited role of the state is a telling indicator of just how much the nature of the political agenda has changed. As a consequence, compared to the days of factory takeovers and land seizures that preceded the 1973 coup, the stakes involved in politics have been dramatically reduced, resulting in a shrinkage of the political arena itself.

Additional features of the 1980 Constitution granted institutional privileges to the military and its allies. For example, it grants the Chilean armed forces tutelary powers within Chile's political arena.[25] Whereas the only reference made to the armed forces in the previous constitution stated that "The armed forces are obedient and non-deliberative" (article 22 of the 1925 Constitution), the 1980 document states that "The armed forces . . . exist in order to defend the nation, and are essential in order to procure national security and to guarantee the institutional order of the republic" (article 90 of the 1980 Constitution). Though the constitution stipulates that the heads of the respective branches of the armed forces are subordinate to the president, the most critical element of that subordination, the power of appointment and removal, is absent for a period of eight years, thereby virtually tenuring the entire command structure of the military until 1997. As a result, the same military leaders who commanded the armed forces during the dictatorship—including Pinochet himself at the head of the army—have continued to do so since March 1990.

To assist the armed forces in carrying out their new tutelary role, the 1980 Constitution (as amended by plebiscite on July 30, 1989) created a National Security Council whose purpose includes, in addition to ensuring national security, examining all matters that may "gravely undermine the bases of the institutional system" (articles 95 and 96). Of the eight positions on the National Security Council, four are to be occupied by the heads of the army, navy, air force, and national police. Two other members were named, indirectly, by General Pinochet before leaving office. General Pinochet's control over this body was enhanced by the creation of a Strategic Advisory Committee, an agency comprised of approximately fifty full-time staff persons designed to keep watch over every aspect of national policy and to give political advice to Pinochet. In addition to its other responsibilities, the National Security Council is charged with designating two of the seven members of the Constitutional Court.

The institutional autonomy of the armed forces enshrined in the 1980 Constitution is further enhanced by a number of policy domains reserved for the privileged action of the military. As J. Samuel Valenzuela notes, in contrast to the diffuse and generally ambiguous character of tutelary powers, reserved domains "remove specific areas of governmental authority and substantive policy making from the purview of elected officials."[26] For instance, the 1980 Constitution prescribes that the defense budget may never fall below the amount spent in real terms by the military government in its last year. Lest there be some misunderstanding, the law also states that funds to ensure these levels of military spending must be provided automatically from 10 percent of all copper sales by the state-owned National Copper Corporation (CODELCO). Elected government officials cannot interfere in the preparation of military budgets or the acquisition of armaments, and thereby are barred from making changes in military doctrine or from altering the curriculum of studies in the military academies. Perhaps most important, military intelligence, which was deeply involved in human rights violations during the seventeen-year dictatorship, is also left entirely in the hands of the armed forces.

The continuing presence of General Pinochet at the head of the army has been a considerable source of concern for both the Aylwin and Frei governments. Though, at the outset of his presidential term in 1989, Aylwin asked Pinochet to resign his command "for the good of the country," Pinochet openly refused to do so. While the other military branches, the navy, air force, and national police, have adjusted their rhetoric and even much of their behavior to the reality of civilian rule, the army and its top leadership have at different times been openly critical of both the Aylwin and Frei governments. The army's hard-line stance has been especially visible in its continuing and vehement objections to investigations of abuses committed by the military during the authoritarian period. In December 1990, while top military leaders, including Pinochet's son, were undergoing judicial and congressional review for misuse of government funds, the army garrisoned its troops, precipitating rumors of an impending coup. Again in May 1993, unhappy with the Aylwin administration's insistence that the constitution be amended to curtail the autonomy of the armed forces, and indignant at a new court interpretation of the 1978 amnesty law that allowed courts to investigate human rights violations, Pinochet called army units to general quarters and surrounded public buildings in downtown Santiago with soldiers dressed menacingly in battle fatigues. The drama of this event occasioned a firm public rebuke to Pinochet by President Aylwin, who insisted that "no demonstration of force from state institutions, individuals, or private groups will lead to solutions."

Aylwin later reflected sullenly that he may have been "overly optimistic" in 1991 when he had affirmed that the transition to democracy was complete in Chile. "Events have clearly shown that key institutional aspects have yet to be resolved in the Chilean transition."[27] Deep unhappiness within the ranks of the army became perhaps most evident during June and July 1995 when, after the arrest of the former head of Chile's dreaded secret police, General Manuel Contreras, public demonstrations of "off-duty" army personnel critical of the Supreme Court's decision to put Contreras and his army accomplice behind bars for the Washington, D.C., murder of Orlando Letelier once again placed in high relief the army's ambivalence toward the institutions of democracy. In sum, an important obstacle still blocking Chile's path to full democratic consolidation is the institutional autonomy granted to the military in the 1980 Constitution.

The sharply increased role of the military within the state set forth in the 1980 Constitution might well have been substantially mitigated if the electoral majorities won by the Concertation for Democracy in 1989 had translated into a proportional number of congressional seats. In such case, key elements of this "perverse institutionalization" might have been removed by way of congressional reform.[28] However, two mechanisms—a heavily biased electoral formula and the presence of Pinochet-designated members of the Senate—have prevented the preferences of the electorate from being fully represented in the composition of the membership in Congress.

Electoral systems in most democracies are biased in the sense of underrepresenting minority parties and candidates. However, the electoral formula adopted by the Pinochet regime departs from this practice. The electoral law provides that, for the elections of both deputies and senators, each congressional voting district (or region in the case of senators) elect two candidates. Parties are allowed to form electoral alliances, or "lists," in order to maximize the vote obtained by a given political tendency. For a single list to obtain both seats in a given voting unit, the list achieving the majority is required to double the combined total of their nearest competitors, thereby allowing (at least theoretically) a list obtaining minority support (33.4% or more in the case of only two lists; the percent decreases the more lists there are) to win one-half of the seats. This system was designed to provide maximum representation of the second-highest lists, which in this case are partisans of Pinochet.

In addition to systematically favoring the candidacies of the minority rightist candidates, the boundaries of electoral districts erected by the military regime made extensive use of gerrymandering. For example, since opposition to Pinochet in the plebiscite of 1988 tended to be much more concentrated in urban areas, urban electoral districts were given far less representation proportionally than rural areas.[29] While Santiago accounts for 40 percent of Chile's population, it is represented by only 26 percent of the nation's deputies. Whereas twenty small rural districts containing one and a half million people elected forty deputies in 1989, the six most densely populated urban districts, also accounting for one and a half million people, elected fourteen deputies. The same distortion occurred in the design of senatorial regions. In practically every case, the lines of districts and regions were drawn in such a way as to overrepresent areas that voted for Pinochet in the 1988 plebiscite.[30]

The results of the 1989 elections demonstrated the effectiveness of the military regime's electoral formula for rewarding the Right and punishing the Left. The law's most egregious effects were reflected in the allocation of seats in the Senate. In the 1989 elections, whereas the Right (National Renovation, the Independent Democratic Union, and various independent candidates) obtained 42.2 percent of the Senate seats with 33.9 percent of the vote, the Left won only 12.5 percent of the Senate with 20.6 percent of the vote. The country's largest party, the centrist Christian Democrats, were left largely unaffected, winning 34.2 percent of the upper house with 32.3 percent of the vote.[31]

It would be misleading, however, to focus the analysis of the impact of the electoral formula exclusively on election results. In some ways a far more important consequence of the regime's electoral formula is the almost inexorable bipolar logic the new electoral rules impose on all the major political actors. Since the rules are designed to reward the two largest political alliances and at the same time punish small or nonallied parties, parties are left with practically no choice but to join together to form large coalitions and alliances. This imposed bipolar logic has resulted in several unintended consequences for the major political parties. First, intense pre-electoral negotiations between party leaders within the same alliance play a decisive role in selecting candidates for office in each district. These often result in arcane intra- and interparty deals, wherein popular candidates are sometimes sacrificed by their own party leadership and prevented from running in the interests of the larger alliance ticket. In some cases, these practices have led to revolts among local party rank and file who view these as opportunistic electoral calculations of national party leadership and an attempt to thwart popular choice.

While this practice has had its costs for the various partners within the Concertation Alliance, it has been especially divisive among the parties of the fractious Right. Tension within the Right has been further heightened by two additional factors. First, a nettlesome populist leader, Francisco Javier Errazuríz, and his Center-Center Party joined forces with the rightist alliance to compete in the 1993 elections, thereby further complicating the already acrimonious relationship between the two major parties of the Right, National Renovation and the Independent Democratic Union. Second, whereas the logic of competition permits the Concertation to aim for both seats in any given electoral unit, the (expanded) Center-Right alliance, termed the Union for the Progress of Chile, could realistically hope for only one seat in each district. The larger number of actors within the alliance, combined with the reduced stakes, have made pre-electoral negotiations and intra-alliance electoral competition among the parties of the Right intensely competitive.

The legislative "fail-safe mechanism" of the Pinochet-inspired 1980 Constitution is its provision for nine designated members to be added to the thirty-eight elected members of the Senate.[32] According to article 45 of the constitution, four of these "institutional" senators are chosen by the National Security Council from among retired commanders in chief of the army, navy, air force, or national police; two are chosen by justices of the Supreme Court from among retired justices, and a third must be chosen by the justices from among retired attorneys general of the republic; one is to be chosen by the president of the republic from among ex-rectors of an officially recognized university; and finally, the president selects one from among former cabinet ministers. Fifteen days after Pinochet lost his bid to stay in power in October 1988, the names of those designated to hold positions were announced to the public. Not surprisingly, all of those chosen were unwavering supporters of General Pinochet.

Repeated efforts by the Aylwin and Frei administrations to remove nonelected members of the Senate failed to gain the support of the

Right. In effect, the former allies of the Pinochet regime have used the presence of their elected colleagues to veto legislation they consider incompatible with the institutional legacy of the military regime. The Concertation Alliance has found itself in a very difficult position: its capacity to respond effectively to antidemocratic features of the institutional framework left behind by the military regime has been severely constrained by the strength of the Right in the Senate. Even with an electoral formula that overrepresented more conservative rural areas, if the Senate had been free of designated members, parties loyal to Aylwin would have controlled 60 percent of the seats in the lower house and 58 percent of the Senate. This would have permitted the government much broader freedom in enacting its legislative agenda. Ironically, however, this feature of the 1980 Constitution and other constraints left behind by Pinochet have forced the new democratic government to govern by seeking to gain the consent of its opponents, thereby strengthening the political system's newfound culture of consensus.

By the early 1990s, Chile had reaffirmed its commitment to a liberal economic regime, but important tutelary powers, electoral discriminations, and reserved domains stood in the path of a consolidated democracy. Returning to the two dimensions that form the focus of this chapter's concerns, economic and political liberalization, we are left in post-Pinochet Chile with considerable asymmetry in terms of the government's capacity to pursue policies in these two areas. Whereas the Aylwin government was almost singularly empowered to pursue liberal economic policies, its capacity to consolidate a democratic political regime was quite constrained.

The 1980 Constitution: Blessing in Disguise?

Perhaps not surprisingly, many of the same features of the 1980 Constitution that have made it difficult to consolidate fully the democratic political regime in Chile have reinforced the choice to continue liberal economic policies. In fact, some have argued that once the opposition to Pinochet accepted the overall institutional framework set forth in the 1980 Constitution, it was left little choice but to follow the conservative bias of the new institutional order.[33] Though this latter claim may be an exaggeration, the provisions within the constitution that overrepresent supporters of the Pinochet regime within the Congress, combined with other reserved domains discussed above, have had the effect of requiring the Center-Left government to seek consensus among an even wider array of political forces, pushing the government to go beyond the parties that comprise the Concertation Alliance.

The Right holds considerable power in the Senate owing to the presence of designated senators, so that the Aylwin and Frei administrations often have had to satisfy the minimal demands of the representatives of

Chile's business and landholding groups in order to pass legislation. While clearly a nondemocratic feature of the new institutional order, this bias has provided important guarantees to capitalists during the transition to democracy. The presence of constitutional restrictions unfriendly to the Center-Left alliance may have given economic policymakers within the Concertation government a necessary weapon to defend themselves from the pressures of populist demands from the Left upon the return to democracy.[34]

Also contributing to this climate of consensus, the 1980 Constitution resolved Chile's perennial problem of what Genaro Arriagada has called the "double minority system" established by the 1925 Constitution. First, whereas the earlier constitution allowed the president of the republic to gain election to office without the support of a majority of the electorate, the 1980 Constitution requires election by a majority of the votes cast (either in the first round or in a runoff election). Even though the 1925 Constitution called for elections (in the case of a no-majority winner) to be decided upon by a majority vote of a joint session of Congress between the two leading candidates, it became a political impossibility to elect anyone other than the candidate with the first plurality. Second, the earlier constitution enabled the president to pass legislation with the support of a simple majority in either house and only one-third plus one in the other. This attribute, combined with other extraordinary executive powers, reinforced a dangerous proclivity of presidents (in many cases elected by a bare plurality) to govern without sufficient popular support, and helped precipitate a deep crisis of legitimacy during the government of Salvador Allende. However, though the current constitution eliminates the possibility of a president elected with minority popular support (with a second-round election), it by no means ensures parliamentary support for the sitting president. Indeed, the president is forced to seek broad alliances with multiple parties in order to enact legislation.

The 1980 Constitution requires the president, who must be elected by at least a majority, to pass legislation with a majority in both houses—and depending on the policy area, substantially more than a majority—thereby requiring broad agreement on policy before legislation is enacted. Though, as we have seen, the requirement of achieving such levels of support has prevented the Aylwin and Frei administrations from removing most elements of perverse institutionalization from the constitution, at the same time it has powerfully reinforced the political logic behind the Concertation Alliance. And this newfound Center-Left alliance, in turn, has provided for, in the words of socialist cabinet minister Enrique Correa, "a more solid political majority for social change than was possible under the government of Salvador Allende."[35] Rather than adopting an openly and completely hostile posture toward the initiatives of the democratic government, the rightist opposition has generally manifested a pragmatic attitude, often engaging in intense parliamentary negotiations to blunt legislation aimed at the interests of capital. Conscious perhaps of the often high levels of popular support enjoyed by both presidents Aylwin and Frei throughout their tenure in office,[36] important elements of the Right have lent their support to government-sponsored reforms ranging from key changes in the tax and industrial relations codes to wide-reaching reforms of local and municipal government.

In sum, while the 1980 Constitution is characterized by multiple elements of perverse institutionalization, at least in the short term, some provisions of the new constitution may have provided a legal and institutional framework to reinforce the policies of economic liberalization. The legal guarantees given to private property and the creation of an independent central bank, as well as other constitutional provisions, enhance the potential for government credibility and consistency. The constitution also sought to resolve several destabilizing propensities inherent in the earlier institutional order, removing the chronic problem of an executive elected with only minority support. These factors, combined with the requirement of parliamentary majorities (and sometimes a supermajority) to pass legislation, reinforce centripetal drives within the political system and contribute to building consensus.

Consensus: A Key Facilitating Condition

Many of the ideological and institutional changes in Chilean politics discussed above suggest that collective learning can occur, making major political actors more tolerant and disposed to compromise.[37] Reflecting on this political sea change, Aylwin's finance minister, Alejandro Foxley, noted that, "the long authoritarian recess created, almost imperceptibly, a new political culture which made possible agreements, accords, and consensus that had simply been unthinkable earlier."[38] The experience of seventeen years of dictatorship profoundly altered belief systems and strategies among politicians in Chile and the capacity of political leaders to engineer compromise. The greater degree of consensus among political forces in Chile, and the enhanced propensity for broad coalitions and alliances, have provided a propitious context for the continuation of the dual processes of economic and political liberalization.

The notion of "consensus" can be a slippery one. Giovanni Sartori proposed a general definition of consensus to be "a sharing that somehow binds." He then usefully identified three levels where such a sharing may hold relevance for the existence of democracy: first, the level of "ultimate values (such as liberty and equality) which structure the belief system"; second, that of "rules of the game, or procedures"; and finally, of "specific governments and governmental policies." He calls the first level of consensus a "facilitating" condition for the existence of democracy, whereas the second level he argues is a fundamental prerequisite. The third level, that of specific governments and government policy, is an area where consensus would be both unnecessary and in some ways undesirable for democracy: the existence of dissenting views over specific policy lies at the heart of democratic government.[39]

In terms of the first level, that of ultimate values that structure the belief system, there is abundant evidence that the transition in Chile has coincided with a substantial narrowing in ideological distance between major social and political actors. Belief systems, especially among opponents to the dictatorship, have reemerged from the experience of authoritarianism substantially transformed. Chastened by the defeat of the Allende regime, and sobered by the global collapse of international Leninism, the Left in Chile is barely recognizable as the heir to its more ideological pre-coup predecessor. The policy agenda of the Left has taken a sharp turn in the direction of liberalism, based on a rethinking of both the value of political democracy and the usefulness of the market.

In this new environment, the centrist Christian Democrats no longer advocate "communitarian socialism" but have resorted to the language of their European cousins proclaiming support for a "socially responsible" market. Comparatively, the Right has traveled the least ideological distance from its pre-authoritarian counterpart, mainly because their goals in economic policy have largely been realized. The near-convergence of these formerly irreconcilable political actors has introduced a moderating dynamic into the political system that has undoubtedly served as a facilitating condition for the return of democracy. The newfound capacity and willingness of political leaders to bridge long-standing animosities and to forge coalitions and alliances among key parties of the Center and Left (within the Concertation), and those of the Center and the Right (within the Union for the Progress of Chile), has supplied a useful lubricant within the political system.

Sartori's second and most fundamental level of consensus, that of basic agreement upon rules and procedures, has been more problematic in the Chilean case. As we have seen, the legal framework established by the 1980 Constitution, though formally acknowledged as the "rules of the game" by major political and social actors, retains authoritarian holdovers that are unacceptable to the parties of the Concertation Alliance. Disagreement over the institutional framework of Chile's democracy will doubtless intensify during the six-year presidential period of Eduardo Frei R. Since the forces of the Concertation failed to gain the seats necessary to remove the legacies of authoritarianism in the December 1993 elections, parties of the Concertation, especially those most disadvantaged by the provisions of the 1980 Constitution, such as the socialists and the PPD, may lose patience with what appears to be an endless waiting game. This in turn could contribute in the not-so-distant future to political instability.

Finally, with regard to the level of policy, the Aylwin and Frei governments succeeded in crafting delicate political understandings and skillfully engineered policies in three critical areas: the economy, the gradual consolidation of political democracy, and human rights. Though sometimes a battleground, in general the terrain of economic policy has been one of broad agreement between Chile's major social and political actors. Pursuing a strategy of "growth with equity," the Concertation government has demonstrated to believers and skeptics alike that responsible and highly successful management of the economy is possible in a democratic context.

In the area of reform of political institutions, success has been more limited. The democratic government has pursued a strategy of incremental reform of the legacies of authoritarianism. Though the Concertation governments gained the support of the Right in securing some progress in this area (such as municipal reform), the more fundamental problems of civil-military relations, nonelected senators, and the reform of the electoral law have not been solved as of mid-1995. It seems likely that these reforms can only be made in piecemeal fashion. In perhaps the most painful policy area for the Concertation government, the area of human rights, Aylwin consistently resisted pressures from the Right and the military to enact legislation putting an end to the investigation of past rights abuses (the so-called *punto final*, or "end point" legislation). Instead, Aylwin insisted on a policy he called *justicia posible*, or "justice of the possible," a measure that required the clarification of the circumstances of the crime, moral rehabilitation of the victim, and material compensation to the victim's family. Under this policy, most of the perpetrators of human rights abuses have not been subject to either trial or punishment. Just as in the area of full democratization, in this third policy area, agreement between the parties of the Concertation and the opposition has been elusive.

Conclusion

I have argued that the democratic government led by Patricio Aylwin, and his successors in the Concertation Alliance under President Eduardo Frei R., have been uniquely positioned to consolidate a free market, outward-oriented political economy. Since 1990 Chile's democratic government has successfully formulated and implemented a set of coherent economic policies that have respected the general market orientation pursued under Pinochet. However, it has been much less successful in removing the legacies of authoritarianism that block the full consolidation of democracy. In some ways, perverse institutional legacies built into the 1980 Constitution have strengthened the new democratic regime's hand in economic policymaking.

The institutional framework set forth in the 1980 Constitution has contributed powerfully, though not always democratically, to the Aylwin government's capacity to pursue coherent policy. The decisive resolution of the status of private property within the constitution helped provide the requisite guarantees without which capitalist investment at current levels would be unthinkable. The systematic overrepresentation of Pinochet's allies in the Congress, especially the presence of nonelected members in the Senate, introduced into the system the requirement of a new level of consensus in order to pass legislation. This latter feature, though again nondemocratic, has reinforced centripetal ideological dynamics already present within the political system and, somewhat ironically, contributed to the overall continuity and effectiveness of the government's ability to pursue coherent economic policies.

Democratic transition in Chile should be understood in terms of a recovery of well-established democratic practices and institutions. Several factors have influenced the government's capacity to formulate and implement coherent policy. The reappearance of strong parties capable of channeling and expressing diverse social and political interests has provided a powerful institutional buffer, at least in part protecting policymakers from populist temptations. However, the presence of strong parties is not enough. The dynamics that characterize the contemporary party system in Chile differ in multiple and salutary ways from the pre-coup period. The ideological distance separating the major contenders within the party system has narrowed markedly, and the newfound capacity among the parties to join alliances and coalitions has greatly enhanced democratic governability. Not surprisingly, coherent economic policymaking is more feasible where political polarization is absent.

The trauma and dislocation caused by the experience of authoritarianism in Chile, combined with other global ideological changes, have contributed to a new political culture in which political compromise and agreement are more likely. This new consensus, at the level of ultimate values that structure the belief system among elites, has enabled policymakers to seek common ground among opposing social and political actors, and has served as a key facilitating condition for economic liberalization in a democratic context.

What of the future of this slightly heterodox, Center-Left Concertation Alliance and its warm embrace of economic liberalization? A fundamental question for the post-Aylwin period is whether the parties of the Concertation can continue to recreate in the mid-1990s the sense of excitement and urgency that characterized the transition to a democratic government at the end of the 1980s. Once the novelty of this historic agreement wears off and the fabric of the implicit social pact upon which it rests becomes thin, will the major parties of the Center and the Left be willing and able to forge new agreements over programs and political leaders that go beyond those created for the transition? As the dominant issue for which the Concertation was created recedes— that is, the goal of defeating Pinochet in the 1988 plebiscite and winning the presidency for the forces pressing for full democratization—the cleavage between supporters and opponents of the authoritarian regime may increase as enthusiasm for maintaining current party alignments diminishes. In this new situation, the political leadership within the various parties of the Concertation will be tempted to try to strengthen their own parties and political identities around issues other than a rejection of the dictatorship, and may, for this reason, welcome more open, unstructured electoral competition.

With the December 1993 election of Eduardo Frei R. to succeed Patricio Aylwin at the head of Chile's second Concertation government, the question arises how the dual reality of relatively unencumbered markets combined with a political regime still harnessed by the constitutional constraints left in place by Pinochet will evolve. Has the political arena undergone a fundamental change, or has the consensus of the Aylwin period been more a necessary truce to see parties through the transition? Will renewed party competition revolve around such specific policy-related issues that the fundamental consensus over basic questions can be retained, thereby avoiding the reemergence of centripetal tendencies in the party system and permitting the recreation of the Concertation during the entire term under Eduardo Frei R.? Most probably, the pressure will mount during the Frei period to strip away, one way or another, these constraints. Despite these pressures, lessons from the relatively recent past may be powerful enough to ensure that party divisions remain moderate, allowing the formation of new alliances between forces around the Center of the ideological spectrum and winning the time needed to consolidate democracy in Chile.

7

Paraguay: Transition from Caudillo *Rule*

Diego Abente Brun

The process of transition to democracy in Paraguay, which began on February 3, 1989, with the overthrow of the dictatorship of General Alfredo Stroessner, has yet to be completed. It was expected to end with the general elections of May 9, 1993, the subordination of the military to civilian rule, and the reorganization of the judiciary and the electoral system. However, as a typical transition from above, its pace and course were dictated more by the willingness or need of the ruling elite to make concessions than by the ability of the opposition to extract them. With no significant elements of pressure, the opposition consented to recognize the hastily arranged postcoup election of May 1, 1989, which assured the ruling party a two-thirds majority in the 1989–93 legislature and the total control of the judiciary, the state apparatus, and the military, and thus went to the 1993 elections at a significant disadvantage.

As a result, the 1993 elections were marred by countless irregularities, from a ruling-party controlled electoral system without the effective control of the opposition, to last-minute changes in the rules of the game and a campaign of public intimidation of voters. Furthermore, the active participation of military officers in the electoral campaign and a judiciary subjected to the political influence of the government demonstrated that polyarchy is still in effect.

Thus in Paraguay the issues of strengthening democratic governance are not yet relevant. Instead, the imperative is that of completing the transition begun in 1989 and successfully addressing its challenges. Before exploring them, however, a brief overview of the 1993 elections is needed.

The Electoral Process and the Emergence of the Wasmosy Government

The elections of May 1993 were to be the first freely contested elections in some seven decades. They were characterized by two cleavages: that of dividing the ruling party's candidate from those of the opposition and the fierce competition within the ruling party for such a candidacy.

On the opposition front, two candidates soon captured the lead: Domingo Laíno, the populist leader of the Liberal Radical Authentic Party (PLRA), and Guillermo Caballero Vargas, a prominent businessman with old ties to the political opposition and a message of change, modernization, and social justice. Laíno won the candidacy of the PLRA, one of Paraguay's two traditional parties, while Caballero Vargas led the formation of a new party, the Encuentro Nacional (EN, National Encounter).

Two major candidates fought the Colorado Party (ANR) primary, Luis María Argaña and Juan Carlos Wasmosy. Argaña had been a principal civil figure in the coup against Stroessner but fell from grace because of constant confrontations with the president, General Rodríguez. A right-wing populist, he was able to appeal to the core membership of the party with a message that in many ways echoed the absolute hegemony enjoyed by the party under Stroessner. On the other hand, Wasmosy, a wealthy businessman who made his fortune in activities connected with the construction of the Itaipú dam in the 1970s, presented himself as the candidate of change representing the idea of a new party ready to adjust successfully to more competitive conditions.

The bitter Colorado campaign confronted an Argaña portrayed by his opponent as nothing but the return of Stroessner and a Wasmosy portrayed by his opponent as a former liberal who had infiltrated the party and was seeking to capture it through his money and close relationship to the military elite. These extreme characterizations represented, if in an exaggerated way, some distinct elements of reality. Argaña's discourse had traditionally been aggressive, and he managed to get the support of a majority of the Colorado faction that followed Stroessner to the end. Wasmosy was clearly the candidate of the government establishment, the business elite connected to it, and especially the powerful First Army corps commander, General Lino C. Oviedo.

By most accounts, the outcome of the primary election produced an Argaña victory. However, by forcing the resignation of several members of the party's Electoral Tribunal and replacing them with others that excluded representatives of Argaña from the vote counting, Wasmosy managed to be declared the winner with a narrow-margin victory over Argaña. The stage was thus set for a three-way race with Wasmosy, Laíno, and Caballero Vargas as the main contenders.

The electoral campaign was full of uncertainties—including a Colorado attempt at cancelling the polls via a judiciary injunction that was dismissed only two weeks before the election—and was marred by several last-minute changes in the electoral code designed to weaken opposition control, by lack of access to and control of the electoral rolls and the electoral apparatus, and by overt military intervention including General Oviedo's proclamation that no matter what, the Colorado Party was to rule *per seculae seculorum*. The outcome of the May 9, 1993, election is shown in Table 3.

Table 3 **Paraguay: Results of the 1993 National Elections**

	Presidential		Senatorial	
	Votes	%	Votes	%
Wasmosy/ANR	473,176	40.09	498,586	42.3
Laíno/PLRA	378,353	32.06	409,728	34.76
Caballero Vargas/EN	271,905	23.04	203,213	17.24
Others[a]	8,198	0.66	20,411	1.73

[a]Includes six candidates of small parties from the Right and Left.

Wasmosy assumed the presidency on August 15 in questionable circumstances: many Colorados questioned his very candidacy, and the opposition questioned the elections of May 9. Yet, for the sake of political stability and social peace, the opposition decided to accept the outcome of the election, hoping to complete the tasks of democratization in the 1993–98 period. Weighing heavily in the opposition's decision was the fact that, in this democratization game, the democratic opposition had gained a distinct advantage. In fact, for the first time in Paraguayan history, the elections of May 9, 1993, produced a divided government. The distribution of congressional seats was as shown in Table 3.

As Table 4 shows, the opposition enjoys a 25–20 majority in the Senate and a 42–38 advantage in the lower house. Besides, as a result of the internal split in the Colorado Party, the product of the primary elections of December 1992, some eight Colorado senators and some six Colorado deputies, Argaña supporters, have been voting with the opposition, thus reducing even further the strength of the government party's representation in Congress.[1] This distinct advantage in Congress, it was hoped, would put the opposition in a strong position to negotiate the later steps of the transition.

The Challenges of the Transition

The Paraguayan process of transition to democracy confronts three main challenges. The first has to do with the resolution of political

Table 4 **Paraguay: Seats in Congress after the 1993 Elections**

	ANR[a]	PLRA	EN	Total
Senate	20 (12)	17	8	45
Deputies	38 (32)	33	9	80
Total	58 (44)	50	17	125

[a]Numbers between parentheses represent the number of Colorado congressmen that support the government; the rest are dissidents.

conflicts between the ruling elite and the democratic opposition. The issue involves the basic question of power: on the one hand, a politico-military-economic elite that does not want to lose power and, in its attempt to retain it, is prepared to tamper with democratic procedures, and, on the other, a political opposition that wants to preserve those democratic procedures as a means of acceding to power in the future. The issue is whether or not Paraguay will have a truly competitive political system in which all actors will have equal opportunity to attain power. This involves the restructuring of the judiciary, the adoption of a new electoral system, and removing partisanship from the state apparatus. Only the first of these has been tackled so far. The second challenge is that of civic-military relations, which implies the consolidation of a system of full military subordination to civilian rule. The third challenge is that of responding to rising social demands to build support for the process and to guarantee the long-term sustainability of the democratic system.

Furthermore, all these challenges must be met in an orderly, or evolutionary, fashion. Paraguay is a conservative country characterized by a history of shifts between periods of order associated with authoritarian rule (1820–70 and 1954–89) and of instability associated with democratic freedoms (1870–1936 and 1946–54). Thus the imperative of completing the transition and facing the challenges associated with it has been made more complex and difficult by the need to maintain what has been known in Paraguay as "governability."

Governability, or the ability of the government to govern and maintain stability and institutional continuity, has a different meaning and strategic value for the government and for the opposition. For the government, of course, governability is an end in itself. The transition need not be completed. Perpetuating a *democradura*, emptying democratic institutions of any substantive content while maintaining their form, is a far more attractive political formula.

For the democratic opposition, though, governability is a means to an end. Governability is important insofar as it leads to a successful completion of the transition. The democratic opposition seeks a climate of governability as insurance against any possible institutional retrogression. Social chaos, continuing economic hardships, or a political power vacuum may well be the pretext for return to an authoritarian regime. At the same time, the opposition must be careful not to allow such an attitude to lead to the freezing of present conditions which, while much better than those of the dictatorship, are still far from the standards of democracy for which Paraguayans are striving.

In short, the democratic opposition in this period needs to achieve acceptable levels of democratization, successfully addressing the challenges it confronts while maintaining acceptable levels of governability—the former in order to avoid a return to authoritarian government and the latter in order to overcome a simple *democradura*. Paraphrasing Robert Dahl, the Paraguayan dilemma may well be summarized as follows: for the ruling coalition, it is a question of finding the cost of a *fujimorazo* higher than that of toleration; while for the democratic opposition it is a matter of lowering the cost of toleration below that, of regression, or, put differently, raising the cost of regression beyond that of toleration.

Its comfortable congressional majority enables the opposition to deal with the government from a position of strength. In fact, even before convening on July 1, 1993, the congressmen elected by the PLRA, the EN, and the Colorado dissidents forged a parliamentary alliance bent on exercising a strong congressional control over the newly elected president. The first test was the election of the leaders of both houses: president, first vice-president, and second vice-president. At that opportunity, the opposition alliance took over all three positions in both houses. In the Senate the presidency went to a member of the PLRA, the first vice-presidency to one of the Colorado dissidents, and the second vice-presidency to a representative of the EN. In the Chamber, the presidency was also given to the PLRA, but the order of the two vice-presidencies was switched: the EN took the first and the Colorado dissidents the second. Committee memberships were decided on a proportional basis, but their chairmanships were also elected only from the opposition alliance.

Yet, just as the opposition enjoyed a comfortable margin, it also inherited the vices of the petty politics of the past. No sooner had the parliamentary alliance begun to bear fruit than the former presidential candidate, Domingo Laíno, began a campaign to sign a so-called Governability Pact between the government and the opposition, which took place on October 14, 1993. Ill-defined and confusing, the pact was first presented as a compromise to defend public liberties and democracy, as if no constitution existed. It was later redefined as a simple dialogue agreement. But by unilaterally engaging in a dialogue with the government, adopting an "appeasement" strategy, and offering it parliamentary support, the pact severely weakened the chances of the opposition to extract quick concessions from the government on the key issues of the reform of the judiciary and the reorganization of the armed forces.

The Struggle for an Independent Judiciary

Soon after the new Congress was inaugurated, the opposition alliance approved legislation rescinding a highly controversial law passed by the Colorado-controlled previous legislature, which had established the functioning of the Consejo de la Magistratura (Council of Magistrates). According to the 1992 Constitution, the judiciary is to be completely restructured, from the highest court to the lowest justice of the peace. The council is the body charged with selecting and proposing candidates for all judiciary appointments, especially members of the Supreme Court and the Supreme Electoral Tribunal, which will serve until age seventy-five unless impeached by Congress. According to the constitution, the latter are designated by the Senate from three names (*ternas*) proposed by the council and with the *acuerdo* (agreement) of the executive. The law approved by the previous legislature, which had not yet been enacted, provided for a system of election of members of the council highly likely to produce a Colorado majority, and at the same time vested in the executive an absolute veto power over the Senate's Supreme Court and Supreme Electoral Tribunal designations. Such a law provided no guarantee of a real change in the judiciary. Therefore, even though in the short term rescinding that law increased the tension between both branches of government, it was indispensable to do so in order to ensure the long-term viability of a democratic system that would be impossible without an independent judiciary.

Upon rescinding that law, and in a climate of division within the opposition, the Congress passed a new law that provided for a fairer system of electing members of the council and for a procedure that equated the *acuerdo* of the executive for the nomination of Supreme Court and Supreme Electoral Tribunal justices with a presidential veto, thus allowing the Congress to override it.

As expected, the executive threatened to veto it in its entirety and to resort to the Colorado-controlled Supreme Court to obtain a ruling of unconstitutionality if the veto was overridden. This triggered a negotiation that led to an agreement known as the Democratic Compromise between the executive and a majority of congressmen, which was signed on January 13, 1994. The compromise called for both branches to find a consensus concerning the members of the new Supreme Court and Supreme Electoral Tribunal.

The success of the Democratic Compromise created a new atmosphere of cooperation between Congress and the executive. But this climate lasted only a short time: in a surprise move, the government delayed the promulgation of the law as much as was legally possible and immediately thereafter issued a decree with a massive number of changes in the judiciary, sending judges considered honorable to unimportant posts and promoting those of questionable integrity to high positions, especially to appellate courts. Appellate courts are very important in the Paraguayan judiciary system because Supreme Court justices are subject to recusation by plaintiffs, in which cases the vacancies are filled by judges from appellate courts. Through this kind of maneuver one can easily manipulate the process in order to ensure a subservient court.

As if all this was not enough, a group of Colorado lawyers with close ties to governmental sectors and to the party sought a ruling of unconstitutionality against the law of the council of Magistrates, questioning the proportional system adopted to allocate the two seats that are to be filled by lawyers.[2] After a long delay, the Supreme Court ruled 3–2 in favor of the Colorado lawyers. The outcry over the Supreme Court ruling led to the calling of elections on October 22 according to the proportional system the court had earlier declared unconstitutional.[3] Immediately the Colorado lawyers threatened to resort to an *amparo,* a judicial measure designed to protect the rights of persons that "consider themselves gravely injured or in danger of being injured by an act or an omission, obviously illegitimate, of an authority or person."[4]

If anything, this situation led to a unification of opposition forces that had before been separated on the issue of the governability pact. The results were encouraging. Not only were elections held on schedule, but also a united opposition slate won a resounding victory. There is no question that the strategy of complacency and weakness previously supported by those supporting the governability pact failed to produce results and that a new strategy, such as the one chosen in the case of the judiciary, needs to be adopted. It remains to be seen if what has been accomplished is going to last.

The Military Question: Will Institutionalism Prevail?

Another early challenge confronted by the Congress was the institutional status of the armed forces. Before finishing its term, the Colorado-controlled Congress had approved a law of organization of the armed forces that provided for the creation of the post of a Pinochet-like commander of the military forces, to be filled by an active duty military officer. The law also gave this military commander the powers of the commander in chief, which, according to the new constitution, belong exclusively to the civilian president and cannot be delegated. Beyond the discussion of the issue itself is the question of why the government was seeking to create such a position. The opposition believed that the post of commander of the military forces was tailor-made for General Oviedo and that the government intention was to give him even more power over the armed forces.

To prevent this, the opposition-controlled Congress rescinded the law and reinstated the earlier one. The executive vetoed the military law bill, the Congress overrode the veto, and the executive then resorted to the Supreme Court alleging that the bill was unconstitutional because Congress could not simultaneously rescind a law, reinstate an old one, and modify it. The Colorado-controlled Supreme Court ruled in favor of the executive.

This allowed Vice-Admiral Eduardo González Petit to retain the post of commander of the military forces to which he was named by former president Rodríguez and confirmed by President Wasmosy. It also opened a yet unfinished debate on a new law of the armed forces which is still being discussed in the lower house.

In a way, the Paraguayan military has demonstrated a remarkable ability to adjust to the new situation and play by the rules of democracy. The institution has accepted a certain degree of subordination to civilian rule, a civilian commander in chief, and the concept of military subordination to civilian rule. Also, confronted with some budget cuts and drastic changes in the chain of food supplies, the military, although grudgingly, has accepted congressional decisions. The military has also accepted congressional rejection of a major salary increase for 1995.

Yet, in other areas, military prerogatives are quite significant. On the one hand, purely institutional concerns, such as the budget, prestige, respect, and so on, are voiced by authorized spokespersons. But, when high-level military officers up for promotion were invited by the Senate Defense Committee to appear before it, the president and commander in chief—in reaction to pressures from the military—denied them permission to appear, on the pretext that the officers were not to "parade" before the Senate. According to the constitution, however, promotions to the rank of colonel and higher need Senate approval.

The military question in Paraguay does not have only an institutional dimension. There is also the constant intervention of the powerful General Lino C. Oviedo, the German-trained cavalry officer who played a key role in the 1989 coup, personally arresting General Stroessner, and who rose through the ranks from colonel to major general in four years. He is now commander of the army and is considered the main architect of the Wasmosy triumph. It is a well-known secret that General Oviedo harbors presidential ambitions, and his meddling in party politics is as evident as it is pervasive. General Oviedo is surely acting in a personal capacity, but if the institution is not strong enough to stop him from getting involved in party politics now, how is the officer corps going to react if and when confronted with a conflict between respect for the constitution and the military institution and loyalty to their commander and his personal leadership? In this climate of uncertain loyalties, Oviedo continues to expand his influence in the armed forces, promoting his loyalists to high positions and demoting his adversaries.

Until recently, it was clear that Oviedo and Wasmosy maintained a close relationship. Yet recent developments suggest that Wasmosy's 1998 plans might not include Oviedo's candidacy, and therefore the question becomes how far General Oviedo can go in his attempt to control political developments in the Colorado Party so as to ensure his candidacy for 1998. Some observers suggest that Oviedo supporters are behind the wave of social unrest discussed in the next section, and that their main objective is to destabilize the Wasmosy government and create the conditions for his impeachment.

At the end of 1994, tensions within the military and between General Oviedo and President Wasmosy rose to unprecedented levels, threatening the rupture of the process. The crisis erupted over the transfer of General Carlos Ayala, commander of the First Infantry Division, a key garrison located in the outskirts of Asunción, to a remote outpost in the Chaco. President Wasmosy canceled General Oviedo's order for the transfer, which led to a virtual insubordination of Oviedo, who placed his loyal troops on high alert and deployed a force of tanks to neutralize the main air force base located in Asunción. Wasmosy received the support of the navy, the police, and the air force, which managed to arm and disperse a significant number of its T-33, Xavante, and Tucano war planes in preparation for combat. The crisis was settled on still unclear terms, though General Ayala was retained as commander of the First Infantry Division.

Less than two weeks later, another crisis developed when once again General Oviedo placed his troops on high alert. It was unclear whether he was preparing to launch a coup or whether he was preparing to resist what he thought was an incoming presidential decision to retire him. The proportions of this move led Brazilian President Fernando Henrique Cardoso to issue a statement warning that a coup was unacceptable and would throw Paraguay into regional isolation including its exclusion from the MERCOSUR (Southern Cone Common Market). This is the first time that a Brazilian government issued such a strong statement in defense of democracy in Paraguay and played a significant role in deterring its interruption. The crisis was overcome when General Oviedo apparently received assurances that his retirement was not being considered.

Although it seems that General Oviedo's base of power suffered a considerable erosion as a result of the latest events, the issue remains his still unprecedented influence and the lack of control over him. Although the number of officers opposing his ambitions seems to be considerable, the strength of the troops he commands, his popularity in a segment of the armed forces, and the wealth at his disposal give him a powerful position. Will Wasmosy be able to send him into retirement? Will he accept it without a major military confrontation? As we enter a period of unstable equilibrium between Wasmosy and Oviedo, this remains perhaps the major cloud hanging over the political process in Paraguay.

The Social Question: Rising Popular Demands

If the political climate evolved from confrontation to some sort of cohabitation to a new climate of confrontation, the social climate followed a different path. The Wasmosy government began its term without major social pressures. However, as time went on, social demands began to increase. First, the discussion of a new labor code produced a high-intensity confrontation between labor and business. The Senate passed a compromise bill that lowered tensions significantly, but the issue is still pending as the bill is up for consideration in the lower house.

Immediately thereafter the discussion of the 1994 budget produced another series of confrontations. Teachers demanded a 40 percent salary increase, and so did doctors and nurses employed in public hospitals, and later all public employees. The issue was resolved successfully through salary increases ranging from 3.5 percent to 15.5 percent.

But the most serious episode of social unrest was yet to come. It began in mid-February 1994 and was connected with the problem of landless peasants and low prices for agricultural products. At that point, and as the harvest approached, the traditional demand for land was coupled with the cyclical issue of the price of cotton. Cotton is grown by a large majority of Paraguayan peasants, some 250,000 to 260,000 families, and is their main cash crop. After three consecutive years of bad prices, adverse climate, and a diversity of pests, the peasantry is looking for a way to recoup previous losses. Even though prices are comparatively good, peasants are asking for higher ones.

Unhappy with the situation, peasants began to occupy roads, interrupting the normal flow of traffic in demand for higher cotton prices. On a number of occasions there were confrontations with police, and, although the level of police repression was not unusually high, the risk of fatalities has been significant. The peasants' demands faced a government that insisted it could do nothing about it and cotton exporters that demanded a more competitive exchange rate.

As the pressure kept mounting, peasants organized a large rally in the capital city of Asunción for March 15. Despite an all-out government campaign aimed at hindering its organization and the transportation of people to Asunción, the march was a great success, and some fifteen thousand peasants gathered before parliament. Students and labor leaders supported the march and closed public roads in solidarity with the peasants. Throughout the streets of Asunción, the outpouring of popular support for the marchers was evident.

At the same time, the major labor confederations called a general strike for May 2, demanding an across-the-board 40 percent salary increase. It was the first general strike in thirty-six years.

In short, Paraguay is witnessing a wave of unprecedented social unrest, the product of long-repressed social demands that are exploding in the climate of political freedoms that characterizes democratic systems. The number of land occupations, road closings, strikes, marches, and other such measures has increased dramatically. The perception among the wealthy is that the situation may be getting out of control. What makes all this even more significant is that it goes along with a generalized sense of frustration with the current economic and social situation. In fact, at the end of January, a well-respected public opinion poll showed that for 75.4 percent of the population the economic situation was worse than it was under Stroessner. Only 33 percent of the people thought that, overall, things had improved after the coup; 34 percent considered that the general situation had deteriorated, and 33 percent felt that the situation remained the same.

In responding to this situation the government has two options: either it resorts to old-fashioned repressive tactics or it seeks reasonable solutions via effective policymaking. The temptation, perhaps even the dream, is to do away with "populist" pressures and pursue an iron-fist Cavallo or Büchi-style policy. Yet currently the government lacks the political support to do so, but it also lacks the political will to do something else. In such a situation, unless the government makes up its mind and does something, the growing disenchantment with the current situation will continue to encourage adventurers and social problems will become increasingly harder to solve.

Conclusions

The problems of governance in transitional Paraguay have three dimensions. One dimension is that of the extent to which the ruling coalition is willing to accept truly democratic procedures when those procedures are likely to throw them out of power. This is an issue of cost and benefits: in Dahlian terms, a question of the cost of toleration and the cost of repression. But it is also an issue of realigning the ruling coalition, as the meaning of "being out of power" varies from case to case. The working hypothesis is, then, that there are some sectors that are prepared to "survive" outside the bubble of state power in contrast to those that are so inextricably linked to a structure of power and graft that they are likely to resort to extreme measures to retain it.

The relationship between the government and the political opposition has revolved around such a dynamic. Until now the opposition's level of flexibility has been remarkable. By and large, the opposition supports the government insofar as it is the expression of the process of democratic transition. It supports it, as well, in an attempt to strengthen and enlarge the group of the ruling coalition that sees itself as able to survive and even do well when out of power. The opposition does not want any interruption of the process, and thus Wasmosy has strong supporters in that group. The opposition's main challenge is to entice government into cooperating in the democratization of the state, basically in the restructuring of the judiciary, the reform of the electoral system, and the reform of the state. Electoral legislation will also have to undergo changes and, most important, the electoral apparatus will have to be reorganized.

The second question revolves around the role of messianic military leaders who distort normal civic-military relations. The Oviedo case is reminiscent of the Aldo Rico or Mohamed Ali Seineldin cases in Argentina. But in Argentina the level of institutionalization of the military acted as a deterrent, while in Paraguay the level is much lower, and Oviedo is not a colonel but a major general and the commander of the army. To help in the removal of this threat the Congress is clearly separating the Oviedo case from all other civil-military issues and furthering an aggressive program of multilevel contacts with military officers. The lower house has invited a number of high-ranking officers to discuss the new military legislation. At the same time, the Senate Appropriations Committee is making a significant effort to improve salary allocation, redoubling investment efforts, and equalizing allocations so as to strengthen the more democratic sectors of the armed forces. The primary responsibility, though, falls on the executive and the armed forces themselves. Will the government do something? Will the armed forces as an institution be able to control this phenomenon? How long will the current unstable equilibrium last?

Complicating an already complex military scenario is the growing influence of drug trafficking, a significant risk factor. Paraguay has long been considered a drug route but not a major one. Lately, though, friction between the U.S. and Paraguayan governments has developed over the effectiveness of Paraguayan efforts at combating that scourge. The late 1994 assassination of retired General Ramón R. Rodríguez, the chief of Paraguay's Drug Enforcement Agency, by some of his own people raised questions about the extent to which the local police and armed forces could be infiltrated by drug traffickers. Well-respected observers believe that some in the military are still involved in illegal trade rings which, while not intended for drug purposes, are prime cover schemes used by drug traffickers. If this threat is not dealt with effectively, a further and formidable obstacle for the successful completion of the transition to democracy is likely to develop.

Finally, there is the question of managing the rising social demands. In and of themselves, social demands could be manageable. But, when mixed with the political elements discussed above, the possibility of their being manipulated for nondemocratic goals is high. Yet, as manipulators cannot be wished away, the government must begin to do away with the underlying problems. As the government continues to ignore the social question, labor organizations keep growing and the business sector becomes increasingly fearful of labor instability, which leads to delaying badly needed investment decisions. Deactivating conflicts by meeting grievances with effective solutions should be the answer, but the government seems not to understand this.

Overall, the prospects for the medium term, although not good, are not necessarily bad. A great deal depends on the intelligence, flexibility, patience, and firmness of three actors: the presidential entourage, the parliamentary opposition, and the highest echelons of the military establishment. The decisions that they must make need to strike a balance between the absolute necessity to establish democratic rules for a democratic game—which means equal opportunity for all parties to accede to power through elections—and the guarantee that the strategic interests of all parties will be duly contemplated.

Therefore, both positive and negative inducements are needed. It is essential to strengthen within the ruling coalition a sector willing to risk democratization, even if that means they lose "power." It is also necessary to raise the cost of any possible authoritarian adventure. International organizations and great powers must send unmistakable signals that any coup will throw the country into total isolation, as the Brazilian government did so effectively and in such a timely fashion at the end of 1994. Cooperation to strengthen democratic institutions is also critical. Finally, there is also necessary a great deal of "thoughtful wishing," that happy expression coined by Abraham F. Lowenthal, for the issue of democratic governance in Paraguay is a complex one and ought to be the subject of a deeper reflection that transcends the day-to-day pressure of politics.

Epilogue: A Civilian President without Civilian Rule

Only a year after writing this chapter, the overall prospects for the transition process look significantly more somber. The Wasmosy government was greatly discredited as a result of its inability to steer the country into a process of economic growth, and as a consequence its authority is constantly challenged by General Lino Oviedo's state of virtual insubordination. Even more than a year ago, the Paraguayan transition continued to be characterized by having a civilian president but no civilian rule, a democratic constitution but not the full rule of law, a powerful ruler but a weak president, and a strong opposition that cannot use its majority to the full extent lest it lead to the further weakening of the president and the interruption of the process.

Only one important development can be counted on the positive side: after much give and take, the new nine-member Supreme Court was sworn in. Made up of four members identified with the opposition, four with the government, and one Colorado of independent background accepted by the opposition, the new court must now proceed to restructure the entire judiciary, a long and complex task. The new three-member Supreme Electoral Tribunal was also set up in a similar fashion, with one Colorado, one liberal, and one independent.

On the negative side, however, the list of developments is long. Social and economic problems continued to increase, and no progress was made in solving the agrarian question. Furthermore, the combination of corrupt and inept financial management led first to the "robbery" of some U.S.$4 million from the central bank vault (only one employee has so far been charged) and then to the collapse of four banks, which thus far has cost U.S.$300 million of taxpayers' money to honor public debts. As the inability of the government to attain a minimum degree of policy coherence became increasingly evident, the government engaged in a systematic campaign to blame the Congress for all the country's ills. A weak and isolated executive resorted to the cheap tactic of portraying everything, from the lack of a clear economic policy to the ineptitude of the public sector, as the failure of the Congress. The hard-liners within the ruling coalition, as if in a well-orchestrated campaign, jumped to the "logical" conclusion that the country would be better off without a Congress, that is, without democracy. As a result, dissatisfaction with the government is at risk of growing into a full-blown alienation from the democratic system.

In a way, Wasmosy's difficulty in coming to terms with an opposition almost eagerly willing to help him out of the critical situation he created is a function of the deep division within his party's ranks between the followers of his vice-president, Angel Seifart, the more democratic wing of the party, and those betting on the 1998 presidential candidacy of General Lino Oviedo. The Seifaristas are more willing to engage in a cooperative relationship with the opposition, while the Oviedistas adopt two-thirds of Wasmosy's already small group of supporters in the Senate and retain little, if any, political support in the party. With such a small power base, Wasmosy lacks the ability to engage in any substantive agreement with the opposition short of a straightforward coalition government, anathema in Colorado circles.

On the other hand, General Oviedo continues to meddle in politics, in defiance of constitutional and legal provisions. He once again challenged President Wasmosy in early September, placing his troops and tanks on high alert when a judge charged him with violating the law prohibiting the military from engaging in party politics and word spread that Wasmosy would retire him. Wasmosy backed down, and Oviedo's lawyers resorted to legal chicanery to impugn the judge and force the case to be moved to another judge who, within hours, dismissed the case.

Wasmosy's political-military problems are a reflection of the internal power struggle within the Colorado Party not only among his would-be supporters (Seifaristas and Oviedistas) but also between these two groups and the rest of the party apparatus. In fact, the upcoming elections for party leaders will confront the official sector with the challenge of winning over Argaña's supporters, the only way to support the claim that the government is the legitimate representative of the party. Yet all existing evidence points to a distinct Argaña lead. In short, Wasmosy, with his supporters divided and in the minority, must confront a solid and united Argañista front that is in the majority.

As this situation unfolds, the challenges become greater and more complex. The opposition must:

1. Support an unpopular and weak president in order to guarantee the completion of the process;

2. Figure out how to deal with President Wasmosy who does not rule, General Oviedo who should not rule, and Vice-President Seifart who cannot rule;

3. Struggle to achieve true civilian rule and the definitive severance of the incestuous relationship between some military leaders and a sector of the Colorado Party without alienating the rest of the armed forces, when the president himself is unwilling to reassert his prerogatives as commander in chief;

4. Withstand the legitimate pressure of the popular sectors that demand clearer policies toward social problems and justify postponing their solution for the sake of stability;

5. Persuade the economic elites that democracy is a workable system for achieving economic reform, while living with governmental excuses to do little to move the country away from statism in order to retain what little support it has among public employees;

6. Be able to go on and on, from no. 1 to no. 5, for the next three years; and

7. Develop a strategy to ensure an opposition alliance capable of achieving a clear-cut victory in the forthcoming elections over the forces of a party that—whether led by Argaña, Oviedo, or Seifart—offers no alternative for real change.

The successful completion of the transition depends on this last item. The EN proposed a united front with the PLRA based on using a method similar to Argentina's FREPASO (National Solidarity Front) or Chile's Concertación Democrática to select candidates. If accepted, this would imply holding primary elections with open rolls in which candidates for a united state would be selected from PLRA and EN lists. Both parties would support the candidates thus elected and present lists based on the proportion of the votes won by each of them.

There has been no peaceful transfer of power from one party to another in Paraguay's 185 years of independent history. For such a transfer to occur, there would need to be both an overwhelming electoral victory and as wide-based and strong a political front as possible. Whether or not that is to be achieved remains to be seen.

8

Uruguay: From Restoration to the Crisis of Governability

Juan Rial

The stability of Uruguayan democracy was historically rooted in an anticipatory style of government that preempted social demands by dealing with them before they had a chance to manifest themselves.[1] The role of the state was preeminent: state intervention was used to "correct" social inequalities and to deflect sociopolitical unrest. This was coupled with a strict separation of church and state, which officially took place in 1919 with the reform of the constitution, but which had gradually been incorporated into the political culture of the country and the mores of its inhabitants since the end of the nineteenth century. Despite the recent efforts of organizations such as Opus Dei on the one hand and movements such as *basismo* (grass-roots Catholic movements) and liberation theory on the other, the Catholic Church could not permeate social habits and political action. An imperfect welfare state[2] buffered tensions and social conflict, while, at the political level, institutional and political engineering created a model based on power sharing between the two major political parties, the Colorado Party and the National Party.

The principle of coparticipation (minority party representation in all paths of institutional life, from the boards of directors of public enterprises to the state bureaucracy) gave the opposition a share in the system but also colonized the state apparatus and impeded the formation of a neutral civil service.[3] The party apparatus is thus hidden inside the state bureaucracy. To maintain this equilibrium born of consensus, interparty pacts were complemented by formulas of political engineering destined to deal with intraparty conflicts and factionalism.[4] Thus, since 1924 Uruguayan electoral laws do not allow ticket splitting, forcing voters to choose all candidates—for local government and for the legislative and executive branches—from the same party (*lema*). The so-called double simultaneous vote (*doble voto simultáneo*) effectively hinders the potential multiplication of parties, making it more convenient for political actors to make alliances within the existing parties than to create new political organizations.[5]

This political system was based on the riches generated by an agrarian economy. The Uruguayan welfare state was financed by economic profits from very favorable external conditions, especially the two world wars and the Korean conflict.[6] When the Uruguayan economy proved unable to adapt to adverse international economic conditions, the politics of extreme consensus that guaranteed democratic stability proved a hindrance and was at the very heart of the country's social and political stagnation. In the 1960s, Uruguayans began to realize that there were limits to equitable social welfare in an underdeveloped economy. The country entered an era of radicalism and ideological polarization as different groups fought to maintain what they perceived as their entitlement to happiness, upward social mobility, and well-being. Organized political violence erupted with the National Liberation Movement (Tupamaros) and other lesser groups.[7]

In 1973, after a long coup that lasted from February to June, the armed forces took control of the country. After 1976 a collegial military-technocratic group attempted to rule the country.[8] The armed forces, however, proved unable to produce an alternative political model and maintained only a very harsh, twelve-year-long "commissarial" dictatorship.[9] Repression alone is never enough. The military was very effective in creating a culture of fear,[10] which served only to paralyze the citizenry; it could not provide the necessary foundation for a new political system. It was therefore relatively easy to restore democracy during the transition process as, despite appearances, many of the country's basic political structures had remained unscathed.[11]

Negotiations between the military and members of the political class resulted in a restoration. As with the nineteenth-century political situation, widely used at the time as a metaphor of current events, the idea was to go back to that point in history where the fracture had taken place and consider the period of military rule as a mere interruption in the normal course of events. Although the main goal of political leaders was to return to a well-known—and safe—political path, they were forced to admit that important changes had taken place during twelve years of authoritarian rule.

The process of negotiation concluded with an election. However, two of the main leaders of the opposition were forced to choose candidates to represent them, as they were forced out of the electoral contest by regulations of the military government still in power. This very special election was won by Dr. Julio María Sanguinetti, who had been the main political negotiator of the transition.[12]

During the first term of Sanguinetti's presidency (1985–90), many tasks of restoration were undertaken. The country returned to the practice of political consensus, while, little by little, the citizenry, recuperating from the strain of the previously pervasive culture of fear, regained confidence in the guarantees of the *état de droit*. In April 1989 this process was completed when the issue of human rights abuses during the military era was put to rest with the passage of the Law-Bill of Amnesty for the Military.[13]

Most of the work of President Sanguinetti centered on managing civil-military relations. Dealing with the legacy of the past consumed four of the five years of his term. As a result, politicians were extremely prudent in their management of the state and in public policymaking. There were no great innovations in economic or social policy. Nonetheless, the reform measures recommended by the so-called Consensus of Washington were cautiously carried out.[14] Governability was guaranteed by the factions of the Colorado Party that followed President Sanguinetti and by a temporary alliance over key issues with Por la Patria, the main sector of the National Party, which was led until his death by Wilson Ferreira Aldunate.

Thanks to this basic agreement, Sanguinetti was able to pass some essential laws that enabled him to govern and begin anew, especially the budgetary law and the law of Amnesty. Other attempts at reform had to be postponed. The president used his veto power to control parliamentary initiatives to increase public expenditures. To forestall pressures from the different political groups that supported him, Sanguinetti was also forced to shoulder much of the burden of administration personally. His tenure in office was characterized by a strong executive that retained control over all important decisions in the hands of the president. Although the constitution states that in certain cases—for example, when discussing and approving budgetary laws—the executive must assume a quasi-parliamentary form by convening the full Council of Ministers, Sanguinetti never implemented these constitutional precepts.[15]

On November 26, 1989, Dr. Luis Alberto Lacalle, a candidate of the National Party, was democratically elected president.[16] Even more important, Dr. Tabaré Vázquez, a Broad Front candidate, was elected mayor of Montevideo, the capital city, where half the country's population lives. With the uneventful alternation of parties in power, the transition process ended. In the same election, the constitution was amended in a measure commonly known as the Plebiscito de los Jubilados (plebiscite on retirees). In a sense, it synthesized and presaged many of the problems and challenges that Uruguayan democracy would have to face during the next period. This addendum to the constitution specifies two conditions for increasing retirement pensions: they must be increased when public sector wages are raised and the index to be used for the increase is the average wage index, which includes private sector salaries. The second condition means that retirees are to receive higher increases than public employees. Moreover, 2 percent of the GNP (gross national product) must be allocated to pay for this reform. The plebiscite on retirees passed with 81 percent of the vote.

The New Challenges Faced by Uruguayan Democracy

Perhaps one of the greatest challenges the country has to face stems from its very demographics. With a total population of almost 3 million, the active economic population is only 1.2 million. While nearly a million persons contribute to an unreformed Social Security system, there are 600,000 pensioners and retirees and nearly 300,000 public servants.[17] The average voter age in the 1994 general election was forty-two. Middle-aged and overeducated, Uruguayans fear and resist change, even though they have experienced many transformations in their everyday life over the last few years.

Thus President Lacalle's government undertook a program of economic adjustments based on fiscal reform. This course of action included an increase in the value added tax (VAT)[18] to finance the deficit-ridden Social Security system, modernization and enhancement of tax collection and tax control procedures, steady reduction of public expenditures, and a monetary policy aimed at reducing the amount of money in circulation in order to control inflation. These policies have achieved some important goals. Compared to 1992, economic growth decreased in 1993 but again increased in 1994.[19] Inflation continues to show a slow decrease,[20] even if the country has not reached the lower levels of inflation of most Latin American countries.

The Economic Commission for Latin America (CEPAL) has therefore placed Uruguay among the countries in a state of "controlled instability." The government deficit in 1995 was only 1.3 percent of GNP.[21] In 1993, real wages of public employees increased 7 percent and those of workers in the private sector 3.3 percent. In 1994, private sector salaries increased 1.1 percent and public sector salaries 0.6 percent. In 1995, real wages decreased 2.2 percent for the private sector and 2 percent for public employees. However, the imbalance of exports and imports (–6 percent and +8 percent respectively for 1993) preoccupies economic groups of exporters and industrialists as the commercial deficit was U.S.$680 million in 1993, U.S.$613 million in 1994, and nearly U.S.$847 million in 1995. Meanwhile, groups of entrepreneurs such as importers and financiers are flourishing.

The economic policies of the Lacalle administration have contributed to the decline of the traditional agrarian sector. On the other hand, as both an effect of Uruguay's participation in Mercado Común del sur (MERCOSUR, Southern Cone Common Market) and the weakness of the U.S. dollar in the region, the internal market has been flooded by imports that have accelerated the country's deindustrialization. As a result of both these factors, Uruguay has increasingly evolved into a service economy.

Thus many of the hopes that had been placed on the process of economic integration have been disappointed. Many entrepreneurs, especially small business owners, and whole groups of workers facing potential layoffs are afraid of the effects this process might have on their interests. This fear has led to a short-term alliance of entrepreneurs and workers in opposing what they perceive as the harsher aspects of the economic policy of the Lacalle government. They also demand some measure of protection against the undesired effects of free trade.

Social inequality has slightly increased over the past few years as there has been a tendency toward income concentration at the top.[22] Sectors below the line of extreme poverty are still minor compared to other countries of the region. However, the vulnerability of previously well-off middle-class sectors has become an urgent problem that must be tackled before it evolves from a social issue into a political problem. The government has launched a series of programs—basically administered through organizations outside and parallel to the state structure—to deal with questions related to extreme poverty: basic health care, education, and housing. But no such programs exist to help and support the sinking middle class, and this is a potential source of political unrest.[23]

The Lacalle administration's original program included reform of the state as one of its main components, but the government was unable to form the political alliances that would have enabled it to implement the proposed changes. Although the administration negotiated a temporary alliance with key sectors of the Colorado Party to pass the law of public enterprises that established the legal framework for privatizing some public enterprises, this coalition could not be sustained after a popular initiative to hold a referendum on the law succeeded in overthrowing some of its articles. In 1992 the Foro Batllista, led by former President Sanguinetti, formed a limited partnership with the Broad Front to oppose the law of public enterprises. The referendum was won by those that opposed privatization by a nearly two-thirds vote.[24]

The Lacalle administration was thus forced to use a dual strategy to achieve its ends. On the one hand, it reduced the size of the state by using a "default" option, banning the hiring of new employees and cutting the salaries of existing ones to make public employment less desirable. On the other hand, it created a structure that ran parallel to that of the state and was not hindered by the constraints and privileges of the public sector. This new structure was put under the administration's direct control and acts in those areas where quick and efficient state intervention is necessary.

Nevertheless, the main problem of the size and cost of the state remains untouched: Uruguay has three hundred thousand public employees, and the average monthly salary per employee is U.S.$240. Although public employment is an underpaid and low-prestige activity, the security it offers makes it a very sought-after occupation in a country where the measurable unemployment rate in 1993 was 8.3 percent and as high as 18 percent when informal activities are included. The squeezing of

Table 5 Uruguay: Economic Performance, 1985–1994

Year	GNP (millions of current U.S.$)	GNP Per Capita (current U.S.$)	Commercial Balance Index (millions of current U.S.$)	Payments Balance (millions of current U.S.$)	Wages Index	Unemployment (%)	Inflation Rate (%)
1985	4.719	1.569	145.8	−64.8	100	12.0	74
1986	5.859	1.937	217.8	256.4	81	10.1	70
1987	7.330	2.409	40.4	44.5	71	9.1	62
1988	7.583	2.478	227.7	73.1	64	8.6	71
1989	7.992	2.598	396.0	94.6	80	8.0	101
1990	8.355	2.700	350.0	80.9	95	8.5	106
1991	10.041	3.226	−31.8	−237.0	111	8.9	85
1992	11.849	3.785	−342.6	120.0	72	9.0	61
1993	13.453	4.272	−680.4	182.8	61	8.3	56
1994	15.543	4.908	−859.1	238.0	46	9.2	45

Source: Central Bank of Uruguay and Instituto Nacional de Estadísticas.

salaries in the public sector has bred discontent among workers: the Lacalle administration has had to deal with increased labor conflicts and strikes of state employees.

There have been several important labor conflicts during the Lacalle administration.[25] However, the most significant challenge in this area stems from major changes within the trade union movement itself. In fact, the labor movement, formerly dominated by the Left and highly centralized in the PIT-CNT (Interunion Workers Council–Workers National Caucus), has suffered three major transformations. First, it has lost the power to raise active and favorable support for its positions and directives among workers and the general public. Second, some trade unions belonging to the federation of organized labor are acting autonomously, disregarding the centralized levels of decision making within the movement and favoring those issues more directly related to the concerns of the sector or enterprise to which they belong. Finally, within the trade union movement, the tendency toward a polarization of the positions that divide moderates from radicals has increased. The PIT-CNT is also facing a financial crisis that clearly reflects the weakening of the power it held over salaried workers: plagued with huge debts, it cannot obtain more money from its affiliates because many federated trade unions have inflated membership lists that do not correspond to the scant levels of support they can raise.[26]

In the future the present structure of the organized labor movement will probably lose most of its current elements. The empty shell will then fall under the control of the more radical factions, further alienating the old organizational structures from newer worker groups. Perhaps new structures will emerge to promote the interests of these workers: the new trade unions may be much more directly linked to the problems and concerns of the workplace itself. Thus the association between trade union and enterprise may be stronger than it is now,[27] while the traditional links between unions and leftist parties or movements may be weakened.

The armed forces are another institution that has endured profound transformations during the last few years. After a series of crises that included military unrest, isolated acts of armed propaganda, the Berríos scandal,[28] the dismissal of the commander in chief of the army, the transfer of two generals to other posts, and the freeze on several promotions of senior and junior officers, the military has entered a phase of internal reorganization. The attempts at professional reform necessarily meet a certain degree of resistance within an institution that still has difficulty in coming to terms with its recent past. However, another source of tension comes from the budgetary constraints the armed forces have to face. These restrictions entangle the issue for military reformers because structural innovations cannot be accompanied by changes in obsolete equipment. The military is carrying on an internal discussion on this matter; it has thus become a conflict of interest among the generals rather than a civil-military issue.

Lieutenant General Daniel García, the commander in chief of the army in the last years of Lacalle's administration, reformed the institution by suppressing the mounted cavalry regiments and transforming them into modern combat units. García was one of the promoters of Uruguayan participation in United Nations peacekeeping forces.[29] This issue has divided the generals while winning acceptance among junior and middle-rank officers, who perceive it as a source of extra income and professional practice. García has also said that the army should be managed as a modern enterprise, and he intends to sell some of its valuable property in order to help pay the cost of internal restructuring. However, these funds will not be sufficient to implement his entire reform program. In 1995, the new army commander, Lieutenant General Juan C. Curuchet, slowed down the process of reform.

The navy has also been undergoing a deep process of transformation. This branch of the military was the first to sign an agreement with the civilian university to modify its own curricula and make them equivalent to those of the university, and was also the first to incorporate women into its ranks. Open to outside influences, the navy has tried to obtain equipment through agreements with countries such as Germany, France, and the United States. Internally less divided than the army, the naval high command wants to accelerate the navy's modernization, thus diminishing the traditional gap between its forces and those of the army.

The air force is no challenge for either of them. It suffers from a chronic shortage of equipment, has no external clout among politicians, and has an unfavorable position vis-à-vis the other two services. Traditionally, the air force has sought to play second fiddle to the army.

Last but not least, the former leftist guerrillas that took arms against institutional order in the 1960s and 1970s are now fully, if negatively, integrated into the system. The National Liberation Movement (Tupamaros) forms the axis of the radical pole within both the Broad Front coalition and the organized labor movement. The bearer of a high-voltage discourse that defends the main tenets of the ideology of the extreme Left, the Tupamaros have nonetheless renounced violence as a convenient political means. The movement has also polarized positions within the leftist coalition, increasing tensions among more moderate groups that want to adopt a more realistic attitude toward the exercise of political power.

The Political Scenario

The framework of electoral rules that regulate Uruguayan political life has only slightly changed since 1925 when the first electoral laws gave guarantees to voters by creating the Electoral Court and the Permanent Civic Register. These laws also implemented the system of "accumulation" designed in 1910 that shaped political parties that are in fact federations of factions covering a wide ideological spectrum and including significant intraparty rivalries among leaders.

Since the constitutional reform of 1967, elections are held every five years for political offices at all levels of government (executive, legislative, and local).[30] Except for the *juntas departamentales* (local councils), proportional representation is used to assign seats in Congress, while executive office, at both the local and national levels, is won by simple majority. The electoral system allows the accumulation of votes among factions (*sub-lemas*) of the same party (officially called *lema* in the electoral jargon of the country) in order to win the presidency (*doble voto simultáneo*, or double simultaneous vote). By this procedure, after counting the ballots in an election, electoral officials must first determine which party has won the election. The candidate of the majority faction of the winning party is then elected to the presidency. The same procedure is used to determine the seats in Congress. Here the first step (called *primer escrutinio*) is to ascertain how many seats have been won by each party through proportional representation. Once this information is known, seats are allocated to each faction using first a quotient and then a modified D'Hondt formula.

Voters cannot choose freely among candidates from different parties for offices at different levels of government. Thus, in the Uruguayan system, parties are seen as self-contained and separate entities: voters must elect one among the different candidates within the same *lema* but cannot trespass the boundaries of the party to select a mayor or a list for Congress from another party. No ticket splitting is allowed under any circumstances.[31] Due to the simultaneity of the different electoral processes, there is a bandwagon effect as the national election influences the local election. This system also gives preeminence to the party leaders, as the first real election is held at the moment of drawing up the list of candidates.

The rules have not changed since 1925, so there is no regulation of political campaigns with regard to the length of the campaign, financing of political parties, or use of the media. The law forbids electoral propaganda forty-eight hours before election day; polls are not regulated except for forbidding electoral propaganda; and only one provision regulates party fund raising. While the government pays each political party U.S.$7 per vote received,[32] there are no limits on political contributions from private citizens, businesses, or interest groups.

Nor is there any provision for monitoring elections using international observers or delegations, as this was not a common practice in the 1920s and 1930s. The normal practice in Uruguay since 1925 has been to have party representatives monitoring the whole process on election day. Until 1980, polling station workers were also designated by political parties. Since then they have been recruited among public employees—usually clerks, teachers, and professors—to speed up the process and make it more efficient. Vote counting is public: any citizen can watch the procedure. After the first counting of the ballots, they can be recounted by the electoral authorities if there are challenges. Exit polls and quick counts, by both parties and the media, are a normal practice. Voting is mandatory, and heavy sanctions for those not participating are strictly enforced.[33] Therefore, voting rates are normally 80 percent or higher.[34]

Uruguay has a presidential system based on two key premises. First, continuous negotiation among all political actors is needed for the system to function; and, second, since the constitutional reform of 1967, the preeminence of the executive branch has increased. Only the executive branch has the right to introduce legislation in the areas of finance and the budget. As in any presidential system, the president has the right to veto acts passed by Congress. However, Congress can override a presidential veto by a two-thirds majority (86 out of 130 votes). This special majority is difficult to achieve in a fragmented party system.

Since 1934 some provisions have been made in the constitution aimed at altering the presidential system. These semiparliamentary mechanisms have not been able to function as intended. According to the constitution, Congress has the power to vote to censure one or more cabinet ministers, who must then leave the government. However, if the vote of censure carries by more than 51 percent but less than

66 percent in the General Assembly, and if the current administration is not in its first or last year of government, the president can retain his minister. If the president chooses this path, he or she must call for a parliamentary election within sixty days. Then the new Congress must confirm or reject the previous vote of censure. The presidential office itself is never jeopardized by this mechanism.

This institutional trend corresponds to the personalization of politics, which has come to be associated not with programs or identities closely linked to political parties but with particular personalities. While this tendency is universal, its impact on more traditional political life in Uruguay cannot easily be dismissed. On the one hand, it has increased the power of the real party leaders and diminished the importance of party structures, as presidential candidates do not depend on these structures to win the election. They rely more on the media to further their interests than on the old party bosses and branches. On the other hand, it creates tension with Congress, as legislators often try to encroach on the role of the executive by invading those areas reserved for the president's initiative in order to obtain some measure of visibility for themselves. The tensions between these two branches of government do not recur in their relationship to the judiciary. Uruguay follows the continental school on this matter: it is an *état de droit*, and the judiciary cannot create laws. Even jurisprudence has only an advisory role, and following its pronouncements is not mandatory.

This tendency toward a concentration of power in the executive branch is tempered by a trend toward direct democracy using the constitutional mechanism of referendum. The original idea of the political elite when writing the constitutional provision on referendums had been to enable the president to bypass Congress and appeal directly to voters when there was an institutional deadlock. However, since the referendum on the amnesty law for the military, the philosophy behind it has changed. Voters began to use this means as a way of colegislating when they did not agree with the actions of the politicians. While this trend has provided an important check on the possibility of an unbalanced exercise of power by the executive, it has also impeded many initiatives that need to be implemented if Uruguay is to outgrow its present stagnation. It has also increased the role and power of the media in the political arena. While this trend has not attained the dimensions it has in Argentina, politics is evolving into media politics in Uruguay. Meanwhile there are important shifts among the interest groups that control the media. Cable TV is being installed in Montevideo and its metropolitan areas, and important groups are fighting to be included in this new way of influencing public life.

After the election of 1994, political and electoral reform became the main priority. It is necessary to address the key issues of governability in the country: (1) In a context of party fragmentation, can the executive branch carry through a program without harmful interference on the part of Congress made only for the sake of publicity or to gain privileges for a political or corporate sector? (2) Can the executive branch have real, as opposed to formal, control of government policies? These issues must be addressed especially in order to prevent a process of "Fujimorization," as the next administration must face some problems that the Lacalle administration could not resolve. Among these are: (1) government reform, which includes trimming down the state bureaucracy and making it more efficient in its central administration as well as transforming many state enterprises into mixed-management operations; (2) reform of the Social Security system, which might entail some form of privatization of retirement funds and a curtailment of existing rights and privileges; (3) designing educational policies that conceive education as an investment and a competitive advantage for the country; (4) designing social policies that alleviate the worst effects of economic reform programs on the lower strata of society; and (5) the challenge of economic integration, even if at a slower pace, through agreements like MERCOSUR.

These and other issues will need governments that can govern. As the challenges the country must face increase, so also does the tendency toward a fearful conservatism on the part of the citizens. The results of the national election in 1994 were very significant: three parties obtained a similar number of votes and seats in the Congress.[35]

The newly elected president, Julio María Sanguinetti, faces a serious dilemma. Strong leadership will be needed to conduct the country through these turbulent times. The institutional setting does not enable politicians to exert this leadership without violating or at least bending constitutional precepts.

Existing institutional arrangements were designed to favor the interaction and mutual accommodation of two political parties. Reality shows that the citizenry today is divided into thirds. In addition to winning a solid one-third of the votes in the last election, the Left won, for the second time, the municipal election in Montevideo with 45 percent of the votes.

Given the new political scenario, Sanguinetti has inaugurated a new style of political action, betting that this new strategy will ensure the governability of the country. Instead of being the omnipresent decision maker in day-to-day matters—a style of government all too frequent in Latin American presidents—he is highlighting his position as head of state while reducing his public appearances as head of the government. In this, the style of his present administration varies significantly from the one he developed between 1985 and 1989.

In this new phase, Sanguinetti apparently allows greater autonomy to his ministers. However, this greater autonomy is curtailed by four factors. First there is the president himself. In certain cases, he directly indicates the boundaries of freedom he concedes to a given minister. In others, he merely suggests what these limits might be or uses one of his political operators—the unofficial "voices" of the president—to do so. The second element of control is provided by the existence of an unofficial head of government who acts on behalf of the president. Usually, this role is fulfilled by the minister of planning or the economic minister. Sometimes the secretary of state assumes the role of an unofficial prime minister. All these members of the executive have one trait in common: they lack independent political backing. They all fulfill roles that help preserve the political capital of the head of state. The third constraint to the autonomy of the ministers is internal: their portfolios lack both human and material resources. Therefore, it is very difficult for any official to introduce major innovations during his or her administration. Attempts at innovation are also reduced by the features of the political scenario: the division of the political arena into thirds forces politicians to act with extreme caution to obtain the necessary support of their peers.

The current situation dictates a coalition government. Sanguinetti has as his chief partner Dr. Alberto Volonté, the candidate of the National Party who received the most votes. Volonté is in fact paying the political cost of providing vital support to the Sanguinetti government while expecting to reap the benefits of such an alliance in the 1999 election.

This political mechanism—a coalition government, the separation of the functions of head of state from the day-to-day management of the state, and the strategic use of areas of autonomy for his ministers—provides Sanguinetti with the space necessary to dissociate himself from his party while preserving his own political capital. He knows he will use it in the coming years to help pass essential reforms and avert a crisis brought on by the unavoidable erosion of the coalition.

The plan of President Sanguinetti is to obtain a series of essential adjustments: reform of the state-controlled retirement system to open it partially to private initiative; reduction of the number of state employees; reform of the educational system to adapt it to new challenges; undertaking some needed public works, such as the bridge between Buenos Aires, the capital city of Argentina, and Colonia, a small Uruguayan city. Sanguinetti's main concern is to manage the administration of the country in an orderly way. This plan, which might seem unambitious, is fraught with difficulties because of the lack of institutional arrangements that could provide him with a majority in parliament and because of resistance from a Uruguayan society condemned to conservatism by its very demographics.

The new style of government of the Sanguinetti administration does not favor his own group, the Colorado Party. Although the internal life of the party is almost nonexistent between elections, it is still the only cohesive political organization that presents a united front on key issues. The oligarchy of power, in Robert Michels' terms, still works.[36] Some Colorado political groups have pointed out that their party has been losing twenty-five votes per day since 1984. Using the words of a well-known Uruguayan political scientist,[37] they say that the Colorado votes "go to heaven," as traditional Colorado supporters die of old age while the party is unable to attract younger voters. Those same groups warn that the Colorado Party may suffer an important defeat in the 1999 election if it does not take the steps necessary to attract these younger citizens with a stronger commitment to change.

The Left has inherited those votes lost by the Colorados. After the breakup of the Soviet Union, the Uruguayan Left went through a series of internal disputes involving its moderate and radical sectors. The internal structure of the Left changed between 1989 and 1994 because of the end of the cold war. The Uruguayan Communist Party ceased playing its traditional pivotal role. However, the Left did not disappear mainly because the existing traditional parties could not and would not incorporate into their own platforms political programs that called for maintaining a strong state that would provide social justice and equality. Therefore, the Left remained in the Broad Front.

Two competing strategies have been devised inside the organization to adapt and grow in the frame of changed circumstances. Tabaré Vázquez, the "new *caudillo*,"[38] the mayor of Montevideo (1989–94) who lost the presidency by sixty thousand votes, sees the possibility of invading a part of the political spectrum normally occupied by the traditional parties. This would be done by creating a new alliance, the Encuentro Progresista (Progressive Encounter), with dissident members of the traditional political organizations. His plan did not work well in 1994. The failure of the Encuentro Progresista to increase significantly the number of votes the Broad Front received on its own opened the door to a new grouping inside the leftist coalition, the Asamblea Uruguay (Uruguay Assembly). This somewhat amorphous group is an electoral movement of citizens more than a group of activists. Their leader, Danilo Astori, a technocrat lacking the popular appeal of Tabaré Vázquez, incarnates a discourse of moderation—a leftist sensibility turned toward social justice in the framework of "politics as the art of the possible" more than an ideological platform. His strategy to invade the space previously occupied by the traditional parties relies precisely on this moderation. He aims at co-opting voters, more than political leaders or structures, from the traditional organizations. His strategy is very effective in a conservative society that cringes at the rhetoric of the extremes after the trauma of the military era.

The rise of Astori has forced Vázquez to lean toward the more radical sectors of the Broad Front. Eventually this move might compromise his chances of winning the internal contest, as any radicalization of discourse makes him lose the support of moderate voters oriented toward an option at the center of the political spectrum. Curiously enough, under very changed sociopolitical circumstances, the conflict that opposes Vázquez and Astori is almost a replica of the confrontation between socialists and communists in the 1960s. Socialists always tried to invade the space of the traditional parties by co-opting dissident members of the establishment and the structures of the traditional organizations. Their efforts were always condemned to failure, as they forgot to include the voters in their political calculations. The failed experience of Unión Popular (Popular Union) in 1962, an alliance of the socialists with the dissident leader of the National Party, Enrique Erro, is perhaps the best example of this type of strategy. On the other hand, the communists, led by their secretary general, Congressman Rodney Arismendi,[39] tried to win the battle for the "hearts and minds" of sectors of the population discontent with politics as practiced by the traditional parties. The transfer of voters from the traditional parties to the Communist Party was permanent.

As for the National Party, it is torn by internal strife. There is an open conflict for party leadership that opposes former president Luis Alberto Lacalle—who wants to win a second presidential term in 1999—and Alberto Volonté, the "new *caudillo*" who emerged as a politician after a successful term as chief executive officer of UTE, the public utility that provides electricity for the country. Volonté has chosen to become the main partner of Sanguinetti in his coalition government. Lacalle also participates in the coalition but has publicly expressed his aversion to it. Political observers consider that he will try to leave the coalition when it is feasible.

This brief description of the situation of the political parties shows that there is urgent need to reform the prevailing institutional design. Contacts are being made to promote constitutional reform, but the outcome of this issue is uncertain.

Many things are still uncertain in Uruguay, a society torn by its desire to keep the achievements of the past while adapting the new circumstances. Uruguay ranks among the highly developed countries in terms of quality of life in the human development index created by the United Nations Development Program (UNDP), with an index of 0.881 in 1994.[40] One of the main goals of Uruguayan society is to preserve that quality of life by defending the social welfare mechanisms created in the past. This goal is extremely ambitious at a time when small countries such as Uruguay cannot make decisions without considering the pressures and conditions imposed by their larger neighbors, the international financial system, and multilateral agencies. Consequently, there is still room for the growth of an old leftist alternative such as the Broad Front. The challenge the political class should meet is how to effect the necessary changes in the state, the institutional arrangements, and the parties without generating social upheavals.

9

Argentina: Democracy in Turmoil

Liliana De Riz

A la memoria de esa experiencia debe su fuerza el orden socioeconómico y político que hoy vemos perfilarse; es el recuerdo aleccionador el que le da a la mayoría la fortaleza necesaria para soportar la ostentosa indiferencia de los sectores privilegiados por las penurias que siguen sufriendo los que no lo son, y ofrecer su acquiescencia a la progresiva degradación de las instituciones cuya restauración celebraron con tan vivas esperanzas hace diez años. Gracias a él, en suma la Argentina que ha logrado finalmente evadirse de su callejón se resigna a vivir en la más dura intemperie.

[The strength of today's socioeconomic and political order is due to the memory of that experience; it is the instructive memory which gives the majority the necessary strength to cope with the ostentatious indifference of the privileged sectors to the hardships suffered by those who are not privileged, and offer their acquiescence to the progressive degradation of the institutions whose restoration they celebrated with great expectations ten years ago. Thanks to it, the Argentina that was finally able to avoid its deadlock is now accepting to live in the most harsh conditions.]

—Tulio Halperín Donghi, *La agonía de la Argentina peronista*

For the third time in twelve years, Argentina has a democratically elected president. This is a remarkable achievement in a country in which political instability was the dominant feature for the main part of its contemporary history. For more than a decade, Argentina has moved away from economic decline and political authoritarianism.

While the principal task for the Radical Party was to restore the rule of law, it rested with the Peronists to straighten out the economy. In the May 1995 elections, Peronist president Carlos Menem was rewarded with a second term in office. Menem's success in controlling the hyperinflation that led the country to the brink of ungovernability in 1989 was the source of his renewed strength.

The economic reforms and their social cost under Menem's first administration have already been well analyzed.[1] So have some of the main features of the Argentine "hybrid" democracy that it brought about.[2] This chapter focuses on the political dynamics underlying Argentina's economic reforms under Menem, the uniqueness of Menem's leadership, the transformations of the country's party system, and the impact of constitutional reforms. All these features are essential to understanding the evolution of democratic governance in the near future.

At present, President Menem must confront the outbreak of financial crises in the provinces in the context of an unprecedentedly high unemployment rate, and he must do so in a drastically changed scenario that lacks the peace and confidence he enjoyed throughout his first term in office and that is now reshaped by the new constitutional rules.

Menem's second term raises some crucial questions regarding the condition of democratic governance in the near future: will he be able to lead a nation with growing social costs resulting from economic reforms? Will he be able to control the political conflict that, far from declining, has exploded inside Peronism? To put it differently: will it be possible for Menem to manage a second presidential term in which the discretionary exercise of power must be replaced by constant negotiations both within and outside party ranks? Will new constitutional rules contribute to reshaping presidential powers? What lessons did the parties learn from twelve years of democracy and economic reforms?

This chapter explores the factors that underlie the answers to these questions. It is necessary to recognize, however, that political reflection, at a time when a society is experiencing a succession of critical episodes, needs to adopt a double and simultaneous reflection: in order to see the present, it is imperative to look back at the past and try to capture those elements that the present reactivates. Nevertheless, current circumstances make tentative assessments prone to be disproven by coming events.

The Politics of Economic Crisis

The Construction of Presidential Authority

President Menem, who emerged from the first primary elections to win the presidency democratically, came to power with the extraordinary resources bestowed on him by the situation of hyperinflation and by having been elected by a political movement that defined itself as the interpreter of national and popular tradition. With this political capital, he crafted a coalition strategy toward the Right of the political spectrum. The uniqueness of his governing style, which was based on a powerful coalition that encompassed the large unions (initially in charge of the Ministry of Labor) and the sectors that emerged as the most representative of economic power, conferred on him inordinate autonomy vis-à-vis his party. This allowed him to create and recreate his cabinet and to react to the situation with strong pragmatism.[3] The members of his administration professed to be free of any conditioning that did not properly stem from the will of the president. Quickly the concentration of political power in the hands of the president reached an extraordinary dimension.

During the first two years of his administration and as a consequence of the absence of cooperation strategies to moderate the distributive struggle, economic stability could not be achieved. The arrival of Domingo Cavallo at the Ministry of the Economy, toward the beginning of 1991, should be seen more as a response to the institutional crisis that had been unleashed by the so-called Swiftgate than as a response to inflationary turmoil. Corruption proceeded to occupy center stage, fueled by a shadowy process of privatizations, which were carried out by government officials who were protected by the great autonomy of action accorded to them by the economic emergency and by an architecture of power that was exclusively accountable to its own vertex, the president.[4] The resulting erosion of the supervisory capacity of the state contributed to weaken the already precarious autonomy of these powers. This situation resulted in lack of accountability and in horizontal control of executive decisions.[5]

The climate that surrounded the departure of the third minister of the economy, Erman González, was not favorable: the sudden increase in strength of the dollar and widespread skepticism, which was a combined product of the recessionary effects of the economic policy that was in place and of almost a decade of failed adjustment attempts, caused the disappearance of the "initial magic" of the government. The Cavallo plan to fix the exchange rate was approved by the Congress. This strategy bolstered confidence in the irreversible nature of the decision made regarding the exchange rate and the free convertibility of the currency.[6] Productivity was established as the defining criterion of wage levels with an eye toward delinking salaries from inflation, as much in the public as in the private sector.

The program was as successful in the economic arena, with an abrupt decline of inflation, as it was in the political one. The government won the congressional elections for the renewal of one-half of the Chamber of Deputies and the gubernatorial elections during the second half of 1991. The results of the elections, interpreted by the administration as an undeniable success, exhibited a decline in the electoral strength of Peronism compared to 1989, the loss of provinces like Salta, Chaco, and Santa Cruz, and the retention of political predominance in others, thanks to the *ley de lemas* (law of the *lemas*), which was implemented in eleven provinces (this electoral system was making its debut in the majority of these elections).[7]

Tax measures, which were approved by the Congress (unlike in the previous administration), together with deregulation of markets, liberalization of imports, and privatizations, created a closed economy with strong state intervention. The state achieved greater autonomy from social and economic actors (the convertibility law assures its own self-disciplining), but at the cost of an extreme personalization of political power. The direction undertaken remained tied to the ability of the executive to maintain its coalition of support and to stay in office.[8] Decisiveness, secrecy, and surprise—the three qualities that define a skillful politician, according to a saying attributed to the deceased Peronist *caudillo* from Catamarca, Vicente Saadi, whom Menem likes to recall—are the hallmark of the style with which this government exercises political power.

The June 1992 elections for senator of the federal capital were won by the Radical candidate. Fernando de la Rúa won 52 percent of the vote by picking up the support of Peronist voters as well as those from the Right and the Left.[9] President Menem's candidate did not manage to gain support from the Center (the bulk of the electorate in the capital). In light of these results, the hypothesis of the alternation in power took shape both inside and outside of Peronism. Economic stability remained at the margin of political competition: it was a common banner of the Radicals and the Peronists. What the elections seemed to show was a change in the social significance of state reform: the demand for a reduced and efficient state was transformed into a demand for the recreation of the state and the reining in of corruption. The resulting privatizations showed the need to create a state that would regulate private monopolies of public service providers and act as a guarantor of essential goods such as health and education. Demonstrations of support for the protests of teachers and pensioners, and for resistance to the practices of the private monopolies (for example, the marches against highway tolls) revealed the widespread uneasiness brought about by the reduced role of the state.

The management of the state itself was in the eye of the storm. An administration whose record included the Yoma case, the appointment of family members to government positions, disastrous municipal administration of the capital, disturbing personal biographies of its civil officials, and a false quorum in the Senate to get a vote on an important law (the *diputrucho*, or false deputy) was punished in the elections in the capital.[10] Presidential reelection, an aspiration of Menem's supporters that was announced early on, became an even harder-to-achieve objective. The results of the senatorial elections in the capital compelled the government to redefine its political agenda. It is in this context that the proposal for political reform was presented as a complement to the economic reform implemented by the government. The sudden injection of political reform into the public debate demonstrated the president's skill in putting the opposition on the defensive: participation, transparency, and representativeness became his banners. Institutional reforms and the means to carry them out—among them, the president's reelection—were portrayed as the instruments to guarantee continued economic stability.

Constitutional Reform

The year 1993 began with the government's announcing a new agenda that had political reform as its core. The first half of the year was marked by the debate over the official proposal in a rarefied climate as a result of certain Supreme Court rulings and the resignation of the minister of justice, Ricardo Arslanian, in open disagreement with the makeup of the Chamber of Annulment, a tribunal that was created by the new Code of Procedures in legal matters.[11]

The political reform bill presented by the minister of the interior, Gustavo Béliz, combined elements contained in a plethora of bills of the ruling party and the opposition.[12] The resignation of Minister Béliz in August, in the midst of a climate of aggression and threats to journalists, highlighted the shady side of the initiative. The text of his resignation reveals the use of corrupt procedures to achieve certain objectives, especially constitutional reform, and the actions of those operating at the periphery of the president's will, who were eager to pay any price in order to continue in power.

The elections of October 3, the second elections for the partial renewal of the national Chamber of Deputies, were preceded by the privatization of Yacimientos Petrolíferos Fiscales (Argentine Petroleum Company), which was carried out with the stated objective of improving the situation of pensioners just at the point of voting (there are approximately 4 million pensioners). The elections took place in a unique political context whose most outstanding aspects were the initiative to reform the constitution and secure the right of the president to be reelected, the scandal in the days prior to the elections involving the Supreme Court over the revoking of a court ruling in favor of a suit against the central bank, and the accusations of corrupt activities that affected those who headed the ruling party ballots in the capital and in the province of Buenos Aires.

The Peronists (PJ, Partido Justicialista) won the 1993 elections with 42.3 percent of the vote, over the 30 percent obtained by the Radicals (UCR, Radical Civic Union). The clear triumph of the PJ came as a rejection of any mechanical link between the severity of the economic adjustment implemented by Minister Cavallo and social discontent. Economic stability was collectively perceived as an achievement capable of neutralizing the impact of excluding growing sectors of the population from the rights of social citizenship, the accusations of corruption, and the scandals that shook the Supreme Court on the eve of the elections. From the perspective of the evolution of the national electoral map, these figures do not substantially alter the tendencies that were recorded up to 1991. However, a more disaggregated analysis of the results shows discontinuities with the pattern recorded since 1983, which is not readily evident from an overall perspective. Peronism managed to win in the capital, where Radicalism has traditionally predominated, with 32.5 percent of the vote compared to the 29.9 percent obtained by the UCR.[13]

In the strategic province of Buenos Aires, which comprises one-third of the electorate, the PJ won with 48.1 percent of the vote over the 25.9 percent obtained by the UCR. The UCR grew with respect to 1991, but its distance from Peronism grew as well. The overall registered tendencies confirm the emergence of a new process: Peronism conquered areas previously reserved for Radicalism, and Radicalism advanced in traditionally Peronist zones.[14] The results of the 1993 elections reveal the presence of a restructuring process of the representational system. This raises some issues: the consolidation of a conservative-popular coalition with a strong electoral predominance in the face of an array of dispersed opposition forces; a greater weight for the third forces to the Right and Left of the political spectrum (now that the parties of the Right are free from the influence exercised by the currently disintegrated UCEDE (Union of the Democratic Center), could they act with greater autonomy with respect to Peronism?); and the formation of a Center-Left coalition.

Interpreted from the perspective of the objective of constitutional reform, the results of the October elections indicated that the reform could be achieved only through negotiations among the main parties. However, the reaction of the government was to rush its reform bill through the Senate, achieving approval by means of a shady process of negotiations within Peronism and thanks to the decisive vote of the senator from the province of San Juan, Leopoldo Bravo. In exchange for this vote, the government abandoned premises that were fundamental to its original bill, such as the direct election of the president, and laid bare the fact that reelection was its only goal. In the Chamber of Deputies, on the other hand, Peronism fell short of rallying the two-thirds vote needed for passage.[15] The centerpiece of the institutional offensive launched by the government was to call for a plebiscite, in which the citizenry could declare itself in favor of or against constitutional reform.

Radicalism appeared before the public on the horns of a dilemma: either reaffirm its refusal to ratify the reform and thus face another electoral defeat in the plebiscite, or agree to negotiate (thereby avoiding an electoral contest) and resign itself to bestowing legitimacy on the reform, knowing as they did that the government was willing to approve a new constitution even without the endorsement of the opposition.[16]

The institutional offensive of Peronism settled into the void created by a party that was in crisis and dismayed by its electoral defeat. The faction led by Raúl Alfonsín decided to negotiate with the government. The negotiations, which took the public by surprise, did not occur in a vacuum: a good part of the Radical leadership began to lean toward a negotiated solution. However, the followers of Fernando de la Rúa in the capital and those of Federico Storani and Juan M. Casella in the province of Buenos Aires, as well as other recognized leaders at the national level, were opposed. Recognized once again as party leader, Alfonsín conducted the negotiations and crafted an agreement with Menem over the contents of the partial reform of the constitution. The immediate corollary of the so-called Olivos Pact was the suspension of the plebiscite. In early December, with 70 percent of the votes in favor, the national convention of the UCR approved the decision to negotiate the reform. The new bill saw the light of day shortly thereafter. The resignation of Supreme Court justices and negotiations over the appointment of new justices, both of which were opposition demands, were the framework of the accord. Once consensus was reached, the text was approved by the Chamber of Deputies and then by the Senate.

However, in the Senate, Peronists and Radicals rejected the modification of the length of a senator's term (from nine to four years), which formed part of the original basic points of agreement. This rejection fueled uncertainty about the binding nature of the accord. The debate began to revolve around the constitutionality of the procedure used to obtain the approval of the law and the powers that the future Constituent Assembly should have. Could the Assembly declare itself sovereign? Are the delegates obligated to respect the basic points of agreement of the Olivos Pact?[17] In a society in which political pacts were always labeled pejoratively as *contubernios* (concubinage, cohabitation), the agreement became the target of criticism that never wavered in reducing the significance of the agreement to the mere political ambition of its signatories. One of the principal arguments used by the critics of the Olivos Pact was that it meant the disappearance of political opposition.

The political pact once again posed an old dilemma in new terms: what is the role of the opposition in a political system that faces the challenge of redefining its constitution? Does an opposition that consents to presidential reelection necessarily give up its role as the opposition? If so, one might conclude that presidential reelection is the only watershed: once it is conceded, the opposition is condemned to disappear from the scene. On the other hand, to forgo the opportunity to negotiate institutional changes entails the danger of being reduced to voices of protest and eventually becoming spectators who lack the necessary power resources to alter the course of reform.[18]

The political pact, which emerged from the presidential ambition to remain in power and the impotence of the opposition, meant, first and foremost, an end to the situation of confrontation between a government that was obsessed with obtaining reelection and an opposition that lacked any goal other than to block it. In effect, the UCR, devoid of leaders capable of giving direction to the party and of convincing the public that they had any vocation for statesmanship, failed to contain the authoritarian concentration of power. Its criticism of the Menem administration never successfully translated into an alternative program of government. The road of negotiating with Menem, which Alfonsín defined as "a response to a confining situation of the party" and as "a return to politics," opened the door to a dialogue with the government.[19]

Menem's decision to negotiate the reform of the constitution with his principal adversary in order to legitimize his ambitions constituted a novelty in the history of Peronism. Negotiations with the main opposition became indispensable for embarking on the transition toward a new presidential term and preempting the possibility that the Constituent Assembly would be transformed into a platform for satisfying, on a symbolic level, a wide variety of social demands.

The willingness of Menem and Alfonsín to come to an agreement created the space for a political convergence: in the executive, by means of the creation of the office of chief of the cabinet; in the election of the presidential ticket, with the ballotage; in the elections of the magistrates, with the incorporation of their representatives; in the control of the exercise of power, with the General Accounting Office of the Nation in the hands of the opposition. Its protagonists became the organizing core of a fragmented society in which the political parties do not function as channels of conflict mediation.

The difficulties that are taking shape on the horizon, forecast by the outbreak of violence in the province of Santiago del Estero, leave no doubts about the precariousness of decisions based on secrecy and surprise.[20] The need to open new topics for discussion, previously blocked by the debate about the pros and cons of presidential reelection, and to legitimize the policies of transformation of the Argentine economy and society were present in the strategy unfolded by the government.

The votes cast by the citizens in the elections for constitutional convention delegates were the only guarantees that the agreements would be respected. In the April 10, 1994, elections, Peronism and Radicalism jointly obtained 57 percent of the vote. The results demonstrated the strong growth of third political forces in tandem with the crisis of the captive vote. In effect, the PJ lost 6 points and the UCR, 11 points, compared to the results of the October 1993 legislative elections.[21] The perception that personal motives acted as the engine of institutional redesign, be it explicitly, as exemplified by presidential reelection, or covertly, as suggested by the renewed protagonism of former president Alfonsín, is at the root of the massive desertion of the Radical vote and the decline of support for the ruling party. This perception also accounts for the apathy of the public toward the constituent debates before and during the sessions of the Assembly.

From the perspective of the novelties that surrounded these elections, the most significant facts are the electoral debacle of the UCR, the erosion of the electoral base of the ruling party (its lowest figure since its 1983 electoral defeat) and the strong growth of the Center-Left represented by the Frente Grande (FG, Broad Front) led by Chacho Alvarez and of the MODIN (Movement for National Dignity and Independence), although to a lesser extent but with a more even distribution across districts. These facts affect the ability to predict the traditional picture of majoritarian alignments.

From the perspective of the constituent process, the results obtained by the ruling party reduced its eventual margin of maneuver to impose rules that would not respect the basic points of agreement with the UCR or that would not achieve sufficient consensus from outside the party in order to be included in the agenda of the Constituent Assembly.[22] Undoubtedly this was one of the factors that encouraged the ruling party to adhere to a pluralistic style of decision making.

The election of convention delegates leveled a strong blow at bipartisanship. At the same time, the geography of the April 1994 vote shows the salience of local issues in determining the vote of each province and precludes drawing hasty conclusions about voting tendencies at the national level.

The process of reconstruction of the system of representation is the context that gives meaning to the reforms introduced into the historic constitution. These reforms can induce innovative political strategies with respect to a past of Peronist-Radical predominance, mutual blocking of initiatives, and congressional gridlock.

The Constituent Process

Each of the points included in the core of the basic points of agreement was a target of criticism. Although not entirely devoid of persuasive arguments, these criticisms were characterized by an analysis that failed to take an overall view of a new institutional architecture that managed to surface in a context of restrictions stemming from the structure and dynamics of party competition. The limitation of reelection to only one consecutive term and the reduction of the presidential mandate to four years were seen as granting ten uninterrupted years to the government of Carlos Menem. By permitting indefinite reelections with a four-year interval, reelection in the medium and short term was conceived as a mechanism of authoritarian concentration of power. The taming of hyperpresidentialism that is sought in the division of the functions between the head of state and the head of government on the one hand and parliamentary controls on the other lost significance.

Distrust concerning the eventual efficacy of parliamentary mechanisms (the chief of the cabinet can be removed by the vote of an absolute majority of the members of each house) and about the powers of the chief of the cabinet stripped these innovations of their original importance. The election of a third senator for the minority was considered a concession to the Radical party owing to the fact that the UCR was the second major political force at the provincial level. By specifying percentages, the ballotage in the presidential election appeared invalidated: it would be applied only when the ticket receiving the most votes did not exceed 45 percent of the vote, or, in the event that it obtained 40 percent of the vote, when its distance from the second force was less than 10 percent. Some argued that this variant of ballotage suited Menem's desire for reelection. The regulation of presidential Decrees of Necessity and Urgency was considered as a legitimation of the authoritarian exercise of presidential power. The Council of Magistrates for the selection of judges appeared as a straightforward politicization of justice.

Topics such as the constitutionalization of political parties, the General Accounting Office of the Nation in the hands of the opposition, the limitation of federal intervention in the provinces, the autonomy of the city of Buenos Aires, and the direct election of the intendant were underestimated in a debate that was obsessed with the issue of presidential reelection. Topics that the pact left open to constituent debate remained unaddressed: the strengthening of the federal regime, municipal autonomy, mechanisms of semidirect democracy, the Office of Public Defender, the public ministry as an outside-of-power agency,[23] and the incorporation of new legal, civic, economic, and environmental rights. Although many of these topics had been raised by the opposition, they remained eclipsed by the prevailing notion of conspiracy, which stripped them of meaning.

Unlike the context in which the constitutional reform was set forth during the Alfonsín administration, the reform during the Menem administration took place in the context of a profoundly modified state. The hasty process of privatizations carried out by the new administration replaced state ownership of public services with unregulated private ownership or, in some cases, with regulatory entities whose boards included representatives of the privatized firms. The institutional deficit for sanctioning the monopolistic behavior of the privatized companies and corruption, made even more serious by the process of privatization of key sectors of production and public service provision, speaks openly of the need for the institutional reform of the state. However, during the six months that preceded the inauguration of the Constituent Assembly, the new reality of the state and the resulting need to endow it with adequate institutional control mechanisms did not form part of the debate, which remained centered around the anti/pro dichotomy on reelection.

The beginning of the deliberations at the Constituent Assembly on May 25, 1994, did not surprise a public that had already interpreted this process as a simple ratification of an agreement between bosses. However, the Constituent Assembly set in motion an unprecedented party dynamic. As a reflection of the new electoral map, the political composition of the Constituent Assembly superimposed on the traditional cleavage of Peronists, Radicals, and minor parties of the political spectrum new criteria of political aggregation: between the "Pro-Pact" and the "Anti-Pact" groups (the latter, comprised of the opposition that fought to eliminate the so-called dead bolt clause and to submit to a separate vote each of the points of the core of the agreement); and between the Menemists and the anti-Menemists, thereby creating an unprecedented situation of great fluidity, especially because the debate on certain topics led to a rise of anti-Menemists within the ruling party and Menemists in the opposition.

A novelty of the Constituent Assembly was the circumstantial alliances formed by different forces, including those situated at the extremes of the ideological-partisan spectrum, regarding issues that were open for debate. Seen from the perspective of the traditional rigidity of Argentine political parties for finding negotiated solutions, the Constituent Assembly served to disentangle the political game by creating multiple spaces of negotiation of institutional issues, around which the parties gradually positioned themselves.

It is in this sense that one can affirm that the Assembly, conditioned by the pact between Menem and Alfonsín, provided a scenario for mutual recognition, the learning of tolerance, and the encouragement of old and new forces of the partisan spectrum to negotiate their differences. The provincial parties found in the Constituent Assembly the space to begin to weave an electoral coalition around a unique presidential candidacy for the first electoral round of 1995.[24] The moderated and moderating tone of Chacho Alvarez on behalf of the Frente Grande and the explicit acceptance of democratic rules on the part of Aldo Rico, head of the MODIN, in spite of the professed antisystem vocation of his party, demonstrate the new political dynamic that surfaced in the constituent process.

The origin of the new constitution was a secret pact between the president and the former president that took the political parties and the public by surprise. Regardless of its merits and defects, this constitution is the first to enjoy a broad consensus of the entire partisan spectrum. Could its origin discredit the reformed constitution? One could interpret the Olivos Pact as the possible agreement in a society whose parties function as electoral machines, lacking the capacity to operate as channels of aggregation of diverse social demands.

President Menem might have emerged euphoric from a reform that authorized his reelection, but the celebration was not exclusively his. The Constituent Assembly brought an array of positive factors. This is its principal novelty: all parties had something to gain from the constituent experience. This is the principal significance of the unanimous endorsement of the new constitutional text.

The Reformed Constitution

The great themes of the constituent process were the structure and functions of the state, the balance of powers, the powers of the executive, territorial representation, the reform of justice, the electoral system, and the relations between the national government and the provinces.

The Reformed Constitution transfers to the legislative power the right to enact special laws that should discipline a series of agencies and regulate the functioning of the new state structure. These rights deal with determining who will comprise the Council of Magistrates (the entity responsible for overseeing judicial power) and the Trial Council, which can remove, without any appeals whatever, lower court federal judges; making decisions about the Decrees of Necessity and Urgency remitted to Congress, based on the opinion of a permanent bicameral commission created ad hoc; defining the scope of the public defender's office; and enacting the rules for electing the attorney general of the nation, a decisive point for assessing whether the Public Ministry will be independent of the other powers.

Constitutional reform opens a unique opportunity to transform the role of Congress in its effective capacity to legislate and control. That opportunity is at the same time a challenge for the political parties, especially for opposition parties. The debates in Congress will serve as a test to discern whether the strength of the protest vis-à-vis the authoritarian concentration of power is transformed into institutional innovation and a subsequent capacity on the part of the new institutional mechanisms to carry out balance-of-power functions vis-à-vis the executive within the framework of a presidential system. The performance of the new institutional architecture will depend on the special legislative regulation that may arise from Congress and on the capacity to resolve, through a wise combination of doctrine and jurisprudence, the problems that might arise in the functioning of the newly created structures.

The institutional reforms have redefined key rules of the political game. The constitutionalization of the Decrees of Necessity and Urgency, prohibiting their application to cases of penal, tax, and electoral legislation, and making them subject to ratification by Congress without time limits, can be interpreted as a moderation of the exceptional powers of the executive. The electoral system adopted in the Reformed Constitution establishes that a candidate be elected in the first round if he or she obtains: (1) more than 45 percent of the validly cast affirmative votes or (2) when the most-voted ticket in the first round obtains at least 40 percent of the validly cast affirmative votes and, in addition, there exists a difference of 10 percent with respect to the validly cast affirmative votes over the ticket that obtains the second highest number of votes.

This is a hybrid form of ballotage (in classic ballotage, the candidate who obtains an absolute majority of the valid popular vote—more than 50 percent in the first round—is president). The two rounds in the presidential election are designed to guarantee the head of state a legitimate mandate based on a majority of votes. In the first round, the voter is guided by sincere vote and opts for the preferred party, while in the second round the voter faces a strategic option and might opt for the candidate who departs the least from his or her expectations. In the variation adopted by the convention delegates, the two objectives mentioned might not be met. Provided that the presidential candidate faces a fragmented opposition, he or she could arrive at the presidency with 40 percent of the votes obtained in the first round, very much below the majority demanded in the classic form of ballotage. In these conditions, the sincere vote of the first round could be neutralized by the useful vote, thereby restricting pluralism. This negotiated formula encourages polarization in the first round, which is, in turn, an incentive for the formation of an opposing electoral coalition.

If the forces of the opposition compete among themselves, they run the risk of not making it to the second round. Without a doubt, this variation of ballotage, which emerged from the negotiation between the UCR and the PJ, encourages electoral coalitions in a society that lacks a tradition of this sort. The institutional reforms do not necessarily generate the intended effects: the decisive variables are the skill with which the political actors define their strategies in relation to the new rules of the electoral game and the interpretation of those rules that the voters make. One can interpret the fragmentation of the party system that is evidenced by the growth of third forces, and the ideological-programmatic depolarization that is reflected in the moderate nature of the forces that place themselves toward the Left of the opposition camp as a symptom of profound changes in the Argentine party system. At the same time, the reforms introduced into the constitution can push in the direction of a Chilean-style electoral convergence as an alternative form of government.

The reformed constitution reveals a society that has escaped institutional impasse and tries to respond to the will of the majority to check the authoritarian exercise of power, to create an honest and independent system of justice, and to render the political leadership accountable to the citizenry. As such, it implies a decisive step in the consolidation of democracy, while simultaneously reflecting a political leadership that seems to have learned from the past. How much of this learning will translate into an improvement in the quality of government remains to be seen. What is certain is that an indispensable step has been taken to put an end to Caesarist temptations and the irresponsible behavior of some legislators.

The May 1995 Presidential Elections

The 1995 elections took place in a climate of electoral anxiety brought about by the prospect of an eventual second round of voting. Menem was faced with a rival in the figure of Peronist senator José Octavio Bordón, presidential candidate for the FREPASO (National Solidarity Front).[25] Bordón has portrayed himself as a modern intellectual modeled in the image of the Brazilian president, Fernando Henrique Cardoso. Representative of the liberal democratic components of Peronism, Bordón tried to capture the vote of the anti-Menemists from both Peronism and Radicalism. His motto, "Por un cambio seguro" (For a certain change), appeared to be far more moderate than Radical candidate Horacio Massaccesi's call to defeat Menem.

Despite the incentives to form coalitions that the ballotage created, the FREPASO and the Radical Party stood alone as independent actors with their own electoral agendas. Their campaigns challenged the present government's policies but failed to produce reliable alternatives. Menem's presidential campaign, on the other hand, was based on the economic performance achieved during his previous government. Menem toured the cities and the countryside, opening schools, hospitals, and roads as if he himself were competing for the office of mayor. He refused to debate with the candidates of the opposition. The media meanwhile focused on the shifting figures yielded by polls while just skimming over the parties' platforms.

It was in this context, on May 14, that the electorate voted for Menem. In the first round, Menem received 48 percent of the vote, surpassing the 46 percent he had obtained in the 1989 elections.[26] In 1995 the Peronist party won, as it had in the previous five national elections that took place since 1985. The Peronists' loyalty to the party has remained unchanged over the last decade, despite Menem's drastic parting from the traditional public policies that Perón had sponsored. This confirms the fact that the Peronists' political identity is not based on programs and policies but rather on a mixture of memories of values such as social justice and a unique leadership style, a combination of charisma and pragmatism, which Perón instituted and Menem copied.[27] The modification in Menem's support is greatly due to non-Peronist voters.

The two-party system that emerged in 1983 was replaced by another composed of three main parties plus other minor ones. In this new arrangement, Peronism continues to be the dominant party.[28] The Radical Party, the second major party since 1987, dropped to third place with 17 percent of the vote.[29] FREPASO, with 28 percent of the vote, swept away the UCR's aspirations to become the second political force in the country. Menem's ticket was 20 points ahead of Bordón's. The minor parties, which represented 15 percent of the total in the 1989 elections, virtually disappeared from the struggle for the presidency.[30] These figures suggest the formation of a broad Menemist electoral coalition that goes beyond the conservative-popular one that supported Perón in 1946. Both the heterogeneity inside the FREPASO—more like a coalition against Menem than a programmatic alliance—and the UCR's lack of national leadership prevented these two parties from organizing a solid front.

The contrast between the results of the presidential elections and the elections for deputies reveals that the Radicals retained broader support in the latter (the difference is about 5 points in favor of the deputies' list of candidates), while the FREPASO was able to impose a national leadership but did not obtain similar support for its deputies (the presidential ticket totaled 8 points more than the deputies' list). In the PJ, there was a difference of 7 points in favor of Menem's presidential candidacy.[31]

The minority parties decreased: from 27 percent in 1993 to only 14 percent in 1995, a figure that is closer to 13 percent of the votes obtained in 1983. The MODIN, which had received 6 percent of the vote in 1993, obtained only 1.66 percent in 1995. The UCEDE continued to decline and obtained barely 3 percent of the vote in 1995.

The distribution of institutional power resulting from the elections gave Menem a clear majority in the lower house: 132 seats out of 257. The Senate is under full control of Peronism, as is the greater majority of the provincial governments.[32] Opposition parties are too weak to benefit from their accrued power under the new constitution to alter the course of government policies. Given these circumstances, will the Peronist Party become a hegemonic party as it was under Perón?

As long as the other parties and coalitions remain weak and disjointed, the traditional Peronista tendency to behave as if no other political force in government counted will continue to strengthen. As a consequence, the internal disputes and the urge to transform them into state issues will persist. The present conflicts between the government and its internal opposition may prove to be more crucial to the evolution of democratic governance than the misadventures of the opposition parties.[33]

The Postelectoral Scenario (Mid-May to Mid-September)

On July 18 Menem began his second term in a climate of general indifference, despite the magnitude of his electoral success. Menem's second term in office was not received with the widespread relief and hope that surrounded his first one. The new government was clouded by two political facts. Eduardo Angeloz, three times Radical governor of the province of Córdoba, resigned as the only means of solving the crisis in his province, and General Antonio Bussi was elected governor of the province of Tucumán, where the Peronist Party had come in first in every election since 1983. The contrast between the magnitude of Menem's electoral triumph and the general atmosphere of crisis that surrounded it characterizes the present situation.

It was not until mid-July that the Argentines learned that the unemployment rate had reached 18.6 percent. As Argentina is a country with a tradition of full employment, open recognition of this figure shook the foundations of society.[34] Opinion polls showed the consistent drop in Menem's popularity: by the end of July it had sunk to 30 percent. The initial confidence in the country's future shifted toward uncertainty. Menem's "magic" lay with the government's macroeconomic performance. At present, past economic achievements are less important than the solutions to new problems, but these new problems cannot be solved by imposing emergency plans on the citizenry. The generalized quest for participation in decision making and establishing control over the exercise of power is narrowing the government's room for maneuver. This is not only because of the Peronists' growing demands for participation but also because the new constitutional framework gives the parties more room to maneuver.

Menem's magic is eroding. This situation has aggravated the latent conflict between the political sector of government and the technocratic staff led by Minister Domingo Cavallo, the guarantor of the economic reforms. The tactical alliance between them was based on economic and electoral success. With electoral success obtained and the opposition "pulverized," the economic problems have caused internal disputes.[35] Cavallo's enemies inside Peronism are openly forcing him to leave, but their strident rhetoric reveals that they have not yet produced a credible alternative program to meet the crisis. President Menem keeps governing in his way, that is, standing apart from Peronism's internal disputes. Everybody knows, on the other hand, that these disputes are the corollary of the present fight for Menem's succession in 1999. Will Menem be able to impose his decisions on a party in turmoil?[36]

The chief of the cabinet created under the new constitution limits Cavallo's action to imposing a decision without negotiating with multiple fronts. For the first time, Cavallo will have to negotiate the 1996 national budget with the chief of the cabinet, Eduardo Bauzá.[37] Neither Menem nor Cavallo can rely on the resources that allowed them to act swiftly in the past. To restore lost fiscal austerity will not be an easy task. Nor will it be easy to form policies to decrease unemployment. The Menem-Cavallo duo's political power is deteriorating in the context of a generalized weakening of the parties. In effect, as a consequence of the extreme personalization of power, the leaders rather than the parties are the winners of each election, and as long as the government is pervaded with corruption, the discredit of the politicians will continue to grow.

In early 1995 the collateral effects of Mexico's financial crisis disclosed the Achilles' heel of the economic program: Argentines do not save enough, and the economy relies on the capital available in the international markets. Latent economic crisis was brought into the open.[38]

Cavallo's dangerous assumption that strong economic growth would be uninterrupted, and its obvious corollary—the lack of anticyclical measures to prevent a crisis in the economy—confront the government with unexpected problems whose solutions can in no way rely on the unanimous consensus that stabilization policies had hitherto enjoyed. Cavallo's recent measures devoted to overcoming the present crisis face resistance from various social sectors and the provincial governments.[39] The conflict inside Peronism, far from ceasing, has peaked.

In mid-August, Cavallo publicly denounced the existence of mafia organizations that exercised an influence on decision making and the amendment of laws. This revelation cast a blanket of doubt on the three powers: neither the executive, nor the legislative, nor the judicial were left unscathed. The minister confronted his moment of greatest political weakness with a direct attack on the corruption that pervades the government. Although he targeted postal services magnate Alfredo Yabrán in particular, his declarations gave voice to the generalized and acknowledged need to put an end to widespread corruption. Since then, the corruption issue has proceeded to take center stage as it had in early 1991 when Cavallo first arrived at the Ministry of the Economy. Bribes, overpriced services for the state, and tax evasion by means of bogus receipts were exposed as mafia operations.

The political crisis unleashed by Cavallo's accusations went to the core of the country's present problems: the weakness of its political institutions.[40] The Argentines leaned out over the abyss, and Cavallo providentially became the one to remove the specter of ungovernability, in both the domestic and the international scenario.[41] President Menem was forced to renew his confidence in Cavallo, who was generally recognized as the man for the job. Nevertheless, this way out of the institutional crisis seems to be more a respite than a solution to the problems it brought into the open. Argentina has to make a transition from a "Menem-Cavallo" government to the government of institutions, a task for which Peronism is particularly ill prepared. It should also be apparent that this transition requires a search for formulas of cooperation that replace decisionism-based strategies, such as those that proved successful during Menem's first term.

Problems and Prospects

It should be evident from the preceding discussion that the success of Menem's economic adjustment policy appeared to be associated in its initial phase with the concentration of power in the executive and its technical cabinet. This has been so not only in Argentina but in most of Latin America, as the studies by Stephan Haggard and Robert Kaufman point out.[42] Great presidential autonomy and an authoritarian concentration of power in the person of the president, at the expense of the systematic violation of the principle of separation of powers, and not just the policy measures adopted, are at the root of the success achieved in controlling inflation. This autonomy stems from the crucial role played by the style of presidential leadership.

An astute and pragmatic politician, recognized for his skill in putting his adversaries on the defensive and his speed in reacting—the manner in which he controlled the December 1990 military uprising consolidated his image of political efficacy and authority—Menem showed an ability to interpret the collective moods of the country.[43] His stabilization policy benefited from the consensus of a public for which nothing could be worse than hyperinflation, the acquiescence of unionism,[44] the discipline of his party, and an opposition that was in crisis and incapable of providing a credible alternative program of government. *Fortuna* and *virtu* are united in the figure of the president, allowing him to set in motion the process of transforming the Argentine economy and society.

During the latter half of President Menem's first term in office the country was midway toward a new economic and political order. Throughout the period after 1989, economic reform was accompanied by important changes in both political and economic debates. The political opposition was keen to point out convergences and not just their differences with the ruling party. The issues of stability, fiscal equilibrium, and trade liberalization were excluded from partisan competition. In the economic debate, the discussion of alternative strategies from a common point of departure was also a novelty, as the work of Pablo Gerchunoff and José Machinea reveals.[45]

President Menem's second term has commenced in a very different political and economic situation in which neither peace prevails nor the will for consensus that is indispensable for consolidating democracy and sustaining economic reforms. As the recent institutional crisis has revealed, in order to ensure the durability of the stabilization policy and the structural reforms, more is required than the president's skill in concentrating power and exercising it at his discretion.

Argentina is now in the process of reconstructing its system of representation. This process is taking place in the context of economic recession, rampant unemployment, and social unrest and with the country being led by a government riddled with corruption and internally split on strategies to overcome the crises.[46]

Argentina's restoration of democracy followed years of terror and fear. Economic reforms have been forced by the severity of the economic crises, above all by the need to put an end to runaway inflation. Will the current political crisis impel the political leadership to "clean house" and undertake the reconstruction of the institutions that are crucial to their own survival? If the answer to this question is no, the ghost of ungovernability will stalk the country once again. The recent political crisis in the province of Santa Fé sowed doubts about the transparency of the country's recent and future electoral processes. This crisis reveals the absence of an independent control of the electoral process, a fact that had already been highlighted in Deborah Hauger's report for the United Nations Development Program in 1992. No electoral judge has yet been nominated in any of the twenty-four electoral districts as was established in the Electoral Code. The minister of internal affairs has practically total control over the electoral process. What is more, this crisis also indicates that the current struggle for the presidential candidacy in 1999 has destroyed republican institutions.[47]

The remainder of Menem's second term remains uncertain. Is the commitment to democratic consolidation and economic renewal strong enough to prevent the country from returning to its past?

Apparently the clock of reform cannot be turned back, not only because there is a general recognition that the political and economic order that emerged in 1946 can in no way be restored, but also because there is a pluralistic civil society calling for dialogue and policies of consensus. Nevertheless, it must not be forgotten that Peronism has always converted its internal conflicts into state crises. What is more, Peronism never left office peacefully. This does not presage a future with the necessary peace and willingness to build the broader consensus that the country's democratic governance requires.

In mid-September 1995, Argentina was still undergoing a political crisis best described as a crisis of confidence in political leadership. A return to the past is highly unlikely. One probable scenario in the near future might be that characterized by isolated and spontaneous outbreaks of violence that open the way to power for such men as retired General Bussi in Tucumán Province. A second scenario might be that of a ruling party willing to negotiate the transformation to democracy with political and social leaders in order to reach a balance between stability and growth, and in this way rebuild a more egalitarian society. In such a scenario, alternation in power would no longer be perceived as a relapse into disorder. Once again this challenge falls on Peronism. The coming months will show which scenario is to prevail.

10

Brazil: The Hyperactive Paralysis Syndrome

Bolívar Lamounier

No more than a jeep with four soldiers would be needed, if the military really wanted to shut down the national Congress. This is how a senator with experience in such matters summed up the situation in October 1993 at the beginning of the public uproar caused by revelations of widespread corruption made against members of Congress by a former advisor to the Budget Committee, himself involved in serious crimes including his wife's murder. The senator's remark was partly a joke, but it was also his own peculiar way of raising that ancient question: what, after all, is the matter with democracy in Brazil?

Perhaps one should begin by saying what it is *not*. Brazil does have regional and ethnic problems, even a little separatist rumbling in the south, but very few analysts would say that these cleavages are capable of threatening either democracy or the country's territorial integrity. There is drug trafficking, but it is not as powerful and organized as in Colombia. There is political antagonism, but it is not as confrontational and violent as it used to be in Argentina or Venezuela. There is no guerrilla movement, let alone anything like Peru's Sendero Luminoso (Shining Path). Why, then, was the first post-transition decade so difficult, and why did apprehensions about democracy continue to surface with disturbing regularity?[1]

Apprehensions with regard to Brazilian democracy have been largely defused, in Brazil and abroad, since Fernando Henrique Cardoso's appointment to the Finance Ministry in May 1993, his election to the presidency in 1994, and the marked improvement in executive-legislative relations during the first part of 1995. All's well that ends well? Not quite. A better understanding of what was going wrong before Cardoso's rise may shed light not only on the Brazilian case but also on unstable or poor-quality democracies in general. One must also ask whether this giant step toward democratic consolidation was not too dependent on a single individual, on the appearance of the right leader at the right time. If Brazilian democracy was faltering because of underlying economic dilemmas and income inequalities, it is clearly too soon to celebrate; if the country's flawed formal political structure was responsible for it, again, nothing has changed. Recognition of the major changes that have taken place since Cardoso took center stage should not, therefore, cause one to forget the larger question of the threats that ineffective policies may pose to Brazilian democracy, or, more generally, of whether poor-quality democracy is not the same thing as unstable democracy.

My argument is that Brazil is an impressive deviant case, so deviant that much can be learned by taking a closer look at it. Some fundamental traits of its economic, social, and institutional makeup are clearly unfavorable to democratic consolidation and high-quality democracy. Worse still, the last stage of the transition from military to civilian rule, in the early 1980s, planted the seeds of a serious, prolonged crisis that I call the hyperactive paralysis syndrome. During this period, most political leaders seemed either unable to understand the syndrome or unwilling to change some features of the underlying institutional context and of their own behavior in order to overcome it more quickly. As a result, economic stagnation, yearly inflation rates in excess of 200 percent a year from 1982 to 1994, ineffective policies, the aggravation of already dismal conditions of poverty and income inequality, increasing ideological polarization even in the late 1980s when the cold war was coming to a close, and the increased salience of corruption to the public agenda combined to keep the country in a situation of continuing doubt about the sustainability of democracy. But democracy did not break down: elections became tremendously competitive, civil society became undoubtedly stronger and more complex, and public debate was intense and rich during this whole period. The question, then, is how it all happened.

Arguments about democratic prospects in Brazil (and generally in Latin America) move back and forth between holistic views (a political culture "inherently" inimical to or a socioeconomic structure "incompatible" with democracy) and the equally untenable opposite extreme: the neorationalist assumption that democracy can live with any political culture and withstand virtually any amount of social inequality and hardship, provided that politicians play the "right game." This chapter steers a middle course and demonstrates that, from the 1980s to the early 1990s, a downward spiral of serious economic dilemmas, deteriorating social conditions, government ineffectiveness, and discredit of representative institutions represented (and perhaps still does) a serious threat to Brazilian democracy.

I will not dwell on the methodological underpinnings of the argument, but three brief remarks are useful. First, the economic difficulties that Brazil has been facing since the late 1970s partially precede and hence cannot be fully explained by the political factors analyzed here. However, I do assume that the hyperactive paralysis of the 1980s entered the picture as a major additional hindrance to monetary stabilization and growth resumption, thus making the loop more complex and dangerous. Second, the reason I dwell at length on the early 1980s is that I regard some features of the democratic transition itself as the factors that triggered the hyperactive process of crisis formation and hence as an important point to be taken into account in the comparative analysis of transitions. Third, because I contend that Brazil experienced a prolonged crisis-formation process that seems to have been broken by Cardoso's rise to the presidency, the question is: why was that process not interrupted at some earlier point? My answer is that the factors just referred to intertwine with the institutional and cultural factors studied below.

Historical Background

What, in short, is wrong with democracy in Brazil?[2] It is worth pointing out that the need to pose this question already indicates some progress toward democratic consolidation. In the 1920s and 1930s it was common for prominent writers and political leaders to peg their disbelief in democratic development directly on a holistic view of the country's cultural formation. In a formerly colonial, slaveholding society, so the argument went, liberal democracy is merely a superstructure, a facade too thin to hide the "hard facts": sharp levels of stratification, bossism from above and deference from below, and a complete lack of public awareness among economic and political elites.

Simplistic as it is, this view sounded persuasive until the 1950s and then began to lose ground, mainly for three reasons. First, a competitive democratic system began to function in 1946 after the downfall of Getúlio Vargas' Estado Novo dictatorship (1937–45) and the Allied victory in World War II. Second, industrialization and urbanization progressively eroded the underpinnings of the colonial heritage argument and even gave rise to a naive "developmentalist" belief that all good things (democracy included) would henceforth go together. Third, and most important, threats to democracy began to appear in a single and definite shape. Throughout Latin America, the threat came to be perceived as a by-product of the cold war context, always involving a combination of external pressure and domestic response to (actual or alleged) revolutionary insurrection. In 1964 democracy did in fact break down, leading to twenty-one years of military rule.

Unlike ideal or typical Latin American dictators, the Brazilian military maintained a substantial part of the previous constitutional framework. Military presidents were formally elected by Congress and were subject to the usual fixed term of office. Likewise, state governors were elected by the respective assemblies. Popular elections continued to be held at regular intervals for the legislature at all three levels—all of this, needless to say, under severe legal and paralegal constraints. The pre-1964 multiparty system was replaced by a compulsory two-party system in 1965, with the Aliança Renovadora Nacional (ARENA, National Renovating Alliance) providing support and the Movimento Democrático Brasileiro (MDB, Brazilian Democratic Movement) harboring the many shades of opposition to the military regime. Military rule in Brazil was thus a peculiar dyarchy: an authoritarian macrostructure that nonetheless allowed considerable space for the reaccommodation of the existing civilian political forces.[3] To describe this system simply in terms of noncompetitive elections is misleading because the electoral arena as such was quite competitive. The distinctive trait was that electoral competition was designed to fill offices largely deprived of their traditional prerogatives and power resources, and constantly subject to a Damocles sword: the so-called institutional acts, a legal reserve of supraconstitutional or emergency powers to which the president and the National Security Council could resort at any time.

This dyarchical pattern, more perhaps than the weakness of the pre-1964 party system, explains why the Brazilian military, unlike their Southern Cone counterparts, were completely successful in their attempt to extinguish all preexisting party organizations. Politicians willing to participate in the electoral game had no option but to join one of the two parties permitted by the new regime. The highly artificial two-party system imposed by the military authorities began to produce unintended effects in the mid-1970s as the so-called economic miracle of the late 1960s waned, resistance to human rights violations grew, and public opinion began to question military rule as such. The MDB quickly became a plebiscitarian symbol of the resistance to military rule: a broad opposition front instead of the narrow and tame parliamentary party that the military probably had in mind when they decreed it into existence. The turning point was the 1974 election when the MDB won sixteen of the twenty-two senatorial seats then being contested. From this point on, the redemocratization process gained momentum and followed what I have elsewhere described as an "opening through elections" logic. By this time, the new (and fourth) military president, General Ernesto Geisel, had already proclaimed his intention to conduct a "gradual and secure" decompression ("abertura gradual e segura").[4]

A major step in the decompression process would take place in 1979 when the government agreed to surrender the dictatorial powers embodied in Institutional Act number 5, negotiated an amnesty law with the Brazilian Bar Association (OAB) and other civil organizations, and suspended the existing legal restrictions on party formation, thus paving the way for the return to a multiparty system. Direct elections for state executives were held in 1982, with five parties already competing and the opposition winning ten of the twenty-two governorships, including those of the three largest states, São Paulo, Rio de Janeiro, and Minas

Gerais. In 1984 massive nationwide demonstrations (the "Diretas-Já," or "Direct Elections Now" campaign) were not sufficient to convince the military to accept the direct election of General Figueiredo's successor in the presidency. The "gradual and secure" process envisaged by General Geisel ten years earlier was thus concluded within the framework of the military regime with the election of Tancredo Neves, a leader of the moderate opposition, by the same Electoral College that used to ratify military nominations.

The Brazilian transition from military to civilian rule was thus an eleven-year-long, partially, and sometimes implicitly, negotiated process. Institutional reform initiatives have proliferated since 1985, and this, as we shall see, is another Brazilian sphinx posing a number of questions: have they been fruitful? Were they inevitable? From a procedural point of view, it is not farfetched to argue that the Brazilian experience since the mid-1980s has been an embarrassment of riches, a wellspring of democratic initiatives. A Congress with full constitution-making powers was elected in November 1986, and a democratic constitution was adopted on October 5, 1988, after almost two years of highly decentralized work. Free and highly competitive elections have been held on schedule since 1985: for the mayoral offices of the capital cities in 1985, for the governorships and federal and state legislatures in 1986 and 1990, and for all (nearly five thousand) mayoral offices throughout the country in 1988 and 1992.

A direct presidential election (the first since 1960) was held in 1989, with full ideological polarization between left-of-center Lula and right-of-center Collor in the runoff balloting. Collor's momentous but orderly impeachment made the headlines throughout the world in 1992. Ideological conflict began to wane, as in most of the world, after the election of 1989, reflecting the collapse of socialism in Eastern Europe and the end of the cold war. The Brazilian military did retain in the 1988 Constitution roughly the same institutionalized political role they have had since the 1930s, but they have asserted it in a moderate way since 1985. Still, a widespread feeling persisted, at least until the election of 1994, that democratic institutions were vulnerable—but vulnerable to what?

From the 1980s to the 1990s: Declining Governability

From the mid-1980s to the early 1990s, Brazil was under the spell of what may be rightly called a hyperactive paralysis. Instead of striving to consolidate interests and issues and negotiate a broad settlement, the political elite was busy doing the opposite, working on a very disaggregated basis, heightening expectations, then finding itself engulfed by the ensuing sea of disappointment.

By hyperactive paralysis I mean a syndrome of declining governability rooted in a pervasive feeling, among the country's elites, of insecurity regarding their cohesion and legitimacy and aggravated by a mistaken attempt on their part to meet the problem by constantly overloading the formal political agenda.[5] From the transition in 1985 up to 1993, the elites, in the midst of increasingly adverse economic and social conditions, continuously tried to regain legitimacy by multiplying the number of issues subject to public debate and decision. In the constitution-making process of 1987–88, for example, they worked literally without programmatic party directives; they also flatly rejected presidential leadership from the very beginning, leadership the Sarney administration was clearly too insecure to provide anyway. The consequence was a waste of time and effort on secondary issues: too many trees and no forest. Worse still, by the end of the decade, Brazil had not only failed to undertake needed economic reforms, but had in fact entrenched a bewildering variety of old-fashioned statist economic concepts as well as corporate interests into the extremely detailed and rigid 1988 Constitution.

The positive side of this story should not go unnoticed: what from one point of view looks like paralysis, from another was an impressive series of redemocratizing and democratic institution-building initiatives: organizing peaceful mass demonstrations for direct presidential elections in 1984 (the Diretas-Já campaign), recapturing that energy and transforming it into the broad coalition that elected Tancredo Neves indirectly in 1985, calling a full-fledged and highly decentralized constitution-making Congress in 1987–88, managing a highly polarized (Collor against Lula) presidential election in 1989, impeaching a president by orderly means in 1992, submitting a change toward parliamentary government (and the restoration of the monarchy!) to a popular plebiscite in 1993, and trying a full revision of the constitution as determined by the 1988 text itself, that is, by simple majority and unicameral vote, instead of the normal three-fifths majority, in two rounds and separately in the Senate and the Chamber of Deputies. Lower-level examples would include direct elections for university chancellors and attempts to involve the local community in the elaboration and approval of municipal budgets.

This ambitious series of democratic experiments has no parallel in Brazil or in other contemporary cases of transition from military to civilian rule. The question is whether Brazilian politicians and other leaders were not biting off more than they could chew: engaging in too much proposing and too much reforming, all of it through lengthy and cumbersome procedures—a questionable course for a country known for the weakness of its political parties, where the final stages of the transition coincided with a violent recession and a jump to three-digit yearly inflation rates, and whose most respected political leader, President-elect Tancredo Neves, through whom civilian rule was being reinstated, fell ill on the day of his inauguration in 1985 and died without taking office.

The net balance of this decade-long experiment does not seem especially brilliant. An inquiry into the roots and consequences of such a manifest instance of hyperactivism should therefore be seen, not as a digression, but as an essential step in this attempt to evaluate democratic prospects in Brazil.

Hyperactive Paralysis in the Making

From about 1984 to early 1993, in a clearly adverse economic environment, it became increasingly clear that there was no party, no coalition, not even an informal group of leaders capable of authoritatively identifying the key issues and stratifying them into a viable agenda. The hyperactive paralysis thus became a self-sustained, progressively autonomous loop. The deeper roots of this phenomenon, as noted below, are to be found in the weakness of the Brazilian party system, in the country's fragile institutional architecture, and even in some remarkably utopian traits of the changing elite political culture. But one must first examine when and how the problem began, that is, the situation Brazil faced in the early 1980s.

The immediate causes of the hyperactive paralysis are to be found in dilemmas arising from the protracted character of the transition itself. The origins of the Brazilian transition date to General Ernesto Geisel's gradual decompression blueprint. That process would unfold over eleven years, from 1974 to 1985, when Tancredo Neves' indirect election to the presidency marked the formal return to civilian rule. Positive insofar as it prevented traumatic confrontations, that slow and implicitly negotiated decompression led to a substantial depletion of political capital on both sides, a simultaneous erosion in public confidence vis-à-vis both the declining military and the ascending civilian authorities. More so than in the Argentine or even the Spanish transition, in Brazil would-be civilian leaders began to lose standing before they were allowed by the military to take over and, needless to say, before they could undertake any serious measure of economic adjustment.[6]

The extent of the damage done to the Brazilian economy by the debt crisis of the early 1980s, a critical juncture in the redemocratization process, must also be taken into account. A key step in the Brazilian transition, as we have seen, was the direct gubernatorial election of 1982, when the opposition parties won ten out of twenty-two governorships, including those of the three largest states, São Paulo, Rio de Janeiro, and Minas Gerais. The proximity in time between this event and the deterioration of the country's economic environment in the wake of the debt crisis is essential to understand the roots of the hyperactive paralysis syndrome. As stated in Lamounier and Bacha:

> The external shocks of the late 1970s and early 1980s hit the Brazilian economy very hard indeed. These shocks included the doubling of the dollar oil prices and the tripling of dollar interest rates in 1979–80, added to a sharp decline in export commodity prices beginning in 1980, and led to the col-

lapse of foreign lending in 1982. Taken together, these shocks meant that real net transfers from abroad fell from plus two percent of Brazil's GDP [gross domestic product] in 1980 to minus seven percent in 1985. This violent reduction imposed a drop of nine percent in the domestic spending ratio to GDP between 1980 and 1985. The transition to democracy thus became much more difficult than anticipated in early 1979, when General Figueiredo promised in his inauguration speech that a civilian would replace him in the presidency in 1985.[7]

The extent of this damage was reflected in the sharp deterioration of the social services provided by the government, in the intensification of redistributive conflicts, and hence in an anxiety for quick results, which would in turn make utopian shock therapies against inflation increasingly attractive to economic policymakers. The first attempt along this line, the Cruzado Plan (February 1986), elicited an overwhelmingly positive popular response, but its failure and each subsequent one led to the public's deeper disappointment in and distrust of the authorities.

A third important factor was the exhaustion of the state-led growth model inherited from the 1930s. Unlike the armed forces in Chile, the Brazilian military did not spare its civilian successors the political costs of public sector reform. On the contrary, twenty-one years of military rule reinforced the pattern of state interventionism inherited from the Vargas era in both practice and ideology. Though disastrous from a redistributive point of view, the state-led industrialization model inherited from that era was a remarkable success as an engine of growth until the late 1970s. This past success story made the political effects of that legacy more powerful in Brazil than elsewhere in the Southern Cone.

Arguably, the vicious circle whose emergence is sketched here could have been broken from the economic side, as in Argentina with the Cavallo Plan. But one must not forget that Raul Alfonsín failed before Carlos Menem succeeded, that the legitimacy of José Sarney's presidency was undoubtedly weaker than Alfonsín's, and that the Brazilian political agenda was already heavily loaded when the Cruzado Plan was launched in February 1986. Though Sarney's popularity and leadership potential did initially soar, the plan's collapse in late 1986 brought back and aggravated the full range of political difficulties the country was facing. Suffice it to recall that the Constitutional Congress, beginning its work in early 1987, had the legal authority to and did in fact try to reduce Sarney's powers and term of office.

The Brazilian situation from that point on is best described as one with two parallel, open, and mutually reinforcing crises—a political and an economic one. Substantially weakening the first civilian government, the Cruzado Plan fiasco of 1986 caused another abrupt fall in the aggregate supply of leadership because Sarney had been able to secure a five-year mandate, due to expire only in March 1990, and also because by this time neither the conservative opposition associated with the *ancien régime*, nor that emerging from the Left under the aegis of the Workers' Party (PT), could seriously challenge Sarney's governing Democratic Alliance (PMDB+PFL).

Like Argentina, Brazil entered the 1990s with a strong-willed president committed to stop inflation and implement market-oriented reforms: Sarney's successor, Fernando Collor de Mello. Unlike Menem, however, Collor was not lucky enough to have his liberal reform package endorsed by a powerful and historically "statist" party, not to mention that, more than a party, he would have needed a miracle to complete his term of office after the charges of corruption made against him by his own brother, Pedro Collor, in May 1992. Collor's failed attempt to curb inflation and implement public sector reform pushed the pendulum at least halfway back to the old Brazilian statist, high-growth-cum-high-inflation economic ideology.

Another useful contrast can be made with developments in the former socialist countries. In most of Eastern Europe and in the Soviet Union, the former "statist" (communist) parties came out of the transition almost totally demoralized. In Brazil, though ideologically declining among average citizens, statism was given a new lease on life by Collor's fall and, more generally, by the marked presence of the leftist and economically antiliberal civil organizations in the process of agenda building and by the growing "ethics in politics" demand. Thus, unlike Eastern Europe, where the statist flag was borne only by apparently moribund communist parties, in Brazil it was also shouldered by some political groups whose legitimacy was on the rise, for example, the Workers' Party, arguably the strongest left-wing party Brazil has ever known.[8]

A further understanding of the progressive autonomy of the hyperactive loop can be gained by comparing the variants of economic ideology and the political resources for economic policymaking actually available in different moments of the transition process.

Implementing a serious economic adjustment was still probably easier in terms of sheer power, and despite the erosion in public confidence referred to above, under the last military administration (Figueiredo) and during the initial four years of the first civilian administration (Sarney). Though increasingly questioned as illegitimate on the political side, the framework provided by the 1967–69 military constitution was more favorable to that objective on the economic and fiscal side. To mention but one example, a massive transfer of tax receipts to states and municipalities would be entrenched in the constitution only after October 1988. The problem was that, at that time, the economic policymaking community was still largely faithful to the Brazilian high-growth-cum-high-inflation ideological tradition. Like Figueiredo and

Sarney themselves, the country's business community and economists were generally not yet convinced that enduring stabilization could not be achieved without serious public sector reforms and fiscal balance. A decade later, having gone through Sarney's Cruzado Plan fiasco, the 1987–88 clumsy attempt to alleviate poverty (and even fix the maximum real yearly interest rate!) by constitutional fiat, Collor's blocking of 75 percent of all financial assets to implement his "single shot" anti-inflation strategy, and perplexity over President Itamar Franco's firing of three finance ministers in seven months, the country's economic imagination had undoubtedly become more sober. The need for major change seems to have dawned even on Franco, a politician bred in the interventionist-nationalist tradition. His decision to appoint Fernando Henrique Cardoso as finance minister (and de facto prime minister) in May 1993 was widely applauded as finding the right combination of intelligent reformism and political experience.

A Fragile Institutional Identity

The essence of the crisis of the 1980s and early 1990s, according to the view set forth here, is the closed loop of hyperactive paralysis: a feeling of illegitimacy begetting ineffectiveness, disaggregated strategies, and utopian reform proposals with a high chance of failure, each failure in turn reducing the chances of effective leadership for a broad negotiated settlement. Nine years after the transition, there could be no question that this vicious circle had seriously discredited most politicians and institutions. As usual, the brunt of public criticism was borne by the legislature, but the executive branch had been affected as well. The underlying terrain was—and in the institutional sense still is—moving sand.

Most analysts agree that the Brazilian political system suffers from some sort of congenital weakness, but too often they look only at the party system or, even more narrowly, at the number of parties, failing to point out the difficulties associated with virtually every cogwheel of the institutional machinery. However, a full understanding of Brazilian political functioning must take into account the inherent shortcomings of the institutional architecture inherited from the 1930s, and whose worst features have been pushed to their ultimate consequences by the above-mentioned dilemmas of the transition, as well as by some emerging political traits.

The institutional model to which I refer is a contradictory combination of highly plebiscitarian and extremely consociational procedures, practices, and symbols. Plebiscitarianism applies to the popular legitimation of the presidential and other executive offices. Consociationalism prevails in the spheres of party, legislative, and federate representation. The overall mechanism is thus based on a multiplicity of mutual vetoes and counterweights that end up providing powerful incentives toward fragmentation, on the clearly illusory expectation that the resulting deadlocks can be neutralized or overcome by the president insofar as the president is the direct incarnation of the "people."[9]

The dangers inherent in the institutional model described above began to be perceived by a number of analysts and practitioners in the 1950s. Irrelevant as public issues during the twenty-one years of military rule, they reemerged during the post-transition Constitutional Congress (1987–88) and continued as a subject of heated debate until the April 21, 1993, plebiscite on presidential versus parliamentary government.

The presidentialist victory settled that issue for the time being but did not resolve the larger problem of the country's insecure institutional "identity," the persistent inability to translate democracy as an abstract aspiration into a consistent and workable set of institutional mechanisms.

The identity crisis to which I refer is partially a consequence of large-scale demographic changes that took place during the twenty-one years of military rule. Less even than Chile, Uruguay, or Argentina, Brazil did not simply "return" to a preexisting format of political competition in 1985 when civilian rule was reinstated. In Brazil the controlled decompression initiated in 1974, and even the limited competition permitted by the military before that year's watershed election, hid an enormous expansion of the electorate and thus an acceleration in the underlying transition from a narrow to a broad-based, mass democracy. Only 13 percent of the Brazilian population voted in the 1945 presidential election; in 1960, in the last presidential election before the military coup of 1964, this figure was still only 22 percent; but in the 1989 election, the first held after the end of the military regime, it had jumped to 55 percent. In absolute figures, it is now an electorate heading toward 100 million, a sixfold increase since 1960.

One is tempted to paraphrase Kant on inequality and say that such a portentous change is "a rich source of much that is evil, but also of all that is good."[10] Massive urbanization and a large electorate mean that demands will exceed any reasonable governmental response and that electoral volatility will increase. But pressure and volatility also mean that individuals are becoming autonomous and demanding citizens, that bossism and deference are probably gone forever, and that the average voter has more information at his disposal and is somehow becoming more involved in the political process. This optimistic note is undoubtedly worth sustaining, but it is easier to sustain when one is confident that the formidable energies released by structural change are being transformed into democratic capital and that the semblance of order formerly ensured by oligarchs and bosses of every description is not simply vanishing but being replaced by institutions suitable to a large-scale society and democracy.

This, indeed, is where the Brazilian shoe pinches. Already in the 1950s when the political system was still quite oligarchical, some right-of-center analysts and politicians were alarmed by rapid party fragmentation and the emergence of antiparty "populist" leaders. In substance, they did not differ much from those Marxists who were then struggling to understand the same signs of instability as a "hegemony crisis." If this was the case four decades ago, one may easily gauge the impact that this huge new electorate would begin to exert in the 1980s.

The problem with the Brazilian institutional framework, as stated above, is its precarious balance between the exacerbated plebiscitarian legitimation of the executive and the extreme consociationalism applying to the format of congressional and federal representation. Clearly, a plebiscitarian element exists in the U.S. presidential model and even in parliamentary governments, personified in the latter case by the leader of the victorious party who becomes a natural candidate for prime minister. The problem in Brazil, and in much of Latin America, is that the plebiscitarian symbols and doctrines about executive offices are a lot more radical, and the institutional environment (judicial and legislative branches, political parties, federation, "civil society") is much too weak to exert effective counterweights. The dangers of executive plebiscitarianism can be serious not only when incumbents are politically too strong but also when they are too weak. If the party system is bipolar, as it used to be in Argentina, Uruguay, or Venezuela, the danger is that the country may be divided into irreconcilable "camps." If it is a mobile plurality in which parties proliferate and subdivide easily, as in Brazil, the president will often find himself in a distinctly minority position, which will tempt him into resorting to dictatorial practices to obtain what he regards as needed legislation. Such practices, in turn, may induce strong antagonism or at least irresponsible behavior on the part of legislators.

Unlike advanced democracies, underdeveloped nations do not as a rule have effective mechanisms to reabsorb the enhancement of personalities that takes place during electoral campaigns. The institutional environment is usually too weak to accomplish this task. Thus, whether the party system is bipolar or a multiparty one, the excessive personalization of political appeals tends to leave serious scars. Since Max Weber, much has been written on the positive functions of "charismatic" leadership, but much less has been said about the negative side of this phenomenon. In Weber's description, charisma rises or declines ("routinizes") as a function of the intensity of belief among the leader's followers: the biblical context of his examples leads him virtually to ignore what happens among those who disliked the leader from the very beginning. But the Latin American and Brazilian experience with such figures suggests that charismatic leadership can easily elicit formidable amounts of positive and negative feelings, love and hate, at the same time and while the leader is still rising. Personal devotion to him or her among parts of the electorate seldom fails to elicit an equally personalized and rancorous rejection among other parts. This phenomenon is perhaps inevitable, but the threat it poses to democracy seems much greater in an institutional framework based on exacerbated plebiscitarianism and consociationalism. In this connection, it is worth recalling that only two of the five presidents of the 1945–64 democratic period—Eurico Gaspar Dutra and Juscelino Kubitscheck—succeeded in completing their terms of office. The landslide that brought Getúlio Vargas back into power in 1950 seemed to indicate that the dictator deposed in 1945 had been forgiven by the "people." Four years later, threatened with a second deposition, he chose to kill himself, but his death did not bridge the deep gap between Getulistas and anti-Getulistas into which the country had been divided.

These well-known dilemmas of the Brazilian presidential system have been seriously complicated by two new phenomena in today's highly urban, inflation-ridden, poll-addicted, and media-intensive society. First, confidence in the incumbent may rise or fall abruptly, sometimes seriously straining the entire institutional framework. Second, the combination of TV campaigning and extreme party fragmentation makes it much easier for candidates without serious party backing to win the presidency, even where a runoff election is required. Sarney's trajectory provides a good example of the first danger. Sarney was chosen by Tancredo Neves as a running mate in a typical ticket-balancing maneuver. Hoisted to the presidency by Neves' death, he was destined to be a weak, faceless president, but his popularity suddenly soared in the wake of the wage and price freeze known as the Cruzado Plan (February 1986). Four years and several heterodox plans later, on the eve of the 1989 presidential election, his performance was rated good by 8 percent of a national sample and by 4 percent among the subset made up of highly schooled respondents.[11]

If Sarney's last three years were disastrous enough, the "real thing" would come with Collor. Capitalizing initially on wildly moralistic appeals and later on the anti-Left, anti-Workers' Party sentiment, Collor climbed from his insignificant Alagoas governorship to the top of the polls and rode on substantial popularity throughout the campaign. With 28 percent of the vote (against Lula's 16 percent and way ahead of the other twenty candidates) in the first round, he was finally crowned by the infallible arithmetic of the runoff election: with only two candidates, one is bound to score an absolute majority. There remained two small problems, however. The party that nominally backed his candidacy (the PRN, Party of National Renovation) had only 3 percent of the seats in the Chamber of Deputies in 1989. Furthermore, the 53 percent of citizens who voted for him in the runoff election, and the much greater majority who told pollsters he was doing an excellent job as president when he decreed the expected "single-shot" package against inflation on his first day in office, began to crumble four months later when the megashock proved ineffectual. The "people" were no longer there to applaud; now the stage was occupied by a diversity of organized groups united by an invisible thread: a profound dislike for Collor.

The "people" had vanished, but the Congress was there. A survey of congressional opinion conducted by IDESP (Institute of Social Economic and Political Research) in August 1991 found that only 6 percent of the deputies and senators were willing to rate Collor's administration as "good" or "excellent," meaning that support for his administration was dwindling even among his ghastly PRN. Not by chance, the president's "political isolation" and the "danger of institutional breakdown" had by then become the daily bread of the Brazilian press, eight months before his brother Pedro's interview in the newsweekly *Veja* set the impeachment machinery into motion. Although Collor's impeachment in 1992 was due to charges of corruption, his steep fall in popular confidence was evident since the second half of 1990 (his first year in office). In mid-1991, 48 percent of a sample of São Paulo and Rio de Janeiro voters interviewed by IDESP said they had more confidence in the legislature than in the president, with 28 percent expressing the opposite sentiment. Coming from a country imbedded in a wildly plebiscitarian presidential tradition, these figures should perhaps be collected by the *Guinness Book of World Records!*[12]

The instability of popular support for presidents and the virtual certainty that he or she will be in a minority in Congress have been stressed above in connection with the weaknesses of the Brazilian system. But do these shortcomings really matter? Do they hinder executive initiatives? In a country known for chronic inflation and unwilling to reduce the existing battery of incentives to party fragmentation, the trend seems to be toward reinforcing rather than attenuating plebiscitarian presidentialism. At the electoral level, it has been reinforced by the highly polarizing procedure of the runoff election. At the legislative level, the constitution not only maintained the old legal figure of the decree law, duly rebaptized, but in fact enlarged its scope, thus making it more arbitrary. The constitution now authorizes the president, in cases of "relevance and urgency," to issue "provisional measures," which become immediately (and remain) effective unless rejected by a legislative majority within thirty days.

This, as the experience since 1988 has amply shown, is the inevitable Caesaristic counterpoint to the idealistically consociational but in fact spineless system of party and legislative representation. Exactly 1,075 such "relevant and urgent" measures have been issued during the seven years since the adoption of the constitution in 1988. The answer to the questions raised above is therefore simple. In a country where consociational democracy and rampant fragmentation have become virtually coterminous, executive initiative and predominance must be somehow ensured. Because changing the underlying institutional architecture is a formidable task, most of the elite chose to believe that arbitrary legislative initiative is compatible with democracy or simply a fact of life.

Brazilian parties are notoriously weak, individually and as a system. Three features stand out as we look at the Brazilian party system. First, the parties lack continuity. Except for the communist parties, both of which claim to be the true descendants of the original organization created in the early 1920s, none of today's parties can claim to descend in direct line from those of the pre-1964 era.

Rapid social change does not explain this instability, which derives from dictatorial interventions and hyperpermissive legislation. Contrary to the other authoritarian rulers of the Southern Cone, the Brazilian military was successful in its attempt to extinguish the pre-1964 party system. Their success in this regard can be compared to a disastrous ecological intervention, as they succeeded in eliminating organizations already advanced toward fragmentation, failed in their attempt to replace them by two artificial ones, and in so doing stimulated a large number of political entrepreneurs to start all over again, this time in a complex and highly mobilized society.

Second, the struggle against the military regime, which in Brazil had a decisive electoral component and coincided with an immense expansion of the electorate, was waged by a "plebiscitarian fraternity"—a broad opposition front bound to collapse after victory, not by a coalition of preexisting parties, each capable of reaffirming its identity and taking responsibility for government programs in the post-transition context. The insecurity brought about by Tancredo Neves' death in 1985 and the disastrous lack of coordination that crippled the Sarney administration (1985–90) and the constitution-making Congress (1987–88) can be largely ascribed to the plebiscitarian and hence amorphous nature of the redemocratizing coalition. Third, as already stressed, the parties are extremely fragmented. Party fragmentation in the Chamber of Deputies, as measured by the Laakso-Taagepera index, has been about 8.5 since 1986—twice the score of the pre-1964 era—leaving aside the question of whether this sort of measurement has any meaning when "real" parties are a large multiple of the "nominal" ones, when internal party cohesion falls below an acceptable level, as is manifestly the case in Brazil.[13]

The belief in the unifying and stabilizing force of the plebiscitarian presidency may not be entirely farfetched in consolidated democracies or in presidential regimes that drastically reduce the consociational component of the overall system, to enable the president to count on the support of a majority or a substantial minority in the legislature. In Venezuela the party system was bipolar for a long time, and congressional elections, held simultaneously with that of the president, are based on hierarchical party lists, excluding the voter's personal choice among individual candidates. In Argentina the provincial multiparty system was subordinated to the antagonism between Peronistas and Radicals, and still contrasts with the three-way division now shaping up at the national level. This degree of coordination from above, which certainly has its own shortcomings, never existed in the Brazilian presidential system. Brazil went from the backward and highly decentralized bossism of the First Republic (1889–1930) to a certainly more modern and democratic, but equally decentralized (and consociational), framework.

The occurrence of two major dictatorial interludes (1937–45 and 1964–85) has misled most analysts into depicting this century-long history as a homogeneously archaic, authoritarian—one could even say proto-institutional—pattern. The fact, however, is that the contemporary framework is an extension of deliberate institution-building efforts undertaken after the 1930 Revolution. It contains strong consociational elements, even though the ethnic, linguistic, or religious cleavages normally associated with consociationalism elsewhere in the world are virtually absent in Brazilian political life. A look at some key features of the Brazilian political system will show its excellent fit with the consociational model as set forth by Arend Lijphart:[14] a preference for proportional, instead of majoritarian, single-member district voting; a multiparty system practically without deterrents against fragmentation; a three-layered federation with autonomous states and local governments; a bicameral national legislature with both houses retaining substantial prerogatives; and a rigid and detailed constitution that can be amended only by broad coalitions and in which a bewildering variety of regional and corporate interests are entrenched.

These mechanisms were constructed to protect specific minorities and facilitate their access to substantial power resources. Brazil's multiparty system, for example, is based on extremely low barriers against party formation and is sustained by substantial power grants, such as free access to prime time, nationwide radio and TV networks twice a year for parties having at least one representative in the national Congress. The proportional electoral system, initially established by the Electoral Code of 1932 and technically improved in 1950, stands out among most proportional representation systems worldwide in that it does not require the voter to endorse a blocked party list. In this sense, it combines the worst of all worlds: it ends up being as "individualistic" as the Anglo-Saxon single-member district system but without the latter's incentives for accountability of the representative vis-à-vis a geographically bounded constituency.

Even a quick listing like this must include a few words on the rules that govern the representation of the member states in the lower house, the Chamber of Deputies. A federation is inherently a consociational mechanism in the sense that a political force unable to make its presence felt at one level may elect representatives at another. It is also consociational in the sense that it guarantees the governing autonomy of and ensures representation for each of its territorial divisions (states and municipalities). But the Brazilian federation is probably unique in the world in the extent to which it overrepresents sparsely populated states (those of the northern and central-western regions) and sharply underrepresents the country's most industrial and densely populated state, São Paulo. Though framed in the heat of the democratic transition, the 1988 Constitution completely disregarded the democratic principle "one person, one vote" and sustained the traditional "federative balancing" principle: large power grants to the small states (now entitled to a minimum of eight deputies each) and a highly restrictive ceiling of seventy for São Paulo, which by sheer arithmetic should be entitled to about one hundred fifteen federal deputies.[15]

The institutional framework described above began to be built in the 1930s, but its worst features were exacerbated in the course of the democratic transition. If the president resigns, dies, or is impeached, he or she is replaced by the vice-president, who is not voted for individually but elected with the president as a running mate on the same ticket. As long as he or she is the legal incumbent and benefits from diffuse plebiscitarian popularity, the president wields an enormous amount of power—best exemplified by the president's authority to issue provisional measures. This is the plebiscitarian half, the upper part of the institutional iceberg. The lower part is the sphere of political parties, legislatures, electoral procedures, the federation. Here the consociational principle, which in practice means powerful incentives toward fragmentation, reigns supreme.[16]

A Changing Political Culture

Brazilian political culture is often depicted as an unchanging authoritarian propensity rooted in Brazil's distant Iberian origins. Elitist at heart, centered on "organic" notions of hierarchy and obedience, founded on a deep-seated denial of individual autonomy, the implication is clearly that such a value system cannot sustain genuine democratic institutions. If this extreme description fit the facts, one would be hard pressed to explain why, despite the imminence of economic catastrophe, the country's elites consistently shun the idea of making "pacts," seem unable to build strong political organizations, and have brought the country to the verge of ungovernability during most of the post-transition decade.

If any simplification made sense, I would rather argue that Brazil is a highly utilitarian, fragmented, individualistic, and in many respects quite anarchical society. If the interpretation of the last decade set forth here is plausible, there can be no question that the Iberian-origins argument vastly underestimates the strength of other factors—such as urban living, the spread of mass communications, and paradoxically even chronic hyperinflation—that tend to erode ancient patterns of stratification. In my view, major changes have already taken place: (1) a wish to preserve democracy has emerged among key elite and middle-class sectors; (2) the rigid segmentation that prevented reasoned public debate across institutional (notably between civilian and military) sectors is gone; (3) among the mass public, allegiance to explicit democratic values seems weaker than in the Southern Cone, but there is a growing subjective feeling of citizenship, in line with the actual expansion of the electorate; (4) there has been an enormous increase in the supply of political information, which means a significant potential for political involvement; (5) the country is no longer divided by rigid symbolic cleavages, as it was around figures like Getúlio Vargas until the late 1950s.

Students of political culture often forget that this concept refers to patterns of orientations toward political objects. The overall patterns of political organization that a society deems viable or desirable—its institutional utopias—are thus the kernel of that concept. The problem with Brazilian political culture is, in my view, that the same emerging democratic ethos seems inclined to lend support to contradictory institutional "utopias." As the recent plebiscite on presidential versus parliamentary government has shown, it is not uncommon for an individual or group simultaneously to combine strongly plebiscitarian views of executive authority with sympathy for parliamentary government and both with *participacionismo*, or wildly utopian dreams of direct democracy. As long as this coexistence among incompatible blueprints prevails, the attempt to translate broad democratic aspirations into workable democratic institutions will probably involve the risk of the sterile hyperactivism described in this chapter.[17]

Democratic sentiment is undoubtedly stronger today than in the pre-1964 era. To understand how democratic values reemerged after twenty-one years of military rule, it is useful to approach them as having a positive and a negative side, as two sides of the same coin.

The positive side is democratic-aspirational: it is a strong wish to consolidate but also to go beyond and somehow enrich the democratic experience. In a country with grim indicators of poverty and inequality, there is a permanent tension between the concepts of democracy as an institutional framework for political competition and democracy as a high likelihood of "just" outcomes, and this is why democracy does not appear in social consciousness as a state of affairs already good and worth "conserving."[18] Elite opinion surveys conducted by IDESP since 1989 show that faith in democratic consolidation is very high among high-status Brazilians; this is especially remarkable if one considers that the respondents have been consistently pessimistic about economic stabilization, growth resumption, and poverty alleviation during the remainder of this decade. In a survey taken in 1989–90, 64 percent of the 450 elite respondents expressed a strong belief that democracy would be consolidated in the course of the 1990s, but 63 percent of them thought it was "very likely" or "almost certain" that the country would undergo "a chronic state of social convulsion" if it failed to reduce poverty and income inequality substantially over that same period. These figures suggest that elite political culture has become strongly democratic, or democratic-aspirational, in the course of the last generation.[19]

The negative side of the coin is what Amaury de Souza and I have elsewhere described as a wholesale rejection of the past.[20] Most Brazilians today seem inclined to take a very negative view of the country's past, interpreting today's evils as the result of five centuries of consistently tyrannical rule. Sharp discontinuities in historical memory due to rapid population growth are compounded by the fact that millions do not know and do not want to learn much about a political past they tend to reject as homogeneously evil. On this point, there is a startling similarity between diffuse mass sentiment and elaborate elite arguments: a dominant or virtually unanimous conviction that the country (meaning past elites) failed utterly in its attempt to reconcile economic growth with social justice.

Needless to say, this negative attitude is also rooted in the marked deterioration of urban living conditions. The perceived association among poverty, crime, mob outbursts, and police brutality reinforces that expectation of imminent "social convulsion," a fear not limited to elite groups. In every social stratum, citizens increasingly ask themselves why so much misfortune has befallen the society, and the answer they find, simplistic as it may be, is that all past generations were monstrously insensitive, greedy, and incompetent. Though comparative data on this point are hard to come by, I am inclined to assert that few countries reject the past so thoroughly (and naively) as Brazilians do.

The impact of this "rejection of the past" attitude on the political sphere is clearly perverse. If the past was elitist and authoritarian, any attempt to simplify or regulate political competition must be an elitist plot against the worthy majority. As the 1993 plebiscite on presidentialism has shown, radical plebiscitarian or populist discourses stand a better chance of gaining the public ear as they convey the notion that the humblest citizen will be "directly" heard. Proposals to reduce extreme consociationalism are too complex to reach the mass electorate but find staunch resistance among part of the elite, especially among left-wing intellectuals, who also tend to see them as an elitist plot.

Carried to its ultimate conclusion, this wholesale rejection of the past makes democracy virtually coterminous with unbridled fragmentation. It feeds on the dubious historical assumption that a rich diversity of parties, associations, and currents of opinion would have emerged had they not been consistently repressed and denied representation by tyrannical elites. Democratic institution building thus comes to be equated with the blooming of these more "authentic" political flowers whose latent existence is assumed and with institutional arrangements designed to maximize their emergence and protect and grant special privileges to the weaker among them. The consequence is an extraordinary paradox: consociational mechanisms originally established to pacify and accommodate regional oligarchies within a patrimonial state (obviously socializing the costs of their peace) come to be acclaimed as the very essence of the struggle for justice within the framework of a modern, mass democracy.

Conclusion

As argued above, the 1994 election seems to have been a turning point toward economic recovery and better governance, but it also has the potential to worsen things considerably. No matter how much Cardoso achieves as president, the crisis of the 1980s and early 1990s was aggravated by serious flaws in the underlying institutional machinery. The succession of failures that Brazil collected over the last decade—the hyperactive paralysis syndrome—resulted from the confluence of an exaggerated reform zeal with a dangerous combination of plebiscitarianism and consociationalism, the latter leading to a highly disaggregated modus operandi. A democracy capable of functioning effectively under average presidential leadership can hardly be expected to emerge in Brazil within the existing institutional framework. An effort must therefore be made to improve democratic governance, and a few strategic reforms will probably be necessary to accomplish this goal.

First and foremost, there is a need to reverse the trend toward exacerbated consociationalism. No one seriously proposes engineering a complete reversal, which would include, for example, the adoption of a two-party system. The military experiment failed in this regard, and there is no reason to assume that such a model, if deemed desirable, could be successfully introduced under democratic conditions. But moderate and effective pluralism will not emerge "naturally" from the present state of exacerbated consociationalism, with its unparalleled battery of incentives to fragmentation. Electoral reform, with the adoption of the German "mixed" or even the Anglo-Saxon majoritarian, single-member district model, should be seriously considered. A threshold equivalent to 5 percent of the national vote for a party to have access to the Chamber of Deputies and to free radio and TV time would seem more realistic than the present highly permissive rules. A somewhat smaller Chamber is also desirable, as well as apportionment of seats in conformity with the "one person, one vote" formula, if the democratic principle embodied in article 14 of the constitution is to be taken seriously.

The second set of problems concerns the excessively plebiscitarian aura surrounding executive offices. The presidentialist victory in the plebiscite of April 1993 limited the range of alternative remedies but did not eliminate the need to find one. Strengthening the party system, an imperative in itself, is also necessary as a means of gradually reducing diffuse plebiscitarianism. Without a stable party system and predictable decision-making procedures within the main parties, the legislature cannot be expected to vote consistently and to make prudent use of its prerogatives. Without stronger parties and more consistent behavior in the Congress, there will be no consensus to do away with the highly arbitrary and potentially Caesaristic right of the president to issue provisional measures. Conflict among the three branches of government is always possible in a democracy, but it seems especially dangerous when the constitution allows the executive branch to exert so much legislative initiative.

A third set of problems concerns public sector reform. The economic difficulties that Brazil has been facing since the early 1980s are largely due to the exhaustion of the state-led growth model, that is, to the overextension to which the government has been led by the immense scope of its regulatory, welfare, and entrepreneurial roles. A substantial part of the corruption unveiled by recent investigations is clearly related to this fact. Market-oriented reforms have been proposed, as in much of the world, but they are usually defended only on economic (or economic-doctrinal) grounds. In the Brazilian case, the weakness of the political system under democratic conditions would seem to be an additional argument for reducing economic interventionism. Doctrines aside, effective state intervention presupposes a true "state" with a substantial degree of cohesion in the government machinery. Cohesion is a variable, not a constant: it does not follow automatically from the definition of the state or from some mystical view of it. Cohesion increases or decreases over time, depending on the country's political process. In Brazil, state cohesion, and hence governability, has declined dramatically over the last decade because of the exhaustion of the state-led growth model and because of the manifest weakness of its underlying political substratum.

There is also a diffuse but nonetheless important set of problems arising from the cultural sphere. Some disturbing new features of Brazilian political culture have been described above. I disagree with the well-known "Iberian-legacy" hypothesis in view of its exaggerated stress on the continuity of a political tradition that is viewed solely as one of hierarchy and rigidity. Brazil has gone a long way toward developing a democratic political culture and has already overcome some of the crucial obstacles in the process of democratic institution building. The franchise has been broadened to a remarkable extent, without the bitter conflicts that marked this process in the United States and in some European countries. Yet I would prefer not to regard the development of a realistic democratic ethos simply as a by-product of political competition. A deliberate effort must be made to increase familiarity with the complexities of the democratic mechanism among key groups. Frequent and preferably informal interaction among various sectors— academic, political, military, the press—should be stimulated. Essential as it obviously is to democratic vitality, press criticism may on occasion give rise to perverse effects, which can be minimized by reasoned and continuous dialogue concerning media approaches.

Last but not least, a strong democratic ethos depends on a firm defense of politics as such. In Brazil, and generally in Latin America, part of the elite and the majority of the mass electorate alternate between wild idealism and rancorous rejection, both rooted in the same lack of even a rudimentary understanding of political behavior and institutional mechanisms. Experiments could be devised to extend the reach of genuine political reflection throughout the body politic. As long as the cold war continued, citizenship training was regarded with suspicion, and rightly so, in view of the Left's frequent attempts to manipulate educational institutions and of the military's wish to impose its own authoritarian brand. Now that the cold war is over, it is time to recall that the 1988 Brazilian Constitution extended the right to vote to sixteen-year-olds (without the mandatory character it has for those over eighteen). The spontaneous effort made by numerous high schools during the 1993 plebiscite campaign should be taken as an indication that training in citizenship ought to begin at the high-school level and include a firm defense of politics. In all of these aspects—mechanisms of representation, the party system, the role of the state, political culture, citizenship training—the consolidation of democracy will not be a "natural" consequence of political competition but more a matter of deliberate effort and crafting, "the state as a work of art."

Notes

Chapter 1   Venezuela: The Rise and Fall of Partyarchy (Coppedge)

This chapter was originally prepared for the Inter-American Dialogue Project on "Democratic Governance in the Americas" and was later published, with permission, in the *Journal of Inter-American Studies and World Affairs* 36, no. 2 (1994): 39–64.

1. For an elaboration of this approach to governance, see Michael Coppedge, "Institutions and Democratic Governance in Latin America," paper presented at the conference on "Rethinking Development Theories in Latin America," University of North Carolina, Chapel Hill, March 1993.

2. This concept is fully developed and contrasted with Robert Dahl's concept of polyarchy in my book *Strong Parties and Lame Ducks: Presidential Partyarchy and Factionalism in Venezuela* (Stanford: Stanford University Press, 1994). This section summarizes arguments developed at length in chap. 2.

3. Daniel H. Levine, *Conflict and Political Change in Venezuela* (Princeton: Princeton University Press, 1973).

4. Franklin Tugwell, *The Politics of Oil in Venezuela* (Stanford: Stanford University Press, 1975); Michael Coppedge, "Venezuela: Democratic despite Presidentialism," in Juan J. Linz and Arturo Valenzuela, eds., *The Crisis of Presidential Democracy* (Baltimore: Johns Hopkins University Press, 1994), 322–47.

5. The church, which has always been comparatively weak in Venezuela, ceased to intervene actively in politics in the early 1960s; see Levine, *Conflict and Political Change in Venezuela.* On relations with the private sector, see Terry Lynn Karl, "The Political Economy of Petrodollars: Oil and Democracy in Venezuela" (Ph.D. diss., Stanford University, 1982). For a different point of view, see José Antonio Gil Yepes, *The Challenge of Venezuelan Democracy* (New Brunswick, N.J.: Transaction Books, 1981).

6. John D. Martz, *Acción Democrática: The Evolution of a Modern Political Party* (Princeton: Princeton University Press, 1966).

7. Daniel H. Levine, "Venezuela since 1958: The Consolidation of Democratic Politics," in Juan J. Linz and Alfred Stepan, eds., *The Breakdown of Democratic Regimes: Latin America* (Baltimore: Johns Hopkins University Press, 1978), 82–109.

8. Terry Lynn Karl, "Petroleum and Political Pacts: The Transition to Democracy in Venezuela," in Guillermo O'Donnell, Philippe C. Schmitter, and Laurence Whitehead, eds., *Transitions from Authoritarian Rule: Latin America* (Baltimore: Johns Hopkins University Press, 1986), 196–219.

9. Robert J. Alexander, *The Venezuelan Democratic Revolution* (New Brunswick, N.J.: Rutgers University Press, 1964).

10. Martz, *Acción Democrática,* 174–92.

11. Donald L. Herman, "The Christian Democratic Party," in Howard Penniman, ed., *Venezuela at the Polls* (Washington, D.C.: American Enterprise Institute, 1980), 133–53.

12. Karl, "The Political Economy of Petrodollars," 17.

13. Mina Silberberg, "Change and Continuity in 'Extra-Clientelist' Politics: Alternative Organizations of the Venezuelan Poor," paper presented at the In-

ternational Congress of the Latin American Studies Association, Los Angeles, 1991.

14. Alfredo Castro Escudero, "Venezuela: La encrucijada de la democracia," *Comercio Exterior* 42, no. 3 (1992): 244–51.

15. There is some evidence that the provision of water and electricity actually improved in 1981–89, which implies that concern about deteriorating "public services" was mostly focused on rising violent crime and shortages of essential goods and services. Andrew Templeton, "The Evolution of Popular Opinion," draft paper presented at the conference on "Lessons of the Venezuelan Experience," Woodrow Wilson International Center for Scholars, Washington, D.C., October 1992.

16. David J. Myers, "Perceptions of a Stressed Democracy: Inevitable Decay or Foundation for Rebirth," paper presented at the conference on "Democracy under Stress," sponsored by the North-South Center of the University of Miami and INVESP (Venezuelan Institute of Social and Political Studies), Caracas, November 1992, 4–5.

17. Ibid.

18. Elías Santana, remarks at the forum on "Venezuela: Recent Events and Future Prospects," sponsored by the Center for Strategic and International Studies and CAUSA, Washington, D.C., May 1992.

19. Templeton, "The Evolution of Popular Opinion."

20. Ibid.

21. Julián Villalba, "Venezuela's Future: Outlook for Investment and Privatization," talk given at the Council of the Americas, Washington, D.C., September 16, 1993.

22. Allan R. Brewer-Carías, "La descentralización política en Venezuela: 1990, el inicio de la reforma," in Dieter Nohlen, ed., *Descentralización política y consolidación democrática* (Madrid: Editorial Síntesis; Caracas: Nueva Sociedad, 1991), 131–60; Miriam Kornblith and Daniel H. Levine, "Venezuela: The Life and Times of the Party System," in Scott Mainwaring and Timothy J. Scully, eds., *Building Democratic Institutions* (Stanford: Stanford University Press, 1995), 33 note.

23. Technocrats recruited from the elite Institute of Higher Administration Studies (IESA), who were pro-market like the "Chicago Boys" of Pinochet's Chile, but less dogmatic.

24. Coppedge, "Venezuela: Democratic despite Presidentialism," 338–40.

25. Juan J. Linz, "The Perils of Presidentialism," *Journal of Democracy* 1, no. 1 (1990): 51–69; and Scott Mainwaring, "Presidentialism, Multiparty Systems, and Democracy: The Difficult Combination," *Comparative Political Studies* 26, no. 2 (1993): 198–228.

26. Personal communication from Luis Gómez Calcaño, February 1994.

27. Margarita López Maya, "El ascenso en Venezuela de la Causa R," paper presented in March at the XVIII International Congress of the Latin American Studies Association, Atlanta, 1994.

28. According to the Supreme Electoral Council, the disputed votes are not enough to alter the final results. *Latin America Weekly Report*, January 13, 1994.

29. "Defense Minister Meets with Colombian Counterpart," *El Universal*, January 28, 1994, 2–19; reprinted in Foreign Broadcast Information Service (FBIS)-LAT-94-020, January 31, 1994, 68.

30. Michael Coppedge, "Parties and Society in Mexico and Venezuela: Why Competition Matters," *Comparative Politics* 25, no. 3 (1993): 253–74.

31. "Venezuelan Bank Collapse Threatens Nation's Future," *Los Angeles Times*, February 14, 1994, A1.

Chapter 2 Colombia: Building Democracy in the Midst of Violence and Drugs (Kline)

1. Archbishop Pedro Rubiano Saenz, quoted in *El Tiempo* (Bogotá), July 4, 1991.

2. Peter Wade, *Blackness and Race Mixture: The Dynamics of Racial Identity in Colombia* (Baltimore: Johns Hopkins University Press, 1993), 20.

3. María Jimena Duzán, "Colombia's Bloody War of Words," *Journal of Democracy* 2, no. 1 (1991): 105.

4. Ibid., 106.

5. Quoted in Douglas Farah, "Colombia's Culpables: Drug Corruption Probe Implicates Entrenched Ruling Class," *Washington Post,* August 23, 1995, A25.

6. Inter-American Commission on Human Rights, *Second Report on the Situation of Human Rights in Colombia* (Washington, D.C.: General Secretariat, Organization of American States, 1993), 36.

Chapter 3 Ecuador: Democracy Standing the Test of Time? (Isaacs)

I acknowledge the helpful comments of the anonymous reviewer and of Alan Angell, Jim Buchanan, and Joan Dassin, as well as the assistance of Pedro Armijos, Serena Hurralde, and Donna Lee Van Cott.

1. See Anita Isaacs, *Military Rule and Transition in Ecuador* (Pittsburgh: University of Pittsburgh Press, 1993), 117–43.

2. Ibid.

3. See Instituto de Estudios Sociales y de la Opinion Pública, *Informe Confidencial,* 1989 and 1993.

4. See, for instance, *Latin America Monitor,* February 1993.

5. See "Parto de los Montes," *Vistazo,* January 21, 1993, 610, and "Punto para Carlos Julio," *Vistazo,* February 4, 1993, 611.

6. For a thorough discussion of the Ecuadorian judicial system, see Laura Chinchilla and David Schodt, *The Administration of Justice in Ecuador* (Miami: Center for the Administration of Justice, Florida International University, 1993).

7. See, for example, *Latinamerica Press,* April 1, 1993.

8. Donna Lee Van Cott, "Modernization Alone Won't Save Ecuador," *Hemisphere* 5, no. 3 (1993): 16–17.

9. See, for instance, *Latin America Monitor,* January 1993, 1096; May 1993, 1144.

10. *Latin America Monitor,* July 1993, 1168.

11. See "45 mil burócratas se van," *Vistazo,* February 4, 1993, 611.

12. See *Latin America Special Report,* June 1993, 93–103.

13. See *Latin America Monitor,* July 1993, 1168. See also *Latin America Weekly Report,* June 17, 1993; December 2, 1993; and December 16, 1993.

14. *Latin America Weekly Report,* August 5, 1993; December 9, 1993.

15. Ibid., June 10, 1993.

16. *Constitución de la República* (Quito, 1982), 23–34. For a discussion of current military activity, see "El otoño del patriarca," *Vistazo,* March 4, 1993, 613, and "Defensores del estatismo," *Vistazo,* April 22, 1993, 616.

17. *Informe Confidencial,* 1993.

Chapter 4 Peru: The Rupture of Democratic Rule (Stokes)

1. We should resist the temptation to fuse the concept of democracy with that of the just society. We should retain a narrow definition of democracy as a system in which the holders of governmental office are chosen in fair elections

in which virtually the entire adult population is free to vote. Robert Dahl, *Polyarchy: Participation and Opposition* (New Haven: Yale University Press, 1971). Real state power, moreover, must reside in the offices thus filled. Philippe Schmitter and Terry Lynn Karl, "What Democracy Is . . . And What It Is Not," *Journal of Democracy* 2, no. 3 (1991): 75–88. Fair elections are ones in which citizens elect representatives whom they prefer, and, in forming their preferences, citizens have available to them information supplied by constitutionally guaranteed nongovernmental sources. See Dahl, *Polyarchy.* For elections to be fair in this sense, free association must also be constitutionally guaranteed.

2. John R. Londregan and Keith T. Poole, "Poverty, the Coup Trap, and the Seizure of Executive Power," *World Politics* 42, no. 2 (1990).

3. Again, for specific reasons the two other traditional party groupings could not offer viable candidates in 1990: APRA was the incumbent party that had presided over (and in part caused) a drastic economic crisis, and the United Left coalition had split into two smaller coalitions in 1989.

4. Quoted in *Latin American Regional Report, Andean Region,* December 1991.

5. Under the 1979 Constitution the president could adjourn Congress after three censure votes or votes of no confidence for the cabinet; new congressional elections would then be held. At the time of Fujimori's threat, the Congress had censured only one minister, and the president failed to accept his resignation, as the constitution required (see below).

6. This period was also one of conflict between the president and the judiciary. Fujimori objected to what he saw as the intimidation of judges by Sendero and corruption by drug traffickers. But there was also a more partisan conflict involved: in 1991 the Supreme Court found insufficient evidence of corruption against former president Alan García. In his televised speech the night of the coup, Fujimori gave as a justification the "covert plans of certain party leaders against the efforts by the people and the government" (quoted in *Latin America Weekly Reports, Andean Group,* May 1992). After the coup, Fujimori purged thirteen of thirty judges from the Supreme Court and appointed the prosecutor in the García case as comptroller-general [*fiscal*].

7. Some evidence suggests that the initial intention of the coup-makers was to install a civilian-military dictatorship that would persist into the foreseeable future. When in mid-April Fujimori announced a twelve-month timetable for the return to democracy, an intelligence officer was reported to have said, "it will be more like 18 years before he relinquishes power" (quoted in *Latin America Regional Report, Andean Group,* May 1992).

8. See *Situación Latinoamericana* 11 (October 1992). The World Bank and IDB initially announced suspension of loans. Days after the coup, Economic Minister Boloña traveled to Washington to try to convince the IFIs and U.S. Treasury to resume disbursements. He failed and returned to Lima to tender his resignation. Fujimori convinced Boloña to stay on (in part by firing his rival, central bank president Jorge Chávez). In explaining his decision to remain, Boloña told the Peruvian press that Enrique Iglesias, head of the IDB, was "looking for a way to support Peru so that our process of re-entry [into the international financial community] would not be blocked" (cited in *Latin America Regional Report, Andean Group,* May 1992).

9. In fact, Peru did not reach several of the goals established in the earlier Letter of Intent. The target for GNP growth, for example, had been 2.5 percent; in fact, GNP growth was –1 percent. Because the IMF and other IFIs frequently extend loans to countries that have not met conditionality, we cannot conclude that their motivations were explicitly political in this case; see, for example, Miles Kahler, "External Influence, Conditionality, and the Politics of Adjust-

ment," in Stephan Haggard and Robert R. Kaufman, eds., *The Politics of Economic Adjustment* (Princeton: Princeton University Press, 1992). Still, as I argue below, whatever their intentions, the IFIs played a critical role in the unfolding political situation in Peru, and that role did not contribute to the survival of democracy.

10. It is indicative of the peculiar quality of this constitution-writing process that the person who suspended the previous constitution was laying down specific rules on reelection in the future, new legal order, before the new constitutional assembly was even formed.

11. The 1979 Constitution allowed presidential reelection after one presidential term elapsed. The 1993 Constitution allows immediate reelection to a second term and then subsequent reelection after one term has elapsed.

12. In addition to drafting the new constitution, the CCD has acted as the legislature since the November 1992 elections and continued to act as such until the new legislature was elected.

13. The judge reasoned that if it were true, as the prosecutor claimed, that the officers had acted alone without the knowledge of their superiors, then they had acted as civilians.

14. See "After the Autogolpe: Human Rights in Peru and the U.S. Response" (Washington, D.C.: Washington Office on Latin America, July 1994), 12–15.

15. Pamela Constable, "Peru Coup Leaders Vow to Fight," *Boston Globe*, June 23, 1993.

16. Caleb Rossiter, *Washington Post*, April 12, 1992.

17. John Omicinski, *Gannett News Service*, April 13, 1992.

18. See the chapter by Jorge Castañeda in this collection.

19. Thomas L. Friedman, "Peru and U.S.: What Course to Take?" *New York Times*, April 15, 1992.

20. Thomas L. Friedman, "U.S. Is Shunning Sanctions against Peru," *New York Times*, April 14, 1992.

21. Presidential approval ratings fell from 64 percent in December 1993 to 54 percent in January 1994; see Imasen, cited in *Latin American Research Review, Andean Region*, February 1994.

22. I use the term *liberalization* here not in the sense of the first step toward a return to civilian rule, as fair elections would signal a return to democracy (as defined in note 1 above). But, as my analysis has made clear, the Peruvian political system is characterized by several authoritarian features, which, without remedying action, would persist even after a return to full democracy.

Chapter 5 Bolivia: Managing Democracy in the 1990s (Gamarra)

1. James M. Malloy and Eduardo A. Gamarra, *Revolution and Reaction: Bolivia, 1964–1985* (New Brunswick, N.J.: Transaction Press, 1988).

2. Ibid.

3. The best studies on these parties and their leaders can be found in Jorge Lazarte, "Partidos políticos, problemas de representación e informalización de la política: El caso de Bolivia," unpublished manuscript, 1992; Joaquín Saravia and Godofredo Sandoval, *Jach'a Uru: La esperanza de un pueblo?* (La Paz: ILDIS and CEP, 1991); and Fernando Mayorga, *La política del silencio* (La Paz: UMSS/ILDIS, 1991).

4. Lazarte, "Partidos políticos."

5. In one specific instance, for example, Fernández offered to build a *matadero frigorífico* (refrigerated slaughterhouse) in Santa Cruz at a cost of U.S.$800,000.

6. Author interview with Max Fernández, La Paz, March 3, 1989.

7. Author interview with U.S. embassy officials, July 1991.

8. Lazarte, "Partidos políticos."

9. Recently, for example, workers defended "Don Max" against charges of ties to the drug industry from Guillermo Lora, Bolivia's oldest Trotskyist leader. Lora was subsequently jailed following a lawsuit for defamation and libel brought against him by Max's lawyers.

10. For an excellent discussion of contemporary trends in the Bolivian party system, see Lazarte, "Partidos políticos."

11. Ibid.

12. For discussions of Bolivia's economic reforms, see Malloy and Gamarra, *Revolution and Reaction;* Juan Antonio Morales and Jeffrey Sachs, "The Bolivian Economic Crisis" (Cambridge, Mass.: National Bureau of Economic Research, Working Paper no. 2620, 1987); Juan Cariaga, "Hiperinflación, estabilidad, y crecimiento," unpublished manuscript, La Paz, 1993.

13. Since 1989 at least three such groups made their appearance in Bolivia. The first, Zárate Wilka, has all but disappeared owing to the government's crackdown following the May 1989 assassination of two young U.S. Mormon missionaries. A second group, the Ejército de Liberación Nacional-Nestor Paz Zamora, which boasted links to Peru's Tupac Amaru group, was also dismantled after the kidnapping and subsequent assassination of Jorge Londsdale, a prominent businessman. The third group, the Ejército Guerrillero Tupac Katari, has been more resilient; it has resorted only to occasional bombings of electric utility stations and the like.

14. Paz Zamora's speech was interpreted as the beginning of his campaign to return to office in 1997. His aim was to make a clear break with the MIR in an attempt to save himself from charges of corruption. Widespread rumors suggested that Paz Zamora intended to found a new party called Movimiento Ciudadano (Citizens Movement). These efforts, however, were soon nipped in the bud by revelations of alleged dealings with drug traffickers.

15. Under the terms of the MNR-UCS pact, Fernández' followers secured one ministry, two undersecretary posts, two embassies, the presidency of one regional development corporation, and the first vice-presidency of both the Chamber of Deputies and the Senate.

16. The MBL was promised one ministry, key congressional posts, and at least one embassy. Araníbar and the MBL extracted a high price, considering that his party won only 5 percent of the vote. Araníbar was later named minister of foreign affairs.

17. Responding to pressures from within his own party, in March 1994 Sánchez de Lozada replaced these entrepreneurs with members of the MNR.

18. Another common explanation given for the slow pace of the new administration is that Sánchez de Lozada prefers to involve himself in every last detail of nearly every policy.

19. MNR, *El Plan de Todos* (La Paz: April 1993), 19–20. Responding to the lack of interest by foreign capital, in January 1994 the government announced that foreign ownership would be increased to 50 percent.

20. In theory, these shares would be handled by pension fund administrators on behalf of the estimated 3.2 million Bolivians who would then apply their shares toward a retirement fund. The constitutional reform of August 1994 lowered the voting age from twenty-one to eighteen.

21. Goodwin Bennett and Dewey Ballantine, "Capitalization and Privatization: Successes and Pitfalls," paper presented at the seminar on "The Currents of Privatization and Capitalization," La Paz: ASOBAN, February 8, 1994.

22. The law was signed by President Gonzalo Sánchez de Lozada on April 20, 1994, and published in the Official Gazette of Bolivia as law no. 1551 on April 21, 1994. The law came into effect on the date of its publication.

23. "Otros 13 generales del Ejército pasarán al servicio pasivo," *Última Hora*, October 18, 1993, 6.

24. "Logias militares derribaron avión del LAB y mataron a Alexander y Otero Calderón," *Bolivian Times*, special edition, January 12, 1994, 1 and 4.

25. Malloy and Gamarra, *Revolution and Reaction*.

26. Indeed, since 1985 the principal political parties have revealed an extraordinary capacity to enter into and out of pacts and accords. The most relevant agreements are the February 5, 1991, and July 9, 1992, accords that encompassed every major political party.

27. The accusations detailed by the FELCN are reported in Eduardo Gamarra, *Entre la Droga y la Democracia* (La Paz: Instituto Latinoamericano de Investigaciones Sociales/ILDES, 1994).

28. In December 1994 Congress approved the law of majorities and minorities to regulate municipal elections. Until the approval of this law, the indirect election of a mayor mirrored the problems of electing a president at the national level. Under the new law, the party that attains even a slim plurality will be granted seven of the thirteen seats on the municipal council, thus ensuring the election of a mayor. In the long run, this mechanism could prove costly, especially in large urban centers such as La Paz where traditional parties fare poorly against populist candidates.

29. To secure congressional approval, the government proposed to amend article 230 of the constitution, which states: "This constitution can be partially reformed through the prior declaration of the need for reform. Reforms are to be determined by an ordinary law approved by two-thirds of the members present in each of the two chambers" (my translation). The MNR believes that the two-thirds requirement constitutes an "unnecessary obstacle" to constitutional reform. Opponents charge that the safeguards found in the constitution are deliberate to prevent any government from modifying the constitution to suit a temporary political trend.

30. In late January 1994 the government sponsored a seminar in which a number of European and Latin American legal scholars joined Bolivian colleagues to discuss the merits of constitutional tribunals. The government has been quite inspired by the sixteen-member constitutional tribunal in Germany. It has also been carefully examining the Spanish court.

31. The basic philosophy in Bolivia that the armed forces will take a leadership role in the fight against narcotics only if and when the police have been overrun by the traffickers may have been altered by the launching of the state of siege. Under the guidelines of these measures, troops have moved into coca-growing regions and have arrested union leaders including the best known and most controversial one, Evo Morales.

32. "Incertidumbre por estado de sitio en Bolivia," *El Nuevo Herald*, April 20, 1995, B2.

Chapter 6 Chile: The Political Underpinnings of Economic Liberalization (Scully)

I am very grateful to several colleagues and friends for their comments and suggestions for revising this chapter, especially E. William Beauchamp, C.S.C., David Collier, Abraham F. Lowenthal, Scott Mainwaring, Bill Maloney, Guillermo O'Donnell, and J. Samuel Valenzuela.

1. William F. Maloney argues persuasively that the set of policies adopted by the military regime during the first decades of authoritarian rule resulted in

unnecessary costs in Chile's transition to a market-oriented, high-growth economy. See "Getting There from Here: Second Thoughts on Chile's Economic Transition," unpublished monograph, Department of Economics, University of Illinois, September 1993.

2. A caveat is in order here. The expansion and diversification of the export sector under Pinochet resulted in little increase in high value-added products, being concentrated instead in (nontraditional) unfinished products. If this general orientation is not redressed, further sustained high growth is improbable over the long term.

3. A useful set of tables on economic performance during the Aylwin administration is available in the appendix to Alejandro Foxley, *Economía política de la transición* (Santiago: Ediciones Dolmen, 1993).

4. See Jaime Gatica, *Deindustrialization in Chile* (Boulder, Colo.: Westview Press, 1989); Eugenio Tironi, *Autoritarismo, modernización, y marginalidad: El caso de Chile 1973–1989* (Santiago: Ediciones Sur, 1990); Pilar Vergara, *Políticas hacia la extrema pobreza en Chile, 1973–1988* (Santiago: FLACSO, 1990); Larissa Lomnitz and Ana Melnick, *Chile's Middle Class: A Struggle for Survival in the Face of Neoliberalism* (Boulder, Colo.: Westview Press, 1991); Cristóbal Kay and Patricio Silva, eds., *Development and Social Change in the Chilean Countryside: From the Pre-Land Reform Period to the Democratic Transition* (Amsterdam: CEDLA, 1992), among others. For a very thorough and provocative review of ten contemporary books on the Chilean political and economic transition, see Gerardo L. Munck, "Authoritarianism, Modernization, and Democracy in Chile: Regime Dynamics and Social Change in Historical Perspective," *Latin American Research Review* 29, no. 2 (1994): 188–211.

5. Taken from "Una estimación de la magnitud de la pobreza en Chile, 1987," *Colecciones Estudios CIEPLAN* 31 (March 1993): 110.

6. Alan Angell, "What Remains of Pinochet's Chile?" *Occasional Paper No. 3*, Institute of Latin American Studies, University of London (1992), 4–5.

7. Tironi, *Autoritarismo, modernización, y marginalidad.*

8. Cited by Kurt Weyland, "Growth with Equity in Chile's New Democracy," Department of Political Science, Vanderbilt University, from *Estadísticas de las finanzas públicas, 1989–1992* (Santiago: Ministerio de Hacienda), 56, 71.

9. *El Mercurio,* July 23, 1993. The same article suggested that, in 1992, two-thirds of total government spending was directed toward social programs. This figure, however, seems inflated.

10. Angell, "What Remains of Pinochet's Chile?" 5.

11. Taken from a national poll administered by MIDEPLAN in November 1992. The Casen poll has been the government's standard social measurement since 1985. Also taken from the *Economist,* June 3, 1995, 17–19.

12. For an excellent discussion of the contemporary transformation of the Chilean state, see Oscar Muñoz, ed., *Después de las privatizaciones: Hacia el estado regulador* (Santiago: CIEPLAN, 1992).

13. Scott Mainwaring and I have discussed extensively in another place what we mean by an "institutionalized party system." We measure party system institutionalization in terms of four attributes: (1) stability in the patterns of interparty competition, (2) the existence of parties that have somewhat stable roots in society, (3) the acceptance of parties and elections as the legitimate institutions that determine who governs, and (4) the existence of party organizations that have reasonably stable rules and structures. Using these criteria, we label Chile as possessing an institutionalized party system (together with Costa Rica, Venezuela, Uruguay, Colombia, and Argentina). See Scott Mainwaring and Timothy R. Scully, eds., *Building Democratic Institutions: Party*

Systems in Latin America (Stanford: Stanford University Press, 1995), especially the Introduction.

14. It is worth reemphasizing here that, though the Aylwin government has not deviated from a basic reliance on free markets, some of its economic policy orientations do differ substantially from the Pinochet period. The most important changes focus on tax reform, labor legislation, and sharply increased social spending.

15. According to Garretón, this "backbone" was formed by "the interlocking of base-level social organizations with the political party structure, both in tension with the state as the focal point for political action." Manuel Antonio Garretón, "Introduction," in Marcelo Cavarozzi and Manuel Antonio Garretón, eds., *Muerte y resurrección: Los partidos políticos en el autoritarismo y las transiciones del Cono Sur* (Santiago: FLACSO, 1989), xvi.

16. As one indication of the moderation of social conflict in Chile, strike rates during the Aylwin administration have been extraordinarily low, both compared to historical rates as well as those of neighboring countries. See Angell, "What Remains of Pinochet's Chile?" 6–9.

17. Scott Mainwaring has shown quite convincingly that the combination of presidentialism with a multiparty format is problematic for maintaining democratic stability; see Mainwaring, "Presidentialism, Multipartism and Democracy: The Difficult Combination," *Comparative Political Studies* 28 (July 1993): 198–228. These notions are also developed in the Introduction to Mainwaring and Scully, *Building Democratic Institutions.*

18. For a more thorough discussion of continuities and changes in the Chilean party system, see Timothy R. Scully, *Rethinking the Center: Party Politics in Nineteenth and Twentieth Century Chile* (Stanford: Stanford University Press, 1992), especially chap. 5; Mainwaring and Scully, *Building Democratic Institutions,* especially chap. 5; also Timothy R. Scully and J. Samuel Valenzuela, "From Democracy to Democracy: Continuities and Changes of Electoral Choices and the Party System in Chile," in Arturo Valenzuela, ed., *Politics, Society, and Democracy: Latin America* (Boulder, Colo.: Westview Press, forthcoming). I take some of the discussion of the next several paragraphs from Scully and Valenzuela.

19. The reasons for this shift within the socialist party have been discussed amply elsewhere. Suffice it to say that it was partly a consequence of the experiences socialist leaders and militants had in both Eastern and Western Europe during their years of exile. See Ignacio Walker, *Socialismo y democracia en Chile: Chile y Europa en perspectiva comparada* (Santiago: CIEPLAN-Hachette, 1990); and Julio Faúndez, *Marxism and Democracy in Chile* (New Haven: Yale University Press, 1988).

20. See Giovanni Sartori, *Parties and Party Systems: A Framework for Analysis* (Cambridge: Cambridge University Press, 1976), 131–216.

21. Robert A. Packenham has written a very stimulating essay tracing the causes of economic liberalization in Argentina and Brazil. He suggests four pattern variables that explain economic liberalization in Argentina (and the absence of it in Brazil). I am indebted to him for his rich analysis. See Robert A. Packenham, "The Politics of Economic Liberalization: Brazil and Argentina in Comparative Perspective," *Kellogg Institute Working Paper* 206 (University of Notre Dame, 1993).

22. These changes are discussed more fully in Scully, *Rethinking the Center,* especially chap. 5.

23. This point should not be exaggerated. The Chilean state continues to play an important role in the economy. For example, the giant copper industry remains in state hands. The state continues to subsidize the forestry industry,

the automobile industry, and, most recently, the coal industry. Unions were also given more power under the Aylwin administration. Packenham ("The Politics of Economic Liberalization") refers to this as the Nixon in China syndrome: his impeccable anticommunist credentials strengthened his hand with potential domestic critics.

24. Issues relating to the process of democratic consolidation in comparative perspective are discussed in J. Samuel Valenzuela's chapter, "Democratic Consolidation in Post-Transitional Settings: Notion, Process, and Facilitating Conditions," in Scott Mainwaring, Guillermo O'Donnell, and J. Samuel Valenzuela, *Issues in Democratic Consolidation: The New South American Democracies in Comparative Perspective* (Notre Dame: University of Notre Dame Press, 1992), 57–104. The term "perverse institutionalization" is his. I have provided a full account of the constraining features of the 1980 Constitution in Timothy R. Scully and Alejandro Ferreiro Y., "Chile Recovers Its Democratic Past: Democratization by Installment," *Journal of Legislation* 18, no. 2 (1992): 317–29.

25. Rhoda Rabkin evaluates the prerogatives granted to the military by the 1980 Constitution: "The Aylwin Government and 'Tutelary' Democracy: A Concept in Search of a Case," *Journal of Interamerican Studies* 34, no. 4 (1992): 119–94.

26. J. Samuel Valenzuela, "Democratic Consolidation in Post-Transitional Settings: Notion, Process, and Facilitating Conditions," in Mainwaring, O'Donnell, and Valenzuela, *Issues in Democratic Consolidation,* 64.

27. *El Mercurio,* June 17, 1993.

28. The ease with which these provisions might be enacted should not be exaggerated, however. Any changes with respect to the armed forces (as well as the Constitutional Court and the National Security Council) require a two-thirds majority in both houses of Congress. To modify other features of the constitution requires a slightly lower majority of both houses, either three-fifths or four-sevenths, depending on the type of law to be modified.

29. For a full treatment of the electoral law and its multiple implications, see "El sistema electoral," Programa de asesoría legislativa, *Análisis de Actualidad* (June 1992). Also see Genaro Arriagada, "Después de los presidencialismos . . . ¿Qué?" in Oscar Godoy, ed., *Cambio de régimen político* (Santiago: Ediciones Universidad Católica de Chile, 1990), 57–91.

30. The overrepresentation of the rural sector was characteristic of pre-coup Chile as well. See Cesar Caviedes, *The Politics of Chile: A Sociographical Assessment* (Boulder, Colo.: Westview Press, 1979).

31. Caution should be exercised in interpreting these results, however, since parties ran in alliances, potentially producing some distortion in the results. Figures are taken from Arriagada, "Después de los presidentialismos," 78.

32. The 1980 Constitution originally provided for only twenty-six senators to be elected, in which case the nine designated would have represented more than one-fourth of that body's total. However, a constitutional reform in July 1989 raised the total number of elected senators to thirty-eight, lowering the relative importance of the designated senators to about one-fifth of the Senate.

33. Eduardo Silva notes his agreement with Brian Loveman; see Silva, "Capitalist Regime Loyalties and Redemocratization in Chile," *Journal of Interamerican Studies* 34, no. 4 (1992): 78.

34. President Aylwin's chief of staff, Edgardo Boeninger, stated two years into the transition that "the main threat is populism, by which I mean the danger of responding to widespread social demands by making promises that outstrip the resources available to fulfill them"; quoted in Rabkin, "The

Aylwin Government," 142. Alejandro Foxley, in an interview with the author, has suggested this to be the case.

35. Cited in Rabkin, "The Aylwin Government," 142.

36. The popularity enjoyed by President Patricio Aylwin's government was consistently high throughout the period of his administration, only once dipping below 50 percent approval. A poll in March 1993 gave Aylwin's government a 57.8 percent approval rating, compared with only 15.6 percent disapproving of the government. Longitudinal survey data covering the previous three years of the Aylwin presidency are provided in "Estudio social y opinion pública no. 19," Centro de Estudios Públicos (May 1993), 41. Eduardo Frei's popularity as president has been at least as high. According to a survey conducted by the Centro de Estudios Públicos, those who rated Frei's performance "positively" or "very positively" comprised 67 percent of the sample. See *Estudios Públicos,* Documento de Trabajo 236 (May–June, 1995).

37. Manuel Antonio Garretón ("La oposición política") argues forcefully that political learning among elites provides a principal explanation for the changed political arena. Nancy Bermeo provides a useful overview of the comparative literature in "Democracy and the Lessons of Dictatorship," *Comparative Politics* 24, no. 3 (1992): 273–91.

38. Acceptance speech made by Alejandro Foxley upon his induction into the Royal Academy of Moral and Political Sciences, Madrid, Spain, March 30, 1993.

39. Giovanni Sartori, *The Theory of Democracy Revisited* (Chatham, N.J.: Chatham House, 1987), 89–91.

Chapter 7 Paraguay: Transition from *Caudillo* Rule (Abente Brun)

1. The procedure for allocating seats in the party's primary was the D'Hondt proportional system. Consequently, Wasmosy's and Argaña's supporters won about an even share of the legislative candidacies. Upon taking office, Wasmosy was able to win the support of a number of former Argaña supporters.

2. The council is made up of eight members. Two are appointed by Congress (one by senators and the other by deputies), one by the executive, one by the Supreme Court, two by the law schools, and two by the lawyers. Of the six members already appointed, three belong to the Colorado Party and three are known as oppositionists. The proportional system is expected to ensure that of the two lawyers elected, one will belong to the Colorado Party and the other to the opposition, thus resulting in a 4–4 tie in the council, which will be forced to find consensus for major designations. The nominal system that the Colorado lawyers want to apply would give both seats to the Colorados, thus producing a 5–3 Colorado majority in the council.

3. According to the constitution, unconstitutionality actions do not have *erga omnes* effects, that is, they cannot result in the complete elimination of the law but only in the suspension of its effects on the individuals that have appealed. In such a context, the unconstitutionality awarded by the court was wholly inapplicable, for the court cannot legislate a different system of election. The most the court could do was to say: the proportional system is unconstitutional, you do not have to be ruled by it; but if you want to vote, you will have to use it because we cannot impose a different system. As the Brazilians would put it, "tem razao mas fica preso." Yet, by raising doubt over the issue, the court has opened the way for other legal actions that could further delay the reform of the judiciary.

4. The constitution excludes judicial acts from the realm of the *amparo,* but the lawyers argue that in calling the election the court has adopted a

merely administrative decision that is subject to a possible *amparo*. The discussion could be endless, but the bottom line is that, given the partiality of the judges, any conceivable recourse can stand, no matter how ridiculous.

Chapter 8 Uruguay: From Restoration to the Crisis of Governability (Rial)

1. This was considered the very essence of Batllismo, a current of thought and political action born and bred in the Colorado Party at the beginning of the century and deeply ingrained in the political culture of the country since then. Named after President José Batlle y Ordóñez (1856–1929) and deeply influenced by French Radicalism, German Krausism, and American Georgism, this ideological tendency postulated the presence of a strong state, conceived of as the great regulator of power relations within society and able to anticipate social demands in order to deflect and channel them. The judicious use of the law and of state intervention would then buffer conflicts, prevent injustice, and preempt revolutionary violence born of discontent. While many of the social and political advances of this small country can be attributed to this school of thought, its critics maintain that it also helped breed a sense of "entitlement to entitlement" in Uruguayan culture that ended by putting a brake on its later development. See Milton Vanger, *Model Country* (Brandeis: Brandeis University Press, 1980); Carlos Real de Azúa, *El impulso y su freno: Tres décadas de Batllismo* (Montevideo: EBO, 1964), and Real de Azúa, *La sociedad amortiguadora* (Montevideo: EBO, 1984).

2. See Fernando Filgueira, "Un estado social centenario: El crecimiento hasta el límite del estado social batllista," in *Peitho*, Documentos de Trabajo 81 (Montevideo: Peitho, 1991).

3. On clientelist practices in Uruguay, see Robert E. Biles, *Patronage Politics: Electoral Behavior in Uruguay* (Baltimore, Johns Hopkins University Press, 1975), and Juan Carlos Fá Robaina, *Cartas a un diputado* (Montevideo: Alfa, 1972).

4. See Oscar Botinelli, "El sistema electoral uruguayo: Descripción y análisis," in *Peitho*, Documentos de Trabajo 83 (Montevideo: Peitho, 1991), and Juan Rial and Jaime Klaczko, "Cómo se vota: El sistema electoral," in *Cuadernos de orientación electoral* 4 (Montevideo: Peitho/CAPEL, 1989).

5. Although the Broad Front, the coalition of parties from the Left, was born in 1971 within this framework, it could be created only by using the provisions of the existing electoral laws that permit accumulation of factions. In 1994 the Broad Front used the political name Encuentro Progresista (Progressive Confluence) but legally kept the designation Frente Amplio (Broad Front). On Uruguayan political parties, see Angel Cocchi, "Un sistema político centenario" and "Los partidos políticos y la historia reciente," in *Cuadernos de orientación electoral* 1, no. 2 (Montevideo: Peitho/CAPEL, 1989).

6. See Henry Finch, *A Political Economy of Uruguay since 1870* (New York: St. Martin's Press, 1981).

7. See Luis Costa Bonino, *Crisis de los partidos tradicionales y movimientos revolucionarios en el Uruguay* (Montevideo: EBO, 1985); Eddy Kauffman, *Uruguay in Transition* (New Brunswick, N.J.: Transaction Books, 1979); Arturo Porzecansky, *Uruguay's Tupamaros: The Urban Guerrilla* (New York: Praeger, 1973).

8. President Juan María Bordaberry, who had decreed the dissolution of the National Assembly on June 27, 1973, was in turn ousted by the military when he tried to institutionalize an authoritarian regime in 1976. See Charles Gillespie, "The Breakdown of Democracy in Uruguay: Alternative Political Models,"

in *Wilson Center for Scholars*, Working Papers 143 (Washington, D.C.: Woodrow Wilson Center, 1984).

9. I have borrowed this term from Carl Schmitt, *La dictadura* (Madrid: Revista de Occidente, 1968), 5ff (originally published in 1921). This idea was developed in Juan Rial, "Transitions in Latin America on the Threshold of the 1990s," *International Social Science Journal* 128 (May 1991), 285.

10. See Juan Corradi, Patricia Fagen, and Manuel A. Garretón, *The Culture of Fear in the Southern Cone* (Berkeley: University of California Press, 1994); Carina Perelli, "Settling Accounts with Blood Memory: The Case of Argentina," *Social Research* 50 (1992), 415–51; and Saul Sosnowski and Louise B. Popkin, eds., *Repression, Exile, and Democracy: Uruguayan Culture* (Durham, N.C.: Duke University Press, 1993).

11. On the transition process, see Charles Gillespie, *Negotiating Democracy: Politicians and Generals in Uruguay* (Cambridge: Cambridge University Press, 1991), and Luis E. González, *Political Structure and Democracy in Uruguay* (Notre Dame: University of Notre Dame Press, 1991).

12. See Juan Rial, *Elecciones de 1984: Sistema electoral y resultados* (San José: IIDH/CAPEL, 1986).

13. See Manuel Alcántara and Ismael Crespo, *Partidos y elecciones en Uruguay, 1971–1990* (Madrid: CEDEAL, 1992), and IIDH/CAPEL, *El referéndum uruguayo de 16 de abril de 1989* (San José: IIDH, 1989).

14. These are the reform measures recommended by the international organizations that monitor third world economies. See John Williamson, "What Washington Means by Political Reform," in John Williamson, ed., *Latin American Adjustment: How Much Has Happened?* (Washington, D.C.: Institute for International Economics, 1990).

15. In an interview with the author (May 1992), Dr. Sanguinetti admitted that this was the only way to prevent continual pressure to increase public expenditures, given the fragmentation of the party system.

16. The National Party obtained 38.87 percent of the vote and the faction of Luis Alberto Lacalle 22.57 percent. See Carina Perelli and Juan Rial, "Las elecciones uruguayas de noviembre de 1989," in Rodolfo Cerdas, Juan Rial, and Daniel Zovatto, *Elecciones y democracia en América Latina: Una tarea inconclusa* (San José: IIDH/CAPEL/Naumann, 1992).

17. Calculations made in 1995 indicate that each member of the active work force must pay an average of U.S.$3,600 dollars to the state in taxes or contributions to Social Security. This amount has been paid by Uruguayan workers since 1991. *Búsqueda 802*, July 27, 1994, 23.

18. The normal VAT rate was 22 percent, increased to 23 percent in 1995. It is one of the highest in the world.

19. It was 7.88 percent in 1992, 2.53 percent in 1993, and 5.08 percent in 1994 (data from the Central Bank of Uruguay). In 1995 the economic team forecasts a recession and 0 percent growth.

20. From 59 percent annual inflation in 1992 to 53 percent in 1993. In 1994 the figure was 44 percent, dropping to 37 percent in 1995.

21. In 1994, an election year, it was 2 percent.

22. In 1990, the Gini Index (which measures income distribution from 0–1, 0 being the most equal) was 0.37; in 1991, 0.43; in 1992, 0.44; in 1993, 0.42; and in 1994, 0.41.

23. If the population is divided into quintiles, the wealthiest 20 percent received 47.5 percent of total income in 1993. The poorest 20 percent received 5 percent of total income, the upper-middle-bracket (20%) received 23 percent of total income, the lower-middle bracket (20%) received 9.5 percent, and the middle bracket (20%) received 15 percent.

24. Carina Perelli and Juan Rial, "El referéndum sobre la Ley de empresas públicas del 13 de diciembre de 1992 en el Uruguay: Un plebiscito sobre la gestión del gobierno," in *Peitho*, Documentos de Trabajo 93 (Montevideo: Peitho, 1992).

25. The level of conflict was more important during Sanguinetti's term. Thus, according to data provided by CEALS (Centro de Estudios y Asesoramiento Laborales y Sociales), 2,139 days of work were lost in 1988 due to strikes; in 1992 there were 1,329 days lost, and in 1993 the number increased to 1,904. It decreased in 1994 and 1995. See Centro Uruguay Independiente, *Relaciones laborales y convenios en el Uruguay. Los sindicatos ante la reestructura* (Montevideo: CIU, 1995).

26. The inflated membership lists allow them to have more votes at the PIT-CNT congresses. The total number of affiliates is about 200,000 in a formal work force of 800,000.

27. In fact, this is what is beginning to occur in modern companies such as PepsiCo International and even some state companies such as UTE (electric company), ANTEL (telecommunications), and ANCAP (oil), where organized labor has negotiated productivity pacts and thus receives a share of the profits. See *Relaciones laborales y convenios.*

28. In 1993 an informant at a police station claimed that he was a Chilean named Berríos (he was investigated for human rights violations and was apparently connected to the Letelier case) and that he had been kidnapped by members of the Uruguayan military as part of an agreement with the Chilean armed forces. Police authorities tried to hush the scandal, and the informant disappeared. However, the press published the case, and some members of the police force and the army were sanctioned. In 1996 the scandal resurfaced. The corpse of a person believed to be Berríos appeared on a Uruguayan beach.

29. Uruguay had a UN battalion in Mozambique until January 1995; another battalion was part of the UN forces in Cambodia until May 1993; and a new battalion was deployed in Angola in 1995.

30. From 1934 to 1967, elections were held every four years.

31. A proposal to reform the constitution in order to allow voters to choose different *lemas* at the national and the municipal level was rejected in August 1994.

32. In 1994 the Congress approved a bill to pay U.S.$7 per vote, up from the previous U.S.$1 per vote.

33. The Electoral Court has proposed easing this rule by making voting voluntary for older citizens. While no resolution has yet been passed on this matter, Congress usually grants amnesty to older citizens who did not or could not vote at any given election.

34. In 1994, voter participation reached 89 percent.

35. The Colorado Party won the election with only 30,000 votes more than the National Party and 60,000 more than the Broad Front (Progressive Confluence). The Colorado Party will have thirty-one senators and thirty-two representatives in the house; the National Party ten senators and thirty-one representatives; the Broad Front nine senators and thirty-one representatives; and the Nuevo Espacio (New Space) Party, one senator and five representatives.

36. Robert Michels, *Los partidos políticos* (Buenos Aires: Amorrortu, 1969), 6ff.

37. Luis Eduardo González used this expression in a television public appearance in 1993.

38. See Carina Perelli, *Gobierno y política en Montevideo: La Intendencia Municipal de Montevideo y la formación de un nuevo liderazgo a comienzos de los años '90* (Montevideo: Peitho, 1991), and Carina Perelli: "La personaliza-

ción de la política: Nuevos caudillos, outsiders, política mediática y política informal," in Carina Perelli, Sonia Picado, and Daniel Zovatto, eds., *Partidos y clase política en América Latina en los 90* (San José: IIDH/CAPEL, 1995).

39. Rodney Arismendi was a member of parliament between 1949 and 1973, when his term of office was interrupted by the military dictatorship. Elected senator in 1989, he never occupied his seat as he died before his new term of office. He was secretary general of the Communist Party from 1955 until almost his death.

40. United Nations Development Program, *Human Development. Report 1994* (Cambridge: Oxford University Press/UNDP, 1995).

Chapter 9 Argentina: Democracy in Turmoil (De Riz)

1. See Mario Damill and Roberto Frenkel, "Restauración democrática y política económica: Argentina, 1984–1991," in Juan Antonio Morales and Gary McMahon, eds., *La política económica en la transición a la democracia: Lecciones de Argentina* (Santiago de Chile: CIEPLAN, 1993); Pablo Gerchunoff and José L. Machinea, "Un ensayo sobre la política económica después de la estabilización," in Pablo Bustos, ed., *Más allá de la estabilidad: Argentina en la época de la globalización y la regionalización* (Buenos Aires: Fundación FEBERT, 1995), 29–92; and Alberto Minujin and Gabriel Kessler, *La nueva pobreza en Argentina* (Buenos Aires: Editorial Planeta, 1995).

2. The best scholarly analysis of Menem's Argentina is Tulio Halperín Donghi, *La larga agonía de la Argentina peronista* (Buenos Aires: Espasa Calpe/Ariel, 1994). Some economists are now developing the concept of "modernización a la intemperie," as referred to by Halperín Donghi and Jose Nun, "Populismo, representación y menemismo," *Sociedad* 5 (October 1994): 93–121.

3. The Ministry of the Economy was initially assigned to the directors of the Bunge and Born group.

4. Shortly after taking office, President Menem obtained approval for the law of economic emergency with the consent of the Radicals. This law granted the executive full powers to modify legislation without the subsequent intervention of Congress and launched the privatization of the state-owned telephone and aviation companies. It must be remembered that President Menem's early assumption of power—a paraconstitutional solution to the governability crisis—opened up an anomalous period. The Menem administration began without the simultaneous renewal of Congress but with the tacit understanding that he would not encounter obstacles during that portion of his term on the part of an opposition that was on the defensive and considered responsible for the disarray and its premature relinquishing of power.

5. I refer to a number of factors: the removal of the deputy prosecutors and of the head of the National Prosecutor's Office for Administrative Investigations, without seeking the required approval by the Senate or submitting the accused officials to due process of political trials; the modification by decree of the statutes of the National Auditor's Office, the agency responsible for monitoring the legality of the administrative procedures for dispensing public funds; the suspension of four of the five members of this office without invoking due cause. The expansion of the number of members of the Supreme Court was one of a series of measures aimed at curtailing the independence of the powers of the state. By repeatedly resorting to *per saltum*, the court lost its character as an extraordinary tribunal and became an ordinary tribunal of the third instance, as cases were taken away from their rightful judges. The political role and resulting political commitment of the Supreme Court are blurred: the *per saltum* in the case of the privatization of Aerolíneas Argentinas is illustrative.

The majority of the members that comprise the court is in favor of the expansion of emergency powers, which have been virtually exempted from legislative controls. A documented analysis of the erosion of these controls is found in Horacio Verbitsky, *Hacer la corte* (Buenos Aires: Editorial Sudamericana, 1993).

6. The convertibility law requires that the money supply have an exact equivalent in foreign currency reserves in the central bank at the official exchange rate (10,000 australes per U.S. dollar). This prevents these reserves from being used for other purposes. In this way the government's hands are perceived to be "tied" and unable to alter the course that was established.

7. See Liliana De Riz, "El debate sobre la reforma electoral en Argentina," *Desarrollo Económico* 32, no. 126 (1992): 163–84. It should be noted that abstentions increased in the legislative elections of 1991, jumping from an average of 15 percent during the 1980s to 22 percent. The phenomenon of the growth of provincial parties to the detriment of the major national parties was accentuated. A new force to the right of the political spectrum, the Movement for National Dignity and Independence (MODIN), led by former colonel Aldo Rico (protagonist of the military rebellion of Easter Week, in April 1987), captured 10 percent of the vote in the province of Buenos Aires and three seats in the Chamber of Deputies. In Chaco a retired general became governor and in Salta, Captain Ulloa. Both men were former governors during the preceding military government. The triumph of Peronism in the elections for governor had the peculiarity of bringing nonparty candidates to power in provincial states. These candidates were chosen by the president without party consultation. They were something of a "new breed," for example, a singer (Ortega in Tucumán), a race car driver (Reuteman in Santa Fé), a businessman (Escobar in San Juan).

8. During the first four years of his term, President Menem issued three hundred eight Decrees of Necessity and Urgency, which sharply contrasts with the ten issued by President Alfonsín. See Delia Ferreira Rubio and Mateo Goretti, "El gobierno por decreto en la Argentina (1983–1993)," *El Derecho* 32, no. 8525 (June 27, 1994).

9. The New Country Alliance, in which historically antagonistic parties such as the PJ (Peronists), the UCEDE (Union of the Democratic Center), and the MID (Movement of Integration and Development) converged, obtained 32 percent of the vote. This figure coincides with that obtained by the FREJUPO (Popular Judicial Front) in the 1989 elections for senator of the federal capital. On that occasion, thanks to the votes of the UCEDE in the electoral college, the FREJUPO reached 52 percent (the UCEDE had obtained 20 percent of the vote). The corollary is the exodus in 1992 of allied votes toward the UCR (Radical Civic Union) and other parties such as the MODIN. The polls showed that 36 percent of those who held a positive image of Cavallo voted for the UCR and 26 percent of those who had a positive opinion of Menem also opted for the UCR. On the other hand, an analysis of the electoral results by electoral constituency shows that Avelino Porto, the candidate of the ruling party, defeated Fernando De la Rúa by a little more than 1 point in Villa Lugano, a district that in 1989 gave 55 percent of its vote to the PJ. Porto managed to win only in Villa Lugano and Socorro (two districts that represent the two extremes of the social scale). The performance of the UCR in 1992, compared with the results of the 1991 legislative elections, confirms the hypothesis that approximately 25 percent of the electorate that voted for Peronism in 1991 leaned toward the UCR, the MODIN, and the Frente del Sur (a leftist political group headed by Pino Solanas) in 1992. The senatorial elections in the capital (and, in particular, the 1992 elections in which De la Rúa ran and was the can-

didate who obtained the most votes in 1989, but did not take office because of the subsequent negotiations in the electoral college) are inconclusive about the volatility of the Peronist vote. These are, on the other hand, occasions when the candidate has greater "weight," and the opportunity exists for opinion votes that are less attached to partisan loyalties than is the case in elections for the partial renewal of the Chamber of Deputies.

10. The Yoma case refers to the trial of the president's sister-in-law—the former director of audiences of the presidency—and of her ex-husband, a fugitive from justice, for the laundering of drug money.

11. Within the framework of procedural reform, the control over the Judicial Federal Privilege was completed. The Judicial Federal Privilege decides which cases can be appealed to the Supreme Court, including the cases that involve officials of the executive branch. Carried out by promoting and transferring judges who ordered the prosecution of government officials, and replacing them with complacent judges, the control made possible a stay of proceedings in these types of cases. The continuance in power or the return of officials under suspicion—for instance, the former minister of public works, Roberto Dromi, was recently reappointed to the cabinet at the level of secretary of state—transformed the fight against corruption, defined by Menem as treason, into a parody.

12. The initiative included changes in the rules governing the party system: direct primaries for the election of party authorities, representation of minorities in the government and administration, the political-legal status of the parties at the municipal level, the establishment of time limits for interventions, setting the minimum age to vote in party primaries at sixteen years, simultaneous noncompulsory but open primaries, and the inclusion of independent candidates unless prohibited by the respective organizational charter of each party. The rules of party financing and municipal-government relations were also modified.

13. These figures suggest the formation of a Menemist electoral coalition that brings together those from the top and those from the bottom of the social scale. A large number of votes from the Right splintered toward Peronism. The Frente Grande (FG), a left-of-center political organization, benefited from the exodus of Radical votes and, to a lesser extent, of Peronist votes. With 13.6 percent of the vote, the FG became the third force in the district. See Liliana De Riz, "La coyuntura argentina," *Nueva Sociedad* 129 (1993): 6–14.

14. The PJ and the UCR represent two heterogeneous and contradictory political forces in their bases of social support. These forces compete on the same hunting grounds, located at the Center of the ideological spectrum. The logic of competition, stimulated by the bipartisan format that emerged in 1983, gradually blurred the traditional identities and profiles and accentuated the phenomenon of the personalization of politics. Given this context, the fluctuation of votes that is clearly evident since 1987 acquires greater sense. The emergence of ideological parties that embrace social protest, such as the FG in the capital and the MODIN in the province of Buenos Aires, creates a broader range of options toward both the Left and the Right. However, the MODIN obtained only 5.8 percent of the vote, and the FG, 3.6 percent (overall, the Left obtained 4.7 percent of the vote of the entire country). See De Riz, "La coyuntura argentina."

15. Article 30 of the constitution requires a two-thirds vote of members of both houses of Congress to declare the need for reform. The commission for Constitutional Affairs of the lower house approved a bill that sustains the interpretation of article 30 to mean that two-thirds of the members of each house present are needed to declare the need for reform.

16. It should be noted that, according to polls taken before the so-called Olivos Pact, the level of support for constitutional reform reached 50 percent. Likewise, data from surveys taken in ten provinces during September 1993 indicated that both the decision to participate in the plebiscite as well as the inclination to vote in support of the reform were about 70 percent. The lowest figure was recorded in Tucumán (64.1 percent) and the highest in Jujuy (74.6 percent expressed support for constitutional reform) (SOFRES [French polling association]–IBOPE [Brazilian Institute of Public Opinion]). The negotiation thus occurred within the framework of a diffuse reformist consensus throughout society. The sectors with the highest concentration of business owners were also in support of these reforms. Although traditionally reluctant to reform the constitution, the private sector ended by accepting the reform as a condition for the continuity of the economic model. Both the church and the armed forces also came to accept what appeared to them as a fait accompli. Even though important sectors of the establishment, represented in the editorials of the newspaper La Nación, maintained a stance of opposition toward reform and, in particular, toward presidential reelection, the crux of their position gradually changed. It shifted from challenging the necessity and opportunity for reform toward debating the constitutionality of the procedures followed by the government and the principal opposition, as well as criticizing the contents of the reform itself.

17. The content of the agreed text that was presented to the Congress establishes a nucleus of basic points of agreement, topics open for discussion by the Constituent Assembly, and guarantees for the enactment of what was agreed upon. Among the basic points of agreement are the direct election of the president and vice-president, the reduction of their term in office to four years, reelection for one term, the elimination of the confessional requirement in order to be president, ballotage, the creation of the position of chief of the Cabinet of Ministers, the direct election of three senators with a four-year term (one senator for the minority), the limiting of Decrees of Necessity and Urgency, the creation of the Council of Magistrates charged with proposing obligatory lists of two and three names for the appointment of judges, Senate approval of nominees to the Supreme Court by absolute majority, and the direct election of the intendant of the federal capital.

18. This is the lesson that was gained from the experience of the plebiscite held in the province of Buenos Aires to decide the reelection of the governor in the face of the opposition's refusal to endorse it at the Constituent Assembly. The opposition—in particular the UCR, in open contradiction to the party's position regarding presidential reelection—ended up a prisoner of its antireelectionist stand. The October 3, 1994, elections gave the victory to the PJ with 61 percent of the vote, securing the right of Governor Duhalde to run again for governor in that province. The opposition bungled the opportunity to negotiate the text of the constitution, contributed to making the elections into a national issue, and had to compete against the ruling party at a clear disadvantage in terms of resources.

19. Interview with Radio Mitre, February 2 and 5, 1994. Raúl Alfonsín justified his strategy in response to those who alleged that the opposition emerged from the negotiations weakened. He affirmed that "the opposition cannot reduce itself to declarations of principles and ideals; it should strive toward the achievement of objectives, a creation of a new type of dialogue with the government." (Radio Mitre, February 5, 1994). One of his main arguments was that, unlike what occurred in 1949 and 1957, this reform would be reached by consent.

20. The violence that erupted in that province took place within the framework of the approval of the law of adjustment of public employment and the amazing contrasts in salaries within the public administration. The mobilizations of protest that proliferated in the poorest provinces were toned-down replicas of what occurred in Santiago del Estero.

21. The PJ obtained 37.7 percent of the vote, a figure below its lowest historic record in 1983, and the UCR, 19.9 percent. With 13.6 percent of the vote, the FG became the third force at the national level. The MODIN went from 6 percent to 9 percent at the national level, achieving a more even distribution in various districts with respect to 1993. The FG prevailed in the federal capital with 37.6 percent of the vote, confirming the pattern of strong voting volatility in that district. In the province of Buenos Aires, the FG managed to become a second minority, slightly above the UCR, with 16.3 percent of the vote. It should be pointed out that the UCR was internally split over the legitimacy of the Olivos Pact and had slogans such as "better to vote for the original than for a copy." This may help explain the important loss of votes, which primarily benefited the FG.

22. The PJ was able to impose neither the clause related to the reelection of governors nor the ban on abortion, two issues over which the PJ encountered the joint resistance of the UCR and the FG.

23. The historic constitution did not consider the Office of Public Defender. Its creation and regulation originated in a law. Since the enactment of law 27, the president appoints the person who fills this office with the approval of the Senate. Political trial and resignation were the only conditions for premature termination of his or her functions. Nevertheless, President Menem removed the last public defender by means of a decree and appointed three attorneys general in his place.

24. Eleven provincial parties surpassed 1.5 million votes in the 1994 elections. Also, with the exception of the MODIN, Fuerza Republicana (the Tucumán Republican Force) of Tucumán, and Frente de la Esperanza (Front of Hope) (San Juan), the tendency toward the electoral strengthening of the provincial parties evident since 1983 is fueled by the discontent of the urban middle class, as confirmed by a demographic analysis of the data. In an indirect manner, this tendency is also shown by the lesser capacity of the UCR relative to the PJ to retain its social base. See Gerardo Adrogué, "Militares en las urnas: ¿a quienes representan?" *Desarrollo Económico* 33, no. 131 (1993): 425–42.

25. The FREPASO is a Center-Left coalition integrated by the FG, the Unidad Socialista (Socialist Union), the Democracia Cristiana (Christian Democrats), and the País (Country), a party created by Peronist senator José Octavio Bordón, former governor of Mendoza Province. Bordón was elected as their residential candidate in the FREPASO's February primaries. Much to everyone's surprise, five hundred thousand citizens cast their votes in the primaries to decide which of the two former Peronist leaders—Chacho Alvarez and Bordón —would be the presidential candidate in the May elections.

26. Under the new electoral rules, only positive votes were considered. The valid votes embrace not only the positive votes but also the annulled votes and the "votos en blanco" (the voter casts a ballot for none of the candidates). It must be kept in mind that voting is compulsory.

27. See Halperín Donghi, *La larga agonía de la Argentina,* and Juan Corradi, "Menem's Argentina, Act II," *Current History* (February 1995): 76–79. Since 1983, Peronist voters have remained steady, between 36 and 38 percent of the total.

28. The electoral results confirmed the evanescence of the two-party system. This was already obvious in the 1994 elections for the Constituent Assembly.

29. In the November 1994 primaries, the Radicals elected Horacio Massaccesi, governor of the Rio Negro province, as their presidential candidate. The fact that only 30 percent of registered Radicals voted in the primaries suggests that the candidate, close to the old guard, and more prone to compromising with President Menem, did not raise enough enthusiasm among many party members. The personal character of Massaccesi's electoral campaign prevented the party from establishing allies in the provincial parties.

30. The 1995 presidential electoral results were: Menem-Ruckauf, 47.7 percent; Bordón-Alvarez, 28.2 percent; Massaccesi-Hernández, 16.4 percent. The rest of the parties accounted for only 3.6 percent of the total. The MODIN did not reach 2 percent. The UCEDE lent its support to Menem's candidacy. The nine left-wing parties together did not reach 2 percent. Annulled and "en blanco" votes represented 4.1 percent of the total.

31. The electoral results for the renewal of the national Chamber of Deputies were: the Peronist Party, 43 percent; the Radical Party, 22 percent; and the FREPASO, 21 percent. The differences between votes for president and votes for deputies in the parties show the increasing tendency among voters to distribute their preferences between candidates belonging to different parties ("corte de boletas"). In the country as a whole, almost 20 percent of valid votes followed this pattern, while the historical median oscillated between 5 and 7 percent.

32. In the fourteen gubernatorial provincial elections, the UCR succeeded in retaining three of the provinces and winning in a new one (Catamarca). The FREPASO did not get any provincial governor (for this reason it is important to keep in mind that the central government established a sequential system of provincial elections). Elections for governor are scheduled in the remaining provinces for September and October 1995. It is also clear that in these elections for governor the UCR's and the PJ's candidates accumulated more votes than the presidential candidates from the same parties. This shows the weight of local politics in voting results. Only in two provinces did the votes for Menem outnumber the votes for Peronist gubernatorial candidates.

33. I refer to Congress' delay in sanctioning key executive legal programs, despite Menem's pressure for the support of Peronist legislators. Under the new constitutional rules, the lower house insisted on the amended executive programs despite Menem's veto, for example, in the case of the copyright law.

34. Since the convertibility plan, the unemployment rate has nearly doubled at the national level. In greater Buenos Aires, laboratory of the deepest, old-fashioned populist policies and led by Governor Eduardo Duhalde, it has nearly tripled.

35. The debate on the government privatization of the Yacyretá hydroelectric complex held in the upper house is a prime example. The Yacyretá case can be seen as an early indication that new constitutional rules will produce important changes in the exercise of presidential power. The minister of the economy is no longer able to impose his decisions on the Peronists. The debate on the privatization of the mail service is another case. Minister Cavallo himself is trying to prevent Peronist deputies from sanctioning it. Cavallo's accusations of corruption in the mail service privatization program brought this issue into the center of the political debates. Cavallo pointed out that if this program were approved by the lower house, a monopolistic mail system would be created that would be suitable for laundering drug money. In that case, Argentina would follow the Colombian pattern.

36. Eduardo Duhalde, former vice-president and current governor of the province of Buenos Aires, has positioned himself to succeed Menem as president in 1999. Elected to a second term as governor of the nation's most popu-

lous province under a new constitution changed to suit his ambitions, Duhalde challenges Cavallo, his rival in the race for the presidency.

37. Some observers have suggested that the former division of roles within the government is changing. As secretary of the presidency, Bauzá mediated in cabinet conflicts representing President Menem. Now, as chief of the cabinet, Bauzá has taken sides on various issues. As a result, Menem's role as mediator has become more clearly defined.

38. Gerchunoff and Machinea, "Un ensayo sobre la política económica." See also Adolfo Canitrot, "Navegamos a ultramar en carabela," *Página* 12 (July 23, 1995).

39. The financial crisis in the provinces is the result of a combination of factors: the provincial governments have been slow to privatize or have refused to do it, their banks are insolvent, their governments employ over half the labor force, and they rely on the central government for their revenues. The federal system in Argentina is such that the central government must regularly bribe the provinces in order to get their political support.

40. Natalio Botana has well described the present political weakness of the regime as a "republic of words," "a republic of suspicions" doomed to disintegrate as the result of both corruption and discord instead of the "modern Republic" that had inspired Mitre, Sarmiento, and Alberdi. *La Nación*, August 28, 1995. In the year that followed the enactment of the new constitution, Congress approved only three of the twenty-one laws that were to be passed. What is more, the deadline for three of the most crucial laws has expired.

41. According to the polls taken by Manuel Mora & Associates following Cavallo's accusations, 79 percent believe that the minister's accusations are true and 66 percent believe that it would be detrimental for Cavallo to resign. On the other hand, 29 percent consider that President Menem was weakened.

42. Stephan Haggard and Robert Kaufman, "The State in the Initiation and Consolidation of Market-oriented Reform," *Série política internacional e comparada* 4 (São Paulo: University of São Paulo, 1991).

43. A new type of relationship between the government and the armed forces was gradually forming throughout the course of the Menem administration. After suppressing the December 1990 Carapintada Rebellion and issuing a presidential pardon to the former commanders, Menem gave the military a function within the framework of the new international policy by sending troops abroad to participate in peacekeeping missions. This "exit into the world" places the military in a new position: it is now under the watchful eye of the rest of the world. At the same time, the emergence of parties of former military officers, such as the MODIN, Acción Chaqueña (Chaco Action), and Fuerza Republicana, synthesize the new type of link established between the military and politics. See Adrogué, "Militares en las urnas;" Argentina has become a successfully demilitarized state to a considerably greater degree than any other South American country. Its military expenses in relation to the gross domestic product have dropped significantly since the advent of the Menem administration. While it reached 3.5 percent in 1989, it represented only 1.9 percent in 1991. See Carlos Escudé and Andrés Fontana, "Divergencias estratégicas en el Cono Sur: Las políticas de seguridad de la Argentina frente a las de Brasil y Chile," in *Universidad Torcuato Di Tella*, Working Paper 20 (Buenos Aires, July 1995).

In this new situation, the armed forces' current demand that the government define its defense and security policy goals, and consequently the nature and scope of the role of the military, is a clear symptom of the unrest.

44. The General Confederation of Labor (CGT) resisted the policies of the Radical government by resorting to repeated general strikes. Today the CGT is no longer the "backbone" of Peronism as it was in the past, but rather one more component of the political system, obliged to lobby rather than stage general strikes. The breakup of the system of collective bargaining and its replacement by either a system of bargaining at individual firms or by salary freezes, and the increasing weakness of the retirement and public assistance systems, have stripped the CGT of its power resources. Its role is now confined to endorsing policies that are decided by the government without the participation of the CGT.

45. Gerchunoff and Machinea, "Un ensayo sobre la política económica."

46. It should be noted that the accumulated increase in gross national product between 1991 and 1994 was about 35 percent. At present, the unemployment and underemployment rates have reached 30 percent. On September 6, 1995, the CGT carried out its first general strike.

47. The September 3, 1995, gubernatorial election in the province of Santa Fé, one of the four main electoral districts, was transformed into another national scandal. The generalized suspicions of fraud raised by the unclear process of provisional scrutiny of the votes led political parties in the province to disavow the results and wait until the definitive count of votes was finished. Encotesa, the official mail service company in charge of the scrutiny, was either the supposed victim of sabotage (a hypothesis that Minister Cavallo himself suggested in an interview on Radio del Plata on September 7, 1995) or responsible for fraud. President Menem ordered Encotesa to publish the preliminary results on September 6. The PJ triumphed with a narrow margin of 4 points over the opposition. Under the current provincial electoral system (ley de lemas), the Peronist winner was the candidate backed by President Menem (a socialist and former mayor of Rosario City). According to the provisional scrutiny, Duhalde and Reuteman's candidate lost by the narrow margin of less than 1 percent. Governor Reuteman declared that he would investigate, despite his having received death threats if he did. He did not hesitate to hold the political sector of the government responsible.

Chapter 10 Brazil: The Hyperactive Paralysis Syndrome (Lamounier)

Support from the Mellon Foundation for background research is gratefully acknowledged.

1. On January 3, 1994, a prominent former ambassador, Paulo Nogueira Batista, wrote that Brazil's illness was "more political than economic" ("A Democracia Ameaçada," Folha de São Paulo); on January 13 the London-based Latin American Weekly Reports opened its Brazil report with the headline "Scale of Corruption Scandal Provokes New Fears of Military Intervention."

2. For an overview of Brazilian politics from the 1930s to 1964, see Thomas Skidmore, Politics in Brazil: An Experiment in Democracy (Oxford: Oxford University Press, 1967) on authoritarianism and democracy; Alfred Stepan, ed., Authoritarian Brazil: Origins, Policies and Future (New Haven: Yale University Press, 1973); and Bolívar Lamounier, "And Yet It Does Move: Formation and Evolution of the Democratic State in Brazil, 1930–1994," in Bolívar Lamounier et al., eds., Fifty Years of Brazil (Rio de Janeiro: Editora da Fundação Getúlio Vargas, 1994), 9–158.

3. On the ambivalent legitimacy of authoritarian rule, see Juan Linz, "The Future of an Authoritarian Situation or the Institutionalization of an Authoritarian Regime: The Case of Brazil," in Stepan, ed., Authoritarian Brazil, 233–

54, and Bolívar Lamounier, "Opening through Elections: Will the Brazilian Case Become a Paradigm?" *Government and Opposition* 19, no. 2 (1984): 167–77, and Lamounier, "Authoritarian Brazil Revisited: the Impact of Elections on the Brazilian 'Abertura,'" in Alfred Stepan, ed., *Democratizing Brazil: Problems of Transition and Consolidation* (New York: Oxford University Press, 1988), 43–79.

4. See Maria D'Alva G. Kinzo, *Legal Opposition Politics under Authoritarian Rule in Brazil* (Oxford: Macmillan, 1988); see also Lamounier, "Opening through Elections," and "Authoritarian Brazil Revisited."

5. This description of hyperactivism is limited to the political sphere; on its interaction with the formidable succession of anti-inflation shocks of this period, see Bolívar Lamounier and Edmar Bacha, "Democracy and Economic Reform in Brazil," in Joan Nelson, ed., *Precarious Balance: Democratic Consolidation and Economic Reform in Eastern Europe and Latin America* (Washington, D.C.: International Center for Economic Growth and the Overseas Development Council [ICEG/ODC], 1994). For a comparison of constitution-making experiences in Brazil, Spain, Portugal, and Chile, see Dieter Nohlen et al., "El proceso constituyente: Experiencias a partir de cuatro casos recientes—España, Portugal, Brasil y Chile," *Boletín electoral latinoamericano* (San José, Costa Rica: IIDH/CAPEL) 5 (Jan.–June 1991), In the Brazilian case, a drafting commission was to be announced by the president-elect, Tancredo Neves, in his inauguration speech (March 15, 1985), but he fell ill on that day and died on April 21. The commission was not appointed by President Sarney until late August. By then it had become an unwieldy fifty-member body, symptomatically entitled "Provisional Commission for Constitutional Studies." One year later, when the commission finished its draft, Sarney recognized it as a government document by having it published in the Diário Oficial, but refused to send it officially as an amendment to the Constitutional Congress.

6. This two-pronged depletion was at work since the 1970s but was bluntly symbolized after the 1982 gubernatorial elections. On one side, the last general, João Figueiredo, under the additional weight of serious health problems, found it clearly painful even to abide by the ceremonial duties of the presidential office; on the other, an angry crowd tried to break through the gates of the Bandeirantes Palace in São Paulo in an attempt to force the just inaugurated oppositionist Governor Franco Montoro to fulfill an alleged campaign promise of creating four hundred thousand jobs.

7. Lamounier and Bacha, "Democracy and Economic Reform in Brazil."

8. On the Workers' Party, see Rachel Meneguello, *PT: A Formação de um partido* (Rio de Janeiro: Editora Paz e Terra, 1989), and Margaret Keck, *The Workers Party and Democratization in Brazil* (New Haven: Yale University Press, 1992).

9. The model inherited from the 1930s was actually a tripod, with the corporatist regulation of capital/labor relations as the third leg; see Bolívar Lamounier, "Institutional Structure and Governability in the 1990s," in Maria D'Alva Kinzo, ed., *Brazil: The Challenges of the 1990s* (London: British Academic Press, 1992), 117–37. On the contrast between "consociational" and "majoritarian" democracies, see Arend Lijphart, *Democracies: Patterns of Majoritarian and Consensus Government in Twenty-One Countries* (New Haven: Yale University Press, 1984). It is worth remarking that Lijphart, a strong advocate of the consociational model, explicitly notes that it is incongruent with presidential government; see Arend Lijphart, "Presidencialismo e democracia majoritária," in Bolívar Lamounier, ed., *A Opção parlamentarista* (São Paulo: Editora Sumaré, 1991), 121–37.

10. Cited by Ralph Dahrendorf, *Essays in the Theory of Society* (Stanford: Stanford University Press, 1968), 178.

11. Data from Ibope polls analyzed in Bolívar Lamounier and Alexandre H. Marques, "A democracia brasileira no final da 'Década Perdida,'" in Bolívar Lamounier, ed., *Ouvindo o Brasil: Uma análise da opinião pública brasileira hoje* (São Paulo: Editora Sumaré, 1992), 139–58. President Clinton's loss of popularity during his first hundred days in office was the subject of a *Time* magazine cover story entitled "The Incredible Shrinking Man." Such an abrupt fall would probably have caused a serious crisis in any other presidentialist country. On plebiscitarian tendencies in the United States, see Theodore Lowi, *The Personal President: Power Invested, Promise Unfulfilled* (Ithaca: Cornell University Press, 1985), and Craig A. Rimmerman, *Presidency by Plebiscite: The Reagan-Bush Era in Institutional Perspective* (Boulder, Colo.: Westview Press, 1993).

12. On Collor's rise and fall, see Amaury Souza, "Collor's Impeachment and Institutional Reform in Brazil," paper prepared for the conference "Wither Brazil after Collor?" University of Miami, North-South Center, February 26–27, 1993; figures in the text are from Bolívar Lamounier and Amaury Souza, "O Congresso Nacional e a crise brasileira," *Research Report* (São Paulo: IDESP, 1991), table 13.

13. On Brazilian political parties, see Bolívar Lamounier and Rachel Meneguello, *Partidos políticos e consolidação democrática: O Caso brasileiro* (São Paulo: Editora Brasiliense, 1986); D'Alva G. Kinzo, *Legal Opposition Politics*; Antonio Lavareda, *A democracia nas urnas: O processo partidário-eleitoral brasileiro* (Rio de Janeiro: IUPERJ/Rio Fundo Editora, 1991); and Maria D'Alva G. Kinzo, *Radiografia do quadro partidário brasileiro* (São Paulo: Fundação Konrad Adenauer, 1994).

14. Arend Lijphart, *Democracies: Patterns of Majoritarian and Consensus Government in Twenty-One Countries* (New Haven: Yale University Press, 1984).

15. Equal representation of the states in the Senate obviously makes the upper house highly disproportionate in terms of the respective populations, but this is not a hotly contested issue. Such blatant deviation from proportionality is understandably supported by politicians from the overrepresented regions. Less understandable is that it also finds staunch supporters among intellectuals from other regions, who resort to the consociationalist argument that the "weaker" regions require a compensation in political power, even if this compensation amounts to a gross violation of the democratic principle "one person, one vote," which the 1988 Constitution also recognizes in article 14. It is also worth noting that some of the intellectuals who accept the disenfranchisement of almost half of the 22 million residents of the state of São Paulo on "consociational" grounds are extreme "proportionalists" when it comes to the electoral system, arguing that the Anglo-Saxon majoritarian and the German mixed models are bound to disenfranchise some worthy ideological minority.

16. In the crisis over salary readjustments of mid-March 1994, the Supreme Court made a decision in its own favor, and thus became directly involved in the continuing conflict between the executive and the legislature. Losing part of its authority to interpret the laws and act as a neutral umpire, the court itself made the crisis especially dangerous. But the underlying tension among all three branches of government can be gauged by the results of a survey conducted by IDESP among 570 judges. Asked to evaluate the performance of thirteen institutions, 23 percent said the federal executive was doing a good job, and 3 percent gave the same positive answer regarding the legislature. See

Maria Teresa Sadek, *O judiciário em debate* (São Paulo: Editora Sumaré, 1994), table 7.

17. On political culture and institutional utopias, see Bolívar Lamounier and Amaury Souza, "Changing Attitudes toward Democracy and Institutional Reform in Brazil," in Larry Diamond, ed., *Political Culture and Democracy in Developing Countries* (Boulder, Colo.: Lynne Rienner, 1993).

18. Commenting on the militants' frustrations over the lack of progress in the struggle to improve the workers' lot, a prominent PT intellectual says that "these hopes and frustrations . . . are the main determinant of internal party cleavages," but he explicitly recognizes that divisions also exist "with regard to key questions, such as the commitment to democracy (*compromisso com a democracia*), the dilemma of central planning versus market economy, and the possibility of resolving economic crises within the limits of the capitalist system." See Paul Singer, "Dilemas estratégicos do PT diante da crise econômica," *Carta Política* 20 (May 1993), 8.

19. See Amaury Souza and Bolívar Lamounier, "As elites brasileiras e a modernização do setor público," in *Seminários e debates* (São Paulo: IDESP, 1992), tables 4 and 5; Lamounier and Souza, "O Congresso Nacional e a crise brasileira," tables 6 and 7; also José Álvaro Moisés, "Democratization, Mass Political Culture, and Political Legitimacy in Brazil," *Working Paper* (Madrid: Juan March Institute, 1993).

20. See Amaury Souza and Bolívar Lamounier, "A feitura da Constituição: Um reexame da cultura política brasileira," in Bolívar Lamounier, ed., *De Geisel a Collor: O balanço da transição* (São Paulo: Editora Sumaré, 1990), 81–103.

Index

IV

Mexico, Central America, and the Caribbean

1

Nicaragua: Politics, Poverty, and Polarization

Rose J. Spalding

In February 1990 Nicaraguan voters elected Violeta Barrios de Chamorro to the presidency, replacing Daniel Ortega of the Frente Sandinista de Liberación Nacional (FSLN, Sandinista Front for National Liberation). This election was widely viewed, by partisans on both sides, as a watershed for democracy in Nicaragua. For supporters of the FSLN, the election demonstrated the democratic character of the electoral apparatus they had designed and the strength of their 1987 Constitution. For those who had bitterly opposed the Sandinista Revolution, the 1990 election finally ended a decade of revolutionary authoritarianism and one-party rule. Throughout the society, there was a general sense that the 1990 election represented a turning point in Nicaraguan history.

The period following the election, however, did not witness the smooth consolidation of democracy. The political institutions needed to build consensus and forge solutions did not coalesce, and the *concertación* process used by the government to fill this institutional void was not an effective substitute.[1] Infighting and political stagnation eroded support for electoral politics. Various groups again resorted to violence to press their political claims. The August 1993 abduction of a government delegation by ex-Contra forces, and the retaliatory seizure of government officials by ex-army forces, offered dramatic testimony of Nicaragua's tangled political life.

This chapter explores the problems that have confronted Nicaraguan democracy in the postrevolutionary period and concludes that several positive developments have occurred. The Chamorro government moved expeditiously to end the decade-long war and shift conflict into the political arena. Through repeated and difficult negotiations involving a shifting array of forces, notable institutional development has taken place. But forty years of dynastic rule under the Somoza family, followed by the Sandinistas' attempt at revolution and the decade-long Contra war, produced a legacy of violence and polarization that poses extraordinary obstacles to the swift consolidation of democracy. These obstacles, compounded by the deepening economic immiseration of the once-hopeful Nicaraguan population and sweeping cynicism about the political elite's intentions, present enduring challenges to the country's democratic system.

Democratic Consolidation

As the literature on democratic transitions routinely notes, elections alone do not produce a fully consolidated democracy.[2] The successful consolidation of democracy requires at least two additional developments. First, a basic consensus about the legitimacy and desirability of a broadly democratic order must emerge within both the leadership and the citizenry. Second, the political leadership must create a set of institutions that can carry out key democratic functions: channel and respond to popular demands, successfully negotiate conflicts, and ensure accountability of the governing elites. If the latter does not occur, the former will surely be jeopardized.

Both the creation of democratic consensus and needed institutional development have been difficult in Nicaragua. The medium-run prognosis for democratic consolidation in Nicaragua therefore remains uncertain.

There are some encouraging developments, several of which date from the Sandinista era. As Frances Hagopian's chapter in this collection notes, the Sandinista government reduced the power of traditional elites through an agrarian reform program and opened political and economic space for newer social groups, rupturing the narrow dynastic order that preceded it.[3] The mobilization of the citizenry, development of a network of mass organizations, and creation of a more participatory political process were all by-products of the Sandinista era (1979–90), especially the early years. Sandinista leaders must also be credited with introducing genuinely competitive elections in Nicaragua and accepting a peaceful leadership transition.

Several external developments, notably in recent U.S. foreign policy, also facilitated democratization. Under the Clinton administration, the U.S. government began playing a less directive role in Nicaraguan politics. This move follows fifteen years of heavy intervention, during which the Carter administration reluctantly acted as a power broker, attempting to remove Anastasio Somoza while blocking an FSLN victory;[4] the Reagan administration tried to dislodge the FSLN militarily and economically by financing a counterrevolutionary war;[5] and the Bush administration maintained Contra army pressure on the Sandinistas while bolstering the electoral opposition.[6] The Clinton administration, in contrast, has been less attentive but also less managerial. Its policy of "active neutrality"[7] has supported greater internal dialogue among opposing parties.

At the same time, social and economic conditions in the country continue to worsen, feeding deep disappointment with the political system. Party fragmentation and institutional impasses have been frequent as unresolved conflicts of the revolutionary era and new intra-elite hostilities continue to play out. Sharp political splits, often overlaying class divisions, confound efforts to forge a durable democratic order. Spasmodic cut-offs of U.S. aid, sponsored by Senator Jesse Helms and approved by the U.S. Congress, undermine both institutional development and economic recovery.[8] These and other problems complicate the process of democratic consolidation in Nicaragua.

The Electoral Framework

In 1987 the Sandinista government oversaw the completion of a new constitution under which the country was governed until reforms were promulgated in 1995. This constitution provided for the direct election, by simple plurality, of the president and vice-president, a unicameral legislature, and a network of municipal councils. In recognition of the ethnic distinctiveness of the Atlantic Coast population, the constitution included provisions for coastal autonomy; governance of the Atlantic Coast region was delegated in most matters to two forty-five-member regional councils.

This electoral system was designed by the FSLN when it was politically hegemonic. Fearing the electoral evaporation of opposition parties and the challenge to its democratic credentials that this would pose, the Sandinista leadership included several provisions that fostered the participation of small, minority parties. In addition to using proportional representation as the basis for allocating legislative seats, electoral rules gave a seat in the National Assembly to all losing presidential candidates who received around 1 percent of the vote. The rules also gave significant power to party leaders; legislative representatives were elected by region from party lists, allowing parties to slate the candidates ranked in order of party preference.

Since the ouster of Somoza, elections have generated high levels of popular participation. The FSLN's work in mobilizing the poor, the politicizing impact of war and economic decline, and the high stakes involved in Nicaragua's elections produced a great deal of interest in voting. Voter turnout was a strong 75 percent in 1984 and an even higher 86 percent in 1990.[9]

Given the relatively brief period of time in which competitive elections have taken place in Nicaragua, and the expected shift toward more routine (as opposed to formative) elections in the future, patterns observed in the past may not prevail in the future. If the strong participation levels found in the February 1994 election for regional councils on the Atlantic Coast reflect broader national trends, then citizen interest in electoral competition has remained fairly strong under the Chamorro government.[10] High levels of alienation detected in national surveys conducted in 1995, however, suggested that political disaffection and withdrawal were on the rise.[11]

Although Nicaragua's 1987 electoral framework reflected general democratic principles, several features posed real or potential problems. Because the long six-year period between elections, for example, did not subject elected officials to frequent review by the electorate, it undercut accountability. The holding of simultaneous instead of staggered elections for the president, legislature, and municipal offices invited traumatic change and instability. Governability was also threatened by the absence of a mechanism that required winning presidential candidates to gain at least a substantial plurality of the votes. Measures like second-round balloting, which did not seem so crucial when the FSLN was hegemonic, became more important as the FSLN lost power and the Unión Nacional Opositora (UNO, National Opposition Union) coalition shattered.

These issues provoked further discussion of electoral rules and gave rise to a movement for constitutional change. After long and acrimonious debate, the legislature moved in 1994–95 to reform several of these institutional features. The constitutional reforms, finally promulgated in 1995 after months of conflict between the legislature and executive, began addressing several of these problems in the electoral structure (see below).

Campaigns and Financing

Although the structure of the election process is constitutionally defined, Nicaragua does not have firmly established campaign legislation or regulations. As in many other areas of Nicaraguan political life, formal law plays a less central role in the process than do political agreements. The rules that govern campaigns have been worked out extemporaneously through fairly inclusive negotiations. The framework for the campaign in 1990, for example, was devised through a "national dialogue" in August 1989 in which representatives of all parties participated in a thirty-six-hour session in the presence of international observers.[12] This dialogue produced an agreement about political advertising and financing that allowed public funding of electoral campaigns. One-half of the public funds went to parties based on the percent of the vote they received in 1984 (a formula that favored the FSLN), and half was divided equally among all registered parties (a formula that favored the smallest parties). Because of the high stakes of the election for international actors, external involvement in

Nicaragua's elections has been high. This involvement has been most visible in two ways: foreign campaign financing and international election monitoring.

Campaign funding in the 1990 election came heavily from foreign sources. The United States was a major contributor with the U.S. Congress authorizing $9 million for this purpose. Although nominally this was nonpartisan aid to fund civic education, training of poll watchers, voter registration, and support for international observers, in practice more than half of the U.S. aid spent went to support the opposition coalition UNO, its labor affiliate, or one of the civic support groups organized by UNO candidates.[13] The FSLN, too, received substantial foreign support, reportedly raising $3.4 million, mostly in the form of material aid (T-shirts, posters, caps) from solidarity groups in France, Spain, Mexico, and Colombia.[14]

Major participation of outside funders in Nicaraguan elections, as allowed under Nicaraguan law, raises complex questions about who is being represented and what distortions are being introduced. Fuller consolidation of democracy will require greater national control over campaign financing and the elections themselves.

Because Nicaragua was at the center of international debate for most of the 1980s, international mediation has been a recurring process there.[15] Much of this effort has been constructive, helping to decrease the level of violence and smooth the transfer of power from one group to another. In the 1990 election, UN and OAS (Organization of American States) activities included overseeing the voter registration process, stationing election monitors at polling places around the country, and conducting a quick count that confirmed the FSLN defeat immediately after the election. The presence of around 240 election-day observers from the UN and another 450 from the OAS,[16] and the ongoing pre-election reports issued by these two organizations, added credibility to the electoral process and encouraged acceptance of the outcome. These interventions helped to raise national confidence in the election; very few questions were raised about the validity of the 1990 results.

At the same time, the active participation of international actors made it less necessary for Nicaraguans to establish their own legitimation formula and resolve their own disputes. Opponents tended to turn to outside actors to validate negotiations and elections; without the imprimatur from the UN and OAS, and ultimately the U.S. government, events were seen as inconclusive. This gave outside organizations an important voice in internal political negotiations. Although the internal election monitoring apparatus, the Consejo Supremo Electoral, has conducted itself with professionalism and gained important supervisory experience, dependence on external validation may prove difficult to suspend in Nicaragua.

The Fragmentation of Political Parties and Coalitions

Nicaraguan parties have long had a tradition of internal division and societal penetration.[17] Although in many respects the exception, even the FSLN experienced repeated fragmentation. It divided into three warring tendencies in 1975 and reunited only in March 1979 as the prospect of victory against the Somoza regime forged a hasty reconciliation; it split again in 1995 following years of internal political conflict and the divisive 1994 party congress. The more traditional parties, including the Liberals, Conservatives, and Social Christians splintered into almost a dozen different microparties by 1990 as party leaders feuded and maneuvered for control. Selective deal making and repression by the Somoza regime had fractured the traditional parties before the revolution; the futility of competition further weakened them during the Sandinista era.

Under the Chamorro government, several "family" clusters of parties, including the various Christian democratic parties and several offshoots of the Liberal Party, have coalesced, modestly reducing the extreme party fragmentation that had occurred. Nonetheless, most parties in Nicaragua remain tiny and frail. As of June 1995, twenty-six parties were registered in the Council of Political Parties. These parties were also only tenuously connected with their elected representatives. According to one Assembly report, of the ninety-two members elected to the legislature in 1990, seventy-eight had resigned, been expelled, or been suspended from their political parties by March 1995.[18]

In order to defeat the FSLN in 1990, opposition parties came together to form UNO, a fourteen-party coalition. Party leaders worked through the difficult task of selecting a presidential and vice-presidential candidate and agreeing upon a slate of candidates, ranked in order of priority, for the legislative and municipal council seats.

This remarkable cooperation proved short-lived. Even at the time when candidates were named, divisions were already palpable. It took two days of balloting, for example, for Violeta Chamorro to be chosen as the UNO candidate, and she narrowly defeated her two main rivals for the nomination.[19] The UNO campaign program was a patchwork of different views designed to hold together a coalition that ranged from the Socialist and Communist parties to the Liberal Constitutionalist Party (PLC, a schismatic offshoot of Somoza's National Liberal Party).[20] As a coalition, UNO functioned only for electoral purposes; its fissure when faced with the task of governing was easily predictable. The tactic of forming a broad coalition, which seemed inspired at the time of the election, proved disastrous. After the 1990 election, it was clear that the FSLN had lost; it was not clear, however, who had won.

The individual party leaders who organized the UNO lacked both the ability to form a clear, coherent vision for the society and the practical political skills needed to negotiate binding agreements with opponents. Urged on by ambitious leaders, like Vice-President Virgilio Godoy and Assembly leader Alfredo César, and by supporters in the United States, like Senator Jesse Helms and former U.S. ambassador to the UN, Jeane Kirkpatrick, UNO hard-liners resisted negotiation with the FSLN and later even with the relatively moderate Chamorro government. The result was a continual battle characterized by intransigent ultimatums, accusations of corruption, coalitional decay, and political stasis.

The FSLN temporarily withstood pressures to splinter, in spite of postelection recriminations and predictions that it would. It did, however, experience a quick erosion of its support and deep fissures within its leadership.[21] The central issue, never quite resolved during the Sandinista decade, was whether the FSLN should be a revolutionary, vanguard party prepared to defend its interests with force, or a mass-based, social democratic party that repudiated violence and pursued a purely electoral strategy. A corollary issue concerned the FSLN's relationship with the Chamorro government. Although some top Sandinistas favored an adversarial relationship with the regime, others endorsed tactical accommodation in the name of postwar recovery and preserving what they could of their revolution. Additional conflicts erupted between those Sandinistas who lived and worked in poverty alongside most of their fellow citizens and the *nueva burguesía sandinista*, composed of wealthier party members, some of whom had appropriated state resources during the final days of the Sandinista government.[22]

Leftist movements in Latin America have long had a tendency to shatter into multiple, small political groupings (see Angell's chapter in this collection). To prevent this disintegration and the resulting political impotence that it brings, the FSLN struggled to maintain a united front. In order to avoid pitting FSLN leaders against each other, the historic July 1991 party congress reelected the seven sitting members of the FSLN's National Directorate as a slate, adding only longtime Sandinista leaders Sergio Ramírez and René Núñez to their number. This apparent unity, however, belied serious tensions within the organization.

By the second party congress, an extraordinary session in May 1994, this internal conflict had erupted publicly. Tensions flared between ex-president Daniel Ortega, who adopted a more radical rhetoric and positioned himself closer to the increasingly militant Sandinista labor front, and former vice-president Sergio Ramírez, who had assumed leadership of the Sandinista bench in the legislature and pushed a more moderate line.[23] This split grew more formalized over time, and by early 1994 the two factions were publishing clashing manifestos and lining up endorsements by prominent Sandinista activists.[24]

The key task of the congress was to elect a secretary general, an expanded National Directorate, and new members of the FSLN Assembly. By a clear margin, the Ortega group dominated the outcome.[25] Ortega was reelected secretary general, defeating conciliation candidate Henry Ruíz 287 to 147. Nine of the fifteen members of the new National Directorate endorsed the Ortega position. Twenty-eight of the forty-five national members of the FSLN Assembly (62%) and fifty-three of the FSLN Assembly's sixty-eight departmental members (78%) reportedly identified with the Ortega faction. Harking back to an earlier era, congress participants voted, by a two-thirds majority, to define the party as a "vanguard" party and retain the distinction between full party members ("militants") and second-level members ("affiliates").

The public debate between Ortega and Ramírez, and the inclusion of an opposition candidate for secretary general over Ortega's objection, were historic firsts for the FSLN. Party spin doctors saw this as evidence that the FSLN was becoming a modern political party with a growing capacity for internal debate and leadership rotation. Indeed, eight of the fifteen members of the 1994–97 National Directorate were new, including, under a quota system set up for underrepresented groups, five women.[26]

On the other hand, the congress sharply repudiated the main internal opposition. In political maneuvering that smacked of a purge, Ramírez lost his position in the National Directorate. A few months later, in a dispute about constitutional reform proposals, he was removed from the legislative seat he had occupied for four years as Ortega's alternate. The National Directorate also dismissed Carlos Fernando Chamorro from the editorship of the Sandinista newspaper, *Barricada*. Chamorro, who had directed the paper since its founding in 1979, had overseen the metamorphosis of *Barricada* into an organ of internal debate in the 1990s. Publicly aligned with the Ramírez tendency, he was found to be inadequately supportive of the postcongress line.

The general defeat of the Ramiristas deepened party control by the more orthodox wing and affirmed Ortega's dominance over the party apparatus. Rejection of the more moderate style of the Ramírez group made the party a more insular body and raised questions about its ability to forge a new national consensus.[27]

To revive its grass-roots organization and prepare for the 1996 electoral contest, the FSLN Assembly called a new round of local-level internal elections in September 1994. Participation levels surprised those who thought the FSLN was fading from the national scene. More than 250,000 party members and supporters voted for a new set of local party leaders.[28] The FSLN remained an important party with a significant support base, but the bruising battles and marginalization of key party sectors took a political toll, particularly among party professionals and intellectuals. The leadership split was formalized in May 1995 with the creation of a second Sandinista party, the Movimiento de Renovación

Sandinista (MRS, Sandinista Renewal Movement), under the leadership of Ramírez.

The PLC, which emerged as the FSLN's main opponent, benefited from this divisiveness and fragmentation. Under the leadership of Managua mayor Arnoldo Alemán, the party constructed an extensive organizational infrastructure through a network of UNO mayors. Building on the political clout provided by a public works program initially funded by the U.S. Agency for International Development (USAID), Alemán emerged as a popular and charismatic leader. The elections for regional councils on the Atlantic Coast in February 1994 suggested that the PLC was expanding its reach. The party showed surprising coastal strength there, winning more than 35 percent of the vote in a seventeen-party competition and the largest number of seats, a total of thirty-seven of the ninety seats in the two regional councils.[29] It outpolled even the FSLN, which came in second with thirty-three seats, down from the forty it had won in 1990.[30]

The coastal population is ethnically distinct from the rest of the Nicaraguan population and represents only 10 percent of the total. Analysts should be cautious about extrapolating from the coastal results to the rest of the population. The surge in the PLC vote in this region and the party's organizational work in Managua and other key municipalities, however, raise the possibility that the main beneficiary of the political and economic morass in Nicaragua will be the PLC. The 1995 electoral alliance agreement of four of the five factions of the Liberal Party[31] positioned Alemán favorably for the 1996 elections; by late 1994 he had emerged as the election front-runner. In a national public opinion poll conducted by the Instituto de Estudios Nicaragüenses (IEN, Institute of Nicaraguan Studies) in November 1994, 23 percent of respondents supported Alemán's presidential bid. Only 16 percent backed his next closest rival, Daniel Ortega.[32] The mayor's ability to produce concrete outcomes, as evidenced by the city's extensive public works program, and his frequently populist discourse, generated a notable base of support for him and, as a by-product, for the Liberal alliance as well.

Executive-Legislative Relations

Like most Latin American countries, Nicaragua has a long tradition of executive dominance and legislative weakness. From the Somoza government through the Sandinista era, the president was able to dominate the legislature under most conditions and circumvent it when necessary.[33] This tradition continued under the Chamorro government. Presidential domination has contributed to, and been exacerbated by, fractious executive-legislative relations.

The Chamorro government began its term with a strong legislative majority that concealed institutional tensions. The UNO coalition swept the 1990 elections at every level. Not only was Chamorro elected president with 55 percent of the vote, but UNO also received 54 percent of the vote in the National Assembly contests, giving it fifty-one of ninety-two seats, and it won control of 99 of the 131 municipalities. With this base of support, UNO was able to secure key leadership positions at all levels of government.

This coalition, however, quickly unraveled. Natural tensions between coalition members who had sharply divergent ideological positions, combined with conflicting responses to the Chamorro government's concessions to the FSLN, provoked open divisions within the UNO camp. These tensions were readily apparent by January 1991 when UNO shattered during the Assembly leadership selection process. Looking for coalition partners with which to secure legislative majorities, and for political cooperation from the country's largest political bloc, the Chamorro government turned to the Sandinistas, who held thirty-nine of the ninety-two seats in the legislature. FSLN representatives joined a moderate faction of UNO to elect Chamorro ally and former Contra leader Alfredo César as Assembly president. This event was widely perceived as a victory for Chamorro and FSLN moderates over the UNO right wing. It fed charges that Chamorro and the FSLN were engaged in a process of "cogovernment."

Political alliances became yet more byzantine when César switched allegiances, assumed leadership of the main UNO bloc, and positioned himself to vie for the nation's presidency. The eight UNO members who worked in cooperation with the FSLN bench (the "Center Group") were denounced by the Assembly leadership as both disloyal and corrupt. In early 1992 the Nicaraguan comptroller charged Antonio Lacayo, the president's son-in-law and minister of the presidency, with buying off these legislators in order to break UNO's power. Chamorro then unceremoniously dismissed the comptroller, charging that this allegation was inspired by partisan affiliations and that it usurped executive powers.

Protesting various maneuvers and countermaneuvers, legislators began absenting themselves from Assembly meetings. The FSLN bloc walked out for three months in 1991 and four in 1992. Taking advantage of their absence, Assembly president César pushed through a series of legislative initiatives in 1992 in spite of the absence of a quorum. In a 7–2 vote, the Supreme Court, itself an object of controversy,[34] found the laws passed in those circumstances to be invalid, and the Assembly was forcibly closed by the president in December 1992.

In the 1993 legislative session, a new Center Group–FSLN coalition replaced César with another UNO leader, Socialist Party leader Gustavo Tablada. Dissident UNO representatives refused to recognize the authority of the new leadership since it was confirmed with the support of the eight former allies they accused of corruption; they called for the expulsion of the Center Group from the legislature and new leadership elections. These UNO representatives then proceeded to boycott the entire 1993 legislative session.

In the face of this turmoil, the legislature barely functioned. Legislators, locked in acrimonious battles, failed to develop effective operational procedures, and the Assembly was unable to conduct day-to-day business. In part because of this internal tumult, it was difficult for Nicaraguan legislators to strike a reasonable balance between working with the president to find solutions to the nation's problems and exercising an independent voice to restrain presidential initiatives. The result was an institutional vacuum that the executive branch readily filled.

The president used extensive constitutional decree powers and the veto to circumvent the turbulent legislature. For example, when the 1991 legislature took up highly charged political issues concerning the misappropriation of state properties by FSLN officials, Chamorro vetoed the measure, presumably fearing that her own tenuous relationship with the still-powerful FSLN would collapse and national reconciliation would fail if punitive measures were applied.

Fundamental economic changes were also made by decree. Desiring a quick move toward a neoliberal economic model in keeping with vigorous recommendations from multilateral lenders and the U.S. government, Chamorro used decree powers to mandate sweeping privatizations, numerous tax increases, and changes in trade laws. Interruptions in the flow of U.S. aid in 1992 and 1993 caused economic crises that also required abrupt policy responses and pushed the executive to act unilaterally. These maneuvers allowed the president to sidestep the institutional impasse and begin restructuring the national economy, but at a cost to the political system.

Constitutional Revision

By 1993 the extreme antagonism of the three major blocs (Chamorro government, UNO, and FSLN) had produced political paralysis. The sense of legitimacy that was afforded to elected officials in 1990 because of the democratic process through which they were chosen was of short duration. Each of the government's actions was considered illegitimate by some sizable political bloc.

Confronted with these problems, most of the political elite agreed in 1993 that institutional change was needed. The extent of the change and the mechanisms by which to achieve it, however, were a matter of dispute. Two camps emerged. Some right-wing critics of the government, led by Cardinal Miguel Obando y Bravo, called for the drafting of a new constitution. Unable to defeat the alliance of eight centrist legislators and the FSLN bench, they pushed for the abolition of the existing Assembly and the election of a constituent assembly that would serve as a transitional legislature.

A second group, composed of more moderate forces, accepted the idea of constitutional reform but proposed that it be designed by the existing legislature and be less extensive. Hoping to overcome the impasse without the political risks and expense of a constitutional convention, the Chamorro government entered into a series of negotiations with this second group.

One of the UNO-coalition members, the Christian Democratic Union, broke the stalemate when it endorsed a program of constitutional reform in October 1993 and opened a new phase of political negotiation. A tactical coalition, now composed of the FSLN, the Center Group, the Unity and Reconciliation Bloc (which had split from both UNO and the Center Group), and the Christian Democratic Union moved quickly to advance the constitutional reform process.

In January 1994 a new legislative leadership, under Christian Democratic Union leader Luis Humberto Guzmán, was elected. Assembly rules requiring the selection of a new leadership every year could theoretically have exacerbated coalition fragility; in this case, however, these rules gave the legislature a much-needed opportunity to recalibrate its forces. After a long sixteen-month impasse, the Assembly resumed meeting in 1994 with virtually all members attending. An ambitious legislative agenda was adopted, including constitutional reform and a law governing the armed forces.

Demonstrating new political capacity, the 1994 Assembly overrode a presidential veto of legislation governing commercial licenses and repealed a tax that had been imposed by presidential decree.[35] Veto overrides (which require only an absolute majority in Nicaragua) could become more common as the legislative function is reestablished.

The constitutional reform process continued through 1994 under a blue-ribbon Assembly working group. Under the 1987 Constitution, the legislature could amend the constitution with approval of 60 percent (fifty-six seats) or more of the members in *two* consecutive legislative sessions. Following intense negotiation, the Assembly produced a series of reform proposals.

In addition to more fully separating the FSLN and the state, the reforms reduced formal presidential powers by giving the Assembly control over tax policy and the power to ratify or reject international treaties or agreements. Presidential selection was restricted through prohibitions on immediate presidential reelection (a provision that affected Violeta Chamorro) and the election of relatives of incumbent presidents (a provision that targeted Antonio Lacayo, Chamorro's son-in-law). Reforms also required a second round of balloting when no presidential candidate obtained at least 45 percent of the vote (a provision that could impede a future FSLN victory) and called for a shortening of the term of office, from six to five years for the executive and Assembly members.[36] In what appeared to be a court-packing plan, the size of the Supreme Court was expanded from nine to twelve, and the Assembly gave itself the opportunity to control these appointments.[37] These measures were designed to address problems of governability and accountability while sharply increasing the power of the legislature relative to that of the executive.

These proposals were approved overwhelmingly by the Assembly at the tail end of the 1994 legislative session and as the first major agenda item in the 1995 session.[38] For the first time, the FSLN legislators split, with the rump Ortega faction joining the Chamorro-aligned Center Group in ineffectual opposition to reform.

The executive responded to the approval of the reforms in the second legislative session by refusing to promulgate them as an official document in *La Gazeta,* placing the reforms in legal limbo. Chamorro government officials argued on technical grounds that the reforms were so extensive that they amounted to the drafting of a new constitution, a process that required the election of a new constituent assembly. They also contended that the new institutions violated democratic principles by ushering in "parliamentary dictatorship."[39] In defiance of the executive, the Assembly then had the reforms published in the newspapers and began conducting its operations as if the new constitution were in effect.

The Supreme Court, historically a weak institution in Nicaragua whose debilities were exacerbated by the death and departure of several members, lacked the political stature needed to resolve the conflict. It finally issued a compromise decision, concluding that the reforms were constitutional but the method by which they were promulgated was not. This decision sent the warring branches back into negotiations, this time mediated by Cardinal Obando y Bravo.

After weeks of intense meetings, the Assembly agreed to concede some of its newly claimed powers, at least until the end of the Chamorro administration.[40] It accepted limits on its budgetary powers and it agreed that key decisions (appointments to the Supreme Court, the Supreme Electoral Council, and the comptroller general and changes in the tax system) could only be made "by consensus" between the two branches. In return, the president promulgated the reforms. Court cases challenging the legality of the reforms and the requirement that key decisions be made by consensus (an elusive state in Nicaragua) promised to keep constitutional conflict alive for some time.

Parties, coalitions, and even the legislature itself remained quite brittle in Nicaragua. Clear working relationships both within the Assembly and between the executive and the legislature have not emerged.

Although the renewed participation of all segments of the Assembly and the size of several legislative victories have strengthened the legislative branch, the fragility of the system and the harshness of the battles between political adversaries suggest that serious contests about the distribution of power remain to be resolved.

Civil-Military Relations

Nicaragua has a long history of executive-military interpenetration. Under both the Somoza dynasty and the Sandinista regime, the military was an integral part of the executive, not a separate entity subordinated to elected authority. The Contra war further complicated this issue by making the military the central political actor in the country and dramatically increasing its grip on national resources. The task of placing the military under civilian control, therefore, has been an important challenge to the Chamorro government. In this area, considerable progress has been made.

The Nicaraguan military was formed from the FSLN guerrilla army after the Guardia Nacional collapsed in July 1979.[41] The new army became the Sandinista Popular Army (EPS); the police became the Sandinista Police. Humberto Ortega, brother of Sandinista President Daniel Ortega and the principal military strategist of the 1978–79 insurrection, was immediately named head of the army; within a year he was also named minister of defense.

Violeta Chamorro shocked the nation with her decision to allow Ortega to stay on as commander-in-chief of the EPS. When she announced the decision right before her inauguration, two of her cabinet appointees withdrew; others on the right began to murmur of some conspiracy orchestrated by her main advisor, Antonio Lacayo, and the FSLN leadership. Chamorro countered that Ortega's active participation was needed in order to achieve the demobilization and downsizing of the armed forces.

Indeed, over the next three years, the Nicaraguan army changed substantially. Two types of changes stand out. First, the resources held by the military fell sharply. Between the 1990 election and early 1993, the number of military personnel dropped from 40,000 to 15,250.[42] The military's budget was also cut, falling 50 percent in 1991 and, after acrimonious debate, another 10 percent for 1992.[43] These reforms made Nicaragua's military one of the smaller ones in the Central American region.[44]

Second, the ideological orientation of the military became less clearcut. Ortega not only withdrew from the National Directorate of the FSLN as required by President Chamorro, but also repeatedly pledged his loyalty to the constitution and the president.[45] As a symbol of the changing orientation, Ortega gave the Camilo Ortega medal, the military's highest honor (named after the third Ortega brother, who was killed during the 1979 insurrection), to the U.S. military attaché in 1992. The general's studied attempts at constitutionalism and conciliation won him condemnation in more radical quarters.[46]

Critics on the Right argued, however, that, without the removal of Ortega, the FSLN was still effectively in power. Cardinal Obando put it bluntly: "He [Humberto Ortega] is the man with the guns, the strongman, and she [Chamorro] will be there only as long as he lends her the rifles. When he says stop, no more, she will be out."[47] Claims that the military had become a law unto itself and followed a leftist agenda were repeatedly made when strikers were not quelled and land invaders were not routed. These claims were bolstered when a Salvadoran guerrilla group's arms cache exploded in Managua in May 1993, revealing the continued presence of foreign guerrilla organizations operating with impunity in Nicaragua. The bid to remove Ortega from power was pushed forcefully by Senator Jesse Helms, who used his position to get U.S. aid to Nicaragua suspended in both 1992 and 1993.

Faced with these pressures, the Chamorro government began to chip away at the FSLN military leadership. In 1992 the Sandinista police chief René Vivas was removed, along with other high-ranking police officers, and the police force was moved under civilian control. In September 1993 Chamorro announced that Ortega too would be removed from his position. Humberto Ortega resisted this maneuver, noting that, under existing law, he could be removed only by the military high command. Looking for a legal solution, Chamorro called for a rewriting of the law governing military appointments and asked for technical assistance from the OAS. Political momentum in Nicaragua, even on the Left, shifted to favor a process that would end with Ortega's replacement.

After extended negotiations with the military high command, Chamorro presented a draft of a new military code to the Assembly in May 1994 and announced that Ortega would be replaced in February 1995. This code, as revised by the Assembly, allowed the military high command to determine which officers would be recommended for advancement to the top leadership post, but gave the president the power to reject unacceptable recommendations. It also declared that no relative of the president or vice-president could be named head of the armed forces, and it fixed the term for the military chief at five years, without the possibility of renewal.[48]

This proposal reopened public debate about the military; especially controversial were provisions in the code that allowed the military to retain its own enterprises.[49] Some political leaders endorsed military-owned businesses as a device that would allow the military to finance its own social welfare fund and relieve the general treasury of this responsibility. Others argued that it allowed the military to become an economic power outside the control of civilian authorities and posed a threat to private producers against which military enterprises would compete. Efforts of the Assembly to tighten control over these military enterprises (require them to pay taxes, limit how their profits could be used, set up a civilian-controlled supervisory process) satisfied a majority of the legislators, but prompted another walkout by UNO hardliners when the bill was approved. A small group of civic leaders in the Civilianist Movement called for the outright abolition of the military.

The Nicaraguan government will have to find an arrangement that both respects the professional integrity of the armed forces and gives the civilian leadership of the country effective control over this organization. This is a difficult task, especially in a country where the military has a revolutionary history and fears the imminent election of an antagonistic government. To its credit, the Nicaraguan military has demonstrated notable political restraint, and substantial progress has been made in developing institutional constraints on its power. The departure of Humberto Ortega and his replacement at the beginning of 1995 by General Joaquín Cuadra reflected this improved institutionalization and reduced the tension surrounding this issue. Debate continued, however, about how best to place this powerful institution under full civilian control.

Recontras and Recompas

Several groups that used violence and warfare to push their political agenda in the 1980s continued to do so in the postrevolutionary era. To complicate the picture further, there has been an upsurge in common crimes, kidnapping, and banditry that sometimes take on a political guise. Although the level of armed conflict in the society dropped dramatically, Nicaragua still struggles with a legacy of violence.

The Resistencia Nicaragüense (Contra) forces that waged war against the Sandinistas in the 1980s were demobilized following Chamorro's electoral victory. Within two months of her inauguration, she declared an amnesty for Contra forces, called on them to disarm, and offered them resources with which to rebuild their lives in carefully selected "development poles." More than 22,000 rebels accepted this offer.[50] Several former resistance leaders were also incorporated into special government boards and institutes.

The development pole strategy quickly failed.[51] Without credit and productive inputs, and far from their home communities, resistance fighters felt defrauded by the government. The continued presence of Sandinista troops in and around Contra strongholds was also an irritant; fighting continued to break out. Within two years, Contra forces were beginning to regroup.

By 1992 the Chamorro government was forced to offer a second amnesty, this time to both rearmed Contras (the Recontra in Nicaraguan parlance) and discharged Sandinista troops that had remobilized (the Re-compañero or Recompa). Fueled by the failure of the government to fulfill its promises, the unwillingness to give up the glamor afforded by participating in the Contra army, and the absence of other alternatives, thousands of demobilized Contras drifted back into decentralized Recontra armies.

Demobilized troops from the armed forces did likewise. The quick reduction in the size of the army sent thousands of militarily trained young men into the ranks of the unemployed. Although the government provided some assistance, particularly for discharged officers, much of this population became impoverished. Economic frustration, combined with political discontent, pulled some ex-soldiers back into armed groups as well.

Both sides engaged in illegal and violent actions. Some discharged troops formed the Fuerzas Punitivas de la Izquierda (Punitive Forces of the Left), which assassinated business leader Arges Sequeira in 1992. Others joined the Frente Revolucionario de Obreros y Campesinos (Revolutionary Front of Workers and Peasants), which raided Estelí, robbing banks and denouncing government indifference in 1993. Recontra forces, too, operated outside the law. Cattle rustling and social banditry escalated into hostage taking in August 1993, when one Recontra group abducted an official peace-seeking delegation in Quilalí.

Following the Quilalí hostage taking by ex-Contras and the retaliatory seizure of forty UNO leaders by former Sandinista soldiers, the Chamorro government declared a third amnesty, seeking to derail and disarm the remaining unofficial forces. The government first threatened to launch a military offensive against those remaining in arms, raising the possibility of renewed warfare; it then offered to incorporate rebels of the Frente Norte 3-80, the last large Contra band, into the local police force. This mixed message worked, and Contra disarmament began again in March 1994.

With great difficulty, the Chamorro government made major progress in demobilizing the organized forces of violence in Nicaragua.[52] But the political polarization and economic woes of the country stood in the way of a permanent solution to this problem. Although armed confrontations of organized groups declined, a general pattern of rural lawlessness and delinquency made political stability elusive. Even though ex-combatants foreswore the use of violence and began to look for political channels through which to pursue their goals, recurring government paralysis and fiscal weakness stymied this effort. The economic disintegration of the country prevented the speedy reintegration of this population into civil society. Unless effective political parties and functioning political institutions emerge to channel their demands, and a growing economy begins to offer them additional opportunities, the challenge of incorporating these disenchanted groups into democratic politics will persist.

Economic Conditions

Many of Nicaragua's political problems are, at root, economic. Poverty is pervasive, and the economy has failed to recover. These conditions have bred disenchantment with the government and with the political system that brought it to power. The economic morass provoked harsh political battles over how increasingly scarce resources were to be allocated. Sweeping poverty contributed to a breakdown of law and order.

Nicaragua's general economic profile has been unfavorable since the late 1970s. The economic successes of the early Sandinista period were followed by years of economic decline as the Contra war deepened and the revolutionary economic model failed to ignite.[53] The transition to a new government in 1990 promised an economic reprieve; indeed, it was the prospect of economic recovery that brought many Nicaraguans to vote for the UNO coalition.

The Chamorro government moved quickly to restructure the economy along neoliberal lines.[54] State monopsonies in trade and banking were eliminated, import barriers were slashed, subsidies were removed, state properties were privatized, and the public sector work force was cut.[55] The U.S. government, through USAID, provided important financial and technical support for this transition.[56]

The Nicaraguan version of neoliberalism did have some traits that would make it more palatable to a postrevolutionary society. The most important concession was that workers were allowed to acquire several of the state enterprises that were undergoing privatization. Thirty percent of the state farm property was turned over to state farm workers; former soldiers and Contra rebels were given another 30 percent.[57] The basic thrust of the new model was, however, distinctly neoliberal.

The new approach produced some positive results. Privatization and the removal of government subsidies dramatically cut the massive fiscal deficit. The elimination of the deficit allowed the government to control inflation; inflation rates fell from 13,490 percent in 1990 to 3.5 percent in 1992.[58] With U.S. aid, Nicaragua cleared its arrears with multilateral banks. Both the IMF (International Monetary Fund) and the World Bank renewed lending in 1991.

However, unlike some cases in Latin America where neoliberal restructuring triggered economic expansion, the Nicaraguan economy generally stagnated. The GDP (gross domestic product) fell 1.5 percent in 1990, 0.2 percent in 1991, and, after rising 0.4 percent in 1992, fell another 0.7 percent in 1993.[59] The economy rebounded some in 1994, with GDP growth estimated at levels as high as 3.2 percent[60] due to improved export prices. It will be difficult to sustain this level of growth in the long run, however, as international prices fluctuate and foreign aid declines.[61]

Various factors contributed to Nicaragua's weak economic performance. The transportation infrastructure had been badly damaged during the war, and energy production had deteriorated; without a government program to repair the highways and port facilities and provide adequate energy supplies, it was difficult for Nicaraguans to compete with other Central American producers. Agricultural credit was slashed when the government cut subsidies to the state bank system; even relatively productive small and medium-sized producers were unable to secure the credit they needed to operate.[62] An array of industries collapsed in the face of cheap imports as the government liberalized trade.[63] International prices for Nicaragua's traditional exports (coffee, cotton) surged periodically but were generally low; without a major government program to support technological innovation, most producers had difficulty finding a new niche in the international economy. Finally, continuing disputes about property titles undermined investment and impeded access to credit, further retarding economic growth.[64]

The opening phase of economic reform in Nicaragua was therefore associated with sweeping unemployment and deepening poverty. Even the relatively understated 1993 World Bank study of poverty in Nicaragua concluded that 50.3 percent of the population lived in poverty, and a full 19.4 percent lived in "extreme poverty," with incomes below the level necessary to obtain the daily minimum caloric requirement.[65] Spreading poverty came at a time when returning exiles and economic elites were engaging in a postrevolution consumption spree. Nicaragua's economic divide visibly widened in the early 1990s.

The broad political consequences of impoverishment are difficult to measure. There is evidence, however, that the legal system has been profoundly challenged. The incidence of common crime rose dramatically. According to a 1993 National Police report submitted to the Assembly, the number of crime reports in the country quadrupled between 1983 and 1993.[66] Criminal charges filed with the police rose another 15 percent in the first half of 1994.[67] Economically motivated kidnappings also increased; according to official reports, thirty-three bands concentrated in the northern interior were living off this activity in early 1994.[68]

Land invasions also became more common. Land seizures were, in part, due to the uncertainties of land claims and counterclaims in the postrevolutionary period, but they were exacerbated by the absence of employment opportunities in much of the Nicaraguan countryside. Economic contraction also triggered recurring strikes in almost every sector of the economy. In 1990 and again in 1993, the strikes escalated into uprisings that closed down the capital city and resulted in deaths.

The Chamorro government developed some small programs to assist the impoverished and unemployed. It created the Ministry of Social Action to consolidate its poverty programs, and a USAID-funded employment program (FISE, Emergency Social Investment Fund) was devised in 1991 for urban areas.[69] Through FISE, foreign funders and, increasingly, the Nicaraguan central government channeled resources to city mayors for public works projects that put unemployed workers to work rebuilding urban infrastructure. With underemployment levels rising to 49 percent in 1992,[70] however, this program had a limited employment impact.[71]

For political, ideological, and social reasons, the Chamorro government was unable to respond forcefully to the country's major economic and social problems. Politically, recurring crises and bitter infighting within the political class undercut agreement on how to rebuild the nation. Ideologically, the shift toward neoliberalism, with its emphasis on market-driven solutions, prevented the government from constructing a strong national development plan. Economically, the fiscal weakness of the state further impeded innovative state interventions. Without the political, ideological, or economic resources with which to address the problem of deepening poverty, the government was immobilized. Responsibility for economic policymaking was largely assumed by multilateral lenders whose guidelines, under the Enhanced Structural Adjustment Facility (ESAF), helped to stabilize but not lift the nation's economy.[72]

The citizenry, watching state inaction in the face of widespread misery, became increasingly alienated. Democratic elections, which were supposed to "save" the country in 1990, failed to improve the lives of many; they were instead associated with continued decline. Public opinion polls indicate the level of dissatisfaction. According to an IEN poll concluded in December 1994, 87 percent of those interviewed did not feel represented by their government, up from 76 percent in 1993.[73] More troubling still, 78 percent responded that the country's political parties were not preoccupied with resolving the people's problems. A full 53 percent of those surveyed expressed no support for *any* of the parties or coalitions operating in Nicaragua.[74] The rejection of both the current government and those institutions that were supposed to generate alternatives suggested that political disenchantment had become widespread.

Civil Society

Unlike many Latin American countries where civil society was undermined by exclusionary authoritarian rule in the 1970s and 1980s, Nicaragua developed a vibrant array of economic, religious, and social organizations.[75] During the 1980s, urban workers poured into the Sandinista Workers Federation (CST), and rural workers aligned with the Sandinista-sponsored Farmworkers Association (ATC). The unionized labor force increased from 11 percent of the salaried work force in 1979 to 56 percent in 1986.[76] Cooperatives were strongly encouraged by the Sandinista government, and the National Union of Farmers and Ranchers (UNAG) was created to mobilize members of co-ops and individual producers. "People's church" groups, women's groups, and neighborhood organizations expanded rapidly in the early years of the revolution.

Many of these associations emerged originally with FSLN sponsorship. They sprang up quickly in the final years of the Somoza dictatorship and had little experience with organizational autonomy. As a result, much of Nicaraguan civil society suffered from dependence on the state, even as it benefited from access to state resources. Because of the alliance between the FSLN and the CST, labor was unable to confront the government forcefully when wages eroded.[77] The Sandinista-sponsored Nicaraguan Women's Association Luisa Amanda Espinoza (AMNLAE) allowed the government to neglect women's demands repeatedly.[78] Although UNAG was able to achieve relatively more autonomy over time, it had serious problems recruiting in many parts of the country because of its association with the regime.[79]

With the electoral defeat of the FSLN, these organizations tended to become more autonomous. Organized labor became more militant; now reorganized under the National Workers' Front (FNT), labor mobilized for repeated strikes as neoliberal reforms were adopted and labor conditions deteriorated.[80] Labor leaders succeeded in getting workers included in the privatization process, and a series of state factories, mines, mills, and farms were handed over to their work forces.

UNAG also experienced a renaissance after 1990. This organization adopted a bold strategy of embracing demobilized Contra peasants, thereby expanding its social and political base. Nicaragua's small and medium-sized producers were badly squeezed by the abrupt shift in the economic model; UNAG has been their main advocate. Although largely ineffective in their call for increased agricultural credit and technical assistance for marginalized producers, UNAG leaders have displayed considerable entrepreneurship, setting up small-scale processing, exporting, and banking operations under the Chamorro government.[81]

New groups also emerged, including several competing community-based organizations and an array of decentralized women's associations. The proliferation of women's organizations was particularly notable; at one point, forty groups competed to define the movement.[82] The opening up of political debate, along with the availability of funding from international organizations, fostered a rapid organizational expansion for women's groups. As in other Latin American countries, the contraction of government services was itself a goad to civic organization, as people looked for ways to address their common problems.

At the same time, a contrary trend has also been under way; many Nicaraguans have withdrawn from social organizations. Cooperatives set up under the Sandinista government suffered a serious erosion, and UNAG's membership declined.[83] The sharp increase in un- and under-employment took a toll on organized labor, in spite of its newfound militancy. As the economy continued to deteriorate, people's attention often shifted to private or family-based survival strategies.

Many nongovernmental organizations experienced internal tensions as well. The interests of workers who became owners of their enterprises diverged from those who continued as workers;[84] the perspectives of UNAG entrepreneurs who could adjust to the neoliberal transition differed from those of marginalized peasant producers who sank deeper into poverty.[85] As a consequence, pressure has built toward organizational fragmentation.

Overall, the results for civil society have been contradictory. Parts of civil society have become stronger and more autonomous, and others have disintegrated. The balance of the outcome is not yet clear, but the political problems posed by a retreat to familism and associational fragmentation deserve further attention.

Conclusions

In some ways, the cause of democracy has advanced in Nicaragua. With the ending of the war, conflicts have shifted away from the battlefield into the political arena. The media have become more open and pluralistic. Institutional development within the government has taken place. The president has increased civilian control over the military by reducing its size and resources and gaining veto power over its leadership selection process. The legislature has pushed for a greater voice in policymaking, using veto overrides and the constitutional reform process to limit presidential prerogatives. The Supreme Court has checked legislative excesses when wayward Assembly members attempted to legislate without a quorum or promulgate constitutional reforms in an unconstitutional manner. The identities of the state and the FSLN have been more fully separated. The FSLN has experienced open public debate and competitive leadership elections. Each of these steps has deepened the process of democratization.

Democratic consolidation, however, remains elusive. A deep political divide, sharpened by revolution and war, persists in Nicaragua. UNO's broad, fourteen-party coalition strategy, which was so effective for electoral purposes, proved disastrous for the task of governing. The tensions, competition, and divisions within UNO, which should have been worked out through electoral competition, surged when the coalition came to power. Miniparties have displayed centrifugal tendencies; key actors have clung tenaciously to established positions; intransigence has been common. Elites governed with little sense of accountability as they staggered from crisis to crisis. The long period between elections further detached the leadership from the citizenry and allowed the political class to view politics as an elite game.

As the economy contracted, the population suffered deepening poverty. Violence continued to erupt both in the form of common crime and open political rebellion. Theft, kidnapping, and assaults created an atmosphere of instability and alarm. The widespread availability of arms and the serious underfunding of the police and judicial systems complicated the job of reducing crime. The complex interweaving of economic and political motivations among the perpetrators made the problem of crime particularly intractable in Nicaragua.

Increasing numbers of Nicaraguans have found their government to be either irrelevant or counterproductive. Much of the legitimacy afforded elected officials by the 1990 vote has been squandered. The result has been increased political anger and alienation.[86]

External actors can contribute to democratic consolidation in Nicaragua. They will need to provide measured support for institutional development, economic recovery, and poverty reduction while refraining from heavy intervention in Nicaragua's internal affairs. The U.S. government should continue to accept the legitimacy of all the major political actors, including the FSLN, and encourage Nicaraguan political leaders to look for authentic local solutions to their conflicts. Foreign donors should also confront the fact that Nicaragua's deeply depressed economy is not finding its own way through neoliberal reform, and develop a consistent aid policy that acknowledges the exceptional severity of the economic problems in that country. Support for a development policy that targets small and medium-sized producers, regardless of their political coloration, would begin to revive the economy and refocus the Nicaraguan political elite's attention on the concerns of the citizenry.

Ultimately, however, Nicaragua's political problems cannot be solved by outside actors. The challenge of democratic governance can only be met through the broad political participation of diverse sectors of the population and the creation of a political apparatus capable of responding to their demands. Unless this occurs, a volatile and disenchanted citizenry in a crisis-prone nation will be the result.

2

El Salvador: Transition from Civil War

Ricardo Córdova Macías

This chapter assesses the achievement of the Peace Accords and of the short- and medium-term prospects for democratic governability in El Salvador. The historic signing of the Peace Accords in Chapultepec on January 16, 1992, between the government and the Farabundo Martí National Liberation Front (FMLN) is undoubtedly the most important political event in the Salvadoran political process of the last several years and one that will have profound repercussions on the country's future.

A central question that some political analysts ask is: Who won at the bargaining table? Did the FMLN win? Did the government win? In these negotiations, there is no single winner: neither the FMLN nor the government won. In twelve years, neither party managed to defeat its opponent militarily on the battlefield, nor did either achieve a resounding political victory for its political program at the bargaining table. One must bear in mind that a crisis of hegemony existed, and therefore neither force had the ability to impose its own program, although each had the necessary power to block the other's.[1]

As is the case in any negotiating process, each party had to make concessions and obtain only part of its demands. Both parties had to move away from their initial positions and make concessions in order to reach the Peace Accords. Besides, a national consensus for peace gradually emerged as the negotiations moved forward, which served as a pressure mechanism on the negotiators to bring about the signing of the historic accords.

The negotiations entailed a series of political, military, and socio-economic agreements. In general, the FMLN managed to impose its demands on the accords in political and security matters but had to yield in the socioeconomic area. In recognition of the impossibility of dissolving the armed forces or merging the two armies, three measures were included to promote military "reconversion": reduction, restructuring, and purging. The overall objective was to achieve the supremacy of civilian over military power and the full enforcement of the lawful state. Some political analysts have seen this as a "democratic revolution."[2] The government, in turn, had to yield in the political and security areas, but it managed to reaffirm its position in the socio-economic area by imposing its view that the government's economic policy was not negotiable. The Peace Accords do not introduce any substantive modification of the socioeconomic structure of the country. By mutual consent, the main socioeconomic problems were excluded from the bargaining table.[3]

The negotiations took place between the two participants in the war: the government/armed forces and the FMLN. Civilian society played a marginal and peripheral role in the substance of what was negotiated. However, it should be made clear that the negotiations were not an arrangement to satisfy exclusively the interests of the two actors involved in the negotiations, but rather they addressed a national agenda for demilitarization and democratization.

After the peace negotiations, some have argued that three transitions are simultaneously taking place in El Salvador: the transitions from war to peace, militarism to demilitarization, and authoritarianism to democracy.[4] That these three transitions are occurring at the same time poses an analytical problem because the abuse of the term *transition* in the academic and political realms has caused the word to lose its precision in terms of the political phenomenon that it seeks to explain. In this sense, I suggest that the Salvadoran political process can be characterized as a *political regime transition.* By *political regime* I mean the set of patterns that determines the means and the channels of access to power, the margins of action of those already in power, and the characteristics of the actors who are admitted to and excluded from this access to power.[5]

One working hypothesis presented here is that the negotiating process ceased to be concerned with who would have power and instead became concerned with the mechanisms and means of access to power. The debate and struggles of the negotiations have centered on the features of the new political regime. As the strategy of the FMLN changed orientation in the negotiations in favor of demilitarization and democratization, the character of the postwar political regime took center stage in the national political debate. The negotiations moved toward redefining the political regime that was gradually being reconstituted since the early 1980s. The fulfillment of the Peace Accords could transform this once exclusionary type of political regime into a competitive and democratic one.

From this analytical perspective, the political transition that was initiated by the signing of the Peace Accords ought to be understood as comprised of two stages. The first stage (1992–94) relates to the observance and implementation of the Peace Accords, which culminated in the 1994 general elections. The second stage opens with the inauguration of the new government and the new political institutions, which reflects conditions and correlations characteristic of the postwar era. The greatest challenge for this transition is that it will have to confront the problems that were not addressed in the peace negotiations, in particular, the socioeconomic problems and the need to deepen the democratic process and consolidate peace.

This chapter discusses these different stages of the Salvadoran political transition. First, it considers the peace process, making reference to the profound modifications that the Salvadoran political system experienced between 1992 and 1994. Second, it analyzes the March 1994 elections within this framework. Third, it analyzes the rebuilding of the party system. Fourth, it discusses the new role of Congress. Fifth, it presents a few considerations regarding some of the challenges for democratic governability in El Salvador for the next several years.

The Peace Accords

The negotiation itself entailed a set of agreements that have implied profound modifications in the Salvadoran political system. Five aspects clearly illustrate these changes: (1) the agreements related to demilitarization and the redefining of civil-military relations, (2) the termination of the military structure of the FMLN, (3) the process of reinserting the ex-combatants in civil society, (4) the agreements related to socioeconomic issues, and (5) the role played by the Commission for the Consolidation of Peace (COPAZ).

The Agreements Related to Demilitarization and the Redefining of Civil-Military Relations

The Peace Accords have redefined civil-military relations. Given that neither the dissolution of the armed forces nor the merging of the two armies was viable, three types of measures were proposed to address the question of military reform: reduction, restructuring, and purging. The overall purpose was to attain the supremacy of civilian over military power and the full enforcement of the lawful state. A brief comment on the seven measures that were set forth to achieve military reconversion will illustrate the complex and significant institutional transformation of the role of the armed forces in Salvadoran politics and its implications for redefining civil-military relations.[6]

First, the modification of the basic doctrine of the armed forces must be highlighted. A constitutional reform that redefines the role of the armed forces—to defend the sovereignty of the state and the integrity of the country—was ratified. This is an important achievement because in the past the constitution assigned multiple roles to the armed forces. In addition to the current role, it included "keeping the public peace, tranquility, and safety, and respect for the constitution and the other laws in force," as well as "insuring especially that the republican form of government and the representative democratic regime be maintained, the norm of alternation of presidency of the republic not be violated, and freedom of suffrage and respect for human rights be guaranteed."[7] In the past, the military was a "supra-institution." It was above other institutions in deciding on a great variety of issues and exhibited a high level of autonomy with respect to the power of the state. Now its role has been strictly limited to defending state sovereignty and the integrity of the national territory.

Second, a reform of the educational system of the armed forces was agreed on. The Academic Council, an entity composed of civilians and military officers, was created and is working on the appointment of an academic staff and reform of the educational system. Third, the armed forces were reduced. As a result of the Peace Accords, it is estimated that by the end of 1992 the armed forces had been reduced from over 60,000 to 31,500 active duty soldiers.[8]

Fourth, the security forces were dismantled. After some disagreements, two security forces were dissolved (the National Guard and the Treasury Police); the preliminary plan for the creation of the National Civilian Police (PNC) was approved; the National Academy of Public Security (ANSP) was created; the director and staff of the Academic Council were appointed by April 1992; and the Academic Council began its administrative operations in May 1992. The general director of the National Civilian Police was appointed at the end of August 1992, and the National Academy of Public Security was officially inaugurated and began classes in September. None of this happened without discussion. While it is true that the security corps were dissolved, it is also true that those active-duty soldiers were transferred to the newly created Special Brigade of Military Security, a military police force expected to have 2,014 troops that will be responsible for the defense of national borders.[9]

The most important aspect of this entire process of reorganization and redefinition of public security is the creation and development of the new National Civilian Police, which is outside the control of the armed forces. This is a new police force based on a new doctrine, new organization, and new mechanisms of selection, education, and training. The creation of the PNC is a fundamental part of the Peace Accords. By the end of 1993, approximately 3,000 police had graduated from the ANSP. It has been estimated that 5,700 officers graduated by the end of 1994. Because of the widespread expansion of the crime problem, the deployment of the PNC began in Chalatenango, Cabañas, Morazán, La Unión, San Miguel, San Vicente, Usulután, and several areas in San Salvador since the beginning of March 1993. However, the very establishment of the ANSP and the deployment of the PNC have encountered serious hurdles: technical problems, lack of resources, sluggishness, lack of political will on the part of the Ministry of Defense to provide the appropriate equipment for carrying out the police work assumed by the armed forces, and so on.[10]

The most burning issue in the discussion about public security has been the reduction of the National Police (PN). The accords envisioned a reduction of the PN that would be inversely proportional to the deployment of the PNC. In practice, there were delays in the demobilization of the PN as officers continued to graduate, while at the same time the obstacles for the deployment of the PNC continued. Finally, the dissolution of the National Police took place at the beginning of 1995. The balance in this area is highly positive because there has been significant progress regarding the duties of the ANSP and the PNC. Moreover, the levels of public security and popular trust have risen in areas where the PNC has been deployed.

Fifth, the National Board of Intelligence was dissolved, and the State Intelligence Agency was created under civilian leadership. Sixth, the obligatory military draft was suspended when armed conflict began to end. The Civil Defense has been dissolved. A new law of military and reserve service for the armed forces was enacted by Congress.

Seventh, the purging process was concluded. In September 1992 the Ad Hoc Commission—made up of three civilians of recognized democratic backgrounds—submitted to President Alfredo Cristiani the list of officers who should be released. Of the 2,200 officers in the armed forces, the commission focused exclusively on 10 percent of the highest-ranking officers.[11] Once in possession of the list, Cristiani encountered problems implementing these recommendations. However, as a consequence of the agreement reached after the third crisis in the implementation of the accords, the president promised the secretary general of the United Nations that he would resolve the issue by the end of November 1992. Later it was suggested that these recommendations would become effective by military order on December 31.

In early January 1993, several military changes took place. On January 5 the president communicated the details of the measures adopted to meet the recommendations of the Ad Hoc Commission to the UN secretary general. The recommendations were applied to 103 officers, one of whom was no longer an active member of the armed forces. Of the 102 remaining officers, it was recommended that 26 be assigned to other roles and 76 be separated from service. In a January 7, 1993, letter to the president of the UN Security Council, the secretary general stated that after carefully studying the measures adopted by President Cristiani: "I am inclined to consider satisfactory the measures adopted and applied by the Government of El Salvador with respect to 87 of the 102 officers mentioned in the recommendations of the Ad Hoc Commission, even when some are not totally consistent with the recommendations. However, with the measures adopted with respect to the other 15 officers, the recommendations are not met."[12] The recommendations with respect to these remaining officers were not carried out until the middle of the year. The response of the right-wing sectors was to accuse the members of the Ad Hoc Commission of acting subjectively and exhibiting biases in their recommendations.[13]

Eighth, there is the question of impunity. In the peace negotiations held in Mexico, agreement was reached on the creation of the Truth Commission, comprised of three individuals appointed by the UN secretary general: Belisario Betancur, Reinaldo Figueredo, and Thomas Buergenthal. The commission was entrusted with the responsibility to investigate the severe acts of violence that had occurred since 1980, "whose mark on society clamors with greater urgency for public disclosure of the truth." The accords recognized "the need to shed light on and resolve any accusations of impunity for officers of the armed forces, especially in cases in which the respect for human rights is compromised." To such ends, both parties "remit the consideration and resolution of this issue to the Truth Commission."

The Report of the Truth Commission was released on March 15, 1993, and became the focus of political debate for several weeks.[14] The report turned out to be quite polemical and has provoked dissatisfaction over a broad segment of the political spectrum, mostly because of the different expectations that each person had about its contents. However, the evaluation of the contents and recommendations of this report should take into account the mandate and methodology of the Truth Commission: "The commission was not established as a legal entity. The Peace Accords gave the commission six months to carry out four principal tasks: to clarify the human rights abuses during the war; to study very carefully the impunity under which the security corps and the Salvadoran military committed such abuses; to offer legal, political, or administrative recommendations to avoid the recurrence of this history of abuses; and, finally, to encourage national reconciliation. Both the guerrillas as well as the government agreed to carry out the recommendations of the commission." The commission received direct testimony from two thousand people concerning seven thousand victims and information from secondary sources related to more than eighteen thousand victims. "Even with this amount of evidence, the commission was able to address only a small fraction of the thousands of abuses committed during the war. It chose a sample of cases that either reflected the most brutal events of the conflict or else were part of a broader and more systematic pattern of violations."[15] Based on these criteria, the commission chose thirty-two cases to be studied.

The seven main recommendations of the Truth Commission were as follows:

1. The first proposal is "that those responsible for serious human rights abuses who hold any public or military office today be removed

immediately and barred from exercising public office in El Salvador for at least ten years. They should also be banned from exercising any military- or security-related responsibility." Based on these investigations, the commission requested that forty military personnel be removed from the armed forces, including the minister and vice-minister of defense, as well as the chief of staff. Similarly, the commission also requested that the various members of the FMLN, including the commanders Joaquín Villalobos and Ana Guadalupe Martínez, be barred from public responsibilities for ten years.

2. The commission called for "the FMLN to renounce forever all forms of violence in the pursuit of political goals."

3. The commission was of the opinion that "the vast majority of abuses studied . . . were committed by members of the armed forces or by groups allied with them." In order to make the military more professional, the commission recommended "the immediate removal of all military officers implicated in human rights violations or other serious violations," "the enactment of measures for civilian control of military promotions, the military budget and all the intelligence services," "the need to establish a new legal mechanism that would permit military personnel to refuse to carry out an order that might result in a crime or violation of human rights," and "the taking of steps to cut all ties between the military and the private and/or paramilitary armed groups."

4. The commission also issued a special call "to carry out a specific investigation on the death squads, for the purpose of further denouncing them publicly and definitively eradicating such activity."

5. The commission found the system of justice to be very inefficient and proposed several recommendations: "the resignation of all members of the Supreme Court, making specific reference to the president of the court, Mauricio Gutiérrez Castro, for his less-than-professional conduct," "a real separation of powers among the executive, legislative, and judicial branches, thereby depoliticizing the court," and, "that the power at the pinnacle of the Supreme Court, as well as its centralized power over the rest of the judicial system, be reduced."

6. The commission "considers that justice requires sanctions against human rights violations, but the purpose of the commission was not to specify sanctions, and it recognizes that the current Salvadoran judicial system is not capable of objectively passing judgment and carrying out such sanctions. Therefore, the commission finds itself unable to recommend judicial procedures in El Salvador against the people mentioned in the report until judicial reforms are carried out."

7. The commission considered that "the victims of human rights violations from both sides be recognized publicly and awarded material compensation," and it issued "a call for the establishment of a special fund toward this end."[16]

The response of conservative sectors to the Truth Commission was astonishing. The armed forces denounced the motive behind the desire to discredit the military institution and declared that the conclusions and suggestions of this report "distort the historical reality and make unfounded and biased accusations." They concluded by affirming that the report is "unjust, incomplete, illegal, unethical, biased, and daring."[17] On the other hand, the issue was raised that the accused were not given the opportunity to defend themselves and be duly processed in a trial. Hurriedly and without consensus within COPAZ, the Legislative Assembly approved the law of general amnesty for the consolidation of peace on March 20, 1993. President Cristiani, in turn, declared in a speech to the nation that the government "committed itself to implement the recommendations that emerged from the report of the Truth Commission; in that sense, the government of El Salvador will fulfill its commitment. . . . Of course, we will do this within the parameters attributed to the executive office and within the bounds established by the constitutional framework."[18]

The president of the judicial Supreme Court stated categorically that he would not resign, and he did not.[19] The Supreme Court energetically rejected the report and the recommendations of the Truth Commission. In the opinion of the court's magistrates, the Truth Commission was created by political agreement to "investigate the severe acts of violence that occurred since 1980." This is a "political agreement between two parties expressly defined and with an especially determined purpose, from which no effect can be derived that might subvert the order established by the constitution, international treaties, and the secondary laws in force in El Salvador." The Supreme Court also denounced the methodology employed to carry out the commission's investigation, which "completely disregarded the principles of due process, under the pretext of avoiding any delays in uncovering the truth, [and] succumbed to arbitrariness, so that with such a methodology, all possibility of defense or hearing for the people who in the opinion of the commission should be mentioned as responsible for the acts under investigation is eliminated."[20]

The debate surrounding the report and recommendations of the Truth Commission has made evident the problems related to the administration of justice in the country, and how limited and minimally effective different attempts at judicial reform have been thus far.

The need to comply with what was signed in the accords has been more traumatic in the case of the recommendations of the report of the Ad Hoc Commission and the Truth Commission. As an editorial in *La Prensa Gráfica* stated, "there may be flaws, holes, and even injustices in those reports. Therefore, the most important factor now is the responsible and careful handling of those reports."[21] The report of the Truth Commission has come to play a dual role. On the one hand, it has historic dimensions, insofar as it has investigated some acts of violence. Reconciliation should be based on knowing the truth about what happened during the years of war. But, in addition, it should be understood that the report is fulfilling a future mission, since its objective is to avoid a repetition of this type of act. The most important task is to put an end to impunity by establishing a precedent so that this type of crime will not be committed again. The report and its recommendations respond to this dual objective in accordance with the four mandates given to the commission by the framework of the Peace Accords. Reconciliation can be achieved only through public disclosure of the truth because "once the past is known, it will be possible to forgive and to try to forget, but always based on the truth, not on forgetfulness."[22] Complying with the recommendations becomes important as we look to the future. For the United Nations, it is thus important, in this regard, that the recommendations of the Truth Commission are obligatory.[23]

According to the recommendations of the Ad Hoc Commission and the Truth Commission, the officials mentioned in both reports were removed on July 1, 1993. The high command was replaced. As an editorial in *La Prensa Gráfica* commented: "It seems important for us to highlight this, and to say it unambiguously and without beating around the bush, because this is not purely an administrative change. This change has political implications and is in line with the institutional renewal under way in the country."[24] With the departure of René Emilio Ponce and Orlando Zepeda, the fulfillment of the recommendations of the Ad Hoc Commission and part of the recommendations of the Truth Commission was completed.

Nevertheless, the political assassinations did not stop there. Between 1993 and 1994, several ex-commandants of the FMLN were assassinated: Oscar Grimaldi, Hernán Castro, Carlos Véliz, and Mario López; attempts against Nidia Díaz were also made on two occasions. In some cases the political nature of the assassinations has been debated. The need to investigate these events led to the creation of the Joint Group for the Investigation of the Politically Motivated Illegal Armed Groups in December 1993. This Joint Group is entrusted with the task of organizing, conducting, and supervising a specialized investigation team.[25]

In making an assessment, it is important to point out that, notwithstanding the modifications in civil-military relations introduced by the constitutional reforms, it is necessary to bear in mind the warning that these "are measures that are centralized at the pinnacle of the executive without creating, thus far, other civilian or state mechanisms that would constitute anything that could be labeled 'civilian government.' The role of the Legislative Assembly is still quite limited and inefficient. The general structure of military power remains almost intact, even though the decentralization of decision making might bring about a potential element of subjection and limitation of functions of the FAES [Armed Forces of El Salvador]."[26] The Peace Accords "reinforce the presidential figure in the relations of the state with the FAES, almost as a guarantee of military control, as the 'counterweight' against the power of an armed institution. Will this type of presidentialism be enough to counteract the political norms and direct exercise of power of the FAES?"[27] This type of questioning raises as a valid concern whether these measures, born of the negotiations, will succeed in changing the historical patterns of behavior of the military institution.

The evaluation that I have made about the level of fulfillment of the Peace Accords in matters pertaining to the armed forces is a bit more optimistic. However, it is important to point out that "a great void in the Peace Accords has to do precisely with the fact that no one has defined precisely who will create—and how—the new defense and/or security doctrine of the Salvadoran state," and that in the case of El Salvador, "responsibilities are transferred to civilian power, but not the institutional capability to confront these challenges. In any case, the task is to define democratically with the contribution of the different sectors of national life the central elements of this security doctrine. Thus we have resolved the issue of who should participate in the formulation of this new security doctrine, but we still need to define how it will be formulated. This is one of the primary deficiencies of the new institutionality that emerged following the Peace Accords."[28]

The Dismantling of the Military Structure of the FMLN

As the FMLN transformed itself into a political party and began to participate in the electoral arena, the political system was modified. For the first time in the contemporary history of El Salvador, the arena of electoral competition encompasses the entire political-ideological spectrum. This has also entailed a change in the existing party system.

On December 15, 1992, the United Nations certified that the FMLN had completed the destruction of its weapons of war and therefore could register as a political party. However, on May 23, 1993, in the neighborhood of Santa Rosa in Managua, a weapons stockpile belonging to the FPL (Popular Liberation Forces) accidentally exploded, prompting the FMLN to admit that it still held weapons. For the FMLN, the existence of these weapons "is the redoubt of the original distrust of the process, but not using the weapons, recognizing their existence, and turning them in constitute a clear demonstration of responsibility and adherence to the political course staked out by the Peace Accords."[29] The political cost paid by the ex-guerrillas was very high, especially because this act was a blow to the very credibility of the FMLN in the new era under way in the country. Lack of trust does not justify having kept these arms as a strategic reserve.

The secretary general of the United Nations declared this incident to be the most serious violation of the Peace Accords. He felt that he had been deceived, since "the inventory presented to ONUSAL [United Nations Mission in El Salvador] by the FMLN was incorrect and failed to include large quantities of war material."[30] He asked them to inform him before June 20 "of the action taken by the FMLN to assure that all arms deposits in El Salvador and neighboring countries be located and their contents destroyed." Subsequently, an agreement was reached to hand over all weapons to ONUSAL by August 4. At the end of August, Dr. Ramírez Ocampo, chief of the United Nations Mission, stated that after the explosion of the weapons stockpile in Nicaragua, the FMLN handed over nine other stockpiles in Nicaraguan territory, two in Honduras, and one hundred nine in El Salvador. Based on these measures, ONUSAL declared, for the second time, that the military structure of the FMLN had been dismantled.[31] After August 4, 1993, any discovery of weapons would be treated as a criminal offense.

The Reinsertion of the Former Combatants

The National Plan for Reconstruction cannot be evaluated here, but it should be emphasized that the support programs for the reinsertion of the ex-combatants have turned out to be slow, bureaucratic, and of limited impact compared to the function that they ought to have fulfilled. The most obvious case is the delay in the legal transfer of land to the army and FMLN ex-combatants. Only 8 percent of the cases have been processed.[32]

This problem is quite serious primarily because it concerns the reinsertion into the civic and institutional life of the country of those who spent years living on and for violence. It also affects the very stability of the peace process. This failure to deliver what was promised to the ex-combatants prompted some demobilized members of the armed forces to take over the Parliament on various occasions to insist that their demands be met. In early 1995 the demobilized members carried out various displays of force in different parts of the country, always as a mechanism of pressure. However, at this stage of transition, one cannot accept these displays of force as mechanisms to voice demands, regardless of their fairness, because they send the wrong message: for demands to be heard, one must resort to measures of force. This cannot be permitted in a lawful state.

The Accords Related to Socioeconomic Matters

The Forum for Economic and Social Concertación is an innovative mechanism of concertación among the government, business leaders, and workers which arose from the Peace Accords. It is innovative in that it created an opportunity for rapprochement, dialogue, and eventual understanding among previously alienated sectors. Now, however, these groups have to work jointly in a productive effort. It was not easy to get the three sectors represented at the forum to sit down together at the table. The private sector refused to participate until September 9, 1992, the official starting date of the forum.

Thus far the only concrete achievement has been the definition of a work agenda and methodology. On December 18, 1992, the agreed agenda for discussion at the forum was disclosed to the public. The launching of the newly created subcommittees—one on economic aspects and the other on social issues—takes into account the issue that most concerns each of the forum's principal actors: economic reactivation for the business sector and labor policy for the labor sector. The agenda itself reflects a far-reaching and broad perspective.

On February 17, 1993, business, labor, and government leaders signed the "Agreement of Principles and Commitments," which was a step forward in creating a favorable framework for the development of the forum's work. Later, however, a series of incidents (strikes, labor layoffs, nonratification of the conventions of the ILO [International Labor Organization], lack of consensus surrounding the new labor code, and so on) occurred, together with some public statements that revealed the profound differences that exist between the government/ business sector and the labor sector. Presently, the work of the forum has been suspended.

The Role of the Commission for the Consolidation of Peace (COPAZ)

The peace negotiations created two new arenas of concertación. The first, the Forum for Economic and Social Concertación, as pointed out earlier, has very few accomplishments to show. This Forum for Concertación among government, business, and labor sectors has reached a dead end because of the existing polarization and lack of political will to seek compromises and respect agreements.

The other arena is COPAZ, conceived in the New York Accords "to supervise the implementation of all the agreements." What was new about this entity was that the responsibility to supervise the accords was transferred to the broadest representation of civil society. The government, the FMLN, and all of the political parties represented in the Legislative Assembly are part of COPAZ. The composition of COPAZ led to an equilibrium, as the government and its supporting parties comprised one-half of the votes, while the opposition controlled the other half. This obligated the two sides to come to an agreement. Some argue that this was intentional—a deliberate way to pressure both sides to conciliate their differences and reach decisions by consensus.

Although COPAZ does not possess executive faculties, it has functioned as a mechanism of participation and control, if not on the part of civil society, at least on the part of the political parties. In general, the balance of COPAZ's achievements is positive because it has served as the arena for seeking national political consensus. Regrettably, in some of its efforts to obtain consensus, COPAZ reached agreements that sacrificed the intended spirit of the supervision of the commitments acquired. COPAZ's role can be criticized on various counts. First, it created a bureaucracy that did little to facilitate the carrying out of some agreements. More than anything, it duplicated the problems from the highest level, passing them along to the commissions and subcommissions that were created. Second, instead of being an arena for the participation of civil society, it became a fiefdom of the "partyocracy," in which the parties arrived at self-serving agreements.

A third shortcoming is that a duality was created regarding the role that the Legislative Assembly was supposed to play. Before approving a law, the Assembly was now supposed to obtain consent from the parties in COPAZ. Of course, the role of COPAZ was intended to be short-lived, but as time went on, COPAZ continued to play this role. This heightened the general uneasiness about COPAZ. The criticism from the Right is that the legal order is being subverted. Through the Peace Accords, they argue, there has been an attempt to impose on the legislative branch "programs that were agreed to by negotiators from the executive, without prior consultations or authorization to do so." COPAZ itself is deemed to be one such mechanism, "which no longer has any reason to exist" but remains in operation, presuming that any law related to the peace process has to be approved by consensus.[33] This is partially true, as, according to its laws, COPAZ must be consulted regarding any important step related to the peace process. Fourth, after the ceremony marking the end of the "armed peace" on December 15, 1992, an offensive emerged proclaiming the need to terminate COPAZ. In January 1993 vice-president Merino suggested that there was an urgent need to revise the pending activities of COPAZ in accordance with its charter and to define how much longer COPAZ's existence was justified.[34]

COPAZ's mandate ended in 1995 as agreed for the final stage of implementation of the Peace Accords. However, carrying out the pending measures of the Peace Accords became the responsibility of the government of Calderón Sol. Delays or breaches of the accords are evident in the following areas: (1) public security, (2) land transfer programs, (3) judicial system reforms recommended by the Truth Commission, and (4) measures for guaranteeing the reinsertion of ex-combatants.

The 1994 General Elections

On March 20, four elections were held simultaneously: (1) presidential; (2) parliamentary, using a proportional representation formula to fill eighty-four seats in the Legislative Assembly; (3) municipal, using a simple majority formula to fill 262 mayoralties (the party that obtains the most votes obtains all the seats of the municipal council); and (4) for the Central American Parliament, using a proportional representation formula in national single districts to elect twenty deputies.

Nine parties ran in these elections. The parties on the Right were the incumbent Nationalist Republican Alliance (ARENA), the Christian Authentic Movement (MAC), and the Party of National Conciliation (PCN). The parties of the Center-Right were the Christian Democratic Party (PDC), the National Solidarity Movement (MSN), and the Unity Movement (MU). The parties on the Left were the National Revolutionary Movement (MNR), the Democratic Convergence (CD), and, participating for the first time, the FMLN. Six parties and one coalition (the Left aligned in the Coalition MNR-CD-FMLN) ran for the presidency.

The Voter Registry

In his October 1993 report, the UN secretary general suggested that there were serious deficiencies in the voter registry. The most serious deficiency was the large number of citizens who were not registered to vote or who did not have a voter identification card. According to a June 1993 survey by the General Board of Statistics and Census, financed by the United Nations Development Program (UNDP/ONUSAL), 27 percent of Salvadorans of voting age (approximately 768,384 people) did not have a voter identification card. The UNDP/ONUSAL survey permitted the identification of two groups with high levels of nonenrollment in the voter registry: (1) the districts that experienced the highest levels of armed conflict in the past and (2) the most densely populated urban areas. This permitted the development of a strategy to promote registration that targeted both groups: (1) ex-combatants: Chalatenango, Cabañas, Morazán, and La Unión; and (2) city dwellers: San Salvador, San Miguel, Santa Ana, and La Libertad. In evaluating this problem, ONUSAL concluded that "non-registration was due more to the lack of citizen mobilization and the technical inefficiency of the Supreme Electoral Board (TSE) than to a deliberate exclusion of certain sectors of the population for political reasons." It also warned that "the problems that limit the possibility of reaching high percentages of registration are numerous."[35]

For these programs to succeed, it was necessary to complement the calls for citizen registration with improvements in the mechanism for issuing voter identification cards. Until June–July 1993, the voter registration process was quite slow. However, since August the main problem was that there was an immense lag in the delivery of voter identification cards, in spite of the notable increase in the production of SIRES (applications for an identification card). Throughout 1993 the delivery of the identification cards gradually improved as follows: the average daily delivery was 92 in January; 388 in July; 1,304 in September; 2,146 in October; 3,009 in November; and 2,637 in December.

Following the close of the registry on January 19 and the configuration of the list of registered voters, the Electoral Division of ONUSAL concluded that "a significant improvement in the conditions of registration has been recorded." This was possibly due to the pressure and support provided by diverse institutions, in particular, by the "strategic and logistical support of the Electoral Division, with the collaboration of other components of ONUSAL." In the judgment of ONUSAL, this is a "more inclusive and cleansed" electoral registry, and, in numeric terms, "the situation of the registry can be considered satisfactory."[36]

It is necessary to pause for a moment to review the complexity underlying these numbers. By the November 19 registration deadline, the result of the TSE-led campaign since July could be considered successful: 787,834 registration applications were filed. Of these applications submitted between July 1 and November 19, 1993, 469,098 represented new registrations; 85,560 were modifications; and 229,800 were replacements.[37] Therefore, the success is more relative, given that this does not refer to 787,834 new registrations covering 786,384 people who, according to the UNDP/ONUSAL survey, did not have voter identification cards. However, it should be recognized that, with regard to new applications, the campaign managed to cover 59.54 percent of the population that did not have voter identification cards.

The electoral census is composed of 2,700,000 persons, of which it is estimated that only 2,350,000 had voter identification cards when the deadline for delivering the identification cards arrived on March 12.[38] This number represents approximately 85 percent of the estimated population of voting age.[39]

The Electoral Outcome

The so-called elections of the century were held within a context of serious technical irregularities, which limited citizen participation. It has been impossible to quantify the impact of these technical problems on voting levels. However, no one is satisfied with the manner in which the March 20 elections were organized. There also were problems with the TSE-crafted tallying system and the manner in which votes were counted. As of this writing, insufficient data is available to question the legitimacy of the electoral results, but we acknowledge nonetheless that there were irregularities. Thus the judgment of the UN secretary general would have to be accepted. He suggested that the March 20 elections occurred under adequate conditions, in terms of freedom, competitiveness, and security; and in spite of the problems, "the results of the elections can be considered acceptable."[40] Based on the problems of the March 20 elections and the recommendations from the political parties and ONUSAL, the second round of presidential voting, held on April 24, was better organized. Having been blamed for the disorganization and the irregularities surrounding the electoral competition, the Supreme Electoral Board was the sole entity to emerge from the March 20 elections with a tarnished reputation.

The low voter turnout in the "elections of the century" is striking. In the presidential elections, 1,307,657 valid votes were cast, which represent 48 percent of the 2.7 million registered voters, or 56 percent of the 2.35 million people holding voter identification cards. One could argue simplistically that the low level of voting is the result of technical problems on voting day, as well as apathy or lack of public interest in the elections. However, the problem is somewhat more complex. It is a clear indicator of the crisis of representation that is besieging the parties—including the Left—and of the limited mobilizing effect of the electoral campaigns.[41] In the second round, 1,197,244 valid votes were cast.

In the first round of the presidential elections, ARENA obtained 49.03 percent of the votes, the Coalition (FMLN-MNR-CD) 24.90 percent, and the PDC 16.36 percent (see Figure 1). These results coincide with the predictions of the opinion polls. Three points deserve highlighting: ARENA received a high percentage of votes and almost reached the 50 percent plus one of the votes needed to win in the first round; the Left was consolidated as the second political force; and the PDC was pushed into third place, although it still received a significant number of votes. In the second round, held on Sunday, April 24, ARENA obtained a resounding victory with 68.35 percent, while the Coalition obtained 31.65 percent of the vote.

With respect to the Legislative Assembly, it is important to compare the makeup of the 1991–94 and the 1994–97 legislatures (Table 1).

The elections reflect a high degree of polarization between ARENA and the FMLN. This is clearly seen in the elections for deputies. While ARENA maintained its thirty-nine deputies, the other political groups saw their representation diminish. As a first-time contender, the FMLN made inroads, gaining twenty-one deputies. The distribution of the votes reveals how the small or centrist parties have suffered the consequences of polarization. ARENA has managed to make the necessary alliances in the Assembly in order to assure itself a simple majority.

As a result of the simple-majority electoral system, it is at the municipal level where ARENA's victory becomes most evident and the defeat of the opposition clearer: ARENA, 207; PDC, 29; FMLN, 15; and PCN, 10 mayoralties (Table 2).

In the case of the 1994 elections, four examples illustrate this disproportion between votes and municipal councils. ARENA obtained 79.01 percent of the municipal councils with 44.48 percent of the vote, while the Coalition of the Left obtained only 5.73 percent of the munic-

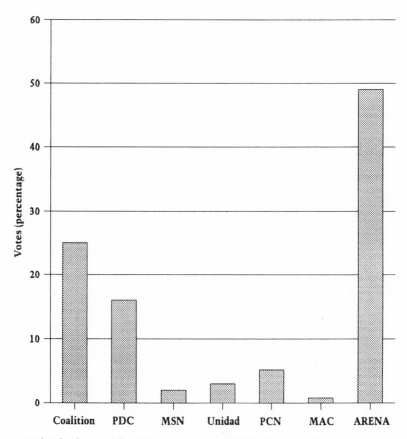

Figure 1 El Salvador presidential election, March 1994 (first round). *Source:* Supreme Electoral Board.

Table 1 **El Salvador: Number of Deputies by Political Parties in the Elected Legislatures in 1991 and 1994**

Political Party	Number of Deputies 1991	Number of Deputies 1994
ARENA	39	39
PCN	9	4
PDC	26	18
CD	9	1
FMLN	NP[a]	21
Unidad	NP	1
MAC	1	0
Total	84	84

[a]NP = did not participate.

Table 2 El Salvador: Votes and Municipal Councils by Political Party, 1994 Elections

Political Party	Municipal Councils	Percentage of Votes
ARENA	207	44.48
MAC	1	0.74
PCN	10	7.96
PDC	29	19.41
CD/FMLN[a]	15	24.48
Total	262	—

[a]Unable to reproduce the coalition achieved at the presidential level, the Left achieved four different types of coalition at the local level for the 1994 elections: FMLN-MNR-CD, FMLN-MNR, FMLN-CD, and CD-MNR. Furthermore, in the majority of municipalities, each party ran alone: the FMLN won running alone in thirteen and in two running in coalition with the CD. To simplify the calculation in this table, I have added all of the votes obtained by the parties of the Left at the municipal level and added the mayoralties won alone or in coalitions.

ipal councils with 24.48 percent of the vote. The PDC obtained 11.06 percent of the local governments with 19.41 percent of the vote, while the MAC obtained one municipal council with 0.74 percent of the vote.

When the results of the three elections are factored into the analysis, there is an unquestionable victory for ARENA, which controls the executive branch, has a simple majority in the Legislative Assembly, and holds more than two-thirds of the municipal governments.

The Rebuilding of the Party System

Regarding the impact of these elections on the transformation of the party system, I would point out that elsewhere I proposed that the incorporation of the Left into the electoral process might modify the party system in one of two directions: (1) a continued "polarized bipolar pluralism," in which the poles would be represented by the Left (FMLN) and the Right (ARENA), without a Center; or (2) a change toward a "polarized pluralism," in which the parties of the Left (FMLN) and the Right (ARENA) occupy the extremes of the political spectrum, while one or two parties (PDC and CD) occupy the Center.[42] The electoral results show a high level of polarization, confirming that the two principal political forces (ARENA and the FMLN) are the two poles at the extremes of the spectrum of political competition. It is still premature, however, to draw conclusions about the future of the political Center. These elections were held under polarized conditions in which the principal actors and themes of the war were salient. The centrist or moderate political options were punished the most by the polarization of this election. It remains to be seen if there is space in the electorate for these options (both of the Center-Right as well as the Center-Left). In the meantime, these forces will have to be rebuilt, resolve their internal problems, and propose more updated and clearer political programs.

The Role of the New Congress

The new Legislative Assembly was inaugurated on May 1, 1994, reflecting the correlation of the March elections discussed earlier. This Assembly confronts three major challenges. The first challenge is the need to reform its structure and functioning in order to meet the challenges of modernization of the country. Second, following the impending withdrawal of ONUSAL and the exhaustion of COPAZ, the Assembly will be the only arena for forming political *concertación* in the country, which will require the deputies to think and act in terms of the national interest more than their partisan interests. Third, in the short term, the Assembly will appoint the *magistrados* (justices) who will make up the new judicial Supreme Court and the Supreme Electoral Board. These appointments are important for selecting capable personnel committed to advancing the new legal-political institutions consonant with the Peace Accords and for confronting the challenges of reconstruction and reconciliation.

The election of the judicial Supreme Court monopolized the attention of national and international public opinion. Congress split in half. The parties of the Right (ARENA and the PCN) were on one side. On the other side, the entire opposition successfully managed to form a unified bloc to carry out the negotiations (PDC-FMLN-MU-CD). Because a two-thirds vote is required to elect the *magistrados,* an impasse occurred, which left the country without a judicial Supreme Court for almost a month, until both sides managed to reach an agreement on the principal issue of discord, the new president of the court. This first experience has shown how complex the process of learning both the parliamentary game and the strategies of coalition building has been for the deputies, and how difficult it has been to achieve compromises among the different legislative factions on such important topics. The one positive aspect is that, for the first time in the political history of El Salvador, the court was formed based not on the suggestions of the executive but rather on debate in the Assembly and on proposals in which the association of lawyers and the National Council of Judicature played an important role. The court's composition is also balanced. This court has a predisposition to take on its properly independent role, thus breaking, up to a certain point, continuity with the past and the partisan politicization of appointments.

The Challenges of Democratic Governability

The second stage of the transition, which opened following the March–April 1994 elections, puts to the test the new political system that emerged following the Peace Accords. Political stability will depend in large measure on the capability of the political system to deal with demands from different social sectors, especially in the current post-election period, in which socioeconomic issues will push their way onto the agenda for discussion.

The probability of a democratic broadening, deepening, and consolidation occurring in the country will depend on the manner in which the following challenges facing the political system are processed and resolved.

1. Overcoming the existing high level of polarization that prevails in the country, as expressed in the last elections.

2. The government's displaying the will and capacity for consensus building. Dialogues with all the sectors of national life are important. The search for consensus is a necessary mechanism of stability in times of crisis such as this transition stage. A governing style that takes into account the opinions of others and tries to look for consensus and arrive at agreements that consolidate peace and reunify Salvadoran society is important.

3. Addressing the social conflicts that result from socioeconomic problems, especially poverty, unemployment, and low wages. Governmental plans should take into account and respond to the needs of the less privileged sectors. Priority should be given to the issue of raising the population's standard of living. This is fundamental for guaranteeing political stability. It is important to emphasize the need to create mechanisms for channeling and responding to the legitimate demands of diverse social groups.

4. Giving more attention to the reconstruction of the areas most affected by the armed conflict, and especially the most remote areas in which reconstruction has not yet been forthcoming. To avoid events that disturb institutional life, such as the takeover of the Legislative Assembly by some demobilized members of the armed forces pressing for their indemnifications, the reinsertion of the ex-combatants into civil and productive life should be assured.

5. Increasing the channels and mechanisms that guarantee real and effective participation of the population in building a new democratic society. This also includes the need to redefine the role of municipal governments in the political system. It is necessary to promote citizen participation and the democratization of decision making at the local government level, which ought to be accompanied by the accountability of the actions of the municipal councils to the citizenry at large. Proportional representation should be introduced at the local government level.

6. Dealing effectively with the phenomenon of crime, which today has the potential of destabilizing the political system and must be controlled. According to recent polls (May 1994), one of every four Salvadorans claims to have been a victim of robbery or assault in the last few months. The same poll suggests that the country's main problem is crime and violence (28%), followed in second place by unemployment.[43] A study by IUDOP (University Institute for Public Opinion) described the environment of general insecurity in which the public lives in the following terms: 70.5 percent of those surveyed can identify the existence of danger zones near their place of residence.[44] What this means is that there is a need to achieve efficiency in the fight against common and organized crime.

7. The necessity for a change in attitude on the part of the communications media. The need in this area is twofold: (1) professionalization and modernization; and (2) recognition of their role as formulators of opinions, that is, that they fulfill an informative and educational role vis-à-vis society.

8. Increasing the training and analytical capacity of civilians in defense/security matters, so that they serve as counterparts in the dialogue with the military in the creation and management of a new security doctrine for the Salvadoran state. Civilian mechanisms that will bring about control over the armed forces and national civilian police ought to be institutionalized within the state at both the governmental and Legislative Assembly levels.

9. Finally, the important role the new political system must play in the future. Each institution of the political system needs to develop an effective and efficient administration to process the demands and needs of the population. Institutional performance becomes critical for enhancing the legitimacy of the political system. Furthermore, each branch of state needs to fulfill its own role. A balance of powers that allows for a system of checks and balances must also be developed. The role to be played by the Assembly will be very important, especially now that ONUSAL is about to leave. The Assembly will remain the only body that can fulfill the role of articulating the consensus on various issues that the democratic transition will continue to demand. The judicial Supreme Court also has an enormous responsibility in pushing for a profound reform that would make it possible to overcome the vices and problems that besiege the imparting of justice. This is an indispensable condition for consolidating a nation of laws.

Final Reflections

Two levels of analysis of governability should be introduced when analyzing the future of the Salvadoran political transition. Although the issue of consensus and its replication should be analyzed, the issue of dissent and how it is managed should not be overlooked. Therefore the analysis must include the behavior of political actors within the logic of the government-opposition relation. This means understanding the implications of dissent so that the new political system might operate on the basis of the relationship between majorities and minorities.

The Replication of Consensus

What is most important in the peace process, as President Cristiani said in his speech in Chapultepec, is the method adopted to settle the war. Regarding the search for consensus, it is worth mentioning that "the worthwhile positive output of a constructive and concerted effort is not just the outcome of the negotiations, but also the method of the dialogue itself, of reaching reasonable mutual understanding, and of searching for wise and effective solutions to the most acute and difficult problems."[45] The negotiations were possible because of the strategic military balance, in which neither party had the ability to defeat its opponent militarily. From a political point of view, this is expressed as a crisis of hegemony, in which the principal actors had veto power or the effective means of neutralizing the initiatives of the others, but they lacked sufficient power to impose themselves or their programs on the rest of the political actors. The conditions for negotiation were created mostly as a result of the impossibility of a military victory by either party. The main lesson of the war, therefore, is that no force by itself is capable of steering the destiny of the country.

I agree with Rafael Guido Béjar that a central political problem for the future governability of El Salvador consists of defining and adhering to the terms that made consensus building possible, which, in turn, allowed society to achieve the Peace Accords.[46] The Peace Accords are the basis of the new social contract for building a democratic society. The 1982 elections and the Pact of Apaneca presuppose an understanding and social pact among the forces of the Right; what the Peace Accords do is extend this understanding and social pact (although with different characteristics) to the forces of the Left. Chapultepec establishes the foundation for a great national accord. In this sense, it is necessary that all of the Chapultepec accords be observed, in terms of both the spirit and the letter of the agreements. Looking to the future, the ability to assure the replication of this consensus is important.

However, some conservative sectors oppose the search for consensus because they think that representative government is assured by the ballot box. Consequently, they do not think it necessary to submit their positions to negotiations or to yield in any way that would constitute an abdication of part of their own convictions to arrive at consensus. They believe that the search for consensus leads to inaction, and from inaction, to national paralysis. In the end, the government is blamed for inefficiency. In sum, the state that seeks consensus confronts paralysis.[47]

The transition under way in the country shows a tension between the concepts of democracy and consensus/*concertación*. Some analysts argue that by having obtained an unquestionable majority of the votes, ARENA became the depository of the will of the people, giving ARENA a strong mandate until the next election and exempting it from the need to reach agreements with the minorities. This is especially true because their economic policy is not considered subject to negotiation. There is a democratic rule that suggests that the majority has preeminence over the minority. The fundamental problem is the relation between majorities and minorities in the postwar political system. Consensus is not the same as unanimity. The search for consensus is a process of political engineering. This process requires that all participants in a decision agree to accept a specific solution, even if some of the participants continue to disagree with the agreement that was reached. What is important is the overall commitment to compromise on the agreed decision, even if it does not satisfy all of the actors. Not everyone is expected to think identically. Consensus is a necessary mechanism of stability in times of crisis and for certain decisions of extraordinary significance.[48] In order to secure the future governability of the country, it is necessary to ensure that the principal political actors achieve minimum strategic and tactical consensus on the most important issues. For this to occur, *concertación* needs to become an important mechanism in the political life of the country.

The Government-Opposition Relation

What has been argued above should not lead to the assumption that, to avoid being blamed for destabilizing the democratic process, building consensus implies hiding or negating the differences that exist among the different political forces. It is important that a consistent opposition exists. It must be fully self-conscious of what it means to be the opposition, and it must learn to use the new spaces and play within the framework of the new democratic institutional system.

The opposition should keep in mind at least three characteristics. (1) Be loyal: accept the rules of the game and reject the pursuit of a breakdown of the system, since there should be no room for political destabilization; (2) be constructive: criticize not for the sake of criticizing but rather for the sake of improving the current status quo; and (3) be proposal-minded: not only criticize but also move toward the formulation of proposals about what ought to be done. Based on these three minimal characteristics, the opposition should support what deserves to be supported and criticize what deserves to be criticized. The replication of consensus on strategic aspects for the consolidation of the peace process does not imply the negation of criticism of government performance. In fact, the democratic process needs a strong and coherent opposition. It is politically incumbent on the opposition vis-à-vis the electorate to differentiate itself from the government and to avoid giving the impression that its only function is to facilitate the laws of the official party in the Assembly. The main task of a pluralist Congress is to supervise the actions of the executive branch regardless of the party in power. The opposition is called to articulate the minimum necessary consensus to carry out this task of oversight.

The opposition should not continue to define itself around the negative theme *opposition*, which is an ambiguous term, lacking proposal-oriented content. It neither attracts nor mobilizes people. The opposition should remain open to debate but also create its own alternative program, which should be concrete and proposal-oriented, not simply a declaration of intentions, and which should demonstrate a profound understanding of the country's new socioeconomic realities.

There is a key question regarding the ability to achieve the type of consensus that has been identified in this chapter. This will depend on the extent to which the institutions (government, Legislative Assembly, judicial Supreme Court, Supreme Electoral Board, and so on), the political parties, and the individuals vis-à-vis the parties/institutions decide to commit themselves to an effective administration of government and to the need to replicate the basic consensus. Indicators of progress will surface as the challenges facing the political system and those discussed above are handled and resolved. Progress in the way in which these challenges are confronted will imply a step forward toward democratic governability; delays and setbacks will imply steps on the dangerous road to ungovernability or authoritarian governability.

3

Guatemala:
Democratic Governability

Edelberto Torres-Rivas

The March 1985 election of the Christian Democratic leader Vinicio Cerezo brought to a halt the thirty-two-year tradition of military governments in Guatemala, which had begun violently in 1954. A few months earlier, at the beginning of 1984, a Constituent Assembly—also elected in a relatively free and open electoral competition and, especially, whose results were not predetermined—approved a new constitution and gave way to a new generation of politicians at the helm of the government. Given the tradition of fraud and deceit, these elections, such as they were, were declared the cleanest since 1949, when Jacobo Arbenz was elected.[1]

The previous paragraph contains almost all of the factors that should be kept in mind in order to understand the Guatemalan situation in the mid-1990s. The democratic nature of the political system in societies with a strong tradition of military dictatorships cannot be stimulated by the reestablishment of electoral procedures, the use of new rules for the partisan game, nor the election of civilian politicians. Legality takes time. In this case, given Guatemala's history, such facts per se do not render the political regime democratic.

It is true that since 1966 the typical coups of military *caudillos* have not recurred, thus marking the end of a long authoritarian-oligarchic cycle. In its place, however, a chapter with modern pretensions began, characterized by a permanent military presence, as the chiefs of the armed forces took over the government in the name of the institution, beginning in 1970 and calling for elections every four years (in 1974, 1978, and 1982). Only conservative parties and candidates participated in these elections, and the general that had been selected to win by the armed forces always won. This model of façade democracies quickly ran its course and broke down irreversibly in 1984.

The electoral processes that began on that date, which mark this debatable return to democracy, were launched with the election of the national Constituent Assembly (June 1984). They were followed by two presidential elections and several others to elect the national Congress and municipal bodies. All of these elections took place in an environment characterized by civil war and a climate of extreme political violence and state terror, especially in the countryside. Seven electoral events comprise this democratizing experience, but they go hand in hand with strategies of war. These two processes proceed in tandem but are in themselves contradictory and incompatible. The logic of democracy is that of a legal and peaceful competition based on a respect for political rights, whereas the logic of war is that of a zero-sum game, in which a political opponent is seen as an enemy to be exterminated.

Democratic Transition by Authoritarian Means

It is debatable whether an effective transition to democracy is occurring in Guatemala because of the extreme weakness of its democratic regime. There is a movement toward something undefinable, which exhibits some characteristics that are important for understanding the nature of the country's political life. First, the transition begins with the decision of the army to abandon direct control of the government gradually. Opting to return to their barracks in an orderly fashion, the army itself made the decision to call for elections in 1984. This is a case of decision from above and not the result of the mobilization of society, that is, popular pressure. Second, the opportunity for the liberalization of the authoritarian regime occurred in the middle of a severe national and regional economic crisis (1979–87), which, together with the effects of the political crisis, made the situation unmanageable for the military.

Third, the liberalization of authoritarian control is further undermined by the effects of the spread of poverty, the growth of the informal economy, the breakdown of public services, and so forth. The weakening of the social bases of civic life occurs simultaneously with the liberalization of political participation: in 1983, by executive decree, the government enacted a more modern and permissive body of laws, for example, the organic law of the electoral Supreme Court, the law of citizen registration, which rationalizes the electoral census register, and the law of political organizations. Finally, civilian candidates of the Center-Right, in some cases from recently formed political forces, won the elections.

More than a transition, Guatemala is experiencing a coexistence of healthy authoritarian forces, institutions, and personalities together with several other weak and inexperienced institutions, party forces, and incipient democratic social forces. Political life has developed upon a secular base of extreme violence. The way in which the armed forces, the police, private armed groups, and other paramilitary forces fought guerrilla insurrection conditioned a similar manner of combating any expression of political opposition. The counterinsurgency is responsible for a ferocity that recognizes no civilized limits. Since the 1980s this ferocity has been aimed especially against the indigenous population.

The economic crisis and political violence of the 1980s have caused an inordinate expansion of poverty. A growing number of people became poor, and the already poor became even poorer. Between 1980 and 1986 the percentage of the population in extreme poverty increased from 39.6 percent to 64 percent,[2] while the percentage corresponding to the wealthiest sectors decreased from 28.9 percent to 17.4 percent. In the countryside the picture is a virtual human disaster: 70 percent of the peasants live in extreme poverty, which, when added to those who lack the means of providing for the basic necessities, amounts to 93.1 percent, almost the entire rural population. This situation affects especially the indigenous population.

What is worrisome, for human reasons as well as for its effects on political life, is that this is a situation that is likely to worsen. If only the data from the decade of the 1980s is taken into account, this means a tragic reversal of seventeen years. The gravity of all this can be understood in a different way: this is the wasting of a generation that came of age without any hope or opportunities to prosper.

The situation in the 1990s seems to encompass a contradiction that is potentially dangerous for democratic governability: none of the socioeconomic deficiencies that in the 1980s fueled armed conflicts and justified, in their own way, the guerrilla struggle has even begun to be resolved. The problem of the land, which remains the pivotal point of any struggle for equity, has yet to be resolved.

Democratic Governability Today

The situation in the 1990s is not stable, and only very slowly do new democratic factors break through. The experience of a civilian government peacefully succeeding another occurred for the first time in Guatemala in February 1991, when President Vinicio Cerezo handed over power to Jorge Serrano Elías. More than emblematic, this fact must be recorded as one of the assets of the democratic experience. However, the Christian Democratic government did not do credit to civilian power in the way that a large majority of Guatemalans enthusiastically had hoped.

Democratic hopes were kindled by the rise of a new generation of civilian politicians who had experienced the hardship of being part of the opposition. A quick review of the Christian Democratic experience (1985–90) reveals various important facts: the blunders of a civilian government when the army retains control of the state from its barracks; the difficulties of efficiently managing a society disrupted by crisis; the political and economic force of the business sector, which, throughout the decade, concentrated in its hands more power and wealth; the temptations of corruption and frivolity in politics; and a certain irresponsibility regarding the historic program of the party and its electoral offerings. An excess of politicking and internal battles seriously weakened the Christian Democratic administration. Human rights were violated in the same manner as in the era of military governments. The experience of power unforgivably wore out the Christian Democrats.[3]

All this explains why in the 1990 presidential elections the Christian Democratic Party lost almost half of its voters, ending up in a modest third place. Jorge Serrano Elías, an engineer by training, won the election in the second round, defeating Jorge Carpio Nicolle, the candidate who won a plurality in the first electoral round. In his inaugural message to the nation, President Serrano again fueled democratic illusions by underscoring the majesty of civilian power over the military and committing himself to ending the long armed conflict that until then had served as a pretext for disregarding human rights and fighting corruption at all levels.

The contradictory situations of the early 1990s explain the current and future problems of Guatemalan society. The second civilian government achieved a certain stability by means of a parliamentary pact with the Christian Democrats and the National Party of the Center, an unheard-of experience in the history of national political *concertación*. But this alliance was restricted to the parliamentary arena and was short-lived. The administration of President Serrano soon showed itself to be inept, which led to a very rapid erosion of presidential prestige. Early on, the governing team showed its proclivity toward administrative inefficiency and its voracity for public resources. The major challenge for building democracy no longer lies in the legality of the one who governs but rather in the need to strengthen the sources of legitimacy on a day-to-day basis. This is what suffered.

A critical situation began in mid-1993, and the way in which it was resolved will have lasting consequences for the future of the country. This situation also explains how, in situations of increasing ungovernability, the breakdown of the most basic agreements is likely. This is the only way to understand the May 25, 1993, auto-coup carried out by President Serrano Elías.

For the reasons analyzed here, Guatemala's political life never manages to escape its long period of anomie. It is necessary to bear that condition in mind because it is only from that perspective that one can understand President Serrano's decision to break the reigning legality in the country in a brutal manner by dissolving the constituent powers of the state—the Legislative Assembly and the judicial branch—and by suspending the constitution.

The Guatemalan legacy is full of examples of military meddling, generally by means of coups d'état, secret conspiracies, and scheming. These means were always justified by the need for order, which civilian incompetence never managed to deliver. The struggle against commu-

nist subversion and the defense of democracy were the reasons and pre-
texts to break violently the military oath to respect the constitution.
The auto-coup of a civilian president is even worse because it is a way
of illegitimizing oneself. It is like trying to rearrange a game board with
an impetuous kick that ultimately only breaks it. There can be no
grounds for the chief of state himself to violate the legitimate bases of
his own mandate through his own conduct, even less under the difficult conditions in which democracy is being built in Guatemala.

In the 1990s, Guatemalan politics gradually acquired an extreme
form of ungovernability. This stems from the surfacing of multiple centers of unresolvable collective demands, which accumulated until they
reached a point of dysfunctional saturation for state power. An obvious
gridlock in the administration of power emerged within the state itself
(institutional instability), which paralleled the increasing disorder that
prevailed throughout society as a whole. The ungovernability, defined
as a function of the political relations between those who govern and
those who are governed, presupposes diverse forms of abnormality.
There is one aspect that originates from society and another that is produced by the elite in the very bosom of the state.

In part, popular dissatisfaction has understandable causes: the crisis
of the 1980s created, exacerbated, and failed to resolve basic problems
of survival for the majority. In part, dissatisfaction increased because
the populace has an "immediatist" view of politics and the performance of democracy. A weak civic culture foments an irrational criticism of everything that is done and exacerbates basic dissatisfaction.
This became evident throughout 1992, a year that was characterized by
repeated, unforeseen, and contradictory actions of social and political
participation, a generalized lack of trust in authorities and representative institutions, and the proliferation of frequently irrelevant centers
of collective discontent.

Popular discontent in Guatemala is based on uncomplicated reasons
because it stems from brutal social poverty. This discontent manifested
itself massively for diverse motives and in different parts of the country. Since late April 1993, as a result of a protest against the disproportionate rise in electricity costs, the government had to rectify its
action. In mid-May 1993, high school students violently took to the
streets to protest the unilateral decision to require the use of a national
identification card in order to use public transportation. In Guatemala,
violent and aggressive means of protest have their counterpart in the
means of repression. This is how the noncivic culture of the society has
been taking shape.

The students once again burned tires and buses, threw molotov
cocktails, and disrupted traffic in rejection of something that in any
normal society would have been quickly and directly negotiated. In an
ungovernable society, the response was equally violent. One of the stu-

dents, thirteen-year-old Abner Hernández, was killed by a bully, a bodyguard of a Christian Democratic leader. As a result, the student disturbance grew and fueled the frustration of other social sectors.

The governments of Serrano, between February and May 1993, and Ramiro de León, since July l993 and throughout his entire administration, give the impression that the executive branch is haunted by an inexplicable paralysis. It is as if they no longer controlled the key strings of the political system and everything was being left to a game of contradictory, partial, and improvised initiatives. The following is a brief outline of some of the elements that led to this complicated disarray.

Political Parties

A first element is the weakness of the political party system, which in Guatemala is explained not only by its precarious temporal existence but also by its programmatic voids and, even more, by its weak social implantation. On the one hand, seventeen parties participated in the elections for the Constituent Assembly (1984), eight of which were created one month before the election and five of which were less than one year old. On the other hand, the big winner on that occasion, the Christian Democrats (founded in 1954), barely obtained 16.3 percent of popular support. The Center Democratic Union, recently created from the splinters of various groups of the Center-Right, obtained 13.4 percent. And the once victorious alliance of the extreme Right, corulers with the military in the 1970s, the Movement of National Liberation and the Institutional Democratic Party (MLN/PID), obtained only 12.5 percent. The remaining votes—mere crumbs—were insignificantly divided up among the other fifteen parties.

Between 1985 and 1990 there were diverse electoral adjustments, but the Christian Democrats were the unquestionable winners. However, in the November 1990 presidential elections, as the incumbent party, the Christian Democrats lost half of their core electorate, obtaining only 17.4 percent of the vote. The National Center Union (UCN) obtained 22.7 percent, and the Movement of Solidarity Action (MAS), a recently founded and perhaps more modern party of the moderate Right, obtained 24.1 percent.[4] In February 1991 the system of a second round to achieve a majority allowed the MAS, with the support of all of the parties of the Right, to elect the first non-Catholic Guatemalan president, Jorge Serrano Elías, with 68.1 percent of the vote. Like various members of his cabinet and some of his deputies, Serrano Elías is a fundamentalist Protestant. His victory reflected the local difficulties in consolidating a political system because victory was the result of party fragmentation, the absence of organic loyalties, and an anomalous "pluralism" that does not rest on programs and principles.

The experience of Guatemala is clear proof that democracy cannot function without political parties: government, a sense of order, and institutional stability will elude consolidation unless political parties rigorously shape the collective private sphere. As in the past, in the present situation (1995), the difficulties in establishing a political system (the space for relationships among parties, the state, and its capacity to mediate with society) strongly fuel, in a new way, the ungovernability that (also) originates in society.[5]

The crisis surrounding Serrano's auto-coup took place on a stage of party weakness, coinciding with the rupture of the political alliance established at the end of 1991 between the MAS, the ruling party, and the two largest political forces in Congress, the Christian Democrats and the Center Democratic Union. Serrano managed to govern with this solid majority for eighteen months and with a wide margin of discretion. In mid-April 1993, the demise of the "hellish trio," as this alliance was called by the opposition, left Serrano's government in an unexpected state of political isolation.

The disintegration of this interparty pact was due to the desire of the aligned parties to run independently and to prove their strength in the May 9, 1993, municipal elections in which candidates for 276 municipal offices were chosen. Here again another modality of the national crisis appears: the electoral process fails to consolidate the party system. In effect, the results of this election led to (1) the deconstruction of Jorge Carpio's UCN, the largest although not the best organized party in the country (which obtained 39.1 percent of the vote in 1990 and only 13.7 percent in 1993); (2) the reduction of the Christian Democrats, the most important party, to only 14 percent of the votes; (3) the intensification of party fragmentation, whose ailments were demonstrated in the fight among a dozen smaller parties and more than forty civic committees; and (4) a rise in electoral abstentionism to almost 70 percent of registered citizens, thereby confirming the mixture of apathy, disenchantment, and fear that prevails among the population.

However, an even more contradictory result occurred for the ruling MAS, the real winner, which obtained 37 percent of the vote. This victory was undoubtedly important but insufficient to reinforce its political presence. Fifteen days after its electoral victory, the auto-coup occurred, immediately leading to the political and moral destruction of the ruling party. How can this thoughtless behavior be explained if not within the framework of a profound moral and political crisis?

Lessons from the May 1993 Auto-Coup

Between Serrano's auto-coup in the early morning hours of May 25 and Ramiro de León Carpio's election on June 5, 1993, three successive coups d'état occurred, as well as an extraordinary and instructive historic experience characterized by at the very least four novelties. One is that the civilian auto-coup was also a National Army coup. The coup could not have happened independently of the army. Because of what it did and did not do, the army simply confirmed its status as the most important element of power in society.[6] General José Domingo García Samayoa and parts of the high-ranking military officials sided with Serrano's decision. Security forces acted immediately to disband the other powers of the state. Five days later, in the face of national and international reaction, they withdrew their support of the president and lent it to vice-president Espina. Finally, on June 4 the army asked Congress to elect a constitutional president after an intervening period of time.

It is wise to mention parenthetically the role that the army has played in this transitional stage. In fact, its importance in contemporary history appears to be already established because it has constituted a well-articulated system of authority, a ubiquitous form of state presence throughout the entire landscape of society. The armed forces are the only national institution that has a messianic sense of its role and, in addition, mighty resources of force. Since the 1960s, encouraged by the doctrine of national security, the armed forces have been the primary element of power, reinforced by a permanent technical and equipment modernization and long periods of control over the government. All of this explains the centrality of the military in national life.

When the military called for elections, it did so from its own point of view in order to redesign its relations with the civilian government, political parties, and other social forces, without ever compromising its political centrality. Democracy building will never be successful in Guatemala unless the role of the army as a state institution changes and adapts to the modern conditions of subordination to civilian power, the impunity and privileges that it enjoys come to an end, it restructures itself in conformity with a peaceful and participatory society, and it exercises only legitimate violence, that is, in accordance with the rule of law. In other words, democracy building will occur only if the army ceases to be the major factor of authoritarian power that it has been thus far.

The second novelty of the auto-coup by Serrano lies in the reactions within the state itself. The suspension of the constitution was accompanied by the order to dissolve Congress and the judicial Supreme Court. However, only two or three cabinet ministers resigned immediately; the rest agreed to continue in office in open constitutional defiance. In the Congress, fifty deputies—eight short of a majority—agreed to ratify the illegal election of vice-president Espina. Like the president of the Supreme Court and many leaders of the political parties, the deputies were opportunistic coup participants. The national Congress did not react like the Peruvian Congress after the auto-coup by Alberto Fujimori; a sector of the Congress was willing to compromise. Therefore, the big losers in this crisis are the political parties, already quite wounded by electoral indifference.

The third novelty, the forgotten power of some institutions and their staffs, was revealed in the actions of the Court of Constitutionality. This court ruled the coup unconstitutional and later rejected vice-president Gustavo Espina's plan to succeed Serrano "constitutionally" because he had participated in the auto-coup. At the same time, the attorney general of the republic and chief of the Public Ministry filed a lawsuit against Serrano, Espina, and Francisco Perdomo (minister of the interior) for corruption, violation of constitutional order, rebellion, inciting the public, disrespectful treatment of the presidents of state agencies, abuse of authority, usurping of functions, embezzlement, misappropriation of funds, and other offenses.

The fourth and final novelty is the force that public opinion, the press, and, above all, social organizations acquired in this situation. These social organizations are organized in the National Instance for Consensus (INC), led by major business elites, and the Multisectorial of the Social Sector, grouping together labor unions, the university, and indigenous organizations led by labor leaders and Rigoberta Menchú. The former mobilized in the National Palace, and the latter in the streets. Together they successfully pressed for respect for the constitution and the rule of law. The Court of Constitutionality set a twenty-four-hour deadline to elect a president. On June 5, 1993, the candidate of the social organizations, Ramiro de León Carpio, was elected constitutional president, and the army-backed Arturo Herbruger was elected vice-president.

Civil Society, Corruption, and the Crisis

In the May 1994 crisis and the events that preceded and followed it, organizations in civil society acquired greater prominence, to the clear detriment of the political parties. In a stable democracy, this contradiction would not exist, as the public spaces where social organizations and parties operate and exercise their influence are different. The labor union movement as well as peasant organizations had long been organizing despite the prevailing repressive environment. However, organizations linked to human rights, such as the National Steering Group of Guatemalan Widows (CONAVIGUA), with its indigenous leader Rosalina Tuyuc, and the Mutual Help Group (GAM), led by Nineth de Montenegro, constitute an extraordinary novelty in the political and social life of Guatemala. The capacity to mobilize and the moral influence that these women-led organizations have in the life of the country are the most important facts with respect to the country's democratic possibilities.

The presence of these social organizations was decisive because it occurred as a convergence of interests that served to unify societal protest. This 1993 experience, which expressed peacefully but decisively the support for legality of diverse and even diametrically opposed interests, echoed the 1920 and 1944 efforts to topple the dictatorships of Estrada Cabrera and Jorge Ubico. The creation of the National Instance for Consensus constitutes an extraordinary experience of popular participation.

The INC was the confluence of political, labor union, popular, business, indigenous, religious, cooperative, and academic organizations of the most dissimilar ideologies. As one national analyst recognized, what is important about the INC is that it surfaced in a society in which decades of war and repression have left profound divisions, intolerance, and sectarianism. "Until May 1993, they were organizations in strong disagreement with respect to opposing interests and divergent social models."[7] The presence of the CACIF (Chambers of Commerce, Industry and Finance), an organization that brings together the business elites of the country, completed the representation and strength of organized society.

The crisis of the auto-coup led to the crisis of purging, put forth by the National Instance for Consensus as the need to punish corrupt politicians, accomplices in the frustrated coup, and especially those responsible for embezzlement and misuse of public resources. Corruption constitutes the most negative factor and probably the major challenge to the democracy currently under construction. As of this writing, the democratic regime is ten years old and has had three civilian governments. Although this is not the moment to assess the decade, it is evident that the political class and public institutions are discredited. The results of a survey at the end of 1993 corroborated the prevailing common perception: only 8 percent of those surveyed approved of the performance of the judicial branch and the Supreme Court in particular, and more than 66 percent considered the deputies to be corrupt and incompetent.[8]

Upon taking office, President de León Carpio offered to carry out a six-month government plan to combat poverty and, under public pressure, incorporated the demand to purge the legislative and judicial powers. As a consequence of the executive's call for the resignation of corrupt deputies, a group composed mostly of Christian Democrats triggered a serious confrontation between the two branches of government. The INC as well as the media supported the president, which led him to propose a referendum or popular consultation on the purging of the legislative branch to be held on November 28, 1993. The Court of Constitutionality ruled that this procedure was illegal, thereby giving rise to a serious problem of authority.

The public rapidly became disenchanted with the new government as it failed to meet expectations. The government never presented the plan to combat poverty and has been unable to reduce the volume of human rights violations, a difficult task that everyone hoped de León Carpio would carry out against the clear transgressors, the military. In September, Jorge Carpio Nicolle, the president's cousin, a businessman, two-time presidential candidate, and secretary general of the UCN, was assassinated. It is now known that the responsibility for the assassination lies with a group from the Civilian Self-Defense Patrol, counseled by political enemies who were until now impossible to identify. Paradoxically, President de León Carpio fiercely combatted such groups when he was the human rights attorney but defended them as president.

The process of political purging initiated an extended conflict of powers between the executive branch and Congress (the latter referred to by public opinion as a refuge of criminals). The tug-of-war—an expression of a civilized modality of political conflict—led to an agreement between the deputies and the president: to submit to public consultation the constitutional reform that would reduce the term of the deputies and other reforms. Reforming the constitution became the way to meet the demand for action against corruption and incompetence in the legislative branch.

Thus the political crisis seemed to find a legal solution. This democratic procedure was called for January 30, 1994. However, the way in which the consultation was set forth, and the intricate technical problems that made it difficult to understand, provoked opposition from various political parties, numerous social organizations, and the principal sectors of the media. This disagreement between a decision from the powers of the state and public opinion precisely reveals one of the characteristics of the political crisis. The result was disastrous for everyone. With abstentionism at 84.1 percent, everyone was a loser, especially the political system. Certainly the government obtained a pro-yes majority, but it corresponds to only 3.6 percent of the population able to vote. Abstentionism has grown considerably, from 39 percent in the first democratic elections of 1985 to 57.1 percent in the presidential elections of 1991. Out of a set of possible explanations for abstention in the January 1994 consultation, the most decisive seems to be the manifest lack of interest of the population in these matters, undoubtedly worried instead about other matters of more serious concern for their daily lives. Is not an abstention rate of this magnitude a form of civil disobedience? A foreign journalist commented that it is frightening that 84 percent of voters have come to the conclusion that their vote cannot extricate the country from its political crisis.

The Indigenous Presence

The appearance of a significant number of legal and public indigenous organizations, which is a result of new forms of consciousness and identity in the 1980s, constitutes an unparalleled challenge in Guatemala's history. The new constitution of 1984 finally recognized that Guatemala is a multiethnic and pluricultural society and therefore has begun to admit that the incorporation of the indigenous population into national life entails the recognition of and respect for their cultural rights and differences.

The importance of this native population does not reside solely in the demographic fact that it constitutes a virtual majority, but also in that it is a culturally diverse population with languages, social relationships, lifestyles, religions, world views, and ideas about society that are different from what has until now been the dominant culture. These differences have endured, with profound changes, for five hundred years.

The rights of the Mayan people (descendants of the ancient Maya) are also linked to land issues. This "minority" has always lived in conditions of extreme poverty, a situation that worsened in the last fifteen years. The greatest indicators of demographic growth, lack of land and work, illiteracy, infant mortality, and deficiencies in housing and basic services (water, electricity, sewage, and so on) are found among the Mayan population. Their ancestral poverty is accompanied by extreme levels of economic exploitation, political subordination, and lack of legal protection, which make for an extremely degrading quality of life.

Permanent, multifaceted violence has been directed against the indigenous population and sustained by a racist culture and brutal policies reminiscent of the colonial era. Based on this mentality, the army carried out its antiguerrilla warfare, targeting the indigenous communities of the Quiché, Baja Verapa, Chimaltenango, and other mountainous areas of the northwest, leaving a death toll of more than sixty thousand between 1980 and 1983.

The cultural and social importance of the indigenous population for democracy building—and, beginning with these dates, for stability—is such that without their participation as full citizens, political life in Guatemala will always be incomplete and weak.[9] In order for this citizenry to take shape effectively, profound changes in society will have to occur. Some of these changes today would be difficult and even unacceptable for the dominant *criollo* (white person) conscience. Because of all this, the sense of order in the governance of democracy has to come from social relations based on respect and political equality, full participation, and opportunities without discrimination against the indigenous population. This begins by recognizing and respecting the differences that exist.

Perspectives for the Immediate Future

First, in compliance with the constitutional reform approved in the January referendum, legislative elections were called for August 14,

1994, to elect eighty deputies, sixteen from the national listing and sixty-four at the district level. Political fragmentation reappeared: eighteen parties and more than a thousand candidates including ten recently released military personnel. The campaign attracted attention because it implied an end to the conflict of powers, which had exhausted the presidential administration and immobilized legislative activity, thereby highlighting the limits of Guatemalan governability. These elections recorded a dangerously high rate of abstentionism, 79.1 percent, and a clear turn to the Right, with the victory of the recently formed Guatemalan Republican Front (FDG), which went from 10.3 percent (in 1990) to 40 percent, and of the National Advancement Party, which also went from 10.3 percent (in 1990) to 30 percent.

On the one hand, these elections constitute a clear political victory for the head of the FDG, the controversial General Efraín Ríos Montt, a hard-liner from a powerful Protestant sect, who, in August 1995, was definitively vetoed as a presidential aspirant because of his previous coup involvement. On the other hand, the elections occasioned the defeat of the two oldest and strongest parties, the Christian Democrats and the National Center Union, which obtained 16 percent and 10 percent of the vote, respectively. In the past year, the volatility of Guatemalan politics has destroyed all expectations. In September 1995 there were eleven presidential candidates from twenty-four political parties. They have organized an electoral front with clear assistance from the URNG (Guatemalan National Revolutionary Unity) guerrillas. There is fear because of the increasing indigenous mobilization in politics, and there is no certainty about the winner in the November 11 elections.

Second, the struggle against impunity is important for the future of political democracy. It is a question of the capacity of the state to punish criminals. The respect for basic human rights, especially for life, has long been violated by the counterinsurgent military. The excesses committed in this out-of-control state undertaking have injured society profoundly. The demand for action against impunity is predicated on the obligation of the state to apply its own norms. The three civilian governments in the first ten years of the democratic regime have failed to prosecute the numerous members of the military responsible for common crimes, for which strong evidence exists. The ultimate test for the rule of law is the punishment of those who violate it.

Third, the greatest popular demand is the achievement of peace. The peace negotiations that occurred throughout the entire year reveal the lack of will on the part of the parties. In March 1994, in Mexico, a calendar was agreed to, but the only deadline that was met was the issue of the resettlement of the populations that were uprooted because of the conflict. Nevertheless, the negotiations have been advancing more rapidly since that date and have endorsed several important accords, especially one relative to the consent of the exiled population regarding a commission that will study the crimes against that population but *without mention of those who are responsible*, and especially an important agreement about the rights of the indigenous population concerning the recognition of their cultural identity and land. There are two more points pending, one referring to the new role of the army in a democracy and the other regarding social and economic politics. The pledge to achieve peace has grown internally but will be possible only with the new government that took office in January 1996.

A preliminary delegation from the United Nations in charge of setting up a UN Mission for Human Rights Monitoring in Guatemala arrived in the country on September 20, 1994. The UN monitoring mission is to include military observers, civilian police, and more than a hundred international civil servants. Whether these tasks are carried out, however, is contingent upon the signing of the peace agreements.

A horrible stage in Guatemala's national history will come to an end with the end of the conflict. Social reconstitution and political democracy will thus have a good chance to succeed. Presently a culture of fear exists, which encourages apathy, fragile trust of public institutions, the loss of relationships of solidarity, excessive self-restraint, and so on. With more than one hundred thousand political deaths in twenty-five years and widespread impunity, the population has resigned itself to live with pain, death, and torture as daily and inevitable facts. In other works, I have called this "the trivialization of horror."

The public and legal forces of the Left are extremely weak, perhaps because the insurrectional Left is also weak, but especially because they have been savagely beaten by more than a quarter of a century of repression. In fact, there are no parties that represent this option. The possibility of incorporating the guerrilla forces into political life, in the Venezuelan (1964) or Salvadoran style (1994), is very complex; Guatemalan society is not prepared to recycle the guerrilla fighters in a legal version that permits their transition to citizens.

The way in which the auto-coup crisis and the 1993–94 confrontations of powers have been resolved rekindles hope because it entailed negotiating within a constitutional framework, through dialogue among civilian politicians, without military meddling and with an open presence of civil society. If these good symptoms persist, political democracy will be able to consolidate itself and thus open the way for a new era of social and democratic development.

uras: Democratization and
...e Role of the Armed Forces

Mark B. Rosenberg and J. Mark Ruhl

Two related issues highlight the state of democratic governance in Honduras. The first issue revolves around the ability of civilian decision makers to effect accountability within the military during the remainder of the 1990s. The second issue is civilian ability to govern responsibly. A lingering third issue concerns the quality of participation in the country's economic evolution. Poverty and depression continue to be major impediments to the country's well-being and economic competitiveness.

The Difficulties of Establishing an Enduring Democratic Order

One of the poorest of Central America's five original republics (U.S.$630 GDP [gross domestic product] per capita), Honduras had little success in establishing and maintaining an enduring democratic order throughout much of the twentieth century. Since 1954 the country has had eleven heads of state, only five of whom have been popularly elected.

The Liberal and National parties are the country's dominant parties, both dating from the turn of the century.[1] In the past the two parties were separated by differing approaches to state involvement in the economy. Today there are few differences in party ideology or platform. Together they command about 96 percent of the popular vote. Their support tends to be cross-class and spread evenly throughout the country. Despite the apparent popularity of both parties, they have offered little effective leadership during the last two decades. Their interest is largely power for power's sake rather than the use of power to effect a larger vision of the common good.[2]

Five elections have been held since 1980, as Table 3 illustrates. With minor exceptions, the five elections that Honduras has held since 1980 have been fair and transparent. They have contributed to what one knowledgeable observer calls an "electoral culture" in the country where "electoral practices are establishing the bases for a firm and coherent process of political democratization in Honduran society."[3]

Table 3 Honduras: Results of Electoral Processes in the 1980s

	1980	%	1981	%	1985	%	1989	%	1993	%
Liberal	495,779	49.6	636,653	52.4	786,603	49.2	776,983	43.2	822,667	51.7
National	423,263	42.4	491,392	40.6	701,440	43.9	917,168	50.9	660,570	41.5
PINU (Innovation and Unity Party)	35,263	3.5	29,419	2.5	23,709	1.4	33,952	1.8	44,772	2.8
Christian Democratic	—	—	19,163	1.6	30,258	1.9	25,423	1.4	17,279	1.1
Blank	19,847	1.9	17,430	1.5	28,115	1.8	18,463	1.0	NA[a]	—
Invalid	24,221	2.4	17,326	1.5	27,616	1.8	27,107	1.5	NA	—
Total	998,522	—	1,214,923	—	1,597,801	—	1,799,126	—	NA	—

Source: Víctor Meza, "Elecciones en Honduras: Un intento de interpretación," *Honduras Especial* 48 (July 1990): 5; "Honduras Liberal Party Emerges Victorious from General Elections," *NotiSur*, December 10, 1993.
[a]NA = not available.

The electoral culture has several components. First, a key factor has been the modernization and revitalization of the National and Liberal parties. Although these parties effectively lost control of the country's political system during the 1960s and early 1970s when the military ruled, they had gradually reinserted themselves into the political arena by the latter part of the 1970s. Through the modernization of the party apparatus (National Party) and internal democratization (Liberal Party) in the 1980s, both parties have been able to maintain and expand their hold on the country's electorate.[4]

Second, the country's two minority parties (PINU, Innovation and Unity Party; and the PDC, Christian Democratic Party) offered electoral opportunities for dissidents who chose to stay within the system, particularly during the early part of the 1980s. Table 3 illustrates the growing acceptance of the traditional parties from 1980 to 1993. They have managed to gain wider support during the decade, capturing 94 percent of the popular vote in the 1989 and 1993 elections compared with just 92 percent in the 1980 constitutional assembly elections.

However, nearly 35 percent of voters abstained from casting a ballot in the 1993 presidential elections compared with just 6 percent in the 1985 elections. Various factors may explain this negative trend. First, the campaign was one of the dirtiest on record. The National Party emphasized the procommunist tendencies of the Liberal Party presidential candidate. The Liberal Party emphasized the connections of the National Party candidate with death squad activity in the early 1980s. Second, both of the minority parties failed to mobilize their supporters, receiving the same portion of support (under 4 percent) that had characterized earlier elections.

Finally, a punishment vote may account for the unexpectedly large margin of victory by the Liberal Party. It appears that voters were generally unhappy with the National Party's neoliberal economic program which has favored the country's wealthier groups. A second dimension of this vote appears to have been voter concern about the polarizing style of the National presidential candidate, who emphasized anti-communism but ultimately reminded voters of the repression and tensions of the early 1980s.

What is obvious from the country's electoral experience during the past two decades is that Hondurans themselves believe in elections and vigorously participate in them. However, as the electoral experience throughout Central America during the last few years indicates,[5] fair elections are only a necessary first step in the development and consolidation of democracy.[6]

Civil-Military Relations

For Honduras the basic issue of civil-military relations has revolved around the inability of both civilian and military actors to adjust their behavior and expectations toward liberal democratic standards of representation and accountability.

The end of open civil war in Central America in the late 1980s, coupled with the demise of the Soviet Union and Eastern Europe and the end of the cold war, have created a serious identity crisis within the Honduran military and perhaps the society more generally. Now the great external and internal threat, defined in ideological terms by a superpower that also provided protection, is no longer a justification for ignoring the countless domestic issues that have not recently, if ever, been addressed.

With the global and regional environment transformed in the 1990s, the Honduran military now confronts the identity crisis that was postponed for more than a decade by regional hostilities. An October 1992 World Court ruling on the disputed border territories between Honduras and El Salvador allowed for both sides to declare victory, thereby defusing long-simmering hostilities that could have spilled over into renewed conflict between the two countries. The ruling undermines even more deeply the Honduran armed forces' claim that El Salvador constitutes a military security threat. It exacerbates the military's identity crisis even further. If there are no external threats to Honduras, why does the country need its armed forces?

Thus, at its core, the fundamental question centers on exactly what role, if any, the military has in contemporary Honduran society.

There are other questions as well:

—Does the Honduran military need an advanced air force with F-5 jet aircraft? Why is the national police force still dependent upon the military?

—What mechanisms are necessary for civilians to exercise control over the military?

—Shouldn't the defense minister be a civilian who is responsive to the president rather than to the military?

These questions, indirectly raised in the late 1970s, were largely left untouched during the 1980s. However, they have resurfaced with greater intensity and interest in the 1990s. They attack the heart of the system of prerogatives and privileges that the military has cultivated since the mid-1950s when the professional armed forces first became a political force in the country. Military accountability in Honduras since then has been a matter left to the military itself.[7]

Some internal accountability norms have evolved over time. There is a vague consensus that senior military officers should not overtly display political ambitions while on active duty. When General Edgardo Melgar-Castro intimated that he might be a candidate for civilian elections in the early 1980s, he was summarily deposed from his position as president of the country. General Gustavo Álvarez lost support within his senior military command when he became too closely associated with civilians through a quasi-corporatist organization linked to the private sector.

Senior officers were also expected to reject any and all civilian efforts to reduce, downsize, or strip the military of its budget and functions. General Walter López was ousted from his position as chief of the armed forces in 1985 when it was feared that he might make too many concessions to the newly elected Liberal Party government of José Azcona. General Arnulfo Cantarero was deposed in December 1990 partly in response to his willingness to go along with cuts in the military budget. Retired officers, even if they have been booted out for disciplinary or political reasons, will be taken care of as long as they maintain a low profile. Almost a dozen officers who left Honduras in the 1980s because of dissatisfaction with military management or promotion issues have quietly returned to the country. Important decisions are normally discussed through a military advisory council that brings together senior officers on a periodic basis. When General Álvarez attempted to restructure this council, he lost support from his senior command. Thus there are some generally held behavioral predispositions within the military that promote accountability. But there has been minimal accountability in areas related to corruption and the violation of human rights.[8]

Challenges to Military Predominance

The post-Sandinista era, however, has brought changes. There have been international and domestic challengers to military primacy. In both cases these challenges have been intermittent and fitful. At the international level, multilateral organizations such as the International Monetary Fund (IMF) and the World Bank issued a joint communiqué in 1991 calling for a reduction in the size of military forces in accordance with the changing security requirements of the post–cold war era. Although delivered at the most general of levels, the Honduran high command felt compelled to reject this call publicly by stating that such issues were outside the purview of these agencies. In any case, the military claimed, "the armed forces were not a heavy load for the state."[9]

The Honduran armed forces rejected the repeated and forceful criticisms of the U.S. ambassador, Cresencio Arcos, who often questioned during his assignment in Honduras (1989–93) the need for such a large military given the declining salience of military security issues in the 1990s. As the ambassador stated in one U.S. journal: "The most useful assistance the US government can offer is to help the armed forces . . . to redefine their role in a less conflictive era. We can accomplish this through our military assistance, through civilian training programs and by stressing constantly the importance of civilian control of armed forces . . . in all Central American countries save Costa Rica, the armed forces and police are still not wholly subordinate to civilian authority."[10] This thinking was also reflected in a drastic reduction in U.S. military aid to Honduras during the 1990s.

The ambassador's insistent questioning of the military's role was rejected on a variety of grounds. In the first place, the U.S. policymaker's willingness to make public statements in Honduras about the military was generally repudiated by the military as intervention in the country's domestic affairs.

One case in particular illustrates the issue. Following the rape and disembowelment of a young female student in July 1991, the Honduran military refused to identify and arrest suspects in the case, largely because they were military officers themselves. However, it was the U.S. ambassador, not the country's president, who first publicly urged an investigation into the military's complicity, engendering a widespread national outcry for justice in the case. Students subsequently marched on the U.S. embassy to thank Arcos for his support. Ultimately a high-ranking military officer and his accomplice were imprisoned for the crime.

At one point in early 1992, the ambassador publicly stated that "society should not allow justice to be turned into a viper that only bites the barefoot and leaves immune those who wear boots."[11] Such was his impact that, as the ambassador's tenure in Honduras neared its end, a caricature in one newspaper, La Tribuna (May 8, 1993), showed three large monkeys (military officers) mocking the ambassador's departure ("se va Arcos!"), implying that they would have the last laugh. The current U.S. ambassador in Honduras has chosen a lower profile on issues of civil-military relations but has been very supportive of civilian efforts to reduce military prerogatives.

A second challenge has come from Honduras' civilian leadership. During the early part of the presidency of Rafael Leonardo Callejas, the Honduran Foreign Ministry took the leadership in crafting a region-wide Central American Security Treaty that called, in part, for the gradual reduction in the size of the region's armies. Although targeted initially at the larger forces in neighboring Nicaragua, El Salvador, and Guatemala, the measure had as an objective the gradual downsizing of the Honduran armed forces once the other militaries had taken similar measures.

The initiative died for lack of support. No regional leader except the president of Costa Rica would support it. Even President Callejas left the ministry exposed to the hostility of his armed forces—he was silent on the matter. He was subsequently criticized in the local media for his "duality" of views. Earlier he had talked about the necessity of regional disarmament.

However, he too publicly discarded the IMF–World Bank call for arms reductions, arguing that Honduran military expenditures barely exceeded 2 percent of the country's GDP. One media analysis rejected the president's figures, asserting that actual military expenditures exceeded 10 percent of GDP or more than 500 million lempiras (about U.S.$100 million).[12]

Through the country's unicameral Congress, a novel constitutional reform measure was proposed in early 1992 to reduce the autonomy of the armed forces. Suggested by deputy Carlos Sosa Coello of the miniscule PINU Party (Innovation and Unity Party), the initiative would have replaced the chief of the armed forces with a minister of defense, an active duty officer with the rank of colonel or higher named by the president. This project was initially repudiated by the military high command as well. However, the military's rejection was later softened because the actual incumbent realized that he could continue in his post for a longer period than under the current rules of incumbency.

The Sosa Coello proposal deserves further study for it illustrates some of the real limits on reducing the military's role in Honduran society. He argued that while President Callejas had control over the military, such control was more a factor of the loyalty that the leader enjoyed within the military high command. According to the deputy, Callejas had consolidated his power over the military, but this could be explained by the "Callejismo in the military." What Sosa sought was an institutional means of control over the military. His reform measure would have created a bureaucratic ministry of defense that would speak for the military. In turn the minister would speak for the president to the military, who under the present constitutional system owes its loyalty to the chief of the armed forces rather than to the president of the republic.

Sosa's reform measure was also prudent because it specified that an active duty soldier, not a civilian, should be the minister. It further referred to the Ministry of National Defense and Public Security. By doing so, the proposal implicitly accepted the sacrosanct position of many military and civilian leaders that a separation of the police from the military was not an acceptable policy option in the Honduran political environment.

Ultimately, General Luis Discua sidestepped the reform measures by engineering an alternative reform of the country's constitution that eliminated the three-year limit on his occupancy of the commander in chief position. Once he had secured another three-year term, he suggested that some Sosa-style reforms of the military might be possible, but not before the year 2000.[13]

Yet another approach to dealing with the military directly targeted the national police, long under the control of the armed forces. The police had been modernized under the hard-line direction of General Gustavo Álvarez during the early 1980s. However, as a recent report by a Honduran human rights ombudsman has outlined, he used the institution as the front line of his "dirty war," the enforcer of national security in a context where the citizen was almost automatically assumed to be a subversive. Álvarez' militarization of the police through the national security doctrine was reinforced by the appointment of senior military officers to police command positions, even when senior police officials were available.

Following the departure of General Álvarez, the police force continued to be a place to rotate senior military officers when other positions were not available. Institutional needs rather than citizen security became the priority. Though the armed forces remains a bloated institution at senior levels, the police were understaffed and underfunded.

In September 1991 the progressive Chamber of Commerce and Industry of Cortes (CCIC) in San Pedro Sula proposed that the military sell off its high-priced F-5 jet aircraft and dismantle unneeded battalions to reinforce the undermanned police. The CCIC also argued that the police should be separated from the military and put under the control of the country's judiciary. According to the proposal, Honduras had about 818 persons for each police agent, while the United Nations recommends one agent for every 300 people. In the country's leading urban centers, Tegucigalpa and San Pedro Sula, there were some 5,161 citizens per police agent. Moreover, Honduran police earned less than the minimum wage (less than U.S.$64 per month).

Juxtaposing the national security imperative against the growing demands for citizen security, the country's private sector had struck a major nerve in the military's system of control. Its police force had always been an institution of low prestige and morale. It had served as the army's dumping ground. According to one army officer, "To serve in the police as an official of the armed forces is to be purged and devalued professionally."[14]

The general deterioration of public order in Honduras coupled with continuing human rights violations did lead to a significant concession from the military in early 1993. In the midst of growing accusations about military involvement in human rights violations, and mounting pressure from popular organizations for action, President Callejas created an ad hoc commission to propose a restructuring of the country's police forces and judicial system.

The commission was chaired by Oscar Andrés Rodríguez, the archbishop of Tegucigalpa and was given thirty days to develop recommendations to reform the country's security forces. Other participants included representatives from the four registered political parties, the Congress, Supreme Court, the military, and the media. Excluded from the group were some of the military's most persistent challengers, including human rights organizations that alleged direct military involvement in politically related assassinations and human rights abuses.

The March 1, 1993, announcement by Callejas of the ad hoc commission was punctuated by a large military mobilization throughout the country's capital and other cities. Explained by the military as a necessary action in the face of reports of imminent terrorist activity by the Morazanista Patriotic Front (FPM, Frente Patriótico Morazanista), their street presence was a threatening message as well to civilian authority. It harked back to the days when General Álvarez freely put troops in the streets to intimidate.

Even before the ad hoc commission could render its findings, President Callejas took an important step by naming a three-person commission to intervene in the National Investigative Directorate (DNI). This measure, urged by the commission, was intended to help the police redirect their efforts. But it was the first step in placing the investigative police under civilian control.

Indeed, weeks later, the ad hoc commission announced a set of historic measures. In a lengthy report presented on April 13, 1993, to President Callejas, the commission called for the creation of a prosecutor general's office and the initiation of a new investigatory police agency that would report directly to the prosecutor general and be located in his office.[15]

With the election of Liberal Party candidate Carlos Roberto Reina in November 1993, civilians have taken a number of steps to limit military influence. President Reina has attempted to back up his campaign promises to cut the military's size and budget, reduce military corruption and human rights abuses, end obligatory military service, and civilianize the police.

These steps have been taken with care and prudence. President Reina has balanced his efforts to curtail military power and privileges with actions that have been reassuring to General Discua and his colleagues.[16] Reina named retired General Walter López as his vice-president and named a Discua ally as his minister of defense. Reina also praised General Discua and his service to the country even while senior military officers were being criticized publicly by the media for corruption. In this context, with strong, vocal support from the public and quiet support from the U.S. embassy, Reina has implemented a number of initiatives begun during the Callejas era, and he has firmly and publicly asserted his right to command the armed forces. He has also excluded the military from any role in decision making on economic policy and other nonsecurity issues.

Among Reina's initiatives: in June 1994, the despised DNI was disbanded and the Public Ministry opened. Only a small group of ex-DNI agents was allowed to join the new investigative force. Months later, in April 1995, judicial proceedings were opened against five military officers who were allegedly involved in death squad operations in the 1980s. In July 1995 the prosecutor general accused ten more retired and active duty officers of human rights abuses.[17]

By late 1994 the country's Treasury Police were transferred from the public security forces (under army control) to civilian authority. Demilitarization of the rest of the police proceeded slowly because of insufficient budgets and initial reticence by National Party members to transfer the force to civilian (Liberal Party) hands. However, although the police commander continued to be an army officer, by mid-1995 there were only three other army officers in the police high command. In September 1995 the national Congress voted to change the constitution to remove the police completely from military control. A second ratification vote will be required in 1996.

Reina's most notable achievement, however, sent a major practical and symbolic message to the military. In the midst of intense military opposition, he took the initiative in May 1994 to pass a constitutional reform that replaced obligatory military service with a voluntary system. When General Discua convinced the president to allow a temporary draft in 1994 during the period between the two required readings of the reform bill, public reaction was highly critical of the measure. About 40 percent of the six thousand draftees called never presented themselves for induction.[18] The voluntary service secured its second passage in mid-1995, although the law does contain a provision allowing a draft lottery if too few volunteers present themselves to meet troop levels set by Congress.

The Reina government also stripped the military of its control over HONDUTEL, the country's lucrative telecommunications monopoly; and both the Department of Immigration and the Merchant Marine, important sources of illicit revenue for senior military officers, were placed under civilian control.

Although the military has generally resigned itself to increased oversight and reduced prerogatives, the gradual assertion of civilian control has had tense moments. Reina was directly and personally threatened with a coup by a senior military officer in August 1994. The military has also challenged his appointment of "leftist" cabinet officers and bridled at the presence of at least one cabinet minister who was vetoed for public service a decade earlier by the military.

In general, however, the military has responded to criticism and demands for reform with the conciliatory, accommodative approach developed during 1992–93 and earlier during the first years of the Lopez-Arellano reform period (1972–74).[19] Senior officers have emphasized their subordination to the president, and they are now busy developing new rationales to justify their existence. Among justifications, they point to their role in environmental protection, disaster relief, and education. They have also stressed the need for involvement in counternarcotics efforts and in support of UN peacekeeping operations such as in Haiti and the Western Sahara. The military has even invited its critics to speak on the proper role of the armed forces in a democratic society at the Colegio de Defensa Nacional and at police headquarters.

The Structure of Civil-Military Relations

As the experience with President Reina illustrates, political will is an element essential to transform the country's pattern of civil-military relations. But there are also serious institutional issues that will have to be resolved if civil-military relations are to continue to be modified.

Military Autonomy and Civilian Control

The most important component of civil-military relations is that the commander in chief of the armed forces of Honduras serves the president of the country at the commander's pleasure. Three articles of the Honduran constitution very clearly give the president of the country little direct control over the armed forces:

> Article 277. The armed forces are under the direct control of the commander in chief of the armed forces, and through his mediation the president of the republic will exercise the constitutional function that corresponds to him in accord with the constituent law of the armed forces.
>
> Article 278. The orders that the president of the republic gives to the armed forces, through the commander in chief of the armed forces, will be obeyed and executed.
>
> Article 279. The commander in chief of the armed forces should be a general or senior officer with the rank of colonel or its equivalent, in active service, Honduran by birth, and he will be elected by the national Congress from a list proposed by the Superior Council of the armed forces.

In essence, it is the Congress that appoints the commander of the armed forces on the recommendation of the military itself. Then this commander has the constitutional right to mediate any orders to his troops that may be given by the president. The autonomy that the military has gained through the constitutional provisions results from concessions made to the military by the framers of the country's 1957 Constitution. They essentially set the military up as a fourth branch of government, in addition to the executive, legislative, and judicial branches.

Moreover, the constitution further stipulates (Article 281) that the head of the country's joint chiefs of staff will replace the commander in chief of the armed forces in the event of his temporary absence. As Honduran sociologist Leticia Salomón points out in her recent research, this stipulation is relatively new, having replaced an earlier article that allowed the minister of defense to substitute for the chief in the event of temporary absence. Salomón and others suggest that this measure is intended as further insulation from any political, that is, civilian control of the military through the defense minister, who of course is part of the civilian cabinet.

Military Leadership

The instability of Honduran civil society is generally mirrored by the same instability within the Honduran armed forces. Since 1972 the armed forces have had nine commanders in chief. Of these nine, only two have been appointed through constitutional means. The other seven have assumed the senior military command position through an irregular process largely determined by intra-institutional forces and coalitions that have had little connection with nonmilitary interests.

Many of the internal tensions within the Honduran armed forces are generated by the parliamentary structure of the military's senior command. Decisions tend to be made collegially through the Superior Council of the Armed Forces, currently composed of the country's top sixty active duty officers. During its formative years, the military was dominated by a senior officer. Throughout the 1960s and early 1970s, Oswaldo López Arellano had personal control of the military. Although his ouster in 1975 was directly attributed to allegations that he was linked to bribery, it coincided with a period of growing demands for participation in decision making by other senior officers. It was during this period that the Superior Council emerged to play the central military decision-making role.

During the early 1980s, efforts made by General Álvarez Martínez to move away from a collegial to a vertical command structure, centralizing power at the very top of the armed forces, led to his ouster by fellow officers in April 1984.[20] Since then the military chief has functioned as a mediator and moderator of competitive military officers and *promociones* (graduating classes). One of the techniques used by the current commander in chief for staying in power has been the explicit development of coalitions within several key *promociones* of the military. As well, the chief military officer depends upon the loyalty of strategic military units, especially those located in and near Tegucigalpa and San Pedro Sula.

The basic issue, however, remains the instability of the armed forces themselves and their tenuous cohesion based upon a pattern of shifting coalitions and personalities. As the military searches for a new mission in the 1990s, the tendency toward internal instability is likely to sharpen as it comes under even greater pressure to downsize.

The Military's Growing Financial Activity

Even as the Honduran armed forces is groping for a new military mission in the post–cold war era, it has not lost sight of its material interests. Through a variety of instruments, the military has become a powerful economic force in the country. As pointed out by one U.S.-based journalist, "military-owned businesses can offer loans and credit cards, sell cement, broker real-estate deals, provide insurance, even embalm and bury the dead."

The military's involvement in the economy is symptomatic of the absence of a strong, cohesive civilian presence in the country. Even though there has been a democratically elected government for more than a decade, the military controlled key agencies until 1994, including the telephone company, the major airports and seaports, immigration services, the merchant marine, and the national police.

At the core of the military's economic domain is the Military Pensions Institute (IPM). Financed with funds appropriated by the government for military retirements, the IPM is an important player in the domestic economy. According to one report, the IPM's purpose is to build its portfolio so that each retired senior officer can have an annual income in excess of U.S.$100,000. Its major assets include the public-access armed forces bank (BANFAA), an insurance company (PREVISA), and a credit card company that makes cards available to the public (PREVICARD). The IPM has also competed in the market for companies being privatized.[21]

Such serious involvement in the country's business affairs has prompted one *Miami Herald* reporter to state that Honduran officers are "more like CEO's than soldiers." In Honduras the military's economic presence is of great concern, especially among private sector leaders who understand that the military's privileged political position can be translated into economic leverage. The IPM's recent successful efforts to purchase a state-owned cement company in the country were particularly troublesome to a number of Honduras' family-oriented investor groups. It is possible that the IPM will target other state-owned enterprises should they become available.

Defenders of the military argue that its pension system is smaller than the teachers' and state employees' funds and that the only way to provide for the military's social security in old age and retirement is through wise investment. What they have not yet pointed out is that the same voices objecting to their involvement in the economy are those that have traditionally sought out monopoly control or state-protected economic advantages to ensure their profitability. These difficulties are likely to continue. Measures to limit military involvement in the economy will likely be met with resistance from the armed forces and from others who benefit from many of the services provided by their well-run companies.

The Military and Human Rights

The political hostilities of the 1980s in Central America spawned a new level of human rights violations in Honduras. Politically motivated disappearances and assassinations were linked to a limited dirty war in the country. The fate of more than 180 people who disappeared during the 1980s is still unclear and a major cause for concern by national and international human rights groups.[22]

One of the shadows hanging over the country relates to the immunity of the armed forces and police to the rule of law. This immunity is most apparent in the field of human rights where violations persist and for the most part go unpunished. According to one U.S. embassy report published in 1993 on human rights in Honduras, members of the country's armed forces enjoy this immunity for a number of reasons:

—The country's Supreme Court has avoided making the difficult decision about the jurisdiction of civilian courts over armed forces personnel accused of offenses involving civilians.
—Civilians have little ability to levy formal accusations before military courts.
—The country's court system has minimal credibility, little capacity, and no sustained history of successfully judging the military.
—Even if the court system had some capacity to address military violations, the armed forces tend to protect those personnel, especially officers, accused of abuses.

There are notable exceptions. A Honduran judge's decision in mid-1993 to give relatively lengthy sentences (by Honduran standards) to two military officials accused in the July 1991 rape and disembowelment of the student mentioned above has been viewed by many in Honduras as a triumph for civilians over the military. However, for this highly publicized case to be completed, it took the intervention of the U.S. ambassador, open mobilization by the public against the armed forces, and the intense interest of the international human rights community.

The military is not alone in enjoying immunity from the legal system. As one report stated, "the same immunity from prosecution and punishment enjoyed by military personnel is extended to other elite groups. Virtually no elected official, member of the business elite, bureaucrat, politician, or anyone with perceived influence or connection to the elite was subjected to legal sanctions for serious abuses."

Conclusion

What happens if a transition to democracy takes place and yet the very beneficiaries of the transition are ill-prepared to take advantage of it? This is exactly the case in Honduras. Although the electoral mechanisms to promote democracy are now firmly in place, and although the country's political elite now seems to accept these mechanisms, it is clear that they are less comfortable with other aspects of consolidating democracy.

Why has the country's political elite been so reticent about taking the steps necessary to reduce the military's autonomy and immunity? First, as has been illustrated, there has been a forty-year tradition of military autonomy in the country. Since the military has at one time been in alliance with or in opposition to almost every significant political organization in the country, there are few organizations that have the capacity or political will to confront the military.

Second, leading Honduran civilian decision makers have been reticent to confront the military directly because that would almost necessarily imply their own greater responsibility. For, as the U.S. embassy has written, most of the country's civilian elites have little sense of accountability either. Thus to promote and enforce control over the military would necessarily lead to greater accountability in other sectors of society. Even if Honduran political institutions have the ability to effect such responsibility, it is clear that the civilian political will to move to this level of behavior is just now beginning to emerge.

Civil-military relations are moving in the direction of far greater accountability for the military. What exists today is a transitional, hybrid regime of civil-military coexistence. Honduras is no longer dominated by its military. The military can no longer dictate policy to civilians, who are showing greater responsibility in their duties as democratically elected leaders. Nevertheless, the military has not yet fully subordinated itself to civilian authority nor accepted that it must obey the rule of law. Such is the civil-military relationship throughout much of Latin America in the 1990s.

5

Costa Rica: New Issues and Alignments

Lowell Gudmundson

While many take Costa Rican democratic stability for granted, recent events in countries such as Venezuela remind us just how complex and precarious the development of institutions able to support democratic, civilian rule is. While Costa Rica has not yet witnessed the sort of crises afflicting other long-standing electoral democracies in the region, Venezuela and Colombia in particular, some of the same tensions and institutional contradictions have emerged. The democratic future of Costa Rica is not surrounded by storm clouds by any means. But a new generation of problems and conflicts may well require the sort of innovative leadership that, between 1940 and 1953, created today's two major parties, whose differences narrowed dramatically in the 1980s.

Four related challenges to democratic governance in Costa Rica are the focus of this chapter:

1. The implications of the dominant party's—the Liberación Nacional (PLN, National Liberation Party)—nearly losing two consecutive presidential elections for the first time, threatening the pattern of presidential alternation and personalist major party leadership, while overturning the PLN's tradition of comfortable parliamentary majorities when holding executive power;

2. The new roles being assumed by a formerly low-profile judiciary;

3. Crime, violence, corruption, and their relationship to drug trafficking and antidrug initiatives;

4. Fears of a collapse of Costa Rica's neoliberal Caribbean Base Initiative (CBI)-based economic growth of the recent past owing to post-NAFTA trading bloc conflicts.

Elections and Realignments after a Decade of Neoliberalism

On February 6, 1994, the PLN won the presidency by the narrowest margin recorded since 1966. The PLN candidate won 49.6 percent of the vote, compared to the incumbent party (PUSC, Social Christian Unity Party) candidate's 47.6 percent. Indeed, the margin of victory,

28,628 votes, was actually smaller than the number of invalid or defaced ballots cast.[1]

Ironically, as recently as 1992 most observers presumed that the post-1948 tradition of presidential alternation in power among the two dominant parties or electoral coalitions, broken only twice (1974 and 1986, both times favoring the PLN candidate), would be the certain result and by a wide margin. The PUSC, led by President Rafael Angel Calderón, nominated as its candidate fifty-four-year-old Miguel Angel Rodríguez, a wealthy businessman with little charisma and no strong ties to the Calderonista following critical to the party's presidential victory in 1990. The PLN relied on the instant name recognition of its candidate, thirty-nine-year-old José María Figueres, son of the immensely popular leader of the 1948 revolt and three-time president who had only recently died. Many considered the upcoming election little more than a formality, assuming that it was the Liberacionistas' turn to take over from the Calderonistas, with Rodríguez playing virtually no role in such a scenario.

This hotly contested campaign was significant for several reasons. The substantial realignments that have taken place both politically and economically over the past decade of neoliberal successes, combined with widespread concern with "character" issues dogging Figueres, led to a virtual dead heat rather than the chronic fragmentation in power for which the Unidad electoral coalition had been notorious in the past. It was precisely this fragmentation, under the ill-fated Carazo administration (1978–82), that aggravated the economic collapse of 1981–82 and threatened to lead to institutional instability as well.

An additional consequence of the unexpectedly close presidential race was the weakening of the PLN's legislative candidates. With only twenty-eight confirmed seats in a fifty-seven-seat legislature, for the first time in memory the PLN needs minority party support to govern. While the PUSC won only twenty-four seats, the Left-Liberal coalition Fuerza Democrática (Democratic Force) held two, and one each was won by regional parties (Partido Agrario Nacional [National Agrarian Party] and Partido Unión Agrícola Cartaginés [The Party of the Agricultural Union of Cartago]). The remaining seat, representing the Atlantic coast province of Limón, was unofficially won by the PUSC candidate by a mere 256 votes and was the object of appeals for a recount.[2]

From the beginning, the PLN's naming of Figueres as its candidate, someone with little experience in government who relied on name recognition almost exclusively, virtually guaranteed a campaign focused on so-called character issues. Thus dirty tricks, innuendo, and character assassination were the order of the day. While many voters wondered aloud about the price such continued personalist politics might extract from historically high levels of voter participation, abstentionism in this contest increased only slightly, to 18.9 percent from 18.7 percent in 1990.[3] However, the disaffection of many PLN members who chose to maintain a very low profile during the campaign rather than support a Figueres candidacy may have been more significant than the abstentionism figures themselves.

The so-called character issues used against both candidates, but particularly against Figueres, dominated the entire campaign. Even before his formal nomination for the presidency, Figueres was accused of involvement, as an eighteen-year-old police lieutenant, in the execution-style murder of a suspected drug dealer in the early 1970s, in a sensationalist tale published under the title *El caso "Chemise."*[4] While libel demands were filed and pursued in the courts, the charges assumed a life of their own and were never effectively silenced, in part owing to the extraordinary role being assumed by a court system that takes under its consideration appeals from the broadest possible spectrum and issues restraining orders far more frequently than substantive rulings. Thus the flurry of negative publicity continued, turning the name recognition advantage into a mixed blessing.

Charges of financial irregularities, long the staple fare of Costa Rican politics, dominated this campaign as well. But, once again, these were handled less effectively by the PLN candidate. The firing of well-known television and print journalists, supposedly for having investigated too vigorously stories of Figueres' early business history and dealings with the national banking system, added further fuel to the flames assiduously fanned by the Rodríguez camp.[5]

The problems for Figueres and the PLN go beyond campaign-generated yellow journalism. His candidacy was undermined by the undeniable prosperity of the recent past, which made a whole series of earlier divisions and electoral strategies irrelevant. Personalism, while long the norm in presidential selection, was now combined with some troubling character traits and enigmas. The same "hot-headed" actions and postures, assumed for their effectiveness in reaching the public via the media as a cabinet minister (agriculture in 1986) and later precandidate, eventually proved counterproductive. And the candidate's own positions, given such a limited public role in the past, were largely unknown. With an electorate habituated to judging presidential candidates, whatever the personalist sins of their selection process, on the basis of their carefully calculated exterior of moderation and statesmanlike rhetoric, Figueres alienated many as a man too quick to answer and just as quick to anger.

The PUSC candidate Rodríguez benefited not only from the contrast in personal styles but from the Calderón administration's capable management of short-term economic policy. He also knew how to capitalize on the fact that the overwhelming dominance of neoliberal, orthodox economic messages in the public arena deprived the PLN of any ability to profit from its traditional profile as a welfare state defender of national and popular interests. The *Calderonista* party and its working-class faithful were his without any need for a direct populist appeal, and thus he felt no pressure to depart from the slogans and images of the neoliberal recipe for success.

Each major party relied heavily on spreading rumors of its opponent's "secret" plans to eliminate this or that popular institution or policy rather than on any substantial differences in publicly expressed positions. The PLN hoped to provoke fears based on Rodríguez' big business background by claiming that as president he would abolish the labor code's guarantees, while the same sort of charges of hidden right-wing, or antipopular intentions were made against Figueres.

The PLN's lack of a working majority in the legislature reduced the early Figueres administration to the pattern of ineffectiveness and fragmentation formerly associated with their opponents in power. Indeed, the extreme personalism of the presidential contest, as well as the ever more scant differences in programs offered by each side, suggested the likelihood of continued gridlock in the legislative branch, the pattern witnessed for the first year of the new administration.

Figueres and the liberal-left Social Democrats within the PLN had questioned the wisdom of signing yet another (third) stabilization agreement with the International Monetary Fund (IMF) during the campaign, a position the newly elected candidate chose to repeat publicly the day after his victory. However, the party and its new president quickly did an about-face once in power, publicly declaring their allegiance to the new neoliberal orthodoxy.[6]

The earlier Left-leaning statements had never reflected a more general, partywide position questioning neoliberal policies. There were party leaders (former ministers such as Otón Solís and Angel Edmundo Solano in particular) who outlined an anti-IMF, anti-neoliberal position, artfully combined with a post–cold war appeal to reasonable, respectful political debate. However, just such a conversion to a peculiar third worldism characterized a few of those near the top of the Carazo administration *after* they left office in 1982 and were no longer particularly relevant to those seeking to win future elections, suggesting again just how weak and isolated such a position is within the current political arena. Solís, elected Assembly deputy in the 1994 election, was the lone PLN dissident in briefly opposing the very public and extraparliamentary agreements on taxation and privatization policy reached by the current and former presidents (Figueres and Calderón) in July 1995 that were designed to resolve both the legislative logjam and the PLN's inability to pursue any economic policy initiatives not agreed to in advance by the opposition.[7]

The problem for the major parties lies in their virtually indistinguishable programs for continued prosperity based on the 1980s recipe of trade liberalization and export-led growth. The profile of the PLN as the defender of statist economic development programs, redistributive taxation, and urban middle-class reform has been sufficiently blurred so as to provide the PUSC with a realistic possibility of appealing to broad segments of the middle-class historical beneficiaries of PLN policies, even as the incumbent party. Conversely, the PLN and Figueres find themselves negotiating economic policy with their most conservative domestic opponents on the one hand, and with an unsympathetic international financial community on the other. Rather than any reinvigoration of its social democratic message and support base, the first year of the Figueres administration reflects a marked shift to the Right with approval ratings falling nearly as fast as the exchange rate and inflation rise.

PLN strategists have suggested that, historically, their presidential candidate in the opposition begins with roughly a 15 percent electoral advantage over the incumbent party candidate. Thus Figueres' razor-thin victory, far from being cause for rejoicing, could as well be seen as the loss of well over 10 percent of the PLN's structural advantage.[8] Subsequently, the inability to push through any legislative program and the unpopularity of the measures ultimately agreed upon with the PUSC opposition have further undermined the PLN's core base of support. Such dissatisfaction with electoral choices, policy options, and perceptions of not being represented may seem little more than minor irritants in the midst of relative prosperity. In any future scenario resembling the collapse of 1981–82, however, they could prove far more significant.

In a post–cold war world of political discourse, the far Right, never overly significant in Costa Rica in any event, has been deprived of some of its rhetorical ammunition. Nevertheless, they continue to denounce any and all movement in the direction of state welfare spending or limitations on the right of private property in the land. Newspaper advertisements continue to be placed by the Movimiento Costa Rica Libre (Free Costa Rica Movement), quite as if the Berlin Wall and those of the Kremlin were as firmly in place as ever. Outside of professional anti-communist circles, however, things have changed at least slightly. The establishment Right is as firmly entrenched and comfortable within one major party as the other, a fact that has deprived the PLN of one of its traditional weapons in the media war. And given the currently untouchable status of neoliberalism and free trade doctrines, the respectable Right has nothing to fear from either major party.

The Left has not recovered from its bitter internal squabble and collapse of the early 1980s, and its influence among both the labor movement and student groups has probably not been at a lower ebb since before the 1920s. The remnants of the historic Left have regrouped under the populist banner of the Fuerza Democrática, electing two Assembly members. Yet even here, personalism reigned supreme as the son of long-term deputy Rodrigo Gutiérrez Sáenz, thirty-six-year-old Rodrigo Gutiérrez Schwanhauser, was elected to succeed his father.[9]

Beyond this minuscule partisan resurfacing, the extent of rank-and-file labor union decline is hard to overestimate. In addition to the proliferation of so-called *solidarista* or mutual-aid/company unions in the 1980s, and the decidedly anti-union policies denounced by the U.S. AFL-CIO as part of the framework of the General Agreement on Tariffs and Trade (GATT), the renewed influx of hundreds of thousands of undocumented Nicaraguans after 1990 has led to a virtual disappearance of blue-collar unionism as a political or economic force. In effect, the Costa Rican Left has been reduced to a role analogous to the provincial "favorite son" candidates for the Assembly, or the first ever "evangelical" candidate for the presidency. Those groups traditionally represented by the Costa Rican Left—banana and port workers' unions on the coasts and a few artisanal and splinter public employee groups in the highlands—have had little or no influence over public policy for well over a decade and have few expectations for change in the near future. Even the more than a month-long national teachers' strike over pension plan cutbacks of mid-1995, while showing what remains of the strongest of all the white-collar public employee unions, failed to budge the newly declared neoliberal PLN leadership and President Figueres.[10]

Politics and Judicial Activism: A Costa Rican Warren Court?

Perhaps Costa Rica's most successful modern political innovation was its development of an effective Supreme Electoral Tribunal (TSE) in the late 1940s as part of the judicial system.[11] The tribunal proved instrumental in reversing a half-century-long tradition of competitive but highly fraudulent presidential elections and consolidating the centerpiece of modern Costa Rican democracy: effective suffrage. Outside of this area, the Costa Rican judiciary has historically been far less distinguished or successful, gaining a reputation for middle-class employment generation, and as a good means to pursue delaying tactics, more than as an effective source of redress for plaintiffs large or small.

More recently, however, the court system has been drawn into a more interventionist, proactive stance regarding a whole series of issues formerly limited to the executive and legislative branches. While no succession crisis or electoral fraud have led the TSE to flex its undoubted muscle, far less universally respected levels of the judiciary have become involved in nearly every major issue of economic policy, in addition to traditional civil or human rights cases.

The new judicial activism is based not on actions taken by the Supreme Court but rather on the involvement of the "Sala IV" or Constitutional Chamber in virtually every public dispute over the past decade.[12] This new development had its origins in two related tendencies of the 1980s: the growth of Costa Rican nongovernmental organizations (NGOs) and activists allied with them and the collapse of the formerly pervasive protectionist economic policy. Each of these new sites of conflict has been transferred to the judicial system far more often than to the other branches of government, where the participants know quite well that with neoliberalism so firmly in command ideologically there is no likelihood of a consensus favoring them.

The NGOs have pursued human, civil, and environmental rights claims, often in association with sister international organizations that they know can exert pressure far beyond their own weight owing to the government's sensitivity to any damaging of Costa Rica's exemplary world image in precisely these areas. Thus appeals for injunctions or judicial orders have regularly surfaced in tourist, coastal, or national park development projects where environmental concerns are involved, as well as with regard to Indian rights and citizenship in the southeastern part of the country, prisoners' rights, and even labor union rights as part of processes related to GATT and the North American Free Trade Agreement (NAFTA).[13]

The goals of the plaintiffs have been twofold: to delay rulings or actions they oppose and, more important, to generate sufficient negative publicity to move the executive branch to action favorable to their position. While not always successful, the willingness of the Sala IV either to hear such cases or to give them extensive publicity even when rejecting them has confirmed both the judiciary's higher profile in politics and the new group of litigants' transparently political strategy for influencing future public policy. The executive branch has recognized this trend and has even responded by creating a new position of ombudsman (defensor del pueblo). Its first director, Rodrigo Carazo Zeledón, son of former president Rodrigo Carazo, was recently roughed up on the streets of the capital and hustled off to jail for presuming to remind a traffic police officer of the antilittering ordinance. Just how much damaging publicity awaits those public and private institutions yet to adjust to the newly central political role of the judiciary will no doubt be spelled out in the case soon to be brought against the Public Security forces.[14]

The use of the Sala IV to protest and resist economic policy decisions threatening formerly protected or tolerated interests is no less frequent. From the heights of power to the depths of poverty, all manner of Costa Ricans have had the opportunity to invoke judicial redress. Ambulatory street vendors have resisted their eviction from the curbsides of the capital by using riotous behavior and by making formal requests for injunctions. Food grain producers, large and small, have organized street and road-blocking protests, but have also used litigation to oppose the elimination or reduction of either price or credit subsidies. Virtually every major economic interest group faced with the loss of its former protection or subsidy during the 1980s has appealed to the Sala IV.

From the very beginning of the economic collapse of 1980–82, when legal cases were brought against the executive for abandoning a fixed exchange rate without legislative action (a case resolved many months later in favor of the plaintiff!), it has been clear that no change in policy would be the automatic result of an eventual favorable ruling. Both the publicity and delaying tactic value of appeals to the Sala IV have proved crucial to the negotiating strategy of a wide variety of interest groups. However, to the extent that appeals to the Sala IV are not directly related to presumably favorable eventual outcomes, judicial involvement can be seen by many to be no more than a means to defend privilege through procrastination and actually lead to politically negative outcomes: atrophy of the partisan (legislative and executive branch) channels for interest articulation and conflict resolution, and a heightened sense of popular cynicism regarding the judiciary. So far at least, popular ire has not fixed upon the judiciary in general, much less the Sala IV in particular, as the cause for nonresolution of problems.

While the Sala IV retains much of its "little guy" popularity as what amounts to a rapid-fire court of appeals, the Supreme Court has lost both credibility and popular esteem owing to persistent rumors of drug money corruption and incompetence. Supreme Court magistrate Jesús Ramírez was reelected to his post in March 1993 in an Assembly vote of seventeen in favor, thirty-seven against, and two abstentions (a two-thirds negative vote was needed to remove him!), despite the fact that he had been named in a 1988 Assembly drug commission probe as obstructing justice in a case against an Argentine accused of drug trafficking.[15]

The most recent band of would-be kidnapping commandos hoped to capitalize on this popular association when they decided to take several Supreme Court judges hostage in mid-1993. While their near-comic lack of professionalism led to their capture en route to the airport with their ransom, this homegrown gang claimed to be Colombian drug dealers out to free their countrymen from Costa Rican jails. Their choice of the judiciary, an emerging center of media coverage and political relevance, for their hostage taking may also reflect a real change only dimly perceived by most as yet.[16]

While the new role of the judiciary in Costa Rica is far less dramatic than similar challenges in Venezuela and Colombia, and far more well established than similar developments in Honduras, the common pattern represents an important political change. Whether the groups involved will long consider judicial means an effective recourse in the face of hostile policies, and given the lack of any clear policy changes in the recent past, is an open question. As a means of exerting pressure for the already powerful organized interest groups, it has proved its usefulness repeatedly; as a vehicle for broader representation or more thoroughgoing change, it may well generate more frustration than political integration. The proliferation of judicial activism during the 1980s would seem more a symptom of the lack of legislative or executive branch remedies to political and economic problems than their chosen vehicle. And in that sense, a comparison with the Warren Court's restructuring of a stalemated U.S. social agenda, leading to a new round of even more virulent partisan conflict, may not be farfetched.

Politics as Media Sweeps: "Cops" in a Costa Rican Context

Over the past decade it has been possible for most Costa Ricans to blame a perceived increase in crime, especially violent crime, on foreigners or foreign-directed enterprises. For the first half of the 1980s, the Contra war was the explanation (as often as not true), while in more recent times the popular wisdom points to drug trafficking organized by Colombian cartels. What has not been possible is to ignore the increase in violent crime and the public spectacles associated with it. United Nations' figures paint a bleak picture: in 1991 Costa Rica had 267 violent crimes per 100,000 residents, compared to 197 in 1983. Crimes against property rose to 944 in 1991, compared to 598 in 1987.[17]

While external forces may have played a leading role, Costa Rican society's reaction to this trend has also changed. No longer is it a simple matter of scapegoating in order to maintain denial and blind spots. Following the U.S. pattern and lead, as well as Reagan-era policies of militarization (increased police numbers, professionalization, technical support, and creation of drug liaison units), local political and media authorities turned to the use of crime and anticrime messages to improve their "ratings." Elaborate reporting on drug busts and raids, lurid detail on manhunts ending in firefights and death, and insinuation of drug money ties to a broad spectrum of public figures and institutions have all become daily fare. In a bizarre twist, some even suggest that Costa Rica's exchange rate and economic stability are possible thanks only to drug-related money laundering, suggesting yet another reason to fear what might happen if the first focus of fear were actually resolved!

The politics of fear in Costa Rica has not, as yet, found so ready a "black and white" divide as in the United States, or at least leading politicians have not yet discovered one. Several of the major public security initiatives have proved counterproductive, as Costa Ricans, fortunately so far, fear the repressive solutions the state offers for their problems of personal security even more than they fear crime itself.

They have had good reason to fear. The masterminds of the assault on the Supreme Court turned out to be ex-police officials formerly employed by the increasingly infamous Judicial Police (OIJ, Organización de Investigación Judicial). Similarly, evidence exists linking former or current antiterrorist and antidrug officers to violent crimes and kidnapping. Four former OIJ agents were actually arrested and charged with the murder of two alleged traffickers in mid-1995. Two years earlier a roundup of youth gang members by the OIJ in San José led to accusations that they had murdered one of the leaders of the gang in custody and to the justice minister, Elizabeth Odio, referring to the unit involved as "a police death squad." Perhaps the most spectacular, and surely the most tragic, example of this strong reaction against an increased state military apparatus came about in response to the crack antidrug unit's accidental killing of an adolescent in a hail of bullets as part of a mistaken predawn raid on a humble dwelling on San José's south side in 1992. Public outrage was so great that the then public security minister was virtually forced to abolish the unit in disgust, after first offering some halfhearted support for his troops. Rambo-style raids and manhunts were widely popularized by the Costa Rican media in the late 1980s, but following these disastrous cases no new initiatives outside the traditional Civil Guard/Rural Guard structure have been proposed, and many calls for abolition of special police forces were heard.[18]

Ironically, there has never been any real shortage in Costa Rica of tragic and bloody violence, often domestic in origin. Among the nation's poor, crimes from simple homicide or assault, to deranged slaughter, to calculated assassinations involving any imaginable level of gore, have long existed. But major media and political interest in violent crime developed only as a function of the involvement of the new public security forces and issues of the mid-to-late 1980s.

Even the casual observer could note the vast increase in drug money, and cocaine in its various forms, in circulation since the late 1980s. According to official figures in 1992, drug seizures totaled 2,000 kilos of cocaine, 920 rocks of crack, 7 kilos of heroin, and the destruction of approximately 300 hectares of marijuana plantations.[19] If, as all sources seem to agree, this is merely the very tip of the iceberg of drug trafficking via Costa Rica, the possibilities for drug-related bribery and corruption are indeed immense.

Despite the media focus on the "war on drugs," the average citizen cared far less about the drug world and its spin-offs than the level of property crime involving firearms. The increased use of deadly force in burglaries and thievery is perhaps the single greatest crime concern of the citizenry, and the courts and prison system are the most ready targets of public frustration. However, while there has been criticism of the OIJ and its tactics, there has been no development of private death squad activity, as in Brazil or Colombia, in the face of what some see as "out of control" street crime.

However, there are several ways in which the fear of crime dynamic can have a harmful effect on democratic governance and civic tolerance. There has long been a relatively fine line, especially in cattle-raising areas of the countryside characterized by land invasions, between private armed "security" and intimidation, especially as public security forces nearly always arrive on the scene well after hostilities begin.[20] Moreover, the unsettling frequency with which former security forces members reappear in civilian life as violent criminals suggests that a Salvadoranlike descent into terror is worth taking precautions against. Finally, the almost knee-jerk reaction of blaming crime on often undocumented Nicaraguans worsens an already tense situation involving not just the many thousands of immigrants but their often visibly and socially distinctive descendants as well, long after they obtain citizenship.

Prosperity and Policy: Too Much of a Good Thing?

Costa Rica was one of the most successful followers of the economic policy doctrines and changes associated with the Reagan and Bush years, whether one uses the CBI, new world order, or neoliberalism as a shorthand identifier. Doubling, and then nearly tripling, its export earnings since 1980, thanks primarily to nontraditional and tropical fruit exports, Costa Rica was Central America's Chile.

Under Calderón the economy was managed with surprising agility and stability, given the disastrous precedent of the Carazo administration and initially low public expectations. Growth rates were maintained in the 3–5 percent range, and inflation was contained at relatively low levels (10–20%) by recent standards. Further steps were taken to lower protectionist tariffs on consumer goods, much as under the administration of Carlos Salinas de Gortari in Mexico prior to the signing of NAFTA, ensuring a high level of short-term popularity among relieved consumers. Auto imports, in particular, surged to new levels, and prices fell significantly. Calderón also continued with and improved upon the immensely popular housing subsidy programs of his predecessor, Oscar Arias, further relieving economic pressure on poor and middle-income groups.

However, the recent experiences with depressed coffee prices, European Community discriminatory tariffs on banana and fresh fruit exports, and fear over the implications of NAFTA point to structural problems with a new world order success story. As exports have boomed, imports have grown even more rapidly. Current account deficits of up to U.S.$500–600 million per year (against exports of U.S.$1.8–2.4 billion) have routinely been covered by a combination of new foreign direct investment capital, "parked" finance capital (owing to historically low rates in the United States), and, some claim, drug money laundering.

The collapse of the world coffee agreement at the high point of free trade initiatives in 1990 has led to the most depressed prices in half a century. Bottoming out at nearly U.S.$50 per hundredweight, prices have now recovered to a range of U.S.$120–140. The object lesson for those raised on a steady diet of the virtues of international competitiveness and trade could hardly be clearer, especially given the highly subsidized and politicized history of the coffee production sector in Costa Rica, as well as the strong identification of its thousands of small producers with the PLN in the past.

Far worse for the proponents of export-led development strategies, the enormous confidence and success Costa Rica has enjoyed with banana, pineapple, and fresh fruit and vegetable exports since the mid-1980s was severely shaken by the European Community (EC) tariffs and restrictions on bananas, imposed beginning in 1993.[21] While negotiations continue, virtually all local commentators assumed that the EC measures were in fact in response to NAFTA and GATT conflicts with the United States rather than anything bilateral involving producers such as Costa Rica. Thus Costa Rica may no longer only benefit from its ever closer trade relationship and dependence on the United States but begin to face new costs and problems as well.

Fears of the direct consequences of NAFTA for Costa Rica center on drawback textile industries, flower exports, and the winter and specialty vegetable trade. If Mexican exports were to displace Costa Rican goods, there could be a significant impact on local growth rates. Only the textile plants would seem likely candidates for rapid relocation, but public expressions of concern, involving even President Calderón immediately after the NAFTA signing, have given greater visibility to perhaps exaggerated fears. Subsequent negotiations with Mexico involving textile reexports gave further cause for concern to an already beleaguered industry.

Only if all three worst-case scenarios were to materialize—the price collapse continues or even deepens in coffee; banana and fruit exports are crippled by tariff penalties; and Mexican goods displace Costa Rica's in labor cost-sensitive sectors formed thanks to the CBI—would economic crisis, much less political instability, be a realistic fear. However, the difference in such an eventuality, compared to 1980–82, is that there would be no PLN waiting in the wings, cautioning patience and claiming a vastly different and more competent economic policy team. The new PLN president was elected with an almost microscopic margin, no clear parliamentary mandate, and a whole series of decimated former welfare state constituencies anticipating more than rhetorical gains. However, a decade of neoliberal success, electoral realignment, and ideological accommodation has put the two major parties in much the same basket, with few distinctive ideas or programs to offer should their bipartisan model of export-led growth falter.

Conclusion

The class bases for Costa Rican electoral competition established in the turbulent period of 1940–53 have been substantially redefined by the neoliberal policies of the 1980s and early 1990s. What for that earlier generation were historical compromises and hard-won gains of almost mystical significance—the labor code, public health care and education, effective suffrage, women's suffrage, progressive taxation, public employment, and state-led economic development—are now either "givens" or seen as hardly relevant for partisan organization in the 1990s. However, bitter social antagonisms and inequalities like those that gave rise to the earlier struggles are being recreated, albeit with far different protagonists this time around.

"New" middle and business classes developed very rapidly under neoliberal, export auspices in the 1980s. They are every bit as convinced of their right to rule as their predecessors were in the late 1940s. However, theirs was an ascent predicated on an opposition to state dominance of economic development rather than as leaders of one or another coalition in search of the "right" form of state intervention. Moreover, the mass base for any sort of challenge to or expansion of the institutional framework is currently not even "imagined" by those groups favored by the 1980s and now willing to consider voting for whichever of the two major parties can most credibly promise more of the same. Organized labor and public employees, two of the major allies at midcentury, are simply antithetical to the ideology of their economic future. And ideology aside, when looking into the face of the common people, not only do they not recognize allies, but they are as likely to see the depoliticized informal sector worker, the evangelical, or the undocumented Nicaraguan as they are to see a member of their imagined community of the nation.

While these historic realignments work themselves out, there will be little to fear in terms of "democratic governance" in Costa Rica, if by that one simply means the continuation of representative democracy. However, that same quiescence ensures that any further social reform will await the clarification of the social antagonisms engendered in Costa Rica by its export-led growth strategy of the 1980s. In that somewhat longer run, there are reasons for concern in that so few of the historical achievements of midcentury bear any direct relationship, either in partisan or class terms, to the challenges of political and institutional incorporation to come. Old-style producers' cooperatives in coffee and plantation laborers' unions in bananas have not found their equivalents in the new context. When they do appear, their incorporation in the political system and institutional context may well pose daunting challenges.

Much was made of the irony of a President Calderón turning over power peacefully to an elected President Figueres in 1994, compared to the violent transfer of power in 1948 involving their fathers. While political peace, participation, and institutional continuity deserve praise, in the case of the most recent election, praise alone would mislead. There is a difference more fundamental than the similarity in last names. Democratic *reform* as well as democratic forms were at issue in 1948. However central an element in governance, democratic form had no such visible companion in the 1994 inauguration ceremony.

6

Panama: Transactional Democracy

Richard L. Millett

In 1994 Panama held what were indisputably its freest and most open elections in the last quarter century. Fifteen parties had achieved legal status, the press and electronic media belabored the incumbent administration and promoted various candidates, and citizens of all regions and social classes were uninhibited in expressing political preferences and criticizing existing situations. The old Panamanian Defense Forces (PDF) had been abolished, and the new Public Force, essentially a police rather than a military establishment, operated under civilian control and did not intervene in the political process. The United States, long a dominant presence in Panama, also stood aside, even when it became clear that the candidate of the Democratic Revolutionary Party (PRD), the party that had provided the political support for the regime of Manuel Noriega, was going to win. While avoiding any interference in domestic politics, the Clinton administration moved steadily ahead with plans to terminate its military presence and transfer full control over the Canal to Panama at the end of 1999. On the surface, at least, Panama appears to have made a successful transition from a long period of military rule and civil strife.

The task of constructing and strengthening democratic institutions in Panama can count on some significant assets. The population is relatively well educated, with an adult literacy rate of 88 percent. More than 80 percent have access to health services and potable water. Despite a nearly 2 percent annual growth rate, the nation is far from overpopulated. While 14 percent of children suffer from malnutrition and 18 percent of the population is unable to satisfy basic needs, these figures are still lower than those in most of the region.[1]

Panama's military, the Panamanian Defense Forces was destroyed in the 1989 U.S. invasion, and the successor institution, the Public Force (FP) is little more than a national police. It operates under a system of civilian control, has no regular combat units, and suffers from low morale and a notable lack of public support. While a proposed constitutional amendment to formally abolish the military was defeated in a referendum in 1992, it has since been adopted by the national Assembly. Whatever other problems Panamanians face, there seems little danger of a military coup.

Panama enjoys a high degree of media freedom. Indeed, few administrations have been as consistently vilified by both the print and the electronic media as was that of President Guillermo Endara. While the majority of the media is controlled by traditional upper-class elite families, there is some diversity, and one of the newspapers that strongly supported General Noriega's regime has continued to publish. The major problem in the media is not restriction on its freedom but the highly partisan content and polemical tone of much of its material.

Labor unions, while not particularly strong, are relatively free. The nation has one of Latin America's strongest traditions of participation in civic, professional, and charitable organizations. Such organizations formed the heart of the National Civic Crusade, created to mobilize opposition to the Noriega dictatorship.

Panama also has open, highly competitive politics. No significant group is denied access to the political process. Panamanian law makes forming new political parties and gaining legal status relatively easy, a situation that has facilitated a proliferation of parties and, despite numerous efforts at alliance formation, produced seven presidential candidates for the 1994 elections. Alliance formation was even less common at lower levels, and in 1994 eleven different parties won seats in the legislative Assembly.

These developments are only a part of the political and social reality of contemporary Panama. Underneath the veneer of democratic institutions and individual freedoms lies a society profoundly influenced by the decades of military rule, deeply divided along class and racial lines, and still attempting to come to terms with its relationship with the United States. While the forms of a democratic system are well established in Panama, the ability of that system to gain the confidence of much of the population and to effectively address pressing national concerns remains open to question.

The sources of most of the problems in Panama's transition to a more democratic system can be easily discerned in that nation's history. Perhaps the most obvious is the extent to which Panamanian sovereignty has been limited by the predominant presence and influence of the United States. This has assumed a wide variety of forms, from direct military interventions, most recently in December 1989, to political and economic pressures on various Panamanian governments, to the potential threat and constant psychological impact of having U.S. military units, always much stronger than any force Panama could muster, stationed within Panama. Panama is also linked to and dependent on the economy of the United States. The U.S.-controlled Canal is the source of much of the nation's actual and potential wealth, and revenues from U.S. civilian and military personnel stationed in Panama account for a significant share of the national income. Add to this the importance of commercial and financial ties with the United States, and the pattern of economic dependence becomes quickly apparent. The ultimate expression of this reality is Panama's use of the U.S. dollar as its national currency.

As great as is the actual U.S. influence in Panama, its psychological influence is even greater. There is a long history of blaming the United States for everything from the excesses of the Panamanian military to the influence of the drug trade. National leaders repeatedly seek solutions to their problems in Washington, attempting to discern U.S. preferences for everything from banking laws to presidential candidates. The fact that President Guillermo Endara was installed in office on a U.S. Air Force base during the 1989 invasion provides Panamanians with a graphic illustration of American influence. Since the 1989 invasion, the United States has made an effort to disengage itself from this process, announcing plans to withdraw military forces from Panama and emphasizing Panamanian responsibilities for confronting their own national problems. Such efforts, though, encounter serious problems of credibility, in part because of past history and in part because some Panamanians apparently want to maintain a high degree of dependence on the United States. Polls consistently show a high percentage of Panamanians favoring the retention of the U.S. bases, but there is little evidence that the U.S. military is seriously interested in any such arrangement. At the moment, Washington seems committed to reducing its presence and curbing its influence. Its open acceptance of the PRD's victory in the 1994 elections lends some credibility to these assertions. Whether this effort can be sustained through the end of the century is less certain.

Panama, in common with much of Central America, has major problems of domestic political leadership. The political scene is deeply fragmented. Fifteen different political parties were legally registered for the 1994 campaign. Although several of these lost their legal status because of their lack of support in the elections, party proliferation remains a problem. This abundance of parties, however, does not indicate widespread faith in or support for the political process. A 1992 poll indicated massive popular rejection of existing political leadership. Only 20 percent of those polled had a favorable image of political parties. Eighty-seven percent believed that politicians take public preferences into account only when they want votes. Seventy percent of the respondents believed politicians wanted to win office largely to advance personal interests, while another 8 percent believed it was simply because they liked to exercise power. Seventy-two percent were dissatisfied with the political system, and another 11 percent had serious doubts. Sixty-six percent believed that the nation might return to a dictatorship, and, by a better than four-to-one margin, the respondents preferred an authoritarian regime with programs of social welfare to a democratic government with problems of social justice.[2]

These attitudes have produced a climate of public apathy and cynicism. Only 38 percent of the voting population participated in the 1992 referendum. Until early 1994, the number of Panamanians indicating dissatisfaction with all potential 1994 presidential candidates exceeded the number supporting any single candidate.[3] The approval rating of the Endara administration was in single digits for its last two years. In a poll taken late in 1992, 59.4 percent of those responding identified the administration as the principal obstacle to Panama's progress, while another 19.5 percent blamed the democratic system itself.[4]

These attitudes demonstrate the serious difficulties confronting efforts to create a viable and credible democratic system in Panama. This does not indicate, however, that the current democratic framework of government is in imminent danger. The possibility of a military coup is minimal, and all major parties give at least verbal support to political democracy. Despite the bitter heritage of the Noriega era, all parties accepted the PRD's return to power in the 1994 elections. The Pérez Balladares administration has made some effort to reach out to other political sectors, including non-PRD supporters in his cabinet. Opposition suspicion of the PRD, however, remains extremely high, and there is evidence that at least some elements in that party would like to return to the corrupt and authoritarian practices of the past. Should that happen, support for the administration would erode, crime and government corruption would steadily increase, and popular support for an authoritarian alternative could ultimately emerge.

Electoral System

Panama has a reasonably efficient and credible system for conducting elections. The process of registering voters, certifying parties and candidates, holding elections, and tabulating results is entrusted to the National Electoral Tribunal, which, under Panama's constitution, enjoys the status of an independent branch of government. While suffering from limited funds and inexperienced personnel, the tribunal did a credible job in running the 1992 referendum on proposed constitutional reforms. Despite official government support for the proposed reforms, they were soundly rejected. Unfortunately, one of the rejected reforms would have strengthened the tribunal's independence and guaranteed it adequate funding.

Funding remained an issue until the eve of the 1994 elections. The tribunal overcame some of these problems by recruiting a large number of volunteers and by cooperating with other groups to ensure widespread electoral supervision. The result was perhaps the cleanest, least controversial election in Panama's history.

While the 1994 elections added to the tribunal's generally high credibility, the electoral process still has some problems. The multiplicity of parties, the common practice of buying signatures to gain legal status for new parties, and the long history of internal divisions and fights for control within parties have made some aspects of the tribunal's work especially difficult. To date, it has handled such problems reasonably well.

More difficult to overcome have been problems connected with the electoral registry. There was general agreement that confusion and errors in the registration process prevented numerous voters from exercising their franchise in 1992. By some estimates, these problems may have involved more than 10 percent of potential voters.[5] Significant efforts have been made since then to improve this situation, but problems remain. Fortunately, these problems are largely due to funding and personnel limitations, and the situation has not generated serious charges of bias on the part of the tribunal. Indeed, if Panamanian politicians agreed on anything, it is that the tribunal functioned fairly and effectively in running the 1994 elections.

The governmental structure of Panama, as well as its political party system, offers obstacles to the development and consolidation of democratic institutions. The nation is still operating under the 1972 Constitution, reformed in 1978 and 1983, which was the product and instrument of the military regimes. The 1992 electoral defeat of the proposed package of changes to this document has frustrated efforts to bring the constitution more in line with the needs of a democratic state. One result has been a movement for convoking a constituent assembly to draft an entirely new basic document.[6] While this may ultimately occur, support has declined since the 1994 elections.

The constitution requires only a simple plurality for election as president. This allowed Pérez Balladares to win in 1994 with just over a third of the votes. The constitution also requires that all candidates for the legislative Assembly be on the lists of approved parties. In districts having only one legislator, a simple plurality is enough to win, but in others, such as metropolitan Panama City, which elect several legislators, the final result is based on a complicated formula involving party lists and modified proportional representation. While this generally ensures a divided Assembly, especially with fifteen parties competing, the system came close to producing a PRD majority in 1994. At the same time it produced major distortions in which some parties wound up with several more seats than their portion of the vote, while others had several less.[7] In addition, with the approval of the Electoral Tribunal, parties may oust legislators who fail to adhere to the "ideological, political, and programmatic platform of the party."[8] However, if parties lose their legal standing, deputies are apparently free to switch to other parties.

The constitution was designed to inhibit the independence of all branches of government, leaving the ultimate moderating power in the hands of the military and its party allies. But, with the elimination of the military, there is no final arbitrating power, producing a system where gridlock, partisanship, and instability are dominant characteristics. In addition to the executive, legislative, judicial, and electoral powers, Panama's constitution also gives broad powers to the comptroller general, who serves the same term as the president and can be removed only by the Supreme Court. He can suspend or delay spending on government budgets if revenues appear insufficient, as well as conduct audits of all national accounts.[9] While these powers have helped curb government spending, they have also added another element to the matrix of political gridlock. A proposal to eliminate the comptroller's powers to prevent spending for budgeted items was included among the package of reforms defeated in 1992. Not surprisingly, the then incumbent comptroller general openly campaigned against the reform package. Under the Perez Balladares administration, the position has become somewhat less controversial, in part because it is filled by a less confrontational individual. But the potential for abuse remains.

The policies of the comptroller general reflect the fiscal conservatism typical of the political elites. Government funding for social programs and for the administration of justice were severely limited under the Endara administration, while priority was given to restoring the nation's international credit. The new administration is more inclined to pay attention to social problems, but is constrained by fiscal realities and by its ardent desire to participate in the General Agreement on Tariffs and Trade (GATT) and to negotiate a free trade arrangement with the United States. As a result, to the surprise of many, it is pursuing fiscal policies almost as conservative as those of its predecessor.

Like many of its counterparts throughout Latin America, Panama's justice system has major defects. It is poorly funded, includes judges with little training, some of whom are holdovers from the period of military rule, and does not enjoy high levels of public confidence or support. The courts are further handicapped by the weakness of the Public Force, Panama's new national police, and the terrible state of Panama's prisons. Before the 1989 intervention, the police, notoriously partisan and corrupt, were an integral part of the Panamanian Defense Forces controlled by General Noriega. The PDF was destroyed in the intervention, leading to a sharp rise in the crime rate and making it necessary to deploy a new national police quickly. As a result, the FP incorporated large numbers of former PDF members into its ranks, bringing with them old habits of corruption and abuse of authority and producing high levels of public distrust. Instances of corruption in the FP are regularly reported in the Panamanian press, and public confidence in the force is extremely low. Panamanians have taken to arming themselves or turning to private security forces whose numbers exceed those of the Public Force and who are better paid and equipped. Even the presidency has created a separate, politicized force, the Institutional Protection Service, to provide for the security of members of the executive branch.

Parties and Problems

The causes of the divisions, weakness, and lack of credibility for Panama's political parties are numerous and complex. In part it is a reflection of the relative ease with which new parties can be created and gain legal status. In part it is the heritage of more than two decades of military domination of politics. For much of this period the normal political process was suspended, the media was restricted, and elections were controlled or manipulated. For years, the opposition to the military was dominated by the charismatic figure of Arnulfo Arias Madrid, founder and leader of the Panamenistas. Three times elected president (and fraudulently denied victory in 1984) and three times ousted from power by the military, Arias combined nationalism, populism, and racism with his opposition to military rule. This won him a large, dedicated following, but made the military his implacable foe, generated grave suspicions about his policies abroad, and hampered efforts to form a political party system based more on issues than on personalities. Despite considerable distaste for some of his policies, the opposition to military rule united behind him as their presidential candidate in 1984, then, following his death, chose a leader of his party, Guillermo Endara, as their standard bearer in 1989. This produced an unstable coalition, headed by an individual who lacked Arnulfo's charisma and whose leadership and administrative qualities were, at best, questionable. At the same time, the manipulation of the results of the 1984 election and the military's effort to annul the 1989 elections contributed both to public cynicism regarding the entire process and to a bitter polarization between supporters and opponents of the military regimes.

The Noriega regime deliberately encouraged divisions within existing parties. Combining offers of political positions to factions that would support the regime with a blatant manipulation of the Electoral Tribunal's power to determine the results of internal party disputes, the regime facilitated divisions within two of the nation's most important political parties, the Liberals and the Panamenistas (currently the Arnulfista Party). The Liberals, who had won or shared victory in at least twelve of Panama's first seventeen elections (from 1904 through 1964), have splintered into several apparently irreconcilable factions and have lost much of their influence. The Panamenistas, by contrast, remain largely united, finishing a strong second in the 1994 elections in which the widow of Arnulfo Arias was their candidate. The party, however, lacks leadership and a coherent program. Its opposition is largely negative, and its appeal combines promises of benefits and jobs for its supporters with elements of xenophobia and appeals to the memory of its deceased founder. It is difficult to imagine it offering a real alternative for the nation's future.

The Christian Democrats, who had gained the strongest popular support and largest bloc of seats in the national Assembly in the 1989 elections, were ousted from the government in 1991. This contributed to internal divisions and a leadership crisis, and the party nearly collapsed in 1994, winning only one seat in the Assembly. The Arnulfistas' other major partner in the anti-Noriega coalition, the National Liberal Republican Movement (MOLIRENA), remained in the government until the end of 1993 when they broke with Endara and the Arnulfistas over the issue of candidates for the 1994 elections. While they fared somewhat better than the Christian Democrats in the 1994 elections, they too saw their support decline significantly.

The declining support for traditional parties led to the creation of seven new parties for the 1994 elections. Most fared badly, but one, the Papa Egoro movement headed by popular actor and singer Rubén Blades, finished third. It had a strong appeal to youth and to Panamanians disgusted with the traditional deal making of national politics. It has remained aloof from coalitions and alliances, but Blades has largely withdrawn from politics, its members represent a wide variety of ideological currents, and its future is uncertain at best.

The opposition's divisions, lack of credible leadership, and association with failed policies of the past have contributed to the ability of the current administration to pursue its policies, but has also placed in further doubt the nation's political future. In early 1995 a poll found no opposition party with more than 12 percent support, a level shared by MOLIRENA and the Arnulfistas.[10] Most of the opposition, with the conspicuous exception of Papa Egoro, has joined together in an opposition bloc but has been unable to offer real alternatives to administration projects. Prospects for the 1999 elections are cloudy at best. President Pérez Balladares is prohibited from running for reelection, and the PRD has no leader approaching his status. The Arnulfistas may again run their founder's widow, Mireya Moscoso de Gruber, despite her lack of visible qualifications. If Blades remains aloof from politics, as seems likely, then Mrs. Gruber will probably be the only 1994 candidate who will run again. No figure is emerging who seems able either to garner broad popular support or to unite the fractious opposition.

Forging electoral alliances, bargaining away positions on the ticket and in future cabinets, and uniting more in opposition to some individual or party rather than in favor of any positive program have long been characteristic of the political process. As the 1994 elections approached, there was frantic maneuvering among the parties to forge alliances that would enhance prospects of victory while promising the most political rewards for each individual party. Only Rubén Blades and his Papa

Egoro movement remained firmly aloof from this process, declaring that, in response to growing popular rejection of this practice, they would make no deals or alliances.

In 1994 most of the proposed alliances ultimately collapsed. Since then there have been numerous efforts to create alliances among anti-PRD parties, while the government has formed a working arrangement with the Solidarity Party. Papa Egoro continues to shun all such arrangements. There seems no reason to believe that the process of political fragmentation in Panama is coming to an end. Transactional politics, negotiating and breaking alliances, often with little regard to ideology, remains a dominant characteristic of the system.

The resurgence of the PRD in 1994 was sufficient to give it control of the government, but it does not seem to be able to achieve majority status.[11] Throughout the electoral campaign, the PRD tried to distance itself from the Noriega regime, stressing, instead, its loyalty to the heritage of General Torrijos. It also modified its criticism of the United States (although it still condemns the 1989 invasion), adopted a more conciliatory tone in dealing with other parties, and declared that it had no plans to recreate a regular military force. Since taking power its actions have generally confirmed these positions. But deep-seated suspicions and animosities remain. The PRD's ranks still include many directly associated with the abuses and corruption of the 1980s. Its protestations of democratic values are given little credibility by other political sectors. And, by its appeal to the poorer, generally nonwhite elements of the population, it arouses fear of renewed class and racial tensions. Freed from its past heritage of military dominance, the PRD now has the potential to become an effective, independent political force. But to do so it will have to deal with the heritage of corruption within its own ranks and also reduce the high levels of distrust it engenders in other sectors of the political spectrum. This will require extremely strong leadership from President Pérez Balladares, but that, in turn, risks charges of arbitrary, even authoritarian, rule on his part. How well he manages to steer the ship of state between these two political reefs will go far in determining the nation's political future.

The proliferation of weapons and the rise of private security forces have led many Panamanians to fear a return to violence in the streets as a part of the political process. Panamanian history provides some grounds for such fears, and it is clear that some of the security forces have political ties, notably to the Arnulfistas or to the PRD. But to date there has been little evidence of a rise in this type of violence. Should the PRD's power be threatened, this danger might increase, but, for the moment at least, Panama has made real progress in reducing the level of violence related to the political process.

Of greater concern to most Panamanians is the sharp increase in ordinary crime, coupled with a rising problem of domestic narcotics use.

While the activities of international narcotics dealers either operating within or transiting through Panama have long been a subject of serious concern, and were an important element in the Bush administration's 1989 decision in favor of military intervention, domestic usage and drug-related crimes have become a much greater problem since 1990. In recognition of this, Pérez Balladares made crime fighting a major theme in his inaugural address.

Prisons are badly overcrowded, with up to 90 percent of those incarcerated still awaiting trial. Many have been detained without trial for periods longer than the applicable sentences for the crimes of which they are accused.[12] Even prominent cases often suffer intolerable delays. It was not until 1993 that the system even began seriously to address the bulk of cases involving Noriega associates imprisoned since the 1989 invasion.

All of this contributes to a general lack of faith in the judicial system, especially among poorer Panamanians who see it as offering them neither security nor justice. The Roman Catholic vicar of the Darién province expressed the problem succinctly when he observed: "Those who are in jail, many of them are guilty of something, but there are guilty persons who never go to jail in this country. There are persons who have influence and, before and after the invasion, have continued with their illegal practices."[13]

The problems in the justice system reflect the deep class, ethnic, and racial divisions in Panamanian society. For decades before the 1968 establishment of military rule, Panama was dominated by a small interlinked elite of families of European descent. Known as *rabiblancos* (literally, whitetails), they controlled the major parties, the economy outside of the Canal, and the media. While the more than twenty-one years of military-dominated governments produced human rights abuses and set back the democratic political process, they did give nonwhite Panamanians increased access to and identification with the government. To many of these people, the Endara administration and most of the political parties associated with it represented a return to *rabiblanco* dominance. Even though much of its leadership has ties to the *rabiblanco* class, the PRD was able to play on this resentment, facilitating its political revival. But neither the PRD nor any of its major rivals has come up with credible scenarios for dealing with the problems of Panama's poor.

Panama does have some advantages; it is far from overpopulated and still has available land for agricultural development. The service-based nature of its economy can more easily adapt to changes in the world economy. Educational levels are relatively high. But income distribution is severely skewed, unemployment remains high, and class divisions tend to run along racial lines. The heart of the problem lies in the Panama-Colon metropolitan areas, and to date no political faction has demonstrated either the will or capacity to confront this situation.

Conclusion

The result of all these factors is a political system whose health is clearly suspect and whose legitimacy is increasingly questioned. The Panamanian Bishops Conference summarized these problems early in 1993 when they issued a lengthy critique of the political situation, noting in part:

> (a) We perceive, as is obvious to everyone, a climate of frustration and confusion. In general, the aspirations of well being and social peace have not been fulfilled and a wave of accusations, conflicts and disputes, which undermine the trust of the population, even among government officials, has been unleashed.
>
> (b) Although statistics indicate a significant economic growth rate, it is obvious that the benefits are not reaching the core of Panama, that is, small farmers, peasants, and Indian peoples.[14]

Panama has made important progress toward democracy in the years since the intervention. The fact that the 1994 elections were widely accepted as free, fair, open, and not subject to significant degrees of foreign influence represents a step forward in the nation's evolution toward a more democratic state and society. Few want a return to the past, and the great majority clearly prefer a peaceful political process to one dominated by force and violence. In the words of former vice-president Ricardo Arias Calderón, "Panama is a transactional, not a confrontational society."[15] But Panama is also a society that is finding it difficult to escape the psychological heritage of years of authoritarian rule. The population is cynical about politics in general, seeing parties and elections as a means of gaining jobs and other favors rather than an effective way of confronting the problems of the nation as a whole. This means party loyalties and votes are often determined by trying to guess who the likely winner will be, then quickly joining with that faction. Alliances are made to gain benefits, and if the benefits are not sufficient, then they are quickly cast aside. The media is successful in undermining the public image of various individuals and groups, but has shown no real ability to marshal support in favor of any positive program.

Panama's 1994 election had a special importance, since the administration inaugurated in September 1994 will be responsible for managing the transfer of the Canal and extensive related properties from the United States to Panama. Most Panamanians recognize that their success or failure in dealing with this will play a determinant role in shaping the nation's economic and political future. The Canal's importance in international commerce is declining, its infrastructure is aging and in need of major modernization, and competition from alternative transit routes, the so-called dry canals, is growing. For the Canal to be viable well into the next century, Panama needs to develop a series of related enterprises providing maritime services, facilitating cargo transfer between vessels and between sea and air terminals. The ecology must be protected, the nation's communication network must be significantly modernized and expanded, and decisions on such basic improvements as widening and installing a second set of locks must be made and, where feasible, implemented quickly. Mechanisms for dealing with this situation have been created, notably a nonpartisan board known as the Inter-Oceanic Regional Authority (ARI) charged with administering the reverted areas. They have hired an administrator and done some planning, but to date they lack the authority and support necessary to pursue their tasks. Public confidence in the ARI seems to be declining, and disputes within its ranks are increasing. International interest in and funds for Canal projects are diminishing, and it will take decisive leadership by the Panamanian government to make significant progress in these areas.[16]

Panama's current administration has shown signs of recognizing the necessity of building a broad consensus in dealing with the future of the Canal and related areas. But charges of political manipulation of the ARI and squabbles over the division of spoils from the reverted areas are increasing. Given the extent to which the political landscape represents a continuation of past patterns of fragmentation and the pursuit of personal and family interests, combined with the high levels of public cynicism regarding the process as a whole, the prospect that the government will be able to deal successfully with the development of the reverted areas and lay a foundation for future economic prosperity are clouded at best. The same judgment can be applied to the ability of the president to maintain control over Congress or even over his own increasingly divided party. In one sense, Panama's problems pale when compared to those of such nearby states as Nicaragua, Guatemala, El Salvador, or even Colombia. But, in another sense, the prospect that this "transactional society" could so easily deal away its best hopes for a prosperous and peaceful future should be the subject of serious concern beyond as well as within its borders.

7

Caribbean Democracy: Decay or Renewal?

Trevor Munroe

The formal institutions, political behavior, and cultural values of democratic governance have relatively deep roots and a long tradition in the Commonwealth Caribbean. Liberal democracy emerged in the aftermath of popular protest in the 1940s and 1950s. The period of decolonization saw the consolidation of the system based on a version of party clientelism and state welfarism that improved the standard of living of the people and facilitated upward social mobility of the underclasses. On this foundation, the postcolonial state, democracy, and constitutional government retained significant legitimacy among the people and performed effectively until the beginning of the 1970s.

Between the Black Power revolt in Trinidad in 1970 and the implosion of the Grenada revolution in 1983, significant social sectors in the region turned toward radical Left alternatives within and outside the framework of liberal democracy and market-driven economies. The successive administrations headed by Michael Manley in Jamaica (1972–80), the People's Revolutionary government in Grenada (1979–83), and the Forbes Burnham government in Guyana represented the highest development (and also the deformation) of these tendencies in the Commonwealth Caribbean. This turn to the Left was influenced by the reality as well as the perception that the democratic governance and state interventionist market economies of the 1960s in the region had deepened, rather than reduced, economic and social inequalities. In this context, the underclasses, the black majority, and the youth benefited less than minority social sectors from the economic growth and social development in the postwar period. Dissatisfaction led to social protest and civil commotion. Reinforced by a global context friendly to anti-imperialism and statism, socialist currents in the Commonwealth Caribbean showed a relative vitality not far out of step with significant tendencies in the third world of the 1970s.

At the outset of the 1980s, majority opinion, as a result of a combination of factors, shifted away from leftist radicalism. Among the more important of these were worsening economic conditions, heightened internal social political conflict, and an international climate increasingly hostile to statism of whatever variety and aggressively promotive of economic liberalization. International Monetary Fund (IMF) structural adjustment agreements and World Bank stabilization programs, initiated in the 1970s, became generalized throughout the Caribbean in the 1980s. This turn to market-driven economics and the rejection of socialism has been accompanied by a mixed record of performance. In general, rates of economic decline were reduced; low-income employment increased; rates of inflation in general dropped; and party political tension and confrontation abated. At the same time, social expenditures fell, debt grew, external aid steadily declined, and, most of all, inequalities again deepened by the end of the 1980s. In sum, under both Left and Right dispensations, the people of the Commonwealth Caribbean have experienced either no significant improvement, declines in standard of living, or some deterioration in the quality of life over the past two decades.

Within this general framework, there has nevertheless been some differentiation between the performance of the larger Commonwealth Caribbean territories and the smaller states (particularly those grouped within the OECS, Organization of Eastern Caribbean States). The latter have done relatively well in comparison to the former in relation to growth, inflation, unemployment, and indebtedness. For example, in 1990 the territories in the region that experienced double-digit inflation were Jamaica, Trinidad and Tobago, and Guyana. In that year as well, these more developed countries (MDCs), including Barbados, also experienced overall negative growth, while the less developed countries (LDCs) continued to experience moderate growth. Debt service ratios in the latter were well below 5 percent, while in the more populous territories it averaged about 20 percent.

Post–cold war democratic governance in the Commonwealth Caribbean can therefore be said to have arisen on a mixed foundation. On the one hand, the region's people have actively participated in more than a hundred national elections based on adult suffrage and given varying degrees of support to more than 130 parties and movements in the period of decolonization and postcolonial development. Military rule was unknown; revolution and extraconstitutional changes of administration were confined to Grenada in 1979 and 1983; one-party regimes were rare. Competitive party systems and constitutional government—popular attachment to freedom and justice—both survived alive and relatively well into the end of the 1980s. At the same time, so did more IMF and World Bank programs per capita than perhaps in any other region in the world. Hence while popular expectations of the state and of the political system remain relatively high, the role of the state has changed and its capacity to deliver has declined. Concurrently the private sector is at best displaying a mixed record in taking the lead to bring about economic growth with social equity. In this context, constitutional democratic governance in the Commonwealth Caribbean, long institutionalized and deeply legitimated, is undoubtedly in malaise and very probably in a process of decay.

Electoral Process and Problems

One clear indicator of malaise and decay is the state of the electoral process in the region. Traditionally, rates of voter turnout have been among the more important measures of confidence in the effectiveness of the Caribbean political system and of the faith of the people in the capacity of government to perform. Conversely, significant decline in rates of electoral participation often signals trouble and occasionally, in specific circumstances, a turn to nonelectoral forms of manifesting popular disaffection. This is the case, for example, in Grenada. The turnout in the 1976 election (65.3 percent), the eve of the 1979 popular insurrection, was significantly below rates of participation in elections going back to the early 1960s and below the average participation in elections from the inception of adult suffrage in 1951. In Trinidad and Tobago, the Black Power revolt of 1970 was preceded by elections in 1966 in which electoral turnout was lower than in any previous election except for the first vote under adult suffrage in 1946.

In this context, popular participation in national elections across the Commonwealth Caribbean reveals a remarkably uniform pattern, despite the continuing diversity from one territory to another. In ten of the thirteen territories in which general elections have so far (until August 1995) been held in the 1990s, voter turnout has registered a decline when compared to the average for the 1980s.[1] In Jamaica the decline in turnout in the March 1993 election represented almost 30 percent of the average turnout in the 1980s elections, whereas in Grenada the equivalent of 20 percent of the turnout in the 1984 election did not participate in the 1990 vote. In other territories the decline has been noteworthy but less dramatic.

The significance of this incipient trend increases when examined against the turnout profile in the period of modern political development in the Commonwealth Caribbean. With few exceptions, across the region, rates of participation in the 1980s were lower than in the 1970s. In only two territories, St. Vincent and Grenada, did participation peak in the 1980s. In nine others participation peaked in the 1970s, and in one, Trinidad and Tobago, in the 1960s. In other words, electoral turnout in the Commonwealth Caribbean has been on the decline from the 1980s and the trend has continued into the 1990s. In fact, the average turnout across the region so far in this decade appears lower than that of forty years ago when adult suffrage and democratic elections were new to the Caribbean and popular involvement relatively limited.

The data, were it readily available for the region as a whole, would probably reveal other trends, consistent with declining voter turnout, which have certainly been confirmed. In the Jamaican experience, non-registration levels, particularly among the youth, have increased; the age cohort from which election candidates and members of parliament are drawn is rising and becoming more out of step with the profile of the electorate. Among those who do participate in elections, voting on the basis of party loyalism has declined dramatically. Public interest in parliamentary proceedings has dropped significantly, and the frequency of parliamentary sittings leaves much to be desired. Undoubtedly, the inability of the state, under conditions of significant downsizing and of economic liberalization, to deliver levels of welfare typical of the 1950s–1970s is undermining both its effectiveness and legitimacy.

The decline in largesse at the disposal of the state has also significantly weakened the Commonwealth Caribbean's political parties. In the years of decolonization, an expanding regional economy and a retreating colonial power provided the basis for party-union coalitions, in the main led by elements from the middle class, to develop and sustain mass support on populist foundations. By the 1980s, patron-client relations premised on partisan distribution of scarce benefits underpinned the loyalty of significant sections of the electorate to one or another established political party in each territory. For the majority, commitment to ideology and program was secondary. In any event, by the end of the 1980s significant programmatic and other differences among regional parties had more or less disappeared.

Despite continued populist orientations, convergence on Center-Right platforms around market-driven prescriptions coincided with declining party access to scarce benefits as economies stagnated and the state liberalized. Hence, by the 1990s, the various designations of the region's parties—"labour," "national," "democratic"—reflected, if anything, historical rather than contemporary differences. Typically, the political party, whatever the label, is now a multiclass coalition, funded largely by big business interests, led by the middle class, and seeking to sustain popular electoral support with declining resources. In two territories, Trinidad and Tobago and Guyana, the two main contending parties are based substantially on divergences between the African and Indian ethnic groups.

Growing popular apathy, alienation, and disaffection are fueled by both the appearance and the reality of self-seeking, corrupt, and partisan abuse of political power. In the Bahamas (1984), Antigua (1990), Jamaica (1991), St. Kitts (1990s) (as well as the Turks and Caicos Islands, a British dependency), government ministers or major party leaders have been judicially implicated or convicted of involvement in illegal corruption. In Jamaica, in 1990, 1992, and 1993 the salaries and allowances of the members of both the legislature and the executive were substantially increased while the working population had to cope with wage restraint and the society with IMF-related austerity programs. Moreover, in a situation of scarce and often declining resources, public funds and the award of government contracts have been used to reward party "clients" in all social classes. More often than not, calls for reform, even from within sectors of the state itself, have fallen on deaf ears and produced little or no change in wasteful, inefficient, and corrupt expenditure from the national budget, thereby further eroding the legitimacy of the system.

Criticism of such abuses is limited from within the structures of governance and invariably ineffective, though growing from the institutions of civil society. One important block to within-system reform lies in the nature of executive-legislative relations in the Commonwealth Caribbean parliamentary-type democracies. In each territory, significant percentages of the members of the legislature are also members of the executive and thereby constitutionally obligated to support the executive on important issues.

On a regionwide scale, for every one member of parliament who is in the cabinet, there are only two who are not. In three cases, Dominica, Montserrat, and St. Kitts, the imbalance in executive-legislature proportions is carried to the extreme whereby more members of the legislature are actually in the executive than outside it. Put another way, almost one-third of the legislatures' members are in effect constitutionally debarred from an independent and critical stance in relation to the executive. Moreover, the power of the executive and of the prime minister in particular over the candidacy, the electoral fortunes, and the legislative tenure of the parliamentary members of the governing party reinforces the subordinate nature of the legislature in relation to the executive. The combination rather than the separation of powers between the executive and the legislature is carried to an extreme in the Commonwealth Caribbean, even as far as parliamentary systems are concerned.

The legislative opposition, for its part, is often tainted with malperformance (having been itself the government previously, in the not-too-distant past), corruption, or partisan self-interest. The ineffectiveness of the opposition is compounded by its underrepresentation in the legislature vis-à-vis its proportion of the popular vote. The "first-past-the-post" electoral system in the Commonwealth Caribbean operates to ensure "an almost unbroken pattern of disproportionality in the relationship between seats and votes won, always in favour of the winning party. Losing parties (and independents) relatedly are disadvantaged as they routinely receive shares of seats significantly lower than their share of votes."[2] Majority parties thereby are reinforced in their confidence that a major theoretical advantage of the parliamentary system—

the legislature's ability to terminate the life of the executive by a vote of "no confidence"—will rarely materialize in parliaments wherein the executive has disproportionately large majorities. Not surprisingly, only three of the roughly one hundred Caribbean governments elected by the first-past-the-post electoral system in the last forty years have fallen as a result of loss of parliamentary majority. The electoral system operates to make the executive "safe" from the ultimate sanction of parliamentary government and to render the vote of the parliamentary opposition less numerous than its presence in the electorate would justify. Indeed, the potential of this disproportion to contribute to opposition discontent and political instability showed itself dramatically in the results of the December 1993 elections in St. Kitts, where the opposition St. Kitts Labour Party received a majority of the popular vote but not a clear majority of the parliamentary seats and was not called upon to form the government.

This electoral system operates even more effectively to keep independent candidates, new parties, and minority tendencies with some national support but no concentrated geographical, constituency base from gaining parliamentary representation. Indeed, the knowledge that the electoral system operates in this fashion is very often enough to ensure that minor tendencies or independent candidates do not enter the electoral arena. The armed insurrection and seizure of the Parliament by the Jamaat-al-Muslimeen religious sect in Trinidad and Tobago in 1990 was no doubt fueled by the perception of the inability to gain effective redress of grievances through existing or independent parliamentary representation. In other territories—in particular, in Jamaica—the relatively closed first-past-the-post electoral system is rendered even more impervious to minority tendencies by varying combinations of violence, force, and fraud. The mobilization of civil society, nationally and internationally, to pressure the executive and to correct electoral malpractice achieved significant gains in Guyana. In Jamaica the issue remains in the balance and provides an important test of the relative power of the state and of civil society in the region.

The Process of Democratic Governance

In this latter regard the media are becoming of increasing significance in the process of democratic governance. The communication profile of the region indicates that the population of the Commonwealth Caribbean has significantly higher access to radios and to television than the average levels for developing countries. In fact there are more than three times as many radios and televisions per capita in the Caribbean than elsewhere in the third world. Moreover, the global average is below that of the region. The significant incidence of cable TV and of satellite dish receivers adds to the means of communication, information, entertainment, and opinion formation available to the population. The alienation of significant segments of the electorate from the political system, the decline in party loyalism, and the growth of issue-oriented public opinion find expression in the relatively dense media network. At the same time, the independent media, primarily through "talk shows" and newspaper columnists which have grown significantly, particularly in Jamaica, provide an increasingly important means of democratic expression as well as a source of public pressure on state authority. Indeed, the quality of this aspect of popular culture is in many ways ahead of the traditional political culture.

These media have provided major mechanisms for the exposure not only of electoral abuses but, more broadly, the violation of human rights in the region. The major area of such abuse relates to the integrity of the person and in particular the gross misuse of police authority. In this regard, the *Country Reports on Human Rights Practices for 1992*, compiled by the U.S. Department of State, identified such abuses (or "credible" charges of violations) in ten of twelve Commonwealth Caribbean countries examined in the review. Allegations of police brutality, of beatings of suspects by prison officials, and of summary executions by security officers are recorded in one territory after another. In Jamaica, the most extreme case in the region, in the first nine months of 1992, 107 people were shot and killed by the police, thirty-three police were charged with murder, and conditions in maximum security prisons and lockups were described as "abysmal." In one instance, on October 22, 1992, the Jamaican police

> rounded up more than a hundred men and sent many of them to the Constant Spring police station lock-up; they were apparently being held only for identification and not upon any specific charge. Nineteen of them were herded into a cell eight by seven feet that had a solid door with holes drilled through as the only source of ventilation. At one point, when the men were led out of the cell for a short time, some of them refused to return; one man said that he had only one lung and could not breathe in the cell. The police forced the men back into the cell with beatings, and then did not let them out again. . . . The men were detained in the cell for a total of 40 hours, and three of them died of asphyxiation. Those detained beat on the door and clamoured to be let out, but the police did nothing.[3]

Public protest and outcry through the national media led to charges being brought against several police officers.

Though the Jamaican case is extreme, throughout the region much disaffection with democratic governance and significant alienation from the political system, particularly among inner-city youth, derives from the unacceptable incidence of police abuse of human rights. This serious problem is compounded by widespread belief that not only politicians but the police force itself is corrupt. A management review undertaken in mid-1991 of the Jamaican police by a team of police officers from the United Kingdom confirmed "the growing and popular perception that there was widespread corruption within the JCF [Jamaican Constabulary Force]," but "because of the limited time available," the team was unable to pursue such allegations "in depth."[4]

The situation was, however, quite different in relation to Trinidad and Tobago. Public outcry in response to allegations against the police became so compelling that the government of Trinidad and Tobago called in officers of the United Kingdom New Scotland Yard to investigate the charges. The report laid on the table of the Trinidadian Parliament on December 10, 1993, is worth quoting at some length:

> Corruption in the police service can be described as endemic. It permeates all ranks. . . . Clear evidence was obtained showing cash demanded not to execute arrest warrants, not to charge criminal offence, not to give evidence at court, or not to be able to locate the prosecution papers. . . . Corruption . . . also includes the protection of drug dealers, their supplies, and their supply routes. This is where the corrupt core of the police service gets its money.
>
> At the top is direct participation in crime or, more specifically, drug racketeering. Some evidence and some good intelligence suggest that police officers have been involved in the importation of cocaine, in growing marijuana, in transporting drugs, and selling them on. . . . Two corrupt groups were identified which stretched from the top to the bottom of the organization.[5]

There is good reason to believe that Trinidad and Tobago is not unique in the Commonwealth Caribbean in respect to corruption in the police force.

The problem with the justice system goes beyond police corruption and police abuse of citizens' rights. Other symptoms of deterioration are "run down physical facilities, increasing delays in processing of cases as growing demands on the system outstrip the capacity of staff and facilities, reduced quality of personnel as worsening work conditions and declining salaries in real terms diminish ability to attract and keep qualified professionals."[6] The consequence of this is growing malaise in the regional justice system, which, particularly in the period of decolonization, has been one of the stronger foundations of democratic governance in the Caribbean. The malaise becomes all the more negative in its consequences as it coincides with increases in crime rates, particularly involving the use of violence against person and property. Violent crime has been disproportionately the province of the youth and reflects more than any other factor the growth of frustration with lack of opportunity and with growing socioeconomic inequities accompanying economic liberalization.

This situation has created a new environment for labor and capital. The latter, freed from state regulation, the beneficiary of privatization, and, often as well, reduced rates of taxation, is in a relatively advantageous position. Labor, on the other hand, throughout the region, has experienced cumulative negative effects of currency devaluation, wage guidelines, and layoffs. By and large, labor organizations have been critical of structural adjustment programs and have been weakened by an overall macroeconomic policy that has transferred resources to capital. The Commonwealth Caribbean trade unions have not, however, suffered the level of subordination that has occurred in other regions of the third world. There has been no significant deunionization nor formal restriction on union rights (beyond wage guidelines). Legislation safeguarding workers' rights has remained, minimum wages have been sustained, and collective bargaining on behalf of labor maintained.

As such, Caribbean unions have undoubtedly managed to avoid the extremes of illegalization and suppression that have sometimes accompanied economic liberalization under some authoritarian third world regimes. One important reason for this lies in the central role played by labor and trade unions in the process of decolonization and state formation in the region. Independence in the 1960s and 1970s arose directly, though not only, from the working-class action and organization of the 1930s and 1940s. Historically, Caribbean unions have not so much been special interests as vital parts of national coalitions. The constitutions, laws, political culture, and industrial relations systems (as well as other labor market institutions) of the postcolonial state accorded trade unions special recognition compared to other countries in the hemisphere, including the United States.

On the other hand, there has been limited or no unionization in the new wage-employment sectors created by export-oriented industrialization policies. Despite being formally covered by labor laws guaranteeing workers the right of free association, very few firms in the export-processing zones across the region have been unionized. In the OECS countries, "only a tiny minority of enclave companies . . . are unionized. The majority rely on intimidatory or paternalistic industrial relations or some combination of the two to keep the workforce in line. With the complicity of the government, some companies are able to stamp out actual or potential union organization of the workforce, using methods which clearly violate national labour laws."[7] Throughout the region as a whole, reflecting a shift in the balance of power, "unilateral actions by employers in matters of layoffs, retrenchment and changes in working conditions without discussion or consultation with workers or their organizations, have become not uncommon experiences in . . . recent years."[8]

Labor's response to this situation has taken traditional as well as relatively novel forms. One stock response has been to resort to industrial action. In major Caribbean Common Market (CARICOM) states, such as Jamaica, Trinidad, Barbados, and Guyana, the 1990s began with significant production time lost because of industrial action, especially disaffection stemming from inadequate wage offers and impending layoffs. Another has been the tendency in rank-and-file labor to take positions on economic and national issues independent of the established parties. The latter are regarded as paying insufficient attention to the interests of workers and of the poor in the elaboration and implementation of structural adjustment programs. This growing tendency in the working class has contributed to the trade unions developing greater independence of political parties even when formally retaining traditional political affiliations. The weakening of partisan political connections has often been accompanied by efforts at more effective joint action and even joint organization among labor unions that nevertheless preserve competitive relations. The established political parties can no longer rely in the old way on affiliated unions to deliver their members as part of the working-class vote in national elections. Labor is increasingly in the ranks of independent, issue-oriented voters or among the growing ranks of nonvoters alienated by one or another aspect of the contemporary malaise in democratic governance.

In this context the trade unions have been slow in coming up with alternatives to the mode of economic liberalization prevailing in the region. Their main energies have been largely consumed in defensive actions aimed at cushioning the impact on the unionized working class of public sector "downsizing," divestment, and privatization programs. Negotiation of significant retrenchment settlements packages has been a primary activity, where layoffs have not been avoided. More generally, the traditional focus on collective bargaining, at both enterprise and industrywide levels, has continued and helped limit short-run negative consequences of liberalization on the unionized labor force. The unions are now more fully recognizing that such defensive actions may be necessary but are certainly insufficient. Hence there are increasing efforts to develop, within the general framework of economic liberalization, alternative approaches more sensitive to the needs of labor on such issues as trade liberalization, the "social contract," wages and incomes policies, taxation, employee share ownership, and housing.

The picture that therefore presents itself is one in which the people of the Commonwealth Caribbean retain commitment to the values of freedom and justice. Indeed, the democratic character of civil society, nurtured by a relatively independent media, facilitated by a self-confident generation of postcolonial youth, and reflected in the growth of nongovernmental organizations (NGOs), is being strengthened. At the same time, nonparticipation in elections and alienation from established political parties and state authorities have grown as socioeconomic inequities, official corruption, and social decay deepen. The people's loyalty to democratic governance in the Commonwealth Caribbean is being severely tested. Against this background, the midterm prospects present a choice between fundamental transformations leading to democratic renewal on the one hand and, on the other, continued slide into sociopolitical decay, ultimately undermining the democratic foundation of the system.

Obstacles to Reform

There are a number of serious obstacles in the way of radical reform and democratic renewal. One such is a constitutional system that, throughout the region, places excessive power in the hands of the executive, in particular in that of the office of the prime minister. The converse of this overconcentration of power are legislatures that are ineffective and electorates that have little institutional means of influencing policy between elections. In its most extreme form, this system allows constitutional dictatorship such as manifested itself in the Eric Gairy regimes of the 1970s and that can lead to extraconstitutional, revolutionary action such as undertaken by the New Jewel Movement in Grenada in the late 1970s.

Some awareness of the self-defeating nature of excessive executive power and of the danger of its associated constitutional systems is evident in the political and social elite of the region. The incidence within recent times of the appointment of commissions to review constitutions and to recommend appropriate reforms of governance bear testimony to this recognition. In some instances, radical proposals have come from such relatively respectable, official quarters in attempts to come to grips with the dominance of the executive, the dependence of legislatures, and the disempowerment of the people. Among these have been proposals to modify constitutions to allow for real separation of powers between the main branches of governance, the modification of the electoral system from first-past-the-post to some variety of mixed or proportional representation, and the recognition of the right of citizens to recall nonperforming members of the legislature.[9]

Very often, evidence suggests significant popular support for some of the recommendations that would represent a real break with traditions of overcentralized power. As such, the proposals for change, by broadening and deepening the democratic channels available to the people, would loosen the grip of the postcolonial political and business elites on the system as well as open up possibilities for new individuals, groups, parties, and movements to gain electoral access to power. By and large, however, the established political elite has rejected radical reform and opted for cosmetic change in the constitutional order. Vested interest in existing arrangements among major party leaders remains, at least for the immediate future, greater than disquiet at growing popular disaffection and, hence, stronger than the impulse to change the prevailing order. To the extent that alienation, abstention, and discontent grow and take obviously harmful, negative forms, to that extent the conservative rigidity of the political elite may diminish as an obstacle to change.

A second hindrance is the as yet underdeveloped level of civil society, despite recent growth. Labor organizations have yet, despite promising beginnings, to detach themselves fully from partisan political affiliation, an important precondition for the development of more effective labor lobbies. Women's groups and youth organizations are even less developed as independent pressure groups. Professional associations, service clubs, the church, and other civic bodies are only now shedding tendencies to be nonpolitical and beginning to focus more pointedly on issues of democratic governance. In this regard, a major concern in these sectors has to do with reducing rampant corruption and redressing socioeconomic inequities, the growth of which is obviously contributing to unacceptable levels of crime, drug abuse, and social tension.

In improving the effectiveness of civil society as a pressure lever for the renewal of democratic governance, the involvement of the international community is proving of continuing importance. The most dramatic recent manifestation of this is related to the October 1992 general elections in Guyana. These would not have been relatively fair and free had not international organizations and pressure of varied forms not reinforced the determination of significant segments of the Guyanese community to clean up the electoral system. The insistence of strategically placed elements of the national community (e.g., the church, the private sector), the persistence of reform demands from the parliamentary opposition, alliance or at least cooperation between the NGO community and the official opposition, as well as obvious popular support for change would appear to have been the main elements facilitating successful international involvement in Guyanese electoral reform. It is likely that similar pressure is going to be required in Jamaica if the thuggery of the 1993 and previous elections is not to repeat itself and if Jamaican civil society is to prevail against a constitutional-electoral order designed to preserve a two-party monopoly against all comers. If the channels of democratic expression are insufficiently cleansed and extended beyond admittedly crucial mass media, disaffection and socially deleterious consequences are bound to continue to grow.

A third obstacle to the preservation and strengthening of democratic governance lies in the model of economic liberalization being applied in the region. By and large this continues to be in the dogmatic, laissez-faire 1980s mode of the Bush-Reagan-Thatcher era. The redress of economic imbalances in the internal and external accounts as well as economic structures of the region is not displaying sufficient regard for past errors or for Caribbean peculiarities. The reality is that the deep support for democratic governance in the Commonwealth Caribbean has grown not only as a result of a historically favorable political culture but also as a result of the successes of statism in the 1950s and 1960s. At the same time, the traditional private sector in the region remains ill-equipped to plunge into the global marketplace suddenly bereft of state assistance in any form. Across-the-board downsizing of the state, including severe cutbacks in expenditure on the social sector, in the context of a private sector at best slow in filling the gap, is a major impediment to the preservation, much less the deepening, of democracy.

The realization that concern with social reform cannot *follow* but has to coincide with economic growth and structural adjustment needs to reflect itself more obviously in the terms and application of agreements between regional governments and the international financial institutions. The idea that the state must be so downsized as to make it stronger, not weaker, in its role as facilitator is not getting through sufficiently to the stage of practical policy implementation. Hence, very often, systems of revenue collection, justice, and vocational training for young people, to name three areas, are often weakened instead of strengthened in the process of economic liberalization and of structural adjustment. In this context, insufficient social responsibility and economic dynamism in much of the traditional private sector is contributing to the problem. Current macroeconomic policies are effecting a massive transfer of economic power and of national income to segments of the private sector. Popular criticism of big business is bound to grow if expansion of investment, production, employment, and social philanthropy concomitant with increased wealth remains insufficiently evident. Moreover, private sector shortsighted self-interest is often accompanied by weak vocal support for political and social reform.

Halting the malaise and deepening democracy in the region is therefore going to require urgent action on the constitutional, political, and economic fronts. Paradoxically, post–cold war circumstances will tend to make the reform agenda less compelling to powerful interests. There is no "communist threat" to encourage significant aid flows from the United States or flexibility in harsh liberalization programs from the multilateral agencies. Revolutionary Left tendencies, or at any rate those based on the traditional Left, are weak throughout the region; hence the prospect of organized civil commotion or popular insurrection is limited in the eyes of the regional elites. Popular alienation and discontent, should the reform agenda not advance, are likely nevertheless to take disruptive forms. One such is the further development of narcotics-related crime and violence not only in the inner cities of the Commonwealth Caribbean but also of North America as flows of illegal migration grow in response to restricted opportunity in the region. Another is increased vulnerability of Caribbean state authorities (with implications for U.S. interests) to subversion by drug-related cartels as corruption grows in the establishment and cynicism deepens alongside apathy among the people. There are fair prospects that the course of decay may be avoided, but it shall require concerted, sustained action on a reform agenda by the coalition of forces with an interest in the preservation and deepening of Caribbean democracy.

My own view is that such coalitions are emerging but much too slowly to prevent further short-run decay in the system and to provide increasingly alienated populations with any significant hope. The main preconditions and requisites are fairly clear. Labor unions and lobbies need to strengthen their independence of political parties and broaden their agenda of concern beyond the workplace to other disadvantaged social groups. The private sector, particularly newly emergent segments of medium and small business, need to act with greater social responsibility and be more vocal on issues of democratic governance. The church, the media, and community organizations need to be encouraged to more consistent civic action around issues of employment, inner-city rehabilitation, skills-training for youth, and political accountability. Independent and more democratic tendencies within the political parties need to ensure their survival and increased activity. Each of these, and other tendencies, is apparent. Their development can and will be speeded up by leadership that is credible, consistent, and courageous. Ultimately, sectoral, national, and regional coalitions for renewal are called for. The platform needs to stress deepening political accountability and eliminating corruption, modification of neoliberal economic programs, and reengineering Caribbean democratic governance. The probability is, however, that these platforms and organizations for renewal are likely, unless present trends change, to emerge more slowly than is necessary to halt sociopolitical decay significantly.

8

The Dominican Republic:
An Ambiguous Democracy

Rosario Espinal

For a country the size and geographical location of the Dominican Republic, plagued by adverse socioeconomic conditions and an authoritarian legacy, it is no minor accomplishment that since 1978 the country has been ruled by elected governments. Elections, even if disputed, have been competitive, and on two occasions (1978 and 1986) they led to turnovers. Control of the executive branch has rotated between the Dominican Revolutionary Party (PRD), which ruled between 1978 and 1986, and the Social Christian Reformist Party (PRSC). Likewise, the composition of the legislature, elected every four years in conjunction with the president, has reflected changes in the strength of the three major parties: the PRD, the PRSC, and the Dominican Liberation Party (PLD). This means that in a context of historical and structural adversities, the Dominican Republic has managed to preserve basic democratic procedures from the late 1970s to the mid-1990s, even if progress toward the consolidation of democracy has been disappointing.

To emphasize this paradox—the preservation of basic democratic procedures and the difficulties in expanding and consolidating democracy—is a good point of departure for analyzing the state of democratic governance in the Dominican Republic. This is so because in discussing Dominican politics one should not lose sight of the adverse economic and political conditions (economic inequalities, the authoritarian legacy) under which the democratic process has unfolded.

Put differently, an assessment of the state of democratic governance in the Dominican Republic confronts one with the dilemma of striking a balance between assessing the historical conditions under which democracy has unfolded and the more normative or idealistic standards of democracy. If the emphasis is on the normative elements (what democracy should be), then it can be easily concluded from the discussion that follows that the Dominican Republic hardly deserves the title of a democratic country. If, on the other hand, the emphasis is simply on the existence of basic political procedures, the Dominican Republic could fall into the category of a democratic regime. The argument made here is that these two positions prevent us from understanding the complexities of Dominican politics, in particular, the ways in which democratic practices coexist with nondemocratic practices.

Three main claims help us understand how some democratic practices have been instituted and prevail in an otherwise undemocratic political regime. The first claim is that the civilian nature of authoritarianism under Joaquín Balaguer (1966–78) facilitated the relatively smooth introduction of democratic procedures, such as competitive elections, in the late 1970s. The civilian nature of authoritarianism also helped preserve the continuity of the party system that began to emerge in the early 1960s. The second claim is that in spite of its antidemocratic nature, personalistic leadership in Dominican politics has provided political stability that has helped preserve some democratic gains. The third claim is that the relative stability of the Dominican party system has allowed for alternability and predictability in the governing process in the context of a state that lacks democratization.

Civilian Rule in the Post-Trujillo Period

It should first be noted that since 1966 the Dominican Republic has been ruled by civilian governments. This is not a minor point in a country ruled for thirty years (1930–61) by Rafael Trujillo, a ruthless dictator, and in which the fall of the dictatorship in 1961 brought about political instability, including the fall of a democratically elected government in 1963, a short civil war in 1965, and a U.S. military intervention.

To understand how the Dominican Republic went from the "politics of chaos" of the early 1960s to the relative political stability and democratic practices of the late 1970s, it is important to understand the fundamentals of the Balaguer regime in the late 1960s and early 1970s. During this period, Balaguer presided over a government committed to two main goals: the maintenance of political order and the promotion of economic growth. To maintain political order, the Balaguer government repressed and banned the most radical and vocal opposition of the Left and the labor movement.[1] It curtailed, but did not eliminate, the more moderate opposition represented by the Dominican Revolutionary Party. Balaguer also presided over a major expansion of the Dominican economy. His program, based on incentives to private capital (both domestic and foreign) and massive public investment, particularly in construction, led to the growth and diversification of business and the middle class. Finally, having learned the techniques of political subordination and co-optation from Trujillo, Balaguer succeeded in preventing military takeovers. Not only was he trusted by the military, but he also kept the military involved in politics, either through mobilization against the Left or through clientelistic networks whereby military officers acquired wealth.

As a result, by the mid-1970s the Dominican Republic was a country in which the most militant opposition to the government had been extinguished and the moderate opposition had begun to reorganize itself. It also was a country with a larger middle class willing to engage in politics, either at the idealistic level in the struggle for democracy or with materialistic concerns by taking advantage of the clientelistic machine of the Dominican state.

In 1978 various factors contributed to the democratic transition. First, the PRD, the main opposition party, presented itself as a moderate and viable option: as a party committed to democracy. In its efforts to gain power, it sought international support from the social democrats in Europe and Latin America. Second, the Carter administration's endorsement of a human rights policy was instrumental in preventing a coup when some of Balaguer's followers tried to distort the electoral results that favored the PRD. Third, and very important, Balaguer showed a willingness to concede defeat—to play by the rule of law when faced with the option of remaining in office through electoral fraud. In brief, the democratic transition of 1978 became viable because of (1) a revitalization of party politics with the democratic renewal of the PRD; (2) favorable international conditions; and (3) the decision of a key authoritarian actor (Balaguer) to accept electoral defeat at the presidential level (results at the congressional level were distorted to give Balaguer's party a Senate majority).

The Process of Democratic Governance

From 1978 to the mid-1990s, the various democratically elected governments have faced similar challenges: what democratic reforms to promote, when, and how. The other major challenge has been dealing with the highly adverse economic conditions. Overall, the policy content of the various administrations during the democratic period reflected both the ideology and commitments of the incumbents and the structural limitations in which they have ruled.

During the two PRD administrations (1978–86), there was, comparatively speaking, the greatest commitment to introduce democratic reforms and promote redistributionist economic policies. But, for the most part, the PRD failed on both fronts. On the one hand, the amnesty law of 1979 was a milestone, yet political reforms practically ended there. Moreover, there was no serious attempt to reform the constitution nor to ban reelection, a much-voiced campaign promise of the PRD. On the other hand, pressed by high public deficits and the growing foreign debt, the first PRD administration, headed by Antonio Guzmán, abandoned by late 1980 its commitment to economic redistributionism. Later, the second PRD administration, headed by President Salvador Jorge Blanco, introduced an adjustment program within the terms of an agreement with the International Monetary Fund (IMF). The program was based on wage and fiscal austerity, and led to a recession in the mid-1980s that contributed to the electoral debacle of the PRD in 1986.[2]

Upon returning to power in 1986, Balaguer proclaimed a commitment to the promotion of institutional-democratic reforms, but practically none was delivered. To fight the recessionary effects of the adjustment program previously instituted by the Jorge Blanco administration, Balaguer sought to promote an economic recovery based on massive investments in public works. As a result, inflation soared and discontent mounted. Thus by 1990 Balaguer agreed to adjust the economy within the terms of a standby agreement with the IMF. The result was a dramatic reduction in the rate of inflation from 101 percent in 1990 to 4 percent in 1991, and stability in the exchange rate at about 12.5 pesos to a U.S. dollar. In addition, Balaguer was able to maintain his massive construction program of urban renewal, now financed by a gasoline tax. Politically, unlike the PRD that saw its popularity decline in the mid-1980s, in part as a result of the adjustment program, Balaguer benefited in the early 1990s from macroeconomic stability. Thus, while the 1994 elections were characterized by massive irregularities and negative campaigning, Balaguer was undoubtedly a strong contender due to the relative economic prosperity prevailing in the country.

Electoral Politics

That elections are central to modern democracy is beyond doubt. Elections allow citizens to choose a government from among contenders and provide for the circulation of governing elites. Elections also provide the winner with a sense of legitimacy and a mandate to pursue a course of action based on programmatic principles and electoral promises.

In the Dominican Republic, elections have played the dual and contradictory role of sustaining and undermining democracy. The five elections held between 1978 and 1995 (in 1978, 1982, 1986, 1990, and 1994) have been competitive, and on two occasions (in 1978 and 1986) there was turnover of parties. This contributed to the vitality of party and electoral politics, with elections in 1990 and 1994 being very tight races. Yet all these elections, particularly those of 1978, 1990, and 1994, were highly disputed.

In 1978, followers of the incumbent, Joaquín Balaguer, attempted a coup when it became evident that the PRD was ahead in the electoral count. The resulting impasse led to two months of uncertainty about whether the PRD would be allowed to take office. To end the impasse, the Electoral Board shifted results around in four provinces to grant Balaguer's Reformist Party a majority in the Senate. Short of being completely out of power, the PRD endorsed the results announced by the Electoral Board and proceeded to take over the presidency with a majority in the House of Deputies.

The 1982 elections were less disputed, yet plagued by rivalries between opposing tendencies within the ruling PRD. A major source of controversy was whether the faction in control of the executive would stage fair elections. President Guzmán's reluctance to introduce a bill in Congress banning reelection was viewed by opposing tendencies within his own party as evidence of his intentions to seek reelection. This issue brought about heated debate within the PRD and helped define the cleavages that would plague the PRD in subsequent years and finally lead to the electoral debacle of 1986.

The 1986 elections were also controversial. Intraparty factionalism in the PRD and the late appointment of the Electoral Board contributed to diminish the credibility of the electoral process. In an effort to provide legitimacy to the electoral contest, President Jorge Blanco, at the request of the opposition, appointed a Committee of Notables, headed by the archbishop of Santo Domingo, to oversee the elections. While important in providing an acceptable framework for elections to take place, this ad hoc committee undermined the power of the constitutionally established Electoral Board and left unchanged its dubious reputation.

The 1990 elections were highly disputed. President Balaguer, known in the past for staging unfair elections, did little to constitute a credible Electoral Board. The board president proved to be a controversial figure, with little capacity to mediate among contending factions. The Dominican Liberation Party, experiencing growing popular support, at the outset accused the Balaguer government of staging fraudulent elections. With a close count (35% for Balaguer and 34% for the PLD), and bombarded by accusations of fraud by the PLD, the Electoral Board did a poor job managing the postelection crisis, thus failing to disqualify accusations of fraud by the opposition PLD.[3]

In 1994, controversy over the fairness of the electoral process became the salient issue. Initially it was expected that the 1994 elections would be less disputed than those of 1990. Electoral laws had been reformed, a new Electoral Board had been appointed with the consent of all major parties, a new voting registration system had been instituted, and international technical assistance had been provided to the Electoral Board. In spite of these improvements, three major issues undermined the fairness of the electoral contest. One was the massive use of state resources by the incumbent president. Another was the negative campaigning adopted by President Balaguer against his main opponent, José Francisco Peña Gómez. Taking advantage of the political crisis in Haiti and the flow of Haitian immigrants into the Dominican Republic, Balaguer led a racist campaign, questioning the commitment of Peña Gómez to the Dominican nation.

Yet the main problem that led to electoral disputes in 1994 was the change of names of registered voters on the lists distributed to polling places. As a result, many voters, and it seemed those mostly from the opposition, were not allowed to vote because their names did not appear on the list. Subsequently, international and domestic pressures for a fair count mounted, and in June the Electoral Board set up a verification commission to investigate the complaints of fraud. The commission issued a report in July documenting significant irregularities in the voting lists distributed to polling places, but it did not provide a clear sense of the extent of name replacement nationwide. Neither did it explain how the name replacement had taken place, nor how it had affected the final results of the elections. The commission's report failed therefore to settle the controversy surrounding the postelection crisis of 1994.

In early August the Electoral Board ignored the complaints of fraud and declared Balaguer the winner. International and domestic pressures for a democratic resolution of the crisis continued, and on August 10 Balaguer agreed to sign an accord, the Pact for Democracy, limiting his presidential term to two years, among other constitutional reforms.

Overall, the experiences in five elections indicate that electoral mistrust has been the rule, not the exception, during the democratic period. Delays in the appointment of Electoral Board members, controversial appointees, inadequate funding of the Electoral Board, excessive use of state resources by incumbents, and manipulation of electoral data and results, have prevented elections from becoming an important factor in the consolidation of democracy. What is worse, the problems persisted in 1994 in spite of the reforms made to the electoral laws in 1992, an improved voting registration system, and the massive technical assistance provided to the Electoral Board.

Parties and Their Electoral Strength

During the democratic process the Dominican Republic has witnessed the fragmentation of its two-party system. From 1966 to 1982 there were two major parties: the Social Christian Reformist Party and the Dominican Revolutionary Party. In 1978 the PRD defeated the PRSC in the first truly competitive elections since 1962, with the electorate almost evenly divided between the two parties. By 1982, however, the PLD, led by Juan Bosch, showed signs of growth (the party received 10 percent of the vote, compared to only 1 percent in 1978). Throughout the rest of the decade the PLD continued to grow. In 1986 the PLD received 18% of the vote, and 34% in 1990, when it almost won the elections. Meanwhile, the PRD declined in popularity, and Balaguer retained more than one-third of electoral support. No doubt, then, a divided opposition was crucial for the electoral success of Balaguer, who secured a victory in 1986, in 1990, and in 1994 with only a relative majority and by a small margin.

If a sign of democratic vibrance is change in political leadership, the Dominican Republic falls short. The four main contenders running in the 1994 elections were the same candidates who ran in 1990: Joaquín Balaguer for the PRSC, José F. Peña Gómez for the PRD, Juan Bosch for the PLD, and Jacobo Majluta for the newly formed Independent Revolutionary Party (PRI). Balaguer and Bosch were in their eighties and continued to exercise almost absolute power in their respective parties. The PRD, a party in which historically there had been more democratic participation, rallied behind Peña Gómez, in part to avoid further intraparty rivalry and fragmentation, which in the past had undermined the party's ability to win power. In turn, the leadership of Majluta and the formation of the PRI was the result of Majluta's unmet expectation to secure successive presidential nominations in the PRD after his defeat in the 1986 elections.

Choosing Peña Gómez as presidential candidate for the 1994 elections presented opportunities and problems for the PRD. On the positive side, he was the most popular leader in the PRD. His poor electoral performance in 1990 reflected more the inability of the PRD to select early on a presidential candidate than it did his own weaknesses. Coming late to the race in 1990, Peña Gómez was unable to reconstitute the traditional constituencies of the PRD, which were in disarray after the poor performance of the PRD governments in the early and mid-1980s. In this context, it was expected that Peña Gómez would be nominated again to run in 1994, and that he would do better. In addition, his selection of former Reformist Party leader Fernando Alvarez Bogaert as a vice-presidential candidate provided him with a partner trusted by conservatives, who had always feared Peña Gómez' populist style and socialist leanings.

Yet the nomination of Peña Gómez presented a major liability for the PRD. With the recurrent political crisis in Haiti, the deep-seated fears among many Dominicans of a massive inflow of Haitians into the Dominican Republic, and Balaguer's well-known historic commitment to reinforce that fear, Peña Gómez was vulnerable to racist attacks. Another problem was that he opposed Balaguer at a time of relative economic stability in the country, after a fairly successful implementation of an adjustment program that reduced the fiscal deficit and lowered inflation drastically.

Whether Balaguer truly won the 1994 elections or the victory was secured through fraud are questions that remain empirically unanswered. Irregularities were documented in the report issued by the verification commission, but the impact on the results remained unclear. Neither do we know the impact of the racist campaigning on the electoral results, or how detrimental this was to Peña Gómez. What we do know, based on a poll conducted in November 1994 by Rumbo-Gallup Dominicana, is that 48 percent of those interviewed believed that Peña Gómez received the majority of the votes cast, while only 37 percent thought that Balaguer won.[4]

Party Organization

Since the mid-1960s, the Dominican Republic has shown remarkable stability of its party system. The PRSC, the PRD, and the PLD have dominated party politics. In different forms and degrees, these three parties have relied on charismatic leadership, which has provided unity and ideological consistency to the parties.[5] In this sense, personalism in Dominican politics has provided a context for political stability that has helped preserve some democratic gains. For instance, Balaguer's decision in 1978 to accept the electoral results proved helpful in the regularization of electoral politics. Likewise, the agreement between Balaguer, Peña Gómez, and Bosch that led to the signing of the Pact for Democracy in 1994 was instrumental in maintaining a constitutional government in the context of a precarious electoral outcome. Yet this personalism has also prevented the democratization of political parties and accounts for the limited importance that political parties have attributed to the democratization of the Dominican state. In this regard, it has hampered the process of democratic consolidation.

With the aging of the political leadership, a major challenge Dominican parties face is internal democratization. Both the PRSC and the PLD are characterized by the excessive personalism of Balaguer and Bosch. Yet Balaguer cannot run for reelection in 1996, and Bosch resigned as party president in July 1994. These two parties differ, however, in their organization and objectives. For Balaguer, the party was a loosely organized, clientelistic machine that was mobilized at Balaguer's whim—at election time or whenever Balaguer's leadership was questioned. In this sense, the PRSC was a vehicle to fulfill Balaguer's persistent aspirations to gain or retain state power. For Bosch, the party was not primarily the vehicle to gain state power but the space to educate a group of cadres, providing both moral guidance and political knowledge about politics and Dominican society. The PLD is a highly organized political machine whose main purpose has been to provide political education to its members as instructed by Bosch.

Attempts to organize the PRSC better, which began in the mid-1980s, might prove helpful in a post-Balaguer period in preventing a rapid demise of the party. Also, Balaguer's choice of Jacinto Peynado as a vice-presidential candidate in 1994 was indicative of his willingness to suggest, even if indirectly, a successor. That is, by choosing Peynado, a prominent party leader and congressional representative, Balaguer made a crucial choice in terms of who could succeed him. In this way, he has allowed for some opening and modernization of his party, while at the same time retaining close control. It is worth noting that while Balaguer can be viewed as an autocrat with no truly organized party, he is an extremely skillful politician for whom the preservation of order is very important.

Regarding the PLD, the situation remains uncertain. While Bosch remained committed to purging dissidents until his retirement from the party's presidency in 1994, the party's unity remains fragile as different groups struggle to impose their vision and agenda. Some hope to retain the basic principles of discipline and morality endorsed by Bosch. Others have learned while in office how to practice the "politics of deals," compromising with Balaguer to secure power sharing. While the presidential candidacy of Leonel Fernández embodies the ideals of the first group, the practice of the party cadres in office reflect more their ambitions to rule with Balaguer's help.

The PRD, which through the 1970s and early 1980s made important progress toward establishing a system of democratic participation, with the formation of comités de base and the holding of primaries, retreated by the mid-1980s. The unfortunate party convention in 1985, where the counting of the ballots to elect the presidential candidate was stopped by a violent assault, marked the end of a period of internal democratization that began in 1979 in response to intraparty rivalry and factionalism. Events evolved as follows. In the late 1970s, factionalism in the PRD led to party reforms aimed at democratizing the candidate selection process. These reforms were pushed forward by Jorge Blanco in order to restrict the power of the Guzmán faction, which controlled the executive and was likely to dominate the candidate selection process. By the mid-1980s, however, with Jorge Blanco as president, rampant factionalism in the PRD worked against the democratic reforms that had been instituted primarily to contain the excessive use of power by factions in control of the executive. Thus, at the 1985 party convention, the counting of the ballots was never completed after a violent assault, and the candidates were selected through an agreement reached by top party officials.

With Dominican parties plagued by undemocratic practices, it is not surprising that projects to democratize the Dominican political system have not become a priority for the ruling parties. Proposals for reform abound, yet Congress and the executive have failed to endorse them or fight vigorously to approve new legislation.[6] With the exception of a minor reform of the electoral system in 1992, no other important political reform has been approved, except the constitutional reforms introduced in haste during the postelection crisis of 1994. They included, among others, the banning of reelection and the runoff election.

It should be noted, however, that in spite of its deficiencies, the democracy that prevails in the Dominican Republic has not yet led to increasing political instability. Along these lines, the argument here is that in a regime lacking profound democratic reforms, personalistic leadership has helped contain a potential process of political fragmentation that could have aggravated problems of governance. That is, in spite of its antidemocratic nature, the entrenched personalism in the Dominican Republic around charismatic figures like Balaguer, Bosch, and Peña Gómez has provided a context for political stability and continuity in Dominican politics, and party politics in particular. This is the reason why the demise of the old *caudillos* poses major challenges for Dominican society: while it may create the conditions for party democratization, which could facilitate the democratization of the political system overall, it could also generate significant political fragmentation and possibly instability.

Dominican Presidentialism and Its Consequences

By electoral design and political practice, the Dominican political system is highly presidential. The president, vice-president, senators, and mayors were all elected by a simple plurality until 1994. In the context of a two-party system, this did not pose a problem. With a multiparty system, however, election by simple plurality led to questions about democratic representativeness. For instance, in the 1990 elections, with only 35 percent of the popular vote, Balaguer's PRSC gained control of the executive and a majority (53%) of Senate seats. In 1986 the contrast was more dramatic: the PRSC won the presidency with 41 percent of the popular vote, yet gained control of 70 percent of Senate seats. While a party that secured a simple plurality at the presidential level did not automatically gain a majority of Senate seats (voters can split their votes since 1990), the tendency in both 1986–90 and 1990–94 was that the party that won the presidency was overrepresented in the Senate. Control of the Senate gives tremendous leverage to the president in the appointment of judges and Electoral Board members, among others.

After thirty years of a military-based dictatorship under Trujillo (1930–61), and twelve years of civilian-based authoritarianism under Balaguer (1966–78), the country inherited a set of political practices that reinforced the power of the president over that of other political institutions. With the arrival of the PRD in office in 1978, institutional changes were expected. The banning of reelection, the institutionalization of Congress, and the independence of the judiciary were promises made by the PRD in the late 1970s and early 1980s. Yet the party failed to deliver on its promises.

The return of Balaguer in 1986 promised few changes, if any, to democratize the political system further. While open repression was not on the agenda, his personalistic and clientelistic practices reinforced the power of the presidency over other spheres of government. Three examples concerning the central government budget, the relationship between the executive and Congress, and the role of the judiciary, help illustrate this point.

It is estimated that in 1993 the presidency spent about eight times more than what was originally budgeted. Meanwhile, it allocated only two-thirds of the amount that was originally budgeted for the Department of Education, one-half of the amount originally budgeted for the Department of Public Health, and one-third of the amount originally budgeted for the Department of Agriculture. Underfunding state agencies and overfunding the presidency was a major mechanism of power centralization under Balaguer. Moreover, the budget for 1994, due to be submitted to Congress during the second ordinary legislature that ended in mid-November 1993, was not submitted until December 28. It was quickly approved by the Senate on December 30, with only two senators from the PRD abstaining from voting, arguing the unconstitutionality of the process.[7]

Before 1978 Congress had acted as a rubber stamp of presidential decisions. In 1978, with the PRD in power, the country witnessed the beginning of congressional independence from the executive (the approval of the amnesty law in 1979 was largely an act of Congress). Yet the intensification of factionalism within the PRD soon led to congressional gridlock. This obstructionism, in turn, did not help improve the image the public had of Congress. With the return of Balaguer to power in 1986, Congress once more assumed a passive role. Balaguer not only maintained fairly tight control over his legislators but also compromised with the PLD, granting them the presidency of the House of Deputies in 1990 in exchange for congressional support (in the Congress elected in 1990, the PLD had forty-four deputies and the PRSC forty-one). Given the historic rivalries between the PLD and the PRD, the opposition consistently failed to form a bloc against Balaguer. Overall, congressional activities leave much to be desired. Congress is not viewed by the population as an important democratic sphere where representatives voice the opinions and interests of those they represent. There is not an entrenched notion of congressional representation in the minds of most Dominicans. According to a poll conducted in 1988 by the daily newspaper *Hoy*, 83 percent of those interviewed said they did not trust Congress to solve the nation's problems.[8]

The Rule of Law and the Judiciary

The judiciary is a sphere of government that, for the most part, has remained unreformed, with the exception of the creation of the Council of the Judiciary introduced as part of the constitutional changes of

1994. After the transition in 1978, the most important measure to comply with basic human and political rights was the amnesty law of 1979. This allowed for the return of political exiles and the release of political prisoners. Freedom of movement to any country in the world was also established.

The administration of justice, however, remained unchanged. The very notion of judicial independence was not entrenched in Dominican political culture and institutions. Political maneuvering in the appointment of judges, the lack of adequate funding for the courts, and the corruption and poor training of many judges were some of the factors that accounted for the inefficiencies in the administration of justice. The president of the Dominican Bar Association said openly to the press that 1993 had been a very negative year for the judicial system. He cited, in particular, police violations of court decisions to release prisoners, corruption scandals involving judges of higher and lower courts, and underfunding of the judicial system; of the 109.8 million pesos assigned to the judiciary in 1993, only 60 percent was actually allocated.[9]

These problems, along with the inefficiencies of the judiciary, reinforce the notion that the rule of law is not fairly applied. Indeed, this notion restricts the very concept of citizenship, insofar as many Dominicans feel that they cannot resolve their problems through the legal system. In lieu of the rule of law, what prevails in Dominican society is the sense that one's interests are ultimately best served through personalistic means.

The emphasis on personalistic over legal means must be understood in historical context. Both Trujillo and Balaguer (who, combined, ruled the country for more than half a century) adhered to a contradictory notion of the rule of law. They both held up the rule of law as the key to full social harmony and the path to civilization. Yet neither under Trujillo nor under Balaguer did the law actually acquire an important status, for it was ultimately subordinated to personal dictates. This can best be understood by quoting Balaguer himself in his inaugural address on July 1, 1966: "Today . . . we return to a regime governed by the rule of law. A state of law means simply that all institutions and all citizens of the country are subject to the law, and no one, neither the government itself nor the least of governors, may from this time forth elude the rule of the constitution or any other legal norm."[10]

Yet a few months later he referred to the constitution in these terms: "Fortunately, constitutions in countries such as ours have been, are, and will be for many years simple pieces of paper. In every country, in every era, at any moment in history, men, not principles, are most important."[11] Clearly, the message sent to all Dominicans was that laws were of limited use, that leaders like Balaguer were above the law. In addition, Balaguer frequently claimed to be one of the few generous Dominicans truly devoted to achieving the well-being of the country and its people. This is how Balaguer cultivated his personalistic leadership: emphasizing his personal qualities and commitment to the country. It is a leadership that even took mythical connotations among segments of Dominican society. Overall, Balaguer exercised power almost totally unconstrained by formal institutions—whether his party, Congress, or the judiciary—without the "checks and balances" that in a democracy should regulate the relationship between different powers or branches of government.

Protest Movements and Social Organizations

In the 1980s the Dominican Republic experienced a rise in protest movements. Early in the decade, the transition to a democratic government gave workers the possibility of organizing and voicing their demands. The number of registered unions increased sharply once the PRD took office in 1978. This was followed by labor's attempts to have employers make concessions in collective agreements. Yet labor soon found resistance from employers, who also pressured the government to control labor unrest. The government, in turn, was caught between labor pressures to improve economic conditions and employers' demands for labor peace. Meanwhile, the government faced the challenge of adjusting the economy in the context of the debt crisis. Short of asking for a "labor truce," the first PRD administration failed to mediate adequately in labor conflicts or satisfy workers' demands for economic improvements.

The second PRD administration faced even more severe problems. The signing of an IMF agreement brought about major social unrest in April 1984 (the well-known food riots), to which the government responded with repression. Thereafter, President Jorge Blanco's popularity fell sharply. The use of repression to fight the riots, the economic recession that accompanied the stabilization program, and allegations of government corruption contributed to the decline of the Jorge Blanco administration and the electoral defeat of the PRD in the 1986 elections.

Nor was the return of Balaguer in 1986 particularly conducive to negotiations between labor and employers, or between labor and government, since Balaguer historically had resisted making concessions to workers. With the rate of inflation increasing dramatically and public services (transportation and electric power in particular) deteriorating rapidly, protest movements spread throughout the country by early 1988. The emergence of a variety of newly formed, popularly rooted social organizations; the activation of professionally based associations (doctors, nurses, and teachers among others); and the accumulated discontent of traditional labor unions contributed to the unrest.

With a government resisting negotiations and a civil society willing to demonstrate, the Catholic Church emerged as the power broker. In March 1988, church leaders called for a Tripartite Dialogue, bringing to the negotiating table representatives from labor confederations, business associations, and the government. Yet representatives from the newly formed Coordinadora de Luchas Populares (Coordinator of Popular Struggles), with fewer credentials as representatives of specific constituencies, and more willing to mobilize, were excluded from the talks.

By bringing together business, labor, and the government, the Catholic Church acquired national recognition as the only institution capable of promoting a national dialogue. Thus, according to the poll conducted by *Hoy* in 1988, close to 80 percent of those interviewed said they trusted the Catholic Church for the solution of major national problems.[12]

After two months of intense negotiations, the parties agreed on an eight-point proposal to be submitted to President Balaguer for his approval. Issues on the proposal included an increase in the minimum wage, price controls, family health insurance, and union protection. The plan was submitted to President Balaguer in May 1988 by a group of representatives from the Tripartite Dialogue led by Archbishop José López Rodríguez. The plan received Balaguer's immediate approval. Yet by mid-June the pact began to fall apart: labor organizations defected, arguing that, shortly after signing the accord, business proceeded to increase prices while the government remained silent.

Thereafter, popular organizations (which had been left out of the talks) intensified their struggles, including a strike called for mid-June 1989. Again the church called for dialogue and negotiation to avoid the strike. The strike took place on June 19–20, but the government remained unresponsive to social demands, allowing only for a very modest increase in the minimum wage.

Once involved in mediating social conflicts, and gaining recognition for doing so, church leaders and institutions, such as the Pontificia Universidad Católica Madre y Maestra (PUCMM), continued in subsequent years to assert their political leadership. Debate and negotiations on economic reforms, modification of legal codes, and the plan for a new identity and voter registration card, took place at the PUCMM.

The prominent role played by the Catholic Church revealed the lack of effective mechanisms of democratic participation in the public sphere, as well as the willingness of the parties involved in the conflict to allow for external mediation. While the former illustrate the limits of democratic governance in the Dominican Republic, the latter suggest the willingness of social actors to accept mediation. No doubt, the initiatives of church leaders helped reduce social tensions at critical junctures. Unfortunately, these opportunities were not used to create more permanent and effective institutions of conflict resolution.

In 1990, the year in which Balaguer was reelected in highly disputed elections, the government endured four general strikes in a six-month period (in June, August, September, and November). In June, newly formed popular organizations (mostly neighborhood-based) succeeded in staging a major general strike. Business used the opportunity to scare the government, and the country became paralyzed. In August the opposition PLD called for a national "civic mourning" to protest Balaguer's inauguration. Popular organizations also joined in the effort, but this time business support was less evident as Balaguer had already called for the signing of a Pact of Economic Solidarity with business. The strikes in September and November proved to be less successful. Business endorsement of strike activities waned. Balaguer had signed an agreement with the major business organizations, promising to slow down public spending and initiate talks with the IMF aimed at signing a standby agreement. Popular organizations, in turn, failed to articulate a common vision. They disagreed over the objectives and duration of the strikes. Some wanted to demand Balaguer's resignation, while others had only socioeconomic claims. Some wanted an indefinite strike; others wanted a forty-eight- or seventy-two-hour strike.

With business now securely on his side, Balaguer simply awaited the collapse of the popular movement as a result of its own internal conflicts. At the end of 1990, Balaguer initiated talks with the IMF that led to the signing of a standby agreement in 1991. By raising taxes, particularly a gasoline tax, Balaguer was able to balance the budget without abandoning his ambitious construction program. By 1992, economic news looked favorable for Balaguer: a significant drop in the rate of inflation from 101 percent in 1990 to about 6 percent in 1992; stability in the newly liberalized exchange market; and a nearly 8 percent rate of growth of the gross domestic product (GDP), one of the highest in Latin America.

Massive public construction, low inflation, stability of the exchange rate, and economic growth proved to be politically beneficial to Balaguer. No major strike was registered in 1993, and a Penn & Schoen poll indicated that popular discontent with the state of the economy declined from 71 percent in 1989 to 58 percent in 1992.[13]

Conclusion

Much can be said, and with good reason, about how fragile or limited democracy is in the Dominican Republic. In fact, in more than a decade and a half of democratically elected governments, virtually no progress has been made in the area of redistributive justice or democratic institutionalization. It should be recognized, however, that since 1978 the

Dominican Republic has witnessed five competitive, even if disputed, elections and two turnovers of power.

Much remains to be done to consolidate democracy in the Dominican Republic. There is an urgent need to make more efficient and effective the organization of elections, which should help to make them more credible to the public. It is also important that the Electoral Board be appointed with enough time before the elections, and that the board receive the necessary funds to conduct the electoral process. The appointees should also be carefully selected to prevent mistrust on the part of the political parties and the electorate. Also, political parties need to democratize from within, overcoming a long history of personalism and entrenched clientelism. Here the selection of candidates by the party membership represents a step in the right direction.

Institutional reforms are needed to secure the separation of power between the executive, the legislative, and the judicial branches. First, Congress should be made more accountable to the electorate. At present, congressional representatives are more responsive to their parties than to the electorate. It is worth considering whether open lists in the selection of congressional representatives might prove to be more democratic than the current system of closed party lists. Making Congress more accountable to the electorate would also increase its power vis-à-vis the president. One must acknowledge, however, that the relationship between Congress and the executive in a presidential system is frequently problematic. For instance, an empowered Congress may lead to frequent gridlock, a problem the Dominican Republic has avoided for the most part given the historic power of the presidency. Yet a weak Congress that acts as a rubber stamp for presidential decisions can hardly be thought of as a democratic institution. To improve the judiciary system, it is important to address problems of corruption, the inadequate training of judges, and politicization in the appointment of judges. Extensive proposals are already available in the country that detail how these objectives can be accomplished. Finally, problems related to extreme poverty and inequality must also be addressed.

Can these and other challenges be met in the 1990s and the beginning years of the next century? Are Dominicans up to the tasks of undoing decades of undemocratic and personalistic politics? There are no precise answers to these questions. What can be said, however, is that in the next few years the Dominican Republic will lose the two most important figures that have shaped politics in the post-Trujillo era: Balaguer and Bosch. Without them, the Dominican Republic will be forced either to democratize or simply look for undemocratic leaders to replace the old ones. This is, therefore, an opportune time to reflect upon the current state of democratic governance in the Dominican Republic and its future. It is also an ideal time to take action in order to avoid a major decomposition of the political fabric that could only generate a power vacuum, which has historically been conducive to un-democratic politics. For what it is worth, it should be noted that in spite of all the inefficiencies of the prevailing democratic regime in the Dominican Republic, according to a poll conducted in 1992, 94 percent of those interviewed said that democracy was very good or good for the country.[14]

The paradox presented in this chapter is that, in the midst of adverse socioeconomic and political conditions, the Dominican Republic has succeeded in maintaining civilian governments for three decades. Moreover, since 1978, elections, even if disputed, have been competitive. The country has also enjoyed freedom of the press, expression, and association. These are not minor accomplishments in a country that until 1961 endured one of the harshest dictatorships in the region, experienced much political turmoil in the early 1960s, and endured political repression in the late 1960s and early 1970s.

Three fundamental conditions account for these accomplishments in the midst of adversities: (1) the civilian nature of authoritarianism in the post-1965 period, which allowed for the maintenance of formal democratic institutions; (2) the willingness of nondemocratic actors, Balaguer in particular, to accept democratic procedures and outcomes, as in the case of the electoral results of 1978; and (3) the strength of the party system that has allowed for alternation and predictability in the governing process. Here the prevalence of personalism in Dominican politics has played a dual role: it has provided a context for political continuity and the preservation of some democratic gains, but it has also hampered the process of democratic expansion and consolidation. It has prevented, in particular, the democratization of political parties and the establishment of institutionalized channels for mediating partisan and societal conflicts. Short of institutional compromise and well-established channels of political negotiation, "outside arbiters" (e.g., the church, the United States) have played a major role in Dominican politics whenever the country has faced a crisis that required dialogue and compromise.

It is expected that the constitutional reforms approved in 1994 under the terms of the Pact for Democracy will help democratize Dominican politics. Yet the banning of reelection and runoff elections presents problems in securing democratic governability. Will the power of the president be even more inflated as a result of the ballotage? Is a four-year term sufficient to carry out a government program? Can the Dominican Electoral Board efficiently administer two consecutive elections? No doubt, the presidential elections of 1996 constitute the first opportunity to assess the political impact of the constitutional reforms of 1994.

9

Haiti: Four Old and Two New Hypotheses

Anthony P. Maingot

In one of those gems of research left hidden as a preface to the work of others, the late Richard Schaedel warned that in Haiti one should never believe things are as they appear and that the path of least resistance seldom turns out to be the best one. "There is no place in Haitian maxims," wrote Schaedel, "for 'seeing is believing.' . . . As in nature so with human beings, one must be careful of traps, camouflage, and apparent bountifulness."[1] Be careful, therefore, with the facile explanation, the unicausal theory, the mindless application of complex paradigms derived from the study of political behavior elsewhere. Fundamentally, do not let the logical and natural instinct toward Manichaean judgments—the "good" and the "bad" Haitian—steer you away from understanding what they all share in common.

This caveat should caution us against too readily accepting some of the more enduring normative propositions regarding the Haitian political system. These propositions often take on mythical dimensions; they are accepted without question, virtually as articles of historical faith. Yet any approximation to an understanding of Haitian politics requires that one consider these and all other plausible propositions. Only after submitting them to rigorous analysis should one attempt to formulate new hypotheses. In this chapter I analyze four widely held hypotheses about Haitian political behavior and suggest two additional ones.

First Proposition

The first proposition goes something like this: dictatorships, and that of François (Papa Doc) Duvalier in particular, have been at least consequences, if not creations, of U.S. policies toward Haiti.

The long and brutal Duvalier period is a good place to begin analyzing this proposition as well as providing new interpretations about Haitian politics. Analysis of the proposition calls for a two-part discussion: first, a description of how and why Dr. François Duvalier came to power, and second, an analysis of the sources or bases of the ongoing power of the Duvaliers.

It was in the historical atmosphere of color animosity between the 10 percent who constituted the colored bourgeoisie (*mulâtres*) and the 90 percent blacks (*noirs*) that Duvalier came to power in 1957, in the first election ever held under direct adult universal suffrage on the island. As Bernard Diederich and Al Burt put it in their vehemently anti-Duvalier book *Papa Doc* (1969), the question in 1957 seemed to be whether Haitians preferred Dr. François Duvalier, a self-styled black idealist, or a haughty mulatto patrician, Louis Dejoie. The latter, they noted, seemed to have the support of the U.S. embassy, U.S. and Haitian business interests, and significant elements in the military. The vote, however, was for Papa Doc: Duvalier 679,884; Dejoie 266,993.

Rather than being due entirely to fraud, the Duvalier victory appears to have been the culmination of a populist movement of black intellectuals that had three crucial stages. The first was not directly related to racial politics but rather anti-imperialism and anti-U.S. occupation. The luminaries of this stage were Jacques Roumain, founder of the Haitian communist party, and Joseph Jolibois Fils, a nationalist leader.[2] The next stage was less specifically ideological and more broadly ethnological: the Les Griots movement of the 1930s was led by the new class of black professionals and bureaucrats created by the U.S. Marine occupation, against which they had reacted. Duvalier, a medical doctor from a humble background, was an important member. They were *authentiques*, that is, opponents of the Roman Catholic Church and of the French language and culture, and advocates of the Voodoo religion and of the wider use of the creole language in society. The Griots represented a "revolution" of Haïtienisme against the politics of *doublure*, where a black puppet is manipulated by the *mulâtre* elite.

The third stage was very specifically black nationalist (*noirist*) in ideology and political orientation. It brought Dumarsais Estime to power through the elections of 1946. Estime was overthrown by a military coup in 1949. Duvalier had been a member of Estime's cabinet and shared its *noirist* ideology. As Robert and Nancy Heinl put it, "Estime's politics . . . amounted to a kind of peasant populism tinged with . . . anti-foreignism and with fierce *mangeur-mulâtre* [*mulâtre*-eating] black racism."[3] That this racial populism was not truly intended to help the masses can be seen in some of the measures taken by Estime to show his nationalism. Various nationalizations of businesses really had as their goal the creation or enrichment of a new black bourgeoisie to counter the *mulâtres*. The historical point is that it was this newly strengthened urban black middle class, deprived of power by the 1949 coup, that would become one of the main sources of support for the Duvaliers. It certainly was not the only one, and perhaps not even the most significant one.

The black, rural "mediating class" was arguably Duvalier's most steadfast ally. If one keeps in mind that Haiti is the least urbanized of the countries in this hemisphere (20%), one understands the potential significance of this class in controlling the mass of the peasantry and thereby defeating the many efforts of urban elites to overthrow Duvalier through the rural guerilla warfare Cuba had made so popular after 1959.

The official element in the mediating class has traditionally been the *chef de section* (section chief). The section is the purely rural administrative unit literally controlled by a chief. The section chiefs go back to the days of the liberation of the slaves and traditionally represented black civilian power against *mulâtre* elite control of the military. It is crucial to know that peasants refer to them as *leta*, creole for "the state." With intimate knowledge of his rural environment and its inhabitants, this chief is a precious political ally or formidable enemy. It was Duvalier's political skill that converted them into his staunch supporters. With the 80 percent in the country secure, he had a free hand to deal with the urban 20 percent, where most of his enemies were. But these chiefs were not the only rural resident force available to the Duvaliers.

The need for a better equipped and controlled rural force became evident during the early stages of the Duvalier regime. There were some six anti-Duvalier invasions staged from Cuba, the United States, or the Dominican Republic. Regardless of where they originated, they all attempted to start "guerrilla" warfare à la Cuba. There is no known case of significant peasant support of these largely *mulâtre*-led invasions. Not only is the Haitian countryside not propitious to guerilla warfare, but these idealistic youth, deeply divided among themselves, were no match for the *chefs de section* and their many underlings. Many of these rural folk became part of one of the most formidable armed pillars of the Duvalier regime, the VSN (Volontaire de la Securité Nationale, Volunteers for National Security). As the Heinls described them, its rural platoons in every village "wore the red sashes of Ogun [the god of war in the Voodoo pantheon], and big straw hats of the old Cacos [rural guerrilla fighters], whose latest descendants they were, and were meant by Duvalier to be."[4] Together with the section chiefs, these VSN militias formed a formidable armed counterforce to the professional military that had been the maker and unmaker of Haitian governments.

It is therefore evident that, contrary to the myth of American origins of the structures of dictatorship, the fundamental bases of the power of the Duvaliers had very autochthonous roots. The first was the traditional network of powerful black peasants, newly recognized and rewarded. The second was the skillful integration of much of the ideology that had preceded Duvalier into the symbolism of the folk religion: Ogun, the Voodoo god of war, and the *cacos*, the black peasant guerrillas who fought both the *mulâtres* and the U.S. Marines during their occupation (1915–34). The VSN were now portrayed as modern-day *cacos,* and, for the first time since the disarming carried out by the Marines, these peasant groups were armed. The presence of this rural network made it much more likely that any change of regime would have to take place through a "palace coup" rather than from any invasion or military campaign, whether supported by the United States or not. Finally, it was Duvalier, not any American advisors, who brought all these elements of culture and history, class and color, nationalism and sovereignty together into a relatively cohesive, albeit repressive, philosophy of the state Haitians now call *macoutisme.*[5]

In a bitter essay written at the height of the Papa Doc Duvalier dictatorship, Haitian ethnologist Rémy Bastien spoke of the *trahison des clercs* that contributed to the rise of Duvalier. "By cruel irony," wrote Bastien, "a sector of the learned minority is responsible for the regression [into barbarism], this time not through failure to act but by deliberate choice."[6] They wanted to believe in a man of the people, with close ties to Voodoo and a known resentment against the traditional bourgeoisie and its Europeanizing ways. Alas, how frequently have we seen elsewhere this miscalculation of the totalitarian motivations of populist leaders. In other words, how difficult it is for even those inside the system to evaluate, judge, and then predict future behavior.

Second Proposition

With this knowledge we can turn briefly to proposition two: "Haiti has been ignored by the world: change will come if it is made a nation of international concern."

If that concern is intellectual, the proposition is absolutely wrong. Both Haitians and foreigners have studied the country more than any other Caribbean island, including Cuba.[7] Part of the problem is that there has been a tendency among serious scholars, despairing about finding domestic remedies, to turn to foreign solutions. In his classic 1941 treatise *The Haitian People,* James Leyburn expressed a common despair: "How conceivably might this problem be dealt with?" His solution lay outside the island, the "moral imperative" of U.S. and European assistance. Over the years, that assistance might not have been at the levels the Haitians would have wished for and certainly less than the nation needed, but it has been substantial. As the Heinls have noted, it was in 1947, with the newly established United Nations, that the era of solving Haiti's problems by foreign survey teams dawned. The Heinls might have added the nineteen years of U.S. occupation, with all its attempts at change. In fact, they do conclude that it was all "built on sand."

Haiti, under Duvalier, was the epitome of that primitive chauvinism that maintains that "our wine is bitter but it is ours." As Dean Rusk once put it, "we made all sorts of efforts to bring about changes in Haiti

. . . persuasion, aid, pressure . . . but President Duvalier was extraordinarily resistant."[8] In fact, during a major crisis in 1963, brought about by international exasperation with Duvalier's brutal excesses, and with American, British, Canadian, and Dominican forces poised to intervene, Duvalier told 150,000 of his assembled supporters: "I take no orders or dictates from anyone." He invoked the masses' belief in the supernatural by adding, "I am even now an immaterial being." In the United Nations, his ambassador was at the same time making one of the most overtly racist appeals to "black people and Africans" everywhere to defend Haiti. Duvalier won. In fact, during his reign Duvalier expelled Catholic archbishops (and was therefore excommunicated by the Vatican) and Episcopalian bishops, the entire Jesuit order, two U.S. ambassadors, several ambassadors from other countries, the U.S. Marine training mission, U.S. Agency for International Development (USAID) mission chiefs, and dozens of other foreign experts.

Therefore, it is not that there have been no foreign concerns with Haiti: it is just that in Haitian politics, when faced with survival, politicians think only of the present and leave the future to the gods. Duvalier Senior was in the tradition of independence leader Pierre Dominique Toussaint L'Ouverture: faced with the 1802 Napoleonic attempt at reconquest of Haiti, L'Ouverture gave his generals the following order: "The only resources we have are destruction and fire. Annihilate and burn everything. . . . Leave nothing white behind you." This position represents tenacious and resolute motivation to confront the enemy no matter what the odds and the costs. In terms of the absoluteness and fortitude of motivations, Duvalier identified himself with Toussaint, Jean-Jacques Dessalines, and Henri Christophe. Few other Haitian leaders merited his attention, and no outsiders—especially not white Americans—deserved to be emulated. His, and his friend Estime's, confrontation with American racism had a lot to do with this attitude.[9]

Third Proposition

In many respects, answers to the first two propositions go a long way toward addressing the third, which has taken on the dimensions of a national myth: "Haiti's problems stem from the elites who prefer tyranny; remove their power and you solve the political problems." This emphasis on an "elite"—variously defined in terms of skin color, cultural orientation, or some vague notion of social class—is an enduring one in Haitian studies. It virtually became an academic given when ethnologist Jean-Price Mars chastised those of Francophile orientation for their disdain of the peasantry. His 1928 book *Ainsi parla l'oncle* set the tone for the critique of the *mulâtre* bourgeoisie. François Duvalier and one of his close associates in the Griot movement, Lorimer Denis, put a bitter political spin on the anti-*mulâtre* sentiment in their 1938 book *Le Problème des classes à travers l'histoire d'Haiti.* Foreign scholars might not have had similar political purposes, but their prescriptions for democratizing Haiti were similar: that "the elite" change its values and attitudes. Mats Lundahl's superb study ends by suggesting that only a change in the elites' "anti-peasant bias" will bring about positive change.[10] He is not sanguine about the prospects. The dilemma of seeing both the problems and the solutions in the attitudes of an elite is evident in the works of twelve Haitian intellectuals gathered by the Woodrow Wilson Center.[11] There is an inherent contradiction between many of these leaders' conclusions that the problem lies with the elites but that if change is to come, it has to be generated by these elites themselves.

The fundamental weakness of this class approach to Haiti's problems, with its emphasis on the elite, is that it never explains, first, how an entrenched elite changes its ideology, and, second, how a rotation or circulation of elites would deal with, much less change, the fundamental underlying problems of the island: lack of political accountability and extraordinary economic underdevelopment. The class origins of various Haitian leaders do not appear to have mitigated their generalized abuses once in power. In fact, some of the most brutal of Haiti's dictators have been anti-elite populists. The difference between Duvalier and all the other previous dictators in the twentieth century, for instance, was the intensity and harshness of his hatred for all his opponents, not just *mulâtres* and foreign whites. His intense hatred for John F. Kennedy is well documented by Robert Heinl who, as commander of the Marine Training Mission in Haiti, was privy to Papa Doc's thoughts on the matter. Estime's regime was also *noirist* but exercised none of the brutal excesses of Duvalier's equally *noirist* regime. Neither showed any concern over the fate of the black working classes in whose name they had come to power.

The peasants' condition continued to deteriorate, as it deteriorates today. In the words of Lundahl, "The Haitian peasant sector is caught in a downward spiral of circular and cumulative causation which slowly depresses the standard of living among the peasants."[12] Put differently, the man/land ratio in Haiti is deteriorating rapidly through population growth coupled with soil erosion and exhaustion, and it is not clear that a circulation of elites can stem this calamity. In Haiti, where the labor supply has been growing much faster than capital, there has been for decades a trend away from capital-intensive crops (largely for export, such as sugar, cotton, cacao) and toward subsistence, labor-intensive cultivation. Haiti is one of the few places in the hemisphere where the number of farms is actually increasing: from 580,000 in 1950 to 616,710 in 1971. Add to this economic dimension the sociocultural dimension of the Haitian peasant's love of land, and one realizes that it is not easy to reverse this trend. Land is such a valuable commodity to the Haitian peasant, as Melville J. Herskovits noted as far back as 1937, that "there are few, among the peasants at least, who do not seek by all means to add to their heritage. . . . The drive to obtain property is an obsession with the Haitian peasants."[13]

There are many reasons for not celebrating this land distribution as some form of peasant democracy. For one, subsistence agriculture, because of the primitive methods used, contributes substantially more to soil erosion than modern cultivation. Subsistence agriculture is also accompanied by another characteristic of poverty, deforestation, not just for cultivation but also for home building, boat building, and, most disastrous of all, charcoal. Again, there is nothing new in this. The black peasant protagonist in Haiti's most acclaimed novel, Jacques Roumain's *Masters of the Dew* (1944), painted a vivid picture of the "gullies" where erosion had "undressed long strata of rock and bled the earth to the bone." Roumain knew where the problem lay: "They had been wrong to cut down the trees that once grew thick up there. But they had burned the woods to plant Congo beans on the plateau and corn on the hillside." With more mouths to feed and heads to shelter, it is a sad irony that this love of the land, combined with current agricultural practices, will bequeath less of it, in worse condition, to future Haitian generations.

Fourth Proposition

The fourth proposition is another popular theoretical explanation that has taken on the characteristics of myth: the emphasis on culture. It is widely believed that either the more "undiluted" culture of the Voodoo-practicing peasants, the more syncretistic forms of culture, or the duality created by the clash of European and African cultures explains Haiti's problems.

It is not surprising that the bulk of the studies about Haiti attempt to explain the role that bad government has played in the island's lack of progress. The question more often than not is whether the explanation for Haiti's intractable problems and bad governance is to be found in the island's culture. It is not just academics who have emphasized culture as the starting point for the analysis, blame, or subsequent solutions to what ails the island. Exiled president Jean-Bertrand Aristide, for instance, maintains that the island's strength lies in its culture. As he told the U.N. General Assembly on September 25, 1991, the "Ninth Commandment" of democracy in Haiti is fidelity to its culture. "No truly deep change can be accomplished democratically," he warned, "without an articulation of the indigenous values that are closely linked with any genuine socio-cultural fabric." This, of course, was precisely what Price-Mars, Les Griots, and the *authentiques* preached in the 1930s and 1940s. It certainly was François Duvalier's theme in his early writings. However, many others have not been as sanguine about the relationship between Haitian culture and the values necessary for the establishment of a democratic society. In fact, that culture has been seen as a grave obstacle to both democracy and economic development.

According to an early Haitian observer, Emmanuel Edouard, the incessant struggle for the state, the major employer of the urban bourgeoisie, had perverted the political culture.[14] To work for the state was "to be in politics" and that meant to be eternally distrustful, false, and conniving. To steal from state revenues, he maintained, did not engender reprobation but outright envy. A bifurcated moral sense was the result: one reserved for public service, that is, matters of state, the other for private and especially family affairs.

This theme of the dual cultural system became a common one in Haitian studies. One of the earliest of the serious outside scholars to point to cultural imperatives for the Haitian status was Melville Herskovits. Herskovits took his cue from Haitian J. C. Dorsainvil's comment that Haitians "to an astonishing degree . . . live on their nerves."[15] Herskovits concluded that what was involved was a need to reconcile two cultural traditions that were often in inner conflict: the African and the French. To indicate its structural nature, he called it "socialized ambivalence": rapid shifts in attitude toward people and situations. The same person, wrote Herskovits, will hold in high regard a person, an institution, an experience, or even an object that has personal significance to him, and simultaneously manifest great disdain and even hatred for it. "In its broader implications," he concluded, "as a matter of fact, it is entirely possible that this socialized ambivalence underlies much of the political and economic instability of Haiti."[16]

Many others have noticed this tendency to rapid shifts in loyalty. Robert Rotberg attributed it to the pervasive attitudes of rivalries, suspicion, and intrigue that characterized rural and urban Haitians alike.[17] Lawrence Harrison, citing Rémy Bastien, puts the blame squarely on Voodoo, its promotion of irrationality and cultural listlessness and inaction. Voodoo, say Bastien and Harrison, is the great bulwark of the status quo.[18]

Whatever explanatory power the cultural approach has as regards economic development, it has to be at least questioned as an explanation of political behavior. Two problems immediately suggest themselves. First, Voodoo is a peasant religion, and peasants do not and never have conducted Haitian politics. The history of maladministration of the island cannot be blamed on them. Second, if Voodoo favors stagnation and the status quo, how does one explain the rise of Jean-Bertrand Aristide and the Se Lavalas movement for structural change that is discussed below?

Evidently, broad cultural explanations do present plausible explanations of Haitian behavior in many areas. They are seldom specific and operational enough, however, to provide explanations about particular cases of political behavior and, fundamentally, how and why—if they are all driven by the same cultural imperatives—the behavior of some leaders differs so dramatically from that of others. The broad cultural explanation does not help one understand what is "generalizable" and what is unique in Haitian political behavior.

Interestingly enough, the same critique can be made of those Marxist studies that stress class conflict or Gramscian ones that interpret key political changes in terms of "hegemonic" crises of the bourgeois power elites.[19] Whatever plausibility this approach might have in explaining macro-level changes, it is difficult to see how it helps in understanding discrete political behavior and leadership, especially as the refutations of the four hypotheses should make it clear to policymakers that the future of Haitian politics will evolve according to its own codes of behavior and not according to what outsiders might design for it. That being the case, it is fundamental to inquire into what those political codes might be. Two hypotheses in particular seem suitable.

Hypothesis One: The Rationality of Individualism

Haiti appears to be an exaggerated case of Mancur Olson's "paradox of individual rational choice."[20] According to Olson, any politician promoting his self-interest will at some point refrain from pursuing collective activities with large numbers of other people. The reason is that beyond a certain group size, the cost of membership outweighs possible rewards to the individual from participation. The larger the group, the more numerous the negotiated interactions and thus, presumably, the claims on a reciprocal loyalty and set of obligations. In many ways, Olson's paradox of individual choices is related to what has been called the law of large numbers. So many individuals compete for the national prize that the impact of the actions of each individual is perceived as insignificant. This often leads the various individuals to be reserved, guarded, secretive, and to base their actions on a "least cost" calculation of risk to self or in-group rather than on considerations of the greater good.

That there is a scarcity of resources in Haiti is a given. It is also well known that any leader has a heavy burden of built-in reciprocal obligations with his or her nuclear and extended family ties and friendship commitments. In other words, there are few opportunities for patronage and even fewer for patronage outside an intimate circle. In Haiti, Olson's paradox of individual rational choice kicks in early and forcefully. To go it alone, individualism, is a totally rational choice. Coalition forming and other forms of strategic interaction with "others" outside the in-group is virtually nonexistent. What do exist are the ad hoc and constantly shifting sets of "alliances." These are invariably short-term and very specifically goal-oriented and circumscribed. The hierarchy of commitments seldom conforms to any formal political or administrative hierarchy. This has often meant institutionalizing in a very formal way what in the United States is called the "kitchen cabinet." In the case of President Aristide, for instance, it is well known that his formal cabinet—both while in power and in exile—has none of the influence and constant contact with him that his group of informal Se Lavalas advisors have.

One consequence of this rationally calculated individualism has been its impact on the nature and use of power in Haiti. Power is used to stop others from doing things, seldom as a vehicle for actually doing things. Since most everyone uses power the same way, very little of a constructive nature is ever accomplished—power is negative rather than positive.

Evidently the question is: if such large numbers desire the highest office, what characteristics are decisive in achieving that goal? But even more important, what characteristics are necessary for safeguarding it once it has been achieved?

Hypothesis Two: The Asymmetries of Motivation

Since Crane Brinton raised the issue in his 1934 book *Anatomy of Revolution*, the literature has pointed to the difference in motivation, the degree of political tenacity and determination (in layman terms "political hunger"), between political moderates and "Jacobins." More recent social-psychological theorizing has emphasized that achievement of any goal depends on two factors: the possession of the necessary ability and the intensity of motivation to reach that goal. Often differential motivation is attributed to class differences.[21] In political theory, it is an established fact that, as Lester Milbrath notes, in every political system there are what he calls "spectator" activists and those he calls "gladiatorial" activists.[22] In Haiti, political activities are limited to the gladiators, so that it is among them that one has to search for the asymmetries in motivation. It is the difference between Papa Doc's determination to hold on to power no matter what the cost in human lives, and the absence of that cruel determination in his son, Jean Claude (Baby Doc) Duvalier. The latter was prone to tell journalists that he should not be blamed for the evils of his father. "I never saw myself as a dictator," he told the French press, "I believe that I was a well-loved President."[23]

Policymakers ought to be able to draw important lessons from the following brief analyses of three phases of recent Haitian political history: the prelude to democratic elections in 1990, the exile of President

Jean-Bertrand Aristide, and his behavior since returning to power. The goal of these descriptions is to illustrate the operation of the paradox of individual rational choice and the importance of understanding asymmetries of motivation in Haitian politics. There might also be some gain from searching for continuities in Haitian political culture by contrasting them with the behavior of François Duvalier described above.

A Girondist Interregnum

The situation that resulted from the overthrow of the Duvalier dynasty in 1986 was essentially one of a plurality of power groups seeking to assert nationwide control. None managed to gain such control, neither the military led fundamentally by General Henri Namphy, nor the civilian Leslie Manigat who attempted to rein in Namphy's pretensions. Namphy would eventually tire of Manigat's "civilianist" inclinations and send him into exile.

Namphy's moment of glory was fleeting, however. Reflecting the divisions in the military, General Namphy was soon overthrown by General Prosper Avril, formerly a close financial advisor of both Duvaliers. Avril did not act alone; the divisions within the military had now reached the noncommissioned officers' ranks.[24] Sergeant Joseph Hebreaux and his colleagues thrust themselves to the fore of Haitian politics, signaling the entry of what Haitians called the *ti soldats* (little soldiers) into the fray. Again, the hope that such democratic populism would help redress the class imbalance in Haitian politics was misplaced. In fact, Haiti was sliding toward anarchy. Paralleling the collapse of military discipline was the rise of a series of paramilitary groups, again without any known central command. Haitians called them variously *groupes sans mamans* (groups without mothers), *zengledo* (bandits), or simply *escadrons de la mort* (death squads).

In Haiti, short periods of hope invariably follow the overthrow of the most recent hated ruler. This hope is invariably also shared by outsiders. "Of the four governments to rule Haiti since the departure of Jean-Claude Duvalier," U.S. Deputy Assistant Secretary of State for Caribbean Affairs Richard Melton said after the coup, "we judge the Avril government as offering the best, and perhaps the last real chance for democratic reform in Haiti for the foreseeable future."[25] That the U.S. government generally believed this to be so is evident in the various letters of the U.S. ambassador to General Avril.[26]

Whatever shortcomings the Avril regime had, it at least attempted to meet the generalized demand for free elections through various attempts at consensus building over the rules of the game. It was all in vain. In March 1990 the pattern of apparently uncontrollable anarchic behavior—strikes, crime, roving gangs—brought down the Avril regime. General Herárd Abraham emerged as a popular figure, especially since he did not put the presidential sash on himself but on a justice of the Supreme Court, Ertha Pascal-Trouillot.

Haiti had just gone through an unusual transition period: no "Jacobin" had made an appearance. It was this fact, in the midst of virtual institutional chaos, that gave the democratically oriented parties, with powerful international support, the opportunity of organizing new elections on December 16, 1990. It is crucial to understand that, while Jean-Bertrand Aristide and his Se Lavalas movement swept these elections, they were conducted in a state of near anarchy among the national political institutions, including a government that was bankrupt. Foreign funding (an estimated U.S.$40 million), foreign supervision (more than a thousand uniformed observers), and foreign management (the OAS [Organization of American States], the Carter Center, the UN) all made it possible.

Enter Aristide

A crucial task still facing scholars of Haiti is to explain the truly impressive post–1986 political mobilization of the Haitian masses, both urban and in the countryside, despite the disarray among the political elite. While Father Jean-Bertrand Aristide never supported the institutionalization of this mobilization into political parties and elections, it is a fact that it was just this organization that made the election of his acknowledgedly popular movement possible. The electoral registration, the Constitution of 1987, and the enormous voter turnouts in 1987 had all been opposed by Aristide. He opposed the elections in 1990 until, five months before they took place, he was convinced that he was the sure winner. An ardent supporter of the radical wing of liberation theology, his intransigent antagonism to the established church, the local bourgeoisie, and the United States were matters of record. His sermons were peppered with suggestions of popular revenge against their class enemies, speeches of distinct Jacobin coloration.[27] His writings showed that, at least theoretically, he appeared to have understood the structural nature of Haitian political culture. Haiti's political situation, he wrote in July 1992, is a product of a long course of traditional politics which he says created a "political paradigm." "The rules," he explained, "are rigid: The more power an individual or institution amasses from money or weapons, the greater the chances of winning: strength comes from an ability to impose one's will on others."[28] Clearly, such historically grounded political paradigms are not changed overnight, as Aristide would discover a mere nine months after his inauguration. In what way do the two hypotheses about Haitian political culture explain Aristide and his dénouement?

Aristide began his administration with an inaugural speech on February 7, 1991, laced with combative symbolism. Four times he invoked the name of *caco* leader and anti-U.S. occupation guerrilla Charlemagne Peralte, asking his audience whether they had Peralte's blood running through their veins. In contrast to Peralte, however, who expected to reach the presidential palace through bullets, Aristide had arrived there through ballots. The constant allusions to struggle confused his friends and intimidated his foes. In light of the short duration of the "honeymoon" given Haitian leaders, no matter how they reached the palace, that confusion shortened Aristide's period of grace. Midway through the Aristide administration, a source in the presidential palace told the press, "an adversary you can argue with is better than a blundering ally."[29]

Aristide's political problem had been evident from the start. Surrounded by ideologues and idealistic Lavalassiens, all political amateurs, Aristide never seemed able to distinguish friend from foe. True to the hypothesis of individualism, he showed no inclination to engage in the profane art of political maneuvering and coalition building. In fact, he seemed to excel at marginalizing those who did not belong to his inner circle, thereby turning allies into opponents. Not surprisingly, it was Aristide's own National Front for Democratic Convergence (FNCD) legislators who began to call for the resignation of Aristide's prime minister, René Préval, and it was this group that was violently threatened with individual necklacing (*pere lebruns*) if they did not desist from their opposition.

By early May the complaints about Aristide's authoritarian style had become a chorus. With his constitutional-institutional space shrinking, Aristide turned to what he did best—haranguing the masses. Day after day, from one end of the island to the other, the president and his prime minister personally dealt with the increasing military mutinies, strikes, food protests, and land disputes. Aristide's efficiency plunged even as his popularity soared. And this created a negative cycle: the lower the ability to cope with "conventional" politics (in the Haitian sense), the greater the appeal to populism, which, in turn, made more apprehensive, aroused, and dangerous the practitioners of conventional politics, that is, those with the motivation to challenge all opponents, internal and external. My hypothesis suggests that in the final analysis, Haitian history has demonstrated that those so motivated hold the ultimate trump cards.

No one in early September 1991, however, expected a significant political crisis. After all, it was believed that the purging of the army along with the support of the United States and the international community to the tune of U.S.$422 million, a prospect that satisfied significant sectors of the business community, was enough to guarantee Aristide's position. He certainly appeared to believe so himself. "Democracy," he told the United Nations on September 25, 1991, "has won out for good, the roots are growing stronger and stronger." One

week later he was on his way into exile, alive only because of the hero-
ics of the French and U.S. ambassadors and the plane made available by
President Carlos Andrés Pérez of Venezuela.

So began Aristide's nearly three years in exile, followed by his return
on October 15, 1994, one month after some twenty-four thousand U.S.
troops had taken control of the island. Again, this entire phase can be
analyzed in terms of the various propositions regarding Haitian political culture. It is evident, however, that in order to justify a claim to
being generalizable, any proposition about political culture has to prove
that the behavior highlighted is not purely contextual and time specific.
The two problems that follow from Aristide's overthrow—how to return
and, then, how to govern once returned to office—provide good opportunities for testing the operation of the hypotheses of the rationality of individual action and the role of the asymmetry of motivations.

Key Problem: How to Return?

For purposes of this analysis, the options open to Aristide for achieving
his return were fundamentally three:[30] (1) lead a countercoup through
alliances with a variety of forces inside and outside Haiti; (2) wait for
the international embargo to bring down the military junta; and (3) call
for a military invasion by foreign troops. Clearly the one option that
would have gone contrary to Olson's proposition of the paradox of individual rational choice is no. 1. Predictably, it was the one not chosen by
Aristide.

Aristide's first choice was to wait for the embargo to work. This was
also the choice of the U.S. government and the international community. The position was summarized by the *New York Times* when it
called editorially on October 29, 1993, to "Tighten the Sanctions on
Haiti" and more dramatically on December 25, 1993, "For Haiti: Sanctions That Bite."

There obviously must have been many strong *positive* arguments in
favor of sanctions for this option to have emerged as the preferred policy of the international community. Indeed, it is precisely this international consensus that was the option's strongest suit. There were, of
course, other features that recommend it, not the least of which was
that it best balanced the tension between international and domestic
considerations. Sanctions in the form of embargoes on weapons and oil
and the freezing of assets allowed the U.S. administration and the international community to buy time (not invade) without appearing to be
indifferent by doing nothing. Similarly, exempting humanitarian assistance from the embargo avoids the impression of callousness.

The basic problem was that it was not achieving its stated goal. The
military junta dug its heels in and made a mockery of the international
community. Papa Doc Duvalier had done exactly the same thing when
President Kennedy tried to overthrow him through an embargo in

1963–64. The irony of the situation was that those who most favored this option also understood its ultimate futility. How, for instance, could Chile's ambassador to the OAS, Heraldo Muñoz, continue to justify sanctions while also admitting that they probably work least well when directed against economies such as Haiti's where subsistence agriculture predominates? Additionally, this strategy was especially difficult to justify once Ambassador Muñoz admitted that the sanctions "have apparently hurt the average citizen without threatening the putschists' control."[31] It was partly the U.S. public's awareness of this result, and their frustration with a Haitian situation they identified with the arrival of herds of "boat people" on U.S. shores, that led to the call for a military solution.

The military invasion option was presented by two editorials in the *Miami Herald*: "Time for the Marines" on December 22, 1993; and "Solution for Haiti: Force" on January 15, 1994. Although not argued on moral grounds in the editorials, foreign military intervention had significant moral merits, as more and more political and legal experts were recognizing.[32]

The major weakness of this option was evident in what the *Miami Herald*'s editorials merely alluded to but did not elaborate on. First, President Aristide's official and public position on the use of foreign troops against the usurpers fell far short of being a policy decision.[33] A foreign intervention when and where there is massive hardship and no recognizable government in existence can be supported, as was the case in Somalia. It is difficult to consider such an action in the face of opposition or silence from the recognized, legitimate government concerning foreign wishes to assist. Although it certainly is a matter of legal interpretation, the Aristide people have been arguing that two articles of the 1987 Haitian Constitution specifically prohibit supporting a foreign miliary intervention. First, article 21 defines "crimes of high treason" to include bearing arms in a foreign army against the republic or serving the interests of a foreign nation against those of the republic. The second is article 263.1, which specifies that no military or armed force other than the army of Haiti can exist on national territory. How does a surgical strike, with or without the support of the legitimate government, modify these provisions?

But even if this Haitian will for an invasion were to have been expressed, the military option still had to address other controversial questions in the United States and in the international community. Subtle arguments about international law were no match for historically rooted opposition to intervention, evident in the international community's opposition to military intervention in Haiti. There was also a question of jurisdiction. It should be understood that, whereas the vote of the OAS to impose sanctions on Haiti was argued on the grounds of the 1991 Santiago Declaration pledging OAS support to restore democracy in the hemisphere, such support did not include military action.

Even though, as Tom Farer, a former member of the Inter-American Court of Human Rights, maintained, Haiti was arguably the most telling case of a country that is recognized to need outside assistance—both to reinstate its democratic mandate and then to defend it—there was no consensus on how this should be done. One need only read the opinions of Michael Manley, former prime minister of Jamaica who had been appointed special envoy on Haiti by the secretary general of the OAS. According to Manley, any forceful intervention to reinstate Aristide "would destroy everything of symbolic importance for Haitian democracy."[34] Manley's recommendation was that Aristide undertake another round of negotiations with every sector in Haiti. It was evident to the military junta that there was nothing in Aristide's political composition and disposition that would make alliances possible. In 1964 Leslie Manigat described two fundamental characteristics of the political opposition to Papa Doc Duvalier: first, the continuation of the internal divisions and betrayals, "even in the face of systematic terror," which had existed before they went underground; second, and perhaps because of their sense of powerlessness, a profound "anxiety to assume power through foreign support." It is the latter attitude that leads them to ignore and minimize the organization and synchronization of internal coalitions and alliances.[35] There was thus a continuity between behavior while in exile and behavior while in power.

The military junta must also have been comforted when the OAS telegraphed its irresolution to the enemies of democracy in Haiti by stating that it reaffirmed the principle that states have the fundamental duty to abstain from intervening, directly or indirectly, for any reason whatever, in the internal or external affairs of any other state in accordance with Article 18 of the Charter. The OAS response to the bloody sabotage of the 1987 elections laid the foundation for the response to the 1991 crisis: statements of regret but reassertions of the principles of state sovereignty as an absolute prohibitor of effective international action. Chile's ambassador Muñoz made his country's position on forceful intervention quite clear—and public—when he noted that even a request from President Aristide, though "it might be well-founded on moral-political grounds," would be "on shaky juridical terrain given the fact that existing law clearly does not allow the use of force, unilaterally or collectively, on behalf of democracy."[36]

The invasion finally came under the auspices of the United Nations Security Council's Resolution 940 declaring that "the situation in Haiti constituted a threat to peace and security in the region." The UN has no authority to act to restore democracy anywhere.

The fact was that even Aristide must have sensed the Clinton administration's exasperation with the deadlocked situation. This sen-

[handwritten: remaining / neutral]

timent was captured by a rare critique coming from the liberal American press, an editorial in the *Washington Post* of December 22, 1993, entitled "The Haitian Deadlock." Aristide, said the *Post*, had demonstrated a troubling, because limited, view of his own role. It was up to him, not to an "imposed colonial situation," to devise a strategy to bring about his own return.

With time slipping by and the military showing no signs of giving up power, Aristide finally appealed to the UN Security Council for a military intervention. Later, his ambassador in Washington, who had actually made the request, argued that it was a patriotic appeal as the military represented "an internal occupying force" alien to true Haitian society.[37]

History records that it was not the United Nations but the exhortations and guarantees of former president Jimmy Carter, and the threat of an imminent invasion by twenty-four thousand U.S. troops, that returned Aristide to power. Those in the Lavalas movement who had long opposed any foreign intervention, and had gotten much political mileage from revisiting the first U.S. occupation, were now engaged in such verbal gymnastics as asserting the differences between a foreign military "intervention" and an "occupation." For the most part, however, they kept quiet about the foreign presence and went about their political business. Be that as it may, the question is whether the two new hypotheses on Haitian political culture help us understand specific decisions made, or not made, by Aristide since his return. I answer this question by analyzing two areas of decision making that seem particularly important given their relevance to the future of the society: first, Aristide's decisions regarding political organization and second, decisions in the area of economic development.

The Political Arena

President Aristide was candid with visiting former president Jimmy Carter that "remaining neutral" in the upcoming political campaigns of 1995 was not going to be easy. First, there was what he twice called "my political roots." In other words, Aristide had always been, and was so publicly identified as, an *engagé* populist radical. Neutrality was a suit that hardly fit the man. But there was another reason why neutrality would be difficult according to Aristide: there was nothing in Haitian political history or political culture that mandated that the president be the referee who would ensure that the process be fair to all. "It will be," Aristide told Carter, "a new experience for Haiti for one President to hand over power peacefully to another."[38] Thus it is good to keep in mind that there is Aristide and there is the context within which even this charismatic leader has to function. Even if one grants the fact that there is a very special interaction between this particular leader and the system, making his every action and word worth analyzing, one still has to contend with the system, which a past prime minister described as "Tough. Vicious."[39]

With two elections to be held in mid- and late 1995, as of June there were no significant fora, debates, or discussions of the platforms of the various parties. Granted that Haiti's political system has always functioned in the midst of rumors and presuppositions, the situation in 1995 had a sense of unreality and tenuousness about it, no doubt partly as a result of the massive U.S. military presence. That presence guaranteed the social calm that—outside of rampant brigandage and organized theft—reigned. It allowed Aristide to dismantle the army with a speed that surprised even his U.S. advisors, and it allowed Aristide's enemies on both the Marxist Left and the traditional Right to vent their frustrations without threatening the stability of the system.

Despite this partial artificiality, there were two trends that were too palpable and evident not to be noticed as major changes in Haiti's politics, if not its political culture. First, the political "center" had shifted toward the populist-reformist end of the spectrum. The traditional parties—those that contested the 1987 and 1990 elections and whose discourse tend toward the more conservative pole—appear to have little following.

This trend was already evident in the 1990 elections but was especially evident in 1995. Sociologist Michèle Oriol calls it *l'effêt coq*: even those inscribed in other political parties voted for the rooster, Aristide's political symbol.[40] One can get some perspective on the present political situation by noting the dilemma facing the once popular leader of the FNCD and mayor of Port-au-Prince, Evans Paul, popularly known as "K-Plum."

It was widely believed that the only competition for the Lavalas OPL (Organization Populaire Lavalas) was in the person of Paul, given his role in the FNCD coalition that provided Aristide with the institutional (not the popular) basis for his electoral victory in 1990. Excluded from the newly organized OPL, Paul organized his own party, the Konvansion Inite Demokratik (KID) (Convention for Democratic Initiatives). Not being one of the inner core of the Lavalas movement, his only political opportunities for national leadership lay outside the OPL, and yet his only chance for political success was to lay claim to the symbols and language of Lavalas, not an easy balancing act even for one as politically skilled as Paul. As Paul's natural constituencies, like those of Lavalas, were the slums (*bidonvilles*)—which daily increase in size and number—it is evident why he ("shamelessly," according to *Haiti Progress*) adopted the Aristide style and language. In the June 25 election, Paul was eventually soundly defeated by the OPL-backed candidate for mayor of Port-au-Prince, Mano Charlemagne. His assertion that the election had been "an electoral coup d'état" was lost by its being part of the protests of the twenty-odd parties that had decided to boycott the elections and by the good face that the Clinton administration's representatives decided to put on them.

All this contributed to exacerbating the second feature evident in Haiti in 1995: extreme polarization and intensity of personal animosities. There was arguably more distrust and suspicion than there was in the election years 1986–87 and 1990. According to Ira Lowenthal, who has followed Haitian politics for many years, in 1995 Haiti was entering "what is likely to be one of the most highly charged and overtly politicized periods in its recent democratic development."[41]

Beyond the normal characteristics of the Haitian system, there was the additional perception that one group monopolized all elements of power: the presidential palace, contact with and support from the United States, the new police force, and the only functioning grassroots organizations in the country. In other words, there is an asymmetry, in both motivational and material terms, that is quite overwhelming. This is where the holding of the 1995 elections and the actions of the agency in charge of running them, the Provisional Electoral Commission (CEP), became the focus of distrust and anger. The partisanship in filling posts was evident when Professor Anselme Rémy, formerly of Howard University in Washington and a known radical Lavalas activist, was appointed chairman of the CEP. He had no previous administrative experience of any kind, and the results were predictably chaotic: the legislative elections of June 25, 1995, were so disorganized that supplementary elections had to be held in August and September. With twenty-five opposition parties boycotting these elections, Lavalas candidates controlled 80 percent of all seats in the House and Senate. It is important, however, to understand that in Haiti few in the opposition were charitable enough to attribute the administrative chaos to Rémy's inexperience. There had to be something more diabolical behind the fiasco. Note, for instance, the thinking of René Theodore, secretary general of the orthodox communist party (now called Movement for National Reconstruction) and once the choice of President Aristide to be his prime minister. When his party was disqualified from participating in the election by the CEP, he explained it this way to Robert Pastor of the Carter Center: "Theodore claimed that the real reason for his disqualification was personal revenge by the President of the CEP [Rémy] and several Lavalas leaders, who opposed his efforts in the late 1980s to persuade the Communist Party—to which they all belonged—to accept the legitimacy of elections."[42]

With such long memories of what has to be considered "normal" Haitian political behavior, it is no surprise that the present system is as charged as it is. Yet it is critical to understand that the sectarianism evident in the system as a whole, and perhaps especially in the OPL's actions, had and has little to do with securing popular votes. This the

OPL has already secured because of Aristide and because of the wide network of grass-roots groups supporting Lavalas. At least at the grass-roots level, both political organization and mobilization have taken priority, tightly controlled by the Pères du Saint-Esprit and specifically by Father Jean-Yves Urfié, publisher of *Liberté,* and follow a defined ideological script, that of radical liberation theology. This combination of politics and religion has paid off handsomely. The fact that in the past the members of this order tended uniformly to condemn elections as merely part of what they called "the American plan" is today overlooked. In a country where so many appear to be suffering from historical amnesia, it is no surprise that the Pères du Saint-Esprit have buried this part of liberation theology and now favor electing Lavalas candidates, secure, of course, in the certainty of the outcome.

The real political competition thus appears to be within the OPL. Except for President Aristide, there is no single popular leader of that movement. In fact, the two other parties that comprise the OPL—the Mouvement d'Organization du Pays (MOP, Organizing Movement of the Nation) and the Parti Louvri Barye (PLB, Barye Workers Party)—are led by politicians with little resonance in the society, today or in the recent past. The competition seems to be for two things: (1) monopoly of the label "Lavalas," and (2) to be anointed by Aristide.

The leading candidate of the Lavalas organizers became René Préval, Aristide's first prime minister after the 1990 elections. It will be recalled that Préval was the constant center of controversy, with non-Lavalas members of Congress repeatedly seeking votes of no-confidence and unruly mobs stopping the vote by filling the galleries and surrounding the parliament building with burning tires. Threats of "Père Lébrun" were flung at Préval's opponents.[43] According to Americas Watch, Préval personally took up interrogating political prisoners while denying them legal counsel.[44] In late 1995, Préval was elected President.

The key organizer within the OPL is Gerard Pierre Charles, who has never run for office and spent most of the Duvalier period in exile in Mexico where he agitated in the Haitian communist party. Because he consistently opposed all form of electoral mobilization, observers tend to base their opinions about him on his previous academic writings, which are decidedly Marxist in slant. However, it is not clear that these writings correctly reflect his present politics as he has now emerged as a fervent advocate of free elections. Interestingly enough, one of his arguments is that "the West," including the United States, should now support free elections.[45] He would not be the first "progressive" leader in the Caribbean to change his stripes when faced with the prospects of actually being in power. In fact, doing so would be very Haitian, just as it is very Haitian that many of his former colleagues on the Left now consider Charles' support for elections a "sellout."

The prominence of political insiders such as Charles with no previous involvement in Haitian political campaigns and few outside political commitments—in other words, keeping the core "pure"—is an attempt to reduce the number of potential compromises and mutual obligations that all reciprocal relations imply. This necessarily means the marginalization of those who do have such experiences. As Jean-Claude Bajeaux of KONAKOM (the Komité Nasyonal Kongré Mouvman Democratik [National Committee of the Congress of Democratic Movements]) told the press, "we were a family and he threw us out of the house. Some real friends of Aristide were left on the outside."[46]

Thus one would have to conclude that Evans Paul is wrong when he says that "confusion is the basis of all political events in Haiti."[47] Everything indicates that the core of Lavalas organizers is highly motivated and shows that motivation through very rational individualism and even sectarianism. This is one way of ensuring political control and party discipline in systems with weak party organization and charismatic rather than institutionalized mobilization. It is hardly the way to engender pluralism, however.

A similar tightfisted modus operandi does not seem to be operating in regard to economic policy. There, indecision—intentional or unintentional—governs.

What Kind of Economic Plan?

Despite the near monopoly of congressional power, it is not evident that this legislature will have the capacity to take economic initiatives as mandated by the 1987 Constitution. Indeed, like the prime minister and the cabinet, they were ignored as Aristide listened to his shadow cabinet of close aides in the palace. "He rarely summons his ministers to meetings," reports the *New York Times*, "but leaves them working blindly in offices scattered about the capital."[48]

The economic program for a returned Aristide government was set in Paris in mid-1993 by a Joint Mission consisting of the Haitian Presidential Commission, the UN Development Program, IMF, World Bank, Inter-American Development Bank, OAS, and USAID.[49] Central to the economic recovery, according to the mission, was reform of the nine largest public enterprises, which were said to be "an important drain on public sector financial resources."[50] This was putting it mildly as it is these enterprises that have been at the center of the debate over corruption, patronage, and inefficiency since the Duvaliers set them up. Not surprisingly, the mission discovered that two of the enterprises, the flour mill and the cement factory (MINOTERIE and Ciment) continued to borrow money from public and private sources, as well as pay salaries, months after they had been shut down. It is fair to conclude that the least of the functions of these enterprises is to contribute to economic development.

Yet it is to the defense of continued state ownership of these albatrosses that the leaders of the Lavalas political movement have dedicated themselves. Aristide's position has been positively ambiguous regarding the original commitment to privatize them. On September 4, 1995, he told an angry group of trade unionists from the nine state enterprises that he "had not signed any document authorizing their privatization."[51] The workers vowed all-out "popular" opposition to what they called the American-inspired sale of the national patrimony by antipatriotic Haitians. This is a case where that powerful myth of the all-powerful role of the United States (hypothesis no. 1) has been revived and made operational. It falls under the general rubric of *le plan américaine.*

That very day the prime minister, Smark Michel, was in Washington attempting to secure the release of the hundreds of millions of dollars promised by the international community, a release conditioned on the liberalization of the economy, including the privatization of state enterprises. Confronted with the evident vacillation emanating from the presidential palace, a member of Michel's delegation dismissed the Lavalas economic nationalists opposing liberalization as a "minority without influence."[52]

This seems to underestimate how the confusion regarding economic development generally and privatization specifically serves the purposes of the highly motivated political clique around Aristide. First, they have the advantage that economic nationalism draws on previous positions taken by Aristide. There is the successful identification of economic reform with "neoliberalism," a favorite target of liberation theology and the Left generally, which thus provides an international cover for the nationalism. Second, economic nationalism ensures continued political patronage. Ideology without jobs might satisfy the most ardent liberation theology follower, but it will hardly do for that army of urban bureaucrats who might not have all the votes but certainly have the power to bring the system to a complete halt.

Finally, there is the not-so-subtle "personalization" of the issue in such a way as to insinuate a color-class basis to the conflict. The attacks have been directed against three members of the government team: Prime Minister Smark Michel, Minister of Finance Marie-Michele Rey, and Governor of the Central Bank Leslie Delatour. All three were earlier singled out by Aristide himself as representing the "mulatto," "bourgeois" sector of his government, evidence of his conciliatory approach.[53] What protects this trio is Aristide's apparent indecision or indifference regarding economics as well as the wide support they enjoy in the multilateral lending agencies; they represent in essence the totality of the technical team of the government. Rey and

Delatour were key members of the presidential commission that negotiated the Emergency Economic Program. They have been branded as
the antipatriotic "merchants" of their country. This theme is not
purely a matter of parliamentary debates but rather of constant street
protests and "popular" pressure that include the burning of tires in
front of parliament and other key offices—all reminiscent of the first
phase of the Aristide administration.[54] In terms of the populist politics
governing the society, it has to be said that these noisy demonstrations
are more than a match for the gentle seminars conducted by Smarck
Michel at local hotels on the relationship between privatization, liberalization, economic modernization, and political democracy.[55]

Not surprisingly, Prime Minister Michel has gone from his broad
economic offensive to defending his reputation: he is not antipatriotic,
he told a press conference, he sees President Aristide every morning,
and the president has given him no instructions to stop the privatization program. "The moment he orders me to desist," he told the press,
"the program will stop immediately."[56] With economic nationalism
slowly but surely becoming an integral part of the evolving Lavalas political campaign for the presidency, it might not be too long before it
becomes the litmus test of loyalty to the cause. It certainly is an issue
beyond the comprehension of the majority of the peasantry who do the
electing; it is key to the urban politicos who do the selecting and governing. In this respect Haitian politics has not moved much from that
urban-rural divide so frequently decried by academics and populist politicians alike.

It appears that it is the Lavalas clique in the OPL that has the motivation to see its program and people in power. Compromise and coalition forming are not necessary given *l'effet coq* and given Aristide's
own propensity either to side with them openly or remain ambiguous.

This propensity toward individualism and sectarianism extends to
relations with the United States. Despite apparent cordial relations between Aristide and U.S. President Clinton, the OPL leadership has resisted any attempts at mending fences with U.S. congressional sources.
In February 1995 the new chairman of the Republican-dominated
Western Hemisphere Subcommittee of the House Foreign Affairs Committee, Representative Dan Burton, led a delegation to talk with Aristide. A U.S. journalist with good access reported that the tone of the
meeting had been "inquisitional," "arrogant and even insulting."[57]

One would normally expect that given the evident—and clearly displayed—shift in the U.S. congressional mood toward helping Haiti, the
Aristide people would welcome any assistance from other, more sympathetic, influential U.S. agencies. Certainly one such agency is directed by former president Jimmy Carter. He visited Haiti one week
after the Republican visit. His reception was anything but warm. "Instead of receiving a hero's welcome," wrote Larry Rohter of the *New*

York Times, "he was immediately plunged into the turmoil of Haitian domestic politics."[58] Douglas Farah of the *Washington Post* noted that the antagonism stemmed from Carter's role in the 1990 election when, say the Lavalas people, "we knew then he was trying to steal the elections for the Americans."[59] Again, hypothesis no.1, this time with added vehemence. Two senior aides to Aristide denied that the president had invited Carter and then added insult to injury by adding the following about former president Carter, General Colin Powell, and Senator Sam Nunn: "He said he was coming and so we will invite him to dinner, but we do not know what he is doing here. We know that we have to watch all three of them carefully, because they are tricky, sneaky."[60]

With their popular base secure, with their president protected by the U.S. and multinational troops, with a basically sympathetic president in Washington, one would expect the OPL elite to at least dissimulate their sectarianism, if only rhetorically. This, however, would contradict the nature of Haitian politics where the stakes are always high because they invariably involve fundamentally one office: the presidency. In this game, the asymmetry of motivations, evident in both actions and speech, divides the gladiators from the observers. The Lavalas elite are all gladiators, and one could only expect them to act and speak as such.

Conclusion

If this refutation of the four major myths concerning Haitian political behavior is valid, then one can expect Haitian political culture to survive the present occupation virtually unchanged. If the two new propositions are valid, one can expect only individualism, not coalitions and conciliation, and eventually the rise of another *caudillo.* Understanding the true nature of the game, this *caudillo* will preach democracy even as he prepares to fend off all pretenders, by whatever means necessary. Similarly, the opposition, splintered and multiplied into a truly absurd number of "parties," will continue to resist forming enduring alliances and coalitions to confront what is essentially a political juggernaut. They, after all, also partake in the country's political culture.

Perhaps Evans Paul illustrates the shifting moral positions that confirm that old adage that where you stand depends on where you sit. While still mayor and hopeful presidential contender, he boasted: "We are in a country where everything is polarized [and many politicians] are opportunists. But sometimes you need opportunists to permit you to implement your program. I think that if we have to make an alliance with the Devil, we do it for the well-being of the country."[61] This is the typical "dirty hands dilemma" posed by Niccolò Machiavelli: "When the act accuses, the result excuses." Unfortunately, Haitian history records mighty few cases where the results ultimately excused. Paul's recent political demise is living example of that.

10

Mexico: The Decline of Dominant-Party Rule

Denise Dresser

During 1994 Mexicans from all walks of life seemed to be following the Chinese dictum "May you live in interesting times." An indigenous uprising, political assassinations, kidnappings, the peso's plunge, and the short-lived hunger strike of former president Carlos Salinas de Gortari transformed the icon of predictable politics in Latin America into the country of uncertainty. The costs of Mexico's latest bout of economic mismanagement have been felt in the pocketbooks of 85 million Mexicans. However, the country's slide from the Mexican miracle to the Mexican meltdown may, paradoxically, intensify the pace of Mexico's incomplete transition from authoritarianism. The events of 1994 have contributed to the rapid unraveling of dominant-party rule and loosened the grip that the Institutional Revolutionary Party (PRI) established since its inception in 1929.

In Mexico the PRI has been a way of life: a system of formal and informal rules, elite circulation, patronage distribution, and clientelist practices. Economic reform during the 1980s and 1990s, however, challenged traditional sources of power by redefining relations among all social, economic, and political forces in the country. Structural reforms including trade liberalization, deregulation, and privatization led to the appearance of new players, to the decline of corporatist structures, and to the weakening of the PRI.[1]

As the result of this broad spectrum of changes, Mexico's governance is in a transitional phase and could fit into Philippe Schmitter's description of "fledgling neodemocracies."[2] Whereas in the past Mexicans were offered economic growth instead of democracy, now the reverse may be true. In order to compensate the population for dramatic declines in income provoked by the devaluation, the government has promised greater political opening. President Ernesto Zedillo's anti-corruption crusade and the promise of a "definitive" electoral reform augur an era of unprecedented power sharing and government accountability.[3] However, despite the optimism fueled by Zedillo's pledges to reform the judiciary, enact a new federalist pact, exercise greater vigilance over government spending, and call former "untouchables" in the political system to account, it is unclear that fully democratic and sustainable institutions can simultaneously emerge and address economic and social problems.

Several actors such as the Zapatista National Liberation Army (EZLN), radical factions of the left-wing Party of the Democratic Revolution (PRD), former president Salinas, and the narcopoliticians are still unwilling to play by the democratic rules of the game.[4] They use their influence to destabilize the political system (through guerrilla warfare and political assassination) and thus jeopardize policy initiatives. Both the democratic empowerment and the democratic accountability of actors in the government and the opposition have yet to be achieved.[5] Although President Zedillo's imprisonment of Raúl Salinas, the brother of former president Salinas, for his alleged involvement in the assassination of a top-ranking PRI official may create new standards of public accountability, the rule of law has yet to prevail at most levels of the political system.

This chapter's main argument is that the legacies of dominant-party rule, including institutional fragility, centralized decision making, and economic and political polarization, constitute serious obstacles to the consolidation of democratic governance in Mexico. Although great progress has been achieved in the electoral arena, the promise of free and fair elections may not be enough to assuage the adjustment fatigue that a third round of economic austerity will undoubtedly create. Mexico faces problems—such as the Chiapas revolt, the growing infiltration of state institutions by drug traffickers, and the antisystemic attitude of many key players—that are broader than those related to the transformation of the country's political regime and cannot be solved electorally.[6] The country is moving toward political democracy, but effective power sharing and government accountability are still scarce commodities.

What remains to be done is nothing short of reinventing the political landscape: institutionalizing new actors, practices, and rules, and engaging in a concerted transformation of the Mexican state. This systemic renewal would entail giving legitimate and regular access to those forces, parties, and groups that are outside the PRI or that, because of the PRI's practices, could never flourish while the PRI dominated the party system. The twilight of the PRI will occur only when consensus building among elites and the people, pact making with opposition parties, and the universal application of the rule of law become a daily part of the country's institutional fabric.

Elections: Free but Not Fair, Important but Not Enough

As Sergio Aguayo, head of the Civic Alliance (AC), declared: "The Mexican elections give us many reasons to celebrate, to lament, and to reflect."[7] The 1994 presidential election marked a significant step forward in Mexico's unfinished transition to a more competitive, democratic system of governance. However, even though the critical importance of elections was widely recognized, one of the major parties (the PRD) did not accept the results and several groups, including the Zapatista rebels, continued to disqualify the rule of law and reject established institutions and political organizations. Although the 1994 elections were generally perceived as clean and free, the structural inequalities of the political system persisted.

The resilience of the PRI was proven once again on August 21, 1994, through not immaculate but relatively decent presidential elections accepted by international observers, the refurbished Federal Electoral Institute, the media, and the Mexican public at large. The PRI demonstrated its time-honed capacity to reinvent itself in adverse circumstances and once again reestablish its predominant position. In the most competitive, scrutinized, and supervised election in Mexican history, the PRI once again managed to extend its longevity, despite the avowed impetus for change fueled by the Chiapas uprising. Hegemonic party rule acquired an unprecedented legitimacy at the ballot box.

The PRI's victory was rooted in a variety of factors.[8] On August 21, Mexico witnessed the reemergence of an inherent conservatism in the Mexican electorate. Since the Chiapas uprising, Mexico had been immersed in a struggle between two divergent currents and forces. Chiapas propelled Mexican public opinion toward the Center-Left, in favor of accountability, change, and renewal, thereby suggesting the demise of Mexican complacency with dominant-party rule. However, the assassination of Luis Donaldo Colosio propelled Mexican public opinion back to the Center-Right, in favor of permanence, stability, and continuity. On election day, broad sectors of the Mexican electorate had trouble envisioning political life in the country without the PRI. The population turned out in droves—the participation rate was an impressive 77 percent of the registered voters—to vote for the reliable, known, predictable option versus the great question mark that the opposition still represents. In a political climate tainted by suspicion, uncertainty, increased public insecurity, and fear of the future, the PRI handily marketed itself as a guarantor of stability and continuity.[9]

Although circumstantial factors may explain the *voto de miedo* (fear vote) in favor of the PRI, expectations also played an important role. President Salinas successfully governed Mexico for six years by fueling expectations of better things to come; he offered visions of a first world Mexico propelled into modernity by the enactment of the North American Free Trade Agreement (NAFTA). Those expectations became a powerful political tool for the ruling party. Many voters were afraid that the Salinista economic reform and its expected benefits would be thwarted by the arrival of the opposition into power.

In addition, August 21 became a great national referendum on President Salinas and the dramatic changes he introduced into Mexico's political economy. Exit polls revealed that satisfaction with his performance translated into votes for the ruling party. Many voters voted their pocketbooks. More than 40 percent of those polled leaving voting booths stated that their economic situation was better in 1994 than it had been six years before. Finally, the 1994 election was won for the PRI by the poor. Large segments of the urban and rural population voted for the PRI, suggesting the effectiveness and popularity of the National Solidarity Program (PRONASOL) and PROCAMPO programs.[10]

An important segment of the electorate voted in favor of "salinastroika"; in favor of structural reforms, trade opening, and the overhaul of the public sector. Beneficiaries of the Salinas revolution rewarded him for "a job well done." The outcome of the August 21 election also suggested that Mexico's basic political axis shifted toward the Center-Right, and that Salinas was capable of providing a certain amount of institutionalization via the ballot box to the kind of Mexico he envisioned. It is not clear whether Salinas won his own election, but he won it for Ernesto Zedillo.

The state of the opposition also explained the outcome of the presidential race. After the presidential debate, when National Action Party (PAN) candidate Diego Fernández de Cevallos jumped from 15 to 30 percent in the polls, it appeared that the Mexican electorate was extremely volatile and could be swayed overnight by a successful media performance. For the first time since its creation, the PAN believed it could win the Mexican presidency. And then, for reasons that have yet to be determined, Fernández de Cevallos disappeared from the political race for more than two weeks. PAN officials offered a host of explanations: illness, weight loss, meeting behind the scenes with the "real factors of power" (such as diplomats and businessmen), and preparing for the economic debate with his contenders that never took place.[11] The candidate's disappearance undoubtedly had a significant impact on the race. What he had won with his televised metamorphosis into a right-wing *caudillo*, the PAN lost with his disappearance after the presidential debate. The party never fully regained the momentum it had acquired in the weeks after the debate, and thus left potential voters stranded. Many returned to the folds of the PRI on election day. Errors in campaign strategy turned out to be decisive.

On the opposite side of the political spectrum, the PRD spent the last months of the campaign trying to recover from the death blow the televised debate had dealt to its presidential candidate, Cuauhtémoc Cárdenas. Once again the Left was caught in debilitating struggles between factions and personalities, and as a result changed course midway through the campaign. The PRD oscillated from radicalism to moderation, and back to radicalism again when guerrilla leader Subcomandante Marcos endorsed the Cárdenas candidacy. Additionally, the perception of having "lost" in 1988 hurt Cárdenas, among voters who viewed his crusade as a futile one, given that in all likelihood he would never be allowed to govern.[12]

Finally, it became clear that the PRI still enjoyed many advantages, subtle and blatant, from its symbiotic relationship with the government. The imperative for Mexico's modernizing technocrats was to hold a clean and fair election. The postelection consensus among opposition forces was that the presidential race was clean but not fair. The election was clean and free insofar as the rules of political competition changed: Citizen Counsellors were incorporated into the Federal Electoral Institute (IFE), national observers and international visitors were present at the *casillas* (polling booths), limits were set on campaign spending, and quick counts and exit polls were allowed. These innovations contributed to imbue the electoral process with an unprecedented degree of credibility.

However, the fairness of the political process, beyond election day, remained a source of contention. The PRI still had many powerful weapons at its disposal that strengthened its staying power in a competitive electoral scenario, including the government's marriage of convenience with the television giant Televisa, the entrenched clientelist network created by both the PRONASOL and PROCAMPO programs, and the capacity to manipulate electoral outcomes. The Civic Alliance reported that the vote was not secret in 34 percent of the *casillas*; people were pressured to vote in 16.5 percent of the *casillas*; and in 65.1 percent of the *casillas*, voters with credentials did not appear on the *lista nominal* (voter registration list).[13] The debate on irregularities continued after the election, and focused mainly on the voter registration list, campaign spending, media coverage, and the political climate prior to election day. Whether democracy can be fully achieved in a country with long-standing one-party rule will depend on whether structural inequalities and deficiencies in the political system are addressed and resolved.

The results of the election may have laid to rest the foremost source of disputes among the country's political actors: electoral fraud. But these results, and the elections themselves, are not enough to create a fully democratic polity. Clean elections are a necessary condition for democracy, but they are not sufficient. Mexico must confront other structural issues. Free elections cannot assure democratic consolidation if the playing field among political parties is not level. A competitive and professional media cannot develop if there is no effective guarantee of freedom of expression. It is unclear that democracy will emerge if there is no commitment to an open debate over policy issues, and if there are no mechanisms by which to hold government officials and other political actors accountable to society and the law.

Democracy is more than elections.[14] The most accepted definition of democracy identifies it with regular elections, fairly conducted and honestly counted. This is the mistake known as "electoralism" or "the faith that merely holding elections will channel political action into peaceful contests among elites and accord public legitimacy to the winners," no matter if they are conducted in an unfair fashion.[15] Elections occur in a discontinuous fashion, and they offer only those choices presented by political parties. True democracies include a gamut of competitive processes and channels (beyond elections) for the expression of interests: associational as well as partisan, functional as well as territorial, collective as well as individual. All are central to its functioning.[16] These processes and channels have yet to emerge and become consolidated in contemporary Mexico.

Fragile Institutions and Traditional Fiefdoms

Decades of dominant-party rule have created serious problems of institutional fragility and lack of representation. The PRI's predominance has hampered what Guillermo O'Donnell considers fundamental conditions for democratic consolidation: "the emergence of regularized and predictable practices, embodied in public organizations that process the demands of politically active sectors, in line with the rules of the competitive game."[17]

Mexico's predominant political style has been presidentialist, clientelist, and patronage-driven. This style has created a world antithetical to democracy, "with little institutional mediations, where personal relationships prevail, and the logic of representation functions intermittently."[18] Although Mexican civil society has become stronger, the political immaturity of social organizations has precluded greater political evolution. Relatively autonomous institutions within the popular sector are still easy prey for clientelism. In addition, the economic debacle of December 1994 has contributed to an even further weakening and discrediting of state institutions and party structures. As elsewhere in Latin America, Mexico's public institutions and several political parties are deeply troubled. Intermediate organizations linking state and society are precarious or in a state of flux.

The country's hegemonic party, the PRI, was conceived to aid Mexico's revolutionary family in the task of institutional construction; the party was designed to build durable links between elites and masses. And for more than fifty years the PRI accomplished its mission. The party functioned successfully since its founding in 1929 as a pragmatic coalition of interests, based on the organized inclusion of the working class, peasants, bureaucrats, and the military. However, as a result of the process of economic overhaul prompted by the debt crisis of the 1980s, the party began to fail in its historic role as interest aggregator, policymaker, and legitimator. Unable to meet the demands of sectors accustomed to a flow of material benefits, the party lost representativeness among its bases. Displaced by a technocratic team intent on implementing economic reform, and wracked by internal factionalism, the party was increasingly marginalized from the decision-making process. Incapable of guaranteeing mass support via uncontested electoral victories, the party began to fail as a legitimator of the regime.[19]

Throughout the Salinas term, groups within the PRI struggled among themselves and against the president in search of a new course. Reform-minded factions attempted to dismantle compulsory sectoral affiliation and promote individual militancy in the face of a more competitive electoral scenario, while traditionalists sought to maintain the party's age-old structures and standard operating procedures. Reformists favored Salinas' economic liberalization policies, while conservatives decried the death of the interventionist state. In order to circumvent party resistance and push forward his economic modernization agenda, Salinas often resorted to discretionary postelection maneuvering that further contributed to deinstitutionalize the country's political landscape.

Mexico's deinstitutionalization was also fueled by the growing tension between increasingly competitive state elections and the imperatives of a presidentialist and centralized governance formula. Extralegal and extrainstitutional forms of conflict resolution in the states of Guanajuato, San Luis Potosí, and Michoacán contributed to the erosion of presidential prestige, institutions, and political parties. Local elections throughout the Salinas term were not normal processes that expressed the views of the citizenry, but rather conflict-ridden events where, independently of what was expressed at the polls, ad hoc decisions were taken and backroom deals were struck, systematically jeopardizing regional stability and regional governance.[20]

It remains to be seen whether elections under Zedillo will follow the same turbulent path, or whether the relatively clean presidential election will set new standards for political behavior. Zedillo recognized opposition victories in several states but has also failed to punish PRI governors who have committed electoral fraud or resorted to repression and intimidation to maintain themselves in office.[21]

The conservative National Action Party has emerged as the short-term beneficiary of the economic collapse and has used popular disaffection with the ruling party to make significant electoral inroads, including the governorship of the state of Jalisco.[22] But the electorate could very well punish the PAN as much as it has the PRI, if Mexico's right-wing alternative fails to deliver economic prosperity. Economic chaos could thus bring about the birth of *alternancia* in Mexican regional politics, whereby in each round of elections parties are voted in or out depending on their performance. Economic decline, however, could also contribute to weaken the links between parties and citizens.

Mexico's current deinstitutionalization will make the country's renewed economic adjustment much more difficult to manage politically. Labor has been called on to sacrifice once again, at a time in which the heavy machinery of PRI-sponsored corporatism no longer seems to function. During the Salinas term, luxury imports bought the political alignment of the middle class; after the devaluation, the middle class is no longer a member of the ruling party's captive audience. Economic adjustment will create a much more volatile and much less loyal electorate, thus opening up windows of opportunity for opposition parties on both the Left and the Right of the political spectrum. Whether parties will be able to bridge the chasm of distrust that currently separates them from an increasingly disaffected population is an open question. Economic decline could also lead to widespread disillusionment with the existing political options offered by parties, and to the strengthening of opposition movements working outside of party channels.

Throughout 1994 the efforts of key political actors, including Interior Minister Jorge Carpizo, the Citizen Counsellors, and the Civic Alliance, to imbue the electoral process with greater credibility bore fruit. Zedillo's expressed commitment to reform the judiciary has been well received by the Mexican public, and the naming of a prominent member of the PAN as attorney general has imbued the government's efforts with a legitimacy they would otherwise have lacked. But the tardiness of these efforts and the difficulty of overcoming decades of distrust and opacity explain the lack of public confidence in state institutions and political parties.

The Mexican party system is only partially institutionalized.[23] The rules that govern interparty competition are unstable, and political elites do not share the expectation that elections will be the primary route to power. The electoral accords agreed upon before the 1994 presidential election suffered from several problems that hampered their effectiveness: they were not sufficiently inclusive or encompassing, and they were not sufficiently binding.[24] Various groups, including factions within the PRD, felt that their interests and concerns were not adequately represented, and therefore contemplated the possibility of ignoring or abandoning them. Groups within the PRI resorted to fraud (albeit intermittently) during the election, and the PRD refused to accept the results although the party had committed itself to do so. As a result, the postelection debate in Mexico revealed the persistence of profound disagreements and polarizing tendencies among party actors. PRI spokesmen talked of the need to "perfect" Mexican democracy, while opposition members continued to call for more substantive changes. The absence of clear rules to govern political competition

among parties has made politics more erratic, governing more complicated, and the establishment of legitimacy more difficult.

Parties are indispensable for democratic consolidation, yet in Mexico parties have failed to "encapsulate" the demands of major interest
groups. As a result, parties often have been eclipsed by politically ambivalent actors and protagonists in civil society, including the EZLN
and its sympathizers, renowned members of the hierarchy of the Catholic Church, nongovernmental organizations (NGOs), business leaders,
and media moguls. In the face of an unstable and conflict-ridden party
system, social movements and interest groups have sought alternative
vehicles for representation.

In the past, political activities in Mexico have been monopolized by
political parties and the state. But since the critical juncture created by
the 1985 earthquake, a nascent civil society is gradually strengthening
NGOs, altering political discourse, and creating a more auspicious environment for political reform. During the past ten years Mexico has
witnessed the emergence of autonomous nongovernmental organizations and informal networks devoted to monitoring elections and promoting governmental accountability.[25] The political activism of these
groups has revealed a burgeoning process of citizen participation and
consciousness, but also reflects public distrust with established political parties, inherited from decades of authoritarian rule.

As Scott Mainwaring and Timothy Scully have argued, when a party
system is not fully institutionalized, a multitude of actors "competes
for influence and power, often employing non-democratic means."[26] In
Mexico, nonparty groupings and individuals in civil society have frequently acted above and beyond specifically political organizations.
Their role has been a dual one: their newfound activism has contributed to the uncertainty of the transition but also to its speed. Their
antisystemic behavior fueled systemic change. However, radical nonparty actors could create intractable problems for the future. Several of
them, including the mercurial Subcomandante Marcos and El Barzón
sympathizers, have individual agendas and interests that are radically
incompatible with the construction of democratic normalcy.[27] Oftentimes the leaders of these organizations espouse apocalyptic and anti-
institutional visions that, if acted upon, could generate polarizations
and ruptures that might jeopardize current achievements. The radicalization of nonparty actors has fueled a climate in which multiple cur-
rencies, including force, violence, and mass movements, compete for
power and influence.

In addition, Mexico still lacks many modern institutional arrangements that could facilitate democratic consolidation by providing predictability and stability in the political arena. In Mexico, most
institutions are not neutral frameworks for containing and channeling
political change but rather PRI-dominated fiefdoms. Existing institu-

tions—the judiciary, Congress, business associations, unions—have been kept frozen in the past and are inadequate to address present problems. In the absence of well-developed institutional checks and balances, patrimonialism and clientelism continue to prevail.

Since its creation, the PRI has depended on patronage to assure its predominance, on the historic distribution of perks and benefits to its constituents. In any process of economic stabilization and adjustment, the most politically influential losers have been the officials of the ruling party and their closest allies, and Mexico is no exception. At the height of his power and popularity in 1991, President Salinas attempted to modernize the party, but internal resistance was too great, and therefore the project was ultimately abandoned. The government-affiliated labor movement was not "democratized" under Salinas. Top-down authoritarian control of unionized workers by labor union bosses persisted, and many of the antimodern features of the government-PRI tandem survived unchecked, including the channeling of public funds for party purposes.

President Zedillo has promised to delink the party from the government and also reform the PRI. However, it remains to be seen whether the president will have the ability to implement a democratizing reform within the party and pressure it into creating linkage formulas beyond clientelism. In order to win the election, Zedillo allied himself with some of the more traditional power brokers within the PRI. Zedillo may be too constrained by political commitments and institutional legacies to push forward a significant political modernization agenda against traditional fiefdoms. In some geographic regions and economic activities, Mexico is still characterized by the existence of powerful *cacicazgos* (fiefdoms) that rallied behind the Zedillo campaign because they perceived him as a weak candidate and knew that their own survival was at stake. In the face of the modernizing directives Zedillo announced once in office, many traditional governors and local *caciques* (power-holders) have closed ranks, opposed the central government's plans, and then proceeded with politics as usual. Mexico seems to be witnessing the growing "feudalization" of the PRI, whereby local power brokers govern their states in the way they see fit, often resorting to violence, fraud, and repression.

The traditional linkages provided by PRI-sponsored corporatism and patronage politics are deteriorating at a fast pace in some parts of the country, but in others the PRI's traditional structure prevails. In states where the PRI has lost ground, alternative forms of mediation between state and society have yet to emerge. The strength and coherent internal functioning of opposition parties and popular movements remain unclear, and as a result Mexican society lacks organizations for effective representation of interests. Patterns of representation in Mexico are still undergoing significant changes, and until they stabilize, the regime is trapped in the dysfunctional category of a "disintermediated neodemocracy."[28]

Centralized Decisions and Insulated Technocrats

Analysts of the politics of economic reform in the developing world have often identified the importance of bureaucratic "insulation" and "expert change teams" as causes of effective policymaking.[29] Yet in the Mexican case, insulated technocratic rule exacerbated the financial crisis. The havoc unleashed by the devaluation was the unfortunate economic manifestation of a political crisis rooted in insulated technobureaucratic rule. Since the country's first financial fiasco in 1982, the imperatives of managing the economy created incentives for state elites to insulate economic policymaking from societal pressure and centralize decision making in the Economic Cabinet.[30] However, these dual paths of insulation and centralization further contributed to Mexico's widespread lack of accountability, a lack of accountability that allowed President Salinas to postpone ad infinitum a much-needed devaluation of the currency.

In a recent article in the *Journal of Democracy*, Guillermo O'Donnell asks: "Do Economists Know Best?"[31] The Mexican debacle would suggest not. Mexico's best and brightest allegedly knew how to reduce inflation, privatize, deregulate, alleviate fiscal imbalances, and implement avowedly optimal economic policies. President Zedillo's campaign slogan was "He knows how to do it" ("El sabe cómo hacerlo"), in a clear reference to his impeccable technical credentials. However, what the best and the brightest did not know was how to use short-term economic achievements as a springboard for sustainable growth.[32] The hypercentralized nature of the political system allowed President Salinas to place personal prestige before economic prudence, and as a result the Mexican population has borne the brunt of a new round of austerity measures unprecedented for their severity.

As Barbara Geddes has argued, to understand why governments undertake or postpone reforms, it is crucial to focus on "the people who make policies, what their interests are, and what shapes their interests."[33] In strong presidentialist systems like Mexico's, ideas held by the president and his economic advisors are fundamental for understanding what political-economic models are adopted. Presidentialist systems allow the chief executive and his advisors to make their own policy preferences into policy objectives.[34] In the Mexican case, President Salinas did not devalue the currency when he could have for political and personal reasons, such as guaranteeing a PRI victory in the August presidential election and assuring his place in history as Mexico's great modernizer. No other institution within the Mexican government, not even the central bank, had the power or the autonomy to question the soundness of his judgment.[35] Salinas placed economic policy at the service of his own political interests, perhaps not even fully aware of the deleterious economic implications of that decision.

Hence the Mexican financial debacle also sheds light on the perils of unbounded presidentialism. From the beginning of his term, Salinas resorted to swift, unilateral presidential action as a means for furthering the economic liberalization agenda. Through the image of a strong and populist presidency, Salinas mobilized the energies and captured the imagination of the population for the modernization effort. By undertaking reforms on a broad spectrum of issues, the president garnered support among constituencies opposed to clientelism and corruption and in favor of change. Salinas was widely perceived as a president *con iniciativa* (with initiative) waging a war of modernity against the old Mexico.

However, the institutional and cultural legacies of his hyperpresidentialist rule have created serious obstacles to democratic consolidation in Mexico.[36] The president's personal style of governance instituted a form of decision making contrary to institutionalization. The president was a promoter of centralized authority and its key beneficiary. He, Salinas, not the political system itself, acquired support from the electorate through ad hoc interventions. Time and time again, in poll after poll, Mexicans gave much greater support to Salinas than to his party and similarly to his decision-making style.[37] Vigorous presidentialism was key to the success of Mexico's adjustment effort, but also a main obstacle to future political evolution: increased presidentialism curtailed the emergence of effective institutions that could both aggregate interests and implement coherent economic policies.

Upon his arrival in office on December 1, 1994, President Ernesto Zedillo was confronted with the institutional vacuum left by his predecessor and with widespread societal expectations about the need for a strong presidency. Given the lack of institutional support, the new president's political clumsiness exacerbated the financial debacle and turned it into a perceived crisis of leadership. In the aftermath of the devaluation, public opinion at home and abroad placed complete responsibility for political management on the presidential chair. For two weeks that chair seemed to be empty, as Zedillo floundered and seemed unable to present a consistent explanation for the devaluation to foreign and domestic investors and the Mexican population at large. In a highly personalistic and presidentialist system, Mexicans expected Zedillo to respond authoritatively via presidentialist strikes, dramatic moves, and bold measures. It was only when Zedillo launched a political attack on one of the "untouchables" in the political system, the brother of former president Salinas, that public confidence in his ability to govern was partially restored.

In the first months after the devaluation, the first priority for the Zedillo government became the herculean task of regaining the confidence of international investors. Given that since 1991 the ruling technocracy gambled on speculative foreign investment as a fulcrum for growth, it had little choice but to make concessions. The devaluation trapped the Mexican government between "the need to rid the economy from its legacy of instability and inefficiency, the domestic political restrictions to do it and powerful and volatile external forces that clouded its vision and compromised its policies."[38] This left the Zedillo team with little room to maneuver given Mexico's need for foreign capital: the only viable option was to negotiate an aid package assembled by the U.S. government and international financial institutions in order to repay its short-term debt. The package contained stringent requirements, including that the Mexican government run a budget surplus and tighten credit through higher interest rates. To fulfill these requirements the Mexican government had no other choice but to offer more austerity at home, leading to dramatic declines in income, rampant unemployment, and volatile politics.

Zedillo's response to the political challenges created by the devaluation was to announce the "modernization" of the Mexican presidency. Zedillo offered to reduce discretionary policymaking, promote a new federalist pact, decentralize power, and bring an end to the symbiotic relationship between the presidency and the ruling party. As an accidental candidate and outsider to the PRI, Zedillo did not feel beholden to the party and therefore believed that the costs of reform would be lower given that he and his close-knit team of advisors were not previously tied to the beneficiaries of state largesse.[39]

However, outsiders oftentimes fail to achieve what they hope precisely because they are outsiders.[40] Time and again, Zedillo has designed and then failed to implement policy objectives because of opposition within the PRI leadership or its rank and file. Zedillo has been unable to elicit widespread support from established party leaders, and as a result his efforts have often been blocked by traditional factions of the political elite. The president and his team have often underestimated the ferocity of PRI and popular opposition to allegedly optimal economic policies, such as the increase in the Value Added Tax (IVA) from 10 to 15 percent. Zedillo's substantive preference has been to achieve economic stabilization, and as a result he has tended to neglect the political and economic needs of the unstable coalition on which his power is based. Mexican political elites have displayed a marked propensity for undemocratic decision making, especially in regard to economic policy.[41] Mexico's postdevaluation crisis has accentuated this trend. The aid package once again placed economic and financial considerations at the center of the public agenda and channeled exclusive responsibility for policy design into the hands of Zedillo and his Economic Cabinet.

Zedillo's insulated governance style has led to a debilitating pattern of erratic policy maneuvers, wherein the president announces a specific policy, is confronted with opposition from affected interests, and as a result the initiative is subsequently abandoned. The president pledged to promote clean elections but then proceeded to support fraudulently elected PRI governors in the states of Tabasco and Yucatán. Zedillo launched an attack against the Salinas family, then later indefinitely postponed investigations into their alleged involvement in corruption and assassination scandals. Zedillo's selectivity in the application of the rule of law has contradicted the spirit of his proposed democratic reforms and shed doubt on his commitment to enforce the law across the board if that means undermining some of his key political allies.[42]

Skillful political management is critical for the successful implementation of far-reaching programs of political and economic reform. However, Zedillo's perceived lack of consistent leadership has sabotaged many of his reformist efforts and heightened conflicts within Mexico's already divided political class. The brief military incursion in Chiapas in February 1995 and the government's fitful position on a definitive electoral reform have deepened rifts between modernizing and traditional factions within the political elite. Negotiations over electoral reform have provoked as much polarization in the ruling party as they have in the opposition. Many members of the PRI feel that the party is paying at the polls for the Economic Cabinet's incompetence, and their loyalty to the new president is tenuous at best.

Neither the "hawks" nor the "doves" in the political elite trust Zedillo. Hard-liners feel betrayed by his offer of amnesty to the EZLN and the restraints imposed on the army. The "doves" resent the strengthening of the military and the witch-hunt launched against Samuel Ruiz, the bishop of San Cristóbal de las Casas, as well as other groups and individuals sympathetic to the Chiapas rebels. Hard-liners demand a firm hand; doves demand further negotiations. By attempting to satisfy both, Zedillo has lost allies in both camps. Traditional factions of the PRI resent Zedillo for breaking the unwritten rules that had governed the country since the PRI's creation. Modernizing groups resent him for not dismantling them quickly or thoroughly enough.

Zedillo's lackluster political performance is a personal flaw, but his insulated governing style reflects the age-old vices of the political system itself. Since the birth of the ruling party, Mexico's presidents and their *camarillas* (cliques) have been able to govern in a relatively unconstrained fashion. The arrival of highly trained economists in political office made policymaking more efficient but not more accountable. Even under the reign of the modernizing technocrats, the traditional ways of doing politics have prevailed. Mexico's political and economic stability has been routinely jeopardized by the lack of rules to govern by and the absence of institutions to govern with.

In the past, because of the unlimited power of the presidency, Mexico had been unable to achieve democratic rule fully; in the future, presidential strength will be required to carry on the critical task of institution building. Zedillo will have to use the presidency to strengthen representative institutions that can order the country's political life and eventually act as counterweights to the presidency and to the PRI. As Wayne Cornelius has argued, a consistent president committed to a profound modernization of the political system will be the key to a successful democratic transition.[43] Zedillo faces the dual task of "modernizing" the presidency and limiting its historically unbounded power, while at the same time controlling his party and demonstrating effective leadership in times of crisis. Strong presidents have traditionally been an obstacle, not a vehicle for democratic evolution in Mexico. But during the transition, presidential strength will be needed in order to rein in the rank and file of the PRI. Zedillo may have to curb traditional patronage politics in the ruling party in order to enact further political liberalization while maintaining the PRI's unity and discipline. He will have to decide whether to foment primary elections; whether the PRI's illegal methods of winning elections should be overlooked; whether he will respect legitimate opposition victories at the state level; and whether he must further consolidate political *apertura* (opening) by beheading the leaders of Mexico's privileged fiefdoms.

Polarization and Political Divergence

Democratic transitions require a convergence among political elites, pacts through which they can negotiate their basic disagreements and establish rules for competition and cooperation that are acceptable to all players.[44] A basic agreement among elites is necessary for the construction and consolidation of a democratic political culture. This agreement is still lacking in Mexico, despite the encouraging results of a peaceful presidential election. Mexico's political life remains clouded by suspicion and distrust among parties, social movements, and political leaders.

The Salinas term was marked by a climate of permanent confrontation between the government and the Left. Salinas attempted to promote a centrist convergence between the PRI and the PAN (a strategy baptized as "selective democracy"), as a way of marginalizing the PRD and deepening the rift between the two oppositions. For more than six years, personal and political animosities between government officials and PRD leaders ran high, and the Salinas government showed little inclination to negotiate seriously with the Left. The behavior of the PRI-government apparatus in several key state and local elections (especially in the PRD stronghold of Michoacán) signaled that it would never allow a Cardenista government to come into power anywhere in the country. The end result was the creation of a climate of uncertainty, distrust, and resentment among the main political actors that ultimately polarized the political process.

Polarization was reinforced by the frequent harassment of opposition forces and individuals including political activists and columnists such as Sergio Aguayo, Jorge Castañeda, Miguel Angel Granados Chapa, and Enrique Quintana. Toward the end of the Salinas term, polarization within the ruling party led to politically motivated violence including the assassination of José Francisco Ruiz Massieu, the secretary general of the PRI. Many of the polarizing vices were reproduced by the Mexican intelligentsia, that is, by intellectuals who argued that Mexico needed a democratic political culture in order to transit into democracy but at the same time criticized and ostracized those who did not share their views.[45]

It took an armed insurgency in Chiapas to generate a preliminary political accord among contending forces. On January 27, 1994, eight political parties signed the Agreement for Peace, Democracy, and Justice that led to a new reform of the electoral code and significant changes in the structure of the Federal Electoral Institute. Mexico's organized political forces initially offered an auspicious response to guerrilla warfare: an institutional, negotiated resolution of the challenges created by the Zapatistas. The Chiapas upheaval led factions within the government and the PRI to recognize the severe limitations of previous electoral reforms that had not included the PRD. Simultaneously, the PRD's leadership recognized the need to incorporate the party into institutionalized politics and abandon (at least temporarily) the temptation of anti-institutional adventures.

Despite the signing of the accord and a peaceful presidential election, political turmoil ensued. The assassination in September 1994 of the PRI's secretary general further deepened conflicts among opposing clans within the PRI. As a result, plans for the modernization of the party were postponed indefinitely. In addition, the "top-down" designation of Zedillo by incumbent president Salinas, the return of members of the old guard to positions of prominence in the Zedillo cabinet, and the military intervention in Chiapas in February 1995 contradicted the conciliatory stance promised by the new government. The PRD continued to question the legality of the election, and the Cardenista faction of the party remained ensconced in its strategy of permanent confrontation and delegitimation. Radical factions in the PRD, in the name of "democratic intransigence," once again resorted to the party's usual confrontational strategy given that they did not want to support any kind of pre-election reform that would constrain their ability to denounce unfavorable election results.

The prevalence of serious disagreements among opposition forces and their ambiguous relationship with the PRI have hampered the possibility of a "pacted transition" toward a more democratic political system. Leaders of the PRD embrace the institutional route one day, only to flirt with openly combative tactics the next. Leaders of the PAN call for the need to inject greater transparency into the exercise of government power, only to engage in behind-the-scenes negotiations with the Zedillo administration. The age-old rivalries and personal animosities that have marked relations between the Center-Right and the Center-Left in Mexico have undoubtedly decreased the speed of the Mexican transition.

Ideological polarization has diminished the prospects for stable party competition in Mexico and opened up greater political space for populist and personalistic appeals among members of civil society. Several key actors seem to be waiting for the party system to collapse so that they can lead a broad, national, extraparty coalition into power. As Philippe Schmitter acknowledges, civil society, in and of itself, may not be an unmitigated blessing.[46] In the context of rapid deinstitutionalization, when members of civil society lose their bearings, the temptation to support "national saviors"—those whom they identify with an idealized past (or future)—is a clear and present danger.

It is undeniable that pressure "from below" has forced the PRI-dominated system to move in a liberalizing direction. However, the potential strength of civil society in Mexico has been hampered by socioeconomic constraints as well as by the cultural legacies of domination by one party. Everyday forms of authoritarian rule, including PRI-sponsored patronage and corruption, suggest that Mexican civil society is still encumbered by what Jonathan Fox calls "the difficult transition from clientelism to citizenship."[47] Numerous groups in civil society are fragmented by opposing agendas, the pressures of co-optation, and the politics of polarization. Schmitter considers the norms of "civility" and "autonomy" as functional prerequisites for a liberal civil society.[48] Yet in many fledgling neodemocracies, such as Mexico, these norms have been quite difficult to achieve. The breakdown of Mexico's authoritarian regime has left a culture of incivility in its wake, a culture where vengeance and retribution often prevail over accommodation and reconciliation. Civil society in Mexico still encompasses a host of illiberal and anti-institutional actors who favor increased polarization over political compromise and the search for a political "center."

Other forms of polarization also threaten democratic evolution, including worsening income disparities. More than 40 percent of the Mexican population continues to live in poverty, and real wages have declined to pre-1980 levels. Extreme inequalities in income and social well-being prevail among states and regions and between urban and rural areas.[49] Between 1984 and 1992 the absolute number of Mexicans living in extreme poverty grew, along with the number of Mexican billionaires included in *Fortune* magazine's list of the world's richest persons. These disparities will be accentuated by high inflation, a dramatic decline in gross domestic product (GDP), and the loss of more than a million jobs in the first six months after the devaluation. In addition, the benefits of greater integration with the United States have been unevenly distributed within the country, deepening regional disparities between a prosperous north increasingly tied to the U.S. economy and a backward south (especially the states of Chiapas, Oaxaca, and Guerrero) plunged into agricultural stagnation. Mexico is increasingly becoming a "dual society" wherein a growing portion of the population is left without the bounties of free trade and economic reform.

Social costs wrought by renewed economic austerity will undoubtedly continue to place severe strains on Mexico's political and economic system. The persistence of severe income inequalities could become a serious threat to political stability because of the simmering conflict in Chiapas. The Zedillo government's offer of amnesty and ongoing negotiations may lure away supporters of the EZLN and contribute to the weakening of its hold over sectors of the Chiapas population. And by unmasking Subcomandante Marcos the hero, and transforming him into Rafael Guillén the delinquent, the government has been able to reduce his popularity among certain sectors of the population, including members of the middle class, business groups, the intelligentsia, and the media.[50] However, sympathy for the EZLN's cause still prevails in the Mexican countryside and could grow as the social impact of the economic crisis extends its scope. In all likelihood, the Chiapas conflict will not be resolved in the near future, and tensions between state elites and *campesino* (peasant) organizations may increase, thus jeopardizing the prospects for governability in the state and elsewhere.[51]

Another form of polarization that threatens political stability and therefore democratic governance is the high concentration of private power and the public-private symbiosis. The government-business alliance constructed by the Salinas government, though crucial for the success of economic liberalization policies, included only the large firms and conglomerates that dominate substantial portions of the Mexican economy.[52] The new understanding between Salinas and the business sector was based on the promotion of concentrated distribution of economic and political power among business elites, which resulted in the growing polarization of the business class.[53] State elites explicitly encouraged a partnership with the "winners" of the economic adjustment process, that is, internationally competitive consortiums, based on shared interests. The Salinas team designed and targeted policies that enhanced the productivity, export, and investment capacity of those groups. However, the government's predominant policy stance toward the "losers" (small and medium-size businesses), the victims of trade liberalization and credit squeezes, was of not-so-benign neglect. For the Salinas administration, microeconomic instability among small-scale and inward-oriented sectors of the business class was the price to be paid for macroeconomic stability. Zedillo has applied the same kind of discretionary logic in favor of select business groups, especially in the export and banking sectors. In the aftermath of the devaluation, these sectors have received privileged treatment through debt restructuring programs and subsidized credit.

As a result, one of the weak spots on the road to economic recovery and political stability remains the small and medium business sector, which has not enjoyed the benefits of government-sponsored privileges. The prevalence of a discriminatory pattern in favor of the large firms has become a major issue of conflict within business circles. Government policy discretion has created bitter disappointment and many vocal reactions from businesses outside of the select groups, many of whom have joined opposition movements such as El Barzón. Sectoral crises and microeconomic instability that translate into anti-institutional ventures led by small and medium-size businesses might well preempt the prospects for a stable polity.

Economic reform in Mexico since 1982 has entailed a transcendental process of coalition realignment, as well as a reshaping of the constituencies sustaining the government coalition in power. The "inclusionist" coalitions of import-substituting industrialization (ISI) have gradually been replaced by the "exclusionist" coalitions of export-led growth (ELG). Under Salinas the cement holding this narrow coalition together was the expectation of economic recovery augured by NAFTA. Under Zedillo a stricken economy will have to generate jobs for a labor force that is growing at more than 3 percent a year. For the neoliberal experiment to survive in the future, Mexican leaders will need to broaden the coalition of beneficiaries of economic reform and lessen both economic and social polarization. To do so, government elites may have to increase spending on social programs and productive projects, even if this entails a return to modest levels of deficit spending.[54] In its efforts to stabilize Mexico's macroeconomic indicators, the Zedillo team has neglected socially beneficial microeconomic intervention by the state. However, it is at the microlevel, among the followers of El Barzón and the EZLN, that some of the greatest challenges to democratic governance are being spawned.

The Democratic Agenda

Mexico's experience as a "hegemonic party system in transition" offers lessons for the future of democracy in the rest of Latin America.[55] As in several other countries in the hemisphere, the quandary facing Mexico today is no longer the initiation of political reform but how to maintain its momentum, assure its consolidation, and avoid political breakdown in a context of renewed economic adjustment. The future of democracy in Mexico, as elsewhere, entails channeling the process of change in a clear direction and assuring effective institutionalization. Mexico still lacks the institutions and attitudes that characterize a true democracy. Few political parties and actors could be described as "democratic" in their everyday activities.

For democratic consolidation to occur, it will be necessary for the main political actors to reproduce and extend the accords that led to the August 21 election.[56] The prospects for democratic governance will be enhanced when the PRI, the PAN, and the PRD recognize the verdict of the polls and commit themselves to legal and institutional routes of political competition. The country's political parties must also transform the sphere in which the majority really counts (the electoral sphere) into a critical locus of decision making regarding the important issues facing the country.[57]

Strengthening the electoral sphere, however, is only one among many necessary steps. Democratic evolution will require that Mexico's political forces fight against clientelist patterns of authority at all levels of society and isolate authoritarian actors. In the past, inclusiveness and patronage had functioned as critical sources of legitimacy. The historic stability of the Mexican political system resulted from the compromises and commitments agreed upon by winning elites. Depoliticization and economic growth were central ingredients of Mexico's postrevolutionary legitimation formula.[58] Leaders of different parties, armies, unions, cliques, factions, and organizations agreed to participate in and support the PRI-dominated system in exchange for material benefits and privileges, including the promotion of their own interests and those of their constituencies. The groups incorporated into the PRI were highly representative of society at the time, and this lent exceptional legitimacy to the PRI.

In the future, democratic governance will require political-ideological redefinitions, including the abandonment of an age-old formula that equated governability with the permanence of the avowed heirs of the Mexican Revolution, the PRI's *familia revolucionaria* (revolutionary family). Democratic progress would entail the collective recognition that the PRI as an electoral machine was probably indispensable given the polarization of the postrevolutionary era, but that today it can be seen only as an obstacle to democratic progress and as a potential source of instability.

The democratic agenda will also need to address the vices of Mexico's educational system. Political learning is crucial for the development of a robust and resilient "civic" civil society. Since the Revolution, the country's educational institutions have not been assigned the task of transmitting democratic values. They have transmitted a vision of history, of myths, of heroic moments that built the ideological backbone of the country's PRI-centric development. The political transition under way must extend to a transformation of the reigning political culture so that it favors competition over political monopoly, all within established and clear rules of the game.

The task for Mexican leaders trapped in an uncertain transition will be to foster the development of a democratic culture while dismantling traditional structures of control and challenging powerful constituencies. The consolidation of democratic governance in Mexico will require a "political education for democracy" that imbues Mexican children with tolerance and respect for alternative worldviews, with respect for legitimate authority, and with the desire to enforce accountability (*rendir cuentas*). Many Mexicans have yet to learn that communities can and should decide their future via the ballot box and other forms of civic participation.

Among the main obstacles to democratic governance is the persistence of inequalities that influence election outcomes. Key among these is the abusive manipulation of election coverage by Mexico's television giant, Televisa. During the 1994 presidential campaign, Televisa orchestrated an "information blackout" of the PAN's candidate after the televised debate that increased his popularity in the polls.[59] Televisa also devoted extensive coverage to the statements made by Roberto Hernández, president of the National Association of Bankers, who warned that interest rates would skyrocket if an opposition party won, thus contributing to the climate of fear and uncertainty that ultimately affected the distribution of the vote.

Voters in Mexico require more than political information. They also need to be exposed to different alternatives and thus develop the capacity to evaluate them. Television is key to this process as it would be difficult to envision a consolidated democracy in Mexico without a truly plural mass media. Political debates in Mexico take place in the press, not on television.[60] Although gains have been made in terms of media access, the issue of biased coverage still needs to be addressed. The media was opened on a temporary basis during the presidential campaign, but opposition parties still need to secure media opening in nonelection periods. In addition, democratic governance in Mexico will require reforms of the government-press relationship in order to inject veracity, reliability, and transparency into Mexico's public discourse and into the country's political debates.[61]

In order to assure a level playing field among parties, campaign financing must be regulated. The 1994 presidential election was marked by the persistence of significant loopholes in rules to regulate campaign financing.[62] Another round of electoral reforms will be needed to eliminate anonymous contributions and impose lower ceilings on the total amount of contributions. Electoral fairness will also require the transformation of the Federal Electoral Institute into an autonomous entity, a fourth power with the capacity and credibility to organize free and clean elections. A future task for the institute should be the determination of clear sanctions for party operatives who commit electoral fraud.

Mexico currently lacks an effective system of checks and balances among the different branches of government. A pending item on the agenda of democratic governance thus should be a constitutional reform that assures the full autonomy of the legislative and judicial powers. In order to achieve a true balance of power, it will not be enough to limit or weaken the power of the presidency; true government accountability will require the strengthening (both politically and legally) of the two other powers. Legislative reform might contemplate the possibility of granting to Congress and the Senate the capacity to supervise and even veto the activities of cabinet members.

An essential ingredient in the Mexican transition should be the transformation of Mexico's formal federalist pact into a concrete reality. The federal government must be willing to move beyond bureaucratic centralism and reinvigorate municipal life. The PAN has applied significant pressure on the Zedillo administration to implement a "new federalism," and the growing number of PAN governors could lead the central government to commit itself to greater decentralization. At the same time, Mexico's federalist strategy ought to include a systematic attack against local and national fiefdoms in order to weaken authoritarian actors who might otherwise benefit from the resources generated by decentralization.[63]

The party system undoubtedly requires urgent reforms. Political parties in Mexico leave much to be desired because of their lack of representativeness, credibility, organization, proposals, and clear identity. A crucial task for their leadership will be to recognize these flaws and undertake organizational, programmatic, and ideological efforts that might enable party consolidation.[64] For the ballot box to become an enduring and effective fulcrum for change, both the PRI and the opposition will need to undergo a process of political maturation.

In the future, the PAN will have to extend its support beyond the confines of the urban middle class and anchor its platform in an economic and social agenda that is more than a carbon copy of the PRI's. Mexico's Center-Right option may also have to combat the widespread perception that the PAN is an elitist and cadre party. PAN leaders will have to decide whether they will continue to support the tacit Center-Right alliance struck during the Salinas years or whether the PAN should be less loyal and more of an opposition.[65] The Zedillo term could witness the radicalization of intemperate sectors within the party—possibly led by the governor of the state of Guanajuato, Vicente

Fox—for whom the costs of perpetuating conciliatory tactics outweigh the benefits of a frontal attack on the Mexican state. The PAN will also have to discern the reasons why the party lost in the regions where it had been in power for the first time.

The Left also faces new dilemmas. Will the PRD survive? Will the party seek a new route under new leadership? Will the mercurial former mayor of Mexico City, Manuel Camacho, play a role in the reconstruction of the Center-Left via a new political party? The Left is at a crossroads. The party can remain ensconced in the purist, combative, and delegitimizing behavior of the past, rooted in the perception of Cuauhtémoc Cárdenas' moral superiority, or it can choose to reposition itself as the flexible, modern, institutionalized Center-Left that Mexico so desperately needs. In order to assure political stability in the context of economic austerity, the Zedillo administration will need to work out some form of peaceful coexistence with the Left. A critical variable for the establishment of democratic normalcy will be to institutionalize the PRD as a credible opposition force that participates in "normal" politics, provides representativeness to the party system, demands greater microlevel government intervention, and exerts useful pressure for deepening the process of political reform.[66] The incorporation of the Left into a governance pact could also contribute to the eventual solution of the Chiapas conflict.

The PRI itself faces significant challenges. Fifty percent of the Mexican electorate did not vote for Zedillo. Participation rose by 12 percent, but the PRI's vote also declined by 12 percent in comparison with the 1991 landslide. Young, educated, and urban voters voted against the PRI, and the ruling party clearly dominated only in the rural areas. In order to survive the brunt of Mexico's economic crisis, the PRI will have to grapple with the changing nature of the electorate and devise an electoral strategy accordingly. A critical imperative for democratic governance in Mexico will be to separate the PRI from the government. The PRI is still a *partido de gobierno* (government party), not a *partido en el gobierno* (party in government). This symbiosis partially explains the persistence of difficulties and anomalies during the August 21 election. The playing field was altered by the quasi-monopolistic privileges of a party that is also a government and that has a bureaucratic reason for existence, given that it provides employment and social mobility to the political class. In order to delink the PRI from the government, it will be necessary to reform most of the country's traditional sectoral organizations, including labor unions, peasant confederations, and business associations.

In addition, what needs to change are the mechanisms by which presidents are selected and cabinet members are appointed. Democracy will not arrive as the result of supposedly optimal policies prescribed by self-appointed technocratic saviors bent on economic stability. True democratization would entail new formulas for presidential selection and elite circulation, including the end of the *dedazo* (the incumbent president's hand-picked selection of his successor). As Peter Smith has argued, in a democracy, competition must involve the allocation of genuine power including, and especially, executive power.[67] Mexico cannot achieve democracy as long as it relies on the long-standing *destape* (the incumbent president's announcement of his successor). A presidential primary within the PRI would provide opportunities for participation and competition among the party's different factions. In tandem with the institution of primaries, electoral laws should be revised in order to make it authentically possible for an opposition, non-PRI contender to win the presidency.

The political backlash created by the devaluation has strengthened the prospects of an opposition victory in the presidential race in the year 2000, but it remains unclear whether the PRI will continue to muddle through and ultimately be rendered irrelevant or modernize itself and prevail. The PRI faces a process of rapid internal decay, accelerated by the assassinations of Luis Donaldo Colosio and José Francisco Ruiz Massieu. As prominent Mexican writer Carlos Fuentes has expressed it: "It is as though the PRI has gone out to kill itself, to commit suicide. There are Priístas killing Priístas. . . . What we see is the internal decomposition of a party, which has, in effect, completed its historic purpose."[68]

In the past, however, the PRI has demonstrated a remarkable capacity to reinvent itself in the face of adverse circumstances, as it did during the 1994 presidential race. The competitive nature of those elections forced the PRI to do something it was rarely compelled to do in the past: behave as a real political party. The PRI devised strategies to mobilize the vote, select better candidates, and construct an effective campaign platform. The real questions are whether the impetus for reform within the PRI will continue in the future and who will lead it. Hegemonic parties do not give up or share power of their own accord; they do so when they are forced to. Therefore, much of the responsibility for dislodging the PRI from power rests on the shoulders of the opposition and on its capacity to construct a coherent and viable option.[69]

Conclusion: Obstacles and Opportunities

The obstacles to democratic consolidation in Mexico abound, including the prevalence of authoritarian actors who control significant levers of power; the widespread confrontational and antisystemic attitude of many key political players; and the persistence in many social spheres of clientelist patterns of domination.[70] Simultaneously, the erosion of corporatist controls and the deinstitutionalization wrought by the weakening of dominant-party rule may ultimately create favorable conditions for democracy. The decline of the PRI is opening windows of political opportunity for opposition parties and societal actors who are taking advantage of the existing political vacuum to strengthen their positions in the political system. As the PRI withers, other forces grow in stature.

Faced with a financial fiasco and unresolved guerrilla warfare, the reaction of Mexico's organized political forces since January 1995 has been mixed. The government offered an institutional, negotiated resolution of the challenges created by the Zapatistas and the unresolved issue of electoral fairness, but has also resorted to the military to deactivate the Chiapas rebels. President Zedillo has recognized opposition victories at the polls, but at the same time he has caved in to pressures exerted by hard-liners in the ruling PRI. Some factions of the political class have decided to work within established institutions, while others still refuse to play by the established rules. Popular organizations and movements are taking to the streets instead of channeling their demands through the ballot box. Democratic evolution in some spheres has been accompanied by political stagnation in others.

A primary variable shaping the outcome and boundaries of the Mexican transition remains the state of the economy. An improved economic profile could buy time for Mexico's battered PRI class and alleviate the pressures for more profound democratic reforms. Economic recovery could once again feed a growing apathy and complacency among business and middle-class groups. Growth-induced social peace would thus reduce the need for substantive changes that extend beyond the electoral realm, as citizens are periodically summoned to the polls by political technocrats. Throughout the rest of the Zedillo term, Mexicans will vote their pocketbooks, and the PRI may lose a host of state elections. If the government is able to channel discontent through the ballot box, Mexico may end up poorer but more electorally competitive.

However, Mexico's economic downturn, with its potential contagion effect throughout the hemisphere, underscores the lessons for Latin American technocrats of resurrecting the formulas associated with "performance legitimacy" and limited electoral democracy. The postponement of further political reform during the Salinas administration rendered the PRI highly vulnerable to economic decline. As the harsh realities of the country's economic fundamentals become more evident, the potential for social conflict and violence among the dispossessed may grow, extending beyond the confines of Chiapas.

Zedillo's tasks, therefore, will be to reignite economic growth, generate employment, reinvigorate the microeconomy, and translate economic recovery into concrete benefits for the population at large. The heightening of social inequalities as a result of the economic crisis constitutes a critical challenge for democratic governance. Unless Mexico's economic reforms translate into social improvements, political pressures against the government will continue to mount, and the offer of greater political liberalization may not be sufficient to appease an increasingly disaffected and impoverished population. As Jorge Domínguez and Abraham Lowenthal have eloquently expressed it: "Democracy speaks to the soul, but has yet to fill the belly."[71]

Mexico's main political actors are walking on the razor's edge. Both government and opposition forces confront the dual challenge of setting the economy on a path toward sustained growth while maintaining the impetus for democratic evolution. At the heart of this challenge is the task of institutional renovation or "stage two reforms."[72] If institutions fail to evolve and accommodate political and social demands until economic growth is restored, instead of sailing into democracy's safe harbor, Mexico might be forced to navigate through the stormy seas of social unrest.

Hence the main task for the country's citizens, parties, technocrats, social movements, and academics will be to collaborate in the construction of institutions that might enable the country to continue on a path toward genuine democratization. Democratic polities cannot exist without democratic institutions.[73] As Philippe Schmitter has argued, the future of democracy will be increasingly "tumultuous, uncertain, and eventful."[74] But in Mexico, as elsewhere in Latin America, uncertainty itself is the essence of democracy. If democracy is indeed the outcome, then the uncertainty and political turbulence fueled by Chiapas, political cannibalism, and the devaluation of the Mexican peso may be a rather small price to pay.

11

Cuba: Prospects for Democracy

Marifeli Pérez-Stable

Cuba is a special case. Summarizing the political situation on the island and appraising the prospects for democratic governance require a recognition of its distinctiveness. The Cuban government is not just another Latin American dictatorship; it once elicited vast popular support. Today, however, Cuba is facing a political crisis that only democracy can relieve, but the government is unlikely to respect civil liberties and hold free elections any time soon. A democratic Cuba is a distant prospect.

In 1959 the Cuban Revolution mobilized an overwhelming consensus around a program of national sovereignty and social justice. That the revolution left no options to its opponents but jail, death, exile, or silence seemed less compelling then to most Cubans than its promise of a new Cuba. Even when, at the height of the cold war, the revolutionary government turned to the Soviet Union and embraced communism, its nationalist and egalitarian appeals proved stronger for most Cubans than the anticommunism to which they had until then subscribed. With its fastidious insistence on checks and balances, separation of powers, and individual rights, representative democracy undoubtedly favors political processes over substantive outcomes. Rejecting representative democracy, the new government relied on the forceful leadership of Fidel Castro and the monopoly of the Cuban Communist Party (PCC) to safeguard national sovereignty and promote social justice. Thus charismatic authority, popular mobilizations, and relative institutionalization formed the basis of Cuban politics.[1]

All political systems must perform two essential tasks: renew popular support (or at least foster open-mindedness on the part of the citizenry concerning the direction taken by the leadership) and rotate elites. For the better part of thirty-seven years, the Cuban government had varying success in meeting these tasks. It managed to maintain sufficient legitimacy and credibility to govern effectively, if not democratically. Nonetheless, a precarious balance between popular support and state repression also underpinned Cuban politics. Since the mid-1980s the political system has demonstrated a declining capacity to renew popular support and, perhaps more important, to retain the population's confidence in the leadership's ability to govern. Moreover, ironclad unity around Fidel Castro and the PCC has precluded the most definitive form of elite rotation: the organization and promotion of an alternate coalition of elites able to suggest different directions for guiding the nation. The current crisis, therefore, lies in the near-exhaustion of the political system. As popular support has declined, the government has increasingly resorted to greater repression. Yet, with Fidel Castro at the helm and with a still significant (albeit minority) proportion of the population supporting the government, the political system is not yet completely depleted.[2]

For the Cuban leadership, and indeed for many Cubans, the past is very much the present. They remain just as committed to the ideals of the Cuban Revolution—national sovereignty and social justice—as they were in 1959, and they cannot, or will not, conceive of new ways of defending them. In the post–cold war world, the U.S. government is conditioning the normalization of relations upon the establishment of political democracy on the island. Since nationalism is its last bastion of legitimacy, the current leadership is loath to implement reforms that appear to be concessions to the United States. U.S. conditions aside, the most compelling reasons for democratization are domestic. How else but by holding free, competitive elections will the Cuban government renew popular support and renovate elites? The key question, therefore, is how long will Cuban leaders be able to govern on the basis of Fidel Castro's authority and PCC monopoly on power without incurring the unbearable cost of deploying massive force against the Cuban people. Having thus far resisted meaningful political reforms, they seem to believe that reinforcing the status quo is their best insurance. The Popular Power elections of 1992–93, explained in greater detail below, are a case in point. Although the elections provided the government with a golden opportunity to signal a willingness to change, it instead used them to reaffirm its well-established patterns of governance.

The Political Reforms of 1992–1993

The electoral law of 1992 made it impossible for anyone but an official candidate to aspire to a seat in the Popular Power assemblies.[3] The elections took place in two steps. In December 1992 a total of 13,865 municipal delegates were elected to two-and-a-half year terms in races featuring at least two candidates. In February 1993 there were 589 deputies elected to the national Assembly and 1,190 delegates to the provincial assemblies elected for five-year terms. Since there was only one nominee per seat, candidates needed more than 50 percent of the validly cast ballots to be elected. Thus citizens had a negative choice: they could withhold their vote for particular candidates, register a blank ballot, or abstain from voting altogether. For the first time, the citizenry elected the members of the national and provincial assemblies; previously the Communist Party had selected them from the pool of municipal delegates or appointed them from the ranks of the elites.

The two-step electoral process resulted in distinctively different outcomes. In December, more than 97 percent of the electorate turned out to vote. Various sources estimated that up to one-third cast invalid ballots (blank or defaced).[4] Since the election was politically uncompetitive, invalidation was tantamount to an antigovernment vote. Initially the government neither refuted these estimates nor gave its own figure. Two months later it admitted to less than 15 percent null or void votes; the final official figure is 10 percent. Undoubtedly the much-delayed and amended official reaction lent credibility to the unofficial estimates, which punctured the myth of overwhelming popular support for the regime.

Cuban leaders were obviously surprised: up to one-third of the electorate sent them a strong and unexpected message. Business could not be allowed to proceed as usual in February, and it did not. The party prepared for the second round as it had not for the first. Indeed, like the two-month official silence on the percentage of invalid ballots, the intensity of the February "campaigning" supported the unofficial estimates of the December outcome. The government's overriding objective was to demonstrate an indisputable popular mandate. First, Fidel Castro, Cuban nationalist par excellence, made a patriotic appeal to vote in favor of all the candidates: *La patria* (the homeland) demanded a demonstration of unity rather than a selective vote. Conveniently, the tightening of the embargo by the United States in the Cuban democracy act of 1992 rounded out Castro's summons to patriotism. Second, the government exerted pressure and intimidation to bring the stray one-third back into the fold and to dissuade other citizens from invalidating their ballots or voting selectively. It updated voter registration lists, increased the number of polling places, and sent the local leadership of the neighborhood committees to visit every home to instruct the citizenry on the allegedly complex voting procedures.

On February 24, more than 99 percent of the electorate went to the polls: 88.5 percent voted the straight ticket, and 7.2 percent cast invalid ballots; in Havana, nullified ballots totaled 14.3 percent. No deputy received less than 87 percent of the votes. Unofficial sources placed the proportion of invalid ballots in Havana between 10 and 20 percent and the percentage of its residents voting selectively at 30 percent.[5] Officially, then, about 18 percent of the voters—the tip of an opposition-in-waiting—did not do what the government had asked them to do: vote for the entire slate.

What did the 1992–93 elections demonstrate? First, in February the Cuban government displayed a certain strength in mobilizing the population which—out of conviction, fear, or a sense of helplessness—

complied with its demands for a show of unity. The election also revealed a profound weakness: the outcome was gained on the basis of ironclad unity behind Fidel Castro and the Communist Party, a formula that today hardly translates into effective, long-term governance. Second, the December outcome was especially telling: when the government did not mount an incessant campaign, up to one-third of the electorate cast a protest vote. Would it not be reasonable to expect that many more citizens would express their opposition in a freely contested election or plebiscite? Third, the deception in the proportion of invalid ballots in December and the "campaign" for the February election confirmed the inability of Cuban leaders to accept less than near-unanimity as a mandate for governance. Finally, the December deception and the February manipulation cast considerable doubt on the electoral system (which clearly prevents meaningful competition) and on the integrity of the government in handling and reporting the outcome.

Obstacles to Democratization

The refusal of Cuban leaders to give public recognition to the political dimension of the crisis they are confronting is the first obstacle to democratization. However belatedly and reluctantly, they are addressing the economic crisis by implementing some market reforms. In short, they are making crucial economic concessions that implicitly acknowledge the collapse of socialism. At the same time, they have steadfastly rejected political reforms that might compromise their power. Cuban leaders are determined to avoid what they consider to have been the decisive blunders in Eastern Europe, the former Soviet Union, and Nicaragua: allowing reformers to fester within the Communist Party; launching political and economic reforms simultaneously; calling an election they cannot win; and, generally, giving the opposition, at the elite or popular levels, the opportunity to galvanize into action.

The political crisis has yet to climax. That Cubans have not actively challenged the government is a second obstacle to democratization. Although their relative quiescence is misleading (it certainly does not indicate support), it sustains the status quo. If a groundswell of popular support once buttressed the Cuban government, today the widespread sense of helplessness—*no hay salida* (no exit)—is a crucial element of its stability. Why should the leadership mend its ways if the Cuban people have so far continued to accept being governed in much the same manner as in the past? The leadership, moreover, has given clear signals of its determination to remain in power. In 1991 the PCC Congress passed a resolution empowering the Central Committee to take whatever steps might be necessary to uphold the government. In 1992 the revised constitution included three new security-related articles:

establishing a National Defense Council, sanctioning the declaration of a state of emergency, and recognizing the people's right to resort to armed struggle in defense of the government if other recourses failed. In December 1994 the Assembly passed a defense and national security law that regulates the functioning of the National Defense Council in the event of war or a national emergency. Civilian and military leaders have made outright references to the possible use of violence to quell dissent. Although the government dispersed the August 1994 demonstration in Havana's *malecón* (waterfront) with relative ease, units of the Interior Ministry's special forces were conspicuously standing by. These measures are an oblique recognition of the political crisis.

U.S. policy toward Cuba, particularly the Cuban democracy act of 1992 and the Cuban liberty and democratic solidarity act proposed by Senator Jesse Helms and Representative Dan Burton and enacted in 1996, is a third obstacle to democratization. The history of U.S.-Cuban relations, before and after 1959, gives pause to many Cubans, not just those in the government. With the cold war over, the United States cannot possibly construe Cuba as a threat to its national security. In relentlessly pursuing an atavistic policy, the United States inadvertently supports the Cuban government's appeals to patriotism: Castro's rhetoric would be hollow if "Yankee imperialism" were to lose resonance for Cuba's citizens. Instead, many ordinary Cubans are persuaded by the official argument that ironclad unity is needed to safeguard *la patria*. In essence, U.S. policy furnishes the Cuban leadership with an easy rationale against democratization, a process that in any case, should be undertaken for domestic considerations.

Thus political stability is an obstacle to democratization. It currently hinges on a delicate balance: the leadership of Fidel Castro; a critical mass of popular support; the fear, apathy, and sense of helplessness of the majority; and the appeal to nationalism that U.S. policy substantiates. Even though his stature is much diminished, Fidel Castro is still the magnet aligning elite unity and whatever popular support the government musters. Sufficient numbers of Cubans continue to endorse the government to the point that many would put their lives on the line in its defense. By the same token, most Cubans are paralyzed in their discontent: repression is effective; the exigencies of daily life leave little energy to engage in other matters; and a viable, credible alternative is not yet in sight. Consequently, maintaining a critical mass of support and keeping the rest of the population relatively quiescent are the most pressing political imperatives of the Cuban government. Finally, U.S. policy fuels nationalism and allows Cuban leaders a credible pretext to resist political reforms. As long as this rather precarious equilibrium continues, the Cuban government is likely to succeed in avoiding democratization.

Prospects for Breaking the Cuban Impasse

Although Cuban elites have so far managed to govern in much the same ways as in the past, they will not be able to do so permanently. The Cuban Communist Party is saddled with a dilemma with which neither the communist parties of its erstwhile allies nor those remaining in power had to contend. It is facing the collapse of socialism and, at some point, the end to its rule without having yet passed the mantle of leadership from the original revolutionaries to a new generation. During the 1980s and early 1990s, the PCC achieved an impressive rotation in the memberships of the Politburo and Central Committee. Many old revolutionaries are no longer active; younger people have taken their places. More recently, the prominence of Ricardo Alarcón (president of the Assembly), Roberto Robaina (foreign minister), Carlos Lage (secretary of the Council of Ministers), and José Luis Rodríguez (economic and planning minister) has underscored the changing face of the Cuban leadership. Ultimately, however, the heart of the matter is Fidel Castro. However impressive it may be, rotation has not amounted to renovation; that is, the new faces have not initiated policies and directions outside the parameters of Castro's leadership and the PCC's monopoly. As long as Castro is in command and the other factors in the precarious equilibrium remain the same, Cuban elites are unlikely to vary their course.

Is Fidel Castro capable of leading the transition? Castro is a pragmatic man; he would not have remained in power thirty-seven years otherwise. Moreover, contrary to his image, he has often negotiated and compromised. Internationally, for example, his government engaged in negotiations with the Carter administration that would likely have concluded in the normalization of relations with the United States had the Democratic Party retained the White House in 1980. Domestically, he accepted a process of institutionalization during the 1970s and early 1980s on terms he had earlier vehemently rejected. But Fidel Castro has never faced a situation dictating negotiation and compromise to end his rule and that of the Communist Party as well as to restore capitalism. That, in essence, is what the transition will eventually mean. Can he do it? The immediate answer is no. His leadership, the combination of sufficient popular support and the relative quiescence of the majority, and present U.S. policy impart upon the present a fragile stability. Neither Castro nor the United States is likely to take the initiative to break the impasse. However, the economic crisis and the government's responses to it could well propel changes by altering the balance between support and quiescence in the Cuban population.

Three main scenarios appear plausible. The most dramatic is one in which the population is in, or near, a state of revolt. Would Cuban leaders make concessions to compromise their rule or, in a desperate attempt to preserve it, would they call out the troops and fire upon *el pueblo cubano* (the Cuban people)? The series of measures mentioned above, which would grant the government extraordinary powers in the event of an emergency, indicates that they indeed have considered the latter option. A popular revolt would almost certainly provoke dissension in the leadership on the advisability of negotiating or giving the order to fire. If Castro believes he still retains sufficient support, he is likely to instigate a hard-line response and call upon the "people" as well as the army or the Interior Ministry to defend *la patria*. If not, he might well negotiate and accept his political demise peacefully. Without his determination, Cuban elites are unlikely to "fight to the death." If Castro calls out the troops, he would face the threat of a civil war: some officers complying with the order to fire, others disobeying it and joining the revolt. This scenario might have two outcomes: Castro is assassinated and his successors negotiate with the opposition and launch a transition to democracy; the civil war expands and the United States, responding to the outcry of Cuban Americans, and perhaps of some Latin American governments, coordinates an Organization of American States (OAS) peacekeeping force. Thus Castro and his allies would go down fighting.

Cuban leaders would avoid this worst-case scenario if the core of genuine support and majority quiescence remain at present levels, as they do in the second scenario, which is, in effect, a prolongation of the current situation. Clearly the political aim of economic reforms is to stem the decline in order to avert a popular upheaval. Indeed, making the U.S. dollar legal tender, authorizing many forms of self-employment, and expanding agricultural cooperatives in 1993 reduced tensions; many Cubans have subsequently expended their energies in pursuit of the dollar to find some means of satisfying their daily needs. If the government slows down reforms, or partially rescinds them, the worst-case scenario of popular revolt could nevertheless still materialize. However, the course of 1994–95 seems to have suggested a third scenario, one of elite struggles over the scope and extent of market reforms.

To succeed, economic liberalization must stop the hemorrhage draining the economy and lay the foundations for recovery. In late 1993, two international reports (by International Monetary Fund officials and a former Spanish economic minister), while praising the reform process, underscored that "time is running out." If the government was to avoid widespread chaos, the reports argued, more thorough reforms were urgently needed. Among these are cutting state subsidies that keep prices artificially low, increasing productivity by reducing unnecessary employment, imposing an income tax, lowering budget deficits, enacting currency reform and moving toward the convertibility of the peso, and fully liberalizing self-employment to alleviate unemployment and increase the supply of goods and services. Without comprehensive reforms, the prospects for economic recovery, the reports emphasized, are bleak.[6]

The government, however, hesitated. In the December 1993 session of the Assembly, Fidel Castro railed against capitalism and the "excesses" of the profit motive and called for workplace assemblies (*parlamentos obreros*) to discuss additional economic reforms. Armed Forces Minister Raúl Castro lambasted "reformist bureaucrats" who did not have the "real interests of the masses" in mind. More comprehensive reforms to strengthen market reforms and promote the private sector were not immediately in the offing.

The incident highlights a significant dimension of Cuban politics. When confronted with a difficult political situation, Castro's natural reaction is to build "consensus" through mass mobilizations, a recourse based on the belief that he still musters sufficient popular support, or at least that he can appeal to the citizenry to consider with an open mind the direction taken by his government. Held in the first trimester of 1994, the assemblies predictably yielded the support of *el pueblo* (the people) for Castro's position: economic reforms must be "politically correct" as well as technically sound, and they must "never" compromise socialism. Convening these "labor parliaments" reaffirmed the entrenched patterns of governance in Cuba, which underscore the weakness of institutions like the Assembly in the making of national policy and do not augur well for the political system after Fidel Castro passes from the scene. The "parliaments" clearly constituted a show of strength by the hard-liners against reformers.

Nonetheless, by the end of 1994, reformers seemed to have gained the upper hand. After the popular "consultations," the government cautiously moved forward on the economic front. It announced price increases on cigarettes, alcoholic beverages, work and school lunches, public transportation, and utilities. Certain goods and services, such as sports and cultural events, gymnasiums, and after-school and vacation activities for children, are no longer free of charge. The government also disclosed plans to phase in a new revenue system that would tax the income of self-employed workers, members of agricultural cooperatives, and private farmers but exempt that of state workers. It put state enterprises on notice of the gradual reduction of subsidies and the consequent possibility of bankruptcy. In the fall, individuals, cooperatives, and state enterprises began selling their products in agricultural markets and special consumer goods stores at freely established prices throughout the island. Initially these measures had a salutary effect: by the end of 1994 they had lowered the budget deficit by more than 3.6 billion pesos and curbed the dramatic slide in the peso's value that "dollarization" had triggered.[7]

Although the tense summer of 1994, when thousands of Cubans joined a demonstration against the government and thirty-two thousand left on rafts, temporarily tilted the balance of power in favor of the reformers, the year 1995 seemed again to swing the pendulum. The government vacillated on the full liberalization of Cuban entrepreneurship. It authorized additional trades for self-employment while undermining the climate for private initiatives by sporadically confiscating "illicit gains" and harassing "profiteers." In July, Castro denounced the mounting levels of corruption, reaffirming that "Revolution is our religion. There will be no transition to capitalism." Economic and planning minister Rodríguez even hinted that some of the monetary policies (that is, "dollarization") might be reversed. In September the Assembly passed a widely anticipated foreign-investment law that reflected official ambivalence toward economic restructuring. On the one hand, it allows for wholly foreign-owned ventures, allows foreign ownership of real estate, and improves the climate for foreign investment. On the other hand, the state retains full control of labor as foreign investors still cannot hire and pay workers directly. Moreover, the Assembly declared the law to be "an opening to defend and develop socialism . . . not a transition to capitalism." Castro also noted: "If there has to be more opening, we will do it, though I do not see an immediate need for that."[8]

The current crossroad raises a crucial question: does the Cuban leadership have the will to implement a full-fledged reform program? The answer, unfortunately, is not clear. So far Cuban leaders have given no indication that they are ready to relinquish state control over most of the economy and give full legal sanction to burgeoning entrepreneurship, which is ultimately the road to take if they are serious about economic recovery. Thus the reform program remains contingent upon the ever-present uncertainties of Cuban politics, particularly the leadership of Fidel Castro. The swinging pendulum between hard-liners and reformers may yet crystallize the third scenario of reformist dissension within the leadership.

The strategy of economic reforms without political change has the Cuban leadership in a dramatic double bind. To maintain political stability, the government needs to reverse the economic collapse and promote a recovery by implementing much bolder market reforms. However, these reforms are likely to impose steeper costs on the government's genuine supporters, who tend to be older, less educated, and poorer, than on the population at large. Consequently, necessary changes in economic policy threaten to undermine their support, an important bolster upholding political stability.

The side effects of reform also corrode the government's achievements in terms of national sovereignty and social justice: corruption grows more rampant, inequalities widen, and preferential treatment of foreigners highlights the second-class citizenship of Cubans. Indeed, true believers have smaller and smaller planks on which to stand. At the same time as it gives many Cubans opportunities for individual betterment, economic liberalization does not garner their political allegiance. Instead, economic reforms weaken the state by making many citizens economically independent and many more dependent on them for their goods and services. They stimulate the further demand that the government grant Cuban citizens the same rights as foreign capital to own property, make profits, and invest. Granting these rights would be the economic equivalent of recognizing the civil liberties of the opposition. In short, economic liberalization is unleashing a political dynamic that could contribute to breaking the Cuban impasse.

This third scenario of a mounting confrontation between reformers and hard-liners has three possible outcomes. The first is dramatically climactic: reformers, with support from members of the armed forces and the Interior Ministry, challenge Castro and his allies outright. Even if they failed, the Cuban government would have to face an unprecedented situation of elite dissension, blatantly revealing its weaknesses and rendering it much harder to continue "politics as usual." If they succeeded, they would probably assassinate Castro (unless he agreed to retire to Galicia) and initiate a true transition. Either of these scenarios bears the potential for violence between elite factions, which could become more widespread if either or both factions succeeded in mobilizing sectors of the population. If this occurred, it might, in turn, prompt a U.S. or OAS peacekeeping intervention. The second outcome is equally climactic but points in a different direction: Castro joins the reformers, supports radical economic restructuring, and presides over the gradual restoration of capitalism as the economy modestly recovers and political reforms safely (for Castro and the PCC) become a longer-term prospect.

Neither of these outcomes is likely at present. There is no evidence that conflicts between reformers and hard-liners will soon climax in a violent confrontation. A popular revolt does not appear imminent. So far, reformers have shown neither the disposition nor the resources to affirm their political independence from Fidel Castro. Even though they have found an invaluable ally in Raúl Castro and the armed forces, the military is loyal to the elder Castro and supports a "go slow" approach. After December 1993 when he echoed his brother's concerns about the reforms, the younger Castro spearheaded the opening of the agricultural markets and consumer goods stores. Underscoring the urgency of the situation, he said: "Today the main political, military, and ideological problem of this country is to increase the food supply." While civilians in the Cuban leadership have expressed dissatisfaction over the military's recent dominance, the armed forces seem to be the only institution capable of following through with the economic transformation.[9]

For the time being, the second alternative seems equally improbable. Fidel Castro appears unwilling to support a radical restructuring of the economy. Even if he did and Cuba attracted significantly more foreign capital, the absence of U.S. and Cuban-American investments, the inaccessibility of the U.S. market, and Cuba's exclusion from the economic integration now taking place in the western hemisphere would probably delay the country's economic recovery.[10] Current elite struggles over reform are more likely to remain contained within the second scenario, that of stasis. This third outcome would thus entail half-hearted approval of stopgap measures, which do not quite relieve the economic crisis but postpone the political day of reckoning. The reforms so far fall safely under this category.

"Muddling through" may well succeed temporarily and thus prolong the fragile stability. While the current equilibrium of popular support amid majority quiescence endures, the Cuban leadership will continue to ignore the political crisis in public, disregard the civil liberties of its opponents, and block free, competitive elections. The economic crisis and the government's handling of it, however, may yet unleash a concatenation of changes that upsets the precarious equilibrium. Whether primarily driven by a popular revolt or by elite dissension, the various scenarios portend the possibility of violence and foreign intervention, neither of which would augur well for the establishment of democracy in Cuba.

Looking Forward: Democracy in Cuba?

The emergence of a democratic Cuba would best be served by a peaceful birth. This would require changes that, at the moment, seem quite remote. First, Fidel Castro and the PCC need to give public recognition to the political crisis. Cuban leaders—Castro first and foremost—were once exceptional revolutionaries, but the revolution is over. Now they are politicians defending the status quo. Although they have more than proven their mettle in the exercise of power, they are proving to be extraordinarily recalcitrant in accepting the other side of the politician's coin: giving up, or at least sharing, power.

Only by allowing the opposition the opportunity to compete fairly and freely for public office would the Cuban government truly signal a disposition to move beyond its long-standing patterns of governance. An organized, legal opposition is absolutely imperative for peaceful transformation. In July 1995 Cuban leaders passed up another opportunity to send such a signal. In an atmosphere of "politics as usual," the government held the elections of the municipal assemblies of Popular Power, reporting a 97.1 percent voter turnout and an 11.3 percent of the ballots invalid (blank or defaced). Unofficial estimates claimed a voter turnout of about 90 percent and a rate of annulled ballots of 10–20 percent.[11]

A second change that would facilitate a peaceful transition is not as remote as the first. The Cuban government might discard the present policy of "muddling through," forge a consensus on radical economic restructuring, and implement far-reaching market reforms. Reality would then give irrefutable testimony to socialism's collapse, the state's declining economic control, and the citizenry's growing economic independence. Indeed, if the current government launches a coherent program of economic restructuring and follows it through, it would likely accelerate the political dynamic of the dramatic double bind mentioned above, altering the fragile stability of popular support and majority quiescence. Unlike China and Vietnam, Cuba is an urban society with a critical mass of educated and skilled workers, and the option of full-fledged economic reforms without political change is unlikely to be viable.

Third, a reformulation of U.S. policy would bolster the chances for a peaceful transition to democracy in Cuba. Current policy complements Cuban intransigence: both governments are precluding negotiation and compromise. The United States is conditioning rapprochement on full democratization, allowing itself little leeway to respond incrementally to partial and incomplete reforms in Cuba. Nonetheless, in September 1994, after the two governments concluded an immigration agreement that ended the uncontrolled exodus and guaranteed immigrant visas to twenty thousand Cubans annually, Secretary of State Warren Christopher suggested the administration was prepared to respond in "calibrated ways" to meaningful changes by the Cuban government. Although the United States limited negotiations with Cuba to the subject of immigration, speculation abounded that the two governments would subsequently broach other subjects.[12] While this had not happened by September 1995, the Clinton administration's May 2 announcement that Cubans seeking illegal entry to the United States would be deported if they failed to prove political persecution constituted another step toward normalizing immigration from Cuba. Unless the United States musters the political will to loosen the stranglehold of codependency that links Cuban nationalism and "Yankee imperialism," it will not succeed in putting the burden of democratization squarely where it belongs, on the shoulders of the Cuban government.[13]

Progress toward democracy is likely to be slow, incremental, and ambiguous. Even after the demise of the current government, democracy will not emerge full-blown. Cubans (and Cuban Americans) need to build institutions, develop attitudes, and establish practices that promote the will of the majority and protect the rights of the opposition. While representative democracy favors political processes, the substance of politics comes from human beings—their ideas, hopes, and fears. In 1959 *el pueblo cubano* responded to the calls of national independence and social justice with such will, energy, and passion that the costs along the way were tempered when compared to the promise of a new Cuba. Today democracy is the only acceptable alternative to the system of governance of the past thirty-seven years. It must bear the burden of national reconciliation, that is, of allowing and encouraging Cubans (and Cuban Americans) to address and live with their differences through compromise and negotiation. Democracy and national reconciliation are also moral imperatives. Their advocates will face two serious obstacles. One is convincing *el pueblo cubano*, which appears to be saturated with moral discourse, that these are, indeed, valid moral imperatives. The other is mobilizing popular momentum in their favor without excluding those who resisted the transition or those who hold minority views on its promotion and consolidation.

For the moment, a democratic Cuba is a distant prospect, a beacon to guide Cubans (and Cuban Americans) of good will through a painful and possibly turbulent transition. Once this great divide is crossed, however, the outlook for the nation may brighten considerably. Cuban society is largely urbanized and educated. Comparatively speaking, socioeconomic inequalities, regional differences, and racial cleavages are not great. The armed forces tend to be professional and disciplined, and they might well welcome civilian control after what promises to be a difficult transition. One can even anticipate that, once the Cuban people have resoundingly repudiated authoritarianism and *caudillismo*, their consensus on democracy will be so strong and widespread as to preempt recourse to other means of settling differences. All of this will depend on an inspired political leadership unequivocally committed to national reconciliation and to giving democratic form to the long-standing aspiration for national sovereignty and social justice.

Notes

Chapter 1 Nicaragua: Politics, Poverty, and Polarization (Spalding)

I acknowledge the helpful comments and suggestions received on earlier versions of this chapter from Jorge I. Domínguez, Ambassador Luigi Einaudi, Laura J. Enríquez, Abraham F. Lowenthal, Jack Spence, and an outside reader. All interpretations and remaining limitations, of course, are my responsibility alone.

1. The Chamorro government twice attempted to forge a new consensus about the social and economic order by bringing together top representatives of various business and labor organizations for negotiations. The first *concertación* process, in October 1990, included representatives of eighteen business and seventeen labor organizations in a month of intense negotiations that allowed the government to begin an economic liberalization process. The second, May–August 1991, produced an agreement that 25 percent of the state enterprises would be sold, on concessionary terms, to their workers. See República de Nicaragua, *Acuerdos de la concertación económica y social y la política exterior del gobierno de Nicaragua* (Managua: República de Nicaragua, 1990); Gobierno de Nicaragua-Central Sandinista de Trabajadores (CST), *Acuerdo* (February 1993). The *concertación* process allowed the Chamorro government to circumvent a divided legislature in which political intransigence was common and to work directly with the economic actors whose support for the economic transition would be vital to its success. See Rose J. Spalding, *The Political Economy of Revolutionary Nicaragua* (Boston: Allen & Unwin, 1987), 171–74. As a result, the administration made some headway on economic policy change, but did little, in the first years, to strengthen the institutional order of the government.

2. Philippe C. Schmitter, "Transitology: The Science or the Art of Democratization?" in Joseph S. Tulchin and Bernice Romero, eds., *The Consolidation of Democracy in Latin America* (Boulder, Colo.: Lynne Rienner, 1995), 11–44; Edelberto Torres-Rivas, "Democracy and the Metaphor of Good Government," ibid., 45–58.

3. On this point, two caveats should be noted. First, although the land reform process was extensive under the Sandinistas, redistributing almost 30 percent of the country's farmland, government data suggest that roughly one-third of the rural landless population was never incorporated into this program. See Eduardo Baumeister, "Estado y campesinado en el gobierno sandinista," paper presented at the 16th International Congress of the Latin American Studies Association (LASA), Washington, D.C., April 4–6, 1991; Michael Zalkin, "The Sandinista Agrarian Reform: 1979–1990," *International Journal of Political Economy* 20, no. 3 (1990): 56–68. Second, some of the deconcentration of land associated with the reform has been reversed in the postrevolutionary period due to the return of some expropriated properties and the extralegal sale of land by financially strapped agrarian reform beneficiaries. See Laura J. Enriquez, "Agrarian Reform in Nicaragua: Its Past and Its Future," paper presented at the 16th International Congress of the LASA, Washington, D.C., April 4–6, 1991.

4. Robert A. Pastor, *Condemned to Repetition: The United States and Nicaragua* (Princeton: Princeton University Press, 1987); Lawrence Pezzullo and

Ralph Pezzullo, *At the Fall of Somoza* (Pittsburgh: University of Pittsburgh Press, 1993).

5. Nora Hamilton et al., *Crisis in Central America: Regional Dynamics and U.S. Policy in the 1980s* (Boulder, Colo.: Westview Press, 1988); Steven Kinzer, *Blood of Brothers* (New York: Anchor, 1991).

6. William I. Robinson, *A Faustian Bargain: U.S. Intervention in the Nicaraguan Elections and American Foreign Policy in the Post–Cold War Era* (Boulder, Colo.: Westview Press, 1992).

7. In contrast to his predecessors, President Clinton's ambassador to Nicaragua, John F. Maisto, had interactions with a range of Nicaraguan actors, including FSLN representatives, and generally avoided overidentification with the far Right. His relative neutrality was of an active sort; he has pushed warring parties into negotiations and pointedly encouraged cooperation.

8. U.S. aid to the Chamorro government was suspended in both 1992, following a request for a review of this aid policy by Senator Jesse Helms and Representative David Obey, and 1993, when the explosion in Managua of an arms arsenal held by supposedly demobilized Salvadoran guerrillas triggered an investigation of Nicaragua's links with international "terrorist" organizations. In both cases the aid was eventually released, but only after delays of several months. The Gonzalez-Helms amendment, which called for another aid cutoff for nations that had not satisfactorily compensated U.S. citizens for expropriated property, would have forced an aid cutoff for Nicaragua in July 1994 and again in July 1995 had not the U.S. State Department issued national interest waivers at the last moment. Senator Helms has been a forceful critic of the Chamorro government and a prime instigator of these aid cutoffs. See Republican Staff Report to the Committee on Foreign Relations, U.S. Senate (1992); for a critical response, see Washington Office on Latin America (WOLA), "The Helms Report on Latin America," *Nicaragua Issue Brief #1* (September 1992). Much of his effort has been on behalf of U.S. citizens (most of whom were, until recently, Nicaraguan citizens) who lost property in Nicaragua. Many of these petitioners are reclaiming properties that were transferred to land reform beneficiaries during the Sandinista era. See WOLA, "US Policy and Property Rights in Nicaragua: Undermining the Search for Consensus."

9. LASA, *The Electoral Process in Nicaragua: Domestic and International Influences*, Report of the LASA Delegation to Observe the Nicaraguan General Elections of November 4, 1984 (Austin: LASA, 1984); LASA, *Electoral Democracy under International Pressure*, Report of the LASA Commission to Observe the 1990 Nicaraguan Election (Pittsburgh: LASA, 1990).

10. The registration rate was reportedly 84 percent, and the turnout rate topped 70 percent: Embassy of Nicaragua, *Nicaragua in Brief* (January 1994): 1; National Union of Farmers and Workers, *Nicaragua Farmer's View* 2, no. 3 (March 1994): 12.

11. In a national survey conducted by the Institute for Nicaraguan Studies (IEN) in February–March 1995, 53 percent of respondents strongly agreed with the statement that "Political participation is not worthwhile because you cannot influence the decisions of the government." Another 22 percent agreed somewhat, for a total of 75 percent who expressed some degree of alienation. See IEN, "La cultura política en Nicaragua: Análisis desde la opinión pública nacional," Managua, unpublished report, June 18, 1995: 11.

12. Hemisphere Initiatives, *Establishing the Ground Rules: A Report on the Nicaraguan Electoral Process* (Boston: Hemisphere Initiatives, Inc., 1989); Shelley McConnell, "Rules of the Game: Nicaragua's Contentious Constitutional Debate," *NACLA [North American Congress on Latin America] Report on the Americas* 27, no. 1 (1993): 20–25.

13. LASA, *Electoral Democracy,* 24–26; U.S. General Accounting Office (GAO), *Central America: Assistance to Promote Democracy and National Reconciliation in Nicaragua* (Washington, D.C.: GAO, September 1990), 13.

14. LASA, *Electoral Democracy,* 26.

15. These processes include the failed Organization of American States (OAS) mediation effort between Somoza and reformers in 1978, mediation by regional powers in the Contadora and, later, Esquipulas peace processes, and the OAS and UN election monitoring in 1989–90.

16. LASA, *Electoral Democracy,* 31.

17. Eric Weaver and William Barnes, "Opposition Parties and Coalitions," in Thomas W. Walker, ed., *Revolution and Counter-Revolution in Nicaragua* (Boulder, Colo.: Westview Press, 1991), 117–42.

18. United Nations Development Program (UNDP), "Contributions to the Analysis of the Nicaraguan Transition," presented to the Consultative Group on Nicaragua, Paris, France, June 19–20, 1995, 18.

19. Chris Taylor, "In Search of the 'Aquino Effect,'" *Barricada International* 300 (September 1989): 3–4.

20. Unión Nacional Opositora (UNO), *Programa de Gobierno de la Unión Nacional Opositora* (Managua: Mimeo, August 24, 1989).

21. For discussion of the debate within the FSLN, see IEN, "FSLN: Del vanguardismo al acuerdo nacional: El debate interno," in *Materiales de estudio y trabajo* 10 (1993); and the interview with Henry Ruíz, "Principal aliado de Lacayo es FSLN," *El Semanario,* June 29–July 5, 1995.

22. During the two-month lame duck period between the electoral defeat of the FSLN and the inauguration of the Chamorro government, some state property was appropriated by or reassigned to Sandinista activists. This distribution of state resources, colloquially labeled *la piñata* in Nicaragua, took many different forms, ranging from the granting of state vehicles to departing functionaries as a form of severance pay to titling over large land grants to a few prominent Sandinista leaders. In his defense of this last-minute titling process, former minister of agriculture and agrarian reform Jaime Wheelock, argued that most of the land titles extended during this time were for land grants that had been made to ordinary petitioners years before under the agrarian reform program but for which the paperwork had never been completed. See Wheelock's *la Verdad sobre la piñata* (Managua: Instituto para el Desarrollo de la Democracia, 1991). Controversy about *la piñata* has continued to flare periodically under the Chamorro government, sharpening the political disputes between the Right and the Left and deepening the divisions within the FSLN.

23. As a losing presidential candidate who received more than 1 percent of the vote, Ortega automatically became a member of the National Assembly, and vice-presidential candidate Ramírez became his alternate. Ortega remained the secretary general of the FSLN, and he assumed responsibility for international affairs and party mobilization; Ramírez was assigned to represent him within the legislature.

24. The Ramírez faction's manifesto, published in the newspapers on February 15, 1994, and accompanied by the names of its endorsers, showed strong support among party intellectuals, professionals, and leaders of the National Union of Farmers and Ranchers (UNAG), an association of agricultural producers. The Ortega wing, on the other hand, was more closely aligned with organized labor and the party's "machine" of organizers, particularly at the departmental level.

25. For information about the congress, see "A Rather Extraordinary Congress," *Envío* 13, no. 156 (1994): 10–13, and Scarlet Cuadra, Guillermo Fernán-

dez A., and Matías Valenzuela, "FSLN Special Congress: Preparing the Ground for '96," *Barricada International* 374 (June 1994): 17–24.

26. The 1994 congress approved a quota system under which women and those under the age of thirty were guaranteed 30 percent and 10 percent, respectively, of the party's leadership posts.

27. Although support for Ramírez subsequently eroded, a national poll conducted in November–December 1993 by the IEN found that, when respondents were asked which political leaders would be best able to achieve some kind of national agreement, Ramírez outpolled Ortega. Whereas 43 percent of respondents gave Ramírez a positive evaluation and 50 percent were negative, only 35 percent were positive about Ortega and 60 percent were negative; see IEN, "FSLN: Del vanguardismo al acuerdo nacional: El debate interno." Public opinion polling in Nicaragua, however, has been problematic, and the results should be approached with some caution. Political analysts have spent years disputing the reasons for the failure of most professional pollsters to predict the outcome of the 1990 elections accurately. See William A. Barnes, "Rereading the Nicaraguan Pre-Election Polls," in Vanessa Castro and Gary Provost, eds., *The 1990 Elections in Nicaragua and Their Aftermath* (Lanham, Md.: Rowman and Littlefield, 1992), 19–22; Leslie Anderson, "Neutrality and Bias in the 1990 Nicaraguan Preelection Polls: A Comment on Bischoping and Schuman," *American Journal of Political Science* 38, no. 2 (1994): 486–94; and John A. Booth, "Assessing Candidate Preference Polling and Other Survey Research in Nicaragua, 1989–90: Comments on Anderson, and Bischoping and Schuman," ibid.: 500–13.

28. "Politics: Left, Right and Center," *Envío* 13, no. 160 (1994): 24–25.

29. In addition to the forty-five members of each council, the five deputies in the National Assembly from the two regions are also eligible to vote in council decisions, bringing the total membership to ninety-five.

30. On the 1994 coastal elections, see Scarlet Cuadra, "Elections to Learn From," *Barricada International* 372 (April 1994): 4–7, and Judy Butler, "Nicaragua's Caribbean Coast: New Government, Old Problems," *Envío* 13, no. 155 (1994): 33–42.

31. These include the PLC, the Authentic Liberal Party (PALI), the Liberal Party for National Unity (PLIUN), and the exiled National Liberal Party (PLN). The Independent Liberal Party (PLI) did not join the alliance.

32. IEN, "La gobernabilidad y el acuerdo nacional en Nicaragua: Investigación sobre la opinión pública nacional," Managua, unpublished report, January 3, 1995: 15. A December 1995 poll by Borge y Asociados suggested even stronger support for Alemán. When asked "For whom will you vote in the 1996 elections?" 41 percent endorsed Alemán and 20 percent supported Ortega. Twenty-three percent stated that they were undecided; 8 percent indicated that they would not vote; and 8 percent gave their support to other candidates. *La Prensa,* December 22, 1995.

33. During the Sandinista era, executive dominance of the legislature was most pronounced in the early years when the FSLN-controlled junta directed the activities of the Council of State. After institutional reforms in 1984 and the adoption of a new constitution in 1987, the Assembly began to develop some independent capability. Its contribution, however, was generally to hammer out the details of legislation proposed by the president. See David Close, "Conflict in Nicaragua's National Assembly," paper presented at the 18th International Congress of the LASA, Atlanta, March 10, 1994; John A. Booth, "The National Governmental System," in Thomas W. Walker, ed., *Nicaragua: The First Five Years* (New York: Praeger, 1985), 29–44.

34. After the 1990 election, some UNO leaders wanted to expand the size of the Supreme Court to reduce the influence of the seven Sandinista government appointees. In a compromise solution, the court size was increased to nine and two of the seven Sandinista appointees resigned, allowing the Chamorro government to name four of the nine court justices. See McConnell, "Rules of the Game," 22.

35. *Latin American Weekly Report*, March 24, 1994, 131.

36. Asamblea Nacional de la República de Nicaragua, Ley no. 192, *Ley de reforma parcial a la Constitución política*, February 1, 1995. The term for municipal officials was reduced to four years, with mayors to be elected directly by the voters and immediate reelection of mayors prohibited.

37. The president still had the power to submit lists of nominees to the Assembly, but the Assembly was empowered to nominate its own slate of candidates as well.

38. The prohibition on immediate presidential reelection or election of close relatives, for example, was endorsed by a vote of seventy-two in favor, six abstentions and none against, through an unprecedented coalition of FSLN moderates (the Grupo Ramírez) and the UNO right wing. See Claudia Chamorro G., "Aprueban inhibiciones," *La Tribuna*, November 25, 1994.

39. "The Constitutional Reforms: Another Opportunity," *Envío* 14, nos. 163–64 (1995): 6.

40. See "Not Yet to the Root of the Crisis," *Envío* 14, no. 169 (1995): 3–9.

41. Steven M. Gorman and Thomas W. Walker, "The Armed Forces," in Walker, ed., *Nicaragua*, 91–118.

42. Gabriela Selser, "New Reductions for EPS," *Barricada International* 330 (December 1990): 14–15; and Lieutenant Colonel Oswaldo Lacayo's report to the National Assembly's budget commission, summarized ibid. 360 (April 1993): 7.

43. Close, "Conflict in Nicaragua's National Assembly," 5–6.

44. According to a 1995 Arias Foundation study, defense spending in Nicaragua in 1994 totaled U.S.$38 million, an amount similar to Costa Rica's U.S.$37 million and substantially below the U.S.$141 million and U.S.$133 million spent in El Salvador and Guatemala, respectively. In terms of personnel, the Nicaraguan military was less than half the size of El Salvador's, and less than one-third the size of Guatemala's. See *Latin American Weekly Report*, April 13, 1995.

45. See, for example, his essay, "El ejército no será brazo armado del sandinismo," in *Nicaragua: Revolución y democracia* (Mexico City: Organización Editorial Mexicana, 1992), 157–73.

46. See, for example, Roger Burbank, "The Pot Boils Over," *NACLA Report on the Americas* 27, no. 4 (1994): 4–7. For a discussion of criticism by leading Sandinistas, see George R. Vickers and Jack Spence, "Nicaragua Two Years after the Fall," *World Policy Journal* 9, no. 3 (1992): 544–45.

47. *Latin American Weekly Report*, August 26, 1993, 393.

48. See Guillermo Fernández Ampié, "Military Code Approved," *Barricada International* 375 (July 1994): 4–5; and "Politics and the Military," ibid. 376 (August 1994): 9.

49. See, for example, "COSEP reitera acusación: EPS en competencia desleal," *La Prensa*, May 29, 1994; "COSEP en contra de empresas del EPS," *Barricada*, June 7, 1994; "Mayorga reta a HOS a debatir el Código Militar," *La Prensa*, June 10, 1994; "Niegan competencia desleal," *Barricada*, June 11, 1994.

50. Margarita Castillo, Melba Castillo, Nelly Miranda, and Reynaldo Sánchez, "El proceso de pacificación y democratización en Nicaragua," paper prepared for the Overseas Development Council, December 1994, 38.

51. Orlando Nuñez, ed., *La guerra en Nicaragua* (Managua: CIPRES, 1991), 461–75; Vickers and Spence, "Nicaragua Two Years after the Fall," 549–52.

52. According to the UNDP, clashes between armed bands and the military rose from 238 in 1991 to 554 in 1993 before declining to 390 in 1994. See "Contributions to the Analysis of the Nicaraguan Transition," paper presented to the Consultative Group on Nicaragua, Paris, France, June 19–20, 1995, 3.

53. According to FitzGerald, total economic losses due to the war were U.S.$1.23 billion between 1980 and 1985. E. V. K.. FitzGerald, "An Evaluation of the Economic Costs to Nicaragua of U.S. Aggression: 1980–1984," in Rose J. Spalding, ed., *The Political Economy of Revolutionary Nicaragua* (Boston: Allen & Unwin, 1987), 213. In addition to the war, the emphasis on funneling resources to the state sector and the relative neglect of private producers and cooperatives had an economic cost. See Alejandro Argüello Huper and Nanno Kleiterp, *Análisis del proceso inversionista nicaragüense de 1979 a 1985* (Managua: Fondo Nicaragüense de Inversión, October 1985).

54. José Luis Medal Mendieta, *Nicaragua: Políticas de estabilización y ajuste* (Managua: Multi-Print, 1993), 93–120; Trevor Evans, "Ajuste estructural y sector público en Nicaragua," in Trevor Evans, ed., *La transformación neoliberal del sector público* (Managua: CRIES, 1995), 179–261.

55. United Nations Economic Commission for Latin America and the Caribbean (UNECLAC), *Nicaragua: An Economy in Transition* (Mexico City: CEPAL, 1994).

56. U.S. Agency for International Development (USAID), "USAID Program in Nicaragua: A Brief Description and Current Status," unpublished report, April 6, 1993.

57. Corporaciones Nacionales del Sector Público (CORNAP), *Avance del proceso de privatización al 31 de diciembre de 1994* (Managua: CORNAP, 1995), 17, 19, 36; Fundación Internacional para el Desafío Económico Global (FIDEG), "Diagnóstico de empresas privatizadas a favor de trabajadores," *El Observador Económico* 19 (July 1993): 22–26.

58. UNECLAC, *Nicaragua: An Economy in Transition*, 57.

59. Ibid.

60. UNECLAC, *Nicaragua: Evolución económica durante 1994* (Mexico City: CEPAL, 1995), 18.

61. See Adolfo Acevedo Vogl, "Algunas implicaciones de los acuerdos con el FMI y el Banco Mundial (ESAF y el ERC-II) para el país y la sociedad nicaragüense," CRIES, *Documento de Trabajo 94*, no. 3 (1994); even Avendaño's (1994) relatively optimistic account identifies major internal and external challenges to sustained growth. See Néstor Avendaño, *La economía de Nicaragua: El año 2000 y las posibilidades de crecimiento* (Managua: Nitlapán CRIES, 1994).

62. According to Nitlapán, the number of bank clients dropped from 80,511 in 1988 to 10,815 in 1993. The amount of credit allocated to large borrowers remained fairly stable from 1989 to 1992, but that for small and medium-sized borrowers fell sharply. Nitlapán, *Evolución reciente del sector agropecuario en Nicaragua: Los efectos de las políticas de estabilización y ajuste estructural (1988–1993)*, preliminary draft (August 1994).

63. Cámara de Industrias de Nicaragua (CADIN), "Estrategia para la reactivación productiva" (Managua: mimeo, 1993).

64. Twenty-five percent of Nicaragua's cultivable land area was claimed by former owners following the FSLN's electoral defeat; Council of Freely Elected Heads of Government, "Report on a Property Issues Conference," Carter Cen-

ter of Emory University, *Working Paper Series* (July 13, 1995), 2. The process of sorting out competing claims and compensating those to whom property was not returned proved slow and costly. See also Proyecto de Ordenamiento y Tecnología, "Informe de actividades, enero–mayo de 1995: Resumen ejecutivo," (Managua: mimeo, June 1995).

65. World Bank, *Living Standards Measurement Survey* (Washington, D.C.: World Bank, 1993), 8. Using a different methodology, the Ministerio de Acción Social painted a bleaker picture: 31 percent of households were classified as "poor" (with one basic necessity not satisfied), and another 44 percent were classified as "extremely poor" (with two or more basic necessities not satisfied). See Gobierno de Nicaragua, *Plan nacional de desarrollo sostenible 1996–2000*, preliminary draft (Managua: Gobierno de Nicaragua, May 5, 1995), 70–72.

66. "Crime Wave Rises," *Envío* 12, no. 149 (1993): 26.

67. *Envío* 13, no. 158 (1994): 24.

68. "No Quiet on the Northern Front," *Envío* 13, no. 155 (1994): 31.

69. In 1991, 75 percent of FISE (Emergency Social Investment Fund) funding came from USAID. In subsequent years, USAID support declined and funding came primarily from the Inter-American Development Bank in 1992 and the World Bank in 1993. By 1994–95 the Nicaraguan government had assumed responsibility for almost 39 percent of the funding. See María Rosa Renzi, *Impacto de los proyectos FISE en las condiciones de vida de los nicaragüenses* (Managua: FIDEG, 1994), 35.

70. UNECLAC, *Nicaragua: An Economy in Transition*, 27.

71. According to Renzi, the number of jobs generated by direct employment in FISE projects represented only 4 percent of total underemployment in 1993; indirect employment represented another 6 percent, for a total employment contribution of 10 percent. See Renzi, *Impacto de los proyectos FISE*, 41–42.

72. In 1995 the Chamorro government committed itself to direct more resources toward small and medium-sized producers and toward poverty alleviation, a position increasingly favored by USAID. See Gobierno de Nicaragua, *Plan nacional 1996–2000*, and USAID, *Nicaragua 2000: A Vision for the Year 2000* (Managua: USAID, March 1995). This shift, coming at the end of the administration and without either clear internal consensus or sufficient external financial support, could at best have a limited impact on prior trends.

73. IEN, "La gobernabilidad y el acuerdo nacional en Nicaragua: Investigación sobre la opinión pública nacional," unpublished report, Managua, Nicaragua, January 1995, 6.

74. This result has been fairly consistent since 1992, when 49 percent expressed this sentiment. Fifty-six percent held this position in 1993. See IEN, "La gobernabilidad y la democracia local en Nicaragua," unpublished report, Managua, Nicaragua, January 1994, 29; IEN, "La gobernabilidad y el acuerdo nacional en Nicaragua," 7.

75. Ilja A. Luciak, *The Sandinista Legacy: Lessons from a Political Economy in Transition* (Gainesville: University of Florida Press, 1995); Michael Dodson and Laura Nuzzi O'Shaughnessy, *Nicaragua's Other Revolution: Religious Faith and Political Struggle* (Chapel Hill: University of North Carolina Press, 1990).

76. Richard Stahler-Sholk, "Labor/Party/State Dynamics in Nicaragua: Union Responses to Austerity under the Sandinista and UNO Governments," paper presented at the 17th International Congress of the LASA, Los Angeles, September 24–27, 1992, 4.

77. Trish O'Kane, "New Autonomy, New Struggle: Labor Unions in Nicaragua," in Minor Sinclair, ed., *The Politics of Survival* (New York: Monthly Re-

view Press, 1995), 183–208; Midge Quandt, "Unbinding the Ties That Bind: The FSLN and the Popular Organizations," ibid., 265–88.

78. Ana Criquillon, "The Nicaraguan Women's Movement: Feminist Reflections from Within," in Sinclair, ed., *The New Politics of Survival*, 209–38.

79. Lisa Haugaard, "With and against the State: Organizing Dilemmas for Grassroots Movements in Nicaragua," *Conference Paper* 54 (New York: Columbia University–New York University Consortium, 1991); Luciak, *The Sandinista Legacy*, 106–22; Baumeister, "Estado y campesinado."

80. Stahler-Sholk, "Labor/Party/State Dynamics in Nicaragua."

81. UNAG, "Aportes para la estrategia de desarrollo agropecuario en Nicaragua," in *Foro Agropecuario Nacional, por la búsqueda de una estrategia de desarrollo para Nicaragua* (Managua: Escuela de Economía Agrícola, UNAN-Managua, 1993), 115–43.

82. Criquillon, "The Nicaraguan Women's Movement," 230.

83. The number of producers "represented" by UNAG declined from 120,506 in 1987 to 69,436 in 1992, a 42 percent drop. See Luciak, *The Sandinista Legacy*, 120–21.

84. Stahler-Sholk, "Labor/Party/State Dynamics in Nicaragua," 20–21.

85. Baumeister, "Estado y campesinado," 260.

86. By 1995, Nicaraguans were questioning whether their government was actually democratic. When asked, in a national survey conducted in February–March 1995, to assess how democratic the government was, only 25 percent answered that it was either "very" (6 percent) or "rather" (19 percent) democratic. In contrast, a full 55 percent said that it was "not very" democratic, and another 19 percent said that it was not at all democratic. See IEN, "Cultura política," 20.

Chapter 2 El Salvador: Transition from Civil War (Córdova Macías)

This chapter is a revised version of a paper given at the conference "Democratic Governance in the Americas," organized by the Inter-American Dialogue, Washington, D.C., September 12–13, 1994. A preliminary version of that paper was presented at the 9th Central American Congress of Sociology, held in San Salvador, July 18–22, 1994.

1. For a global perspective on the process of peace negotiations in the Salvadoran case, see Ricardo Córdova Macías, *El Salvador: Las negociaciones de paz y los retos de la postguerra* (San Salvador: Instituto de Estudios Latinoamericanos, 1993).

2. See, for example, Terry Lynn Karl, "El Salvador's Negotiated Revolution," *Foreign Affairs* 71, no. 2 (1992): 147–64, and George Vickers, "El Salvador: A Negotiated Revolution," *NACLA* 25, no. 5 (1992): 4–8.

3. The only issue that was broached was land distribution for the ex-combatants and the landholders (*tenedores*).

4. See, for example, "La izquierda en la encrucijada," interview with Rubén Zamora, *Tendencias* (San Salvador) 15 (February 1992).

5. Guillermo O'Donnell and Philippe C. Schmitter, *Transitions from Authoritarian Rule: Tentative Conclusions about Uncertain Democracies* (Baltimore: Johns Hopkins University Press, 1986).

6. For a preliminary evaluation of the process of military reconversion in the case of El Salvador, see Ricardo Córdova Macías, "El Salvador: Transición política y reconversión militar," in Gabriel Aguilera, ed., *Reconversión militar en América Latina* (Guatemala City: FLACSO, 1994),

7. See article 211 of the 1983 Constitution of El Salvador.

8. See "Desmovilizan batallón Arce y queda ejército con 31.5 mil hombres," *La Prensa Gráfica*, February 8, 1993, and "Fuerza armada queda con 31,500 efectivos," *Diario de Hoy*, February 26, 1993.

9. "20 mil 770 miembros del Ejército han reducido," *La Prensa Gráfica*, July 15, 1992, 3.

10. For an outline of the problems surrounding the establishment and deployment of the PNC, see William Stanley, "Risking Failure: The Problems and Promise of the New Civilian Police in El Salvador," report produced by Hemisphere Initiatives and the Washington Office on Latin America, September 1993.

11. "De 2,200 militares sólo 200 ha evaluado Ad-Hoc," *La Prensa Gráfica*, September 8, 1992.

12. January 7, 1993, letter addressed to the president of the UN Security Council by the secretary general, United Nations, January 13, 1993, general distribution, S/25078.

13. See "Discusión de diputados sobre Comisión Ad Hoc," *La Prensa Gráfica*, January 15, 1993, 39, and "Critican a Comisión Ad Hoc por actuar con subjetividad," *Diario de Hoy*, January 16, 1993.

14. *De la locura a la esperanza: La guerra de 12 años en El Salvador* (United Nations: New York–San Salvador, 1993).

15. Ibid.

16. Ibid.

17. "Posición de la Fuerza Armada de El Salvador ante el informe de la Comisión de la Verdad," *Diario Latino*, March 24, 1993, 11.

18. "Mensaje dirigido a la Nación por el excelentísimo señor Presidente de la República, licenciado Félix Alfredo Cristiani el día 18 de marzo de 1993," *La Prensa Gráfica*, March 19, 1993, 57.

19. "Corte cumplirá período constitucional: Gutiérrez C.," *La Prensa Gráfica*, March 18, 1993, 3.

20. "Respuesta oficial de la Corte Suprema de Justicia al Informe y Recomendaciones de la Comisión de la Verdad," *Diario de Hoy*, March 28, 1994, 20–22.

21. March 15, 1993.

22. "La Comisión de la Verdad," *ECA* (San Salvador) 512 (June 1991): 529.

23. "Objeciones hace la ONU aplicación de amnistía," *La Prensa Gráfica*, March 22, 1993.

24. "Los cambios en el Alto Mando," *La Prensa Gráfica*, June 26, 1993.

25. See the letter dated September 7, 1993, addressed to the president of the Security Council by the secretary general.

26. Rafael Guido Béjar, "El sistema de relaciones civico-militares y la democracia en El Salvador," *Sociológica* (Mexico City, UNAM) 19 (May–August 1992): 139–40.

27. Ibid., 139–40.

28. Macías, "El Salvador: Transición política y reconversión militar," 216.

29. See "Comunicado oficial de las FPL sobre arsenal encontrado in Nicaragua," *Diario Latino*, July 3, 1993, and "El FMLN comunica a la Nación," *La Prensa Gráfica*, June 16, 1993.

30. "Estructura militar del FMLN finaliza: ONUSAL," *La Prensa Gráfica*, August 19, 1993.

31. Ibid.

32. "ONUSAL culminará labor tras comicios de marzo," *La Prensa Gráfica*, January 17, 1994.

33. "Cree el señor diputado que sigue viva la momia de COPAZ," *Diario de Hoy*, March 25, 1993.

34. "Merino sugiere agilizar el cumplimiento mandato COPAZ," *Diario Latino*, January 20, 1993.

35. Report of the UN secretary general, October 20, 1993.

36. Report of the UN secretary general, February 18, 1994.

37. In fact, the TSE managed to register fewer than the goal of 673,649 new registrants that had been proposed in its July plan.

38. By March 1994 the TSE had issued 2,288,370 voter identification cards and had 422,317 data cards to convert into identification cards, making a total of 2,710,687 people registered in the electoral census. If we take the 2,288,370 delivered identification cards as a base, the question is how many of these data cards could have been converted into identification cards, which implies that the number of possible voters—with identification cards in hand—would have been greater. For ONUSAL, 2,350,000 people had voter identification cards by the time of the elections.

39. For a review of the problems involved in the creation of the electoral census, see the third report of the Electoral Division, presented by the UN secretary general in his report, March 16, 1994.

40. Report of the UN secretary general, March 31, 1994, 7.

Some raise the issue of the credibility of the electoral process, although they do not question the election results. For example, Dr. Héctor Dada, director of the FLACSO Program, suggested in a television interview on Channel 12, April 13, 1994, that the elections were acceptable but not credible. It would be necessary to point out how the problems related to updating the electoral census and the irregularities on election day, even if they did not change the outcome of the election at the presidential level, nevertheless had an impact on the election of certain deputies, especially at the municipal level where winning candidates obtained a reduced number of votes.

41. In the March 1991 elections for deputies, 1,051,481 valid votes were cast, and in March 1994, the valid votes increased by 250,000, an increase of approximately 20 percent.

42. Ricardo Córdova Macías, "Procesos electorales y sistema de partidos en El Salvador, 1982–1989," *Foro Internacional* (Mexico City, El Colegio de México) 32, no. 4 (1992): 519–59.

43. CID-Gallup, *Opinión Pública, El Salvador* 20 (May 1994).

44. IUDOP, *La delincuencia urbana: Encuesta exploratoria* (San Salvador: mimeo, February 1993).

45. In "Adiós a las armas: Paz para El Salvador," *El Día* (Mexico), January 17, 1992, 6.

46. Rafael Guido Béjar, "El centro político y la reproducción del consenso," *Tendencias* (San Salvador) (September 1993): 20–24.

47. See, for example, "Otra palabreja que se pone de moda: 'Consenso,'" editorial in *Diario de Hoy*, February 15, 1994.

48. See "Los consensos y las mayorías," *La Prensa Gráfica*, June 28, 1993.

Chapter 3 Guatemala: Democratic Governability (Torres-Rivas)

1. The process of constructing a political democracy began in Central America during the 1980s. The dates mentioned establish a decade of important and continuing political changes.

2. There is much information of doubtful accuracy about the distribution of income, poverty, and so on. The statistical information used here is taken from FLACSO-IICA, *Centroamérica en cifras* (San José, Costa Rica: FLACSO-IICA, 1991).

3. Edelberto Torres-Rivas, *El tamaño de nuestra democracia* (San Salvador: Istmo, 1992), 107.

4. It is important to mention that more than half (in 1985) and one-third (in 1991) of the population with the right to vote failed to register to vote. What is equally harmful for democracy is the declining level of participation, that is, the relation between the citizens qualified to vote and those who register.

5. Edelberto Torres-Rivas, "Los problemas del orden y la gobernabilidad en Centroamérica," in *El desorden democrático* (San Salvador: Istmo, 1995).

6. One speaks of novelty because the army did not act as an institution; instead, it divided and accepted the decision of the civil forces. The support of one part of the army was decisive, but the initiative was civil. See Víctor Gálvez B., *Estado, participación popular y democratización* (Guatemala City: FLACSO, 1994), and especially R. Poitevin, *Los problemas de la democracia* (Guatemala City: FLACSO, 1993).

7. Gabriel Aguilera, *Democracia y la cuadratura del círculo: La crisis política en Guatemala,* working paper (Guatemala City: FLACSO).

8. Survey of 310 citizens over the age of eighteen and from different social strata conducted by Generis Latina S.A., December 27–28, 1993. *Crónica,* January 7, 1994, 4–5.

9. Jorge Solares, "Guatemala, etnicidad y democracia," in Gabriel Aguilera et al., *Los problemas de la democracia* (Guatemala City: FLACSO, 1992), 49–51.

Chapter 4 Honduras: Democratization and the Role of the Armed Forces (Rosenberg and Ruhl)

1. See James A. Morris, *Honduras: Caudillo Politics and Military Rulers* (Boulder, Colo.: Westview Press, 1984).

2. See Mark B. Rosenberg, "Honduran Scorecard: Military and Democrats in Central America," *Caribbean Review* 12, no. 2 (1983): 12–14.

3. Víctor Meza, "Elecciones en Honduras: Un intento de interpretación," *Honduras Especial* 48 (July 1990): 1.

4. D. Schulz and D. Schulz, *The United States, Honduras, and the Crisis in Central America* (Boulder, Colo.: Westview Press, 1994).

5. See Rachel Sider and James Dunkerly, *The Military in Central America: The Challenge of Transition* (University of London: Institute of Latin American Studies, Occasional Papers no. 5, 1994), 16–22.

6. See John A. Booth and Mitchell A. Seligson, eds., *Elections and Democracy in Central America, Revisited* (Chapel Hill: University of North Carolina Press, 1996).

7. See Matías Funes, *Los deliberantes: El poder militar en Honduras* (Tegucigalpa: Editorial Guaymuras, 1995).

8. See Americas Watch, *Human Rights in Honduras: Central America's Sideshow* (New York: Human Rights Watch, 1987).

9. *La Tribuna* (Tegucigalpa), October 4, 1991.

10. Cresencio Arcos, "Managing Change in Central America," *Foreign Service Journal* 68, no. 4 (1991): 13.

11. Quoted in Tracy Wilkinson, "Emboldened Hondurans Take Aim at Army's Power," *Los Angeles Times,* July 11, 1993.

12. *Tiempo,* September 20, 1991.

13. *Latin American Weekly Report,* October 15, 1992.

14. *La Prensa,* October 15, 1978.

15. See Leticia Salomón, "Honduras: Las fuerzas armadas y retos de la consolidación democrática," in Leticia Salomón, ed., *Los retos de la democracia* (Tegucigalpa: Centro de Documentación de Honduras, 1994).

16. See Mark J. Ruhl, *Redefining Civil-Military Relations in Honduras* (Carlisle, Pa.: Dickinson College, 1994), 24.

17. See "Honduras: Government Initiates Legal Proceedings Against Military Officers Accused of Human Rights Abuses," *NotiSur*, August 4, 1995.

18. See Richard Millett, "An End to Militarism?: Democracy and the Armed Forces in Central America," *Current History* 94, no. 589 (1995): 71–75.

19. Rachel Sieder, "Honduras: The Politics of Exception and Military Reformism, 1972–1978," *Journal of Latin American Studies* 27, no. 1 (1995): 99–127.

20. In her analysis of civil-military relations, Leticia Salomon describes the parliamentary decision-making model as a "thousand-headed serpent." See Leticia Salomon, *Política y militares en Honduras* (Tegucigalpa: Centro de Documentación de Honduras, 1992), 100. Álvarez Martinez recognized the difficulties of controlling this monster and gracelessly proceeded to cut heads, reducing the number of seats on the Superior Council from more than forty to just twenty-one. His other efforts to centralize decision making also helped to erode his support and resulted in his unexpected ouster.

21. Although Reina could do little about the IPM, he did eliminate the free electric and telephone service being provided to the institute.

22. See Center for Justice and International Law and Human Rights Watch/Americas, *The Facts Speak for Themselves: Preliminary Report on Disappearances of the National Commissioner for the Protection of Human Rights in Honduras* (New York: Human Rights Watch, 1994).

Chapter 5 Costa Rica: New Issues and Alignments (Gudmundson)

1. *Tico Times*, February 25, 1994, 5.

2. Ibid.

3. Ibid.

4. The case occupied media attention, including televised legal testimony of the candidate, for months. A brief account can be found in *Central America Report*, December 10, 1993, 375.

5. *Central America Report*, January 7, 1994; *Rumbo*, February 1, 1994, 8–10.

6. On the party's ideological conversion and commitment to neoliberal principles, see *Central America Report*, June 16, 1995, 1–2.

7. On the agreement with former president Calderón and the PUSC, see *Central America Report*, May 26, 1995, 4–5; June 16, 1995, 1–2; *Tico Times*, July 28, 1995, 5.

8. *Rumbo*, February 1, 1994, 4–5. PLN figures Alberto Fait and Víctor Ramírez quote a study to the effect that nearly 80 percent of Costa Ricans vote by family tradition, 43 percent PLN and 35 percent PUSC. Twenty percent of voters are noncommitted, of whom 7 percent are poverty-stricken and always anti-incumbent, 5 percent working poor who may vote for an incumbent but only once; and 8 percent real independents. From these calculations they estimated an opposition PLN presidential candidate began with a roughly 15 percent advantage over an incumbent PUSC candidate, while Figueres won by barely 2 percent of the vote.

9. *Rumbo*, March 1, 1994, 28.

10. Coverage of the teachers' strike dominated the local media during July and August 1995. For an analysis of its significance for democratic politics, see *Tico Times*, July 28, 1995, 1, 4–5.

11. For an analysis of the failures of the forerunner of the TSE in the 1948 Civil War, see Fabrice Edouard Lehoucq, "Class Conflict, Political Crisis and the Breakdown of Democratic Practices in Costa Rica: Reassessing the Origins of the 1948 Civil War," *Journal of Latin American Studies* 23, no. 1 (1991): 37–60.

12. For background to the creation of the Sala IV in 1989 and analysis of its subsequent actions, see Jaime Murillo Víquez, *La Sala Constitucional: Una revolución político-jurídica en Costa Rica* (San José: Editorial Guayacán, 1994).

13. Examples of environmental opposition to beach hotel developments via the Sala IV appear in *Central America Report*, February 17, 1993, 48; and involving the AFL-CIO unfair labor practices complaint, September 10, 1993, 272; November 5, 1993, 336; and November 26, 1993, 359.

14. *Central America Report*, April 16, 1993, 101.

15. Ibid., March 26, 1993, 87.

16. Ibid., May 7, 1993, 128; *Latin American Regional Reports: Caribbean and Central American Report*, May 13, 1993, 4.

17. *Central America Report*, October 1, 1993, 294–95.

18. For a fascinating review of these questions, see Mercedes Muñoz Guillén, "La seguridad de Costa Rica hoy," *Avances de Investigación: Centro de Investigaciones Históricas* (Universidad de Costa Rica), 68 (1994). For Minister Odio's comment, see *Central America Report*, October 1, 1993, 294–95. Additional examples are detailed ibid., May 7, 1993, 128, and July 16, 1993, 207–8. The arrests of former police agents are covered in *La Nación*, July 30, 1995, 1, 10A; July 31, 1995, 10A.

19. *Central America Report*, March 12, 1993, 66.

20. A typical example of this is described in *Central America Report*, July 16, 1993, 205.

21. For a summary of the conflict, see *Central America Report*, August 6, 1993, 225.

Chapter 6 Panama: Transactional Democracy (Millett)

1. *Central America Report*, January 14, 1994.

2. *Latin American Political Advisors, análisis de riesgo político: Panama*, July 1992.

3. A poll published in *Panama America*, September 9, 1993, indicated that 70 percent of Panamanians, only eight months before the elections, still did not support any of the potential presidential candidates.

4. *La Prensa* (Panama), October 14, 1992, 1A.

5. Margaret E. Scranton, "Consolidation and Imposition: Panama's 1992 Referendum," *Journal of Interamerican Studies and World Affairs* 35, no. 3 (1993): 88 and 90.

6. For an example of such arguments, see Miguel Antonio Bernal V., *Reformas o constituyente* (Panama: Ediciones Nari, 1992).

7. For example, Solidaridad, which had less than two-thirds of the votes of the Christian Democrats and less than half the vote of Renovación Civilista, won four seats, while Renovación won three and the Christian Democrats only one.

8. *Constitución Política de la República de Panamá de 1972: Reformada por los Actos Reformatorios de 1978 y por el Acto Constitucional de 1983*, article 145.

9. *Constitución Política de la República de Panamá*, articles 275 and 276.

10. Foreign Broadcast Information Service (FBIS), *Latin America: Daily Report*, February 6, 1995, 30.

11. An early 1995 poll showed the PRD with 40 percent support, a slight drop from its standing four months earlier; ibid.

12. U.S. General Accounting Office, *Aid to Panama: Improving the Criminal Justice System,* GAO/NSIAD 92-147 (Washington, D.C., May, 1992).

13. FBIS, *Latin America: Daily Report,* January 13, 1993, 20.

14. Ibid., January 12, 1993, 35.

15. Interview with Ricardo Arias Calderón, June 1987.

16. For details on the Canal's problems, see "The Future of Panama and the Canal," special issue of the *Journal of Interamerican Studies and World Affairs* 35 (Fall 1993).

Chapter 7 Caribbean Democracy: Decay or Renewal? (Munroe)

1. Cf. *Reports of Director of Elections* for CARICOM states, and Patrick Emmanuel, *Governance and Democracy in the Commonwealth Caribbean: An Introduction* (Cave Hill, Barbados: ISER, 1993).

2. Emmanuel, *Governance and Democracy in the Commonwealth Caribbean.*

3. Americas Watch, *Human Rights in Jamaica* 5, no. 3 (April 1993).

4. Green Paper No. 2, *Management Review Jamaica Constabulary Force* (Ministry of National Security and Justice, 1992).

5. *Trinidad Guardian,* December 11, 1993, 9–10.

6. *USAID Project Identification Document,* unpublished paper, Jamaica Sustainable Justice Reform Project, 1991.

7. World Market Factory, "A Study of Enclave Industrialization in the Eastern Caribbean and Its Impact on Women Workers, Summary Report," paper prepared by Maria Giovanni coordinated by the Centre for Caribbean Dialogue, 1988.

8. Zin Henry, *Labour Relations in the Caribbean Region,* background paper for Labour Relations in Caribbean Countries Conference, Castries, St. Lucia, November 1–4, 1988.

9. Wooding Commission (Trinidad), Report of the Constitution Commission, 1974; Stone Committee (Jamaica), Report of Committee Appointed to Examine Ways of Strengthening the Role and Performance of Parliamentarians Appointed by the Prime Minister on June 14, 1990 (Ministry Paper No. 11, April 25, 1991); Phillips Commission (Grenada), Report of the Grenada Constitution Review Committee, 1985.

Chapter 8 The Dominican Republic: An Ambiguous Democracy (Espinal)

1. For a discussion of Balaguer's labor policies, see Rosario Espinal, "Labor, Politics, and Industrialization in the Dominican Republic," *Economic and Industrial Democracy: An International Journal* 8, no. 1 (1987): 183–212, and Wilfredo Lozano, *El reformismo dependiente* (Santo Domingo: Editora Taller, 1985).

2. For extensive analysis of the PRD governments, see Rosario Espinal, *Autoritarismo y democracia en la política dominicana* (San José: IIDH/CAPEL, 1987). For a review of the literature on this period, see Ramonina Brea, Isis Duarte, Ramón Tejada, and Clara Báez, *Estado de situación de la democracia dominicana (1978–1992)* (Santo Domingo: Pontificia Universidad Católica Madre y Maestra, 1995).

3. Rosario Espinal, "The 1990 Elections in the Dominican Republic," *Electoral Studies* 10, no. 2 (1991): 139–44; Jonathan Hartlyn, "Crisis-Ridden Elections (Again) in the Dominican Republic: Neopatrimonialism, Presidentialism,

and Weak Electoral Oversight," *Journal of Interamerican Studies and World Affairs* 36, no. 4 (1994): 91–144.

4. "La mayoría de los dominicanos cree Peña Gómez ganó elecciones," *Rumbo*, December 14–20, 1994.

5. For an extensive analysis of political parties in the Dominican Republic, see Jacqueline Jiménez Polanco, *Los partidos políticos en la República Dominicana* (Madrid: Editorial de la Universidad Complutense, 1993).

6. See Jonathan Hartlyn, "The Dominican Republic: Contemporary Problems and Challenges," in Jorge Domínguez, Robert Pastor, and R. DeLisle Worrel, eds., *Democracy in the Caribbean* (Baltimore: Johns Hopkins University Press, 1994).

7. *El Siglo*, December 30, 1993.

8. *Hoy*, February 1, 1988.

9. *El Siglo*, December 30, 1993.

10. Joaquín Balaguer, *Mensajes presidenciales* (Barcelona, 1979), 13.

11. *Listín Diario*, December 6, 1966.

12. *Hoy*, February 1, 1988.

13. Penn & Schoen Survey for *Última Hora*, May 1992.

14. Ibid.

Chapter 9 Haiti: Four Old and Two New Hypotheses (Maingot)

1. Richard P. Schaedel, "Preface," in Theodore L. Stoddard, ed., *Religion and Politics in Haiti* (Washington, D.C.: Institute for Cross-Cultural Research, 1966), xiv.

2. Hector Michel, "Solidarité et luttes politiques en Haiti: L'action internationale de Joseph Jolibois Fils, 1927–1936," *Revolution et Société en Haiti* 49, no. 176 (1993): 7–53.

3. Robert Debs Heinl and Nancy Gordon Heinl, *Written in Blood* (Boston: Houghton Mifflin, 1978), 552.

4. Ibid.

5. See Gérard Barthelemy, *Les Duvalieristes après Duvalier* (Paris: L'Harmattan, 1992).

6. Rémy Bastien, "Vodun and Politics in Haiti," in *Religion and Politics in Haiti*, 62.

7. See Michel S. Laguerre, ed., *The Complete Haitiana: A Bibliographic Guide to the Scholarly Literature, 1900–1980*, 2 vols. (New York: Kraus International Publications, 1982).

8. Heinl and Heinl, *Written in Blood*, 622.

9. Note the dramatic version given by Elizabeth Abbott: "Only toward whites did Duvalier and Estime differ, though only in degree. Estime disliked them, while Duvalier was neutral. Both had humiliating experiences with them, but Estime's had been incomparably worse. He had been invited to Washington for an international conference, greeted by a twenty-one-gun salute, then refused accommodation with the other heads of state because the host hotel had just discovered he was black. He finally found lodging in a Negro hotel and left the States humiliated, embittered, and confirmed in every anti-white prejudice he had ever had." *Haiti: An Insider's History of the Rise and Fall of the Duvaliers* (New York: Simon and Schuster, 1991), 58.

10. Mats Lundahl, *Peasants and Poverty: A Study of Haiti* (New York: St. Martin's Press, 1979), 644–46.

11. See Richard M. Morse, ed., *Haiti's Future: Views of Twelve Haitian Leaders* (Washington, D.C.: Wilson Center Press, 1988).

12. Lundahl, *Peasants and Poverty*, 18.

13. Melville J. Herskovits, *Life in a Haitian Valley* (New York: Alfred A. Knopf, 1937), 297.

14. Emmanuel Edouard, *Essai sur la politique intérieure d'Haiti* (Paris, 1890), 42, 99–100.

15. Herskovits, *Life in a Haitian Valley*, 297.

16. Ibid.

17. Robert Rotberg, *Haiti: The Politics of Squalor* (Boston: Houghton Mifflin, 1971), 17–19.

18. Cf. Rémy Bastien, "Vodun and Politics in Haiti"; Lawrence E. Harrison, "The Cultural Roots of Haitian Underdevelopment," in Anthony P. Maingot, ed., *Small Country Development and International Labor Flows* (Boulder, Colo.: Westview Press, 1991), 223–46.

19. The two best examples of Marxist political sociology on Haiti are Gérard Pierre Charles, *Radiographie d'une dictature: Haiti et Duvalier* (Montreal: Editions Nouvelle Optique, 1973), and the more Gramscian, Michel-Ralph Trouillot, *Haiti: State against Nation* (New York: Monthly Review Press, 1990).

20. Mancur Olson, *The Logic of Collective Action: Public Goods and the Theory of Goods* (Cambridge, Mass.: Harvard University Press, 1971).

21. See the literature summarized in Herbert H. Hyman, "The Value Systems of Different Classes," in Reinhard Bendix and Seymour Martin Lipset, eds., *Class, Status and Power* (New York: Free Press, 1966), 488–99.

22. Lester Milbrath, *Political Participation* (Chicago: Rand McNally, 1965).

23. Abbott, *Haiti*, 365.

24. For detailed discussion of the "fratricidal" infighting among the military at the time, see the memoirs of Prosper Avril, *Verités et révélations*, vol. 1 (Port-au-Prince, 1993).

25. Ibid., Annexes.

26. Ibid.

27. On his confrontation with the hierarchy of the Roman Catholic Church, see Conference Episcopale d'Haiti, *Présence de l'Eglise en Haiti: Messages et documents de l'Episcopat, 1980–1988* (Paris: Editions S.O.S., 1988). For a particularly revealing insight into his more "Jacobin" orientations, see Gregorio Selser, "Haiti: El drama permanente de su pueblo. Entrevista con el Sacerdote Jean-Bertrand Aristide," *Caribe Contemporáneo* 22 (January–June, 1990): 49–63.

28. Jean-Bertrand Aristide, *Aristide: An Autobiography* (Maryknoll, N.Y.: Orbis Books, 1993), 168.

29. See Anthony P. Maingot, "Haiti and Aristide: The Legacy of History," *Current History* 91, no. 562 (February 1992), 65–69, on which this section draws.

30. This section draws on Anthony P. Maingot, "Grasping the Nettle: A 'National Liberation' Option for Haiti," University of Miami, North-South Center, Agenda Paper no. 6, March 1994.

31. See Heraldo Muñoz, in Viron P. Vaky and Heraldo Muñoz, *The Future of the Organization of American States* (New York: Twentieth Century Fund Press, 1993), 83.

32. See Laura W. Reed and Carl Kaysen, eds., *Emerging Norms of Justified Intervention* (Cambridge, Mass.: American Academy of Arts and Sciences, 1993); and Anthony P. Maingot, "Haiti: Sovereign Consent vs. State-Centric Sovereignty," in *Beyond Sovereignty: Collectively Defending Democracy in the Americas*, ed. Tom Farer (Baltimore: Johns Hopkins University Press, 1996), 189–212.

33. "Aristide Says He'd Support Surgical Strike to Oust 'Thugs,'" *Miami Herald*, January 5, 1994, 1.

34. Michael Manley, "No existe solución rápida para Haiti," *El Nuevo Herald*, November 26, 1993, 14.

35. See Leslie Manigat, *Haiti of the Sixties, Object of International Concern* (Washington, D.C.: Washington Center of Foreign Policy Research, 1964), 89–93.

36. Heraldo Muñoz, "Haiti and Beyond," *Miami Herald*, March 1, 1992, 6C.

37. *Le Nouvelliste*, September 25, 1995, 1.

38. Council of Freely Elected Heads of Government, Carter Center, Emory University, *Mission to Haiti No. 2*, February 23–26, 1995, 7.

39. Words of Robert Malval, Aristide's prime minister during the transition from exile to power; quoted in *New York Times*, August 4, 1993, 4.

40. See *Les Collectivités territoriales entre 1991 et 1993* (Port-au-Prince: Project intégré pour le reinforcement de la democratie en Haiti, 1993).

41. *Issues in the Redesign of USAID/Haiti's Democracy Enhancement Project*, January 3, 1995. A team from the United Kingdom's Foreign and Commonwealth Office returned from Haiti with a similar opinion. Discussion with Ms. Cathy Ward, research officer, Miami, February 2, 1995.

42. See Robert A. Pastor, *Mission to Haiti No. 3: Elections for Parliament and Municipalities, June 23–26, 1995* (Atlanta: Carter Center, July 17, 1995), 3, n. 5.

43. See Nina Shea, "Human Rights in Haiti," in Georges A. Fauriol, ed., *The Haitian Challenge: U.S. Policy Considerations* (Washington, D.C.: Center for Strategic and International Studies, 1993), 20–32.

44. Americas Watch, *Haiti: The Aristide Government's Human Rights Record* (Washington, D.C., November 1, 1991), 24.

45. See Gerárd Pierre Charles, "Fundamentos sociológicos del proyecto democrático haitiano," in Pablo González Casanova and Marcos Roitman Rosenmann, eds., *La democracia en América Latina* (Mexico: Centro de Investigaciones Interdisciplinarias en Humanidades, 1992), 559–71.

46. *New York Times*, September 20, 1995, 6.

47. *Le Nouvelliste*, September 25, 1995, 1.

48. *New York Times*, September 20, 1995, 6.

49. UN Development Program, *Haiti-Emergency Economic Recovery Program* (Port-au-Prince and Washington, D.C., July 14, 1993).

50. State enterprises are (1) Electricité d'Haiti (EDH); (2) Telephone and Telegraph Co. (Teléco); (3) Port Authority (APN); (4) Airport; (5) Ciment d'Haiti; (6) Minoterie d'Haiti; (7) Enterprise national des oléaginen; (8) Banque Nationale de Crédit (BNC); and (9) Banque Populaire d'Haiti.

51. *Le Nouvelliste*, September 15, 1995, 1.

52. Ibid., September 7, 1995, 1.

53. President Aristide during the meeting with the private sector, Miami, January 15, 1994; reprinted in International Liaison Office of the President, *Democracy: The Solution to the Haitian Crisis* (West Palm Beach, Fla.: Desktop Publishing, 1994), 24–28.

54. *Le Nouvelliste*, September 19, 1995, 1.

55. Ibid., September 25, 1995, 1.

56. *Le Matin*, September 29, 1995, 1.

57. *New York Times*, February 27, 1995, 2.

58. Ibid., February 24, 1995, 1.

59. *Washington Post*, February 24, 1995, 1.

60. Ibid.

61. Evans Paul quoted in *U.S. News and World Report*, October 24, 1994, 55.

Chapter 10 Mexico: The Decline of Dominant-Party Rule (Dresser)

This chapter is a revised version of a paper given at the conference "Democratic Governance in the Americas," organized by the Inter-American Dialogue, Washington, D.C., September 12–13, 1994.

1. For an analysis of the major economic, social, and political trends experienced in Mexico since 1988, see Luis Rubio and Arturo Fernández, eds., *México a la hora del cambio* (Mexico City: Cal y Arena, 1995); and María Lorena Cook, Kevin J. Middlebrook, and Juan Molinar Horcasitas, eds., *The Politics of Economic Restructuring in Mexico* (La Jolla, Calif.: Center for U.S.-Mexican Studies, University of California, San Diego, 1994).

2. Philippe Schmitter, "Democracy's Future: More Liberal, Preliberal, or Postliberal," *Journal of Democracy* 6, no. 1 (1995): 15–22.

3. For a sampling of Zedillo's political offers, see Ernesto Zedillo, "Primer informe de gobierno: Texto al H. Congreso de la Union," *La Jornada,* September 2, 1995.

4. For an analysis of the growing influence of drug traffickers on state institutions in Mexico, see Silvana Paternostro, "Mexico as a Narco-democracy," *World Policy Journal* 12, no. 1 (Spring 1995): 41–47.

5. For a discussion of these problems in the Latin American context, see Scott Mainwaring, Guillermo O'Donnell, and J. Samuel Valenzuela, "Introduction," in *Issues in Democratic Consolidation: The New South American Democracies in Comparative Perspective* (Notre Dame: University of Notre Dame Press, 1992), 3.

6. Democratic consolidation according to Mainwaring, O'Donnell, and Valenzuela (*Issues in Democratic Consolidation,* 5) entails much more than changes in a country's political regime.

7. Remarks delivered at the National Endowment for Democracy Forum on Mexico, October 7, 1994.

8. For an analysis of these factors, see Jennifer L. McCoy, "On the Mexican Elections," *Hemisphere* (Fall 1994); Carter Center, Emory University, "The August 21, 1994 Mexican National Elections" (Atlanta, January 1995); and John Bailey, "The 1994 Mexican Presidential Election Report," *CSIS Western Hemisphere Election Study Series* 12, Study 13, October 8, 1994.

9. Jonathan Fox, "The Mexican Elections: What Does the 'Fear Vote' Mean?" paper presented at the New England Council on Latin American Studies Meeting, Harvard University, September 24, 1994.

10. During the Salinas administration, overarching subsidies for consumers and guaranteed support prices for agricultural producers were replaced by targeted antipoverty programs like PRONASOL and by direct-subsidy programs for small-scale agricultural producers like PROCAMPO. For an analysis of these programs, see Wayne A. Cornelius, Ann L. Craig, and Jonathan Fox, eds., *Transforming State-Society Relations: The National Solidarity Strategy* (La Jolla, Calif.: Center for U.S.-Mexican Studies, University of California, San Diego, 1994).

11. This mysterious disappearance, coupled with the PAN candidate's quick concession of defeat on election night, raised questions among the electorate about a possible backroom deal with the PRI, or the PAN's fear of its own victory. Perhaps Fernández de Cevallos and his strategists in the PAN truly did not want a presidential victory in this election and were wary of the consequences of such a victory. A Panista triumph would have been unacceptable to the rank and file of the PRI, who might have taken to the streets to protest the ultimate *concertacesión* (concerted concession) engineered to bolster Salinas' reputation as an avowed democrat. Perhaps Fernández de Cevallos feared that

Notes to Pages 163–167 • 217

the PRI would not have allowed the PAN to govern, and therefore that the PAN's historic responsibility was to assure stability and wait six more years until the year 2000.

12. For an analysis of Cuauhtémoc Cárdenas' campaign for the presidency in 1994, see Adolfo Aguilar Zínser, *Vamos a ganar: La pugna de Cuauhtémoc Cárdenas por el poder* (Mexico City: Editorial Oceano, 1995); and Andrea Dabrowksi, *Perdimos la palabra* (Mexico City: Editorial Posadas, 1995).

13. Alianza Cívica, "La calidad del proceso electoral del 21 de agosto 1994," *La Jornada*, September 20, 1994.

14. Many members of Mexico's political class, however, declared that after the August 21 election Mexico had finally joined the ranks of other western democracies such as Switzerland. In a scathing critique, historian Alan Knight branded these individuals "neo-Maderistas" because, like Mexico's short-lived president, they were misguided enough to believe that free elections are enough to guarantee democracy. See Knight's remarks in the *Memoria* of the conference "The Electoral Aftermath: Mexico's Alternative Political Future in Light of the August 21 Elections," Austin, Texas, September 2–3, 1994.

15. Philippe Schmitter and Terry Karl, "What Democracy Is . . . and Is Not," in Larry Diamond and Marc Plattner, eds., *The Global Spread of Democracy* (Baltimore: Johns Hopkins University Press, 1993), 42.

16. Ibid., 42–43.

17. For a theoretical analysis of these obstacles, see Guillermo O'Donnell, "Transitions, Continuities, and Paradoxes," in Mainwaring, O'Donnell, and Valenzuela, eds., *Issues in Democratic Consolidation*, 17–56.

18. Ibid.

19. See Denise Dresser, "Embellishment, Empowerment or Euthanasia of the PRI? Neoliberalism and Party Reform in Mexico," in Cook, Middlebrook, and Molinar Horcasitas, eds., *The Politics of Economic Restructuring*, 125–42; and Mónica Serrano, "The End of Hegemonic Rule: Political Parties and the Transformation of the Mexican Party System," in Neil Harvey and Mónica Serrano, eds., *Party Politics in an "Uncommon Democracy": Political Parties and Elections in Mexico* (London University: Institute of Latin American Studies, 1994), 1–24.

20. See José Antonio Crespo, *"Urnas de Pandora": Partidos políticos y elecciones bajo Salinas* (Mexico City: Centro de Investigaciones Económicas, 1995).

21. In 1995 the governor of the state of Guerrero, Rubén Figueroa, was involved in the assassination of seventeen peasants, and the governor of the state of Tabasco was accused of spending more than forty times the legal limit in his bid for the governorship. Neither was sanctioned or removed from office.

22. For the first time in Jalisco since its creation, the PRI lost the February 12, 1995, gubernatorial and municipal elections to the PAN. The PRI lost the race for governor by nearly a twenty-point margin. For an analysis of this election, see "Mexico's Dysfunctional Neoliberalism," *North-South Focus* (University of Miami, North-South Center), 4, no. 1 (1995).

23. Scott Mainwaring and Timothy R. Scully, eds., *Building Democratic Institutions: Party Systems in Latin America* (Stanford: Stanford University Press, 1995), 20, and Ann L. Craig and Wayne Cornelius, "Houses Divided: Parties and Political Reform in Mexico," ibid., 249–97.

24. José Woldenberg, "Antes de los comicios," in *Violencia y política* (Mexico City: Cal y Arena, 1995), 99–195.

25. For the democratizing role of domestic and international NGOs, see Daniel Moreno, "ONG: Los nuevos protagonistas," *Enfoque*, June 25, 1995; Luis Hernández, "En el país de Gulliver: ONG, democracia y desarrollo," ibid.;

Denise Dresser, "Treading Lightly and without a Stick: International Actors and the Promotion of Democracy in Mexico," in Thomas Farer, ed., *Beyond Sovereignty: The Collective Defense of Democracy in Latin America* (Baltimore: Johns Hopkins University Press, 1995).

26. Mainwaring and Scully, *Building Democratic Institutions*, 24.

27. El Barzón is an organization of small agricultural producers burdened by accumulation of debt. Its affiliates organize nationwide protest marches and sit-ins designed to pressure the banks and the government into debt restructuring and relief. The Zedillo government's restructuring plan for small debtors, the Agreement to Support Debtors (*Acuerdo para el apoyo a deudores*), has sought to deactivate the growing popularity of the Barzonistas but has had little impact. See Sergio Sarmiento, "Y ahora El Barzón," *Reforma*, August 26, 1995.

28. Ben Ross Schneider uses the term *disintermediated democracies* in reference to polities that lack effective organizations for continuous representation of interests; see "Democratic Consolidations: Some Broad Comparisons and Sweeping Arguments," *Latin American Research Review* 30, no. 2 (1995): 215–35.

29. See John Waterbury, "The Heart of the Matter? Public Enterprise and the Adjustment Process," in Stephan Haggard and Robert R. Kaufman, eds., *The Politics of Economic Adjustment* (Princeton: Princeton University Press, 1992), 182–220; and Stephan Haggard and Robert R. Kaufman, *The Political Economy of Democratic Transitions* (Princeton: Princeton University Press, 1995).

30. This argument is based on James M. Malloy, "Economic Crisis and Democratization: Latin America in the 1980s," *The Latin America and Caribbean Contemporary Record* 8. For an analysis of the Mexican case, see Miguel Centeno, *Democracy within Reason: Mexico's Technocratic Revolution* (University Park: Pennsylvania State University Press, 1994).

31. Guillermo O'Donnell, "Do Economists Know Best?" *Journal of Democracy* 6, no. 1 (1995): 23–28.

32. Ibid., 26.

33. Barbara Geddes argues that in order to understand government behavior, it is indispensable to include government interests motivated by the desire to stay in office; see "The Politics of Economic Liberalization," *Latin American Research Review* 30, no. 2 (1995): 198.

34. This argument is drawn from Manuel Pastor Jr. and Carol Wise, "Peruvian Economic Policy in the 1980s: From Orthodoxy to Heterodoxy and Back," *Latin American Research Review* 27, no. 2 (1992): 83–117.

35. For a similar argument see Andrew A. Reding, "It Isn't the Peso. It's the Presidency," *New York Times Magazine*, April 9, 1995.

36. Among the negative fallouts of the PRI's landslide victory in August 1994 is the reinstatement of the legislative machinery that allows unbridled presidentialism. Presidentialism in Mexico is not an exclusively anthropological or sociological phenomenon, but is rooted in a host of institutional arrangements that provide the executive with almost unlimited discretionary power.

Because of its wide margin of victory, the PRI will not have to engage in power sharing with the opposition. The ruling party retains control over Congress and the Senate and thus will be able to push through legislation without having to make concessions to the opposition as it did after the 1988 election. The PRI will continue to benefit from an electoral formula that assures the party's overrepresentation. The PRI obtained the lowest average votes in its history, but it still retains the greatest amount of representation in Mexico's legislative branch. Legislative elections will be held once again in 1997, at which point the PRI could lose its current majority.

37. Jorge Domínguez and James A. McCann, "Whither the PRI? Explaining Voter Defection from Mexico's Ruling Party in the 1988 Presidential Elections," *American Political Science Review* 89, no. 1 (March 1995): 34–48.

38. Moisés Naim, "Mexico's Larger Story," *Foreign Policy*, no. 99 (Summer 1995): 112–30. For further elaboration on the international dimensions of the Mexican crisis, see Leslie Elliot Armijo, "Mixed Blessings: Foreign Capital Inflows and Democracy in 'Emerging Markets,'" paper prepared for the conference on "Financial Globalization and Emerging Markets," Watson Institute of International Studies, Brown University, November 18–19, 1995.

39. For an analysis of the Zedillo cabinet, see Roderic Camp, "El equipo de Zedillo: Continuidad, cambio, o revolución?" *Este País* 51 (June 1995): 46–54.

40. Geddes, "The Politics of Economic Liberalization," 209.

41. For an analysis of this trend in Latin America, see Malloy, "Economic Crisis and Democratization."

42. Lorenzo Meyer, "El estilo impersonal de gobernar," *Reforma* 4 (May 1995).

43. Wayne Cornelius, "Mexico's Delayed Democratization," *Foreign Policy* 95 (Summer 1994): 53–71.

44. Michael Burton, Richard Gunther, and John Higley, "Introduction: Elite Transformations and Democratic Regimes," in John Higley and Richard Gunther, eds., *Elites and Democratic Consolidation: Latin America and Southern Europe* (Cambridge: Cambridge University Press, 1992), 1–37.

45. Such was the case of the Grupo San Angel, a roundtable of intellectuals and politicians formed before the August presidential race, which expelled two members who refused to endorse the group's "consensus document" on the state of Mexican politics prior to the election.

46. Philippe Schmitter, "On Civil Society and the Consolidation of Democracy: Ten General Propositions and Nine Speculations about Their Relation in Asian Societies," paper presented at the conference on "Consolidating the Third Wave Democracies: Trends and Challenges," Institute for Policy Research, Taipei, Taiwan, August 27–30, 1995, 14.

47. Jonathan Fox, "The Difficult Transition from Clientelism to Citizenship," *World Politics* 46, no. 2 (1994): 151–84.

48. Schmitter, "On Civil Society," 3.

49. Wayne Cornelius, "Designing Social Policy for Mexico's Liberalized Economy: From Social Services and Infrastructure to Job Creation," in Riordan Roett, ed., *The Challenge of Institutional Reform in Mexico* (Boulder, Colo.: Lynne Rienner, 1995), 142–43.

50. For an analysis of the leadership of the EZLN and its key role in the uprising, see Carlos Tello Díaz, *La rebelión de las cañadas* (Mexico City: Cal y Arena, 1995).

51. See Luis Hernández Navarro, *Chiapas: La guerra y la paz* (Mexico City: ADN Editores, 1995).

52. Blanca Heredia, "Businessmen and Democracy in Mexico: Can Rational Profit-Maximizers be Democratic?" paper presented at the conference on "Business Elites and Democracy in Latin America," Kellogg Institute, South Bend, Indiana, May 3–5, 1991.

53. According to a 1994 study by the Economic Research Institute of Mexico's National Autonomous University cited by Wayne Cornelius, the privatization policy pursued from 1982 to 1994 resulted in 50 percent of the country's assets being held by just five conglomerates; see Cornelius, "Designing Social Policy," 141.

54. Cornelius, "Designing Social Policy," 146.

55. I borrow this characterization from Mainwaring and Scully, *Building Democratic Institutions*, 1.

56. This section draws on the proposals contained in Woldenberg, *Violencia y política*, which includes the proposal for a new electoral reform designed by the Citizen Counsellors of the Federal Electoral Institute.

57. Woldenberg, *Violencia y política*, 225.

58. Héctor Aguilar Camín and Lorenzo Meyer, *A la sombra de la Revolución Mexicana* (Mexico City: Cal y Arena, 1989).

59. Alianza Cívica, "La calidad del proceso electoral."

60. Raymundo Riva Palacio, "The Media and Democracy," *El Financiero Internacional*, November 1–7, 1993.

61. Woldenberg, *Violencia y política*, 266–78.

62. Ibid., 275.

63. Alonso Lujambio, "Federalismo integrador vs. presidencialismo excluyente en la transición mexicana a la democracia," unpublished paper, n.d.

64. Woldenberg, *Violencia y política*, 262–65.

65. For an analysis of the PAN's dilemmas, see Soledad Loaeza, "Partido Acción Nacional and the Paradoxes of Opposition," in Harvey and Serrano, *Party Politics*, 41–60.

66. Cornelius, "Mexico's Delayed Democratization."

67. Peter Smith, "The Political Impact of Free Trade on Mexico," *Journal of Interamerican Studies and World Affairs* 34, no. 1 (1992).

68. Carlos Fuentes, cited in "Political Reform Must Be President Ernesto Zedillo's Priority," *Mexico and NAFTA Report*, December 8, 1994, 3.

69. See Jonathan Fox and Luis Hernández, "Lessons from the Mexican Election," *Dissent* (Winter 1995).

70. Guillermo O'Donnell ("Transitions") identifies these traits as fundamental obstacles to democratic consolidation.

71. Jorge Domínguez and Abraham Lowenthal, *Democratic Governance in the Americas: Sounding the Alarm* (Washington, D.C.: Inter-American Dialogue Brief, 1994).

72. Moisés Naim, "Latin America: The Second Stage of Reform," *Journal of Democracy* 5, no. 4 (1994): 32–48.

73. Mainwaring and Scully, *Building Democratic Institutions*, viii.

74. Philippe Schmitter, "Dangers and Dilemmas of Democracy," *Journal of Democracy* 5, no. 3 (1994): 57–74.

Chapter 11 Cuba: Prospects for Democracy (Pérez-Stable)

1. For historical background and full exposition of the arguments presented in this chapter, see Marifeli Pérez-Stable, *The Cuban Revolution: Origins, Course, and Legacy* (New York: Oxford University Press, 1993), and Pérez-Stable, "Cuban Nationalism and Political Democracy toward the Twenty-First Century," in Archibald R. M. Ritter and John M. Kirk, eds., *Cuba in the International System: Integration and Normalization* (New York: Macmillan, 1995).

2. *El Nuevo Herald* (October 10, 1994) reported the results of a September 1994 survey of four hundred Cubans (eighteen years or older, residents of Havana) conducted by Mexico's Televisión Azteca, which, even though not representative of the Cuban population, serve as an interesting indication of the mind-set of an important sector. About two-thirds of respondents characterized Fidel Castro as a "dictator," and more than three-quarters said he was either "arrogant and self-possessed" or an "unjust oppressor." At the same time, 25 percent expressed a "good" opinion of Castro, and more than 60 percent

considered that he "loved" his people (28%) or "sort of" loved them (35%). When asked if they supported or opposed the Cuban leader, 66 percent of interviewees responded "opposed," 22 percent "supported." The quarter of the population in Havana, where discontent and opposition are reportedly more widespread, that apparently supports Castro or retains some goodwill toward him is part of the core of popular support which, I argue, still buttresses the government. Televisión Azteca has a reliable record of public opinion research in Mexico.

On December 18, 1994, the *Miami Herald* reported the results of a forty-six-question poll conducted by CID-Gallup of Costa Rica in the period of November 1–9 with 1,002 adults in the western two-thirds of the island. The Cuban government forbade the pollsters to ask questions about Castro and other political personalities. Three of the responses are especially relevant to my argument. First, 58 percent considered the revolution had more achievements than failures. Second, 21 percent considered themselves "socialist" or "communist"; 48 percent identified themselves as "revolutionary," which should not be interpreted as support of the government but rather of the ideals of national sovereignty and social justice. Third, 46 percent responded "don't know," gave no answer, or said "nobody" when asked who would guide or help people who disagreed with the government, which supports my point of a widespread sense of helplessness.

3. For a detailed analysis of the 1992–93 elections, see Marifeli Pérez-Stable, "Legislative and Electoral Dynamics: Reforms and Options," in *Transition in Cuba: New Challenges for U.S. Policy* (May 1993), 39–65. Funded by the U.S. Department of State and the U.S. Agency for International Development (USAID), *Transition in Cuba* was a project of the Cuban Research Institute of the Latin American and Caribbean Center at Florida International University.

4. *CubaFax Update,* December 31, 1992.

5. Spanish News Agency EFE, February 25, 1993.

6. *CubaINFO,* January 11, 1994, and Carlos Solchaga, "La reforma económica en Cuba," *Actualidad Económica,* October 17, 1994, 7–13.

7. See *Cuba en el mes* (February 1995): 30, for the reduction in the budget deficit. The *Economist* (November 19, 1994) reported the dollar exchanged for 40 pesos in contrast to 120 a year earlier. *El Nuevo Herald* (August 26, 1995) reported an exchange rate of 10–15 pesos per dollar.

8. *Associated Press,* September 5 and 6, 1995, and the *Washington Post,* September 6, 1995. The law facilitates the repatriation of profits, clarifies the settlement of business disputes, permits the establishment of duty-free zones, and speeds up the review process of investment proposals. Interestingly, it also welcomes investments from Cuban exiles, even though the government prohibits Cubans on the island from starting their own businesses. All economic sectors are open to foreign capital except education, health, and defense.

9. *Cuba en el mes* (September 1994): 34–35.

10. Between 1990 and 1995, Cuba attracted up to U.S.$2.1 billion in foreign investment in 221 joint ventures. In 1994–95, more than a hundred U.S. corporations visited the island and signed letters of intent to invest upon the lifting of the embargo (*Wall Street Journal,* August 7, 1995). In October 1994 a British-based investment group, Beta Funds International, launched a U.S.$50 million fund for Cuba; its Havana Asset Management Limited (HAM) is the first investment company to focus exclusively on Cuba (*Reuters,* October 13, 1994). The amount of foreign investment represents roughly 10 percent of the losses in foreign aid and investment Cuba suffered after the collapse of the Soviet Union. See Carmelo Mesa-Lago, *Are Economic Reforms Propelling Cuba to the Market?* (Miami: University of Miami Press, 1994), 21.

11. *Miami Herald,* July 13, 1995. Although Foreign Minister Robaina had earlier suggested that individuals in an unofficial capacity (that is, not representatives of organizations and governments) might be allowed to observe the elections, these observers never materialized. For Robaina's suggestion, see *Contrapunto* 5, no. 11 (November 1994): 8.

12. Ending the privileged entry of Cubans into the United States, while regrettable on humanitarian grounds, is a laudable step forward. Normalizing immigration from Cuba is a prerequisite for the eventual normalization of relations between the two countries. The Clinton administration, however, took two steps backward when it simultaneously eliminated dollar remittances and curtailed most travel to the island. These measures do not take into account the political crisis the Cuban government is facing. The United States should promote people-to-people contacts, particularly between Cuban Americans and their relatives in Cuba, and it should broaden the wedge between the Cuban people and their government by renewing dollar remittances. Whatever immediate benefits the government derived from the dollar influx, they were clearly dwarfed in comparison to the costs they imposed on an already strained state control of the economy and society. On July 26, 1995, Castro blasted Track II of the Cuban democracy act, which seeks to promote broader people-to-people contacts so as to "corrode the revolution from within." His stinging rebuke lends credence to the thesis that the Cuban government fears engagement more than isolation.

13. Cuba's symbolic, political concessions were not facilitating a change in U.S. policy. For example, in November 1994 the government allowed a first-time visit of the UN High Commissioner for Human Rights. A potentially more significant event took place in June 1995 when Castro met with former political prisoner and long-time opponent Eloy Gutiérrez Menoyo. Although neither man has disclosed the substance of their meeting, Gutiérrez Menoyo has declared that he is confident he will soon be able to take up residence in Cuba, open offices of his organization, Cambio Cubano, and function as an opposition group. See *El Nuevo Herald,* August 18, 1995. Indeed, if the government recognizes Cambio Cubano as a legal opposition, it would open real—not just symbolic—political space. Were the meeting not to produce that or other comparable outcomes, it would remain at the level of symbolism.

Index

V

Conclusion

Conclusion: Parties, Institutions, and Market Reforms in Constructing Democracies

Jorge I. Domínguez and Jeanne Kinney Giraldo

While discussing local events, some younger would-be reformers of Ilhéus (in Jorge Amado's novel *Gabriela: Cravo e canela*) observed that the traditional elites "support a state government that plunders us and then practically ignores us. While our local government does absolutely nothing . . . [and] in fact it actually places obstacles in the way of improvements." The reformers resolved to make changes; as one said to another, "you'll earn twice as much if you get into politics and change the existing situation."[1]

Though Amado wrote this forty years ago, his fictional characters still identify key themes in the political experience of a great many ordinary people in Latin America and the Caribbean in the mid-1990s. Government is unresponsive and at times an obstacle, traditional political leaders deserve no support, and political reform is an illusion because those who promise change are likely to change only the beneficiaries of corruption. The record reviewed in this book offers much justification for political cynicism and despair.

In the late 1980s and early 1990s, voters in many countries elected to office politicians who promised change but then disappointed the electorate. Elected on platforms committed to change, Fernando Collor de Mello in Brazil and Carlos Andrés Pérez in Venezuela were impeached for corruption and removed from office. Never before had a constitutionally elected president been removed from office in this manner and for this reason in either country.

More generally, the late 1980s and early 1990s was a time of troubles in many Latin American and Caribbean countries, a period when social, economic, and political circumstances were redefined. One sign of disaffection was the pattern of electoral outcomes. In those years, incumbent political parties were defeated at least once in Argentina, Uruguay, Brazil, Bolivia, Peru, Ecuador, Venezuela, Guyana, Barbados, Trinidad and Tobago, Jamaica, Panama, Costa Rica, Nicaragua, El Salvador, Honduras, and Guatemala, as were the incumbent politicians associated with the authoritarian government in Chile in 1989 and in Haiti in 1991.[2] The voters in these countries were unhappy with long-standing rulers and with would-be reformers.

Voters have blamed governing parties for the region's prolonged economic crisis. Dire living conditions still prevail years after the great depression that hit this region in the 1980s. By the end of 1994, on average and in real prices, the gross domestic product (GDP) per capita of the countries of Latin America and the Caribbean had yet to surpass the 1981 level. Among the Latin American countries, only Argentina, Chile, Colombia, Costa Rica, the Dominican Republic, Panama, and Uruguay had surpassed the 1981 level. In the Anglophone Caribbean, the record was better: the Bahamas, Belize, Guyana, Jamaica, and the countries that belong to the Organization of Eastern Caribbean States (OECS) had exceeded the 1981 level.[3]

Latin America and the Caribbean, in short, have been battered by the winds of change, anger, hope, and dissatisfaction. One might expect voter apathy and alienation from political parties to rise, politicians and civic leaders to redesign basic national institutions, market reforms to fail, and political regimes to fall.

In this chapter we advance four propositions that run somewhat counter to these expectations. Though there is much voter anger, new and many old parties have continued to mobilize support. Several new political parties have become credible opposition contenders even in countries where no "new" party has seriously challenged the political establishment in decades. In other cases, long-established political parties have "reinvented" themselves.

Second, while an orgy of constitutional reform-mongering designed to improve democratic governance has occurred, it has had little impact. Attempts have been made to redesign the relationship between executive and legislative branches, improve the performance of the judiciary, and decentralize certain tasks of government, but these attempts have either not gone far enough or proven counterproductive. In too many countries, the performance of state institutions remains poor and democratic governance is weak.

Third, contrary to the expectations of many in years past, democratic regimes in Latin America have proven more effective at introducing market reforms than had been the case with authoritarian regimes. Even more surprising to certain skeptics, in several cases these governments have effectively used the procedures of democracy to advance and secure such reforms.

And fourth, although the stability of constitutional government in the region is still a matter of concern—especially in view of the coup attempts that took place in the 1990s, some sponsored by constitutionally elected presidents—barriers against *successful* coup attempts have gradually been constructed. Since 1976, outside of Suriname, Haiti, and

Peru, all attempts to overthrow a constitutional government chosen through general fraud-free elections have failed. Important changes within the armed forces, in the relationships between the armed forces and the rest of the society, and in the international community have decreased the likelihood of successful military coups.

Crises and Opportunities for Representation

Latin American countries are facing a crisis of representation linked to the challenges of two major transitions: from authoritarian to constitutional governments, and from statist to more market-oriented economies. This second transition also affects most of the countries of the Anglophone Caribbean. Representative networks were battered by the authoritarian regimes; in some countries, they broke down. In nearly all new democracies, parties face a mass electorate that is larger, more urbanized, more educated, and more exposed to mass media than was the case under past constitutional governments. Moreover, the economic depression of the 1980s and the nearly simultaneous transition toward a more market-oriented economy strained old networks of representation and created demands for new forms of representation. Many parties have reconsidered their long-held adherence to statist ideologies. Labor union power has weakened nearly everywhere, while business and "liberal" ideologies have gathered strength. The cutbacks in government consumer subsidies and in funding for many public services have hurt the poor and weakened the political allegiances of many middle-class sectors.

As a result of these changes, organizations that seek to represent the interests of citizens have been simultaneously destroyed, created, and recreated. Many of these organizations have been political parties, but a wide array of social movements have also been involved, and many parties have drawn strength from such movements.[4]

This section examines four kinds of representational challenges facing countries undergoing the dual transition from authoritarianism and statist economies. In countries where the transition from authoritarian regimes to constitutional governments coincided with the end of civil war, new democracies face the challenge of incorporating parties that have been formed out of guerrilla and paramilitary groups. Second, in countries where parties have historically been strong, democratizing pressures and efforts to undertake economic reform have led to the creation of new parties that challenge the monopolies or oligopolies on representation that one or two parties have long held. In other countries where parties have been historically weak, such as Brazil, the major representational challenge is the construction of more programmatic and responsible parties. And fourth, older political parties in many countries have scrambled to adapt to changed circumstances, with varying degrees of success. On balance, the transformation of old parties and the appearance of new parties may improve the prospects of effective representation in the medium to long term.

Explaining the Defeat of Parties

One manifestation of the crisis of representation is the defeat of parties on election day. The most common reason for the defeat of parties at moments of transition from authoritarian rule has been the perception that they are "tainted." In elections that found a democratic regime, parties associated with, or conciliatory to, an outgoing military regime are punished at the voting booth. With the ambiguous exceptions of Mexico[5] and Paraguay, whose elections in the 1980s and early 1990s have been marred by irregularities that protected the incumbents from the full wrath of the voters, the parties most closely identified with an authoritarian regime lost the elections that marked the transition toward constitutional government. This fate befell parties as different as those of the Chilean Right, which lost the 1989 elections at the end of the dictatorship of Augusto Pinochet despite an excellent record of economic growth in the late 1980s, and the Sandinistas in Nicaragua in 1990.

In countries where no major parties supported the military regime, voters chose the opposition party most distant from the unpopular incumbents. This was one important reason why in 1983 Argentina's Radical Civic Union (UCR) beat the Peronistas for the first time since the latter political movement was founded in 1946; why in 1980 Fernando Belaúnde beat the APRA Party (American Popular Revolutionary Alliance) in Peru; and why in 1982 Hernán Siles Suazo became president of Bolivia at the head of a leftist political coalition.

Elections have also punished political parties that were elected as the standard-bearers of political reform but sinned through corruption once in power. The defeats of the Dominican Revolutionary Party (PRD) in 1986, the Christian Democrats (PDC) in El Salvador in 1989 and in Guatemala in 1990, APRA in Peru in 1990, and Acción Democrática (AD) in Venezuela in 1993 can be seen at least in part as voter retribution for such perceived failures.

A third source of electoral defeat for parties has been the response to bad economic conditions.[6] This was certainly a factor in the defeat of the Radical Party in Argentina in 1989, as well as in the defeats of the Christian Democrats in El Salvador in 1989 and in Guatemala in 1990, of APRA in Peru in 1990, and of Acción Democrática in Venezuela in 1993. The economic issue weakened every incumbent Brazilian president since the end of military government in 1985, though Itamar Franco's popularity rose at the very end of his presidency thanks partly to the successful inflation containment policies of his finance minister and eventual successor, Fernando Henrique Cardoso. It also weakened

Guillermo Endara's presidency in Panama, paving the way for the 1994 election victory of the Democratic Revolutionary Party (PRD) once associated with deposed General Manuel Antonio Noriega.

Given the overlap between these three explanations, which is most important to explain the defeat of parties? We believe that "association with authoritarian governments" has more explanatory power than the response to bad economic conditions. Except for the two ambiguous cases already noted (Paraguay and Mexico), no incumbent party tainted by association with prolonged authoritarian rule won an election during the transition from such rule. In contrast, some parties associated with incumbent governments have been defeated despite managing the economy well (in Chile and Jamaica in 1989 and in Uruguay and Costa Rica in 1994), and not every government that has mismanaged the economy has been defeated (Acción Democrática retained the presidency in the 1988 elections). Association with authoritarian rule has been punished more systematically than bad economic outcomes, while good economic management has not always been rewarded.

With the evidence available, however, it is more difficult to determine the relative importance of corruption and bad economic conditions. In Argentina in the early 1990s, for example, the positive economic results under President Carlos Saúl Menem meant more in the public opinion polls than the numerous charges of corruption leveled against people in or close to the administration. In Venezuela, in contrast, the positive performance of the economy under President Pérez during the same years did not bolster his popularity as much as Menem's. It did not save him from later impeachment and conviction on the grounds of corruption, nor did it save his party from election defeats that were also caused in part by the economy's eventual downturn.

The defeat of incumbent parties for any of these three reasons is understandable. Indeed, it is the essence of democratic politics that voters should turn out those officeholders of whose conduct or performance they disapprove. If the reasons why these parties have been defeated give cause to worry about the fate of constitutional government in the region, then the way these parties were defeated gives reason for hope that the instruments of constitutionalism can serve the people's needs.

However, another manifestation of the crisis of representation in the 1990s is the decline of electoral participation in the Anglophone Caribbean and in Venezuela, countries with well-established constitutional governments where such participation had been high historically. Citizens find no electoral vehicle that responds to their concerns to bring about meaningful change. In the early 1990s, as Trevor Munroe notes, voter turnout declined in ten of the thirteen Anglophone Caribbean countries in which general elections were held compared to the average for the 1980s. Voter turnout declined as well in Venezuela, a country with a once consistently high voting rate; its electoral abstention rate rose to 44 percent in 1993, a time of peril for its constitutional life.

Explaining the Birth of New Parties: From Warrior to Peacemaker

By definition, all new parties are born in dissent. Their leaders and followers claim that existing parties no longer represent them. The revolt against established parties has at times begun literally in rebellion. Never before in Latin America's twentieth-century history have so many political parties been spawned by paramilitary or guerrilla organizations. The new parties examined in this section differ in many ways but share one important trait: their founders once used violence to attempt to overthrow the government or dispose of their adversaries. The transformation of military movements into political parties is best explained as a slow, rational process in which exhausted leaders and followers conclude that politics is more cost-effective than war as a way to gain power.

On the Left, Venezuela's Movimiento al Socialismo (MAS) traces its origins in part to the Venezuelan Communist Party's decision to abandon the guerrilla warfare conducted against Venezuela's governments in the 1960s, after which some key leaders of that effort founded the MAS. By the 1980s and 1990s, as Alan Angell makes clear, the MAS had won a respected place among Venezuela's political parties, and it played an important role in Rafael Caldera's 1993 presidential election victory.

In Colombia the M-19 guerrilla group agreed to demobilize in 1989. Its leaders founded Alianza Democrática (AD) M-19, which won 12.5 percent of the vote in the 1990 presidential elections, the largest share of the vote for any party of the Left in Colombian history, as Harvey F. Kline notes. This party went on to win the second largest bloc of seats in the elections for the Constituent Assembly that met during the first half of 1991, though it had weakened greatly by the time of the 1994 national elections.

Revolutionary victory in Nicaragua in 1979 and the Sandinista defeat in 1990 gradually permitted and eventually required the transformation of the Sandinista Front for National Liberation (FSLN) from a military force into a political party. As Rose Spalding shows, the FSLN as a party has had a tumultuous history since 1990, but it has remained within the framework of constitutional politics.

In El Salvador the FMLN (Farabundo Martí National Liberation Front) began its transformation into a political party upon the signing of the peace agreement in 1992; allied with others on the political Left, as Ricardo Córdova Macías shows, it became the country's second-largest political force in the 1994 elections.

On the Right, it is only a slight exaggeration to argue that El Salvador's Nationalist Republican Alliance (ARENA) was born from a wedding between death squads and a segment of the business community. Roberto D'Aubuisson was the key figure in death squad activities in the late 1970s and early 1980s, and he would become ARENA's equally key leader until his death.

In Argentina, Colonel Aldo Rico led an unsuccessful military mutiny against the constitutional government in April 1987. When national congressional and gubernatorial elections were held in 1991, as Liliana De Riz shows, Rico's Movement for National Dignity and Independence (MODIN) won three seats in the Chamber of Deputies and 10 percent of the vote in the crucial province of Buenos Aires; its subsequent strength has varied but remained generally modest. Moreover, provincial parties in Chaco, Salta, and Tucumán nominated retired military officers who had served as governors during the previous military government; these candidates won the governorships.

The fate of these parties depends in part on their ability to resolve the often bitter internal debates over electoral strategy that occur frequently among new participants in the democratic process. In Colombia the M-19's decision to pursue electoral coalitions with traditional parties instead of focusing on party building seems to have backfired; by 1994 its electoral weight was insignificant. In El Salvador the FMLN split over these issues after the 1994 elections, as did the FSLN in Nicaragua in 1995. The importance of the new parties should not be underestimated, however. In the mid-1990s, the MAS was part of the governing coalition in Venezuela. The FSLN and the FMLN remained among the largest political forces in Nicaragua and El Salvador. And ARENA governed El Salvador.

Why did former military combatants lay down their arms to compete in elections? The general reason is *not* the end of the cold war, which had nothing to do with the creation of the MAS, ARENA, or MODIN, or the M-19's decision to end the armed struggle. Nonetheless, international factors did affect the costs and benefits of war for both the rebels and the government. The decision of some guerrillas in Venezuela in the late 1960s to abandon the armed struggle was part of a wider international debate within the political Left about the proper means to contest power. And the turn away from war by the FMLN and the FSLN was indeed framed by the end of the cold war in Europe.

Apart from these lesser considerations, a familiar but powerful explanation serves best.[7] In Thomas Hobbes' *Leviathan*, political order is established as exhausted individuals recoil from a state of war that is "nasty" and "brutish." In all the cases under review, terrible experiences of prolonged war eventually led the combatants to a rational decision to lay down their arms. Through prolonged war they learned that they could not win. The end of warfare in Latin America led, however, not to Leviathans but to constitutional governments. In the logic of stalemate, neither side could dictate its preferences to the other. Each settled for the second-best solution: to contest each other peacefully.[8] Putting something on the negotiating table became a more effective route to achieve their goals.

Latin America's warriors-turned-peacemakers stumbled unknow- ingly onto Robert A. Dahl's axiom that, from the government's perspec- tive, "the more the costs of suppression exceed the costs of toleration, the greater the chance for a competitive regime."[9] From the perspective of the armed opposition, the axiom might be rewritten: "The more the costs of rebellion exceed the costs of participation, the greater the chance for a competitive regime."[10] Moreover, governments changed their strategies to provide institutional guarantees and other incentives for guerrillas to make peace and participate in politics. Lawful political space expanded; the insurgents responded rationally. Where the terms for peaceful participation remained insufficiently attractive, as in Gua- temala and for some guerrilla forces in Colombia, the war staggers on.

Explaining the Birth of New Parties: A Protest against Partyarchy and Ideological Betrayal

In recent years, new parties have been more likely to be born and to attract nationwide support when two processes converged: (1) the pre- existing party establishment gave signs of seeking to strengthen its rul- ing monopoly or duopoly, reducing the space for alternative political forces to express themselves within these parties; and (2) the key polit- ical party that had received support from the Left abandoned its prior policies and veered sharply toward promarket or other right-wing poli- cies, seemingly "betraying the public trust" and generating a secession on its Left. Political entrepreneurs acted when space on the party spec- trum was abdicated through ideological betrayal ("pull factor") and when they no longer found room to play a role within the existing par- ties ("push factor"). Facing blocked opportunities to voice dissent, the would-be founders of new parties and their followers exited.[11] The new parties gained electorally as citizens expressed their discontent with the status quo by voting against establishment parties.

Argentina, Mexico, Uruguay, and Venezuela exemplify these trends. In these four cases, the emergence of new parties has been in part a response to what some perceived as the arrogance of the national par- ties and the predominance within older parties of an apparently self- perpetuating leadership—a classic crisis of representation. Writing about Venezuela, Michael Coppedge uses the word *partyarchy* to de- scribe this phenomenon. In Coppedge's analysis of partyarchy, parties fully penetrate organizations in civil society. We use the term a bit more loosely, simply to identify countries where the number of parties long perceived as capable of winning a presidential election is either one (Mexico) or just two (Argentina, Uruguay, and Venezuela), and where party leaders made use of this monopoly or duopoly to create a "cartel of party elites" (in Mexico, Uruguay, and Venezuela) or were perceived to be attempting to create such a cartel (in Argentina in 1994). Under partyarchy, party leaders and organizations seek to regulate electoral competition within each party and between the two dominant parties, to enforce party discipline in legislative assemblies and executive posts, and to rely on intra-elite negotiation to address various important issues.[12]

In Uruguay the constitution was modified in the late 1960s to concentrate greater powers in the presidency and to constrain political rights. Under President Jorge Pacheco Areco, the governing faction of the Colorado party turned to the Right. The government became generally repressive in response to the Tupamaro urban insurgency and began to adopt market-oriented economic policies. Because Uruguay's labor movement had been independent of the traditional parties, it served as a key vehicle to launch a third-party challenge to an entrenched duopoly (the Colorado and Blanco parties) long protected by the electoral law. In 1971 the law-abiding Left reorganized into a broad coalition, the Frente Amplio (FA), to capture 18 percent of the national vote, most of it from the city of Montevideo. By the 1994 national election, the Frente Amplio had made significant gains in the interior provinces; its share of the national vote rose to just under one-third, in a virtual three-way tie with the Blanco and Colorado parties.

In Argentina, President Menem led the governing Peronista Party toward promarket policies in the 1990s, dismantling the legacy of Juan Perón on which Menem had run for the presidency. Critics responded in various ways. Argentine provincial parties acquired a new lease on life.[13] Historically they had done well in gubernatorial and legislative elections, but in 1994 they also obtained important representation in the Constituent Assembly at the expense of both the Peronistas and the Radicals, as De Riz shows. Support for provincial parties, MODIN, and the left-leaning Frente Grande (FG) coalition blossomed in response to the 1994 agreement between President Menem and former president Raúl Alfonsín to modify the constitution, which was widely perceived as an effort to advance their own ambitions. To prevent the continuity of such a duopoly, many voters turned to third parties.

Something similar happened in Mexico, where national elections became much more competitive in the 1980s and 1990s, as Denise Dresser reminds us. After 1982 the long-ruling Institutional Revolutionary Party (PRI) abandoned decades of statist policies to shift toward promarket policies, but it was still reluctant to recognize opposition election victories. In response, the center-right National Action Party (PAN) ran on a platform calling for democratization and was able to increase its national appeal beyond its historic bases of support in various states of northern Mexico. Within the PRI, party elites raised the barriers to internal dissent even as they were abandoning decades of statist policies; denied a voice within the party they had called home, dissenters exited to form a new party. The new center-left Party of the Democratic Revolution (PRD), led by Cuauhtémoc Cárdenas, combined these dissidents from the PRI with supporters drawn from other small parties of the Left (including Mexico's communist party). The PRD considered itself a national party though it obtained disproportionate support from central and southern Mexico.[14] Both the reinvigoration of the PAN and the rise of the Cardenista opposition can be traced to protests against the PRI's monopoly on public office.

In Venezuela in 1989, President Carlos Andrés Pérez shifted away from his populist and statist past toward promarket policies markedly different from those that Acción Democrática had normally espoused. For the most part, the hitherto main opposition party, COPEI (Christian Democratic Party), supported the new economic orientation. In the early 1990s, opposition to these economic policies merged with a revolt against partyarchy that had been gathering strength during the previous decade. Opponents felt that they had no choice but to look outside the two long-dominant parties or to abstain; abstention rates in Venezuelan elections, historically very low, rose significantly. A plurality elected former president Rafael Caldera to the presidency in December 1993 after he had denounced the party establishment and its economic policies, broken with COPEI, and founded the National Convergence (CN), which aligned with the MAS and other parties. Another noteworthy result was the explosive growth of Causa R, a new political party that rose from a social and regional base and quickly became a national party. Causa R emerged in the labor movement of the State of Bolívar, led by union leader Andrés Velásquez, who was elected as state governor and served as the party's presidential candidate in 1993. By the 1993 national elections, Causa R had built a strong presence in the Venezuelan labor movement nationwide and drew support from other regions of the country to capture just under a fourth of the votes cast, a virtual tie with Acción Democrática and COPEI.

The combination of partyarchy and doctrinal abandonment set the stage for the rise of new parties. If partyarchy alone were the explanation, similar challenges should have developed in Colombia (see Kline's chapter) and Honduras (see the chapter by Mark B. Rosenberg and J. Mark Ruhl), where the Liberal and Conservative and the Liberal and National parties, respectively, enjoyed duopolies of representation and where party programs did not typically differ much in ideological content. In these countries, however, the question of "ideological betrayal" never arose. Parties remained reliable: once in office they did not change the behavior displayed in the pre-election campaign.[15] In these countries, despite discontent with the party establishment, no strong new parties emerged in the absence of ideological betrayal.

In the same vein, merely dropping previous programmatic commitments does not suffice to trigger the emergence of a third party seeking to represent interests within civil society. Third parties did not gain much support in Costa Rica in the 1980s, when Liberación Nacional (PLN) governments under presidents Luis Monge and Oscar Arias veered away from the party's historic statism toward freer market policies but did not seek simultaneously to increase barriers to representation. As Lowell Gudmundson tells us, court litigation became the channel for dissent from the new economic policies.

In Argentina, Carlos Menem ran for office without hinting that he planned to abandon decades of Peronista commitment to statist economic policies, but he did. In response, the Frente Grande coalition was formed on the Left to claim the political space that the Peronistas had ceded, but voting support for the Peronistas (though it declined slightly in 1991 relative to the 1989 elections) remained strong in the two nationwide congressional elections following his policy about-face. As De Riz shows, the Peronista share of the vote dropped only in response to the Menem-Alfonsín pact to modify the constitution. The Frente Grande had received only 3.6 percent of the vote in 1993 (before the Menem-Alfonsín pact), but it gained 13.6 percent in 1994 (after the pact), when it also carried the capital city of Buenos Aires; the MODIN's share of the vote rose from 6 percent before the pact to 9 percent after it. In the 1995 presidential elections, the Frente Grande transformed itself into the Frente País Solidario (FREPASO). Its candidate, former Peronista senator and governor José Octavio Bordón, won 28 percent of the votes, finishing second to Menem and ahead of the Radicals—the first time in a century that the Radical Civic Union had failed to come in first or second in a presidential election. (The MODIN's share of the votes fell below 2 percent.)

In short, neither a change in economic policy commitments nor the existence of partisan monopolies or duopolies suffices to trigger the emergence of new parties or party coalitions. Together, however, these two factors greatly increase the likelihood that such parties or coalitions will arise and grow.[16] A hypothesis to explore in the future is the following: when parties are formed around groups organized in civil society (Frente Amplio in Uruguay, PAN in Mexico, Causa R in Venezuela), they are more likely to endure and succeed than parties that are formed principally by dissidents who find their paths blocked within existing parties (Convergencia Nacional in Venezuela, FREPASO in Argentina), with Mexico's PRD exhibiting traits of both processes. There is preliminary support for this view in the December 1995 gubernatorial elections in Venezuela, in which Causa R received 13 percent of the votes cast, the MAS 10 percent, and Convergencia Nacional less than 9 percent.

Explaining the Birth of New Parties: Constructing Political Society

In other countries, representation has suffered not because of the tight grip of one or two strong parties on public office but because of the predominance of many weak parties. Brazil, for example, has been bereft of "real" political parties. As Bolívar Lamounier and Frances Hagopian explain, the combination of powerful traditional elites, entrenched regional interests, the incentives created for politicians by the electoral laws, and the norms and habits of politics have left Brazil with weak, incoherent, unprogrammatic, undisciplined, and fractious parties. In contrast, as Lamounier put it at the Inter-American Dialogue's conference on democracy, "real" modern parties should be internally democratic, pragmatic, and able to recruit cadres and respond quickly to problems with well-defined initiatives.

Since the late 1970s, two real parties have been founded in Brazil. The PT (Workers' Party) grew out of the militant unionism developed in the late 1970s in the metallurgical industries of the highly urban state of São Paulo in protest against the ruling military dictatorship and in search of better economic conditions. It has become the largest explicitly socialist party in Latin America, incorporating a variety of small Brazilian left-wing parties within its midst and providing a partisan home for many social movements that arose in connection with Roman Catholic ecclesiastical base communities, neighborhood associations, and women's movements. In Brazil's 1990 and 1994 presidential elections, the PT's candidate, Lula (Luis Inácio da Silva), came in second. The PT's formal members have genuine opportunities to engage in internal party life and debate and choose party programs and policies. The PT has what Lamounier has called "a definite *esprit de corps.*" It is Brazil's first-ever large mass political party that does not depend on just the popularity of its leader or the efficacy of a patronage machine.

The second real party is the Brazilian Social Democratic Party (PSDB). Founded in 1988 from a schism in the Brazilian Democratic Movement Party (PMDB)—a classic incoherent combination of traditional clientelism, patronage, and factions—the PSDB sought to formulate a centrist "modern" alternative to other parties, with strong appeal to the urban middle class. The PSDB designed a program for effective democratic governance to which its officeholders were ordinarily bound. In 1994 PSDB founding leader Fernando Henrique Cardoso was elected president of Brazil in large part because of his previous success as finance minister. Like the PT, although to a lesser extent, the PSDB is characterized by programmatic coherence, officeholder discipline, and internal party life.

Since the 1994 elections, then, Brazil for the first time has had "real" parties in government and in opposition, in addition to the traditional clientelistic patronage machines. Nonetheless, the strength of those traditional machines was also evident in that election. In order to elect Cardoso to the presidency, the PSDB had to form an alliance with the Liberal Front Party (PFL), a classic patronage party. Thus it remains to be seen how much long-term impact the PT and the PSDB will have on the traditional style of politics in Brazil, especially because skewed electoral laws still limit their representation in Congress.

Explaining the Reinvention of Old Parties

The region's crisis of representation and its economic depression of the 1980s did not overwhelm every preexisting political party, nor was the creation of new parties the sole response to these problems, however. Many existing parties have made efforts to adapt to changed circumstances, a strategy of reinvention. In most cases, defeat—either of the party or of democracy as a whole—permitted challengers within the party to marginalize discredited factions and leaders, at times relieving them of their power. Defeat also made it easier to reexamine old dogmas and discard failed policies. Defeat alone is insufficient, of course, for the successful reinvention of parties. A reinvented party's programmatic reorientation can be consolidated only if the party is rewarded with electoral victory.

During the 1980s, as Timothy R. Scully demonstrates, the Chilean Christian Democrats and the socialists (including the socialist offshoot PPD, the Party for Democracy) rebuilt and repositioned themselves, and forged an alliance (the Concertación Democrática, CD) to win the 1988 plebiscite that ended the dictatorship and then to win the next two presidential elections in 1989 and 1993. The breakdown of democracy in 1973, the failure of the protests of the mid-1980s to unseat the military government, and the collapse of heterodox economic policies in neighboring countries affected the balance of forces within the parties of the Center and the Left and eventually resulted in the ascendance of new leaders who embraced a market-conforming political platform.

Also during the 1980s, the People's National Party (PNP) in Jamaica reconstructed its program and renewed its cadres, after the party's failed statist economic policies led to a crushing electoral defeat in 1980. The reinvented party won the parliamentary elections of 1989 and subsequently effected a transition of the prime ministership from Michael Manley to P. J. Patterson. The party recognized that its statist economic policies during the 1970s failed and had also resulted in its election defeat in 1980.

In Argentina, in response to their 1983 presidential election defeat, the Peronistas reinvented themselves. Founded in the mid-1940s by Juan Perón as what he called a "movement" more than a party, the Peronistas (Partido Justicialista, PJ) at last held internal party elections in the 1980s to choose candidates for office. These new internal procedures made it easier to remove many old-time leaders who had lost the support of the rank and file. In the early 1990s, in addition, the Menem government adopted an entirely new profile of economic policies.

In Panama in the early 1990s the PRD successfully recovered from its long cohabitation with General Noriega. As Richard L. Millett indicates, after its 1989 defeat the PRD modified its policies toward the United States, dropped its support for reestablishing the armed forces, adopted less confrontational stands toward other political forces, and adopted a market-friendly economic program. It won the 1994 presidential elections.

In Chile, Jamaica, Argentina, and Panama, the reinvention of the parties rested on a shift from statist to promarket economic policies, a shift made possible by the shock of defeat, which in turn permitted the removal of discredited leaders. In many cases a comfortable margin of victory for the reinvented parties in a later election facilitated the consolidation of the reinvention and the policies associated with it. Leaders who changed the historical policy commitments of their party were likely to lose some part of their previous constituency; the larger the victory, the less risky was this change. In Jamaica the margin of victory of the People's National Party in 1989 meant that the "renovating" leadership did not need to rely on the vote-mobilizing capabilities of the more radical wing of the party. In Chile the weakening of the Communist Party removed the incentive for leaders of the Center-Left to back away from their commitment to more market-oriented economic policies. In Argentina and Panama the Peronistas and the PRD, respectively, faced ineffectual opposition parties. In short, a significant victory over the opposition was as important to party renewal as the prior defeat of the party itself.

Representational Challenges to the Party System

Many of the new parties under review have been linked to social movements, but the relationship between political and civil society remains problematic in many countries. In Brazil, Chile, Mexico, Nicaragua, and Venezuela, for example, many groups in civil society have sought to increase their autonomy with regard to parties in order to avoid partisan manipulation. In Venezuela and Colombia, new social movements have pressed for the decentralization of the state as a way to weaken central party leaderships, and new local leaders have run for office successfully as independents. Though understandable, these combined trends may well make it more difficult to secure both effective political representation and sustained political cooperation on a nationwide basis.

In addition, there remain important representational voids that not even the new parties have begun to fill sufficiently and that are just as important for effective democratic governance. We call attention to three of them.

As Deborah J. Yashar points out, the representation of indigenous peoples has been woefully inadequate throughout the region. Organized ethnic protest has been emerging since the 1970s in countries with large indigenous populations. In Bolivia, new, small political parties have so far been able to channel these energies and provide some means for representation. But, as Eduardo A. Gamarra indicates, Víctor Hugo Cárdenas, the Aymara leader elected in 1993 as Bolivia's vice-president, may be more popular outside Bolivia than in his own country. He can obtain considerable international sympathy and support on behalf of those whom he claims to represent, but his actual backing within Bolivia, even among indigenous peoples, remains modest for a variety of reasons, including the internal diversity of the indigenous community and the limited accomplishments of his administration. Bolivia has also witnessed the phenomenon of Palenquismo, not organized ethnic protest but populist appeals to indigenous peoples by television and radio personality Carlos Palenque.

In the southern Mexican state of Chiapas, the Zapatista National Liberation Army (EZLN) combines ethnic and regional grievances with a larger national program and the disposition to use armed violence to advance its ends. Because of its reliance on violence, this insurgency has been the most worrisome example of ethnic protest.

In Ecuador the Confederation of Indigenous Nationalities (CONAIE) organized and spearheaded important nationwide protests in the 1990s in opposition to proposed land tenure law changes and other measures that, in its judgment, adversely affected the interests of indigenous peoples. CONAIE also learned to collaborate with some labor unions to organize general strikes. This may well be Latin America's strongest indigenous-based social movement independent of a political party.

Until the 1980s, nationwide political protest by indigenous peoples had been extremely rare in Latin America. To understand the change leading to the rise of such protest, Yashar highlights four features that apply with special force during the 1980s and 1990s: (1) the political opening associated with democratization; (2) the erosion of existing avenues of representation and the increase in material hardship that often accompany the implementation of neoliberal economic policies; (3) the nurturing and enabling effects of institutions such as the changed Roman Catholic Church and other religious communities; and (4) the growth of an international movement of foundations, scholars, and activists to provide support for indigenous organizations in Latin America. There is still the need to explain further, however, why Quechua speakers in Ecuador organize on behalf of the rights of indigenous peoples who happen to be poor, while Quechua speakers in Peru organize on behalf of the rights of poor people who happen to be indigenous.

Why does the likelihood of organized protest on behalf of ethnocultural and linguistic goals vary so much?

A second problem of inadequate representation is evident with regard to gender.[17] Universal suffrage came later to Latin America than to Western Europe and North America, and women's effective participation in politics has continued to lag. In the 1980s and 1990s, some women politicians have emerged on the national scene, but they are still rare. Some of the new and renovating political parties on the Left, such as Brazil's PT, the Chilean socialists, and Nicaragua's Sandinistas, consciously design their internal rules to attempt, with varying degrees of success, to create an active role for women in discussions and leadership.

A third problem of inadequate representation is the oldest and best known: the question of social class and democratic politics. In this collection, Jorge G. Castañeda examines the compatibility between new promarket economic policies and the distributive pressures that, he argues, inevitably emerge in democratic regimes. Latin American and Caribbean countries have not been good at meeting these goals in the past. The risk of neoliberal reforms is that the prospects for many people are likely to worsen unless there is a conscious commitment to address problems of absolute poverty so that "common folk" can become true "citizens." It is not just the troubles of the powerful, in other words, but the inattention to the troubles of the unempowered that has created a crisis of representation. Effective democratic governance demands that the voiceless be heard.

Reforming State Institutions

In response to the crisis of representation, the legacies of authoritarian rule, and the inefficacy of government economic management in all countries in the early 1980s, government institutions came in for close scrutiny after the demise of authoritarian rule. The result was a widespread and intensive effort to reform the institutions of the state. This section describes the strategies pursued and analyzes their limited success.

We focus on three major areas of attempted institutional redesign. One is the effort to break the gridlock between, and improve the democratic responsiveness of, the executive and the legislature. The second is the effort to reform the administration of justice: to combat crime and corruption, to depoliticize the courts, and to improve access to the court system. The third is the attempt to bring about territorial decentralization and to devolve responsibilities to subnational governments while seeking to improve their capacity to handle their new duties.

Reshaping Executive-Legislative Relations

With the return of constitutional government in Latin America, scholars and politicians advanced proposals for institutional reform designed to help solve the problems that they believed had contributed to the previous breakdown of democratic institutions. In many cases the nature of legislative-executive relations was blamed; in particular, fixed presidential terms and the stalemate between the legislature and the president in presidential systems were seen as crucial factors in democratic breakdown.

The most commonly heard prescription was parliamentarism. Its scholarly advocates believed that incentives for cooperation between the two branches would be increased by tying the legislators' tenure in office to the success of the executive.[18] Legislators who would face the prospect of losing their ballot positions in new elections called by a stymied prime minister would be more likely, the proponents of parliamentarism believed, to organize in disciplined parties and form effective government coalitions. Similarly, executives in parliamentary systems would face votes of no-confidence and thus would have more incentive to negotiate with legislators than would a president elected separately from the legislature and unaccountable to it. Despite these arguments, parliamentarism was not adopted in any Latin American country.

In the Anglophone Caribbean, the problems were different. In their existing parliamentary systems, the first-past-the-post electoral system and the small size of parliaments gravely weakened the capacity of the legislature to represent political minorities or to balance the executive. Elections produced large parliamentary majorities, denying even large minority parties adequate representation in parliament. Moreover, parliament was left with few means to check unbridled executive power. As Munroe reports, almost one-third of the region's members of parliament are also cabinet members. In effect, they are constitutionally debarred from independent and critical stances in relation to the executive because they are also in the executive. These problems remain unsolved for the most part.

Although politicians in Latin America and the Caribbean have been unwilling to undertake a wholesale change of state institutions (from presidentialism to parliamentarism, or vice versa), they did make a variety of institutional changes. Argentina (1994), Brazil (1988), Colombia (1991), and Peru (1978 and 1994) convened constituent assemblies to rewrite their basic charter. In Bolivia, Chile, Nicaragua, Paraguay, and Venezuela, legislators undertook constitutional reforms. In Ecuador a commission of experts drafted a new constitution based on widespread consultation and subsequent submission to a referendum.

There have been two waves of constitutional reforms. The first wave accompanied the transition to democracy and was aimed at solving the problems that were believed to have plagued previous experiences with democracy, especially gridlock and exclusionary practices such as the effective disenfranchisement of large numbers of citizens. Exclusionary practices also came in for sharp criticism in the long-established constitutional polities of Colombia, Venezuela, and the Anglophone Caribbean, where the most widely voiced demand was for an opening of the political system to greater participation (a cry heard also in Mexico). The second wave of constitutional reforms responded to long-standing problems of democratic governance that came to public attention as governments attempted to implement market reforms: corruption, excessive concentration of power in the presidency, and irresponsible behavior by legislators.

The goals for reform advanced by the two waves were broad and potentially contradictory: (1) to break the stalemate between the executive and the legislature; (2) to encourage the democratic responsiveness of the executive by checking its unbridled powers; and (3) to increase the democratic responsiveness of the legislature. This third point had two aspects: to encourage responsible, programmatic behavior by legislators and to increase the effective representation of voting minorities.

In order to break the stalemate between the executive and the legislature, several kinds of reforms were passed to strengthen the executive. The most widely adopted reform was the ballotage, that is, a "second round" in presidential elections in order to ensure that the president would be elected by a majority. Since the late 1970s, this has been introduced in Argentina and Nicaragua (where a candidate needs only 45 percent of the vote to avoid a second round), and also in Brazil, Chile, Colombia, the Dominican Republic, Ecuador, El Salvador, Guatemala, and Peru. A second reform was to give special powers to the executive to make macroeconomic policy. Such reforms first occurred in gridlocked democracies: Uruguay in 1967, Colombia in 1968, and Chile in 1970. They would be introduced in Peru in 1979 and 1993, Brazil in 1988, and passed by plebiscite in Ecuador in 1994.

A third change, introduced in Peru in 1993 and in Argentina in 1994, was to permit the president's immediate reelection, ostensibly to strengthen the incumbent's capacity to govern. The fact that incumbent presidents Fujimori and Menem benefited from the reform, however, led many to see this change as a resurgence of personalism in contexts where partisan, judicial, and legislative checks on the executive remain weak.

A different approach to breaking stalemates between the president and the legislature focused on the electoral law and the incentives it provides to legislators. The electoral law is often cited as an explanation for the stable governmental coalition in Congress in Chile and for unstable coalitions in Congress in Brazil. Brazilianists point to electoral law incentives that hinder cooperation, foster party indiscipline and disloyalty, and induce preferential attention to pork-barrel politics over policy issues. In contrast, Scully calls attention to Chile's quite different electoral law of the early 1990s, whose "almost inexorable bipolar logic" has provided strong incentives for interparty cooperation at the polls and in the legislature.

In order to check the president's powers, politicians in various countries have granted greater prerogatives to legislatures. In Colombia, the Congress was authorized to censure ministers. In Nicaragua in 1994, the Assembly acquired greater authority over tax policy. In Argentina the 1994 constitutional reform created a cabinet chief accountable to the legislature and curbed the president's power to rule by decree. Bans on presidential reelection, already in place in most countries, have been added to several constitutions. In 1994 Nicaragua and the Dominican Republic banned immediate reelection; in 1991 Colombia banned re-election at any time. This strengthening of congressional prerogatives is largely a reaction against the abuse of presidential power that occurred as chief executives attempted to stabilize and reform the economies of these countries. (This happened only to a limited degree in Brazil, where the 1988 Constitution increased a great many of the legislature's powers but at the same time made the president's decree powers, established in the prior authoritarian constitution, even more arbitrary.)

Meanwhile, some reformers tried to end exclusionary practices and foster the legislature's democratic responsiveness by increasing representational pluralism. In many countries, expansion of the suffrage was expected to provide a constituency for reformist parties of the Center and Left. The ballotage in Argentina and Colombia was designed to encourage the proliferation of presidential candidates, and consequently of parties as representative vehicles, by permitting "sincere" voting (in which voters support the candidate they truly prefer) in the first round. Colombia's use of national districts for the election of senators allows voting minorities not concentrated in a particular region to gain representation in this chamber. Venezuela's shift to voting in part for individual candidates, not just for party slates, seeks to promote greater pluralism and weaken control by party leaders as well.

The most striking characteristic of these reform processes as a whole, however, has been their failure to improve the quality of democratic governance. Constitutional reform has proceeded the least in the Anglophone Caribbean, but the Latin Americans, frankly, have relatively little to show for their efforts, either. The greatest disappointments are evident in Brazil, Colombia, Ecuador, and Honduras, where little seems to have changed, and in Chile, where the electoral laws and the standing and structure of Congress remain well below acceptable levels for democratic constitutionalism. There, executive powers are excessive, one-fifth of the Senate is unelected, and the electoral law overrepresents conservative rural districts and impedes the effective representation of voting minorities.

How can this failure be explained? Some of the problems are genuinely intractable. Even if "smart people" were omnipotent in implementing reforms, they would still find it extraordinarily hard to determine how to balance the trade-off between accountability and effectiveness. The somewhat contradictory goals present early in the reform process were just as evident at the end.

In some cases, the diagnoses and prescriptions advanced by reforming elites turned out to be faulty. Ecuadorian academics, Anita Isaacs reminds us, expected radical changes even though the modifications enacted in 1979 were for the most part limited to the extension of the suffrage, party registration, and ballotage, stopping well short of reforming the institutional relations between the executive and the legislature. Ecuadorian elites erroneously focused their attention on creating incentives for short-term *electoral* coalitions (such as the ballotage), failing to realize that these incentives did not facilitate longer-term *governing* coalitions. Similarly flawed was the exercise in Brazil. Brazilian constitutionalists in 1988 did not address the electoral law's incentives for politicians to focus on pork-barrel politics and its disincentives for party discipline. Lamounier argues that this neglect can be traced to the mistaken notion that fragmented ("pluralist") representation in the legislature and concentrated power in the executive are the best ways to reconcile democratic government and effectiveness. (Although Brazil has long suffered from representational imbalance and electoral fragmentation, the 1988 Constitution continued to over-represent the northeast while failing to establish a minimum vote threshold that parties must meet to win representation in Congress.) In both Ecuador and Brazil, constitutional reform did little to solve the problem of governmental gridlock; president and congress continued to confront each other, the former often resorting to rule by decree.

In many cases, necessary reforms were not passed because they threatened the interests of elites. Munroe shows that the first-past-the-post electoral laws common throughout the Anglophone Caribbean protect the interests of the dominant parties best because they exclude third parties from ever gaining significant parliamentary membership.

More generally in Latin America, Hagopian's study of traditional elites shows that the interests of such elites are best served by existing electoral arrangements that reinforce the clientelistic nature of parties. Clientelistic party systems are characterized by fragmentation, personalism, a patronage or rent-seeking approach to the state and public policy, and a lack of party loyalty on the part of legislators and voters. Party indiscipline is especially evident when politicians desert the parties on whose tickets they ran, as a majority of Brazilian members of Congress have done since the restoration of civilian government in 1985 and as a comparable proportion of Ecuadorian members of Congress have done since a similar transition in 1979; in each of these two countries, as many as a third of the members of the legislature change parties during one term of office.

In clientelistic party systems, parties fail to articulate the interests of their constituents at a programmatic level, which fuels voter apathy and, in some cases, social violence. Collective action is difficult when power is dispersed among many parties (as in Brazil and Ecuador, for example); even where parties are fewer (as in Colombia and Honduras), internal factionalization and lack of discipline within large parties frequently results in an equally paralyzing de facto multipartyism. Members of congress pursue pork-barrel objectives at the expense of legislation or administrative oversight, permitting the excessive concentration of powers in the presidency. Traditional elites can make such conditions work well for them.

In clientelistic systems, presidents can employ patronage to co-opt the opposition, weaken congressional supervision over executive policies, and lull legislators into permitting the use of presidential decree powers. For these reasons, presidents, too, often prefer the constitutional status quo, therefore. For example, as Kline notes, Colombian presidents since 1946 have routinely ruled under "state of siege" provisions authorized by the constitution, relying on decrees rather than laws for the governance of the economy.

In this book, Hagopian argues that traditional elites are less predisposed to respect democratic institutions and processes and more likely to abuse the state for ends that are both antidemocratic and antimarket. Lamounier, Kline, Isaacs, Edelberto Torres-Rivas, Rosario Espinal, and Rosenberg and Ruhl document the long-standing clientelistic features of party systems in Brazil, Colombia, Ecuador, Guatemala, the Dominican Republic, and Honduras, which have had the effects summarized above. As Rosenberg and Ruhl put it, the two principal parties in Honduras have offered little effective leadership because their interest is largely directed at meeting the needs of their respective clienteles. Power is rarely exercised to effect a larger vision of the common good. In all such cases, democratic representativeness suffers, and effective constitutional reform to improve governance becomes highly unlikely.

Nevertheless, there have been some modest improvements, especially in countries with little experience of congressional assertiveness or efficacy. Ironically these improvements have resulted less from constitutional changes than from a more even balance of power between executive and legislature. For the first time ever, the Congress of El Salvador plays a role of oversight and legislation in the 1990s, with all of the country's political forces represented in its midst. During these same years, the Mexican Congress began to question the executive more systematically. Also in the 1990s, albeit (as Spalding shows) after excruciating difficulties, Nicaragua's Assembly began to legislate to address some of the country's ills. After the 1993 national elections, as Diego Abente Brun points out, Paraguay found itself with a divided government for the first time in its history; at issue was the capacity of president and congress to deepen a still-incipient process of constitutionalizing the government while maintaining acceptable levels of governability.

History also shows the importance of political learning in improving democratic governance. Consider the problem of resolving executive-legislative gridlock. The cases of Costa Rica in the 1950s and El Salvador in the 1990s exemplify the capacity of politicians to learn to cooperate for the purpose of fostering civil peace and establishing constitutional government. In each of those cases, civil wars came to an end and constitutional governments were installed. Venezuela in the 1950s and Chile in the 1990s provide related examples: various parties were able to cooperate to end dictatorship, install constitutional government, and fashion effective relations between president and congress.

Bolivia in the mid-1980s is equally remarkable. As Gamarra shows, Bolivia had had a textbook example of a weak, fragmented party system that permitted the military and, later on, drug traffickers to influence the exercise of power. In 1985, Bolivian politicians responded with inventiveness and creativity to a runaway hyperinflation. They have been able to form three kinds of partisan coalitions: one to contest elections, another in Congress to identify the next president (in the past three elections, the winner of the plurality of votes became president only once), and a third also in Congress to fashion reliable congressional governing majorities. The very same parties that had brought the country near its grave made possible its resurrection.

Each of these five countries was in the midst of effecting an epochal transition from economic chaos (Bolivia), civil war (Costa Rica and El Salvador), or dictatorship (Chile and Venezuela). In each case, politicians successfully responded to the problems of their times. These examples suggest that institutional changes are most effective and lasting when they are backed by strong political coalitions and serve the interests of the dominant political forces at a critical juncture.

Reforming the Court System

Judiciaries throughout Latin America are in dire need of reform, but little headway is being made. The problems with the court system occur at nearly every level, for four general reasons: (1) the corruption of judges; (2) the politicization of the courts; (3) the gutting of judicial independence by the president; and (4) the operational incapacities of the court system itself. In the 1980s and 1990s, reform efforts have attempted to expedite the administration of justice to combat crime and corruption, depoliticize the courts, and improve societal access to the court system. This section looks first at the four explanations for the malperformance of the court system and then turns to reform efforts.

In some countries, especially Bolivia and Colombia, the judiciary has been corrupted by drug traffickers. In Colombia, Kline recalls, drug leaders have been convicted infrequently because they have bribed, threatened, or killed judges. In response, the Colombian judicial system acknowledged its incapacity and came to rely more on plea bargaining: any person could receive a reduced sentence upon surrendering and confessing one crime. The problem of judicial corruption from drug trafficking has spread to other countries.

Meanwhile, the extent of politicization of judicial appointments by political parties is a threat to impartiality. In Ecuador in 1983 and again in 1993, Isaacs reports, congressional majorities deeply politicized the appointments to the Supreme Court, gutting its independence and threatening constitutional order.[19]

The threat to judicial independence comes not only from the legislature but, even more frequently, from an executive eager to reduce all obstacles to the implementation of presidential policies. In Argentina in the early 1990s, De Riz reminds us, President Menem increased the size of the Supreme Court to add his appointees and at the same time reduced the scope of Supreme Court jurisdiction over cases bearing on the "economic emergency." The Supreme Court's deference to the executive seriously compromised its legitimacy in the eyes of much of the public and the legal community. In other places—such as the Dominican Republic, as Espinal tells us—presidentialist personalism in the appointment of judges is routine and has greatly weakened the independence of the judiciary.

Presidents have also meddled with the courts to avert the politically costly prosecution of their allies. In February 1994 President Fujimori used his legislative majority to prevent the Peruvian Supreme Court from trying military officers accused of extrajudicial executions, the killings of nine students and a professor from La Cantuta national teachers' university.[20] In Argentina, President Menem replaced the independent judges who were slated to try some of his associates on corruption charges with more compliant court officers.

Finally, the operation of the courts is itself defective. In Bolivia, for example, Gamarra notes that the most serious problem facing the judicial system is the non-Spanish-speaking population's lack of access to the courts. By law, all proceedings must be conducted in Spanish, even though this is not the primary language of a substantial proportion of the population. As a result, many people look for justice outside the courts.

Operative deficiencies are also apparent in Colombia, according to Kline: in the early 1980s, only one in ten reported crimes ever led to a verdict, and in the early 1990s that figure had dropped to one of twenty. Similar statistics, regrettably, are common throughout the region. In many countries the court system is severely underfinanced, as Millett and Isaacs point out for the cases of Panama and Ecuador, respectively.

Despite these enduring and serious problems, there are glimmers of reform. In many cases, sustained efforts are under way to allocate greater resources to the courts, to improve the training of judges, and to professionalize the circumstances of their work. Colombia's 1991 Constitution created a National Prosecutor's Office (Fiscalía Nacional) with the authority to investigate and prosecute cases and to coordinate the activities of all military and civilian agencies gathering evidence on crimes. Thus the new constitution broke with the Napoleonic Code tradition in which some judges investigate crimes and others adjudicate them; the reforms freed the court system from investigative responsibilities. During the first two years, the judicial system processed 50 percent more cases than under the old system. This change holds promise for expediting the administration of justice.

Argentina's constitutional reform of 1994 also holds promise. In the so-called Olivos Pact between Alfonsín and Menem, a new council was created to nominate all judges prior to their appointment. The constitutional reform created a new General Accounting Office to audit the government's accounts and thus combat corruption. These agreements enhanced the independence and professionalism of the judiciary system, created more effective means to combat corruption, and attempted to depoliticize the judiciary. Parties in El Salvador, Nicaragua, and Paraguay have also been able to reach agreements and appoint balanced supreme courts. The willingness of political actors to compromise raises the hope that one of the root causes of judicial politicization, legislative-executive conflict, might be reduced.

Most ambitious has been Costa Rica's experiment with judicial activism to facilitate societal access to the court system, as described by Gudmundson. Since the 1980s the Fourth or Constitutional Chamber (Sala IV) of the Supreme Court has become involved in an ever-widening number of disputes. Nongovernmental organizations (NGOs) have gone to the Fourth Chamber to challenge the neoliberal economic policies implemented by Congress and the executive. The Chamber has also become involved in tourist, coastal, and national park development projects and in disputes about the rights of indigenous peoples, labor unions, and prisoners. Virtually all important economic interest groups have litigated to oppose the elimination of protection or subsidies. Plaintiffs often try to generate publicity and controversy to provoke the executive to modify its policies. Although effective at channeling discontent in the short run, this approach could lead to the atrophy of legitimate political channels for interest articulation and conflict resolution, and a heightened sense of popular cynicism regarding the judiciary.

The Territorial Decentralization of State Powers

In the 1980s and 1990s most Latin American countries placed territorial decentralization on their national agendas.[21] Many see it as a way to unburden the national government by turning over some of its responsibilities to local entities that may understand local conditions better and, reformers hope, may be more effective; at times, it is but one way to cut the national budget.

For others, decentralization is widely regarded as a means to increase the participatory nature of regimes, especially in countries that have come to elect local officials only in the 1980s or 1990s, such as Colombia and Venezuela. For many groups in civil society which have had trouble articulating their interests at the national level because of a reluctance to form close ties with political parties, local government holds hope for meaningful participation in community affairs. Parties of the Left, as Angell notes, hope that territorial decentralization will allow their officeholders to prove their competence in government at the local level, paving the way for a claim to national office; Causa R in Venezuela's Bolívar State, the Frente Amplio in the city of Montevideo, and the PT in São Paulo exemplify this strategy. Finally, local governments can provide new participatory opportunities for the informally disenfranchised, including indigenous groups and the poor; their increased participation at the local level might have positive implications for democratization at the national level.

Government and opposition may have contradictory objectives with regard to decentralization, however. The example of Chiapas illustrates this tension. For the Mexican government, territorial decentralization in Chiapas is a means to pacify the region and co-opt some indigenous elites. For the Zapatistas who began an insurgency in January 1994, the objective is to establish bases from which to launch wider political challenges, as they did in 1994 and 1995.

Despite these high (and somewhat contradictory) hopes, the results are discouraging. In most countries, local governments possess neither the funds nor the technical expertise to assume the new responsibilities assigned to them. Under these circumstances, subnational governments can undermine the efforts of national executives to carry out economic reforms. In Argentina and Brazil, for example, fiscal powers and prerogatives were extended to states and municipalities without corresponding responsibilities; the resulting deficits and debt contracted by subnational governments have hampered the consolidation of economic reforms.

Decentralization can also undermine democratization by reinforcing the power of local elites, their practices of clientelism (to which Hagopian calls attention), and the power of their military or paramilitary allies, as in Brazil, Colombia, El Salvador, and Mexico. Especially in the rural areas, these countries suffer from the inability of the central state to enforce the law equitably throughout its national territory. Instead of increasing the accountability of local elites to civil society, decentralization would decrease even further their accountability to national authority, and it might permit the consolidation of petty tyrannies. Decentralization is also likely to remove certain issues from the national agenda, which has been more likely to be hospitable to initiatives from the political Left. Decentralization may some day empower ordinary citizens to take better charge of their government, and permit a wider range of innovation at the local level, but there is still a long way to go before these promises are realized.

Economic Reforms, the Market, and Democratic Consolidation

Free markets and free politics are celebrated throughout much of the region, and thoughtful arguments are advanced about why they "go together" in Latin America and the Caribbean in the 1990s. Yet many scholars and political activists also argue that the rapid implementation of "neoliberal" market reforms has disrupted democratic representation, hurt the poor, and increased social conflict.[22]

Market reforms (especially deregulation, privatization, and the termination of business subsidies) can serve the goals of democratic politics. Statist economic arrangements often permit and foster close connections between economic and political elites, reducing the prospects for wider participation and fair contestation. Statist economics privilege business groups whose profits depend on political connections, not necessarily on efficiency or quality. Market reforms can break the ties between political and economic elites, reduce the opportunities for corruption and rent-seeking behavior, and create a level playing field for economic actors. Insertion into international markets provides external actors with the leverage needed to defend constitutional government in the region; such leverage helped to thwart Guatemalan president Jorge Serrano's attempt to overturn the constitution in 1993. In the 1990s, external actors have also used their economic leverage to prevent authoritarian reversals and to widen political openings in the Dominican Republic, Mexico, and Peru.

Some governments—most notably in Argentina, Chile, and Costa Rica—are establishing a "happy partnership" between market reforms and nationalism, replacing the historic alliance of populism and nationalism, as a means to consolidate both constitutional government and a market economy. In Chile, for example, defenders of constitutionalism and market openings appeal to nationalist sentiments suggesting that a proud nation would surely wish to meet these standards of "civilized" peoples; similar arguments are made for the integration of the poorest sectors into the national economy.

Democracy, in turn, can help to consolidate a market economy. In countries where levels of societal contestation and political instability have often been very high and organized opposition forces have been strong, democracy can reduce many transaction costs. There may be fewer disruptions from labor strikes or insurgencies if the would-be supporters of these strategies can find more cost-effective alternatives to advance their interests within democratic politics. In addition, democratic regimes can involve the political opposition in support of a market economy more effectively than can authoritarian regimes. In Argentina and Chile in the 1990s, for example, key decisions— Argentina's convertibility law governing monetary and exchange rate policies and Chile's tax laws—have resulted from negotiation between executive and Congress. By giving the opposition a voice and vote in the creation of fundamental long-term market-conforming policies, democratic regimes can set the foundations for credible and stable long-term rules. In these circumstances, rational investors can expect that today's rules will endure tomorrow even if the opposition wins the general elections. The procedures of democracy help to consolidate the market economy.

But the connection between democracy and the market is complex. Many of the devices designed to maintain fiscal discipline barely meet the test of democracy. For example, a closed and technocratic style of decision making reinforces the unresponsiveness of the state to societal demands and may well be authoritarian. At times presidents rule by decree, deliberately bypassing the legislature. These concerns were raised most often in Argentina and Bolivia in the 1990s. Even strong parties such as those in Chile, which have adapted well to the challenges of governance, must still prove their ability to articulate societal interests; there is so much "consensus" in Chile that dissenting interests and values may be neglected.

The turn toward a market opening has coincided with spectacular cases of corruption that led to the impeachments of presidents Collor in Brazil and Pérez in Venezuela. Concern about corruption also looms high in nearly all other countries. During the early stages of the privatization of state enterprises, for example, there are substantial opportunities for government officials to favor certain business groups. Mexico illustrates a related problem: because PRI politicians can no longer rely as much on state resources to pay for their campaigns, they resort to private funds in a political environment where rules governing campaign financing are weak and often unenforced.[23]

In the short run, moreover, the shift in economic models has contributed to the crisis of representation discussed earlier because parties must overhaul their economic programs and find new ways to gain support from their often surprised constituents. New parties and social movements have arisen to protest these policies, invigorating democratic contestation, to be sure, but also challenging the scope and durability of market reforms. Populist parties and corporatist forms of interest representation had in years past tied labor and other groups to the political system, but in the 1990s these forces have weakened precisely at the moment when public support must be found to help guarantee the stability of economic reforms and constitutional government, especially in Brazil, Mexico, and Venezuela. And, as noted earlier, Yashar traces the rise of indigenous mobilization throughout the hemisphere in part to grievances exacerbated by neoliberal reforms and left unarticulated by eroded representational networks.

The change in economic models has also altered the roles of the political Right, the political Left, and the traditional elites, shaping the quality of politics and the stability of constitutional government. The political Right has increased its participation in party politics in many countries, as Edward L. Gibson demonstrates. Parties of the Right, or parties with strong support from the Right, have proven far stronger than some eminent scholars had thought as recently as the early 1980s that they would be.[24] As the 1990s opened, for instance, elected parties or coalitions with strong support from the Right governed in every Central American country. This development portends well for the stability of constitutional rule, at least in the short term, because conservative interests (most often those of business) are well represented through the party system.

The marriage between democracy and the market also makes it possible for many economic actors to pledge their allegiance to constitutional government. Few incentives now exist for business to knock on the barracks door to alter national economic policy. The military is often judged to be too incompetent to manage the economy, given its generally poor record in government in the 1970s and early 1980s. Labor unions are weak, and macroeconomic policies benefit property owners. Business participates in politics, often supporting parties of the Right (though sometimes also other parties), mainly through the deployment of resources at election time (such as purchasing television time during campaigns), not through party building. The connection between business and parties may be close in El Salvador (with regard to ARENA) and in Mexico (with regard to the PRI), but it is tactical at best in most countries.

One obstacle to building parties of the Right has been the tendency of formerly populist parties in Argentina, Bolivia, Mexico, and Venezuela to usurp neoliberal platforms. One question for these parties is whether they can incorporate the Right as leaders and as constituents and still retain lower-class support. In the mid-1990s, perhaps surprisingly, the answer (except in Venezuela) seemed to be yes—a true feat of partisan skill.

The stability of constitutional government in the short term depends on the representation of the Right, but the long-run consolidation of democracy depends on the representation of nonelite interests, often by parties of the Left as Hagopian argues in her chapter. The development of a social democratic Left in Latin America, as Angell shows, has been encouraged by the same events that have weakened the Left in general: authoritarian repression, the collapse of communism, the decline of labor unions, and the narrowing of economic options. Widespread corruption and inattention to social needs have become key issues for these parties. The parties of the social democratic Left are very strong in Brazil, the Dominican Republic, Nicaragua, Panama, Uruguay, and Venezuela, and strong in Chile and El Salvador. For them, constitutional government holds the only route to national power in the 1990s. The Left's lack of governing experience in most countries and the absence of a clear economic alternative are liabilities, however.

Finally, as Hagopian notes, most traditional elites have opposed market reforms because such reforms threaten their control of resources and their access to government policymakers. To the extent that reforms succeed in shifting control over clientelistic resources from traditional elites to the executive, or reduce the salience of such resources by means of privatization and deregulation, the reforms are likely to advance the cause of both freer markets and freer politics. Traditional elites undermine democracy and markets by skewing electoral laws in order to block the emergence of political rivals who articulate mass interests, by placing limits on market and other policy reforms as a condition of their support for constitutional government, and by deforming the mechanisms of political representation with clientelism. These practices have pernicious effects on the extent and effectiveness of democratic governance. The alienation of citizens from the political system and the obstacles to market reforms are greatest where traditional elites are the strongest, as in Brazil, Ecuador, and Guatemala.

In sum, market reforms in many countries have strengthened the Right's allegiance to constitutional government[25] (especially evident in the export business sectors), while they have revivified the prospects for parties of the Left[26] that can channel some of the discontent aroused by such policies. Traditional elites, in contrast, are the enemies of both markets and democracy.

Empirically, in the mid-1990s voters signaled their preliminary approval of the shift toward a market economy. They abandoned the punitive electoral behavior noted at the beginning of this chapter. They began to reward officeholders who had managed the economy and other fundamental tasks well. Colombia's Liberal Party won three consecutive presidential elections in the 1980s and 1990s, in part in response to good economic management. Chile's Concertación Democrática coalition (including Christian Democratic, socialist, and other parties) won a second consecutive presidential election in 1993 thanks to its consolidation of a transition to a democratic regime and its excellent economic management. El Salvador's ARENA party, credited with securing internal peace and reactivating the economy, won a second consecutive presidential election in 1994. Ernesto Zedillo won the fairest-ever Mexican presidential election in 1994 in part because his party, the PRI, was perceived to have rescued Mexico from the economic depression of the 1980s. Fernando Henrique Cardoso was elected Brazil's president in 1994 mainly because of his successful control of inflation during his term as finance minister. Alberto Fujimori was reelected president of Peru in 1995 because he was credited with taming inflation, reactivating the economy, and controlling a virulent insurgency. And Carlos Menem, having presided over the termination of hyperinflation and the revival of economic growth, was reelected president of Argentina. In these and other instances, rational voters supported new market-oriented policies, thereby wedding the future of constitutional government to the success of the market economy.

For the "happy partnership" between democracy and markets to prosper, however, more needs to happen. Poverty must be reduced if citizens are to have the needed resources for effective participation; only with a widespread capacity to participate is democratic consolidation achieved. The reform of social services—their financing, organization, and effectiveness—awaits attention throughout the region. And the capacity of the state to raise revenues to rebuild infrastructure, and to improve the quality of health and education, requires ongoing effort. Special care must be taken to ensure that privatization decisions and implementation are transparent, not opportunities for corruption. Other issues include the balance between direct and indirect taxation, as well as the efforts of middle-class groups to resist reforms that hurt their interests (most notably in Uruguay, as Juan Rial points out, to protect and increase middle-class pensions through the use of a plebiscite). Successful defense of past rent-seeking achievements limits the resources available for other urgent needs.

The worry, best expressed by Castañeda, is that the political system will be unable to handle the pent-up demands that are bound to be expressed as the memories of authoritarian governments and hyperinflationary crises recede. Creating the understanding that democracy cannot solve everything is essential for a democratic culture, but it is not sufficient for stability; sooner or later constitutional government must provide some answers to the material problems of the poor. To justify his authoritarian methods, former Peruvian strongman Manuel Odría used to argue that people cannot eat democracy. For democracy to be consolidated and for the poor to resist the temptation of would-be authoritarians, democratic polities with market economies must make it possible for the poor to eat.

The Armed Forces and the Consolidation of Democracy

Since the mid-1980s there have been three types of military assault on constitutional government; they are discussed here in increasing order of concern. One, evident in the early 1990s in Haiti, as Anthony P. Maingot notes, is for the high command of the armed forces to overthrow the civilian government. In the 1980s this was the principal means to rotate rulers under authoritarian regimes, as in the case of Panama throughout the Noriega years. As Abente Brun notes, it was also used to terminate General Alfredo Stroessner's regime in Paraguay. This practice had been common in much of South and Central America from the mid-1960s to the early 1980s, but no successful military coup led by the high command has occurred in other South or Central American countries since 1982, when one group of Guatemalan military officers overthrew another. In the 1980s and early 1990s, the less professional the military, the more likely that its high command would publicly lead an overthrow of the government—the opposite of the pattern that prevailed in the 1960s and 1970s.[27]

In several countries with professional armed forces, however, there have been military mutinies against constitutional governments in the late 1980s and early 1990s. These revolts were led by disgruntled middle-ranking officers in Argentina, Ecuador, Guatemala, Panama, and Venezuela;[28] each of these countries except Panama has seen at least two coup attempts in these years. The motivations for the coups varied. In Argentina and Panama, they were related to the downsizing of the security forces, and in Argentina to the prospect of trials for human rights violations. In Argentina, Ecuador, and Venezuela, ambitious and popular officers led the coup effort. In Guatemala, opposition from some business elites to tax and other economic policies played a role. A common aspect of these mutinies was that the military chain of command broke down; the mutinies were aimed at the high command as much as at the constitutional government. Consequently, the capacity to maintain civilian control was shaken because the generals could no longer ensure the loyalty of the lower ranks of the armed forces. Military deprofessionalization was associated with the increased likelihood of coup attempts. All of these attempts failed in the end because they were opposed by the military high command and because civilian politicians, for the most part, closed ranks in support of constitutional government. But will the high command and the civilians be able to retain control in the future?

Finally, a grave threat to constitutional government may come from a coup led by an elected civilian president supported by the high command of the armed forces against the congress, the courts, the political parties, and all vehicles that help civil society seek advocacy and representation for its interests. Pioneered in Uruguay in the early 1930s and repeated in Uruguay in the early 1970s, this pattern is associated in the 1990s with Peru's president Fujimori. Thus far only Guatemalan president Jorge Serrano has attempted to emulate him, without success. (Susan Stokes discusses Fujimori's case in detail.) In these cases, presidents have claimed that extensive corruption in congress generates gridlock as well as the pursuit of illicit objectives at the expense of the public interest. Presidents thus call on the military to establish a temporary civilian dictatorship. This pattern of coup-making is particularly worrisome, even if it has succeeded just in one country, because the problems of corruption and gridlock are real, and the disenchantment with the performance of constitutional government has been considerable in many countries.

The aftermath of Fujimori's coup in Peru has made his suspension of constitutional government especially appealing to antidemocrats. The economic reforms initiated in Peru in the early 1990s before the coup finally began to bear fruit, while good police work led to the capture of Abigael Guzmán, the founder and longtime leader of the Sendero Luminoso insurgency. Though both outcomes could have occurred without a coup, Fujimori claimed that his decisive anticonstitutional act brought them about. Right after the coup, the Organization of American States (with strong backing from the U.S. government) pressured Fujimori into calling internationally supervised elections for a constituent assembly (which would double as a parliament) and to agree not to prolong his presidential term without a free election. In April 1995 Fujimori was reelected president by a strong majority. Despite some irregularities, the election was fair enough.

This combination of circumstances recalls the potentially great appeal of a Caesar who proclaims the need for a temporary interruption of constitutional government to save the country and constitutionalism in the long run. The problem, of course, is that such interruptions often last for a longer time. Fujimori's economic and military policies, together with his acquiescence to international pressure in returning to the procedures of constitutional government, may have had the paradoxical effect of making a "Fujimorazo" much more appealing than either Fujimori or the international community ever imagined: he seemed to have fulfilled the promise of a short and effective dictatorship.

On balance, however, the barriers against *successful* military coups did rise in Latin America in the 1980s and 1990s and remain high in the Anglophone Caribbean. In general, the "demand" for coups has been constrained by the generally disastrous performance of military rulers in the late 1970s and early 1980s. The economies of Latin American countries collapsed when military presidents governed. The military lost the reputation for competence beyond its specific professional sphere, though the Pinochet government in Chile regained such a reputation during the second half of the 1980s. The demand for coups has also been reduced by the strength of parties of the Right, as noted above; many business elites no longer rely on military coups to advance their objectives because they are effective under civilian rule. The "supply" of coup-makers has also been limited because military officers recall their frustration, their unpreparedness, and the loss of their own military professionalism when they attempted to run the government. If the memories of military misgovernment fade and the performance of constitutional governments remains weak, however, the prospects for such coups might increase again.

Another reason for the decline in the frequency of coups is that in many cases the armed forces can have their demands met without resorting to such tactics. The military retains significant prerogatives in countries as different as Chile and Nicaragua, Cuba and Honduras, Brazil and Peru, Colombia and Guatemala. Military courts defy civilian jurisdiction over the criminal activities of some military personnel. The military continues to control police forces and intelligence agencies in a great many countries, without significant civilian oversight. Retired and, at times, active duty military officers continue to control important state enterprises directly or indirectly; in Chile a portion of earnings from copper exports is explicitly reserved for military use. In these ways, the armed forces in many countries retain an independent source of revenue to shield them from budget austerity. In some countries, military commanders also maintain significant subnational influence through their alliance with local power elites. In countries where civil violence is particularly high, the armed forces exercise even greater power; despite transitions to constitutional government and despite elections, much of Colombia, Guatemala, and Peru has remained under direct military rule. For the rural citizens of these countries, no "democratic transition" has taken place. Such military prerogatives remain important obstacles to the realization of democratic practice.[29]

There is considerable debate about the appropriate roles of the armed forces in contemporary Latin America. In Argentina and Uruguay, civilian governments have eagerly promoted military participation in international peacekeeping and peace-enforcing operations under the auspices of the United Nations in order to focus the armed forces on these new professional issues. The hope is that the military will be less likely to interfere in domestic politics if so occupied.

One persistent concern about any military operation, including military involvement in combating drug trafficking, is the need for effective means of civilian control. For the most part, such mechanisms remain insufficiently developed, and in some countries they have yet to exist because too many civilian "defense experts" have been specialists not in controlling the military but in aligning with them to make coups.

There is a related concern about military involvement in the development of infrastructure or the improvement of public health. Such normally praiseworthy activities may blur civilian and military lines of authority, reviving the notion (proven false during the economic crises of the late 1970s and early 1980s) that military officers can handle the routine affairs of government more effectively than civilians. In short, the task of establishing civilian supremacy over the military remains daunting, and the likelihood of coup attempts remains high. Nonetheless, the prospects for continued constitutional government are better than at any time since the great depression of the 1930s.

The International Defense and Promotion of Democracy

Never before has there been such a strong international commitment to the defense and promotion of constitutional government in Latin America and the Caribbean. Such a new commitment is yet another barrier to successful coup attempts. Propelling the international activity on behalf of constitutional government is a change in the attitude of many Latin American governments toward intervention. This shift is best exemplified by Resolution 1080 of the Organization of American States, enacted in Santiago, Chile, in June 1991; it requires OAS member governments to address the interruption of constitutional government, should it occur.

There is also a marked change in the behavior of the U.S. government. Twice since the end of the cold war in Europe, the United States has deployed tens of thousands of troops to a near neighbor, motivated at least in part by the need to establish or restore viable constitutional government. In Panama in 1989 and in Haiti in 1994, U.S. troops deposed a military ruler and installed a civilian president. In Panama, international observers found that Guillermo Endara had won the 1989 presidential elections but was prevented from taking office because the military government stopped counting the ballots when it became evident that its candidate would lose. In Haiti, Jean-Bertrand Aristide was duly elected and took office, but was subsequently overthrown.[30] While the renewed commitment to constitutional government is encouraging, the lowering of barriers to the use of force across international boundaries is a source of concern.

The U.S. and other governments in Latin America, the Caribbean, Canada, and Western Europe, as well as the United Nations and the OAS, have also played valuable roles in ending wars in Nicaragua, El Salvador, and Suriname, making possible a transition toward more open politics. Through election observation, moreover, foreign governments and transnational NGOs have fostered a climate for freer elections in the Dominican Republic, Guyana, Paraguay, Peru, and Mexico. These international actors have supported trends away from electoral abuse and fraud, assisted with the logistics that permit freer and fairer elections, and denounced violations of the electoral process where they occurred. In Guatemala the international community played a decisive role in foiling President Jorge Serrano's attempted coup against constitutional government. And in the early to mid-1990s, the international community, including the Clinton administration, helped advance peace and constitutionalism in Guatemala, El Salvador, and Nicaragua, as well as defending constitutional government in Venezuela.

The defense of constitutional government has had some noteworthy limitations. Transition to civilian rule in Haiti was not accomplished without military force. And Peruvian president Fujimori's coup against constitutional government was not reversed; its thrust was mitigated through international pressure and negotiation in ways that, inadvertently, may have increased its appeal. On balance, however, the international community has had a good record defending constitutional government in the 1990s.

There is also the hope that the increased international engagement of certain countries will promote constitutional government within them. Mexico's participation in the North American Free Trade Agreement (NAFTA) may help consolidate the economic reforms enacted in the late 1980s and early 1990s, assist the country's recovery from the late 1994 and early 1995 currency devaluation shock, and foster a more open political climate. As Dresser's chapter shows, the administrations of presidents Carlos Salinas and Ernesto Zedillo were required to change many undemocratic political practices in order to safeguard Mexico's participation in NAFTA. Under international scrutiny, Mexico created mechanisms to protect human rights, reduce the likelihood of election fraud, and recognize opposition victories for subnational offices. Similarly, Paraguay's engagement in international trade and other economic relations through MERCOSUR (with Argentina, Brazil, and Uruguay) may help to open the political system further, years after the end of Alfredo Stroessner's dictatorship. Freer markets in the global economy, as in domestic economies, may contribute to the consolidation of freer politics in the long run.

By the same token, however, international factors may also create pressures that destabilize domestic politics. NAFTA, for example, is making it very difficult for Mexican maize producers to compete with imports from the United States, fueling discontent in already volatile rural areas and giving credence to the enemies of NAFTA (and of the government) within Mexico.

These perspectives offer a window into the future of Cuba, which Marifeli Pérez-Stable reviews in this collection. Will the future of Cuba be like the past in Panama in the 1980s and Haiti in the early 1990s, where massive U.S. military intervention occurred after unarticulated civil societies and weak and fragmented opposition movements within and outside the country were unable to launch a successful process of democratization? Will it be like Nicaragua and El Salvador in the 1980s, where extensive civil war with external participation lingered for years? Or will the future of Cuba be like the 1980s and 1990s in much of Central America, Mexico, and Paraguay, where an engaged international community aided a peaceful transition toward more open politics? The third scenario would require, of course, that Cuban leaders be more willing than they have been in the past to negotiate new rules of governance with the domestic opposition. From the perspective of democratization, the prospects are not good; the current political regime seems likely to endure, though it has already become much friendlier to international market forces. For the reasons Pérez-Stable reviews, however, we believe that the third scenario has the better chance of achieving Cuba's successful transition to democracy because it would impose the lowest costs on its people and its neighbors.

Conclusion

"Like all men in Babylon," Jorge Luis Borges wrote, "I have been a proconsul; like all, a slave. I have also known omnipotence, opprobrium, imprisonment."[31] In many ways, this characterizes the experience of many prominent Latin American politicians in the 1990s. Some, like Argentine president Carlos Saúl Menem, spent years in prison under military government. Others, like President Fernando Henrique Cardoso of Brazil, spent years under official opprobrium and exile during his country's period of military rule. As Latin America and the Caribbean approach a new millennium, the task is to banish forever slavery, opprobrium, and imprisonment without succumbing to the temptations of the omnipotent proconsul. The power of presidents and ministers to govern is at times vast and injurious to democratic practice, for it presumes falsely that the executive alone has been elected by the people.

In this work we call attention to the importance of institutions and procedures that remain fundamental for democratic practice. In particular, we have focused on parties and their key role as bridges between state and society. And we have pondered the issues and concerns that arise within governments regarding executive, legislative, judiciary, and military institutions. These institutions and relationships are at the heart of the future of constitutional government in the Americas.

With regard to the prospects for military intervention in politics, we have echoed the alarm of others and have noted the extent to which the military may remain involved in politics short of staging a coup. Nonetheless, we are heartened by the decreased frequency of successful overthrows of constitutional government.

Thus the task at hand is to improve effective democratic governance. We are especially encouraged by the capacity of many to organize peacefully to participate in political life, but we are discouraged by continuing evidence that the design and redesign of the institutions of constitutional government have fallen well short of the needs of these countries. Between these two trends lies the future of democracy in the region.

Notes

This is not a freestanding chapter. Instead, it calls attention to, and to some degree summarizes, themes that emerge in the chapters in this collection and in other work that has been part of the Inter-American Dialogue project on democratic governance. Because the introductory chapter by Jorge Domínguez and Abraham F. Lowenthal highlights certain policy issues, this chapter concentrates on more scholarly questions. This chapter relies occasionally on textual references to other chapters, but our debt to the authors in this collection is much greater than these citations suggest. The views expressed here are ours alone. The Inter-American Dialogue and the authors are at liberty to claim that all the errors in this chapter are ours and all the insights are theirs. We are also grateful for comments on an earlier version from Alan Angell, Michael Coppedge, Rosario Espinal, Peter Hakim, Harvey F. Kline, Abraham F. Lowenthal, Marifeli Pérez-Stable, Rose J. Spalding, Michael Shifter, and Deborah J. Yashar. An earlier version was presented at meetings of the Harvard University comparative politics faculty group and of the University's Sawyer Seminar, sponsored by the Mellon Foundation; we are also grateful for the comments from the participants, Eva Bellin, Daniel Goldhagen, Torben Iversen, Stanley Hoffmann, Stephen Krasner, Anthony Pereira, Theda Skocpol, and Deborah J. Yashar. We thank Linda Lowenthal for very fine editing. All mistakes are ours alone.

1. Jorge Amado, *Gabriela: Clove and Cinnamon*, trans. James L. Taylor and William L. Grossman (New York: Crest Books, 1964), 75, 80.

2. Reelections had occurred uninterruptedly only where there had been no competition (Cuba), or where doubts have existed about the fairness of electoral procedures (Antigua, the Dominican Republic, Mexico, and Paraguay). Only in Colombia (except in 1982) and elsewhere in the eastern Caribbean have fair elections resulting in repeated incumbent party victories been the norm.

3. United Nations, Economic Commission for Latin America and the Caribbean, *Preliminary Overview of the Economy of Latin America and the Caribbean, 1994*, LC/G.1846 (December 20, 1994), 39.

4. On this linkage function of social movements, see Kay Lawson and Peter Merkl, eds., *When Parties Fail* (Princeton: Princeton University Press, 1988).

5. The Mexican case is complex for two other reasons. Civilians have ruled in Mexico, and, despite important irregularities in Mexican elections, the evidence from public opinion polls shows that a plurality of voters have preferred to vote for the Institutional Revolutionary Party (PRI) than for any of the opposition parties. See Jorge I. Domínguez and James A. McCann, "Shaping Mexico's Electoral Arena: The Construction of Partisan Cleavages in the 1988 and 1991 National Elections," *American Political Science Review* 89, no. 1 (1995): 34–48.

6. See also Karen Remmer, "The Political Economy of Elections in Latin America, 1980–1991," *American Political Science Review* 87, no. 2 (1993): 393–407.

7. This and the next two paragraphs draw on Jorge I. Domínguez, "Transiciones democráticas en Centro América y Panamá," in Jorge I. Domínguez and Marc Lindenberg, eds., *Transiciones democráticas en Centro América* (San José, Costa Rica: Editorial Instituto Centroamericano de Administración de Empresas, 1994), 19–62.

8. For a discussion of bargains that may lead to democratic outcomes, see also Adam Przeworski, *Democracy and the Market: Political and Economic Reforms in Eastern Europe and Latin America* (Cambridge: Cambridge University Press, 1991), chaps. 1–2.

9. Robert A. Dahl, *Polyarchy: Participation and Opposition* (New Haven: Yale University Press, 1971), 15.

10. For a more elaborate discussion of the costs and benefits facing guerrillas and governments, see Matthew Soberg Shugart, "Guerrillas and Elections: An Institutionalist Perspective on the Costs of Conflict and Competition," *International Studies Quarterly* 36, no. 2 (1992): 121–51.

11. For the general concepts, see Albert Hirschman, *Exit, Voice, and Loyalty* (New Haven: Yale University Press, 1970).

12. Barriers to entry by new parties in the electoral law are, however, often low; in some cases, they have been lowered in recent years. This is why dissident politicians can form new parties instead of seeking to overthrow the government by force.

13. For a discussion of the historic role of Argentina's provincial parties, see Edward Gibson, *Conservative Parties and Democratic Politics: Argentina in Comparative Perspective* (Baltimore: Johns Hopkins University Press, 1996).

14. See Domínguez and McCann, "Shaping Mexico's Electoral Arena."

15. For a classic discussion of the utility of "reliability" and "responsibility" in parties, see Anthony Downs, *An Economic Theory of Democracy* (New York: Harper & Row, 1957), 96–113.

16. We recognize an anomaly. If this argument were right in every instance, a major third party should have emerged in Jamaica in the early 1990s in response to the People's National Party's turn from statism toward promarket policies and the continued resistance of the two dominant parties to changing the electoral law to lower the threshold for third-party membership in parliament. Our argument with regard to the Latin American cases requires, therefore, permissive electoral laws—proportional representation. This is exactly what the Anglophone Caribbean does not have.

17. For further discussion, see Jane S. Jaquette, "Rewriting the Scripts: Gender in the Comparative Study of Latin American Politics," in Peter H. Smith, ed., *Latin America in Comparative Perspective: New Approaches to Methods and Analysis* (Boulder, Colo.: Westview Press, 1995), 111–33.

18. See Juan J. Linz and Arturo Valenzuela, eds., *The Failure of Presidential Democracy* (Baltimore: Johns Hopkins University Press, 1994); Juan J. Linz, Arend Lijphart, and Arturo Valenzuela, eds., *Hacia una democracia moderna: La opción parlamentaria* (Santiago: Ediciones Universidad Católica de Chile, 1990).

19. For an overview of supreme courts, see Joel G. Verner, "The Independence of Supreme Courts in Latin America: A Review of the Literature," *Journal of Latin American Studies* 16, no. 2 (1984): 463–506.

20. For a general discussion of human rights issues during democratic transitions, see Manuel Antonio Garretón, "Human Rights in Processes of Democratization," *Journal of Latin American Studies* 26, no. 1 (1994): 221–34.

21. For a general discussion, see R. Andrew Nickson, *Local Government in Latin America* (Boulder, Colo.: Lynne Rienner, 1995); Jonathan Fox, "Latin America's Emerging Local Politics," *Journal of Democracy* 5, no. 2 (1994): 105–16.

22. For a theoretical argument about the economic advantages of democracy over autocracy, see Mancur Olson, "Dictatorship, Democracy and Development," *American Political Science Review* 87, no. 3 (1993): 567–76. See also the special issues on "Economic Liberalization and Democratization: Explorations of the Linkages" in *World Development* 21, no. 8 (1993), and on "Economic Reform and Democracy" in *Journal of Democracy* 5, no. 4 (1994).

23. For a related argument, see Barbara Geddes and Artur Ribeiro, "Institutional Sources of Corruption in Brazil," *Third World Quarterly* 13 (1992): 641–61.

24. See, for example, Guillermo O'Donnell and Philippe Schmitter, *Tentative Conclusions about Uncertain Democracies: Transitions from Authoritarian Rule* (Baltimore: Johns Hopkins University Press, 1986), 62–63.

25. The greater allegiance of the Right to democracy can be found to varying degrees (listing from south to north) in Argentina, Chile, Colombia, Panama, Costa Rica, Nicaragua, El Salvador, and Mexico.

26. Opposition to some of the negative consequences of market reforms has strengthened the long-term prospects for parties of the Left to varying degrees. Listing from south to north, this is evident in Argentina, Uruguay, Brazil, Panama, Nicaragua, El Salvador, and Mexico.

27. For discussion of the earlier pattern, see Alfred Stepan, "The New Professionalism of Internal Warfare and Military Role Expansion," in Abraham F. Lowenthal and J. Samuel Fitch, eds., *Armies and Politics in Latin America*, (New York: Holmes and Meier, 1986), 134–47.

28. This pattern has been common elsewhere as well. See Samuel P. Huntington, *The Third Wave: Democratization in the Late Twentieth Century* (Norman: University of Oklahoma Press, 1991), 234.

29. A number of scholars stress the prerogatives retained by the military after the transition to constitutional government and the threat that this poses to democracy. See Alfred Stepan, *Rethinking Military Politics* (Princeton: Princeton University Press, 1988), 68–127. See also Brian Loveman, "'Protected Democracies' and Military Guardianship: Political Transition in Latin America, 1978–1993," *Journal of Interamerican Studies and World Affairs* 36, no. 2 (1994): 105–89; and Felipe Agüero, "The Military and the Limits to Democratization in South America," in Scott Mainwaring, Guillermo O'Donnell, and J. Samuel Valenzuela, eds., *Issues in Democratic Consolidation: The New South American Democracies in Comparative Perspective* (Notre Dame: University of Notre Dame Press, 1992). In contrast, Wendy Hunter shows how democracy has helped to limit military prerogatives in Brazil. See her "Politicians against Soldiers: Contesting the Military in Postauthoritarian Brazil," *Comparative Politics* 27, no. 4 (1995): 425–43.

30. To be sure, the main U.S. motivation for intervention has not always been the promotion of democracy. In Panama the main motivation was to curtail drug trafficking and financial laundering, while in Haiti it was to make it easier to stop the flow of immigration and to return undocumented immigrants. Another important difference between the two interventions is that in Haiti the United States had sought and obtained prior authorization from the United Nations Security Council and a commitment that other countries would eventually join a peacekeeping effort; in Panama the United States acted unilaterally.

31. Jorge Luis Borges, "The Lottery in Babylon," in his *Labyrinths: Selected Stories and Other Writings*, ed. Donald A. Yates and James E. Irby (New York: New Directions Books, 1964), 30.